S0-BLN-301

FROMMERS

BUDGET TRAVEL GUIDE

HAWAII '91
ON $60 A DAY

by Faye Hammel

PRENTICE
HALL
PRESS

NEW YORK • LONDON • TORONTO • SYDNEY • TOKYO • SINGAPORE

FROMMER BOOKS

Published by Prentice Hall Press
A division of Simon & Schuster Inc.
15 Columbus Circle
New York, NY 10023

ISBN 0-13-326794-6
ISSN 8755-9250

CONTENTS

MAPS

A Disclaimer

Although every effort was made to ensure the accuracy of the prices and travel information appearing in this book, it should be kept in mind that prices do fluctuate in the course of time, and that information does change under the impact of the varied and volatile factors that affect the travel industry.

Readers should also note that the establishments described under Reader's Selections or Suggestions have not in many cases been inspected by the authors and that the opinions expressed there are those of the individual readers only. They do not in any way represent the opinions of the publisher or authors of this guide.

HAWAII ON $60 A DAY

This book was written for the express purpose of disposing of a couple of myths. The first is that a South Seas idyll—that longed-for journey to enchanted islands that everyone dreams of at one time or another—is beyond the means of the budget traveler. We're here to tell you that all that is ancient history. Less than five jet hours and less than $200 away from the West Coast lie the islands of Hawaii, a name to conjure dreams, a place to explore on a shoestring budget.

People will tell you, of course, that the 50th American state is one of the most expensive areas on earth to visit. It is—and it isn't—depending on which Hawaii you care to see. If you choose prepackaged and preconceived Hawaii, you'll undoubtedly stay at plush hotels, dine at expensive restaurants, be herded around in sightseeing limousines with people just like the folks you left back home—and pay a pretty penny for it. But if you agree with us that travel is a do-it-yourself activity, if you'd rather leave the plush and nonsense to others and strike out on your own to find out how the islanders really live, you'll find that a vacation in Hawaii is one of the best travel bargains anywhere. For, contrary to legend, Hawaii has dozens of comfortable, clean, and reasonable hotels; scores of restaurants where the food is exotic and inexpensive; and most important, an almost endless list of free and low-cost entertainment—from beaches to bon dances, from museum browsing to mountain climbing, from hiking to dancing the hula. Add to that an incredibly cheap airfare, and you've got the ideal place for a budget vacation—even in these costly times.

WHAT $60 A DAY MEANS

As in most of the other books in this series, our aim is to show you how to keep your basic living costs—*room and three meals only*—down to somewhere around $60 a day. There's nothing fantastic or gimmicky about that goal. Since the costs of transportation, shopping, sightseeing, and entertainment are all in addition to that figure, our book prescribes reasonable methods of vacationing on a budget.

We think you'll agree that by keeping these room-and-meal expenses low, you can make a substantial dent in the overall cost of your trip. But more important, we believe you'll have more fun—and enjoy a more meaningful vacation—by relying on your brains rather than your pocketbook. Hawaii is one of the few places where you can still live comfortably on a limited budget, even in the face of economic factors that are raising prices everywhere. In fact, many people who used to travel abroad for their holidays are finding Hawaii one of the best bargain areas anywhere. And considering that this is an enormously popular resort area, $60 a day per person is very little to pay. We'll give you specific tips on how to do it elsewhere in this chapter. But first, back to our debunking.

MYTHS AND PARADOXES

The second myth was neatly put by a friend of ours, a sophisticated woman who travels regularly to Europe. "Why go all the way to Hawaii," she asks, "just to find yourself at a beach?" Now no one in his or her right mind would dispute the glory of Hawaii's beaches, some of the best in the world. But anyone who looks on Hawaii as merely a seaside resort is missing some of the most profound, exciting, and exotic travel experiences available anywhere.

The essence of Hawaii, its special mystery, lies in its startling and subtle paradoxes. Take its people, as fascinating a mixture of humanity as you'll find on this planet. The children and grandchildren of Stone Age warriors, New England missionaries, and Asian plantation workers mingled and intermarrried to create nothing less than a new race. Scratch an islander and you'll find a Hawaiian-Chinese-Portuguese, a Japanese-American-Tahitian, or perhaps an English-Filipino-Korean. The typical islander—if such a creature exists—long ago gave up counting the racial strains in his or her background; it got too complicated. Hawaii's people, American in ideals, optimism, and drive, still retain the serenity of Polynesia and Asia. They avidly follow the scores of baseball games played by fellow citizens 6,000 miles away in Boston or Philadelphia, yet many of them dream of going to visit "the old country"—Japan, China, the Phillipines. And as if in answer to the bigots who cringe at "mongrelization," the interracial democracy of Hawaii has produced the most attractive Americans anywhere. Hawaii's children are unbelievably exquisite, a mixture of the best the races can give to each other.

But the paradoxes don't stop here. They are even more astonishing on a sheer topographical level; Hawaii has the kind of scenery that all but overwhelms the senses. Steep cliffs tumbling down to coral beaches, tropical rain forests and woods that run a hundred shades of green, black-sand beaches and pounding blue surf, scores of tropical blossoms, vying for attention at every turn—this is the landscape. Even more awe-inspiring, the volcanoes that created these islands from the vast nothingness of ocean are still alive. The land is still being born. Drive mile after mile on the Big Island of Hawaii and see where the lava flows have scalded their way to the sea and how slowly life renews itself over the years. Then go to Kauai and see what the centuries and the forces of erosion have done to a much older and extinct volcano. You will have a sense of the youth—and age—of the earth that you can get nowhere else.

The paradox that is Hawaii continues on a third level as well. In less than 200 years it has gone from Stone Age to Space Age, from a primitive island kingdom ruled by stern gods of nature to the fastest-growing state in the U.S., ruled by booming laws of economics. Industry soars, hotel and apartment construction grows apace, population and tourism increases astronomically, Space Age science and education become established, and wherever one looks, something new is being built, planned, developed. "Full speed ahead" are the words on every front. Still, despite the aggressive energy of the times, Hawaii somehow manages to retain its gentleness, its warmth, its relaxed nature. The spirit of aloha remains untouched, a calm center in the eye of the hurricane of progress. Which is perhaps why so many people who've been everywhere and back can't seem to get enough of Hawaii.

LIVING ON $60 A DAY

The trick in Honolulu is to stay at a small apartment-hotel or condominium complex, complete with a built-in money-saving device: a kitchenette. This doesn't mean, however, that you'll spend your vacation slaving away at a hot stove. It means only that you'll fix breakfast, maybe pack a sandwich or some marvelous fresh fruit for a picnic or a light supper, and dine out once a day (preferably at lunchtime, when prices are always low and values best). Many of Hawaii's visitors live just this way—but they live in expensive apartment-hotels. We've scoured the state looking for *budget* apartment-hotels and have come up with a surprisingly large number of them.

To stay within the boundaries of a $60-a-day budget, you should be part of a twosome, which means that you will have a total of $120 per day to spend on room and meals. To stay on the low side of this budget, you will want to choose a room that rents for $60 or less, double. If you wish to live a little higher, then choose a room that goes above $60. Whatever will be left over from your planned $120-a-day-for-two living expenses can be used for your meals; in our chapter on restaurants, we'll show you how to eat inexpensively and well, figuring about $15 for dinner, about $5 or $6 for lunch, roughly $3 to $4 for breakfast. Of course, whatever you save by eating in means that much more in the kitty for other pleasures.

THE SEASON, THE COMPETITION, AND THE PRICE

You should bear in mind another important fact about hotels in Hawaii: their rates usually vary according to season and business. The hotel industry is highly competitive, and room prices go up or down as conditions dictate.

In general, you'll get a much better bargain if you avoid the winter season—mid-December to mid-April. That's when *everybody* seems to want to go to Hawaii, and many visitors—especially those from cold areas like western Canada and Alaska—often stay a few months at the budget apartment-hotels. Many hotels routinely impose a surcharge of as much as $10 to $20 per room during that period. The summer months of June, July, and August are also busy, but many hotels maintain "low-season" rates in those months, and during the months of October, November, and May all kinds of choice rooms are yours for the picking. If you think you'd like to spend the Christmas–New Year's season in the islands, make reservations as far in advance as you possibly can; many hotels accept reservations as much as six months to a year in advance for this insanely popular period. The months of January and February are also extremely popular. Reservations are a good idea, in fact, any time of the year. Budget accommodations do exist, but they are much sought after even now that the supply of hotel rooms has overshot the demand—few of the new hotels that have been built in Waikiki in the past few years have been in the economy category.

The high-season markup also extends to car rentals and other visitors' services as well. The motto seems to be, alas: "Get what the traffic will bear."

The Hawaiian "season," incidentally, has little to do with the weather, except the weather back home. In the islands the weather is usually good year round. Hawaii's climate is subtropical, with springlike temperatures averaging about 75° Fahrenheit and seldom going more than six or seven degrees above or below this point. In midwinter you can occasionally get some "raw" days in the low- to mid-60s and in midsummer some humid ones in the 80s. (August is probably the most humid month of the year; if your room does not have cross-ventilation to allow the trade winds to come through, air conditioning is essential at that time.) Cool waters drifting down from the Bering Sea make the islands 10 degrees cooler than other places in the same latitude—and the trade winds provide balmy breezes. As for rain, we must admit that we have experienced some dreary, rainy days here, especially in the winter—any time from November to March. But most of the time showers are brief and seldom heavy enough to spoil the pleasures of a vacation.

A BIT OF GEOGRAPHY

Most people think of Hawaii as synonymous with Honolulu and Waikiki Beach (they probably know they're on the island of Oahu), but they're a bit vague about the names of the other islands. Actually, there are 122 islands in the Hawaiian chain, a great volcanic mountain range spreading 1,500 miles across the floor of the Pacific, from Hawaii on the southeast to Midway and Kure islands in the northwest. Many of these are just jagged rocks or sand shoals, however, and the term "Hawaiian Islands" usually refers only to eight: Oahu (on which you find Honolulu), Hawaii or the Big Island, Maui, Kauai, Molokai, Lanai, Kahoolawe, and Niihau. The first five are the ones of greatest interest to the visitor, and the ones we'll describe in this book. Of the last three, Lanai is a pineapple plantation island, owned almost completely by Castle & Cooke, the parent company of the Dole Pineapple Company, with resort development just getting underway with the opening of two new luxury Rockresorts. The Lodge at Koele and the Manele Bay Hotel; Kahoolawe, uninhabited, is a target range for American planes and ships; and Niihau, where an ancient Hawaiian community survives, is private property, not open to the public.

ISLANDER ORIGINS

The Hawaiian Islands were settled about a thousand years ago by Polynesians who came most likely from Tahiti, crossing the Pacific in outrigger canoes and performing feats of navigation undreamed of by their European contemporaries. They were Stone Age people, blissfully unaware of the modern world until Captain Cook inadvertently discovered the islands in 1778 (he was seeking the Northwest Passage) and received a god's welcome. He named them the Sandwich Islands, in honor of the Earl of Sandwich. Then came fur traders, merchants, whalers, adventurers from all over, to the crossroads of the Pacific and its languorous pleasure ports. In 1820, from Boston, arrived other travelers, those who would settle the islands and, more than any others, determine Hawaii's pattern of civilization. These were the missionaries, earnest men and women intent on converting the "childlike" heathen to the no-nonsense Calvinism of New England. The missionaries never went home; their children stayed to inherit the islands and their riches, to create the great business empires that still rule Hawaii. The Polynesians, sickened and dwindled, had refused to work the white man's sugar and pineapple plantations. But the poor of Asia came, tens of thousands of them—contract labor pursuing the dream of a better life. (In the great mainland cities at the same time, the dispossessed of Europe were finding their America.) Somehow the welcoming aloha of the islands found a way to absorb them all. Now the era of settling the land is over, and today's "immigrants" are Japanese, Filipinos, and many, many mainland *haoles* (whites or foreigners): Westchester businessmen, California schoolteachers, tourists from all over who fall in love with the islands and forget to go home.

REQUIRED READING

Don't—this is a must—get on the plane without having read James Michener's great epic novel of the islands, *Hawaii;* not to do so would be as bad as forgetting your bathing suit. Michener has taken a leading figure from each of the groups who settled in the islands—the Polynesians, American missionaries, Chinese, Japanese—and through their stories, told the story of Hawaii. The book, which is available in paperback, will illuminate your trip as nothing else will. A newer book, *Hawaii: An Uncommon History,* by Edward Koesting, published by W. W. Norton & Co., has received high critical praise and is well worth your time. So, too, certainly, is Gavan Daws's *A Shoal of Time,* a history of Hawaii from 1778 (Captain Cook) until statehood (1959), published by the University of Hawaii Press. *Hawaii, an Informal History,* by Gerret P. Judd (Collier Books) is another worthwhile study. For a fictional account of the Japanese in Hawaii, read Kazuro Miyamoto's *Hawaii, End of the Rainbow* (Tuttle). Scores of photographers were given one-day assignments in Hawaii and the result was a fascinating tome that may cause you to exceed your airline baggage weight limit: *A Day in the Life of Hawaii,* (Workman Publishing). *A Hawaiian Reader,* a delightful anthology of pieces on Hawaii past and present written by, among others, Jack London, Robert Louis Stevenson, and W. Somerset Maugham, also makes absorbing reading before, during, or after a stay in the islands. This one's in paperback too.

KNOWING SOME HAWAIIAN

You don't have to learn the language, since everyone speaks English. But the islanders do pepper their vocabulary with lots of Hawaiian words, and almost all place names are Hawaiian. So it's a good idea to bone up on a few pronunciation rules and learn a few words. The original Hawaiians spoke a Polynesian dialect but they had no written language; the missionaries transcribed it in order to teach them to read the Bible, and they made it as easy as possible. There are only 12 letters in the alphabet: the five vowels and seven consonants: *h, k, l, m, n, p, w.* Every syllable ends in a vowel; every vowel is pronounced no matter how many there are in the word (these have a frightening way of piling up one after another); and the accent is almost always on the penultimate syllable (the next to the last), as it is in Spanish. Consonants receive their English sounds, but vowels get the Latin pronunciation: *a* as in farm, *e* as in they, *i* as in machine, *o* as in cold, and *u* as in tutor.

Lists of Hawaiian words can be obtained in most tourist offices, but check out our Appendix—"A Hawaiian Vocabulary"—first. Do bear in mind that the name of the state is pronounced Ha-wye-ee (it does not rhyme with how-are-yuh). You are a newcomer, a *malihini* (mah-lee-hee-nee), and longtime residents of the islands are *kamaainas* (kama-eye-nahs). The *haoles* (properly pronounced ha-o-lays, but more commonly how-lays) are the whites, originally foreigners.

The mysterious *lanai* (lah-neye) that landlords are always boasting about is nothing but a balcony or porch. *Kau kau* (cow-cow) means food; you'll go to a lot of *luaus* (loo-ows), Hawaiian feasts; and people will say thank you—rather, *mahalo* (mah-hah-low)—for your *kokua* (ko-koo-ah), your help. It's *kanes* (kah-nays) for men, *wahines* (wah-hee-nays) for women. You probably already know that a *lei* (lay) is a necklace of flowers. And just as you expected, everyone says *aloha* (ah-low-hah) —one of the most beautiful words in any language—meaning hello, good-bye, good luck, and *salud!* It also means love, as in "I send you my aloha."

THE ALOHA SPIRIT

The warm, welcoming hospitality of the islanders is perhaps the thing that most impresses the visitor, who usually goes back home and reports to friends: "I couldn't get over the people—they're the nicest I've met anywhere." One celebrated visitor expressed it very well. Mrs. Jacqueline Kennedy Onassis, returning home after a visit to Hawaii with her family some years back, wrote to the editors of the *Honolulu Advertiser and Star Bulletin* (who had asked the public to give the Kennedys privacy and assigned no reporters or photographers to follow them around): "In this strange land everyone constantly goes out of his way to be kind to the other. From Governor Burns, who so kindly watched over us and asked people to help make our visit private, to the driver of a vegetable truck who went out of his way to lead us several miles, when we merely asked for directions, everyone in Hawaii has been the same. Now I know what the Aloha spirit means. I hope it is contagious—for it could change the world."

A FEW MATTERS OF USAGE

It's preferable to refer to the residents of the 50th state as "islanders," rather than as natives or Hawaiians—unless they happen to be of Hawaiian descent. You are from the mainland, not the States; islanders are very sensitive about this. Another integral segment of the Hawaiian population are Japanese-Americans. They're as proud of being Americans as any descendants of the *Mayflower* passengers. During World War II, in fact, the Nisei volunteers so distinguished themselves in the bloody battles of southern Europe that their unit—the 442nd Regimental Combat Team —was designated "probably the most decorated unit in United States military history." One of its veterans is Daniel K. Inouye (of Watergate and "Irangate" investigation fame), chosen as Hawaii's first representative in Congress, now its senior senator. The late Spark M. Matsunaga, formerly its junior senator, was also a veteran of the 442nd. Both Matsunaga and Inouye started their careers in the territorial house in the 1954 elections. Recent state leaders of Japanese ancestry have included the superintendent of schools, the house leader, the chairman of the senate's powerful ways and means committee, and a number of judges. Remember, too, that although statehood was achieved only in 1959, residents of Hawaii have been American citizens since 1898, when, five years after the Hawaiian monarchy was overthrown in a bloodless coup with U.S. Marines standing by (a triumph for the haole sugar and other commercial interests), the Republic of Hawaii was annexed by the government of President McKinley.

INCIDENTAL INTELLIGENCE

One of the nicest things about going to Hawaii is that you don't have to get one single shot, you don't have to fiddle with passports or visas, or have the slightest worry about unsanitary food or polluted drinking water. Standards of sanitation are very high, and the islands have an excellent supply of pure water. As far as health goes, Hawaii is way ahead of the rest of the United States: A male child has a life expectancy of 74 years compared to 66.5 on the mainland; a female child has a life expectancy of 78.1 years compared to 73 for women in the other 49 states.

TELEPHONE AREA CODE

All of the Hawaiian Islands share one area code number: it's 808. The only area code numbers we list in the text are the 800, toll-free numbers.

A WORD FROM OUR READERS

As the years have gone by (this book is now in its 26th annual edition), we have printed hundreds of Readers' Selections and Readers' Suggestions. If you come across any particularly appealing hotel, restaurant, beach, shop, bargain—please don't keep it to yourself. Let us hear about it. And we also welcome any comments you may have about the existing listings: The fact that a hotel or restaurant is recommended in this edition doesn't mean that it will necessarily appear in future editions if readers report that its service has slipped, that bugs have gotten out of hand (something that, alas, happens now and then in this climate), or that prices have risen unreasonably. Send your comments to us, Faye Hammel and Sylvan Levey, c/o Frommer Books, 15 Columbus Circle, New York, NY 10023. We regret that we cannot personally answer the many hundreds of letters we receive each year. You can, however, be sure that your letter is carefully read and that we are grateful for your comments. Please note that we reserve the right to make minor editorial changes for the sake of brevity and clarity.

To those of our readers who follow the Readers' Selections listed at the end of most chapters, we should also add a word of caution: We cannot personally vouch for these selections, since we have not seen and tried most of them for ourselves. Our general experience, however, has been that 90% of them are excellent. We also try to give a cross-section of opinion on various establishments that we do cover, knowing that somebody's great little discovery may be somebody else's great little disaster. But that's all part of the fun of traveling and discovering.

PRICES

We don't have to tell you that no matter what the level of inflation may be prices do rise, and they may be slightly higher at a given establishment when you read this book than they were at the time this information was collected (and when future projections were made by the establishments) in mid-1990. This may be especially true of restaurant prices. Be that as it may, we feel sure these selections will still represent the best travel bargains in the islands.

And please don't be one of those nonunderstanding types (we understand there are some!) who become furious with proprietors whose current rates have gone up above the prices mentioned here. Remember that the prices we give here are the most specific the proprietors could project as we went to press. Remember, too, that this book is revised each year to keep prices as accurate as possible; always be sure you are reading the very latest copy available.

SAFETY

Yes, it's true; there is crime and violence in Hawaii, as there is everywhere else in the world. Only, because Hawaii was indeed a trouble-free paradise for so many years, people tend to ignore basic safety precautions. Our advice is: *Don't.* Don't go hiking on deserted trails except in a group; don't go wandering on isolated beaches alone; and don't go jogging in the cane fields alone at the crack of dawn, as one crime victim did. (There are many marijuana farms in secluded areas, and the owners do not take kindly to strangers.) Stay in well-lighted areas at night, travel with a friend if possible, lock your car and remove valuables from your trunk, and use your common sense—just as you would at home. Follow these precautions, and you should find a visit to Hawaii no more dangerous than one to your own hometown.

FROMMER'S DOLLARWISE® TRAVEL CLUB—HOW TO SAVE MONEY ON ALL YOUR TRAVELS

In this book we'll be looking at how to get your money's worth in Hawaii, but there is a "device" for saving money and determining value on *all* your trips. It's the popular, international Frommer's Dollarwise Travel Club, now in its 31st successful year of operation. For information about the Club and order forms listing all Prentice Hall travel guides, turn to the last four pages of this book.

ABOUT THIS BOOK

And now, here's how to plan to handle the details of low-cost Hawaiian living.

Chapter I describes the easiest and the cheapest ways to get to the islands and gives you information on packing to save money.

Chapter II outlines the Fast Facts about Honolulu.

Chapter III gets you off the plane, onto the island of Oahu and into the city of Honolulu, and outlines the best hotel bargains in Honolulu, especially in the heart of the tourist scene, Waikiki Beach.

Chapter IV takes you to Honolulu restaurants, on and off the beaten tourist path, where an appetizing meal costs less than you would expect—and to the inexpensive nightspots all over town.

Chapter V discusses the pros and cons of guided tours, taxis, bus trips, and auto rentals, and delves into the cheapest way of getting around the fabulous city of Honolulu.

Chapter VI is devoted to shopping in Hawaii—where to buy items ranging from muumuus to orchids to macadamia nuts, concentrating on bargains, of course.

Chapter VII tells you about the enormous range of activities and entertainment available in Honolulu at little or no cost—with a rundown on beaches, sports, free classes, concerts, films, folk festivals, art galleries, and learning the hula, to mention just a few.

Chapter VIII provides an alternative to the expensive guided tour: seven do-it-yourself bus and walking trips in Honolulu, only one of which should cost you more than $1.20 for transportation.

Chapter IX takes you out of Honolulu, for a low-cost, never-to-be-forgotten drive around the island of Oahu.

Chapter X gives you the basic orientation on traveling in the neighbor islands: Kauai, Hawaii, Maui, and Molokai.

Chapter XI introduces you to the Garden Isle of Kauai and gives you the essentials on hotels, restaurants, car rentals, and the night scene.

Chapter XII takes you sightseeing in Kauai.

Chapter XIII describes the biggest island in the 50th state—Hawaii. Essentials again: hotels, restaurants, car rentals, nightlife.

Chapter XIV takes you sightseeing on the Big Island.

Chapter XV provides all the basics about the island of Maui.

Chapter XVI shows you the sights on Maui.

Chapter XVII takes you to Hawaii's newest tourist destination: Molokai.

Chapter XVIII presents alternative and special-interest travel information.

The *Appendix* offers a Hawaiian vocabulary.

ADDITIONAL SOURCES

For further information on traveling and living in Hawaii, you can contact the **Hawaii Visitors Bureau (HVB),** which has offices in the following cities:

Los Angeles—Room 502, Central Plaza, 3440 Wilshire Blvd., Los Angeles, CA 90010 (tel. 213/385-5301).

San Francisco—Suite 450, 50 California St., San Francisco, CA 94111 (tel. 415/392-8173). (*Note:* The California offices request that you write to the main office in Honolulu—see below—instead of contacting them.)

Chicago—Suite 1031, 180 N. Michigan Ave., Chicago, IL 60601 (tel. 312/236-0632).

New York—Room 1407, 441 Lexington Ave., New York, NY 10017 (tel. 212/986-9203).

In Hawaii, the **HVB** offices are as follows:

Oahu—Suite 801, Waikiki Business Plaza, 2270 Kalakaua Ave., Honolulu, HI 96815; or P.O. Box 8527, Honolulu, HI 96815 (tel. 808/923-1811).

Hawaii—75-5719 W. Alii Dr., Kailua-Kona, HI 96740 (tel. 808/329-7787); or Suite 104, Hilo Plaza, 180 Kinoole St., Hilo, HI 96720 (tel. 808/961-5797).

Maui—Maui Visitors Bureau, Suite 100, 172 Alamaha St., Kahului, Maui, HI 96732 (tel. 808/871-8691).

Kauai—Suite 207, Lihue Plaza Bldg., 3016 Umi St. (or Kauai P.O. Box 507), Lihue, Kauai, HI 96766 (tel. 808/245-3971).

READERS' TIPS ON BOOKS AND MAPS: "Your reading list should include *Plants of Hawaii National Parks* by Otto Degener, $4.50, paperback, available in most of the larger bookstores and in the National Park Service visitor centers. Far more than a botanical guide, it contains fascinating essays on Polynesian and modern uses of various plants. One can learn to make poi, tapa cloth, and many other things. It also goes into the history and religious practices of the Hawaiians. We used it every day. It is a gold mine" (David and Marilynn Rowland, Oakland, Calif.). . . . "The best, most comprehensive, and altogether most fascinating work on Hawaii is Frederick Simpich, Jr.'s *Anatomy of Hawaii,* Coward, McCann & Geoghegan, Inc., 1971. Mr. Simpich's discussion of early Hawaii, modern Hawaii, the land, the military influence, the social scene, tourism, politics, and island psychology and sociology is the most concise and interesting I have read anywhere" (Hobbs A. Brown, Mesa, Ariz.). . . . "As an addition to your recommended reading on Hawaii, I would suggest that 'on the spot' account by Lucien Young, U.S.N., in *The Real Hawaii, Its History and Present Condition, Including the True Story of the Revolution (American Imperialism—Viewpoints of U.S. Foreign Policy, 1898–1941),* reprint edition published by Arno Press, N.Y., 1970, covering the author's personal observations of the political situation in 1892 and 1893 and later years. It provides another perspective (and background) to Michener's *Hawaii* and du Plessix Gray's *Hawaii: The Sugar-Coated Fortress*" (Donna Inguerson, Calgary, Alberta, Canada). . . . "For those who like books about the islands, might we suggest *Above Hawaii* by Cameron, with pictures from the satellite and then present-day and 50-year-ago pictures of the same site—really gorgeous photography" (Mr. and Mrs. B. D. Riley, Rockford, Ill.). . . . "For a background to the islands, we recommend Insight Guides' *Hawaii* by APA Productions, 1980, 413 pages, $15.95 in paperback. Hundreds of color photos. Sensitive and accurate text. A combination guide and history" (Larry Sprecher, Beaverton, Ore.).

"Get a copy of *Dangerous Sea Creatures:* I got a copy at the local library here. It identifies dangerous sea animals that are venomous and toxic that bathers may encounter, especially on the leeward side of the island (the cone shell is very common there). They won't hurt anyone as long as they're left alone" (M.B., Mililani, HI).

"For northerners like me, a trip to Hawaii means a chance to see southern stars. You don't even need pitch-black skies: I got my first view of Alpha Centauri (earth's nearest stellar neighbor) and the Southern Cross from the beach at Kaanapali. For identification, I used the star map in *Sky and Telescope* magazine, which is published monthly and is available in newsstands. Each issue carries a sky map for that month. . . . Much of the bird life on the islands differs from what we have on the mainland. Some are native, like the apapene, which we saw many of in Volcanoes National Park. Some have been introduced, such as the Indian mynah, Hawaii's answer to the starling. *Peterson's Guide to Western Birds* has a short, convenient section on Hawaii. I also recommend a short book on Hawaiian birds published by the Hawaii chapter of the Audubon Society, available in book shops and souvenir stands throughout the islands" (Brent Warner, Charleston, W. Va). . . . "I enjoyed reading *Aloha, The Magazine of Hawaii and the Pacific* when I was in the islands and decided to take a subscription. One year's subscription is $14.95. I think other readers might also enjoy it. It is published every other month. Write to them at P.O. Box 3260, Honolulu, HI 96801" (Mrs. Beatrice Solomon, Philadelphia, Pa.).

"For books on hiking, camping, bicycling, and other outdoor activities in Hawaii, contact Hawaii Geographic Maps & Books, P.O. Box 1698, Honolulu, HI 96806-1698, or phone toll free 800/323-3723 and request their brochure and books/maps list. They publish *Hawaii Parklands,* which contains 112 pages with 98 color plates, and informative and useful text about parks on six of the major islands. It is an excellent source of information about Hawaii and is available in softcover ($15) or hardcover ($25)" (Willis H. Moore, Hawaii Geographic Society Publications, Honolulu, HI). [*Authors' Note:* Agreed. Photographs are superb.] . . . "Buy the reference maps published by University Press of Hawaii. These are topographic road maps, very detailed and accurate. We bought them at the airport and used them constantly. You might want to buy two maps—one to use and one to frame—it would make a nice inexpensive memento of your trip to Hawaii" (Cheryl Reese and Becky Gardner, Richmond, Wisc.).

"I would hope that you could include Euell Gibbons's *Beachcombers' Guide* and *The Rising Sun* by John Toland, or Gordon Prange's *At Dawn We Slept,* as further enlightenment. These last two are essentially historical rather than political and give quite a challenge and stimulus to some of the historical and geographical highlights to one's interest" (Bob Thompson, Stockton, Calif.).

"For those who really want to get the feel of the history of Hawaii, but who have already read Michener and don't want to get into history books, there is no better source than the three beautifully written novels by O. A. Bushnell, which begin with Captain Cook and carry through until the end of the monarchy. They are exciting, enjoyable, and tremendously informative in a painless way. They are: *The Return of Lono* ($4.95, paper); *Kaawa* ($10, hardback only); and *Molokai* ($5.95, paper). Many public libraries carry all three volumes, but for those who would like to buy them, they are available from the Book Department of *Aloha, The Magazine of Hawaii,* P.O. Box 3260, Honolulu, HI 96801" (William S. McDonald, Houston, Tex). . . . "Thor Heyerdahl's book *Early Man and the Ocean* has an excellent section on Hawaii, pages 164 to 184. Reading these will make visits to the Bishop Museum and the Academy of Arts much more enlightening" (Mrs. Lydia Marie Matz, Lehigh Acres, Fla.).

"I would like to recommend the five beautiful pictorial books by Robert Wenkam; his photography is superb and his thoughts about the people and the environment are really excellent. *Honolulu Is an Island* is surely a book to reminisce with. *Hawaii* has 150 full-color photographs of Kauai, Oahu, Maui, Molokai, Hawaii, and Lanai. *Maui: The Last Hawaiian Place, Kauai and the Park Country of Hawaii,* and *The Big Island Hawaii* are the other three. These books cost about $25 each, but they are available in libraries and it's enjoyable to read them and look at the photographic beauty of Hawaii" (Margaret Niezgoda, Calumet City, Ill.). [*Authors' Note:* Agreed: These are books to treasure.] . . . "I picked up a most interesting historical novel of Hawaii, covering the period from approximately 1820 to 1850, called *To Raise a Nation,* by Mary Cooke, at the airport on the way home. I wish I had read it on the way to Hawaii instead" (Carole McIvor, Calgary, Alberta, Canada). . . . "The best **maps** of Oahu Island are now available from the State of Hawaii, Department of Transportation, Highway Planning Branch, Honolulu. These maps are available to the public at nominal cost. There are also maps available from the Map Information Center, Denver, Colo., prepared by the U.S. Geological Survey" (David C. Moore, Phoenix, Ariz.).

GETTING THERE

What will it cost you to travel to Hawaii? We wish we could tell you precisely, but our crystal ball is cloudy. Ever since the federal government reduced its tight regulation of the airline industry, competition—and massive confusion—has set in. Fares can vary from airline to airline, and even within one airline, depending on when you're going, how long you're staying, whether you make land arrangements through the airlines, and how far in advance you book your ticket. Or fares can vary depending on what new, low-cost gimmick one airline might introduce to beat the competition. But you can rely on this: The airlines want your business, and the 2,400-mile route from California to the Hawaiian Islands is a highly competitive one. A little smart shopping on your part and that of your trusted travel agent will usually turn up a good deal.

1. The Fares

To get the very best deal on a ticket to Hawaii means that you're going to have to do some intensive shopping. Either you or your travel agent—if you have one who will do the work—should get on the phone, call the airlines that serve Honolulu and your area (see below), and find out what the best possible prices are. Don't bother inquiring about first-class, business-class, or full coach fares; what you want are economy-class fares. Continental Airlines, for example, on a one-way trip from Los Angeles to Honolulu on a specific date last summer, offered one-way, first-class fares of $890, business-class fares of $705, full coach fares of $503, and economy fares of just $286! Economy-class fares cover a wide range, depending on the date you wish to travel; they could go from as low as $286 to as high as $502. Remember that you will probably get better rates if you're willing to travel in the middle of the week rather than on weekends, in the fall or at off-peak times rather than during holidays or peak winter vacation months, and paying in advance. These pay-in-advance fares, which are known in the trade as the APEX fare, are very volatile; prices may change from day to day. Depending on bookings, airlines will often open up more discount seats. Some travel restrictions and ticketing penalties apply on deeply discounted fares.

Since Continental Airlines is now the second largest U.S. carrier serving Hawaii (it has been flying there for over 20 years), with over 160 flights weekly and 1,500 employees based in Honolulu, it's an excellent choice. Its major connecting hubs are Denver, Newark, Cleveland, Los Angeles, Boston, and New Orleans; Honolulu is its main Pacific hub. Continental recently made news when it was awarded a new route by the Department of Transportation to fly nonstop to Tokyo; daily 747 flights depart from Houston to Honolulu nonstop, then on to Tokyo nonstop, with a daily reverse flight also on a 747. Continental has also recently expanded its service from Honolulu to Cairns and Brisbane, Queensland, and to Guam. As for fares, Continental frequently offers low-cost promotional fares. And you can save a bundle by booking one of their package deals: Last year, for example, a seven-night stay in Waikiki was available for $419, round trip from Los Angeles, including air fare! Packages to Maui or Kauai are also available. Note that fares vary and restrictions apply, but overall, this is one of the best travel bargains we know. Continental's toll-free number is 800-525-0280; in Honolulu, 808/836-7730.

In case you're wondering about flying on one of the new airlines that seem to crop up every six months or so with bargain fares to the islands, we can only repeat to you what a very wise person in the travel industry has stated: "To be perfectly sure that the airline doesn't go out of business and leave you holding your tickets, fly only on reputable carriers that you know have been in business for at least five years." Sounds like good advice to us.

NAMES AND NUMBERS

These are the airlines that fly into Honolulu: toll-free numbers are given first, when applicable, and then the local (808) numbers when applicable. **American West Airlines,** 800-247-5692; **American Airlines,** 800-433-7300, 526-0044; **Canadian Airlines International,** 800-426-7000, 922-0533; **China Airlines,** 800-227-5118, 536-6951; **Continental Airlines,** 800/525-0280, 836-7730; **Delta Air Lines,** 800/221-1212; **Garuda Indonesia,** 800/826-2829, 945-3791; **Hawaiian Airlines,** 800/367-5320, 537-5100; **Japan Airlines,** 800/525-3663, 521-1441; **Korean Air,** 800/223-1155 (East Coast), 800/421-8200 (West Coast), 923-7302; **Northwest Airlines,** 800/225-2525, 955-2255; **Pan Am,** 800/221-1111, 831-6215; **Philippine Airlines,** 800/435-9725, 536-1928; **Qantas,** 800/227-0290, 836-2461; **Singapore Airlines,** 800/742-3333, 524-6063; **Trans World Airlines,** 800/221-2000; **United Airlines,** 800/241-6523, 547-2211.

DISCOUNT TRAVEL AGENCIES

Sometimes known as "bucket shops" from their English counterparts, these are agencies that, working with wholesale companies, are often able to offer airline discounts. We found five agencies on the West Coast that offer flights to Hawaii at discounts ranging anywhere from 20% to 40%—depending on the season you fly, and upon availability. You may do as well on your own or with your regular travel agent, but it wouldn't hurt to give these people a call and see what they might have for you. Remember that it's very difficult to return these tickets, and many restrictions apply: so once you've bought them, for good or bad, they're all yours. The following agencies offer discount flights to Hawaii: **Sunline Express Holidays,** 210 Post St., San Francisco, CA 94108 (tel. 800/877-2111 or 415/398-2111); **All Unique Travel,** 1030 Georgia St., Vallejo, CA 94590 (tel. 707/648-0237); **Euro-Asia, Inc.,** 4203 East Indian School Rd., Phoenix, AZ 85018 (tel. 602/955-2742); **Community Travel Service,** 5237 College Ave., Oakland, CA 94618 (tel. 415/653-0990).

GROUP TOURS

Some excellent values are available on group tours, for short periods of one or two weeks. Many package options are available, including condominium vacations and multi-island packages. We usually prefer the do-it-yourself brand of travel, but if you do want a group trip, consult your travel agent or airline for a variety of choices.

JET LAG

If you're going all the way through from the East Coast to Honolulu or the neighbor islands in one stretch—about 10 air hours—you'll be crossing at least six time zones, and your normal body rhythms are going to be thrown out of sync. Here are some tips from the experts in avoiding jet lag. First, they advise that several days before your departure, you gradually accommodate your eating and sleeping times to be closer to those of your destination. You'll be heading west, so go to bed a little later each night and sleep a little later in the morning. When you come home, reverse that pattern. Second, avoid smoking, drinking, and heavy eating in flight—another reason to bring your own picnic lunch! You may have heard of the Argonne Anti-Jet-Lag Diet, which alternates feasting and fasting for several days before departure, and is effective for many people. To get a free copy of the program (more than 200,000 cars have been sent out to date), send a stamped, self-addressed envelope to Office of Public Affairs, Argonne National Laboratory, 9700 South Cass Ave., Argonne, IL 60439. Our personal prescription for avoiding jet lag is to stop off at one of the airport hotels in either Los Angeles or San Francisco en route. For years we've enjoyed staying at the **Los Angeles Airport Marriott,** which has a pool set in a magnificent garden and a variety of restaurants, including the very reasonable Fairfield. If you call far enough in advance (tel. toll free 800/228-9290), you may be able to get a Family Plan rate (for at least two people) during the week; weekend rates are always available, and both of these are approximately $69, about half the regular price. After a swim in the pool (or a workout in the exercise room), and a good night's sleep, we board our plane the next morning and arrive in Hawaii refreshed.

THE TRIP BY SHIP

Forget about it. There is no crossing to Hawaii that costs less than the lowest air fares. Only luxury ships now call at Honolulu Harbor.

ANOTHER TIP

Try not to arrive in Hawaii on a weekend, when Honolulu is crowded with visitors from the outer islands. Everything is easier and less crowded on weekdays, especially checking into hotels, and air fares are lower during the week as well.

TIME TRICKS

Don't forget that you'll be flying into yesterday when you head for Hawaii from the U.S. mainland. You pick up an extra five hours in flight (six during daylight saving time) if you're starting from the East Coast, three hours if you begin on the West Coast. Going home, of course, you lose the hours and can find yourself leaving this afternoon and arriving tomorrow morning.

2. Inter-Island Travel

THE FARES

Hawaii has three major inter-island carriers: **Hawaiian Airlines, Aloha Airlines,** and **Discovery Airways.** Hawaii and Aloha are the veterans in the field, having been around for many years. Discovery began service in 1990. The fares are close, give or take a few dollars. Because fares change often, and because all three inter-island carriers offer periodic promotion fares and tie-ins with hotel and car-rental packages, it pays to do some personal research on this, either by calling the airlines directly or by consulting your travel agent before you book. Expect fares to be their highest during peak winter and summer travel periods. Hawaiian offers flights to the major islands for $54.95. The first and last flights of each day are $39.95. If you're going directly to one of the neighbor islands and bypassing Honolulu, you can save money by flying from the West Coast on Hawaiian, which has service from Los Angeles, San Francisco, Seattle, and Las Vegas. The first flight to a neighbor island is free; you can change planes in Honolulu. If you wish to stop in Honolulu first, the fee is $20. Hawaiian is the only major airline to stop at Molokai. Special fares are available for senior citizens, children, and the military. Hawaiian's mileage program, known as "Gold Plus," offers passengers mileage credits that are good for free inter-island transportation, transportation on Hawaiian to the mainland, and also transportation on other cooperating airlines from mainland United States. Gold Plus members may also join Hawaiian's Premier Club and enjoy such extra niceties as free inter-terminal transportation, special check-in and boarding privileges, use of club lounges and free telephones, and priority baggage handling (membership is around $75 for one, $100 for a member and a spouse).

On Aloha Airlines, the regular fare on its all-jet fleet is $54.95. Sunset and sunrise flights are $39.95. A fare of $43.95 is offered for senior citizens and the military, $39.95 for children ages 2 to 11. Aloha also offers first-class service; the fare for this is $74.95. And your Aloha mileage counts toward mileage plus when you fly United Airlines or Canadian Airlines. Aloha is highly regarded by frequent business travelers and rates very low in the area of passenger complaints, according to U.S. Department of Transportation surveys.

Discovery Airlines had just begun service at the time of this writing, and were offering special promotional fares. By the time you read this, rates, which had not yet been determined, will be competitive with Hawaiian and Aloha. Both first-class and coach service are offered. Discovery flies BAe 146 jets, leased from British Aerospace. Its check-in and gates are in the main terminal building, not in the inter-island building.

There are no longer standby flights on any of the airlines.

Should you wish to call the airlines direct, here are their toll-free numbers: Hawaiian Airlines, 800/367-5320; Aloha Airlines, 800/367-5250; Discovery Airways, 800/874-3131.

SCHEDULING SECRETS

Now that the big jets fly directly to Maui, Kauai, and the Big Island, it's not necessary to both arrive at and depart from Honolulu; you can be more flexible with your itinerary. You might, for example, start in Honolulu, travel from there to Kauai, then to Maui, from there to Molokai, and on to Kona, where you pick up your plane for your return flight to Los Angeles or San Francisco. Another routing that we have found very pleasant is to fly directly to Kona from the West Coast, then on to Maui, Molokai, and Kauai, making the last stop Honolulu, and departing from there to home. (Plan it this way if you want peace and quiet first, excitement later.)

---

3. Packing to Save Money

Another important way to save money on your Hawaiian trip is to give careful thought to the clothes you take and the way you pack. First rule is *not* to go on a big shopping spree in advance. If you need to fill out your wardrobe, do it in Hawaii, where the stores are packed with colorful island resort clothes at prices cheaper than those you'll probably pay at home (see Chapter VI).

Second important rule: Pack a light suitcase and take only one piece of luggage per person (you can also carry a small travel bag for reading matter on the plane, then use it later as a beach bag). If you can carry your own bag, you are your own person and not dependent on expensive porters and bellboys and taxis. Having a light bag, a bag with wheels (or at least one of those wheeled luggage carriers), is practically essential, since it is sometimes difficult to locate porters at the airports, and in small hotels you are usually expected to carry your own luggage. If you happen to arrive at a new place without hotel reservations, being able to manage your own luggage will enable you to look around instead of grabbing anything that gives you a chance to put your bags down. Therefore get yourself the lightest suitcase you can buy (the cloth ones are good, roomy bets), and leave at least one-third of the space for bringing back the things you'll buy in Hawaii. It's best to buy all your luggage before you go: It will be more expensive in Hawaii. (If however, despite your best intentions you find you've got just *too much* to carry home, head for one of the inexpensive gift stores (like ABC in Honolulu) and buy yourself one of those soft, standup bags (usually under $25) that you can cram multitudes into.

Most important, don't burden yourself with several large bags. By what we dub the Hammel-Levey Amendment to Parkinson's Law, the contents of a suitcase have a way of expanding to fit the space available.

CONTENTS

What will you need to take with you? Easy does it. It's much simpler to pack for Hawaii than it is for Europe or almost anyplace else. You need only spring or summer clothes and then of the simplest kind. There are no extreme variations in temperature between day and night, so you don't need the usual all-purpose travel coat or overcoat you'd take to Europe or Mexico—unless you're coming from the eastern United States and plan to spend a few days in San Francisco on the way back; then you'll have good use for it. A light raincoat is helpful, and so is a folding umbrella—and let's hope you won't need them! Women will find a stole or shawl useful at night. The only heavy garment that you will require is a warm sweater or hooded parka for exploring the volcano regions on the islands of Hawaii and Maui. Good canvas or other heavy-soled hiking shoes and socks are a must for hiking or for trekking over recent lava flows on Hawaii.

FOR MEN

We're not going to give specifics on what to take, since you know what you like. We will tell you, however, that island dress is extremely casual, and many of our readers say they've never worn a suit in the islands! Some of the fancier places do require a jacket for dinner, however. It's easier to travel with drip-dry shirts and underclothing, but not necessary since the islands are dotted with quick-service launderettes (many apartment-hotels have their own), so you can have a stack of clothes washed and ready to wear in a few hours. Plan on buying a colorful aloha shirt when you're in Hawaii (it's worn outside the trousers and cut a little fuller than the usual sports shirt). You can use it back home for beach or country wear.

FOR WOMEN

Before you begin to pack your bag, you'll want to know a little bit about what women wear in Hawaii. Allow us to introduce you to the muumuu, the most comfortable garment known to woman. Try one and see. They're loose enough to provide their own inner air conditioning, require a minimum of underwear underneath (the girdle industry must be nonexistent in Hawaii), and look pretty enough to flatter almost everybody—especially large women, who look positively graceful in them. (You'll see more than a few of these hefty Polynesian ladies, by the way, a carryover from the days when the alii, the nobility, cultivated fat as a royal status symbol.)

The thing we love most about Hawaiian fashion is that many women wear muumuus or other long dresses outdoors, especially at night. Even though many island women are now extremely fashion conscious and favor the same kinds of spring-summer fashions that might be seen in New York or Paris or San Francisco, the muumuu is still going strong, especially on "Aloha Fridays," when many women wear muumuus to work. It seems Hawaii discovered the maxi back in the days of the missionaries. You'll see full-flowing muumuus (the colorful Hawaiian version of the Mother Hubbards the missionaries forced on the natives); long, slim adaptations of classic Chinese tunics; or, prettiest of all, holomuus, long muumuus, slightly fitted at the waist. (The holoku—a fitted muumuu with a train—is worn mostly on formal occasions.) We strongly urge you to buy a long dress while you're in the islands. You can use it later for an at-home gown, and you'll have a great time walking through the streets with it swishing gracefully at your ankles. Be sure that the muumuu at least touches the instep if you want to look like a kamaaina. And unless you already own a couple of shifts, it's not a bad idea to wait until you get to

Hawaii to pick up a few of the local equivalents: the short muumuu, or island-style sundress. The selection is tremendous (see Chapter VI), and the prices are at all levels. Of course, many women visitors live in pants and shorts in Hawaii, and there's no reason why you shouldn't. It's just that muumuus are so much more a part of the island scene.

So pack your bathing suits (or get a bikini in Hawaii), your favorite casual clothes, a sturdy pair of sandals or sneakers (maybe some hiking boots if you're going to go out on the trails), a lightweight woolen sweater, stole, or throw to wear in the evenings, a warm jacket if you're going up into the mountains. Leave your stockings at home; only businesswomen seem to wear them. You'll live in sandals or Japanese zoris, or go barefoot the way many islanders do, especially indoors. (Island kids, by the way, wear shoes as little as possible, usually not even to school, with resulting household crises when they need to find their shoes to go to a movie or restaurant.) The idea, in summer, is to fortify yourself against the heat by wearing open shoes and sleeveless dresses. Leave all your city cottons and little dark dresses at home. In the winter months, when Hawaiian weather can be springlike, pants and tops are practically a uniform. And T-shirts are worn everywhere, year 'round. Wash-and-dry clothes are helpful but not crucial since the launderettes are so handy. As for jewelry, the only kind most people wear is island craft, shell or coral necklaces and the like, which can be picked up in any gift shop. The most beautiful jewelry of island women is the natural kind: blossoms in the hair, flower leis around the neck.

A final word on Hawaiian clothing: We don't want to give you the impression that island women never get dressed up. They do, especially for fancy social events. In downtown Honolulu, businesswomen wear more conservative summer clothing, and many men wear regular business suits with tuck-in shirts. But that's for work—not fun.

SUNDRIES

It's not necessary to bring a travel iron from home: most hotels have boards and irons for guests. Get plastic bottles for your liquid toilet articles; they won't break and they take up less space. Seal perfume bottles with wax for plane flights. Get little packets of cold-water soap and scatter them in odd corners of your suitcase. The plastic clotheslines, complete with miniature clothespins and soap, sold in most department stores, are very, very handy. Those inflatable or plastic hangers are good to have too, since you can't always count on finding wooden hangers on which to drip-dry your clothes in an inexpensive hotel. Disposable wash-up tissues are nice to carry with you, particularly on long plane or auto trips.

HOW TO PACK

Everyone's got his or her own theory on this, but ours is simply to put all the heavy things on the bottom—shoes, books, bulky objects—and lay everything else neatly on top. Then, roll underwear, socks, soft articles into the corners and empty spots (inside shoes, for instance). We think it also helps to have plastic bags for organizing underwear, handkerchiefs, sundries. You'll need one large one at any rate for carrying damp bathing suits. Folding tissue into your garments does help avoid wrinkles. And here's a tip we learned on how to pack a wide-brimmed sun hat. Place the hat upside down in the bag, then fill the crown with soft items, and tuck other soft items under the brim. This way you avoid either having to wear the hat on the plane trip home or possibly ruining it by folding it (we've ruined quite a few in our time).

SAFETY FIRST

Let's hope your suitcase won't get stolen, lost, or misdirected on the airlines to Australia. But it doesn't hurt to take a few sensible precautions, especially if you're flying in a huge group where bags often get shipped to the wrong hotels and you may have to go without them for several hours. Always tag your bags, inside and out, with your name and home address. Inside each bag, put a note that gives your address in Hawaii; if your bag should arrive at somebody else's hotel, it can easily be sent to yours. Carry with you your valuables, medicines, prescriptions, cameras, and so on —anything that you can't easily replace if your bag is among the missing.

READERS' TRAVEL SUGGESTIONS: "First-time visitors to Oahu (and even those who have been there before but are somewhat vague on their geography) will find a little folder titled 'Map of Waikiki—Hotels and Points of Interest,' available free at any **HVB** office, invaluable as they attempt to sort out the vast wealth of free tourist literature they encounter on street corners and in hotel lobbies. Major and minor hotels are indexed both alphabetically and by map reference number. All streets, no matter how short, are shown and clearly labeled; and the longer ones have street number indicators to help you locate the exact block where a nonhotel attraction (such as a restaurant) is located" (Leilani Moyers, Patterson, N.Y.).

"Keep in mind that winter is the rainy season and it's quite possible that you won't be able to 'sun at the beach' for a few days in a row. We went to the movies, tours, and malls. Luckily, when that was running out, the weather improved. But it's a good thing to keep this in mind so you won't be in for a big disappointment when you see it pouring in Paradise. . . . And remember not to overpack! We did, and as a result we had to 'stuff' souvenirs into our luggage and one cup broke. Bring shorts, one pair of pants, and T-shirts. Anything you forgot you can buy cheaply at drugstores such as Long's, Holiday Mart, or Pay N Save" (Tracy White, Madison, Wisc.). . . . "Bring binoculars—we had a pair of mini-binoculars and used them constantly to watch everything from the mountain goats at Waimea Canyon on Kauai and birds from our lanai to humpback whales on the Big Island. And bring a good 35mm camera with adjustable lens if at all possible: We only had an automatic 35mm and could not capture how awesome the scenery really was!" (Cheryl Reese and Becky Gardner, Richmond, Wisc.).

"Agricultural inspection is now performed by X-ray machine and not by hand as in the past. I had returned to the islands after a four-year absence, and when it was time to go home, packed my film in my suitcase. My heart sank as I saw the agricultural inspection being done by machine and the suitcases were not opened, as they had been in the past. Luckily, my film was not noticeably hurt, but I worried until the pictures were developed and in my hands" (Cindy A. Lewis, Denver, Colo.). . . . "I estimated to people who asked me how much it cost doing it 'your way' that we spent about $1,000 per person per week, including *everything* (souvenirs, air fare, film, and developing 29 rolls of film, food, etc.). Of course, if the air fare is prorated over 23 days, it becomes cheaper per day" (Patricia Ann Schultz, St. Joseph, Mich.).

"I visited Hawaii several years ago, and this year I decided to brighten up the winter by subscribing to the Honolulu Sunday newspaper. Perhaps other readers would enjoy this paper, either to help plan a trip or to read during a cold winter. You can get all the information about subscribing by mail to the *Sunday Star-Bulletin and Advertiser* by writing to Hawaii Newspaper Agency, Circulation Dept., P.O. Box 3350, Honolulu, HI 96801" (John Meyer, Sterling, Ill.). . . . "A word of caution: Although we were very careful about leaving anything valuable in our car, we had no choice on one occasion, and someone broke into the trunk of the car and took two canvas bags containing all of our newly purchased snorkeling equipment, plus beach and swimwear. The policeman said the trunk can be opened with a screwdriver without damaging the lock. This theft occurred one block from the Pioneer Inn in Lahaina while we were on a sunset dinner sail" (H. Emil Johnson, Darien, Conn.).

"We made the mistake of going to Oahu in late June. Unless you like zillions of teenagers, don't travel to Hawaii then. It seemed that every high school graduation class in California, bar none, was there. They took over everything. The only escape was the Hale Koa, the military hotel" (Don and Nancy Gossard, Bellevue, Wash.). . . . "It is amazing how finely the Hawaiians have honored their ability to handle great mobs of tourists so that you seldom feel taken advantage of or intruded upon. A great deal of this is probably due to the pride people take in doing their work and in their state, from the lowest paid waitress to the captain of the DC-10 that takes you there. We are sure that Hawaii has its grim sides, since no place is paradise, but with a little common sense the visitor can enjoy the islands to a greater degree than most other places" (Robert and Jean Carroll, Helena, Mont.).

"We brought two round plastic containers from home to fill with ice to put in our insulated lunch bag to help keep our lunches cold. We didn't have to purchase straw mats for the beach as a lot of people did, as I had packed a large sheet for our "beach blanket." Certainly, a lot easier to pack for our trip home. A folding suitcase we had packed came in handy for all the souvenirs we had bought. Our most indispensable item turned out to be a ten-foot length of rope. Since most of our previous traveling has been camping, it just seemed like a natural thing to pack. It was used to secure the trunk of a small car when all the luggage wouldn't fit, to hang wet bathing suits outside, and last, to tie a suitcase when the lock broke" (Beverly Russo, N. Massapequa, N.Y.).

"T-shirts are very much a part of the island scene, worn by every age, it appears. I think it would be more interesting if people wore a T-shirt with the name of their hometown, or area, on it, instead of the local Hawaiian ones; that way tourists could say 'Hi' to anyone wearing a name from their own hometown and probably end up enjoying a great chat. We did see the odd person wearing a 'hometown' T-shirt, and noticed the way passersby obviously read it" (Joy E. Deeks, Victoria, B.C., Canada).

"A terrific packing idea is an inflatable raft. It takes up no room in the suitcase, but can be used to lie on the sand and float in the water" (Mr. and Mrs. R. Bivona, Massapequa, N.Y.). . . . "For an inexpensive souvenir to take back home, just bring a cassette radio recorder and some blank tapes; you can record Hawaiian music from the local radio stations" (Roz and Jim Morino, Colma, Calif.).

"In three weeks in the islands I broke my watchband, my sunglasses' earpiece, my tote pocketbook strap, and my camera carrying-case strap. Therefore, my suggestion is to purchase carrying cases with secure handles, preferably straps that continue all around the bag, including the bottom. This is important for any type of vinyl or plastic bag that will be used for carrying more than a hanky. . . . I carried my film (40 rolls) in film-shield bags, which are lead-lined. They can be found in camera stores. Because I made several inter-island flights and went through numerous X-ray machines, the film was protected from the rays. They try to insist it won't damage the film, but professional photographers recommend using the bags because of the cumulative effect of the rays. Where possible I had them hand-examine the film carriers. Some places I was required to remove them from my baggage for examination because the lead lining made them show up as a black, unidentifiable blob on the machine" (Jane Kenney, Kingston, N.H.).

"It's nice to go to the airport early and ask for seating arrangements, as the first row of seats behind the first class has more leg room, is less noisy, and has less vibration from the engines. We left three transistor radios at home, but wanted one so badly that we bought one in Honolulu. We recommend one for the packing list" (Mr. and Mrs. Rodney Phillips, Seattle, Wash.). [*Authors' Note:* More and more letters arrive every year agreeing about transistor radios. Many hotels include neither radio nor television, and the cost of renting a radio is about $3.50 a week. As for going to the airport early to get good seats, it's usually not necessary: try asking your travel agent to reserve seats for you or do so yourself by phoning the airlines a few days before your flight. Unless you've done so, three or four of you traveling together during a busy season may have to be split up, or you may not get to sit in the cabin (smoking or nonsmoking, movie or not) that you prefer.] . . . "I would like to suggest to your readers that they either bring with them or buy as soon as they get to the islands a can of good insect repellent. We were at Waimea Falls Park in June (which wasn't really all that great) and even though we never saw any, we were eaten up by insects. Our tram guide had sprayed himself and at the time I couldn't imagine why, until later when we started itching and scratching. This also happened to us on Kauai when we took the evening Wailua River Cruise to the Fern Grotto. At least that time we saw them flying around" (Muriel P. Maloney, Huntington Beach, Calif.).

"My husband and I agree that a tape recorder is a must for trips. We taped the songs and commentary at the Fern Grotto cruise on Kauai and plan to use the tapes as part of a background to our slides. We also taped our impressions of each day's events before we went to bed. It's so much easier and quicker than keeping a diary, and a great deal of fun to replay" (Joann Leonard, Los Angeles, Calif.). . . . "Let me thank the reader who suggested taking a featherweight, *hooded* nylon waterproof shell jacket—that saved my day many, many times. It was for those sudden showers that it was invaluable during our trip. I had made a special shopping trip before I left home to buy the jacket and found it much better to carry and use than a plastic raincoat; it folds into such a neat package that I could tuck it into my purse. Another helpful item we took with us was a pair of binoculars, and we were the envy of lots of fellow travelers viewing the Waimea Canyon on Kauai, Haleakala on Maui, and the volcanic action on Hawaii —it was very active at that time. They have telescopes at some of the places, but the lines are long! Binoculars need not be expensive or heavy to carry; there are many compact glasses available" (Mrs. Lee Morgan, Vacaville, Calif.).

"In the ten days we were in the islands, my husband didn't have to wear a suit once. Visitors might be safe to bring one, but one is more than enough" (Terry and Lou Cicalese, South Ozone Park, N.Y.). . . . "One item that made our trip particularly enjoyable was a plaid insulated bag. It easily fit into my suitcase on the way over. We thoroughly enjoyed shopping for foods in Hawaii. The produce department was great fun. Each day we packed a lunch, which stayed fresh in our insulated container until we found a delightful place to stop for lunch. This bag saved us considerable time and money. We used it to transport leftover foods when we island hopped. And on the way home we stuffed it with souvenirs" (Marilyn C. Haley, Watertown, Mass.).

And now, after a budget flight, we land in the islands. It's time to tour Hawaii on $60 a day.

II

HONOLULU FAST FACTS

Here's a capsule list of names and numbers to help you find your way around town. Some is a recap of what you'll find explained in more depth in other chapters, and some of it is new.

AAA HAWAII: The local office of the American Automobile Association is at 590 Queen St. (tel. 528-2600; road service, 537-5544).

AIRPORT: Honolulu International Airport, about five miles from Waikiki, is easily reached by TheBUS no. 19 or TheBUS no. 20 from Waikiki and Ala Moana Center, without luggage. With luggage, try Airport Motor Coach (tel. 926-4747). For visitor information at the airport, call 836-6413.

ANIMAL HOSPITAL: Twenty-four-hour emergency care for pets is provided at **Care Animal Hospital,** 1135 Kapahulu Ave. (tel. 737-7910).

AREA CODE: All telephone numbers in the state of Hawaii have one telephone area code: 808.

BABYSITTERS: Check first at your hotel desk. You can also try **Aloha Babysitting Service** (tel. 732-2029).

BANKING HOURS: Normal hours are 8:30am to 3 or 3:30pm, until 6pm on Friday.

BUSINESS HOURS: Most office workers in Hawaii are at their desks by 8am, sometimes even earlier, and it's *pau hana* (finish work) at 4 or 5pm, the better to get in an afternoon swim or a round of golf. Hawaii may be the only place where even executives can be reached by 8:30am!

BUS INFORMATION: Call **MTL,** which operates TheBUS, at 531-1611.

CAMPING PERMITS: For information about camping permits for city parks, phone 523-4525; for state parks, phone 548-7455.

CAR RENTALS: Major car-rental companies, which rent automobiles on all four major islands, include **Dollar Rent-A-Car,** 1600 Kapiolani Blvd, Honolulu, HI 96814 (tel. 944-1544 or toll free 800/367-7006). **Alamo Rent-A-Car,** 3055 N.

Nimitz Hwy. (tel. 833-4585 or 924-4444, or toll free 800/327-9633); **Budget Rent-A-Car,** 2379 Kuhio Ave. (tel. 922-3600, or toll free 800/5270-0700); **Tropical Rent-A-Car Systems,** 550 Paiea St. (tel. 836-1041, or toll free 800/367-5140); **Avis Rent-A-Car,** Honolulu International Airport (tel. 834-5836, or toll free 800/831-8000); **Hertz Rent-A-Car,** 233 Keawe St., Room 625 (tel. 836-2511). See Chapter V for details.

CLIMATE: Among the best in the world. Hawaii's climate is tropical, which means that temperatures average about 75° Fahrenheit, rarely going more than six or seven degrees above or below that point. In summer months, the temperature is usually in the 80s; winter months, November through March, can bring slightly lower temperatures and occasional rain and storms.

CONSUMER PROTECTION: To reach the Office of Consumer Protection, phone 548-2540.

DENTISTS: **Dental Care Centers of Hawaii** offers 24-hour emergency service. It has many locations around the island; addresses can be found in the telephone book. The after-hours number to call is 488-5200. . . . **Hawaii Family Dental Center** is conveniently located at Sears at the Ala Moana Shopping Center, and has a number of doctors on hand who can provide speedy treatment at reasonable cost. Phone 944-0011.

DISABLED SERVICES: **Handicabs of the Pacific** provides private transportation and tours (tel. 524-3866). For free brochures describing accessibility features of Hawaii's major hotels, shopping malls, beach parks, and sightseeing and visitor attractions, on all islands, write to **Commission on Persons With Disabilities,** 5 Waterfront Plaza, Suite 210, 500 Ala Moana Blvd., Honolulu, HI 96813 (tel. 548-7606). Enclose a legal-size, self-addressed, stamped envelope for each brochure desired.

DOCTORS: House calls are available from **DOC** (Doctors on Call), 24 hours a day, seven days a week (tel. 926-4777), charging $75. For health-care information and physician-referral service, call **Ask-A-Nurse,** a free, 24-hour service of Queen's and Castle Medical Center. Dial 533-NURS for assistance. From the outer islands, phone toll free, 800/342-5901. Hearing impaired: 523-9609.

DRINKING AGE: Sorry, kids, the legal drinking age in Hawaii is now 21.

DRY CLEANERS: Quick service is available from **Al Phillips the Cleaner** in the Waikiki Market Place, 2310 Kuhio Ave. (tel. 923-1971). Open 7am to 6pm daily, 10am to 4pm Sundays.

EMERGENCY: Dial 911 for fire, ambulance, or police; if you cannot reach 911, dial 0 and the operator will assist you.

HAWAII VISITORS BUREAU: The **HVB** is located at 2270 Kalakaua Ave., 8th floor (tel. 923-1811). There is also a booth at Ala Moana Center.

HOLIDAYS: Just about all businesses and banks will be closed on the major holidays: Christmas, New Year's, Easter Sunday, Thanksgiving Day. In addition to the legal holidays observed throughout the United States—Memorial Day, July 4th, Labor Day, Columbus Day, Election Day, and Veterans Day—there are specific Hawaiian holidays on which many business establishments close: Prince Kuhio Day (March 26), Kamehameha Day (June 11), and Admission Day (the third Friday in August).

HOSPITAL EMERGENCY ROOM: **Queen's Medical Center,** 1301 Punchbowl, has 24-hour emergency-room service and offers outstanding trauma care (tel. 547-4311). On the windward side, it's Castle Medical Center, 640 Ulukahiki in Kailua (tel. 263-5500).

LAUNDRY: Should your hotel not provide washers and dryers (most do), try **Waikiki Laundromats,** with four central locations. They also provide irons, ironing boards, and hair dryers. Addresses are 2335 Kalakaua Ave., across from the International Market Place; Outrigger West Hotel, 2330 Kuhio Ave.; Outrigger East Hotel, 150 Kaiulani Ave.; and Edgewater Hotel, 2168 Kalia Rd. These are open daily from 7am to 10pm. The location at the Coral Seas Hotel, 250 Lewers St. (tel. 923-2057), is open around the clock.

ON CALL: This is a new telephone service that provides information on a variety of subjects, including visitor information. First you dial 296-1818; when that answers, you have a multitude of choices, including Visitor Information for Honolulu and Waikiki, 1638; for the rest of Oahu, 1639; for Maui, 1640; for the Big Island, 1641; for Kauai, 1642; for the rest of the state, 1643. Other choices: World News, 1504; Stock Report, 1505; Business News, 1506; Road Conditions, 1663; National Sports, 1407; Weather (local), 1671; Horoscope, 1763; Special Island Events, 1631; Major Honolulu Events, 1632. Note that this service is free on Oahu only when you have a pushbutton phone; it is not free from a pay phone or if there is a hotel surcharge. If you are interested in the rest of the services available, look for a GTE insert in your hotel-room phone book. If not, ask at the desk.

PHARMACIES: In Waikiki, try the **Outrigger Pharmacy** at the Outrigger Hotel, 2335 Kalakaua Ave. (tel. 923-2529), or the **Kuhio Pharmacy,** Outrigger West Hotel, 2330 Kuhio Ave. (tel. 923-4466); at Ala Moana Shopping Center, **Long's Drug Store,** 1450 Ala Moana (tel. 941-4433). **The Pillbox Pharmacy,** 1133 Eleventh Ave. (tel. 737-1777), is open six days a week until 11pm (Sunday from 7 to 11pm), and provides 24-hour emergency service (for prescriptions only).

POISON CENTER: 941-4411.

POST OFFICE: The main post office in Honolulu is at 3600 Aolele St. (tel. 423-3930), open 8am to 7:30pm Monday to Friday, from 8am to 2:30pm on Saturday. In Waikiki it's at 330 Saratoga Rd., next to Fort DeRussy (tel. 941-1062), open 8am to 4:30pm Monday to Friday, 9am to 11:30am on Saturday.

PUBLIC PHONES: Cost of a local call is 25¢ from any one part of an island to another. Inter-island calls are billed as long distance. Be aware that most hotels impose a surcharge on all calls.

SAFETY: In general, the U.S. is about as safe as most other countries, but there are "danger zones" in the tourist areas that should be approached only with extreme caution.

As a general rule, isolated areas such as gardens and parking lots should be avoided after dark. Elevators, rest rooms at bus and train stations, and public-transport systems in off-hours, particularly between 10pm and 6am, are also potential crime scenes. You should drive through decaying neighborhoods with your car doors locked and the windows closed. Never carry on your person valuables like jewelry or large sums of cash; traveler's checks are much safer.

SHOPPING MALLS: Most shopping malls are open Monday to Friday from 9 or 10am to 9pm, on Saturday until 5pm, and for a shorter period on Sunday, usually until 4pm. Individual establishments at these malls will vary their hours, some closing earlier than others.

SUNDRIES: **ABC Discount Stores** offers a little bit of everything one might need under one roof, from suntan lotion to sandwiches, from groceries to gifts, from liquor to laundry detergent, from postcards to photo processing and film, and much more, all at bargain prices. There are 30 ABCs in town, and most of them are open from 7am to midnight. Walk a block or two from where you are and you'll find one. The **7-11 Food Stores** now have almost 50 shops on Oahu; two convenient locations are at 1901 Kalakaua Ave. and 707 Kapahulu Ave. They carry everything from grocery and toiletry items to pantyhose, hot food, soft drinks, etc. Open 24 hours.

SURF REPORT: 836-1952.

TIME ZONES: From the East Coast of the United States to Hawaii, one crosses five time zones. That means that when it's noon Hawaiian Standard Time, it's 5pm Eastern Standard Time, 4pm Central, 3pm Mountain, and 2pm Pacific. Hawaii does not convert to Daylight Saving Time as the rest of the nation does, so from May through October, noon in Hawaii would mean 6pm Eastern, 5pm Central, and so on.

VISITOR INFORMATION: **Hawaii Visitors Bureau,** 2270 Kalakaua Ave., 8th floor (tel. 923-1811); they also have a booth at Ala Moana Center.

WEATHER REPORT: In the Honolulu area, call 833-2849; for the rest of Oahu, phone 836-0121; for the Hawaiian waters, dial 836-3921.

III

HONOLULU: ORIENTATION AND HOTELS

1. HOTELS IN WAIKIKI
2. HOTELS IN DOWNTOWN HONOLULU
3. HOTELS IN WINDWARD OAHU

As you've already learned, most planes and ships going to the Hawaiian Islands land first on the island of Oahu and deposit you in or near the capital city of Honolulu. For those of us on a budget, that's a marvelously appropriate choice, because Oahu happens to be the cheapest of all the Hawaiian Islands—and one of the most fascinating to boot.

THE ISLAND ITSELF

Oahu means "the gathering place" in Hawaiian, and no other name could be so apt. Although it's merely the third largest of the islands in size (40 miles long, 26 miles wide), it boasts the most people (three-quarters of a million, and more arriving all the time), the most skyscrapers, the most construction, the most schools, hospitals, radio and television stations—and the most tourists. Honolulu, the capital city, is the center of island life, the metropolis of which youngsters from the other islands dream, a tremendous military stronghold (approximately one-quarter of the island is owned by the military, and defense is a major industry), a bustling boom town, and a cosmopolitan center plunked down in the middle of the Pacific Ocean.

Just about ten minutes away from downtown Honolulu is **Waikiki Beach,** a favorite resort of Hawaiian royalty long before the word "tourist" was invented. For the visitor, this is an ideal situation; it's as if Mexico City were just ten minutes away from Acapulco, Paris a short bus ride from the Riviera. You can, with such geography, have the best of both worlds—as much beach or city, laziness or excitement, as you choose.

The island is dominated by two mountain ranges: the Waianae, along the west coast, and the Koolaus, which form the spectacular backdrop to the city of Honolulu. On the other side of the Koolaus is **Windward Oahu,** which is what islanders are referring to when they talk of going to the country. Commuters tunnel through the mountains to pretty little suburbs that are developing here as the population booms

For the visitor, it's the closest thing you'll see—if you don't get to the neighbor islands—of rural Hawaii: tiny plantation villages, miles of red earth planted with pineapple and sugarcane, a breathtaking succession of emerald beaches, and gorgeous trails for riding and hiking. But we'll get to that later. First, let's get you settled in Waikiki, which in all likelihood will be your center of operations in Honolulu.

ARRIVAL

Honolulu International Airport is one of the world's largest and busiest airports. It is about five miles out of town. Although it's easy enough to hop right on TheBUS no. 20 Hickam-Waikiki that goes from the terminal to the beach area (fare: 60¢), there is one major problem: The bus has no special section for luggage; your bag must not take up any extra space. So unless you're traveling extremely light, or picking up a car at the airport, your best bet is to take the Grayline Airporter bus that leaves from the lower level of the airport, $5 one way. Regular taxi fare into town runs around $20. Getting back to the airport is also easy: Airport Motor Coach (tel. 926-4747) and Waikiki Express (tel. 942-2177) will pick you up at your hotel about two hours before plane time and deliver you to the airport for a charge of $5.

If you're planning to rent a car, the rates are usually cheaper at places in town than at the airport. Better yet, make your arrangements in advance at one of the less-expensive car agencies in town (see Chapter IV).

GETTING YOUR DIRECTIONAL SIGNALS

In order to get your bearings, you should know that no one ever refers to directions in the old-fashioned north-south, east-west way out here. Since the islands sit in a kind of slanted direction on the map, those terms just wouldn't make much sense.

This is how it's done in Hawaii. Everything toward the sea is **makai** (mah-kye); everything toward the mountains is **mauka** (mow-kah). The other directions are **Diamond Head** (roughly eastward) and **Ewa** (roughly westward), named after two of the major landmarks of the city. Once you move out beyond Diamond Head, roughly eastward directions are referred to as **Koko Head** (Aina Haina is Koko Head of Kalani Valley, for example). Once you learn how to use these simple terms, you'll be well on the way to becoming a kamaaina yourself.

HOTELS

Now, with the preliminaries done, we arrive at the initial, all-important, make-or-break project of your Hawaiian vacation—finding a good but inexpensive hotel. As we've discussed in our introduction, inflation is rampant in Hawaii—as it is everywhere else. Many of the cozy little guesthouses that used to enable budget tourists to live comfortably on peanuts some years ago have been torn down as part of the master plan for upgrading Waikiki. In their place, new, more expensive structures have been built. (Some of the remaining establishments are in such a state of neglect that we won't bother mentioning them here.) However—and this is good news—because of the tremendous number of accommodations in Waikiki, it is still possible to find plenty of good rooms that are reasonably priced.

For the purpose of a $60-a-day budget, we will presume that you are part of a traveling twosome, and that between the two of you, you have a total of $120 to spend on a room and meals. If you want to stay on the low side of this budget, check out our selections under "Bargain Beauties." This section covers rooms that go for $50 a night or less for two. If you can afford to spend more, then consider the listings under "The Good Buys." These rooms begin at $50 and go to $60 and $70 and up. Whatever is left over from the money you spend on your room can go for food. Of course, if there are more than two of you traveling in a party, or if you are staying in Honolulu for more than a week or two, you can realize considerable savings on these figures.

Whichever your budget, you will be living sensibly and pleasantly—and far

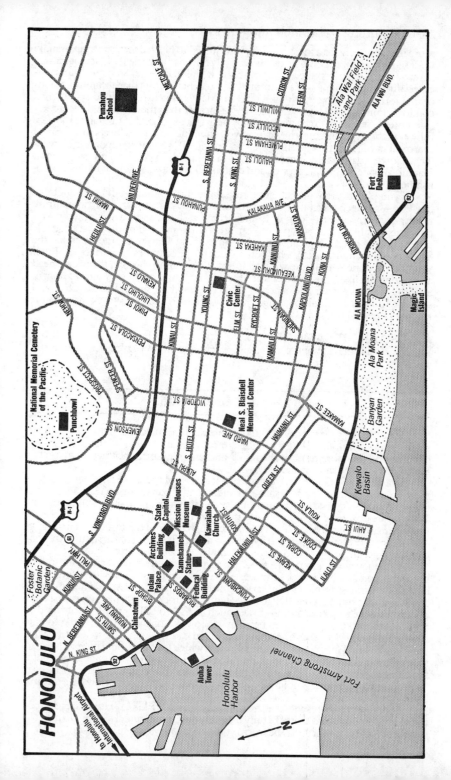

more inexpensively than most tourists, who are led to believe that a hotel in Waikiki under $100 a day just doesn't exist. It certainly does exist, particularly at that Hawaiian wonder of wonders: the apartment-hotel with kitchenette. So many tourists—especially family groups—are enamored of kitchenette units that accommodations of this sort have sprung up all over Waikiki. Many of them are individually owned condominium units. Almost always, they're cheaper than the rooms in the large seaside hotels; they have excellent locations near the beach and mountains; they are fully available to transients; they permit you to reduce expenses by cooking at least one meal in (dishes and utensils are always provided); and most important, they offer what we regard as the most relaxing and enjoyable type of accommodation in Hawaii. We offer names, addresses, and descriptions of several dozens of these establishments below.

If you plan to arrive in Hawaii during the summer season—June through Labor Day—advance reservations are a good idea. They are essential anytime during the peak winter season—roughly from December 20 to April 15. (During the winter, returnees often reserve up to a year in advance at some of the most desirable places). While not so imperative at other times of the year, reservations remain the best way of obtaining exactly what you want at the price you can afford to pay. But if you haven't done your homework, all is not lost. Thumb through the pages ahead and phone the likely possibilities from the airport. Or park your traveling companion and suitcases at a seaside bench in Waikiki (get off the bus at Kuhio Beach) and set out to do some serious scouting. That way you won't collapse with exhaustion at the first hotel you find.

A WORD ABOUT CAMPING

For details on camping permits and where to camp on Oahu, see Chapters II and IX.

---

1. Hotels in Waikiki

Practically all tourists stay in Waikiki, mecca of the malihinis. This is a relatively small area of Honolulu, but within it are concentrated most of the town's best beaches, and therefore most of the hotels and entertainment facilities. Downtown Honolulu is only a short bus ride away.

As a point of orientation, remember that most of the fancy hotels are located right on the beach and on Kalakaua Avenue, the main drag; between Kalakaua and the Ala Wai Boulevard (which marks most of the makai and mauka boundaries of Waikiki) are dozens of tree-lined pretty streets containing the bulk of the smaller and less expensive hotels. Waikiki itself is small enough that you can easily walk from any one of these hotels to the beach; they are also near each other, so you should have no trouble in getting from one to another if you have to do some hotel hunting.

A further word about prices: As we've pointed out above, prices are often cheaper if you stay for a week or more. Also, they can go up or down according to business pressures, so prices may vary slightly from these figures, gathered in mid-1990, but give or take a few dollars, they will be your best hotel buys on the island. Almost all hotels up their rates—by as much as $10 to $20 per unit—during the busy winter months. But remember that in slow seasons you may be able to get rooms at lower prices than the going rates; you can do especially well on weekly rentals. The hotel may eliminate maid service (which is costly), but you may be able to get a very decent apartment for a low price. Please note that we are not responsible for changes in prices: We simply quote the figures and projections hotel owners give us. In addition, and unless otherwise stated by us, all rooms listed below have private bath.

Since most tourists spend far less than a month in Waikiki, we have not covered the apartment buildings that take only monthly or seasonal rentals; if you do plan to stay for at least a month, it may be worth your while to investigate them, too. And, of course, many of the apartment-hotels listed here will accept guests for several months or more.

HOTEL TAX

We're sorry to have to break it to you. Hawaii's hotel room tax is now a hefty 9.43%.

THE BARGAIN BEAUTIES

Although the price range in this category is modest—averaging around $50 for a double room—the variety of accommodations is surprisingly wide. They range from simple motel-like apartment buildings to graceful small hotels featuring pools, lovely tropical grounds, air conditioning, private phones, and resort-living comfort. We've divided these hotels, and the ones in "The Good Buys" section to follow, into three general areas: **Diamond Head Waikiki,** that part of town closest to Kuhio Beach and Kapiolani Park; **Central Waikiki,** the area centering, roughly, around the International Market Place; and **Ewa Waikiki,** the section near the Hilton Hawaiian Village Hotel and Reef Hotel and the closest area to downtown Honolulu. Two additional subdivisions of the last will be called **Near the Ala Wai** and **Near Ala Moana.** Remember that all these areas are within a few blocks' walking or a short bus distance of each other and all are comparable in terms of comfort and convenience. And they're all near the beach.

Diamond Head Waikiki

We'll begin with an old standby in this part of town, the **Royal Grove Hotel,** 151 Uluniu Ave., Honolulu, HI 96815 (tel. 923-7691), one of the prettiest of Waikiki's small hotels. The six-story pink concrete building is about three minutes away from Kuhio Beach, but if you're really lazy you can dunk in the tiny pool right on the grounds. All told, the Royal Grove has about 85 rooms and a widely varying price range: You can get a studio (single or double) from $30 to $50, a studio with kitchenette starting at $36.50, a kitchenette unit with private lanai at $46 to $55—all air-conditioned. One-bedroom apartments average $65 to $90, and it's $10 for an extra person in the room. The accommodations become fancier as prices go up, but all are nicely furnished and comfortable, have tub-shower facilities, and the kitchens are all electric. Subject to availability, you get a day's charge off the weekly rate if you stay for seven consecutive nights or longer between April and November 30. Round-the-clock desk service, twice-weekly or weekly maid service, a health-food shop/restaurant, and a good pizza parlor with outdoor tables are other pluses. Winter sees Canadian and Midwestern families here for long stays. Over the years, readers continue to write to comment on the friendliness of the owners, the Fong family, who frequently have potluck dinners and parties so that everyone can get acquainted. Lots of aloha for a small price at this one.

The Fongs also rent a number of units at the lovely **Pacific Monarch Hotel and Condominium,** just across the street, at higher prices. These are comfortable, spacious, and wonderfully set up for family living. Inquire about these when you make your reservations.

The **Continental Surf,** 2426 Kuhio Ave., Honolulu, HI 96815 (tel. 922-2755), is an attractive 140-room, 22-story, high-rise, with a big, airy lobby and comfortable rooms. The rooms all have color TV, telephone, and individually controlled air conditioning, but no lanais. The decor is tasteful Polynesian, using earthy browns and golds. A complimentary Budget Rent-A-Car is included (subject to availability) in the room rate, and parking on the premises is available for a nominal fee. Considering all this, prices are reasonable: from April 1 through December 12, standard and superior rooms cost $47 and $54, single or double; the rest of the year, they are $61 and $68. Half the hotel's rooms have nicely equipped kitchenettes: these rent for $62 during the off-season, $76 in peak season. One-bedroom suites with kitchenettes rent for $94—for up to four people—during the low season, $121 during the high season. An extra person is charged $15 a day, but children under 12 may stay free with their parents if they use existing bedding. The Continental Surf has no pool, but the beach is just two blocks away. For reservations, call toll free 800/367-5004 from mainland United States and from Canada; the free FAX number is 800/477-2329.

Some of the most reasonable prices in this close-to-the-beach area are offered by the modest little **Waikiki Prince Hotel,** 2431 Prince Edward St., Honolulu, HI 96815 (tel. 922-1544). James Patey, the personable manager, took over this older, six-story, 30-unit hotel, about six years ago, and he has been working steadily to improve it: furnishings are acceptable; there is air conditioning and color cable TV in all the rooms; there are new drapes, bedspreads, pots and pans in the 20 rooms that have kitchenettes. The location, however, needs no improvement: It's right behind the Hyatt Regency Hotel, just two short blocks from Kuhio Beach. The hotel is very popular with foreigners (about 75% of the clientele), especially with the Japanese; it received a four-star rating within the budget class from a leading Japanese tourist guide. And many students stay here when school is out. There are no phones, but a buzzer system gets you your messages; rooms are cleaned every three or four days, towels are changed every day. Rates, which include the 9.43% hotel tax, are as follows: from April 1 to December 19, a small room with no kitchen is $31 a day, $215 a week; a small room with kitchenette is $37 a day, $250 a week; and a larger studio with kitchenette is $43 a day, $290 a week. From December 20 to March 31, the rates are $36 and $245, $40 and $270, and $46 and $305 respectively. The rates are for either single or double occupancy.

Hopefully, by the time you read this, the Waikiki Prince will have acquired a 24-room building, which will have similarly affordable prices; it will be just three blocks from the beach.

On a quiet, narrow one-way road in the center of Waikiki is a $50 hotel. The **Lealea Hale Apartment Hotel,** 2423 Cleghorn St., Honolulu, HI 96815 (tel. 922-1726), is a three-story building in well-preserved condition and boasting bedrooms with double or twin beds, full kitchen, lanai, air conditioning, bath with shower, for $50 double occupancy from April 1 to December 20. The rest of the year, these rooms are all $65. Weekly rates can be as low as $315, which makes this place a real bargain. No pool, few amenities, limited extra-cost parking, but still this is one of the better budget bets in Waikiki.

The **Waikiki Circle Hotel,** 2464 Kalakaua Ave., Honolulu, HI 96815 (tel. 923-1571) is one of the few bargain spots left in Waikiki. Yes, it's a circular hotel, and it is right across the street from Kuhio Beach. We'd call this older hotel mostly suitable for undemanding types—it's simple, but clean and well maintained. All rooms are air-conditioned, have TV and telephones, and private lanais with wide-angle views (the rooms are more or less pie-shaped) from Diamond Head to the Koolaus. There are 100 studios priced from $40 up, but they are $4 higher from mid-December to the end of March. This lowest price is for one person on floors 2 to 4. Floors 5 to 9 are $39, and floors 10 to 14 are $41. Add $3 for a second person, $4 for a third (maximum occupancy permitted). A budget-conscious restaurant is located off the lobby, and there is parking beneath the lobby.

If a homey management makes up for an old-but-livable building, check out **Hale Waikiki Apartment Hotel,** 2410 Koa Ave., Honolulu, HI 96815 (tel. 923-9012). Vera Brady—the term "house mother" fits her better than manager—has been helping guests enjoy their Waikiki stay for 10 years. One guest we met has been returning here each year for 15 years. Summer prices are $38.50 to $45, winter rates are $50 to $65. If you stay a week or longer, the rates are negotiable—downwards. An iron gate is kept locked most of the time. Once inside, a long walkway lined with greenery fronts the low-rise building. Each unit accommodates two people comfortably, with a kitchenette and a bath with shower. There is no phone, but you can install your own (the room is already wired for a phone) if you plan a long stay. There is maid service twice a week, ceiling fans rather than air conditioning, and shared laundry facilities on the premises. You might have to scurry here to find parking, but the central location, just one block from the beach and big hotels, makes up for it.

There are youth hostels in Honolulu. There's been one in graceful Manoa Val-

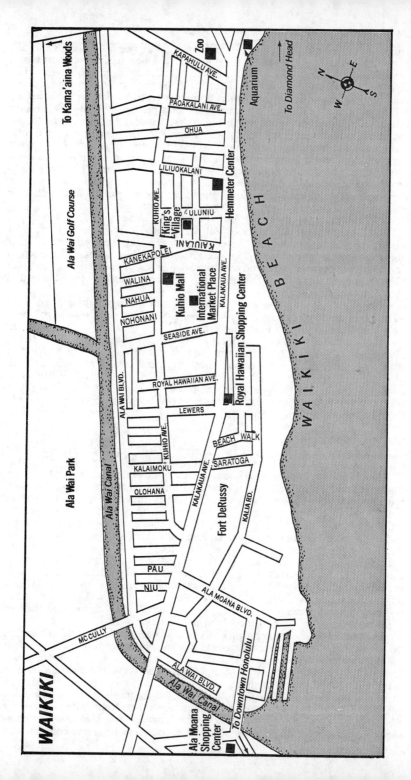

ley, near the campus of the University of Hawaii, for 20 years, and there's a smaller one, **Hale Aloha,** which is just the ticket for beach buffs, since it's two short blocks from Waikiki Beach at 2417 Prince Edward St., Honolulu, HI 96815 (tel. 926-8313). The Waikiki hostel is for AYH or IYHF members only (you can become a member by paying a $25 fee), and offers dormitory accommodations at $12 a night for 20 women and 30 men. Two common rooms provide kitchens, TV, and the relaxed comraderie for which youth hostels are famous. Dorms are closed and locked from 10 am to 5 pm daily in accordance with the hostel tradition of promoting the outdoor life. Couples might consider renting one of the four studios here at $26 per night, which features private bath and shower, mini-refrigerators, private entrance, and 24-hour access to the rooms; some have TV. Jack Butrymowicz, Hale Aloha's houseparent, is a veritable font of information on low-cost vacationing and travel. Stays are limited to three days; parking is $2 a day on a space-available basis.

The **Honolulu International Youth Hostel,** 2323A Sea View Ave., Honolulu, HI 96822 (tel. 946-0591) in Manoa Valley is the major facility, with 18 beds for women and 20 beds for men. Rates are $9 per night for members, $12 for nonmembers. Common rooms, a kitchen, Ping-Pong table, games, and a patio under the stars create a relaxed mood here, and again, houseparents, Thelma and Susan Akau are helpful sources of information. Facilities are locked between 9:30am and 5pm daily.

Note: Hostels are for "the young at heart, regardless of age," although students —Australian, European, Canadian, Japanese, as well as American—do predominate. Simple chores are expected of all guests.

Waikiki Beachside Apartments is located at 2556 Lemon Rd., Suite B101, Honolulu, HI 96815—an address that is a bit far from Waikiki's beaches. So that is the tip-off, that this is just a listing center for rentable condos at a number of addresses in Waikiki. During the winter season, these are available for $300 a week; off-season, they're $210 a week. Weekly rentals are preferred, but for an extra day or two, it will be $30 or $45 a day. These are all one-bedroom apartments with kitchen; a one-week deposit is required.

Central Waikiki

Choicely located a block from the beach and a block from the main drag in Waikiki, the **Outrigger Coral Seas Hotel,** 250 Lewers St., Honolulu, HI 96815 (tel. 923-3881), is one of the original hotels in the empire of Outrigger Hotels Hawaii. The rooms and lobby were recently renovated and are more comfortable than ever. Spacious rooms boast color TVs, direct-dial phones, either two queen-size or three twin beds, in-room safes, showers, colorful decor; all have private lanais and air conditioning to keep things cool. Small kitchenettes (with microwave oven, utensils, and refrigerator), are available upon request. From April 1 through December 18, doubles or singles without kitchenettes are priced from $50 to $75; those with kitchenettes are $65 to $85. Add $10 during peak season. An additional person is charged $15. Children under 18 are free when sharing beds with parents. Some larger rooms, starting around $80, can comfortably accommodate four, a real family find. A Dollar Rent-A-Car is free. The beach is down the street, and right in the hotel is Perry's Smorgy Restaurant, which offers such good buffet bargains on all three meals that you may never bother cooking in your room at all.

An important thing to remember about the Outrigger Coral Seas: If there are no rooms available here, the management can probably place you in an equivalent room elsewhere in one of their 21 Waikiki hotels: At least count, they were handling something like 7,000 rooms! Throughout this text, you will find descriptions of many of their budget and medium-priced properties. Also quite special is the fact that The Hawaii Free Ride is usually available at all Outrigger hotels. This means that you can have the use of a free compact, automatic shift car from Dollar Rent-A-Car for every day of your stay, *but only if you request the car at the time you make your reservation.* Certain restrictions apply, and insurance, taxes, refueling service charges, and other expenses are your responsibility. However, considering that renting a car will probably cost you $25 or $30 a day or more if you do it separately, this is an extraordinary offer.

For reservations at the Coral Seas, or any other Outrigger hotel, call toll free 800/733-7777 from mainland United States or Canada; Australia, 0014-800/125-642. The toll-free FAX number is 800/456-4329.

Another of those ubiquitous Outrigger outposts, the **Outrigger Waikiki Surf,** 2200 Kuhio Avenue, Honolulu, HI 96815 (tel. 923-7671), is well set up for comfortable living. The rooms are spacious, with compact kitchenettes if you ask for them, usually twin beds (a few doubles and queens are available), air conditioning, color TV, and a long, narrow lanai that is shared with the next room. Accommodations vary with the price, but all are comfortable. From April 1 through December 18 rooms without kitchenette range from $45 to $60; rooms with kitchenette are $60 to $70. An extra person is charged $15. Suites with kitchenettes for up to four persons are $65 to $75. Rates go up $5 to $10 during peak season. Cars from Dollar Rent-A-Car are free. The comfortable chairs in the lobby afford a view of passersby on the sidewalk. The bustle of Kalakaua is just one long block away, the Pacific two. For reservations call toll free 800/733-7777 in the U.S. and Canada; 0014-800-125-642 in Australia. Toll-free FAX is 800/456-4329.

One of the lowest priced of the Outrigger chain is the **Outrigger Waikiki Surf West,** 412 Lewers St., Honolulu, HI 96815 (tel. 923-7671). It shares the lobby and front desk with the main Waikiki Surf, just across the street, and has its own large pool area. All rooms have recently been renovated, with kitchenettes, air conditioning, television, telephones, bath with shower, and lanais. There are 100 rooms and suites, with prices beginning at $45 to $65 per night for one or two people from April 1 through December 18, $5 more the rest of the year. The suites run from $75 to $85 for up to four persons, up to $90 in winter. For reservations call toll free 800/733-7777 in the U.S. and Canada; 0014-800/125-642 in Australia. Toll-free FAX number is 800/456-4329. Calls from Dollar Rent-A-Car are free.

The same chain's **Outrigger Waikiki Surf East,** 420 Royal Hawaiian Ave., Honolulu, HI 96815 (tel. 923-7671), seems to be the lowest priced of the 20 Outrigger hotels in Waikiki, but we can't figure out why. It is quiet, rooms are tastefully and newly appointed, and there are many amenities. Perhaps it's the size; there's no wasted space here. When you register at the desk, be careful not to fall into the pool! Single or double occupancy is $45 to $55. For this you get a refrigerator, cooking top or microwave, TV, air conditioning, toaster and dining ware, stall shower in the bathroom, and a sliding glass door leading to a lanai large enough for dining or sunbathing. If you get a corner room there are two lanais. It's $5 more in peak season. Cars from Dollar Rent-A-Car are free. It's a five-minute walk to the beach, the International Market Place, or the heart of the Waikiki action. Outrigger's toll-free reservations number is 800/733-7777 in the U.S. and Canada, 0014-800-125-642 in Australia. Toll-free FAX number is 800/456-4329.

The **Outrigger Edgewater,** at 2168 Kalia Rd., Honolulu, HI 96815, corner of Lewers (tel. 922-6424), has long enjoyed one of the best locations in Waikiki. Halfway between the ocean and Kalakaua Avenue, the hotel is a two-minute walk to either the peace of sun and surf or the bustle of restaurants, shops, and nighteries. It's a big hotel, with a fairly big swing in prices. Rooms without kitchenettes go from $50 to $65, single or double, depending upon space and view. Kitchenettes are $70 single or double, and family suites cost $115. Rates are from $10 to $20 higher from mid-December to April 1. An additional person is charged $15. Cars from Dollar Rent-A-Car are free. Rates subject to change. Rooms are pleasantly furnished, with color TV including in-room movies, direct-dial phone, and air conditioning; the bathrooms have stall showers but no tubs. Your lanai will be furnished, but nothing will separate you from your neighbor's porch. This is a homey place, with lots of space to stroll around the building, plenty of lobby area and public rooms. The Trattoria Restaurant, right on the grounds, is a Waikiki favorite for northern Italian food, Chuck's Steakhouse is another popular old timer, and the Patisserie is a favorite French bakery. This is another of those Outrigger Hotels Hawaii, which means that, for toll-free reservations in U.S. and Canada you phone 800/733-7777; in Australia, it's 0014-800/125-642. Toll-free FAX is 800/456-4329.

Ewa Waikiki

The **Outrigger Reef Lanais,** 225 Saratoga Rd., Honolulu, HI 96815 (tel. 923-3881), is still another member of that popular hotel chain, tops in location with the beach just a hop-skip-and-a-jump away, since there is a public right-of-way to the ocean just across Kalia Road. The hotel is 100% air-conditioned, and although it lacks some of the frills of its sister hotels, it's still a good value for the price. Guest rooms are nicely decorated, with either twin or queen-size beds, and feature color TV, direct-dial phone, in-room safe, shower (no tub); some rooms have kitchenettes, which include a microwave oven, refrigerator, and utensils. Rates are the same for both singles and doubles: During regular season, rooms without kitchenettes go for $50 to $75; those with kitchenettes are $65 to $85. Add $15 for an additional person, $10 more during peak season. There is no pool on the premises, but guests may use the one at Outrigger Village, right around the corner on Lewers Street. The presence of the ever-popular Buzz's Steakhouse on the premises is a definite plus. For toll-free reservations, call 800/733-7777 in the U.S. and Canada; in Australia, 0014-800/125-642. Toll-free FAX is 800/456-4329.

One of our favorite streets in Honolulu is Beach Walk, a tiny street running from Kalakaua smack into the ocean and relatively—for Waikiki—quiet. Here you'll find **Hale Pua Nui,** 228 Beach Walk, Honolulu, HI 96815 (tel. 923-9693), many of whose guests are returnees, coming back year after year to this lovely little complex of some 22 large studio apartments. The location is tops—just a half block to the beach at the Outrigger Reef Hotel, and just around the bend from Fort DeRussy, where the swimming is excellent. The studio apartments are of good size, with either twin or double beds. They are tastefully furnished with new carpets, drapes, bedspreads, phones, artistic touches, have cross-ventilation and acoustic walls and ceilings, are thoroughly equipped (even to ironing boards), and have kitchenettes. During peak season, June 16 to September 15 and December 16 to March 15, the rate is $55 single or double; during regular season, March 16 to June 15 and September 16 to December 15, the rate is $40. There is a maximum of three persons in a room; each additional person is charged $5. An excellent value!

The owners of the **Aloha Punawai** at 305 Saratoga Rd., Honolulu, HI 96815 (tel. 923-5211), try hard to keep a low-profile hotel. But we are breaking their secret because there are not many places in Waikiki where you can stay for $40 a day single, $45 a day double, and even $35 and $40 a day if you stay a week. For this price you get a clean, comfortable apartment with a furnished kitchen, bath with shower, and a lanai. The same unit with air conditioning is $5 more. There is TV but no telephone, although the apartments are TV and cable-ready for those on longer stays who wish to have a phone installed. Minimum stay is three days. Stay a month and the rate goes down to $25 and $30 a day. There are also small one-bedroom apartments at $10 more, and large one-bedroom apartments for $15 more. Towels and linens are provided; there is maid service three times a week. Saratoga Road is near Fort DeRussy, and the hotel is only a block from the beach.

The modest-looking **Kai Aloha Hotel,** 235 Saratoga Rd., Honolulu, HI 96815 (tel. 923-6723), is the kind of place whose faithful fans return year after year. They prefer the homeyness of this simple little hotel, the friendliness of the management, and the feeling of intimacy rare at the more impersonal concrete high-rise hotels. The location, very close to the beach and shopping area, is convenient, and the lush tropical plantings add an island flavor. Every unit has either a modern kitchen or kitchenette; apartments have full-size refrigerators, and the studios, half-size ones. All units have a color TV, a garbage disposal, toaster, and ironing board. There are coin-operated laundry facilities available on the premises. Every unit has air conditioning, although on our last visit the trade winds alone made the rooms delightfully cool on a very hot day. Lanai studios, all with their own little porches, are $47 to $55 double; the one-bedroom apartments are $55 to $63 double. The latter can comfortably accommodate families of four or five, with twin beds in the living room as well as living-room furniture. There is a charge of $10 for each additional person, and children are welcome. Rates are subject to change.

Near the Ala Wai

A clean white six-story building stands at the corner of Ala Wai Boulevard and Nohonani Street, anything but imposing, yet well worth considering because the **Holiday Surf Apartment Hotel,** 2303 Ala Wai Blvd., Honolulu, HI 96815 (tel. 737-8078), offers delightfully appointed studios and one-bedroom units starting at $51 in the off-season (mid-April to December 14), and $72 in the winter. Most units have small lanais that accommodate two chairs. Most of the bathrooms have stall showers, but some do have tub-shower combinations. There are no telephones in the rooms, but guests may make free local calls at the lobby office phone. Kitchens are fully equipped. From here to the beach it's three long blocks, about a ten-minute walk.

Some of the lowest rates in Waikiki are being offered at the **Outrigger Ala Wai Terrace Hotel,** 1547 Ala Wai Blvd., Honolulu, HI 96815 (tel. 949-7384), at the very beginning of the boulevard, not far from Ala Moana. This 43-year-old apartment building, was converted into a hotel a few years ago, and while there's nothing at all fancy about it (don't expect tourist amenities like a pool or restaurant), it does offer clean and comfortable units—with kitchen facilities, air conditioning, and all the necessities—at very decent rates. There are two buildings, the newly renovated, 16-story Tower Building (which has TV in its units), and the low-rise, walk-up Garden Building. Garden studios go from $45 to $50, garden one-bedrooms are $50 to $55. Tower units range from $65 to $85. Cars from Dollar Rent-A-Car are free. Rates are subject to change. For reservations, phone the central office for Outrigger Hotels Hawaii, at toll free 800/733-7777 in the U.S. and Canada, 0014-800/125-642 in Australia. The toll-free FAX is 800/456-4329.

The **Waikiki Sand Villa Hotel,** 2375 Ala Wai Blvd., Honolulu, HI 96815 (tel. 922-4744; toll-free reservations for U.S., Puerto Rico, and Virgin Islands, 800/247-1903) is looking better than ever these days, with a $3 million top-to-bottom renovation completed. The lobby now has a Hawaiian plantation-style ambiance, accented with a Chinese pink slate floor; the 220 air-conditioned rooms now include color TV, a refrigerator, and an in-room safe for valuables. And the prices are still moderate: most of the year, double-occupancy rates are $49 standard; additional persons $10 each. Superior and deluxe doubles are $55 and $69, respectively. In the winter season, these prices go up to $59, $72, and $84, respectively, for the three categories. There is no charge for children under 8 in your room.

The best views are of the Ala Wai Canal, the golf course across it, and the Koolau Mountains, but even the opposite views are not "socked in" by neighboring buildings. The rooms are adequate in size, and the decorations are handsome. Two tables —one inside and one out on the cozy lanai—afford a choice of breakfast spots. There's phone service, and the bathrooms have both tub and shower.

Opening off the lobby is the also completely redecorated Noodle Shop Restaurant, an attractive spot for three meals a day, and best known as the place where Hawaii's "Crown Prince" of comedy, zany Frank DeLima, got his start. Hopefully, by the time you read this, the hotel's new swimming pool and porte-cochere (temporarily stalled in the government permit process) will be in place.

The toll-free number is 800/247-1903; the FAX number is 923-2541.

Near Ala Moana

A good budget choice here, in the big Ilikai and Hilton Hawaiian Village complex of hotels, stores, restaurants, and beaches is the **Hawaii Dynasty Hotel,** 1830 Ala Moana Blvd., Honolulu, HI 96815 (tel. 955-1111), a high-rise hotel with an inn atmosphere. The accent is on comfort, with medium-size rooms and oversize beds. Twin beds are as big as most doubles, and the doubles are enormous. Rooms are tastefully furnished, with combination tub-showers in the bathroom, TV, and individual air-conditioning units. There are no cooking facilities but there is a 24-

hour restaurant. A laundry room is available. The pool on the second floor is one of the largest in Waikiki. Now for the prices: doubles at $47 standard, $50 deluxe, $55 superior-deluxe, plus a high-season surcharge of $12 from December 21 through April. An additional person is $12. There are some suites at $130 per day for up to four persons. For reservations, call toll free 800/421-6662 outside of California, 800/352-6686 in California.

The **Big Surf Hotel,** 1690 Ala Moana Blvd., Honolulu, HI 96815 (tel. 946-6525), has what are probably the lowest-cost hotel accommodations in Waikiki. Located just over the bridge into Waikiki, it has recently been converted from a condominium building. There is no pool, no restaurant, and the only telephone is a coin phone in the small lobby. Prices start at $26.61 for a single person; that is not a misprint. For this you get a single bed in a small room with a hot plate. There is a private bath with shower, but no TV. A couple would require one of the larger studios with twin beds and lanai at $35.79. For parties of up to five people, there are one-bedroom suites with full kitchen and, yes, color TV; price: $59.64.

Most of the accommodations have been recently renovated and, though simple, are adequately furnished. Don't expect spaciousness at this price. The hotel is a few minutes' stroll around the Ilikai lagoon to the beach, and just a few minutes in the other direction to the Ala Moana Shopping Center. Parking is available for $2 a day.

About a block and a half away is the Diamond Head of the Ilikai Hotel—the **Hawaii Colony Hotel,** 1946 Ala Moana, Blvd., Honolulu, HI 96815 (tel. 955-0040), which offers some of the lowest prices in Waikiki for studios with kitchenettes: from $40, single or double. But before you get too excited, let us say that this is a bare-bones deal with no phone, no maid service (towels and linens are supplied), and no reservations taken. Because their low rates invite long-term guests, availability here is sporadic. Two three-story, aging frame buildings flank a decorative pool and garden; the studios are entered from open hallways. The units are carpeted and air-conditioned, and each has a TV.

A desk at the entrance opens to both the small hotel lobby and the sidewalk, where it becomes **Hotel Exchange,** an organization that makes deals with hotels at substantial discounts and is able to pass on some of the savings to you. Hotel Exchange works with 180 hotels on Oahu and all the neighbor islands. They will take advance reservations with an approved credit card (phone them at 942-8544), or you can simply walk in and see them if you're already in town and not happy where you're staying. Savings can average $5 to $10 a day at many leading hotels.

The **Driftwood Hotel,** 1696 Ala Moana Blvd., Honolulu, HI 96815 (tel. 949-0061), across from the new luxury Hawaiian Prince Hotel is also on the other side of the price spectrum from it: $35 to $65, single or double. The lower rate is for a standard room and bath (shower only) including TV and telephone. The higher rates are for rooms that have been renovated, with new carpeting and draperies, some with new furniture. If you are on a limited budget and choose the lower rate, be advised that the furnishings are not glamorous, but certainly adequate. There is a swimming pool, laundromat, and parking on the premises of this 71-unit hotel. Parking is $5 a day. The hotel is less than two blocks' walking distance from the Ala Moana Shopping Center and Ala Moana Beach Park. The FAX number is 949-4906.

Just Beyond Waikiki

Our last recommendation in this category is technically just over the Waikiki border, but not far enough out to be inconvenient. The **Central Branch YMCA,** 401 Atkinson Dr., Honolulu, HI 96814 (tel. 941-3344), is a five-minute bus ride from Waikiki on TheBUS no. 8 Ala Moana to Ala Moana and Atkinson Drive. It's a beautiful place, with an outdoor swimming pool and lovely grounds. The newly painted rooms are small but adequate—"Y-style." Singles with community bathroom and showers are $29 daily; with bathroom and shower, $36.50 daily. Add $10 a day for a rollaway bed and you have a double. The Y has a reasonably priced coffee shop and no end of recreational activities. The single male tourist could hardly do better than stop here. No reservations are accepted.

THE GOOD BUYS

Prices in this category range, roughly, from $50 to $70 and up for a double. Again, savings can be realized by those staying for more than a week and by groups of more than two people traveling together.

Diamond Head Waikiki

Up near the Honolulu Zoo, an old hotel not only has a new look, but it also has a new name: now it's the **EWA** (East-West Adventure) **Hotel Waikiki,** 2555 Cartwright St., Honolulu, HI 96815 (tel. 922-1677). A $3-million-dollar renovation has lightened and brightened this small hotel. Italian-marble floors and counters, light-green grass cloth on the walls, sand-colored carpets, and pastel color schemes everywhere, in the lobby and the rooms, make this hotel very attractive. Wouldn't you know it, rates have gone up. Every room now has a kitchenette, along with telephone, color TV, air conditioning, in-room safe, and a tub-shower combo. Most rooms have twin beds, some have queens. Studio rooms are $75 and $85 for one to three people; lovely one-bedroom suites are $110 to $120 for one to four people. There is guest parking ($3 a night), no swimming pool, and no dining facilities. But with the ocean and restaurants two short blocks away, this is no problem. For information and reservations, phone 800/367-8047.

Located in a great spot three minutes away from Kuhio Beach, the 90-room **Kaiulani Kai,** 2425 Kuhio Ave., Honolulu, HI 96815 (tel. 922-7777) has for several years been "one of the best little buys in Waikiki." However, now that a new Japanese management has taken over and transformed the tall, modern pyramidlike building designed by Scandinavian architect Jo Paul Rognstad, changes are in the wind. New prices are $70 for a studio with kitchenette, $80 for a deluxe studio with kitchen, and $100 for a one-bedroom suite with kitchen for up to four people. However, the transformation has turned the hotel into a little jewel, its lobby and guest rooms all done in shades of mauve and pink, with gold fixtures. Rooms are not large but they are attractive, with twin beds, small lanais, and a tidy two-burner kitchenette, with refrigerator underneath the range. Bathrooms are marble, kitchen and bathroom floors are tiled, and so are the lanais. And the lobby is beautiful, with its marble floors, indented ceilings in the Japanese style, and gorgeous flower arrangements. There's free coffee service in the lobby. Prices subject to change. The toll-free reservation number is 800/367-9473 in the continental U.S.

Very welcome in this area is the **Quality Inn,** 175 Paoakalani Ave., Honolulu, HI 96815 (two blocks from Kalakaua, one block from Kapahulu, near Kapiolani Park; tel. 922-3861). It's cheerful, sparkling, and radiates aloha, which you'll notice the minute you approach it. It's smart looking, with a waterfall at the entrance, a golden lobby, and friendly people behind the desk. Prices are lowest in the Diamond Head Tower: $63 to $111 double, with $12 for each additional person. There are no kitchenettes, but you'll still enjoy your lanai and the view. In the Pali Tower, all rooms have partial kitchenettes; here the rates are $83 double in low season, $137 in high season. The air-conditioned rooms are standard size, equipped with call-out phones, dressing areas, and stall showers large enough and deep enough for a bath, too. There are two small pools on the third floor. Call toll free, for reservations: 800/367-2317. The FAX number is 924-1982. Rates are subject to change.

The **Waikiki Grand,** 134 Kapahulu, Honolulu, HI 96815 (tel. 923-1511), is one of the most popular places in town for the flocks of Japanese tourists who've discovered Hawaii, and for us that's an extra inducement to stay at this attractive hotel. You can get all the comforts of this hotel at its standard low-season (April 1 to December 19) rate of $60, single or double. At this price you'll get a room with a view of the center of Waikiki and the mountains in the distance; you'll have to go to $75 for a breathtaking view of Diamond Head in the other direction. Deluxe rooms with kitchenettes are $80, single or double. An additional person is $10; add $10 in high season. Super views or not, the rooms are pleasant if small (very little closet space), feature tub-showers, direct-dial telephones, and air conditioning. There's a pleasant swimming pool in a secluded court, a Japanese restaurant is on the premises, Kapiolani Park and its activities are across the street, and good old Kuhio Beach is just around the bend.

Each room of the **Kaimana Villa Condominiums,** 2550 Kuhio Ave., Honolulu, HI 96815 (tel. 922-3833), has a private lanai facing Diamond Head. From the higher floors (7 to 19) of this 114-room building, you feel you can almost touch it. Located two blocks from the beach and from shopping and nightlife, this is the place for those who like space: over 600 square feet per unit, each tastefully appointed. Amenities include your own washer and dryer, dishwasher, clock radio, air conditioning, color TV, a full kitchen, and daily housekeeping services. There are direct-dial phones, and 24-hour front desk service. A modest front lobby has lounging facilities that extend to a covered outdoor area. One-bedroom apartments rent for $70 from April through December 19, and for $85 the rest of the year, double occupancy; an extra person is charged $15. Two-bedroom apartments, which can accommodate up to six people, are $120 to $145 for two.

For reservations, phone toll-free 800/367-6060, or write to 2490 Kalakaua Ave., Honolulu, HI 96815.

Tucked away behind the post Hyatt Regency Hotel, and just a short block from Kuhio Beach, is a newer hotel called **Waikiki Hana,** 2424 Koa Ave., Honolulu, HI 96815 (tel. 926-8841). Actually, the building is not new, but a new management took over several years ago and totally renovated and refurbished an older hotel, creating a sparkling, wicker-chaired lobby and 73 modern rooms that are just as attractive, each entered from the outside. They are furnished smartly in light woods with rose walls, blue quilted bedspreads, color TV, phone, and air conditioning. Refrigerators may be rented for $3 a day; only the top-of-the-line rooms have a kitchenette, which consists of a combination sink, refrigerator, and electric hot plate. Considering that this is a full-service hotel with an excellent location, rates are not bad: from April 1 to December 21, $44 to $58 for a standard double, $63 to $66 for a superior, $72 to $75 for a deluxe, and $84 to $87 for a superior deluxe (with kitchenette). In winter, rates are $10 more per night, still making this one of the better values on the beach. For reservations, write Hawaiian Pacific Resorts, 1150 S. King St., Honolulu, HI 96814, or phone toll-free number 800/367-5004 from the continental U.S. and Canada. The toll-free FAX number is 800/477-2329.

One of the most elegant buildings in this part of Waikiki, once called the "jungle," is the **Waikiki Park Heights,** 2440 Kuhio Ave., Honolulu, HI 96815 (tel. 923-2288). Over 20 stories high, it contains 150 one-bedroom apartments with kitchenettes (some with full kitchens). The lobby is magnificent, dominated by lava rock walls, fountains, and tasteful groupings. Sounds like $100 plus a day? Would you believe $69 a day from April 1 to December 19, and $89 the rest of the year? Most units can accommodate four people at that price, and have ocean views, to boot. All are air-conditioned and furnished with towels, linens, and a vacuum cleaner. (Get the message?) The cooking facilities are fully equipped for making this your home away from home. On the premises is Hy's Steak House, dinner only and a splurge for budgeteers. There's a swimming pool, laundry facilities in the basement, and available parking. Two blocks away is Kuhio Beach. For reservations, phone toll-free 800/922-4496.

Manor International Resorts, a company that offers discounted hotel rooms at a number of Waikiki hotels, is located in the rear of the lobby. Prices are similar, but could be as low as $50 a day, all year round. They can be reached at 923-2228 or 926-8253.

The **Honolulu Prince,** 415 Nahua St., Honolulu, HI 96815 (tel. 922-1616), is one of Waikiki's older apartment-hotels that has seen many years of comfortable, casual living. A new management has remodeled all the guest rooms, and values are still good. Our favorite units here are the spacious one-bedroom apartments with full kitchens and separate bedrooms, nicely furnished and laid out. These rent for $95 for up to four people. The studios, furnished with either two doubles or a king plus a sofa bed, are also good buys at $59 standard, $65 superior. Four people can also be accommodated in the two-bedroom kitchen apartments, with two double beds and a sofa bed, and plenty of room to putter around in, for $110. Most units have lanais, all have television and telephone, and are air-conditioned. Maid service is provided every other day. No pool, no frills, but good value. Reservations: 800/ 92-ASTON (922-7866).

The towering **Royal Kuhio** condominium building, 2240 Kuhio Ave., Honolulu, HI 96815 (tel. 923-1747 or 923-2502), is one of the growing number of such places that has a great number of apartments in the "hotel pool"—which means they are available to visitors for short- or long-term stays. These apartments are quite attractive, nicely decorated, with a bedroom with twin beds that can be closed off from the sitting room or opened to make one big area. The sitting room has sofa beds, and rollaways are available for extra people. The kitchens are all-electric (with dishwashers), the closet space is ample, and every apartment has its own color TV and lanai. A pool and sundeck area, billiard room, Ping-Pong, a shuffleboard court, and a huge laundry room and recreation area all make for easy living—not to mention the location close to the beach. There is weekly maid service. During the off-season, two people can get a one-bedroom apartment for $70, a mountain-view apartment for $95; rates go way up for a deluxe ocean view. Rates may be rising soon. Reservations: Paradise Management Corp., Suite C-207, 50 S. Beretania St., Honolulu, HI 96813. The toll-free number is 800/367-5205.

Central Waikiki

A place that has just about everything going for it is the **Marine Surf**, 364 Seaside Ave., Honolulu, HI 96815 (tel. 923-0277). Located about a block and a half away from the beach, the Marine Surf is a 23-story condominium hotel featuring smartly decorated studio apartments, each of which boasts two extra-length double beds, lots of drawer space, color TV, air conditioning, phone, dressing room, and bath with both tub and shower. Best of all, each studio has a full electric kitchen, just in case you're not prepared to eat every night at Matteo's Italian Restaurant, one of the finest in town, right on the lobby floor. Rooms, which have been completely renovated, are serviced daily; and a personal safe is available in every unit. Those too lazy to walk to the beach can swim and sun at the lovely pool on the fourth floor. Now for the rates: During the long spring-summer-fall season (April 1 to December 20), standard rooms are $60, superior are $65, and deluxe are $70, single or double. A one-bedroom penthouse suite is $110. During the winter, rates are $75, $80, $85, and $130, respectively. The extra-person charge is $12 for up to four in the studios and up to six in the penthouse suite. There is no charge for children under the age of 18; cribs are $12 per day. On-site parking is $3 a day. A rate increase is expected. For toll-free reservations, call 800/367-5176 in the continental U.S.; in Canada, 800/ 663-1118. The FAX number is 926-5915.

You could call Patrick Winston's 10 units in the **Hawaiian King Hotel** at 417 Nohonani St., Honolulu, HI 96815 (tel. 923-3894) a hotel-within-a-hotel—they're really something special. Winston, a delightful young man who takes a caring, personal interest in his guests, many of whom return year after year, purchased his first unit in the Hawaiian King when it became a condominium hotel back in 1981. He was the interior designer-contractor who furnished the entire project. Six of his units have gone through complete $20,000 renovations. One unit is called the Blue Hawaiian Suite since it is furnished with blue rattan and blue carpeting along with an accent coral color. His largest unit (780 square feet) is called the Corporate Suite; it contains a separate room with a complete work station including a typewriter, calculator, and other business supplies, along with a large living room with an area for conferences. The Mount Fuji Suite has white marble-and-black accents along with Oriental furniture, futons, a small waterfall, and shoji screens. His other one-bedroom units have also been upgraded from ceilings to floors and have new carpeting and furniture, ceramic tiles, floor-to-ceiling mirrors, stereos and cable remote televisions, and kitchens with microwave and convection ovens, and washer/dryers. From April 15 to December 15, rates are $75; during the winter, $95. The corporate rate is $65 year round, with space availability during the peak winter season. Rates are for two; a third and fourth person pay $10 more each. Winston states: "I am dedicated to concepts that ring out time and again in your literature and that is quality lodging at a price, with the Aloha spirit ringing in loudly."

The Hawaiian King is a five-story building centering around a lovely pool and garden area, on a quiet street, about two blocks from the beach. All apartments are air-conditioned; there's a laundry on the premises as well as a cocktail lounge and minimart, and 24-hour front desk and telephone switchboard service. A good bet even if you don't get one of the special rooms; even better if you do.

On that same pleasant Nohonai Street, about halfway between Kuhio Ave. and the Ala Wai Blvd., is the **White Sands Waikiki Resort,** 431 Nohonani St., Honolulu, HI 96815 (tel. 923-7336). The low-rise garden hotel, a longtime favorite in these parts, is a time-sharing establishment, so it is not always easy to get an opening here, and reservations cannot be confirmed until two weeks before your arrival date. However, when you consider that rooms are nicely furnished and that you get a kitchenette and a private lanai with even a standard room at $52 single, $59 double, it's worth a try. Superior rooms are slightly larger and the price only slightly higher: $59 single, $65 double.

Each apartment is furnished differently but well. Beds are large and comfortable, decor is Polynesian. Rooms have phones, color TVs, air conditioning, and daily maid service. There is free, but limited parking on the premises. The deluxe swimming pool is in an inner court and is surrounded by gardens, shady nooks, and pathways to explore this tranquil acre in the heart of Waikiki. Coffee is served gratis in the lobby in the morning and rum punch at sunset.

Outrigger Hotels Hawaii has a number of establishments in central Waikiki, and of these, the newly renovated (to the tune of $5 million) **Outrigger East,** 150 Kaiulani Ave., Honolulu, HI 96815, is the top of the line in the chain's mid-priced category. The 445-room, 18-floor hotel is a short block from Waikiki Beach, and has just about everything a visitor needs, from four restaurants to a beauty shop, travel and tour desks, laundry facilities, and on-site parking ($5 a day). Rooms have been smartly furnished, each with either two double beds, a king or a queen; all have color TVs with pay movies, in-room safes, direct-dial phones, refrigerators; a few have kitchenettes. During the regular season, April 1 through December 18, standard rooms are $75, moderate rooms $80, deluxe rooms $85; studios with kitchenettes for two are $85, and suites with kitchenette for up to four are $110 to $120. During the peak winter season, rates in these categories are $85, $95, $105, $110, and $115 to $135, respectively.

All rates include free cars from Dollar Rent-A-Car; senior citizen discounts are often available. The Outrigger chains handle something like 7,000 rooms in 22 hotels in Waikiki, so you can be sure their reservation number works 24 hours a day. Phone toll-free number 800/733-7777 from mainland U.S. and Canada; the toll-free FAX number is 800/456-4329.

For those watching their dollars closely, the **Outrigger Surf,** 2280 Kuhio Ave., Honolulu, HI 96815 (tel. 922-5777), on the corner of Nohonani Street, a short walk from the beach, is one of the most suitable. We like it because it has the greatest number of standard units, with kitchenettes throughout; these are $55 during regular season, $75 during peak season; moderate and deluxe kitchenette units are $60 and $65 regular, $80 and $90 peak. Additional persons are charged $15 each. There are also suites with kitchenettes that can sleep up to four persons, at $85, $95, and $115. Adding even greater value is the use of a Dollar Rent-A-Car for each day of your stay. Phone toll free 800/733-7777 from mainland U.S. and Canada; the toll-free FAX number is 800/456-4329.

Outrigger Surf is a tall, modern building with 16 floors of comfortable studios, each with a lanai, color TV, carpeting, air conditioning, in-room safe, beds in studio arrangement providing a living-room look. There's a stall shower in the bathroom, his-and-her closets for storage, a two-burner range, and base cabinet type of refrigerator for light cooking. The lobby is small but comfortable, and green Astroturf surrounds the lobby-level pool. The Waikiki Pasta Company is right at hand. For toll-free reservations, phone 800/733-7777 in the U.S. and Canada, 0014-800/125-642 in Australia. Toll-free FAX number is 800/456-4329.

The **Outrigger Waikiki Tower Hotel,** 200 Lewers St., Honolulu, HI 96815 (tel. 922-6424), is adjacent to the Outrigger Edgewater Hotel (described above), which means that it shares a prime, close-to-the-beach location, right across Kalia Road from the Outrigger Reef Hotel. Access to restaurants is just as easy as to the beach; there's the Waikiki Broiler downstairs, Trattoria and The Original Chuck's Steak House at the Edgewater, and popular Denny's across Lewers Street. The lobby, recently renovated, is open to the breezes and chock full of convenience desks and shops. Rooms are pleasantly decorated (they have also been recently renovated), each have a color TV, direct-dial phone, central air conditioning, lanai, in-room safe, shower, and bedding consisting of either a king, queen, or two twins. Whether or not you get a kitchenette here, you will get a refrigerator, and that goes a long way to cutting costs on food. During the regular season, nonkitchenette rooms are $70 standard, $75 moderate, $80 deluxe; during peak season, these are $80, $90, and $100. Kitchenette units include a microwave oven, refrigerator, and utensils; these run for $75, $80, and $85 regular; $85, $95, and $100 peak. An additional person is charged $15. The Waikiki Free Ride (free use of a Dollar Rent-A-Car) should be available here, too. For toll-free reservations, phone 800/733-7777 in the U.S. and Canada, 0014-800/125-642 in Australia. Toll-free FAX: 800/456-4329.

The **Outrigger Village,** 240 Lewers St., Honolulu, HI 96815 (tel. 923-3881), is the first hotel we've ever seen with a swimming pool in the center of the lobby! The lobby is a quadrangle built around the pool and there's no ceiling in the center, so you can swim and sunbathe while checking out the new arrivals. The hotel is decorated from lobby to rooms in a bright blending of contemporary and Polynesian styles. Each of the 439 units has air conditioning, TV, telephone, in-room safe; most have lanais. Rooms are all similar, although those on the lower floors are cheaper; the prices, in regular season, bottom to top, are $70 to $80, single or double. Kitchenette units—standard, moderate, and deluxe—go for $75 to $85. Family suites are $85 to $150 for up to four persons. These have half-size refrigerators and hot plates. Additional person: $15. During peak season, rates go up $10 to $20. The Village boasts its own restaurant, cocktail lounge, video dance palace, and several attractive shops—and a superb location right in the middle of everything and close to the beach. The Waikiki Free Ride is available here as well. Rates subject to change. For reservations from the mainland U.S. and Canada, phone toll free 800/733-7777. From Australia, it's 0014-800/125-642. Toll-free FAX: 800/456-4329.

The **Outrigger Malia Hotel,** 2211 Kuhio Ave., Honolulu, HI 96815 (tel. 923-7621), is a bright and beautiful place. The rooms in the Malia wing, the taller of the hotel's two sections, contain two double beds with Polynesian-print bedspreads in soft, muted colors and wall-to-wall carpeting. All rooms in the hotel have color TV, telephone, and lanai, both tub and shower in the bathroom, as well as small refrigerator, and ironing board. Disabled people will be glad to know that there are 16 rooms in this wing specially designed for them, with wider doorways, grab bars in the bathrooms, and twin-size rather than double beds for greater wheelchair mobility. Rooms rent for $55 to $90, depending on season and floor.

Then there's the Luana wing, with its junior suites. These contain a sitting room with two couches and a bedroom with two beds. The lanais in the suites are much larger than those in the bedrooms in the Malia wing. Junior suites, which can accommodate four guests comfortably, go from $85 to $95. An extra person pays $15. Pluses for guests at both wings include a Jacuzzi whirlpool, a rooftop tennis court, and the excellent Wailana Coffeeshop, open 24 hours a day (see Chapter IV). And, of course, the beach is just three blocks away. To top it all off, you may be able to get the Waikiki Free Ride here. For reservations, call toll free 800/773-7777 in the U.S. and Canada, 0014-800/125-642 in Australia. Toll-free FAX: 800/456-4329.

You get a really large room at the **Coral Reef,** a modern high-rise hotel at 2299 Kuhio Ave., Honolulu, HI 96815 (tel. 922-1262), directly behind the International Market Place and a short walk from Waikiki Beach. The 247-room hotel boasts every facility—swimming pool, garage, restaurants, shops—and nicely furnished, air-conditioned rooms that have either one or two double beds (or a double and a single), private lanai, and cable TV. Prices run from $58 for doubles all the way up to

$109 for one-bedroom suites on the higher floors. An extra person in the room is charged $10. Rates are subject to change. For reservations, write Aston Hotels & Resorts, 2255 Kuhio Ave., Honolulu, HI 96815, or phone toll free 800/922-7866 in the continental U.S. The FAX number is 922-5048.

They call it a "Deco–Post Modern" building. We call it a reminder of the plantation days. But whatever you call it, the **Hotel Honolulu,** 376 Kaiolu Street, Honolulu, HI 96815 (tel. 926-2766), is an oasis in time and space. Located where the street dead-ends just makai of Kuhio Avenue, the two buildings of the hotel compound overlook a parking lot, isolating them even more from traffic. A beautiful orchid collection, tropical birds, and hundreds of potted plants give a garden atmosphere to the entry, hallways, and suites. According to their literature, "Our best Gay clubs. . . . Hula's, Hamburger Mary's, C.C.'s, and an interesting variety of restaurants and shops are in our same block, just around the corner."

Best choice for budgeteers here is the smaller, two-story building called the Bamboo Lanai, where small studios go for just $49 year round. The studios are adequate in size, nicely furnished, but with a limited view. They have a small but fully equipped kitchenette; the bathroom has a tile-enclosed shower and a closet. Larger studios and one-bedroom suites in the three-story main building, which is air-conditioned, are more elaborate and more expensive. The studios have a sitting area, queen-size bed, complete kitchen, full bathroom, ceiling fans and cross-ventilation, and a lanai; they rent for $59 from May 16 to November 15, and $64 the rest of the year. The one-bedroom suites are quite large, with king-size bed, lanai, complete kitchen, and full bath, and each one is distinctively decorated in various styles: Japanese, Chinese, bamboo, safari, Chippendale, Deco, and the like. These run from $79 to $89 during the regular season, $7 to $10 higher in winter. Rates are for two: an extra person is charged $8.

Phones are available on the lobby level, as is a big-screen color TV (individual TVs are available only on request), laundry room, and all-day free coffee. There is covered off-street parking. Beach mats and towels are supplied for the beach, just two blocks away; there is also a rooftop garden sun deck, very popular for evening barbecues and drinks.

For toll-free reservations, phone 800/426-2766.

Ewa Waikiki

Outrigger Maile Court, 2058 Kuhio Ave., Honolulu, HI 96815 (tel. 947-2828), is designed for the easy life and located at the "Gateway to Waikiki," across the road from the well-known Nick's Fishmarket Restaurant—which means it's within easy walking distance of the beach and all the attractions of Kalakaua Avenue. There's a very pleasant feeling here, evident as soon as you walk into the open-air lobby, so pretty with its maroon-and-beige rugs and dusty-rose and rattan sofas. With almost 600 rooms, this 44-story resort has a variety of accommodations to offer: 410 hotel rooms, 178 studios, and 81 two-bedroom suites. Rooms are of modest size, but most have views (some, from the higher floors, are spectacular), all have attractive furnishings, cable color-TV, and individually controlled air-conditioning. There are clocks, radios, tub-showers, phones, but no lanais. Even the hotel rooms boast small refrigerators; studios and suites add a two-burner electric range for light cooking. Prices are $70 to $80 for hotel rooms, $80 to $100 for studios, $140 to $165 for one-bedroom suites (perfect for two couples or a family, with two bedrooms, two bathrooms, and two refrigerators). Children under 12 stay free if they use existing beds; rollaways and cribs are $10 each. Free cars are available from Dollar Rent-A-Car. There's lots to keep you busy in-house: a pool and a Jacuzzi on the large, 360° sun deck. For reservations at Maile Court, phone toll free from mainland U.S. and Canada, 800/733-7777. Toll-free FAX: 800/456-4329.

A favorite old-timer in Hawaii, the **Hawaiiana Hotel,** 260 Beach Walk, Honolulu, HI 96815 (tel. 923-3811), just keeps getting more and more mellow year after year. One of the few low-rise garden hotels left in Waikiki, the Hawaiiana is wonderfully located just half a block from a good swimming in front of the Outrigger Reef

Hotel and Fort DeRussy. Ninety-five rooms are situated around a gorgeous tropical garden and two swimming pools in the two- and three-story buildings, so you can just step out of your door for a swim in the pool or a complimentary breakfast of juice and coffee out on the patio. Comfortable chairs at poolside are occupied most of the day by guests too content to go out and do much else. All rooms have recently been remodeled and furnished in the tropical Brown Jordan rattan furniture. Each room has a color TV, electronic safe, electric kitchen, excellent beds, air conditioning, and phone; most have a lanai. During the summer season, April 20 to December 17, rates are $75 to $85 single, $80 to $90 double, extra person $8, for studios with kitchens. One-bedroom suites are $120 with kitchens for up to four guests. Nine new Alii Ultra deluxe rooms are $150. During the winter, rates are about $5 higher. Several package deals offer good value; inquire with the management. Rates are subject to change. Niceties include free newspapers in the morning or afternoon, Hawaiian shows twice a week, free use of washing and drying machines, free parking at the rear of the hotel on Saratoga Road. For reservations, phone toll free 800/367-5122 from mainland U.S. and Canada.

Those of you who remember the old Kalia Inn will be surprised to find that it's now the **Outrigger Royal Islander,** 2164 Kalia Rd., Honolulu, HI 96815 (tel. 922-1961). The lobby, small and open to the street, is much as it used to be, but all of the 98 units have been done over and are quite pretty, not large, but tastefully decorated with tapa-print spreads and shell lamps, with Hawaiian-type pictures on the walls. Each room has a private lanai, air conditioning, color TV, direct-dial telephone, refrigerator, and a modern bathroom with shower. Standard and moderate rooms are $55 to $80, single or double. Families will do well in the one-bedroom apartments and suites, which range from $105 to $120 for up to three people. The Outrigger Royal Islander has a super location, right near the Halekulani and Outrigger Reef hotels, across the road from a very good beach. There's a McDonald's right in the hotel. For reservations, phone toll free 800/733-7777 from mainland U.S. and Canada. Toll-free FAX: 800/456-4329.

Still going strong after 21 years, the **Ilima Hotel,** 445 Nohonani St., Honolulu, HI 96815 is eminently comfortable, offers many facilities and services, and a recent $1,200,000 renovation has not upped the rates unreasonably. A walk of less than 10 minutes will take you to the beach. You can really kick off your shoes and feel at home here; floors are carpeted, and the studios include two double beds, a fully equipped kitchen, color TV, radio, full tub and shower, plenty of storage space, and a private lanai. There's a swimming pool at ground level, two sun decks on the 10th floor, as well as an exercise room and sauna. Generosities not usually found in most hotels include free parking and free local phone calls! If you stick to one of the standard studio units, 4th floor and under, you can get by with $56 single, $63 double. Views and prices increase as you go up to the moderate rooms on the 5th floor ($60 and $69), the superior ones on the 6th through 9th floors ($69 and $78), and the deluxe ones on the 10th through 16th floors ($78 and $89). Small one-bedroom apartments for three run from $96 to $122; large one-bedroom apartments for four are $110 and up; two-bedroom suites for up to four are $130 and up. A crib or rollaway is $6 extra; an extra person is $8. For reservations, call toll free 800/367-5172; in Canada, 800/663-1118. The FAX number is 924-8371.

Although it looks better from the outside than it does inside, **Ambassador Hotel of Waikiki,** 2040 Kuhio Ave., Honolulu, HI 96815 (tel. 941-7777), is still good value for the money. Even the lobby, being glass-enclosed, does not spell home. But this is a comfortable hotel with all the conveniences. All of the rooms in this high-rise building are approached from outside walkways, and the studios from the 2nd through 7th floors boast private lanais, contemporary furniture, air conditioning, and deep *furo*-type shower-tubs. You can relax at the big pool and sun deck on the second floor, eat at the Café Ambassador, and you're fairly close to all the attractions of Waikiki. Rates for studio rooms range from $72 to $96 single, $80 to $104 double, and there are also deluxe one-bedroom suites, with full electric kitchens, from $115 to $140. Studios with kitchens on request.

The **Waikiki Gateway Hotel,** 2070 Kalakaua Ave., Honolulu, HI 96815 (tel

955-3741), is well known as the home of Nick's Fishmarket, one of Honolulu's favorite restaurants. It's also well known as a good value choice; the 185-room hotel has recently been renovated, and its rooms each have a private lanai, telephone, cable color TV, air conditioning, an under-the-counter refrigerator, in-room safe, and a luxurious bath with tub and shower. From April 2 to May 24 and again from September 5 to December 21, standard rooms (on the 3rd to 7th floors) are $49; superior rooms (8th to 15th floors) are $59; deluxe rooms with partial ocean view are $69; a junior penthouse suite is $85; and a penthouse suite is $100. The rest of the year, these accommodations go for $60, $70, $80, $100, and $140, respectively. An additional person is charged $15. There's daily maid service and a guest laundry. The beach is less than a 10-minute walk, but if you'd rather swim at home, try the beautiful pool backed by a volcanic rock wall and a spacious sun deck. Toll-free reservations: 800/633-8799 in mainland U.S. and Canada; the FAX number is 955-1313.

Near the Ala Wai

The **Coconut Plaza,** 2171 The Ala Wai, Honolulu, HI 96815 (tel. 923-8828), offers the gentility and intimacy that go with the word "plaza." Although it fronts on the Ala Wai Canal, it could be in Switzerland or on the Mediterranean. Sedate brass nameplates, a waterfall, and proud palms give a special ambience to the stone entry. Up front, near the waterfall, is a small, free-form pool. The hotel's garden-like restaurant, ZukeBISTRO (California-Cajun cuisine), fronts on a lush inner courtyard. Rates start at $60 for a standard studio and move up to $80 superior, $100 deluxe. Yet there's no skimping at the lower prices. All studios are beautifully furnished, with tile floors and woven-fiber walls, and have a private lanai, television, air conditioning, telephone, and a kitchenette with microwave oven. In the morning, guests are invited to enjoy a lovely complimentary continental breakfast: fruits, juices, banana bread, breakfast rolls, and tea or Kona coffee. A nice way to start a Hawaiian day! For information and reservations, phone toll free 800/882-9696 in continental U.S. The FAX number is 923-3473.

The **Hawaiian Monarch,** 444 Niu St., Honolulu, HI 96815 (tel. 949-3911), is a skyscraper hotel situated very close to the Ala Wai Canal and halfway between the Ala Moana Shopping Center and the beaches of Waikiki. It's a well-run establishment, with a mixed international clientele, complete with all the amenities of tourist life: a huge sun deck and regular pool, plenty of shops in the arcade, and a cozy bar in the main lobby. Parking is available at a nominal fee.

The Hawaiian Monarch is part hotel, part condo, and the hotel rooms, which occupy the 7th to 24th floors, all have individually controlled air conditioning, color TV, telephone, tub-shower combinations. As part of the hotel's recent $400,000 face-lift, they have been newly redone in modern tropical decor with whitewashed rattan furniture, pastel island-style pictures, and new bedspreads and chairs decked out with color-coordinated fabric. All rooms now have a refrigerator and coffee bar. Rooms are small but comfortable. The nicest views are those overlooking the Ala Wai Canal. From April 16 to December 21, standard rooms are $59; superior rooms are $65; deluxe rooms are $70. A studio suite with kitchenette is $75; with kitchen, $79. The rest of the year, the rates are $74, $80, $85, $90, and $94, respectively. A third person in a room is charged $15; children under 18 are free, using existing bedding. For reservations, call toll free 800/92-ASTON (922-7866) in continental U.S. The FAX number is 955-3506.

Near Ala Moana

Located near the Hilton Hawaiian Village and a block from the popular Fort DeRussy Beach is the attractive **Inn on the Park,** 1920 Ala Moana Blvd., Honolulu, HI 96815 (tel. 946-8355). This is a 230-unit, completely renovated hotel/condominium, with smallish but pretty rooms attractively decorated with floral spreads setting off the modern furnishings and decor. Very helpful for those wishing to eat breakfast in and fix a light lunch are the refrigerators and wet bars in most of the units; kitchenette units are also available This place would be most suitable for two, or perhaps three persons in a room: families might find it a bit tight. There's a modern lobby with a convenience store, and a nice pool and sun deck on the 5th floor, next to the Inn Beer Garden Lounge, which provides jazz entertainment.

Accommodations here are in three classes: standard (city or mountain view); superior (ocean view); deluxe kitchenette (city view or ocean view, the latter on request only). In standard or superior accommodations, refrigerators and lanais are available on request only. Rates in low season, April 16 to December 21 range from $59 to $79 per night; in high season, from $74 to $94. For reservations, phone toll free 800/92-ASTON (922-7866) in continental United States. The FAX number is 955-3506.

A skyscraper for this area, **Days Inn Outrigger Hobron,** 343 Hobron Lane, Honolulu, HI 96815, at Discovery Bay (tel. 942-7777), has 600 attractive accommodations to its credit. The 44-story condominium hotel is very popular with tour groups. There are 310 hotel rooms, 140 studios, and 150 deluxe studios. Most of these rooms look similar, the major difference being in height. All rooms have attractive blond-wood furniture (desk, vanity, chair), multicolored drapes and bedspreads, air conditioning, and TV; they are small but well appointed, and many offer very good views of ocean, city, mountains, and the nearby Ala Wai Yacht Harbor. Most rooms have twin beds; only four on each floor have queen-size beds, which must be requested in advance. There are also differences in housekeeping facilities: the hotel rooms have refrigerators only; the studios have mini-kitchenettes. Prices are $45 standard, $55 moderate, $60 to $70 deluxe. All rates are $15 more from December 19 to the end of March. There are a few one-bedroom suites with kitchenettes at $90 for up to four persons, year round. Rates are subject to change. There's a pool on the mezzanine level, a sun deck plus Jacuzzi whirlpool and sauna on the fifth floor. All the excitement of the Ilikai and Hilton Hawaiian Village complexes is about five minutes away. For toll-free reservations, phone toll free 800/456-4329 in continental U.S., Alaska, and Canada.

The **Waikiki Marina,** 1956 Ala Moana Blvd., Honolulu, HI 96815 (tel. 955-0714), is a handsome hotel, just a few steps away from the Hilton Hawaiian Village and Rainbow Bazaar Complex, boasting a large swimming pool and sun deck, plus central air conditioning, and cable color TV. The most inexpensive accommodations here are the standard hotel room, which go for $48, single or double, from April 1 to December 15, and $58 the rest of the year. If you want to cook in, however, you can request a kitchenette for an additional charge of $5 per day. Deluxe mountain- and ocean-view rooms are $53 and $58 off-season, $65 and $73 in season. Suites, which include kitchenettes, run for $73 standard, $78 deluxe (mountain view), and $83 deluxe (ocean view), off-season, $81, $87, and $93, in season. An extra person is $12. Studios are adequate in size, with sliding glass doors opening onto a lanai. Inside is a kitchenette with a base refrigerator and a two-burner range, a tub-shower combination, television, and phone. Rates are subject to change. For toll-free reservations, phone 800/367-6070. The FAX number is 949-0096.

Although the **Pagoda Hotel,** 1525 Rycroft St., Honolulu, HI 96814 (tel. 941-6611), is about a ten-minute ride from Waikiki, you won't be isolated here: Not only are you near the Ala Moana Shopping Center, but right on the grounds is one of Honolulu's most spectacular restaurants, the Pagoda, with its colorful displays of flashing carp. Two buildings flank Rycroft Street. One is called the Pagoda Terrace; the other is called the Pagoda Hotel. Rooms here used to be of somber decor, but a renovation has made them cheery and bright. The best buys are in the Pagoda Terrace, where a studio apartment is nicely set up for housekeeping, with a full-size refrigerator, four-burner range, and all the necessary equipment goes for $65, single or double. A one-bedroom kitchenette suite for up to four people is $80; a two-bedroom suite, also for up to four people, is $95. The Pagoda Hotel offers moderate rooms at $70, deluxe rooms at $80, for one or two people; refrigerators only, no kitchenettes here. The rooms have air conditioning, color TVs, and full baths—and two swimming pools are here for dunking. For toll-free reservations, phone 800/367-7070 from mainland U.S. and Canada. The FAX number is 922-8061.

2. Hotels in Downtown Honolulu

Tourists who prefer to stay in downtown Honolulu (an easy bus ride from Waikiki) rather than in the beach area will have somewhat tougher sledding; there are so few hotels outside Waikiki that most tourists never hear about them at all. They are primarily occupied by business people. But there are a few in our budget category, and because this area is ideal for serious sightseeing, you may want to consider them.

There are only 41 units in the **Nakamura Hotel**, 1140 S. King St., Honolulu, HI 96814, just off Piikoi Street (tel. 537-1951), but you may be lucky enough to find a room on the spur of the moment since it's out of the tourist mainstream. We say lucky because rates are only $32 single, $40 double, $42 twin (subject to change), in this clean and quite comfortably appointed building; and because each and every room has wall-to-wall carpeting, a large tiled bathroom with a tub-shower combo, good drawer and closet space, even a telephone. We prefer the rooms facing the mountains; even though they do not have air conditioning, they do have those refreshing trade winds. In the air-conditioned rooms, the machine also has to drown out the traffic on King Street (so keep those jalousied windows closed). All these rooms are too small for a third person, but there are a few larger rooms in which a third person is permitted for an additional $4. Mrs. Winifred Hakoda, the personable desk clerk and day manager, advises that no late arrivals (after 10pm on weekdays, after 9pm on Sundays and holidays) are accepted.

Also pleasant is the tastefully modern and newly refurbished **Town Inn**, 250 N. Beretania St. Honolulu, HI 96817 (tel. 536-2377), a Japanese establishment where you'll mingle, so the management promises, "with important personages and travelers of every race." All this cosmopolitanism costs $37.70 single, without air conditioning, $39.88 with; $39.88 double without air conditioning, $42.06 with. Don't expect to sleep on the floor Japanese style; the bedrooms are as Western as the air conditioning. There's a Japanese restaurant, Miyajima, on the premises.

For men, the **Nuuanu YMCA** is a good downtown bet at 1441 Pali Hwy., Honolulu, HI 96813, near South Vineyard Boulevard (tel. 536-3556). It is a modern, $1.3-million facility with 70 dormitory rooms; singles go for $25 a day. Weekly rates are available, and advance reservations are accepted. There's a cafeteria here, and excellent athletic facilities are made available to residents.

For women tourists who'd like to stay at a Y, Honolulu has a terrific answer: the **Fernhurst YWCA**, an attractive tropical residence at 1566 Wilder Ave., Honolulu, HI 96822, about halfway between downtown Honolulu and Waikiki (tel. 941-2231). Women can stay overnight, or for up to six months, as the residence accepts both short- and long-term visitors, many of the latter from afar. So staying here is a good way to get to know people from many countries and backgrounds. The accommodations are double rooms, nicely furnished, each joined to another room by a common bath. At times single rooms are available. For a double occupancy, each person pays $20 a night with YWCA membership ($23 without), and that includes two meals a day—surely one of the best buys in town! (Y membership is required for stays longer than three nights.) The room-and-board charge for a single room is $25 a night with membership, $28 without. Linens may be rented for a nominal fee if you do not wish to provide your own. Pluses include a swimming pool, garden, laundry room, and a lounge area. Also available for use: typewriters, piano, TV, sewing machine. Advance reservations are accepted with a one-night deposit. Fernhurst recommends that you write first and inquire about future accommodations.

3. Hotels in Windward Oahu

Windward Oahu, as you'll recall from the introduction to this chapter, is the area on the other side of the mighty Koolau mountain range, which serves as a backdrop to Honolulu. The scenery is comparable to what you'll find on the neighbor islands. This is "the country," where many local people spend their vacations, but it's far off the usual tourist track. Although this is a good jumping-off spot from which to visit many of the attractions of the windward side, it's essentially a place where you sit on the gorgeous beach surrounded by sea, sky, and fragrant blossoms and do absolutely nothing at all.

Schrader's Windward Marine Resort, 47-039 Lihikai Dr., Kaneohe, HI 96744 (tel. 239-5711) is just about a half-hour drive from both Waikiki and downtown Honolulu, but this older, rural hotel on the shores of Kaneohe Bay is a world unto itself, dedicated to opening the field of marine recreation to its guests. Its own pier services the North Bay Boat Club and Sailing School, with daily boat trips available and a variety of sailboats, windsurfers, kayaks, and jet boats on hand. Beginners can learn how, and experts can just take off.

Five buildings here share a compound bordered by a stream on one side and Kaneohe Bay on the other. There's a swimming pool and a therapy pool (that's a Jacuzzi whirlpool with unheated water). Picnic tables and barbecues abound.

There are about 50 units—one, two, and three bedrooms. Rates start at $70 for a one-bedroom, not waterfront, for one or two people; an additional person is $7.50. Two-bedroom units start at $95 for up to four persons; add $30 to $35 more for waterfront. Each unit has a living room, bathroom, and lanai. All have full-size refrigerators; some have kitchen facilities as well. Furnishings are modest but comfortable in this older establishment; daily maid service is provided. You might have an old-fashioned tub instead of a shower. But you can count on color TV, air conditioning, and computerized phones. For reservations, phone toll free 800/367-8047, ext. 239, from the U.S.; 800/423-8733, ext. 239, from Canada.

Dreaming of a cottage right on the beach? They're not easy to come by in modern Hawaii, but Pat O'Malley of **Pat's Kailua Beach Properties,** 204 S. Kalaheo Ave., Kailua, HI 96734 (tel. 261-1653 or 262-4128) may be able to help you out. Pat offers more than 40 fully furnished houses and cottages along Kailua Beach, from a million-dollar beachfront estate to "beachy" cottages on or close to the water. About half of these come within our budget, costing $50 to $70 a day. Each is different, but all are fully furnished and provide cooking and dining utensils, bedding and towels, and television. Some are duplex. The interiors of the cottages we saw were well maintained; some have been recently renovated. The exteriors of some are weather-beaten, giving them a rustic look. Settings and views are lovely, and many have delightful yards and gardens.

A one-bedroom, one-bath beachfront home recently owned by a prominent Hawaiian family is priced at $70 a day and can sleep two adults and two children. Overlooking Kailua Beach Park, less than 100 yards from the surf, are one-bedroom, one-bath units from $55 to $75 that can sleep three to four people. Three blocks from the beach is one unit at $50, which can sleep three people.

Call Pat O'Malley for information and reservations: ask about the deposit requirements. The FAX number is 262-8275.

Ke Iki Hale at 59-579 Ke Iki Rd., near Waimea Bay but officially in Haleiwa, HI 96712 (tel. 638-8229), offers families a chance to be right on the beach at the North Shore. A bedroom on the beach (and we mean right on it) is $90 a day; a few steps back from the sand, it is only $65 a day with a living room and kitchen to boot. A family of six might opt for the two-bedroom apartment at $135 a day or $770 a week; not bad per person. There's a public telephone on the premises, but not a TV in sight. About 10 units are located in five buildings on the acre-and-a-half site. Furnishings are in good taste. Remember that Waimea Bay is ideal for swimming in the summer months, but during the winter its sky-high waves are for experienced surfers only.

More basic accommodations overlooking the ocean at Waimea Bay can be found at **Vacation Inn & Hostel,** 59-788 Kamehameha Hwy., Haleiwa, HI 96712 (tel. 638-7838). Backpackers like the hostel facilities at $12 a day. There are several rooms fitted out with four bunks to a room, a common living room with TV, a bathroom, and a kitchen. The quarters are cleaned each morning. Moving one step up, you can rent a single or double room, with common bath, kitchen, and TV room, for $35 single or double. Private studio apartments, $60 and $75 nightly, $360 and $450 weekly, can sleep up to four and are comfortably furnished, with TV and kitchenette; they all have good views of surf and beach. Some of these units are right on Three Tables Beach, which is next to Waimea Bay; others are higher up in a building on the mountain side of the road and command great ocean vistas. A protected area is safe for swimming for children. Boogie boards and snorkels are part of the North Shore life-style, so they are supplied free to guests. Chaz Wagner and Sharlyn Foo are warm hosts, who will help you locate the closest laundry facilities to your unit, point out a nearby supermarket, and maybe even find you a bicycle. They also rent many vacation homes and condos "in all shapes, sizes, and locations." Rates on request. Again, remember that Waimea Bay is perfect for summer swimming, but the water is rough in winter.

Located right next door to the Polynesian Cultural Center, the **Laniloa Lodge Hotel,** 55-109 Laniloa St., Laie, HI 96762 (tel. 293-9282), is a modern, motel-like building offering lots of comfort and a good location not far from many of the attractions of the North Shore. Right at home is a sandy ocean beach and pool; a short drive away is all the swimming, surfing, windsurfing, diving, horseback riding, championship golfing, and the like available in the Sunset Beach and Haleiwa area. Waimea Bay offers some of the world's best swimming (in summer) and best surfing (in winter); Waimea Falls Park is delightful, and Haleiwa has many shops and restaurants and an artsy-craftsy atmosphere. Rooms at Laniloa Lodge overlook the pool and courtyard, have private lanais, color cable TV, and air conditioning; the Lodge is within walking distance of the Brigham Young University Hawaii Campus and the Mormon Temple. Rates, subject to change, are $70 single or double, $75 triple, $80 quad. No charge for children under 8. Room/car packages, weekly, and temple-patron rates are available upon request.

SOME FINAL WORDS ON LODGINGS

If you'd like to exchange your own home or apartment for a place to stay in Honolulu, it can probably be arranged. Get in touch with the **Vacation Exchange Club,** 12006 111th Ave., Unit 12, Youngstown, AZ 85363 (tel. 602/972-2186), a worldwide home-swapping group. You can be listed in their directory for $24.70 (or receive their directory without being listed for $16) a year and find out what's available in Hawaii (a recent listing, for example, offered a three-bedroom, two-bath house, along with two cars and two bikes, in the posh Kahala region, for a three-month exchange), as well as many other places in the world. Rentals are also available. Vacation Exchange Club provides information only (it is not a travel agency); the actual arrangements are all up to you.

Another organization that provides a similar service is **Intervac US International Home Exchange,** P.O. Box 190070, San Francisco, CA (tel. 415/435-3497). Membership fee to be listed in one of their directories is $35 plus postage and handling; subscription to the publication only is also $35 plus. All told, they have something like 7,300 home listings, with about 100 in the Hawaiian Islands—on Oahu, Maui, Kauai, and the Big Island.

Teachers have more time for vacations than most of us, so it was inevitable that a service like **Teacher Swap Directory of Homes** would come about. They have an excellent list of international locations, as well as quite a few in Hawaii. The price is $32 for both a listing and the directory, $40 for the directory only. Write to Teacher Swap, Box 4130, Rocky Point, NY 11778 or phone 516/744-6403.

The **Honolulu Airport Mini Hotel** at Honolulu International Airport is something every traveler should know about—just in case. In case your plane departure is delayed, or you have to wait several hours to make a connecting flight, or you arrive late at night and there's no inter-island plane service until the next morning—or you simply need a place to go if you've checked out of your hotel early and have a late-night flight. That's where the Honolulu Airport Mini Hotel comes in. This clean and pleasant facility offers 17 private rooms at $22.50 per person for eight hours, including a shower. Resting facilities are $4 an hour with an extra $7.50 for a shower, including towels and toiletries. Facilities include a mini-spa, a small tread-mill, exercise bikes, and the like. "Travelers travel under stress," says owner Mona Dunn. "When they walk in this door, the stress ends." Each guest receives personal attention and a real feeling of aloha. There's a coffee pot perpetually brewing, plus a kitchen where flowers or medication can be refrigerated. Honolulu Airport Mini Hotel is open 24 hours a day. Reservations are advised for sleeping space; they are usually booked after 10pm. So popular has this establishment become that we may soon see versions of it in other airports in the country. It is located mid-terminal on the main level (tel. 836-3044). The FAX number is 423-2029. A refreshing idea.

Next door to the Honolulu Airport Mini Hotel, the same owners have opened the **Airport Business Center,** a boon to any business traveler. It contains a photo-copy center, FAX machines, a postal service, and a notary and secretarial service. Computers and small offices are available for rental. You can make long-distance phone calls here, buy travel insurance, store your small luggage, arrange for cellular phones and digital beepers. For information, phone 423-1991, or FAX 423-2029.

Bed and Breakfast

The bed-and-breakfast concept is gaining in popularity all over the United States, and Hawaii is no exception. Evelyn Warner and Al Davis started **Bed & Breakfast Hawaii** years ago, "not as a big business operation, but as a low-key, inti-mate way for people to visit Hawaii." They offer accommodations in private homes and apartments on all the islands, for rates ranging from $35 to $50 single, $40 to $90 double, including continental breakfast. If you think you'd like to live in a pri-vate home in the islands, this might be for you. Working mostly with Dollar Rent-A-Car, they can often pass on substantial savings on car rentals to their guests. Write for a free brochure to Bed & Breakfast Hawaii, P.O. Box 449, Kapaa, HI 96746 (tel. toll free 800/657-7832, local 822-7771, FAX 822-2723). For $8.50, you receive a di-rectory of homes and apartments with rooms for rent called *Bed & Breakfast Goes Hawaiian.*

Mary Lee, the woman who runs **Bed & Breakfast Honolulu,** 3242 Kaohinani Dr., Honolulu, HI 96817 (tel. 595-7533, or toll free 800/288-4646), does not believe directories do the trick; in more than six years of operating her business, she's found that almost any place a guest picks from a directory will probably be unavaila-ble at the time the request comes in. So Ms. Lee installed an 800 number and she, or one of her family, will engage you in a personal conversation and help you find accommodations—either a room in a home or a studio in an apartment building. She charges a $5 reservation fee for each unit she reserves. She currently offers more than 200 "homestays" and studios on all the major islands, even including Lanai! Prices range upward from about $35 single, $45 double. Mrs. Lee also handles car rentals and inter-island flights, and she can get you good discounts on each.

More than 100 different bed-and-breakfast facilities are available through **Oahu Prestige Realty & Management,** 1750 Kalakau Ave., Honolulu, HI 96826 (tel. 949-1881). It does not matter whether you want a condo, a cabin, or rooms in a private house. They have varied facilities all over Oahu, and even some on the other islands, with the exception of Molokai. The best time to phone is after 1pm Hawaii time, when you'll be more likely to find someone in the office. Most facilities run $35 to $80 a day for two or three people; if you wish to rent an entire house, prices will be higher. A 20% deposit is usually required.

The lovely suburb of Kailua, not far from Waikiki, is the home of Doris Epp, who runs **Pacific-Hawaii Bed & Breakfast,** and most of her Oahu rentals are in that area. It's one of our favorites, too, since both Kailua and Lanikai beaches are superb —and it's also one of the new meccas for windsurfers. Mrs. Epp also has a few list-ings on Maui, the Big Island, and Kauai. Rates begin at $40 a day for a room for two with bed and bath, and go up to complete homes or estates that can accommodate up to 16 guests at $375 a day. She requests a fee of $3 for her directory and mailing costs, plus 20% of the cost of the stay for confirmation, promising a complete refund if the room does not meet your expectations or you do not take occupancy because of a serious emergency; she's serious when she says, "satisfaction guaranteed." Write to her at Pacific-Hawaii Bed & Breakfast, 970 N. Kalaheo St., Suite A218, Kailua, HI 96734.

If you'd like a bed-and-breakfast accommodation on the windward side, close to Hanauma Bay and Sea Life Park (and about a 25-minute drive from Waikiki), get in touch with Mrs. Joan Webb, or her daughter, Barbara Abe; two Englishwomen who have a beautiful home, with garden and swimming pool, in Hawaii Kai. They rent two rooms: the larger one, with access to the pool area, has a queen-size bed, color TV, a small refrigerator, and a private bath, for $55. The smaller room, also cozy, has a double bed, color TV, and shares a bath with the hosts. It rents for $45. Joan and Barbara enjoy whipping up full island breakfasts for their guests, and join them at the dining table around a meal of fresh fruits, juices, homemade breads, English muffins, cereals, and beverages. They are generous with sightseeing advice and tips, and also provide beach mats and towels. Write to them at P.O. Box 25907, Honolulu, HI 96825, or phone 396-9462.

Discount Discoveries

Club Costa, founded in 1982, offers discounts ranging from 10% to 50% on hotels or condominiums on the four major Hawaiian Islands through its Worldwide Vacation Retreats program, a feature of its deluxe family membership, which also includes rebates on airfare, cruises, and packaged tours. The club is strongest in Hawaii and represents approximately two dozen properties on Oahu (many mentioned in this book). Family membership is $49. If you'd like to explore this further, write to Club Costa, 7701 College Blvd., Suite 200, Overland Park, KS 66210, or call toll free 800/444-3998 (in Kansas and Alaska, the number is 913/451-3462).

READERS' HOTEL SELECTIONS: "You list the **Royal Grove Hotel** as an 'old standby' in Waikiki and you are correct. This vintage hotel has the Aloha spirit all right. My wife and I were moving our business to Hawaii. We had booked a stay at the Royal Grove for a month. We lucked out and found a permanent home in four days. Tim Fong, who runs the hotel, extended the Aloha spirit to include a credit for the half-month we did not spend at his hotel. Tammy, who works with Tim, helped us get a good parking rate across the street. Surfers like to stay here, too, because Tim is an expert surfer, so watch out for surfboards in the lobby when you enter. It's the 'Best Buy for your Buck' in Waikiki. Our rate was $575 monthly for a studio with kitchen" (Capt. A. Plaut, *Sailorman Star Magazine,* Wahiawa, HI).

"I have several vacation rentals available in Lanikai, Kailua, just a block from the beach. These one- and two-bedroom apartments begin at $65 nightly, and a stay of three days is preferred. The one-bedroom has twin beds (which can turn into a California king), a queen-size sofa couch, a full kitchen, color TV, built-in bookcases, and a homey atmosphere. You share the deck with the upstairs (long-term) tenant. Write to Rusty Kunz, 1332 Mokolea Drive, Kailua, HI 96734, or phone 878-2137" (Rusty Kunz, Kailua, HI). . . . "My family moved to Oahu a year and a half ago. For the first month we stayed at the **Waikiki Marina Hotel,** which was wonderful, for under $50 a day for a family of four. We received a discount because my husband works for the Defense Department. Many (if not most) of the hotels and local establishments offer substantial discounts for military or defense workers" (M.B. Mililani, HI).

"The **YWCA** is for women only, all ages, from all over the world, so a most interesting place. Pool, garden, lounges, phones in rooms. We paid $20 per person, per day, for a double room, shared a bath with two people next door, *and this price included buffet, breakfast, and dinner, every day but Sunday!* Can't beat this! Reservations needed" (Mrs. Dorothy Astman, Northport, N.Y.). [*Authors' Note:* See text for details on the Fernhurst YWCA, one of our long-time favorites.]

"The **Marine Surf** in Honolulu proved to be a godsend. We stayed in the penthouse apartment (one bedroom with two king-size beds and bath, living room with sleeper-couch, kitchen, and *huge* lanai) for $130 a day. The Marine Surf is only 1½ blocks from Waikiki, adjacent to all shopping, including grocery stores, has in-house parking and a pool. The staff was friendly and efficient. This hotel is perfect in location, service, and for use by a large traveling family" (Michael P. Gaertner, Huntington, N.Y.). [*Author's Note:* See text for details on the Marine Surf.]. . . . I would like to strongly recommend the **Colony Pacific Monarch Hotel**

A Word of Caution

It is always advisable to put your valuables into your hotel's safe or an in-room safe. We once had a letter from two women who'd visited a major, highly reputable Waikiki hotel. They were asked if they wanted to use the safe and refused. While they were out of the room, a burgler entered using a hotel key, and stole their airline tickets, traveler's checks, cash, and all valuables! If you don't want to use a safe, then at least take your valuables with you. Never leave them unprotected in a hotel room, to which any number of people—staff, service personnel, guests past or present, and others—could have access.

where we have vacationed for many years. It is at 142 Uluniu Avenue, Honolulu, HI 96815 (tel. 923-9805). It is ideally located one block from the beach and King's Village and close to many fine restaurants. The skytop pool, Jacuzzi, and sauna with weatherproofed picnic activity area add to the many pleasures available. Lanais are equipped with table and chairs so that you can have a relaxing meal while watching the beautiful views (many of them oceanfront) and the sunset. Rooms have kitchenettes and include a welcome kit of coffee, tea, etc. Rates are structured by season. The studios with kitchenettes and walkout lanais are $80 to $88. One-bedroom apartments with full kitchens and large lanais are $110 and $120. Maid service is included. . . . **Hale Koa** at Fort DeRussy is still a marvelous place for active and retired military. In addition to lodgings, they have excellent meals and discount on entertainment. And their Sunday brunch is the best ever, surpassing that at many of the elegant hotels" (Dr. John Lopresti, Jr., Bricktown, N.J.).

"This time we booked our trip through **Pleasant Hawaiian Holidays,** and with one minor exception, we have nothing but the highest commendations for this outfit. In fact, I feel sure that we might never have received the palatial rooms and views we got with an outfit with less clout in the islands. Transportation to and from the airport on Oahu, flights, car rentals, and hotel accommodations went virtually without a hitch. These people surely know their business! The minor disappointment was the orientation breakfast (it seemed that at least 1,000 people were there) with long commercials about bargain side trips and shows. We were a captive audience for more than 60 minutes. Next time, we'll probably go with Pleasant again, but the one thing we won't do, as third-timers in the islands, is sit through another orientation session!" (James H. Cox, Middleton, Ky.). . . . "We booked through **Pleasant Hawaiian Holidays** and were not disappointed. In fact, by going to the orientation breakfast, we were able to get a few tours on two-for-one-specials and the Papillon Helicopters on Kauai for $20 off per person. We highly recommend the Pearl Kai sunset cruise and the Society of Seven nightclub tour, both on Oahu, and everyone should experience a helicopter ride, at least on one island" (Margaret A. Pyzik, Naperville, Ill.).

Might I suggest to your readers that they visit Hawaii as I did? I spent six weeks in Honolulu as a student at the **University of Hawaii** at Manoa. The cost of dorm room and board was very economical. Many tours, at special prices, were provided through the university. Our summer student identity cards even got us 'kamaaina' rates at various clubs and attractions. We were often roomed with local students and were thus able to share our different cultures. This is not just meant for single students; there were some dorm facilities for couples. The course selection is wide, ranging from golf and tennis to more academic studies. By the end of six weeks, I was referring to the dorm as 'home' (Susan McEwin, Stratford, Ontario, Canada). . . . "There was a big robbery in our hotel, which occurred only because people on the 12th floor kept their lanai doors open, thinking no one could get in. The robber crawled from the stairway, went from one lanai to another, entering and stealing from purses. Please keep your doors locked at night! We were lucky, as ours was locked" (Dorothy and Mike Capellani, Chicago, Ill.).

"On our last trip to Hawaii, we decided to go on June 17 and later wished that we had not. No one had told us that Honolulu, along with Miami, is *the* place to go when school is out. We and our daughter stayed at a Waikiki hotel that is usually very nice. This time it was loaded with high school students who took over the pool day and night and the beaches. They partied and ran from room to room until 3:30 or 4am, jumped up and down in the elevator until it broke down twice. People then had to use the stairs which were littered with broken beer and whisky bottles" (Mrs. Fred J. Criss, Portland, Ore.) . . . "We stayed at the **Hawaiiana Hotel** in Waikiki and loved it. The warmth and friendliness of a small hotel definitely has it over the impersonal atmosphere of a high-rise. When we checked out, however, I foolishly left behind a gold necklace on the shelf of the room safe. Two days later, when I realized what I had done, I called the hotel. The desk clerk said he would check. A day later I called again, and he told me he had found it and would mail it to me. I can't tell you how much his honesty impressed me! It would have been so easy to tell me it wasn't there and keep it. I would never have known. My only complaint about this terrific hotel is the noise from the street. Please advise readers to request a room in the middle of the complex, as it stretches between two busy streets" (Frances S. Kielt, West Hartford, Conn.).

"The **Royal Grove** was everything you said it was, and more. . . . There is no question where we would stay if ever again we would be in Waikiki. Why, the bus stop is less than 50 yards from the front door!" (Charles B. Ash, Prescott, Ariz.). . . . "People in Hawaii were absolutely incredible. We stayed at the **Outrigger Edgewater.** I would never dream of staying anywhere else" (Diane Presser, Marietta, Ga.).

"We spent five weeks in Oahu, having previously arranged to exchange homes with a couple who lived in a delightful home in Manoa Valley. Surprisingly, many island people do like to have excursions to the mainland, and home exchange is an ideal way of providing the basis for a really inexpensive vacation. A government employees' bulletin circulates in Honolulu and elsewhere, and at the University of Hawaii; this provides a good place to advertise" (David Brokensha, Santa Barbara, Calif.) . . . "Some hotels will give a 25% to 50% discount off their published room rates for military personnel and their families. We stayed at three- and four-star hotels at half the normal room rate. I believe that many of your readers are in the U.S. military and would be happy to know about this benefit!" (Joe and Robin Gruender, Wright-Patterson AFB, Ohio).

HONOLULU: RESTAURANTS AND NIGHTLIFE

Can the average tourist still find romance, happiness, and a good inexpensive meal in Hawaii? Well, we won't make any rash promises on the first two counts (that's up to you), but on the third we can be quite positive: Despite inflation everywhere, Honolulu's restaurants still do very well for the tourist. Although the price for dinner at one of the really elegant restaurants can easily zoom into the stratosphere, most of the good restaurants are in the middle range, which means soup to nuts averaging $12 to $20. And there are also quite a few—praise be—where a good dinner can average around $15. That's where we come in. Even if you wish to spend as little as $20 to $25 a day on food, you should have no trouble figuring about $14 or $15 for dinner, $5 to $6 for lunch, and $3 to $4 for breakfast. To keep on a really tight budget, plan to eat breakfast and at least one meal a day at home; that's when your kitchenette apartment more than pays for itself. Remember that lunch is always cheaper than dinner—often for much the same meal. Early Bird specials offer excellent dinner bargains all over town.

THE FOOD ITSELF

The food of Hawaii, like its people, reflects a wide cultural diversity—a lot of American, quite a bit of Japanese, a little less of Chinese, a smattering of Hawaiian, Korean, Filipino, and you-name-it thrown in for good measure. You quickly get used to the ubiquitous sign "Japanese Delicatessen" and to the fact that saimin (a Japanese-type noodle soup with a seaweed base) is just as popular as a hamburger and is often served at the same counter. You soon learn that the exotic-sounding *mahimahi* is Hawaiian for dolphin, a bland and pleasant-tasting fish—not to be confused with the intelligent mammal of the same name, the porpoise. You'll be introduced to poi, the staff of life of the early Hawaiians, at your very first luau, and you may develop a liking for this purple-gray goo that's one of the most nutritious foods known to man, so high in vitamin B and calcium that it's fed to babies and invalids. Just ignore the old joke that it tastes like library paste; the Hawaiians, and quite a few malihinis, think it's delicious.

Hawaii's fruits are among the islands' special glories. Pineapple, while not exactly invented here, might just as well have been. It's well priced in the markets, served everywhere, and as good as you'd imagine. Pineapple juice is kind of a national drink, something like tea for the English. If you hit the mango season in July, when the local trees are bursting with this succulent fruit, you're in for a great treat. Guavas, coconuts, papayas (one of the most common breakfast foods) are all superb, as are guava juice and passion-fruit juice, which you'll often see listed under its Hawaiian name, *lilikoi* (lilikoi sherbet is wonderful). Macadamia-nut pancakes, as well as coconut ice cream and syrup, are special treats that taste better in Hawaii than anywhere else in the world. We should warn you coffee addicts right here and now —the kind of coffee you'll get everywhere is Kona coffee, grown on the Big Island of Hawaii, and it's so good that you may find yourself drinking innumerable cups a day.

Don't miss the chance to try Hawaii's game fish, caught fresh in local waters, and served up in fish houses under "Catch of the Day." If you're lucky, the catch that day will be ahi (a kind of tuna and a personal favorite), or aki (another tuna), marlin, ulua, opakapaka, rock cod, or a special island delicacy called ono. That word has, in fact, slipped into local parlance as meaning "delicious"—or even "great"—as in "ono ono." At this writing, "Catch of the Day" was selling for about $16 to $20 in most restaurants; save this for a "big splurge" meal.

As for the preparation of these foods, you may not find haute cuisine, but you will find good eating. It is no hardship at all to eat in the budget establishments. Standards of sanitation are very high, and you need have no worries that your food will be anything less than clean, tasty, nourishing, and more often than you'd expect, surprisingly delicious.

---

1. Restaurants in Waikiki

The most exotic, and the most numerous, budget restaurants are located outside Waikiki. But that doesn't mean you can't have a very good time eating in the beachside area. We'll tell you first about our particular favorites, almost four dozen places we call the "fun" restaurants; then move on to the "old reliables," where you can always have a good and inexpensive meal with a minimum of fuss and bother. We've also thrown in a few big splurges—for those moments when you don't mind going slightly beyond your food budget.

THE "FUN" RESTAURANTS

The **Old Company Restaurant,** 2256 Kuhio Ave. (corner Seaside Ave.; tel. 923-3373) is in a two-story building that looks like a home; when you step off noisy Kuhio into the street-level dining room (there's another dining spot on the second floor), it's like entering someone's living room. Books and objets d'art fill the dividers. Comfortable captain's chairs, polished wood tables, low rafters, plants, and carpeting contribute to the homey feel. Lunch is fun here, since it features an all-you-can-eat fruit, soup, and salad bar for $6.75. Sandwiches run the gamut from grilled cheese at $3.15 to steak at $5.85. And dinner prices are modest, too: barbequed ribs or teriyaki chicken, for example, at $9.95; the seafood combination plate, $10.65. All regular dinners include a trip to the fruit, soup, and salad bar, plus vegetables and rice or potatoes (four choices). Dinner is served from 4pm to midnight. There's a bar with three television screens for viewing sports events, and live entertainment nightly, from 9pm on.

Lunch is on from 11am to 4pm, breakfast from 6am to 4pm. Arrive before noon and you can take advantage of the Sunrise Special: pancakes, egg, and bacon, for only $1.99.

If you can bring yourself to walk past the huge stuffed moose head with a lei around its neck—the first thing you see when you walk in—you'll love **Moose McGillicuddy's Pub-Café,** 310 Lewers St. (tel. 923-0751). It's big and airy—in fact, it's open to the street, with lots of plants and shiny ceramic-tile floor. This place is very popular among the local folks, since portions are large and prices very reasonable. Their Early Bird Breakfast Special, served from 6:30 to 9:30am is one of the best buys in town: two eggs, bacon, toast or rice or potatoes, orange juice, all for $2.49. Lunch and dinner menus are the same, and feature gourmet hamburgers (most under $5), hearty three-egg omelets served with fries, rice, or Texas toast ($5.50), hot soups, sandwiches, and salads. We specially like their pupus: nachos, deep-fried zucchini in beer batter, fried potato skins with beef, chicken or bacon, fish 'n' chips, yummy hot Texas chili ($3.95 to $5.95). Along with your meal you can have terrific margaritas and daiquiris at $4. A rock 'n' roll band plays nightly for dancing in the upstairs pub. McGillicuddy's is a lively spot, the crowd is congenial, and the menu descriptions an entertainment in themselves: look up, for example, the description of "Euell Gibbons' Memorial Omelette." A half-price happy hour is on from 4 to 8pm. There's another Moose at 1035 University Ave. (tel. 944-5525). That's where the UH kids hang out, and it's lots of fun. Both Mooses are very noisy. There's a third one in Lahaina, Maui, and it's noisy, too. Open every day, from 6:30am to 2am.

The budget crowd is kept well in mind at the **Waikiki Broiler,** in the Outrigger Waikiki Tower, 200 Lewers St. (tel. 922-6424), a cozy place brightened by shell-shaped ceiling lights and modern paintings on the walls. The dining room overlooks the pool area of the Outrigger Edgewater Hotel; in fact, two of the tables are practically in the pool! The Broiler offers low-priced dinner entrees like fish and chips, teriyaki chicken breasts, and mahimahi, from $6.95 to $11.95—in addition to such higher-priced offerings as lobster tail, scampi, and prime rib, the specialty of the house, $12.95 and up. At lunch, there are special sandwiches served with soup or salad (around $5), burgers, and a chef's special salad. Breakfast is served all the way from 6am to 2pm; waffles or buttermilk pancakes are a good bet at $1.95.

And there's a long daytime happy hour too, from 6am to 9pm, when exotic drinks are sold for the price of standards. Extend that to 2am on Saturdays and Sundays. Plus entertainment in the evening.

Just because you're saving money, it doesn't mean that you can't dine in style. If, for example, you'd like to have breakfast at one of the most glamorous tropical settings in town, at coffeehouse prices, simply take yourself over to the **Tahitian Lanai Restaurant** of the Waikikian Hotel, 1811 Ala Moana Blvd. (next to the Ilikai Hotel; tel. 946-6541). Seat yourself at an umbrellaed table overlooking the pool, the tropical lagoon, and the Waikiki surf out beyond (or in the atmospheric lanai dining room), and prepare yourself to feast both eyes and palate. Palm trees ring the pool, waitresses are clad in Polynesian costumes, and junglelike island decor is everywhere. While you're soaking it all up, you can order, as we usually do, coconut waffles or fresh banana griddle cakes for $3.65, two eggs for $2, and Hawaiian banana muffins for $1.50—recommended! If you're a little hungrier, you could have, perhaps, "Half a Benedict"—eggs Benedict served with hash browns, banana muffins, or a scrumptious popover, $5.25 (a "Whole Benedict" is $6.90). Coffee is robust, and served continuously. Come as early as 7am; they stop serving breakfast by 11am.

Lunch and dinner are also good buys at the Tahitian Lanai. Lunch, served from 11am to 2:30pm, features salads, sandwiches, and hot entrees that range from cottage-cheese blintzes at $4.95 to shrimp curry at $9.25, with chicken Kamaiina, cooked teriyaki style, somewhere in the middle at $7.25. From 2:30 to 5:30pm, there's a midafternoon lunch menu with lots of tasty hot meat sandwiches (hot pastrami on rye, grilled Reuben, Monte Cristo), from $4.75 to $6.75. And from 6 to 10pm, you can get a complete dinner for $9.95 to $16.95, featuring entrees like chicken curry or broiled mahimahi along with fresh fruit cup, French onion soup or tossed green salad to start; either steak fries or rice pilaf; banana muffins; dessert and coffee or tea. Look, too, for their daily "Jet Fresh" specials at lunch and dinner, which change depending on the seasons and the availability of fresh or live seafood items; you might be able to get fresh Pacific crabs from Chile, live Maine lobsters from Boston, or even fresh green lip mussels from New Zealand.

Another top choice for a glamorous breakfast is the **Hau Tree Lanai** of the New Otani Kaimana Beach Hotel, 2863 Kalakaua Ave. (opposite Kapiolani Park; tel. 923-1555). This is one of those sparkling, over-the-water spots, where the atmosphere and food contend for honors. It's so nice to dine here under the hau tree, watching the waves wash up to the shore, in the very setting that Robert Louis Stevenson once favored. A new menu here has way-upped the prices (lunch entrees go from $10 to $14.50, dinner entrees up to $23), but splurge on breakfast, at least. The standard American breakfast called the "Kamaaina" consists of two eggs; a choice of meat, potatoes, or rice and toast, for $8.50. Even more fun: the "Japanese Gourmet Breakfast" at $13.50; that's a bowl of miso soup, rice, seaweed, filet of fish, an egg, fresh fruit, pickled vegetables, and green tea—a meal big enough to last you for quite a while. Breakfast is served from 6:30 to 11am, lunch from 11:30am to 1:30pm, dinner from 5:30 to 9:45pm.

Another good move is to visit **Scoop Du Jour** at Sans Souci Beach at the same hotel, an ice cream parlor with a history. A few years back, a famous hamburger stand on the beach was declared in violation of the building laws and had to be dismantled. Hundreds of beachgoers signed a petition to save it, but to no avail. In its place rose Scoop Du Jour, where you can get very good saimin, jumbo hot dogs, meat sandwiches on onion roll or whole wheat packed with alfalfa sprouts and lettuce, and submarines, from $2.70 to $4. Sorry, no hamburgers—the grill would be a building violation—but ice cream sundaes are triple scoop with more chocolate syrup than you've probably ever had. Hours vary, but are roughly 9am to 5pm.

It doesn't surprise us a bit to see the lines in front of the **Lewers Street Fish Company** at 227 Lewers St., in the Outrigger Reef Towers Hotel (tel. 971-1000) at dinnertime; this restaurant has just about everything a hungry tourist could want: great, tasty food, an attractive ambience with sparkling tiled floors, a piano bar, a 40s decorative scheme; and prices that are downright appetizing. Most dishes are under $14, and there are quite a few that are a lot lower, like island fish and chips at $5.95; crispy fried chicken at $6.95; seafood spinach lasagne with garlic bread, a house specialty, at $6.95; beer-batter calamari at $9.95. Fresh fish from their own fishing boats is featured ("subject to season, weather, and the condition of our captain"), and it is handsomely presented on an oversized, fish-shaped platter, with a choice of rice or waffle french fries or fresh garlic pasta (we'd take the latter), and freshly baked bread. For a special treat, try their gourmet black pasta or gourmet lobster pastas; all pastas are homemade and seasoned with herbs and spices from the island of Molokai. Start your meal with an excellent seafood chowder and end with one of the everchanging desserts, each only $2.50.

Lewers Street Fish Company serves dinner only, nightly from 5 to 10:30pm. There's piano entertainment 6 to 11pm, except Monday.

The same management responsible for Lewers Street Fish Company runs two other Waikiki eateries that are equally good bets. We're excited about the **Waikiki Seafood and Pasta Company**, in the Outrigger Surf Hotel, 2280 Kuhio Ave. (tel. 923-5949); it's so pretty, with its dining room ceiling totally covered by plants, a smart New York–style deli and a bar up front. The food is inexpensive and delicious; pastas are made on the premises (you can ask to visit the "Pasta Factory"), so you know they're fresh. Gourmet pasta dinners run from $5.95 to $12.95. And the fresh pasta comes along with house specialties like garlic basil chicken, chicken parmesan, and chicken Italiano, $7.95 to $9.95. Fresh fish, seafood, and American favorites like mahimahi sauté, calamari steak, teriyaki beef kebab, and baby back ribs are priced from about $7.95 to $10.95, with only a few items higher. Desserts? Just $2.50. Again, good food, good value, and a fun atmosphere. Dinner only, nightly from 5 to 11pm.

Pieces of Eight, in the Outrigger Coral Seas Hotel, 250 Lewers St. (tel. 923-6646) is a bit pricier than the others, since it concentrates on steak and seafood, but prices are still reasonable, considering. One of Waikiki's oldest steak and seafood houses, it's won many dining awards since it opened in 1967. The cannon located on the piano bar goes all the way back to the time of King Kamehameha II, and was presented to him by a Russian sea captain in 1822. This is the place for fresh fish of the day, Pacific oysters, beer-battered shrimp, mahimahi almondine, top sirloin, filet mignon, and steak and seafood combos. Most entrees run from $9.95 to $12.95. Add $2.50 more and you get your turns at the salad bar; salad bar alone is $5.95. In typical steakhouse fashion, there's one major dessert: homemade cheesecake, $3.

Pieces of Eight serves dinner only, daily from 5 to 11pm. The bar is open from 4 to 11:30pm.

If you like tasty Mexican food, good prices, and a lively, noisy atmosphere, then you'll enjoy **Malia's Cantina,** 311 Lewers St. (tel. 922-7808). Malia's award-winning chili is, indeed, a winner, and so are the Mexican pizza and nacho macho among the appetizers ($4.50 to $8.95). Dinners are served with Malia's beans and Mexican rice, made fresh several times daily, and run from $7.25 to $11.75; house specialty is a succulent chicken fajitas at $8.95. Good salads, too, that could be a meal in themselves. The mood here is upbeat, with a large bar covering one side of the restaurant (reportedly, Malia's has the widest selection of tequilas in the islands), paneled walls and wooden floor, a large photomural of Diamond Head, around 1910. There's free live music Tuesdays through Saturdays, and happy hour from 11am to 6pm. Open daily from 11am to 2am. Everything on the menu is available for take-out.

Bring on the Buffets

Buffets are very, very popular in Honolulu, and ideal for the budget-minder. Just about the best values are offered at the **Perry's Smorgy Restaurants,** which have been serving hearty, American-style buffet meals for as many years as we can remember. The food is generally very good, there's no limit to how much of it you can eat, and at prices like $7.95 for dinner, $5.45 for lunch, and $3.95 for breakfast (prices subject to change), how can anyone go wrong! Choose any of three Perry's (or try them all); one at the Outrigger Waikiki Hotel, with gorgeous oceanside views and tables for watching the world go by; another at the Coral Seas Hotel at 250 Lewers St.; and the newest location, in a lush, garden setting (the site of the old Banyan Gardens Restaurant) at 2380 Kuhio Ave. at Kanekapolei. At all three, the help-yourself buffet is the same. The table is stacked with about 30 different selections: many fruit and vegetable salads; gelatin combinations; hot vegetables; rice or potatoes; homemade corn muffins and dinner rolls; and lots of hot entrees including southern fried chicken, beef and vegetable stew, mahimahi, and Italian spaghetti. Dinner adds a hand-carved round of beef au jus and golden fried shrimp. Fresh island pineapple and local Kona coffee are served at each meal. Breakfast features french toast, blueberry and banana muffins, hotcakes, smoked ham and sausages, a fruit bar, and more. You can have as many refills as you like, but no take-home packages, please. Breakfast is served from 7 to 10:30am, lunch from 11am to 2:30pm, dinner from 5 to 9pm.

The atmospheric **Peacock Room and Garden Lanai** of the Queen Kapiolani Hotel, at 150 Kapahulu Ave. (tel. 922-1941) is a great place to eat your fill, and then some. Buffets are served at lunch, dinner, and breakfast. You can have a Hawaiian-luau luncheon buffet any day except Thursday and Sunday, featuring all the traditional luau ingredients, for $9.50, which includes entertainment. On Thursday it's a Japanese luncheon buffet at $8.95; Sunday, a lavish brunch at $10.95. Or come by for dinner. The prime rib buffet, $12.95, is served Saturday and Sunday; it's a crab leg and roast beef buffet dinner at $12.95 on Monday and Thursday; Japanese buffet at $13.95 Wednesday and Thursday; and a seafood buffet on Friday. There's live entertainment nightly from 6:30 to 8pm. Dinner service is from 5:30 to 9pm. Lunch is on from 11am to 2pm. And for those of you who can't wait to start buffeting, the breakfast spread runs from 6:30 to 10am weekdays, to 9:30am Sunday, and costs $7.50. Reservations are advised for all dinners. Prices and schedules may change slightly, so check in advance.

For a buffet meal that's also a fine dining experience, the **Parc Café** at the Waikiki Parc Hotel, 2233 Helumoa Rd., across from the Halekulani Hotel (tel. 921-2727) is just the ticket. The atmosphere is charming, the service attentive, and the food of a quality not usually found on buffet tables. Consider the dinner buffet, which features the likes of Peking duck salad, celery rémoulade, fresh fish of the day, pastas and Far Eastern favorites. The carving station offers roast beef or pork, charbroiled top sirloin, plus poultry and lamb freshly done in the rotisserie. For dessert, you can choose strawberry shortcake, chocolate mousse, guava chiffon cake, among others, or make your own frozen yogurt sundaes with a choice of 14 toppings. Priced at $16.50, the buffet is served daily from 5:30 to 10pm. Sunday brunch, served from 11am to 2pm, is another lavish feast at $16.50. The rest of the week, the luncheon buffet features a create-your-own sandwich bar, a Cobb salad station, pastas, chicken from the rotisserie, the do-it-yourself yogurt bar, and more, for $9.50, from 11:30am to 2pm. And then there's the breakfast buffet, with a table full of goodies like exotic fresh fruits; danishes, muffins, and croissants; a variety of eggs and breakfast meats; cereals; pancakes and delicious french toast with both maple and guava syrups. A great place to conduct quiet business or a morning tête-à-tête. Breakfast is on from 7 to 10am.

It started with a few tables around the pool at the newly expanded Princess Kaiulani Hotel. But every year the tables increased, and now the **Pikake Terrace Buffet & Broiler** at the Princess Kaiulani, 120 Kaiulani Ave. (tel. 922-5811) is a dominant feature of the hotel's poolside and public areas. It lives up to its name with sumptuous buffets served morning, noon, and night in an open-air fantasia. Breakfast buffets, 6 to 10am daily, are $10.95 for adults, $4.95 for children 12 or under, and offer all you can eat of juices, fruits, cereal, crêpes, meats, and eggs cooked-to-your order. Lunch buffets, 11:30am to 2pm, are $11.95 for adults, $5.95 for children. Choose from a huge salad table, a hot entree table with half a dozen choices, a chef's table with a roast carved to your order, and a dessert table that tempts you to take one of each. The salad buffet alone is $7.50; the chef's table alone, $9.95. At dinner, 6 to 10pm, you have the choice of an expanded buffet at $17.95, or an elaborate menu, featuring such dishes as roast beef at $15.50 and filet mignon at $17.50. You can enter the area from the hotel, or use the informal walk-in entranceway to the pool area from Kalakaua Avenue.

Although the **Plantation Café** in the recently renovated Ramada Renaissance Ala Moana Hotel at 410 Atkinson (close to the Ala Moana Shopping Center; tel. 955-4811) serves more than just buffets, it's hard to resist these luscious treats. The restaurant is opulent with a huge glass wall opening on to a richly planted area, but prices are not out of line. The $9.95 breakfast buffet, served from 6 to 11am, is sumptuous and includes fruits, juices, eggs, meats, and pastries galore. Lunch features a soup-and-salad bar for $6.50, from 11:30am to 2pm. (If you opt for the regular menu, try the nasi goreng, Indonesian fried rice with chicken, shrimp, veggies, and eggs, $10.50; there are also Chinese, Indian, and other exotic dishes in the same price range.) On Aloha Friday there's Hawaiian entertainment at lunch. Come dinnertime, 6 to midnight, the chef's talents are displayed with out-of-the-ordinary soups and tantalizing appetizers such as the fettuccine Alfredo. Entrees are $8 and up, but again, we think you'll choose the all-you-can-eat buffet starring prime ribs at $14.95.

Vegetarians and health-conscious types take note: Waikiki now has a branch of the internationally acclaimed **Country Life Vegetarian Buffet**. It's at 421 Nahua Street; for details, see ahead, under "Nice and Natural."

More Fun Choices

Save this one for a big splurge and enjoy every moment of it. Months of renovations at the Ilikai Hotel, 1777 Ala Moana Blvd. (tel. 949-3811), have created a dining spot where eloquence and sophistication keynote the decor, music, and cuisine. The **Ilikai Yacht Club** provides sheltered outdoor views of the Ala Wai Yacht Harbor and, inside, a feeling of being served on a yacht. Large blue-glass columns are fish-filled aquariums. Upholstered chairs with a mahogany look seat you at the ample marble-topped tables You start your dinner with a choice of hot appetizers (perhaps a kettle of clams at $7, or poached salmon with spinach and chives at $5.50) or cold (the Alaskan King Crab served with salmon caviar at $6.50 is outstanding). The regular soup is seafood chowder, hearty with big chunks of fish, $3. The price of entrees includes a garden salad, home-baked breads, and fresh vegetables. On the low side of the menu, you might have fettuccine Alfredo at $13, or fettuccine with scallops and shrimps at $17. One of our favorites is the breast of chicken Nantua, stuffed with crab and served on a bed of spinach with lobster sauce; it comes with a rice mixture and assorted fresh vegetables, $17. Desserts are indescribable; the chef creates new wonders every day.

The Ilikai Yacht Club serves dinner only, daily from 5:30pm, with the kitchen closing at 10pm.

To dine more modestly at the same hotel, try one of the most atmospheric "coffeehouses" in town: that's **Pier Seven** at the Ilikai, 1777 Ala Moana Blvd. (tel. 949-3811), where all of the booths and tables have a view of the ocean and of the passersby on the boardwalk. A window booth gives you the added advantage of a bank of tropical greenery and the marina beyond. There, an early dinner provides a front-row seat for the sunset and the Ilikai's nightly torchlighting ceremony. There are a few dinnertime bargains, like the salad bar at just $5.95. Among the low-priced entrees is a steamed-vegetable platter at $7.95; ginger chicken is $9.75. Sandwiches and burgers are well worth the $5.25 to $9.75 tab as they are robust and served with all the trimmings. And we'll vouch for the clam chowder, among the richest New England-style chowders we've tasted. Pier Seven is open every day from 6am to 10:30pm. A stylish spot.

It's not hard to figure out why the **Shore Bird Beach Broiler,** beachfront at the Outrigger Reef Hotel, 2169 Kalia Rd. (tel. 922-2887), quickly became one of the most popular restaurants in Waikiki. First of all, you can't beat the location: The large, attractively decorated open dining room is right on Waikiki Beach. Second, the food is good; and third, the price is right: that's because you're the chef, broiling your own portion of teriyaki chicken or ribs, seafood or filet mignon kebab, New York steak, ground or top sirloin. Prices run from $6.95 (for island filet) to $11.95. While the fire is doing its work, you can have a few drinks, then fill up on salad bar, chili, rice, and fresh pastas. Coffee, tea, or iced tea is included with the meal; dessert (including their own cheesecake made fresh every day) is extra. Perfect for sunset drinks and dinner. Early Bird specials from 5 to 6:30pm. The broiler is hot from 5 to 10pm; from 10pm on the heat is provided by nonstop video disco on a 10-foot screen, a laser light show, and music and dancing continuing until about 2am. They also have an all-you-can-eat breakfast buffet at $5.95, served from 7:30 to 10:30am daily.

Everyone likes **Caffè Guccinni,** 2139 Kuhio Ave. (tel. 922-5287), both for the Italian meals and the delectable desserts. This is a modest place, with a counter inside, tables outside, and the menu posted beside the counter. Dinner specials, which average $8.50 to $10.50, include various pasta dishes on the regular menu (we're partial to the manicotti stuffed with five kinds of cheese), and two or three daily specials, like veal, calamari, quiche, and Italian sausage. There's a full liquor and wine bar. Happily, both meals feature those wonderful desserts that made Caffè Guccinni famous. We're always hard put to decide among the merits of a heavenly crème brûlée or chocolate torte, a Sicilian cannoli, or a light and lemony cheesecake. The best solution is to bring a group of friends and share. Desserts are all $3. (If you've eaten elsewhere, come here just for dessert.) Along with your feast, have some of the best espresso and cappuccino in the islands, or an ice cream "shake with a shot." Everything is homemade in owner Jocelyn Battista's own kitchen, including fresh pasta and bread daily. Open daily from 3 to 10:30pm.

Here you are in the tropics, but you love the desert, too. What to do? Ride that lonesome trail to **Peppers Waikiki Grill and Bar,** 150 Kaiulani Ave. (tel. 926-4374), a hybrid of the islands and the southwest, sprouting both cacti and palm trees, and serving some of the best Tex-Mex food in town. It's a casual, sophisticated spot, dominated by a lively bar (watch out for those frosty margaritas!) and yet, with its well-spaced booths and tables, conducive to good conversation. The secret ingredients here are the wood-fired smoke oven that gives a true barbecue taste to the chicken and ribs, and the mesquite grill that turns out super burgers and steaks. Mexican dishes—tacos, fajitas, burritos, and the like—run from $6.75 to $10.95; smoke-oven baby back ribs begin at $10.45; and there are excellent salads like the Cobb salad and the chicken taco salad, from $6.25 to $7.25. Nachos, sandwiches, quesadillas, yummy potato skins, and the like offer inexpensive and tempting possibilities for grazing. For dessert, try hula pie, a specialty of Hawaii, or fried ice cream, a specialty of Mexico (no, it's really not fried, but in such a *simpático* spot, it's hard to quibble). Peppers, in the very heart of Waikiki, serves the same menu from 11:30am to 2am every day of the week.

"Waikiki's only San Francisco–style seafood house" is what they call **Blue Water Seafood** at 2350 Kuhio Ave. (tel. 926-2191), a big, busy place decorated with a nautical flair—captain's chairs and lots of brass. Most complete dinners are priced from $6.95 to $14.95 (lobsters higher), and include rice, french fries, sliced tomatoes, and freshly baked bread. Entrees of note are fresh fish caught daily, top sirloin steak, scallops, mahimahi, teriyaki chicken, and steak and seafood combinations. Blue Water is also open for breakfast and lunch, serving meals from 7am to 10pm daily. A breakfast buffet is $3.75. From 10pm to 4am, it turns into a night spot.

Tony Roma's—A Place for Ribs is getting to be as popular in Honolulu as it is on the mainland, with three restaurants to choose from. One is at the gateway to Waikiki at 1972 Kalakaua Ave. (tel. 942-2121); another is at 4230 Waialae Ave., across from Kahala Mall; and still a third is in Westridge Center, convenient for visitors to Pearl Harbor. The restaurants are big and comfortable, decorated in western style, with lots of wood and leather, walls of brick, shuttered windows, oil paintings on the wall. The staff is energetic and friendly. All entrees are served with rice, baked potato, or french fries and coleslaw. The house specialty, of course, is ribs: at dinner, a generous serving of St. Louis–style ribs is $10.45; barbecued baby back ribs, $10.95 (lunch orders are a few dollars less). Barbecued chicken is a bargain at $6.95, and so is filet mignon on a skewer at $8.95. Don't miss the famous onion rings at $2.50 for half-a-loaf. Daily specials are $10.95 at dinner, $6.95 at lunch on weekdays. There's a special keiki menu for kids under 12. Cheesecake or mud pie, the only desserts, go well with espresso or cappuccino, as well as with French, Irish, or Mexican coffee.

In addition to all this, Tony Roma's features many of Hawaii's premier entertainers—with no cover charge. It's open 365 days and nights a year, from 11am on. To have those ribs and onion rings delivered wiki-wiki to your hotel or condo, call 947-RIBS in Waikiki, 737-RIBS in Kahala.

A meal at **El Crab Catcher,** at 1765 Ala Moana Blvd. (tel. 955-4911) in the Ilikai Hotel area, need not be expensive, if you know where to sit and what to eat. We like to head for the Seafood Cafe, set off from the main Coral dining room by a beautiful marine aquarium of rainbow-colored fish. Pupus, light entrees, and generous tropical drinks are featured every day from 11:30am to midnight, and they are terrific. House specialty is crab-stuffed mushrooms, topped with melted Jack cheese, $5.95. Shrimp, scallops, fresh fish, oysters, and clams are presented in various ways, from $6.95 to $9.95. The Chinese shredded-wonton chicken salad is heaven, and the Crab Catcher sandwich—snowcrab, cheese, tomato, and sprouts baked on cheese bread—is equally delightful ($7.95). In the Coral dining room, the Light Cafe Selections offer such tasty entrees as chicken teriyaki, combination seafood platter, and lobster primavera for around $13. Fresh Hawaiian fish of the day is around $10. Higher priced entrees begin at $17.95 and include crab-stuffed Hawaiian fish and scampi sautéed. With all entrees, El Crab Catcher serves baked breads, fresh vegetables, and broiled red potatoes. Dinner is served from 5:30 to 10pm every day. Dress is casual.

We're great fans of Japanese noodle houses: They're just the ticket for those times you want a simple, tasty, nutritious—and extremely low-cost—meal. So we were delighted to find the **Tsuruya Noodle Shop** at 325 Lewers St. (tel. 922-3434), a sparkling clean little place with a horseshoe-shaped counter in the middle, four tables with comfortable leather chairs, and some mirror-framed paintings on the walls. We chose the hot soba broth called Sansai, with a "mountain of vegetables and garnishings," and the teriyaki chicken teishoku—grilled, marinated chicken and salad, which came with miso soup and pickled vegetables—two hearty meals for $5.15 and $5.50, respectively. Cold soba (buckwheat) noodles are also available, as are various other Japanese dishes, and side orders of shrimp tempura, cooked in "100% vegetable oil." Your food is served promptly, on a lacquered tray in a beautiful bowl. Take-out orders are available. Tsuruya Noodle Shop is open every day, from 11am to 10pm.

A meal at **Kobe Japanese Steak House,** 1841 Ala Moana Blvd. (tel. 941-4444), is a show in itself. First, there's the beautiful Japanese country inn surroundings and artifacts everywhere; second, the splendid sushi bar; and third, and most important, the communal tables where you and fellow diners can chat and watch your meal being prepared teppanyaki-hibachi style, by a master chef who stands at the grill in the center of it all. Stay on the low side of the menu here: Choose teriyaki chicken, sukiyaki sirloin, or teppan shrimps, or a steak and teriyaki combo, and you can have a complete meal for $11.90 to $28. First, the chef sautés some teppan shrimp and serves you a delicate soup; then he stir-fries your order with mushrooms, onions, peppers, and bean sprouts. Vegetables, rice, and tea come with the meal, and you top it all off with delicate green-tea ice cream. Japanese beers and warmed saké make a perfect accompaniment to a fun meal. The grill is hot dinnertime only, from 5:30pm on daily.

The **New Tokyo Restaurant** at 286 Beachwalk, just off Kalakaua Ave. (tel. 923-5411), is getting to be an institution in Waikiki, attracting tourists and locals alike. The anteroom, with its Asian ambience and aquarium display of live seafood, is both decorative and functional, getting you in the mood for seafood. For lunch, you might have the grilled fish marinated in soy sauce for $3.95, or the assorted tempura vegetables with tempura fish at $5.25. Combination lunches run $3.75 to $6.25. At dinner, prices are more as they are in Tokyo, starting with noodle dishes from $8.25 to $10.75, and old favorites like sukiyaki and shabu, $19. Lunch is served from 11:30am to 2pm, dinner from 5 to 9:30pm daily.

Despite its name, **Waikiki Sidewalk Café,** 2526 Kalakaua Ave., near Kapahulu Ave. (tel. 926-5105), is really just a tiny Japanese fast-food restaurant with only a dozen small tables and even fewer counter seats. The name belongs to a permanent building sign that once identified a different restaurant. A Japanese sign proclaims a different name, as this is a restaurant run by the Japanese for the Japanese. But visitors from elsewhere love this place, too, both for the food and the low prices. You choose your dish by looking in the window and studying its colored plastic replica. Underneath each is its Japanese name in English letters, its ingredients and price. Good bets are the Kake Udon, saimin-like noodle soup, $4.50; Oyako-Don, a chicken and egg entree, $6; Gyu-Don, beef and rice, $6. The Japanese visitors eat these dishes from breakfast to supper, so the menu stays the same from the 7am opening to the 10:30pm closing time, seven days a week.

A touch of Thai lives in Waikiki. One flight up at 407 Seaside Avenue is the **Siam Inn** (tel. 926-8802), a pretty little place in which to make, or renew, acquaintance with the subtle (and not-so-subtle) spiceries of Thai cuisine. Dine inside in a setting of white walls covered with colorful murals of Thai scenery, crisp green tablecloths, and tile floors; or outside on a little balcony under potted trees. When last we lunched there, the daily specials, $6.95, were Bangkok chicken, served with rice and the chef's special soup, and the chicken masaman curry—slices of tender chicken on a bed of avocado, peanuts, and coconut milk, served with curried rice and cucumber sauce (mild or hot). Other luncheon possibilities are also very reasonable (there are 12 dishes under $6.50), and include a variety of noodle dishes featuring chicken, beef, pork, or shrimp. Your waiter will ask if you wish your meal mild, hot, or very hot (advice to newcomers to Thai cooking: mild is the safest). Dinner prices are also reasonable, with all the chicken, beef, pork, and shrimp dishes at $7.95, fish specialties at $15.95, and rice dishes from $5.95 to $6.45.

Siam Inn opens at 11am Monday through Saturday and at 5pm on Sunday; dinner is served until 10:30 nightly.

The Godmother, at 339 Saratoga Road (tel. 922-6960), is a bit of Old-World Italy in an indoor-outdoor lanai setting; its logo is a shapely signora in black tights, a Mafia-style jacket, and slouch hat, carrying a violin case. Dinners are a good buy since they are served with salad or soup and homemade bread, and there are many on the low side of the menu, like veal or chicken piccata, with rice or pasta, $14. Pasta specialties include lasagne, ravioli, and spaghetti dishes, priced at $10 and an especially flavorful spinach fettuccine al Cestare: noodles sautéed in garlic butter, with hot sausage, onions, mushrooms, and fresh tomatoes, "an offer you can't refuse."

The Godmother opens for happy hour at 2pm; it serves dinner from 6 to 11pm and closes at 2am daily; piano bar and entertainment from 8pm to 1:30am Wednesday to Sunday.

There's a cute little corner of Mexico at the corner of Kalakaua and Saratoga, and **Popo's Mexican Restaurant,** 2112 Kalakaua (tel. 923-7355), is the name. Popo's has both decor (white walls, tile floors, stucco, serapes, native pottery) and food that is *muy auténtico,* and the prices are right. Come at lunch and you can have dishes like a good and snappy chile relleno for $7.50, or machaca—shredded beef sautéed with bell peppers, tomatoes, eggs, and onions—for $7.75. Combination plates are mostly $8.75 to $9.25, and regular entrees of enchiladas, burritos, and so on are $10.50 to $11.95. The native-born Mexican chef does tasty flautas and chalupas, too. Dessert? Guava sherbet with coconut and honey is great, and, of course, there are margaritas, sangría, and Mexican beer at the ready. A *simpático* choice. Lunch is 11:30am to 2:30pm, dinner 5 to 9:30pm daily.

A *Honolulu Advertiser* columnist once named **Emilio's Pizza** as "the best new pizza place in Honolulu." Well, we knew it all along. Emilio's isn't new anymore, but it's still as cozy as ever, with interesting framed pictures and glass shelving lending a homey atmosphere to its quarters at 1423 Kalakaua, near the corner of King Street (tel. 946-4972). This is pizza with a professional touch—deep-dish Sicilian style. They make their own tasty dough fresh every day, and their own sausages and sauces. They also make several specialty dishes like fettuccine Alfredo with artichoke hearts, spaghetti carbonara, meat and vegetarian calzone, and lasagne (most are $7.50), as well as hearty sandwiches, soups, salads, garlic bread. But about those pizzas. . . .

There is a choice of 14 fresh toppings, which are piled abundantly on deep-dish crusts, making a 10-inch pie a filling meal for two to three people. Prices run from about $7 for the 10-inch cheese pies with one topping, up to $18.50 for the mind-blowing combo with six toppings. Customers are welcome to bring their own beer or wine; there is no corkage charge. Emilio's is open from noon to 11pm Monday through Thursday, to midnight on Friday and Saturday, from 5 to 10pm on Sunday. And, yes, they will deliver to most hotels and condos in Waikiki.

At the International Market Place and Kuhio Mall

Few tourists who set foot in Waikiki leave without at least one visit to the **International Market Place** in the heart of the beach area at 2330 Kalakaua Ave., where throngs of merchants offer everything from grass skirts to wooden idols to T-shirts and pearls-in-the-shell. Immediately adjoining it, and fronting on Kuhio Avenue, is **Kuhio Mall,** another lively bazaar. Just about in the middle of the two of them is the attractive **International Food Court** (follow the yellow-brick line), where some 30 fast-food stands offer a variety of tempting foods that you eat at central tables. You can certainly make a meal here, lunch or dinner, for $5 or under: some of our favorites include **Peking Garden, Beef & Burger,** the **Mad Greek, Aloha Yakitori, Choi's Kitchen, Bautista's Filipino Kitchen, Yummy Korean BBQ,** and **Mario's Pizza and Pasta. Cinn-a-Yums** dispense enormous, fattening, delicious cinnamon buns with various toppings. Open daily from 8:30am to 11pm.

Elsewhere in the Market Place is a bit of Mittel Europa in Waikiki. That's the **Hofbräu,** a German biergarten-deli, where the guests sing along and drink along as the Hofbräu Band belts forth nightly polkas, waltzes, and the like. While you're humming along, you can dine (lunch or dinner) on inexpensive plates like bratwurst, knockwurst, Polish kielbasa or smoked pork loin for $6.75 to $19.95.

Sandwiches, served on country rye, with kosher pickle, include pastrami, ham and cheese, and assorted German meats, around $4 to $5.

The culinary adventurers among you will want to experience something different indeed: the **Mongolian Bar-B-Que** at Kuhio Mall. Seems that a very special dish in the northern part of China is strips of beef, barbecued with vegetables and spices, and this is one of the few restaurants we know of in Honolulu that serves it. You select your own meats, sauces, vegetables, and spices and pass them on to the chefs, who then cook them in an open-fire pit. The full Bar-B-Que is $13.95, with seconds free ("quick" meals—the chefs make the selection—and "mini" meals are $5.95 and $4.95). Also available: sandwiches on homemade sesame buns, lunch plates, soups, salad, beers, wines, and cocktails. Truth to tell, we find the Bar-B-Que a mite strange tasting, but many local people have become addicted to it. It's one of those things you have to experience for yourself to judge.

Ashley's, 2301 Kuhio Ave. (tel. 923-2288), upstairs at Kuhio Mall, is a small restaurant with a lot going for it. It's a pleasant setting, partially open, with old Hawaiian prints on the walls and a view of the street from your table. The biggest draw is the $3.99 spaghetti meal; everything is made daily from scratch, and the clam, marinara, and meat sauces are fresh and tasty. Along with the spaghetti comes an all-you-can-eat salad and fresh-fruit bar; cheese toast is $1 more. Complete dinners, served with steamed vegetables and a choice of french fries or rice or baked potato, offer excellent value as well: teriyaki chicken, a steak-and-shrimp combo or a steak-and-chicken combo, as well as top sirloin, are priced from $7.99 to $9.95. Ashley's is open every day from 4 to 9pm.

We can never resist the luscious aromas wafting from the **Hung Yun Chinese Kitchen,** at no. 110 in Kuhio Mall, entrance on Kuhio Avenue. Bear left and follow your nose past the waterfall. It's just a little service counter place with a few tables, but it's the least expensive spot we know to sample a variety of Chinese dishes at penny-pinching prices. Some entrees, like curry chicken, chicken with black beans, beef broccoli, and sweet-and-sour pork are just 99¢ per portion: other plates, including shrimp and rice, green onion beef, and spicy Szechuan eggplant, are all of $2.95. Open every day during mall shopping hours.

Keep in mind that Kuhio Mall also has several good fast-food outlets, among them **Pizza Hut** and **Taco Hut.**

At the Waikiki Shopping Plaza

Time was when budget dining at the **Waikiki Shopping Plaza,** at 2250 Kalakaua (corner of Seaside), was limited to the basement snack shops (see "Old Reliables," ahead), while its upper floors harbored some of the more glamorous and expensive international restaurants in town. But then the **Marco Polo Eating and Drinking Establishment** (tel. 922-7733) took over one of these attractive enclaves, and all that changed. Marco Polo offers steak and seafood at reasonable prices. Entrees—which include soup or salad, rice pilaf or potato, and homemade bread— run mostly from $9.95 to $13.95. Steak and shrimp are $12.95, prime rib is $13.95. Marco Polo also offers a daily luncheon special like beef curry, mahimahi sandwiches, or omelets, as low as $4.95. It boasts an intimate, multilevel setting, lively bar, and happy hour prices from 11am to closing. Open for lunch Monday to Friday from 11am to 2pm, for dinner every day from 5 to 10pm.

For a touch of opulence at the Waikiki Shopping Plaza, try **Lau Yee Chai** (tel. 923-1112), the famed Waikiki Cantonese restaurant, whose magnificent furnishings, irreplaceable today, come from the original Waikiki Lau Yee Chai, which opened in 1929. The main dining room, big enough to hold 500 people, is decorated with gleaming lacquered furniture, rich wood carvings, a huge brass gong, and real gold in the exquisite wall panels. The golden calligraphy characters spell out poetry in the Cantonese dialect. Considering the splendor befitting a Chinese emperor, the prices are surprisingly democratic, and the food is very good. Most Cantonese entrees run between $6.50 and $8.50, and in this price range you could have mushroom chicken, lemon chicken, scallops with vegetables, almond chicken or duck, stuffed duck, beef with tomato, or shrimp with vegetables. Should you favor shark's-fin soup (a rarefied taste), it's $6.95. For those who favor the hot and spicy flavors of Szechuan cooking, there's a full menu, and you can eat your fill of dim sum at lunchtime.

Lau Yee Chai is open every day, serving lunch from 11am to 2pm, dinner from 5 to 10pm.

For the Steak Set

When the whole family wants to eat steak and you don't want to break the budget, there's a terrific answer: find the nearest **Sizzler Restaurant.** There are 11 of them in the Hawaiian Islands, including one right in Waikiki, at the corner of Kalakaua and Ala Moana (tel. 955-4060), and it's open 24 hours a day. The Jamboree Breakfast, served from midnight until 11am, offers eggs, bacon, and all the hotcakes you can eat for $2.99. For lunch and dinner, Sizzler serves steaks that are a good size and good quality, amazing values for the money, an order of sirloin is $7.69. New York–cut steak, $9.25. Along with your steak comes Sizzler toast, plus a choice of baked potato, french fries, or rice. All Sizzlers now have salad bars, soup, and serve beer and wine. There's also seafood, including steak and shrimp at $11.99. Salad, desserts, and coffee and iced tea are extra, but refills on the beverages are free. There are more Sizzlers elsewhere on Oahu, including one at Koko Marina.

At the Royal Hawaiian Shopping Center

Right in the middle of Waikiki at 2233 Kalakaua, the **Royal Hawaiian Shopping Center** houses a number of good restaurants: our favorites are The Great Wok of China, Spaghetti! Spaghetti!, and the Bavarian Beer Garden.

Wok cooking is becoming almost as popular in the United States as it is in China. To see a master perform the art at your own table, take your chopsticks to **The Great Wok of China** (tel. 922-5373), a spacious and handsomely decorated room. The kitchen is largely Cantonese but various dishes also represent Mandarin and Szechuan cuisines. You'll be seated at tables for eight, with two woks in the center; you place your order for, perhaps, the Celestial Celebration Chicken at $9.75, the Shanghai Vegetarian (vegetables and tofu) at $7.70, or whatever the Wokmaster's Special is for that night, at $9.75. While the chef is busy in the kitchen with his cleaver cutting up the ingredients for your main dish, you'll be served, first, a delicious bowl of hot-and-sour soup, followed by a Chinese chicken salad—tiny shreds of chicken with lettuce and a sesame-based dressing—very tasty. Then the chef goes to work at the wok, tossing up a succulent (and happily, smokeless) meal. Of course, there's a pot of tea, and fortune cookies for dessert. Dinner is served daily from 5:30 to 10pm. At lunch, daily from noon to 2pm, you can sample inexpensive dishes like freshly roasted Chinese barbecue on a bed of stir-fried pasta for only $4.45. The 4-to-6:30pm happy hour features low prices and free pupus. Cooking classes are often held here on Friday at 11:30am.

Everybody seems to like spaghetti, so it's good to know that you can eat your fill—from a spaghetti buffet and salad bar—for $4.99, at a stylish restaurant called **Spaghetti! Spaghetti!,** 2233 Kalakaua Ave. (tel. 922-7724). This is a large, multilevel restaurant with attractive furnishings, a huge and busy bar, and, on the buffet table, a choice of four different pastas, four freshly made sauces, and a variety of salad ingredients. Salad bar alone is $3.50; with soup, it's $4.50; and with the pastas, $4.99. A $2 slice of garlic bread rounds out the meal nicely. Also available are soups; hot meat loaf, mahimahi, and other sandwiches; chicken in a basket; and a giant burger for $5.95. You can top off a not-exactly-slimming meal here with cheesecake or a super Baskin-Robbins mud pie. Spaghetti's open from 11am to 11pm.

If you'd like some hearty German fare, then go to the top of the Center and visit the **Bavarian Beer Garden** (tel. 922-6535). Here you can dine on authentic German cuisine in a gemütlich atmosphere. There's ballroom dancing every night to live music, and Oktoberfest celebrations every day. Traditional dishes like wienershnitzel, sauerbraten, Bavarian meatloaf, pan-fried bratwurst, and beef roulade are nicely done. Prices begin at $4.50 for wieners and $5.50 for European cold cuts and go up to $13.50 for the wienerschnitzel. There's a good selection of imported wines, beers, and schnapps. The Bavarian Beer Garden is open every day from 5pm to midnight; dinner is served until 11pm.

More Fun Choices

Discovery Bay, a two-level shopping area topped by a huge condominium, at 1778 Ala Moana Blvd., opposite the Ilikai Hotel, houses one of Honolulu's most enjoyable French restaurants: **Bon Appetit** (tel. 942-3837). It's master chef Guy Banal's contribution to the cause of haute cuisine. Dinner here can be rather expensive if you order off the à la carte menu, so save yourself some francs by having their complete gourmet dinner: three courses for $21.95. The menu changes daily; the day we were there, course one was duck and morels mushroom soup with vegetables, and course two was Maui tomatoes with shrimp salad and avocado dressing. Course three was a choice of venison casserole or broiled island fish with lobster champagne sauce. You dine seated on royal-red chairs, at windows overlooking Ala Moana Boulevard. There is an excellent wine list, and a popular wine and appetizer bar as well, the biggest in town. Bon Appetit serves dinner only from 5:30 until 10pm. Closed Sunday.

The cheerful little **Harbor Pub and Pizzeria,** just below the Chart House at 1765 Ala Moana Blvd. (tel. 941-0985), is usually filled with a "fun" crowd in the evening. It's a favorite watering hole for people employed at nearby hotels and offices. The fare is not terribly varied here, but what there is, is just fine. All sandwiches —roast beef, breast of turkey, submarine, and tuna melt—are around $5. The specialty is pizza: plain cheese pies are $7.95 small, and the Harbor combo, with everything, is $10.50 small. This is the sort of place where everyone talks with everyone else, and the atmosphere is friendly and fun. Hours are 11am to 1:30am daily.

THE OLD RELIABLES

Now we come to the standbys, the places you can always count on for fast service, and good, basic food. And if there's anything more basic than a McDonald's we've yet to find it. There are about half a dozen **McDonald's** in Waikiki; the most central is the one at 2204 Kalakaua Ave., in the heart of the beach area. At all McDonald's you'll find the usual standbys like Big Mac sandwiches ($2.05), Filet-O-Fish ($1.65), and the like, but since this is multi-ethnic Hawaii, you'll also find such local favorites as saimin, Portuguese sausage, a scrambled-eggs-and-rice breakfast, fruit punch, and guava juice. And if you get the hungries late at night, it's good to know that these places usually do not close until midnight on weekdays, 1am on weekends.

The Japanese counterpart for McDonald's is **Mos Burger,** with over 850 outlets in that country. Now the first one outside Japan has opened at 2186 Kalakaua Ave., just a few doors from Lewers Street. It offers a quarter-pound hamburger for $1.95, a cheeseburger for $2.25—standard U.S. fare. However, they also feature a teriyaki burger, $2.45, and a teriyaki chicken sandwich at $2.50. Unique also is their $2.50 beef bowl, a plastic throw-away "casserole" filled with rice and topped with beef and onions in chipped beef style. Most beverages—Western style—are 85¢. Open 9am to 11pm every day.

Woolworth's, in the Bank of Hawaii Building on Kalakaua (tel. 923-1713), atmosphere is pleasant, and the prices are right. Beef stew, chopped steak, and filet of fish are $5.95 at both lunch and dinner. Sandwiches are $4.50 to $6.25, served from morning on. Japanese and Chinese dishes are also served, and you can have Southern fried chicken to go. Note, too, Woolworth's Far Eastern snack bar in the back of the store, where you can sample all kinds of strange goodies. We'll give you more details in our section on Japanese restaurants ahead. You'll find a larger, equally bustling and cheerful Woolworth's restaurant at the Ala Moana Center. Open 7am to 10pm every day.

Eggs 'n' Things, at 1911B Kalakaua (tel. 949-0280), near Ala Moana Boulevard, is a longtime favorite in Waikiki. This is a spic-and-span white-tile dining room with decorative wall plaques containing amusing sayings. Note the unusual hours: It is open from 11pm until 2pm the next day, seven days a week. Various early- and late-riser specials are available. House specialty is the three buttermilk pancakes with eggs any style and a choice of meat (from $5.25 for corned beef hash or Vienna sausage to $6.50 for steak). Also special are the 10 kinds of crêpes Suzette ($5.25 to $6), even more varieties of omelets ($5 to $7), 10 ways to enjoy pancakes ($3.25 to $6.25) and eight different approaches to waffles ($3.25 to $6.25). Lots of side orders and fruit juices, too. Great for those who are truly devoted to breakfast.

Branches of the Denny's chain in Hawaii are always crowded, and with good reason. The food is hearty, the atmosphere is pleasant, and the tab is realistic. The **Denny's** in the Imperial Hawaii Hotel at 205 Lewers St. (tel. 923-8188), is a large, coffeeshop-style operation that's always open. There are comfortable booths, silent ceiling fans, and abundant greenery. And the glass façade affords a panoramic view of the passing parade. Lunch or dinner entrees are priced the same all day. Such entrees as chicken-fried steak or fried chicken, broiled rainbow trout, meat loaf, New York steak, or steak and shrimp range from $4.15 to $7.95, and are accompanied by vegetables and potato, roll and butter. Our breakfast favorite here is the french toast with strawberries ($4.20), but eggs Benedict is another winner. Other popular Denny's can be found in the Miramar Hawaii Hotel on Kuhio Avenue, at 1909 Ala Wai Blvd., and on the mezzanine level of 2586 Kalakaua.

There are two **Jolly Rogers** in Waikiki: the newer one is in the Outrigger East, at the corner of Kuhio and Kaiulani; the original has been holding forth at 2244 Kalakaua Ave. for just about as long as anyone can remember. The newer place has green carpets and a cheery atmosphere; there's a cocktail lounge, too, where a trio entertains nightly. The other place gives you the choice of a few sidewalk tables right out on the busy avenue or, more peacefully, tables inside under umbrellas; there's also the **Crow's Nest** above the restaurant with nightly entertainment and a happy hour every day from 4 to 8pm, when mai tais are priced at $2. Both restaurants offer a casual ambience and American coffeehouse-style food, quite tasty, at good prices. Complete dinners—served with soup or salad, potatoes or rice, and dinner roll—include such entrees as chicken Polynesian or baby beef liver with onions or bacon, and most are under $10.50. There are daily specials like roast beef or steak and shrimp. Burgers, salads, and sandwiches are also available. Breakfast is a special treat, since that's when you can get the "MacWaple." Reader Teresa Tydings of Olympia, Washington, wrote us about this one: "It consists of a waffle covered in sliced, spiced hot apples topped with macadamia nuts. Positively sinful." The doors are open from 6:30am until midnight, cocktail lounge till 2am.

While shopping at the **Waikiki Shopping Plaza,** 2250 Kalakaua Ave., corner of Seaside, can be expensive, and most of its upper-level restaurants are pricey, its below-street level is a veritable bonanza for the budget-conscious diner who wants something a little bit different. Start in the Japanese sector at **Ramen** for freshly made Japanese noodles. You can have them seated at the open tables or at the Japanese counter flanked by Japanese lanterns. Prices start at $4.75 for shoyu ramen and go to $6.25 for gyoza—Japanese noodles Chinese-style—and shrimp tempura; a combination plate is $6.75. You'll see Japanese visitors enjoying ramen at all hours of the day; in fact, this is one of the few Plaza spots that opens early, at 10am. There are no tables at the next Japanese fast-food outlet, **Okazu-Ya Bento** ("Bento" means take-out). Here they custom-design your take-out lunch or dinner, filling the large plate with Japanese favorites at tiny prices: yaki soba, meatballs, chicken cutlet, cone sushi, from 45¢ to $2.25. All items are in view in a glass showcase, Japanese style, so you can just point, or take their daily special at $3.25. To round off this Japanese trio, there's **Plaza Sushi,** a tidy little restaurant that serves a mostly Japanese crowd (prices from $6.50 to $11.50 daytime, $8.50 to $18.50 at night).

Want more variety? You can have a deli lunch at **Plaza Deli,** perhaps a baked ham or roast beef sandwich at $3.95. Daily soup and sandwich specials are $3.50. **Plaza Burger** is versatile, serving a quarter-pounder for $1.95, plus a taco dinner at $4.50, and fried-chicken dinner at $5.50. The **Chinese Kitchen** has lots of goodies, like lemon chicken, sweet-and-sour fish, and roast duck, from $3.50 to $5.20. **Plaza Pizza** is one of the welcome few places around town where you can get pizza by the slice

($1.95) plus daily specials; and of course there has to be a **Plaza Ice Cream,** with soda chairs and tables, offering cooling cones, sodas, and sundaes.

Your best all-around choice here is the huge **Plaza Coffee Shop,** where changing lunch specials go from $5.75 to $5.95 and include the likes of boneless barbecued chicken, corned beef and cabbage, and filet of mahimahi. Similar specials are $9.75 to $11.95 at dinner.

An always dependable establishment at the oceanfront in the Reef Towers Hotel is the **Islander,** at 247 Lewers St. (tel. 923-3233), famous for its fresh-baked orange bread, served hot with dinner or as french toast or dessert. Copper trim and copper fixtures against a cocoa color scheme accent this impeccably clean and attractive place, open most of the day (6am to 11pm). Breakfast is served all day; $2.29 buys a waker-upper of egg, two slices of bacon, and two pancakes. Lunch and dinner menus and prices are largely the same. At dinner, along with your entree—perhaps teriyaki steak, mahimahi, or roast pork, at prices ranging from $6.25 to $11.95— you get homemade soup or salad, potatoes or rice, plus hot orange bread. Don't miss one of their great desserts, and if you order pie, ask them to heat it up for you.

At last count, there were something like 29 **Jack in the Box** restaurants in Honolulu, and six of them right in Waikiki: one next to the Hyatt Regency Hotel, another in the Outrigger Hotel, a third at the corner of McCully Street and Kalakaua, a fourth in the Holiday Isle Hotel, one in Kuhio Market Place, and one in the Waikiki Grand Hotel on Kapahulu. Which means that you need never go far to find one of these bright, cheerful spots, where you can start the day with a croissant breakfast ($1.95 and $2.05), served from 5 to 10:30am. From 10:30am on throughout the day you can nibble on finger foods like egg rolls and shrimp or taquitos ($3.49 and $2.49) and, of course, those good Jumbo Jacks at $2.09. Very popular on their menu are beef or chicken fajitas served on pita bread ($2.95) and a grilled chicken-filet sandwich. A filling bowl of saimin is served all day.

Unless somebody told you, you wouldn't think the **Wailana Coffee House** was a budget place, because it looks so imposing and expensive, located as it is in the exclusive Wailana condominiums at 1860 Ala Moana Blvd. (corner John Ena Road), opposite the Hilton Hawaiian Village dome. But go! It's never closed, and the prices will surprise you. The nicest thing about the Wailana is that lunches and dinners are the same price—the tab does not go up after 5pm as it does in so many other places. So any time of the day you can have the homemade soup and sandwich lunch for $4.50, or the delicious "broasted" chicken, juicy and tender, served with a generous helping of french fries, coleslaw or salad, roll and honey, for $6.75. Other good buys are the old-fashioned beef stew at $6.50, the top sirloin at $10.50. All of these entrees are served with either soup, salad bar, or fresh-fruit cup, as well as a choice of starch. The salad bar is available from 11am to 11pm. Breakfast is served around the clock, so you can come by anytime to try their delicious classic french toast or their Irish breakfast, which features a three-egg omelet stuffed with corned-beef hash and topped with cheddar cheese, plus grilled fresh pineapple spears and hash-brown potatoes—guaranteed to put you on top of the morning at $6.50. Prices are subject to change.

There's another Wailana Coffee House in mid-Waikiki, with the same menu; it's called the **Wailana Malia** and it's located in the Outrigger Malia Hotel, 2211 Kuhio Ave. (tel. 922-4769). Both restaurants are open 24 hours a day. Another Wailana winner for Waikiki!

Subway Salads & Sandwiches, which dishes out divine submarine sandwiches in foot-long and six-inch sizes, just keeps growing and growing. A new branch seems to appear just about every time you turn around: The last time we counted, there were 12 in Honolulu, including one in Waikiki at 2310 Kuhio Ave. (tel. 923-0400), and one downtown at 207 S. King St. (tel. 536-3957). All are very clean counter operations (some have tables and chairs), nicely decorated with posters showing scenes of the New York subways in the early days. The club (turkey, ham, and roast beef), seafood and crab, steak and cheese, meatball, B.M.T. (pepperoni, Genoa salami, and bologna), and pastrami are all stuffed with your choice of extras, such as lettuce, tomatoes, onions, peppers, pickles, or black olives. Prices range from $1.99 for the six-inch veggie sub to $6.59 for the foot-long seafood and crab extravaganza. They bake their own bread, cinnamon rolls, and cookies daily. All Subways are open from 10am to 2am daily.

The **Waikiki Circle Hotel Restaurant** at 2466 Kalakaua Ave. (tel. 923-1571), is oriented toward the budget traveler, from its $2.65 breakfast specials to complete dinners beginning at $7.95. You enter through the open lobby of the circular building, but before you do, read the menu and specials of the day on large posters that practically scream "save money." The bargains are not at the expense of quality, either, but the ambience is plain—just tables and chairs. Low prices continue all day, from breakfast served from 6:30am to 2pm, lunch noon to 2pm, dinner 6:30 to 9:30pm. Lunchtime offers sandwiches from $3.45 to $6.25, salads from $1.45 to $4.95. Come dinnertime there is a daily special, perhaps brisket of beef with cabbage, at $5.25. From baby beef liver at $5.95 to filet of beef with shrimp tempura at $7.95, regular dinners include rolls, tossed green salad, vegetables, and rice or potatoes. There is also a bar and lounge.

Pizza Perfect

Jack Zajac is a man who loves to cook. So you can be certain that the gourmet pan pizzas and other Italian fare he whips up at the **Great Canadian Pizza Company**, in the Royal Grove Hotel at 151 Uluniu Ave. (tel. 923-3875), are something special. He bakes his own dough, creates his own sausages and sauces, uses no salt or MSG. If you order a slice, it will be baked to order for you—not just reheated in the usual way—so sit down to wait at one of the few outside tables or relax indoors. Slices run $2.50 to $3.45; we can vouch for the vegetarian—it's smothered with tomatoes, green peppers, mushrooms, onions, and cheeses—and is terrific. Whole pies range from $6.45 to $9.45 small, $8.45 to $13.25 medium, and $11.45 to $18.25 large. Jack also has daily specials, like baked spaghetti or lasagna or veal parmigiana, moderately priced. And he does homemade soups, a different one every day, and even pastries; try the pineapple cheesecake for a special treat. Open daily from 11am to midnight. Free delivery.

Pizzeria Uno, 2256 Kuhio Ave. (tel. 926-0646), is a great favorite with the younger crowd. Although it serves all sorts of good things—burgers, spare rib platters, chili, salads (seafood, spinach, Caesar, and antipasto)—the specialty here is definitely pizza of the unique variety. This is "Chicago's original deep dish pizza." We're especially fond of the Sea Delico, with the flavor of shrimp and crab; the steak and cheese; and the chicken fajita pizza, sizzling strips of marinated chicken breast, with a blend of cheeses, peppers, and onions. Pizzas come in two sizes: individual, priced from $4.25 to $6.25; and a larger size that serves two or three, priced from $8.75 to $12.50. Beer is at hand, by the glass or pitcher. The full-service bar also dispenses some of the best piña coladas in town. Pizzeria Uno is open every day, from 11am to midnight.

Nice and Natural

What a treat to find a handy health-food store, restaurant, and juice bar right in the heart of the busy Waikiki scene. **Ruffage Natural Foods** is at 2443 Kuhio Ave. in the Royal Grove Hotel (tel. 926-1118), just a block from the beach. It specializes in organic food and those that are as free as possible of processing, all modestly priced. They serve freshly squeezed juices; good fruit and vegetable salads; lunch and dinner dishes on the order of coconut curry with brown rice or vege-tostados ($2.95 to $3.95); sandwiches like zucchini-cheese or tofu-tuna, on multigrain bread, stuffed with tomatoes and sprouts and practically a meal in themselves ($2.75 to $4.50); yummy shakes and smoothies. At the front of the store is an authentic Japanese sushi bar, where you can get a complete sushi lunch for $6.95, a complete sushi dinner for $9.95, or order by the piece (yes, they have vegetable sushis). Ruffage's atmosphere is health-food counter, but the food is fresh and very good. Take it out and go to the beach, or dine there at one of the several open-to-the-street tables. While you're there, pick up a few organically grown papayas to take back to your hotel for breakfast. Ruffage is open daily from 8am to 9pm; sushi hours are 11am to 2pm, and 5 to 11pm.

If you've already eaten at a Country Life restaurant in New York, Los Angeles, Paris, London, or Osaka, you already know how good these places are. And if you haven't, you're in for a discovery. **Country Life Vegetarian Buffet,** 421 Nahua St. (tel. 922-5010), had just opened in Waikiki at the time of our last visit, and it's a delight for vegetarians and health-conscious people. No animal products of any kind (and that includes cheese, dairy, eggs, or animal fat) are used, which means no cholesterol; delicious desserts are made with fruit concentrates, dates and honey, which means no sugar. The buffet table features entrees like pecan loaf with cashew gravy, baked potatoes with soy sour cream, lasagne, taco salad, tofu-and-rice croquettes. There's a generous salad and fresh-fruit bar; freshly baked whole grain breads and homemade spreads; and guilt-free desserts on the order of carob brownies, pumpkin pie, and blackberry cobbler. Country Life restaurants are a project of lay members of the Seventh Day Adventist Church: The only proselytizing they do (if you ask) are on the benefits of good nutrition, as they are sincerely anxious to help people improve their health. Manager Bill Ridley will even provide you with an excellent collection of vegetarian recipes for a modest price. Modest, too, is the price for the meals: You pay by weight, $3.99 a pound at lunch, $4.99 a pound at dinner. The average meals runs from about $2.50 to $7.50.

Country Life Vegetarian Buffet serves lunch from 11am to 2:30pm Sunday through Friday; dinner from 5 to 8pm Sunday through Thursday. They offer validated parking at any Outrigger Hotel. They are located in the Honolulu Prince Hotel, next to the Outrigger West, and just behind the International Market Place.

---

2. Restaurants Around Town (Outside Waikiki)

Once you leave the Waikiki area, your choice of restaurants—in all categories —becomes much greater. The following are all within easy driving or bus distance of Waikiki, and they're listed according to the type of food they serve and/or the geographical area in which they're located.

AMERICAN/CONTINENTAL RESTAURANTS

These aren't necessarily your basic steak-and-baked-potato/hamburger-and-fries/fried-chicken-and-mashed-potatoes places. Not in Honolulu, U.S.A., where teriyaki beef is as American as apple pie. So many ethnic specialties have come into the local repertoire that Japanese, Chinese, and Polynesian dishes (among others) are listed right along with steak, hamburger, and fried chicken. In a few pages we'll concentrate on the "foreign" restaurants—those that specialize solely in ethnic food. Right now, it's a little bit of everything.

Close to Waikiki

Honolulu is home to the world's ninth **Hard Rock Café,** 1837 Kapiolani Blvd. (tel. 955-7383), which, like its sister restaurants in Europe and on the mainland, is a restaurant-cum-museum of rock-music memorabilia and 1950s artifacts. Nonstop rock blares forth on Muzak; management prides itself on the fact that one can see and be seen by everyone in the place at all times, no matter where one is seated. Gold records and musical instruments—either donated by their famous owners or purchased at auctions—adorn the walls; a real '50s station wagon is suspended from the ceiling over the bar! Larger-than-life busts of Mick Jagger and Keith Richards dominate the foyer, where souvenirs such as T-shirts, lapel pins, baseball caps, cigarette lighters, etc., bearing the HRC logo are for sale. Like all of the other Hard Rock Cafés, this one will not accept reservations; lines are common but seem to be part of the fun. The menu features house specials like watermelon barbecue ribs, lime barbecue chicken ($9.95 each); burgers served with home-cut fries, green salad, and your choice of made-from-scratch dressing, $5.75 to $6.95; sandwiches such as grilled chicken breast and avocado, Swiss cheese and tomato, or smoked turkey for $4.95 and $6.95; and thick, cold shakes at $2.50. All are cheerfully whisked to your table by the foxy young staff members. Hard Rock Café is proud of the fact that it "absolutely uses no preservatives or additives." It's open daily from 11am until midnight, the bar is open until 1am Monday to Thursday, until 1:30am Friday and Saturday, until midnight on Sunday.

We always wonder why Honolulu's tourists haven't yet caught up with **King's Bakery and Coffee Shop,** 1936 S. King St. near McCully (tel. 941-5211), which has been a popular local rendezvous for years. Even though it's open 24 hours a day, seven days a week, it's always jammed, and you sometimes have to wait a few minutes for a seat at the counter, tables, or booths—that's how well liked it is. Certainly it's not because of the decor, which is perfectly plain with plastic-topped tables. It is because of the good service, the good food, and the fact that breakfast, lunch, and dinner menus are the same and are served around the clock. This means you can always count on a plate of hot, lusty beef stew, Hawaiian chopped steak, crispy fried chicken, sautéed mahimahi, or breaded veal cutlet, from $3.80 to $5.50. Daily specials at $4.95 to $5.10 include pot roast pork, short ribs, and mushroom chicken, served with a tossed green salad, vegetable, rice or potatoes, butter, and roll. We mention the roll because this is also a bakery, and a good one. People come from miles around to shop for King's bread and rolls and their delicious pies and cakes. After you've had your fruit pie, or cream-cheese pie, you may be tempted to join the crowd at the bakery counter and take some home with you—and don't forget the very special sweet bread, $1.85 per loaf. (Try it for french toast!) Send some home to your friends—King's has them already packaged—and they'll bless you forever.

You can also get the standard sandwiches here at low prices, plus soups, salads, and soda-fountain concoctions. King's also has two other locations, at the Kaimuki Shopping Center, 3221 Waialae Ave., and at Eaton Square, on Hobron Lane.

The **Pagoda Floating Restaurant,** 1525 Rycroft St. (tel. 941-6611), is one of those rare places where the scenery alone is worth the price of admission. The glass-enclosed Koi Room on the first floor, which specializes in seafood, and the more elegant La Salle (see, below, under French/Japanese restaurants) overlook a lotus-blossom pond stocked with almost 3,000 brilliantly colored Japanese carp. Walkways lead to individual pagodas seemingly afloat in the pond. Although the pagodas are reserved for groups of eight or more, the view from the main dining rooms is quite beautiful. At dinner, most entrees go from $9.50 to $20. The house specialty, mahimahi is $9.50. Lunch is always a buffet, priced at $8.95 daily, $11.95 Sunday, and served from 11am to 2pm; dinner is from 5 to 10pm. Try to plan your visit to catch the grand show at carp-feeding time—8am, noon, or 6pm. Bring the kids and the cameras.

A new Honolulu restaurant has turned the lowly crab into a featured attraction. **Crab Factory Sada,** 1360 S. King St., just Ewa of Keeaumoku Street (tel. 941-0054), imports fresh crabs from Pribilof Island, Alaska, and serves them in your choice of Western or Japanese cooking styles. It's a bit of a splurge, but a crab lover's idea of heaven. For steamed crabs you pay by the pound—snow crabs, $10.50; king crabs, $25; Dungeness crabs, $15. On the set menu, the crabs are broiled, and the price is $25. Porthole windows and a nautical decor set the mood; white tablecloths and bright red napkins contribute a festive air. Crab Factory Sada serves dinner only, from 4 to 11pm daily. There is a large adjacent parking lot.

At the McCully Shopping Center

The **McCully Shopping Center,** 1960 Kapiolani Blvd., one of Honolulu's newest, has quite a variety of restaurants. And it's easy to reach from Waikiki, just a block over the McCully Bridge (corner of McCully and Kapiolani). One of the most popular places here is also one of the most reasonable: **Sunny's Seafood** (tel. 949-4559), which serves great take-out fish and seafood plate lunches for under $4.20. Possibilities include the butterfish sweet miso, sashimi, ahi teriyaki, and salmon fry. Recently we sampled the mahimahi plate, which came with two scoops of rice, salad including tasty crab poki with seaweed, plus the mahimahi. The fish-market counter is right there, so you can see the fresh catch of the day while you wait. It's open Monday through Saturday from 10am to 7pm, Sunday from noon to 6:30pm. Arrive at least half-an-hour before closing.

Tummy's Inn (tel. 946-0074), is another prime spot for penny-pinchers. Prices are low all day for breakfast, lunch, and dinner until 9pm (Friday and Saturday to 10pm, Sunday to 6pm). For $4.75 you get a generous portion of country-style barbecued baby-back ribs; chicken teriyaki or beef stew are $3.95; and hot open-faced sandwiches, served with whipped potatoes, are mostly under $4.

In a medium price range, our favorite here is **Salerno** (tel. 942-5273). That authentic Italian aroma greets you the moment you enter. Lunches, 11am to 2pm Monday to Saturday only, feature 10 pasta dishes from $6 to $9.50, plus entrees like veal parmigiana, $8.50 and saltimbocca, $14, the latter served with eggplant, mushrooms, prosciutto, and white wine. *Delizioso!* Dinners are served daily, from 5 to 10pm. You can save $2 by choosing a small portion, or go for regular sizes of such entrees as chicken marsala or calamari scampi (giant squid) at $10.90.

In the Ala Moana Area

Kengo Royal Buffet does have a royal-looking entrance at 1529 Kapiolani Blvd. (tel. 941-2241), just Diamond Head of Keeaumoku Street. But if you're driving, you should enter the parking lot from Kona Street, which runs parallel to the Ala Moana Shopping Center. Hearing how popular this place was, we recently went there for an early lunch, at 11:15. By that time, the parking lot was already filling, and the restaurant was so packed that we had to be seated in the bar and lounge area. This was fine, and we were soon inching our way along the two buffets: one features such Japanese specialties as sushi and salads; the other, haole favorites like fried fish, pork chops, and roast beef. Soup (we sampled an excellent clam chowder) is served at your table, as is your beverage. The price of the luncheon buffet is $8.50. At dinnertime, the price goes up to $15.95, but many more items—especially luscious seafood dishes like shrimp tempura and lobster in black-bean sauce—are added. The atmosphere competes with the food for attention: There's a comfortable paneled lobby with what appear to be family portraits, attractive carpeting, and a plethora of ceiling lamps, cane-bracketed. A royal buffet indeed.

Kengo Royal Buffet serves lunch every day from 11am to 2pm, dinner from 5 to 9:30pm.

After a few years under another name, **La Paloma,** 1216 Kapiolani Blvd. (tel. 538-1066)—a restaurant that veteran readers of this book may well remember—is back, and owners Laura and Jo Martinez are on hand. The place is nicely decorated with stucco and brick walls, lots of white wrought iron, bright-red tufted booths, abundant hanging plants, and fresh flowers on the tables. The same menu is in effect all day, offering quite a variety of delicious southwestern and south-of-the-border specialties. You might start off with chile con queso with flour chips or Rio Grande Pizza Snacks (a veggie-and-cheese mixture on sopapilla puffs). The homemade soups here are exceptional; we especially like the albondinga soup, a vegetable and meatball concoction. There are tamales, too, as well as chile rellenos, chimichangas, burritos, and a variety of enchiladas; these go from $4.95 to $10.95. From the grill, you might select fajitas, barbecue ribs, pollo a la parrilla (tender chicken breasts that you roll in tortillas with sauce), or grilled Texas shrimp, $10.95 to $12.95. The individual tamale pies, some $5.95, are a treat. Desserts are unusual and luscious—we'll go with the caramel flan with Kahlua and whipped cream every time. Laura, Joe, and family are *muy simpático* hosts, and the food is nothing less than terrific!

La Paloma is open from 11:30am to 10pm Monday to Friday, from 5 to 10pm Saturday and Sunday.

The **Original Pancake House,** at 1221 Kapiolani Blvd. (tel. 533-3005), is a pleasant place to have breakfast or lunch on your way to or from the Ala Moana Center. We especially like to sit out in the pretty little garden, where one is sure to be visited by English sparrows, doves, Brazilian cardinals, and mynahs, all looking for a handout. Pancakes and crêpes include cottage-cheese pancakes (one of our favorites!), at $2.65; cherry crêpes, made with liqueur, at $5.50; blueberry pancakes, at

$4.50; and the house special, apple pancakes (allow 20 minutes), at $6.75. Among the many omelets, all served with three buttermilk pancakes, our favorite is the potato—made with green onions and bacon bits and served with a flavorful sour-cream sauce, $3.50. There are also hot sandwiches such as teriyaki steak, and french dip in the $2.95 to $4.70 range, and daily specials like mahimahi, chicken-fried steak, spaghetti, and beef stew, priced at $4.75. The restaurant is open from 6am until 2pm every day.

There is another Original Pancake House in the Waikiki Marina Hotel, 1956 Ala Moana Blvd., across from Fort DeRussy (tel. 947-8848), open 6am until 10pm, Sunday until 2pm; and a third at 1411 Dillingham (tel. 847-1496). Dinner specials might include lemon chicken, seafood platter, steak and mahimahi, and more.

One of our favorite places to pick up wonderful, portable food for a picnic or the beach—or just to take back to our hotel—is **Chicken Alice's,** at 1470 Kapiolani Blvd. (tel. 946-6117). The stellar attraction here is Alice Gahinhin's flavorful fried chicken. It's ever-so-delicately spiced and definitely habit forming. And you can't beat the price—$4.75 for a small box containing 12 pieces; $11 for the large box, 30 pieces; $22 for some 60 pieces (in case you're throwing a party or have a very large family to feed). Chicken is also available by the piece. We also like the combination Korean plate: kal-bi (tender barbecued ribs), chicken, rice, and kim chee, for $5.25. The plate lunches here are king-size, to say the least. Chicken Alice's is open from 9am to 10:30pm every day.

Although J.C. Penney's, the huge department store at Ala Moana Center, is right up to date with its fashions, the prices they charge at **Penney's Restaurant,** on the third floor, went out of style years ago—which makes it a great place for us. It is a good deal for breakfast, lunch, or dinner. At lunch, for example, hot plates are mostly under $4.75; we like their teriyaki plate at $4.10. A roast beef sandwich is $3.25. At 4pm some dinner items are added to the menu, like grilled beef liver or choice sirloin steak. Entrees, from $4.25 to $7.50, are served with potatoes, vegetable, dessert, and beverage. Try to avoid the peak lunch hour unless you don't mind queuing up for a few minutes' wait. Open from 7:30am to 8pm on weekdays, on Saturday from 8am to 5pm, and on Sunday from 8:30am to 4pm. Early arrivals must use the special third-floor entrance.

Call **Hackfeld's,** on the ground level of Liberty House at Ala Moana Center (tel. 945-5243), an elegant bistro; the food has a French-continental accent, and the artful presentations make dishes as pleasing to the eye as they are to the plate. Prices are the most reasonable at lunch, when entrees run from $8.95 to $10.95 and include dishes like coquille of scallops and escargots, Thai curry, and New England crab cakes, all served with a choice of soup of the day or salad. The dinner menu, with entrees priced from $10.25 to $13.25, is also intriguing. Try escargots maison or fettuccine Alfredo among the appetizers, the wonderful Burnt Crème (or any of the French pastries and tortes) for dessert. In between are dishes such as the fresh catch of the day, teriyaki steak, chicken fettuccine, and veal gourmande, all served up with soup of the day or salad, plus garlic pasta, fresh mashed potatoes, potato pancakes, or steamed rice.

Hackfeld's serves lunch from 11am to 2:30pm Monday through Saturday; dinner, Monday through Friday only, from 5 to 8:30pm. Closed Sunday.

The kamaainas are mad about **Zippy's,** and it's no wonder. The food is plentiful, and the prices are as reasonable as you'll find anywhere in Hawaii. There are 17 Zippy's restaurants on Oahu (they're all listed in the phone book), including one convenient for us at Ala Moana Center. Two of their most popular specialties are chili and fried chicken. In fact, many local clubs and children's athletic teams sell tickets for the chili to raise funds, and they sell like . . . Zippy's chili! A big bucket of this taste treat (seven servings) is $8.30. Fried chicken is $13.50 for a 12-piece bucket. And everyone seems to love Zippy's plate lunches: big platters of beef or pork, teriyaki, breaded beef cutlet, fried chicken, spaghetti with meat sauce, hamburger steak, or mahimahi, including rice or fries, are priced from $3.90 to $6.25. There's good news for the diet-conscious, too: Zippy's huge salad—we especially like the taco and chef's salads—are all $5.15 and under. Zippy's are self-service restaurants where you place your order at one window, pay, and collect it in very short order at the next windows. Eleven of them have table-service dining rooms as well, and all have a Napoleon's Bakery (their local TV commercials feature a somewhat addled emperor who is never sure whether it is he or the pastries that the announcer asserts are "flaky"). Waiting to fatten you up are luscious haupia and dobash cakes; wonderful doughnuts, danishes, and cupcakes; freshly baked Portuguese-sweet, French, and raisin breads; and great pies, from apple to macadamia cream. And most Zippy's eateries are open 24 hours a day. Ala Moana and Pearlridge Zippy's close when the shopping centers close.

Note: For a rundown of other restaurants at the Ala Moana Shopping Center, see Chapter VI.

Close to Town

For years the Flamingo restaurants have been offering terrific quality for the money. One of the original Flamingos, Café Flamingo was torn down to make way for Restaurant Row. **Flamingo Kapiolani,** 871 Kapiolani Blvd. (tel. 538-6931), was recently reopened after extensive renovations. The pink booths, paneled wainscoting, and all-around newness makes this a fitting ambience for their excellent food. They're well known for their oxtail soup ($6.40), roasts, and specials. The day we were there, the lunch special was boiled brisket of beef ($6.85). The dinner special was pot roast with noodles ($7.75). Lunch features half-a-dozen sandwiches from $4.25 to $5.90, 10 plates from $5.50 to $9.50. At dinner, there are a dozen items, from spaghetti at $6.20 to lobster at $18.50. The same management also runs the **Flamingo Chuck Wagon** at 1015 Kapiolani, where lunch starts at $5.70, and a lunch buffet offers a salad bar, fried chicken, barbecued beef, and a daily special for $6.50. At dinnertime, you can eat as much prime rib or fried chicken as you like, served chuckwagon style, for around $12. In the business district downtown, the **Flamingo Coffee Shop** and **Arthur's Restaurant,** at 173 Merchant St., are big local favorites. Luncheon in the coffee shop starts at around $2.75, for chili; and at Arthur's, at $6.95, for sandwiches. Flamingo's at the Windward City Shopping Center in Kaneohe (tel. 235-5566) and at Pearl City, 803 Kamehameha Hwy (tel. 456-5946) are very popular with local families.

News dominates the conversation at **Columbia Inn,** 645 Kapiolani Blvd. (tel. 531-3747), a favorite hangout for the staffs of Honolulu's two daily newspapers just a few doors away. The news about food is also good at this large, wood-paneled spot with its leather booths. At lunch you can choose from 28 complete lunches between $6.05 and $12.55, and that includes boiled brisket of corned beef and cabbage, oysters cooked in garlic butter, pepper steak with rice pilaf, all accompanied by fish chowder or fruit salad, dessert, and beverage. Order à la carte and the range is $5 to $11.30. At dinner there are some two dozen choices for $10 and under, beginning at $7 for a complete meal (higher-priced meals go up to $15). Columbia Inn is open from 6am to 12:30am daily—but full meals are served only from 11am to 4pm (lunch) and 4 to 10pm (dinner).

The Queen's Physicians Office Building, one of the largest in the islands, has a secret: It has its own cafeteria-type coffee shop, **The Queen's Cafe,** 1380 Lusitania St. (directly behind the Queen's Medical Center near Beretania Street and Punchbowl), which offers both healthy food and low prices. It is hiding on the street-level floor behind the elevators. Parking in the office building's garage will only be about $1 for the time it takes you to eat breakfast or lunch—the only meals served. Breakfast muffins are a big favorite here. The most you can spend for a special breakfast order of french toast, pancakes, or eggs is $2.25. At lunch, help yourself to soup from the kettle, order a sandwich of roast beef, ham, turkey, cheese, or tuna, and your lunch will run $2.75 to $3. There is a salad bar on the healthy side and burgers on the fun side. Open 7:30am to 2:30pm.

Even before it was immortalized in song by Hawaii's favorite funny man, Frank DeLima, **Grace's Inn,** 1296 S. Beretania St. (tel. 537-3362), and the staple food of Hawaii—the plate lunch—were all but synonymous. Grace caters more than her share of baby luaus—a Hawaiian tradition—the celebration of the first birthday of a *keiki o ka aina* (child of the land), weddings, office parties, and any other occasion you can think of. Her food isn't fancy or unique, but its popularity is mind-boggling. Chicken or beef katsu, teriyaki beef or pork, sweet-and-sour pork, seafood mix, and mixed beef curry, ribs, and teri pork plates, with the traditional two scoops of rice and salad, go for $4.15 to $5.55. Specialties such as fried noodles and fish tempura and big bowls of curry stew are likewise reasonably priced. There are a few tables inside, but the bulk of Grace's trade is take-out. The lady is definitely doing something right. Grace's Inn is open every Monday to Saturday from 6am to 10:30pm, Sunday from 7am to 10pm.

When a restaurant has been going strong for over 37 years, you know it must be doing something right. Such a place is the **Wisteria,** 1206 S. King St. (tel. 531-5276), very popular with the local crowd. The dining room, newly renovated, is bright and airy. The atmosphere is pleasantly businesslike, the service swift and professional, and the deep leather booths comfortable. The menu leans to the Japanese side, but there are also quite a few American-style specialties. If you're in the mood for Japanese food, you can choose from various sushi dishes at $5.60 to $7.50, or select from a wide range of donburi, tempura, and sukiyaki specials (sukiyaki dinners of chicken, beef, or pork are $5.80 to $9.65). Treading on more familiar ground, you might order such American-style dishes as roast chicken, baked meat loaf, or seafood creole, from $4.95 to $6.95 at lunch. The house special is an excellent sizzling rib steak, $9.95. Our Japanese meal (we chose the daily specials of tempura soba and chicken araimo) included egg-drop soup garnished with scallions in dainty black bowls, pickled vegetables, rice, and a pot of tea. Two of us had more than enough to eat for $11.50. The Wisteria is open daily from 6am until 10:30pm, on Friday and Saturday until 11:15pm. The cocktail lounge is open from 11am to 1am.

Everything about **TGIFriday's,** at 950 Ward Ave., corner of King (tel. 523-5841), is delightfully different—from the *big* menu with some 160 items to the art nouveau leaded-glass hanging lamps and lovely antique furniture and accessories. It's obvious that no expense was spared.

The food, too, is far from run-of-the-mill. It was here that we first discovered potato-skin plates, a TGIF specialty. The skins are baked, then fried to a delightful crispness and "loaded," that is, slathered, with a quarter pound of cheese and crumbled bacon, plus a sour-cream dip ($5.85). Another tasty treat is chicken nachos (like the Mexican original but substituting chicken for refried beans), $5.45. The blackened chicken, Cajun style, is fun at $8.95. Omelets can be custome designed, and there are tacos and burgers of all descriptions, and sandwiches on the order of chicken, french dip, or steak, priced from $5.95 and up. We like their steak on a stick too: three skewers of beef marinated in teriyaki sauce and served with a crisp dinner, salad, potato, and chef's vegetables, $7.95. TGIFriday's is open every day from 11am until 2am. Weekends' opening time is 10am. This is a super place to dine or have a drink. Friday's is insanely popular, and since reservations are not accepted, it's first-come, first-served.

Hawaiian Bagel—how's that for a marriage of concepts? This wholesale-retail delicatessen with a few tables for those who can't make it out the door is at 753 B Halekauwila St. (tel. 523-8638), in a new contemporary-style building located in the run-down but picturesque Kakaako section of Honolulu. The sights and scents are surpassed only by the tastes. Needless to say, proprietor Stephen Gelson is not a full-blooded Hawaiian. Nor are the bagels, blueberry muffins, and homemade rye bread. But the little restaurant and take-out bakery-deli is a hit with the local folk. And our readers love it, too. We quote from a letter from Samuel Meerkreebs of Washington, D.C.: "We were met with such gracious, kosher, aloha spirit that we had to write you on behalf of Hawaiian Bagel. We were not informed that it closed at 3pm on Saturday. When we arrived around 3:30, the door was locked and things were all put away. Mr. Gelson finally opened the door and explained they were closed. I mentioned that we had come from the Hyatt, had called earlier, and added, "My wife will kill me after bringing her all the way out here!" Steve left and brought back a 'care package' containing bagels, blueberry muffins, and cream cheese, and refused any money. His actions were different from the crass, commercial demeanor we had encountered around the island. A hearty mahalo for having the Hawaiian Bagel in your book; it was a pleasure to run into a 'mensch' along our holiday path."

They carry 10 varieties of bagels, including onion, sesame seed, and poppy seed, priced at 35¢ and 37¢ each, $4.20 to $4.44 a dozen. The sandwiches are typical deli variety: roast beef, lox or whitefish and cream cheese, corned beef, liverwurst, turkey, pastrami, and the like, at $4.35. In true deli tradition, they even serve celery tonic. You may want to take home a fragrant, round loaf of fresh-from-the-oven rye bread. Hawaiian Bagel is open weekdays from 6am to 5:30pm, until 3pm on Saturday. There is parking on the premises.

Auntie Pasto's, 1099 S. Beretania St., corner of Pensacola (tel. 523-8855), resembles a little trattoria in Florence or Rome, with its brick interior, café curtains, and checkered cloths. The food here is marvelous, and at lunchtime the place attracts a lively crowd, many of whom work at the shops and medical clinics in the neighborhood. Special lunches, $4.50 to $5.50, include frittata (an open-faced omelet), a mortadella scramble, pan-fried sausage and vegetables, and a club sandwich served with pasta salad. Also very popular are Auntie's big sandwiches (meatball, salami, subs), $3.95 to $5.75, and her super pastas, especially those with clams and spinach, from $4.25 to $6.50. At dinnertime, pastas are priced a little higher, and there are also some flavorful specialties like stuffed calamari, veal parmigiana, and osso buco, all from $5.95 to $10.95. Auntie does business Monday through Friday from 11am until 10:30pm; Saturday, Sunday, and holidays, 4pm until 10:30pm.

At Fisherman's Wharf

Want some local color in your vacation life? You can join the fishermen and other local types who frequent the **Kewalo Ship's Galley Restaurant** at 1125 Ala Moana Blvd, at Kewalo Basin (tel. 521-6608). It's been here for at least 27 years, first under the name of Sampan Inn, then Seaside Inn. Owner Zenen Ozoa made news a few years back when he agreed to pay the state of Hawaii $150,000 over the next five years to keep operating the restaurant. He promises he won't raise his prices very much, although he does have plans for reconstructing the place and adding a seating area outdoors near the waterfront. At this writing, it still looks like a very worn 1950s diner, complete with jukebox, and with 1950s prices to match: fresh fish every day at $5, honey-dipped chicken at $4.75, $1 hamburgers and $8 sirloin steaks. Daily specials offer even better buys. Doors open at 6am to accommodate the fishermen and stay open until about 2am, when popular entertainers or who-knows-who are likely to drop by.

At Ward Warehouse

Just opposite Kewalo Basin is the delightful **Ward Warehouse** shopping complex, and there are several charming restaurants here that match the appeal of the shops. The **Chowder House** (tel. 521-5681), for one, is a bright, bustling, and inexpensive seafood house, where you can watch the boats of Fisherman's Wharf through the glass wall behind the bar and have a light seafood dinner for as little as $8.25. We've lunched on a good-size fresh salad, two slices of French bread, and filet of red snapper with french fries for that price. Most of the other seafood dinners are $12.95 (prices stay the same in the evening; there's only one menu). Fish sandwiches, also served with fries, go from $5.50 for mahimahi, $5.25 for red snapper; there are salads, seafood, cocktails, fish fries, and three kinds of chowder, all reasonably priced. Open from 11am to 10pm daily.

Upstairs at Ward Warehouse, the same management operates the much fancier **Orson's Restaurant** (tel. 521-5681), a lovely dining room with spacious ocean and mountain views and a delightfully open and breezy feeling. Although there are a number of seafood specialties in the higher-price ranges, there's plenty to choose from under $10: filet of mahimahi, sautéed calamari, filet of red snapper meunière, for example, as well as several pasta dishes and a good variety of fish and seafood sandwiches, from $5.25 to $8.95. Orson's is open from 11am to 10 or 11pm daily. Both restaurants use the same menus for lunch and dinner.

Japanese food tends to be expensive, so it's great to know that you can go to the delightful **Restaurant Benkei** at Ward Warehouse (tel. 523-8713) and feast on a bountiful buffet table of Japanese delicacies for just $7.95 at lunchtime, $14.95 at dinner. The restaurant is decorated in Old-World Japanese style and pleasant tables look out over the street. (If there are 20 people in your party, you can command the upstairs teahouse-style room.) The buffet table always features miso soup, an array of chicken, beef, and seafood dishes, plus sashimi, noodle dishes, and a tasty array of Japanese salads. Tea and dessert come with your meal. If you opt for the set menus, which begin at $7.95 at lunch and $10.50 at dinner, you can choose from a variety of seafood tempura, fried and broiled fish, sashimi, steak salad, and Japanese-style steak—all served with appetizer, rice, pickles, and soup. Restaurant Benkei is open from 11am to 2pm for lunch and from 5:30 to 9:30pm for dinner every day.

If you like spaghetti and you like low prices, then you're going to love the **Old Spaghetti Factory** at Ward Warehouse (tel. 531-1513), which has to be the most stunning budget restaurant in town. It's worth a visit just to see the setting, which might be described as "fabulous Victorian," the rooms brimming with authentic European antiques and Oriental rugs, ornamental lamp shades, overstuffed chairs, many mirrors, and huge chandeliers. You may dine in an authentic trolley car or, more likely, at large, comfortable tables on colorful plush velvet seats, some with backs made from giant headboards. So popular is this place that you can always anticipate a wait for lunch and dinner, even though the main dining rooms seat 350 and the bar upstairs about 125! The menu is modest, concentrating mostly on spaghetti, and the food is not as dazzling as the surroundings; but you will eat heartily and well for very little. Complete dinners, from about $4.25 to $7.10, include a good green salad with choice of dressing, sourdough bread with marvelous garlic butter (a whole loaf is brought to your table with a knife, and there are seconds), beverage, and spumoni ice cream in addition to the main dish. It's fun to have either the Pot Pourri, a sample of the four most popular sauces, or the Manager's Favorite, which serves up two different sauces. Our favorite sauces are the clam and the browned butter with mizithra (a Greek cheese). Lunch runs from about $3.25 to $5.35, has smaller portions, and does not include beverage and dessert. Beer, wine, and cocktails are available. Note the hours: lunch from 11:30am to 2pm Monday through Saturday; dinner from 5 to 10pm Monday through Thursday, till 11pm on Friday and Saturday, from 4 to 10pm on Sunday.

Dynasty II, an elegant Chinese restaurant at Ward Warehouse, offers a popular weekday lunch buffet from 11am to 2pm. You can eat all you want, and the price is only $8.45. For a splurge, you might want to come back here for dinner. Appetizers like stuffed crab claw at $4.75 and entrees like the Peking duck at $38 (the whole bird), deep-fried crispy chicken at $7.50, and the king prawns sautéed with seasonal vegetables, $13.75, have earned this restaurant many awards. Even before you dine, you will be impressed by the impeccably coutured maître d', the Oriental carpets, and the distinctive serving ware. Dinner is served 6 to 10pm every day.

At Ward Centre

The elegant **Ward Centre** shopping/dining complex at 1200 Ala Moana Blvd. and Auahi Street, a block from Ward Warehouse, boasts a number of first-rate restaurants. We could spend weeks eating here and not needing to go anywhere else.

The quality of the food and the charm of the surroundings make **Crêpe Fever** (tel. 521-9023) on the street level, inside the Le Pavillon shopping area, quite special. Red-tile floors, oak tables, pastel pennants overhead, plus tables in the pretty garden outdoors, set a sparkling background for a menu that is not limited to just crêpes. It has a lot to offer vegetarians, sophisticated "grazers," and those who just want to eat delicious, healthy food at very reasonable prices. Our favorite lunch here used to be the homemade soup served in a bowl of scooped-out cracked-wheat bread with salad; it's a satisfying lunch for $4.75. But ever since owner Sandee Garcia came up with her Grain & Green salad bar, it's been a toss-up. Here you build your own vegetarian meal from a selection of complementary protein combinations that changes every day; grains, legumes, greens, beans, and seeds are provided in a variety of ways that might have a Mexican or Italian or Indian accent. Have a medium-size bowl at $3.50 or a huge bowlful for $4.80. Begin with a cup of that wonderful homemade soup and you've got a super meal. Now for those crêpes: They're filled with the likes of chicken and ham, tuna-salad melt, and lemon spinach (with cream cheese), and so are croissants, and either can be had with brown rice or salad or both for an under-$6 meal. Desserts are yummy too: cheese blintzes topped with sour cream, fresh strawberries and cream, and bananas and cream crêpes, $4.25 to $5.50. Since Crêpe Fever serves the same menu continuously, Monday to Saturday from 8am to 9pm Sunday to 4pm, you can have breakfast anytime: three-egg omelets, waffles, and (especially good) their french toast—thick slices of bakery wheat bread, garnished with bananas, $3.95.

Right next to Crêpe Fever, the same management is in charge at **Mocha Java,** an espresso fountain bar with a variety of hot and iced gourmet coffees, plus real milk shakes, and homemade cakes and sundaes. Take anything from here as a dessert for your Crêpe Fever meal: perhaps a simple but satisfying choice like espresso over a scoop of vanilla ice cream at $2.25. Wine, beer, and a full bar menu are available. This one is open Monday to Saturday from 8am to 10pm, weekends until 11pm.

The most picturesque restaurant here must surely be **Keo's at Ward Centre** (tel. 533-0533), one of the latest creations of Thai restauranteur Keo Sananikone. Keo runs five restaurants in town (see ahead, under Thai Restaurants, for a description of the cuisine), and this one is exquisite, with lovely plantings, flowers, a fountain splashing into a languid pool, pink tablecloths, black bentwood chairs, seating indoors and out—just beautiful! Enjoy the European-Asian café ambience at either lunch or dinner for reasonable prices: Most entrees run between $7.95 and $11.95. While you're here, you can pick up a copy of *Keo's Thai Cuisine,* so you can try your hand at creating these delicate wonders back home. Open Monday to Saturday from 11am to 10:30pm, from 5pm on Sunday.

There comes a time when the wandering traveler, far from home, suddenly develops an irrepressible longing for, say, a corned beef on rye, a bowl of matzoh ball soup, or a big plate of brisket of beef. Happily, a remedy is at hand right here in Honolulu: **Big Ed's Deli** (tel. 536-4591), which packs in the crowds at its counter and large table section at Ward Centre. Big Ed serves up all kinds of delicatessen delights, super sandwiches, salads, deli platters, and hot meals. You can start your meal with a wonderful borscht ($1.85 for a large bowl) or a chicken matzoh-ball soup for $2.25. House specialties include roast brisket of beef with potato pancakes and vegetables, and stuffed cabbage, $7.50 and $6.95. Or have a sandwich: corned beef, pastrami, liverwurst, beef tongue, and roast beef are priced from $4.25 to $5.35. Salad and delicatessen platters—our favorite is smoked salmon with Maui onions—range in price from $4.75 to $8.95. Beer, wine, and cocktails are available, and the atmosphere is cheerful and hearty. Open from 7am to 10pm Sunday to Thursday, to 11pm Friday and Saturday.

Monterey Bay Canners (tel. 536-6197) offers a tremendous variety of seafood specialties, many of which we've not seen elsewhere. It's a big, bustling, nautical-type place, very popular with the local people, so service can sometimes be slow. If you're lucky enough to get a table by the window, you can overlook Kewalo Basin, where the commercial fishing charters are berthed. Lunch is a good bet here since there is often a $5.95 soup-and-sandwich deal; or, you could order a bay shrimp sandwich with bacon and avocado for $6.45. Dinner, too, has a number of entrees on the low side of the menu, like mahimahi at $10.95 or ono at $13.95. And at both lunch or dinner, you can order the catch of the day—which might be opakapaka, ono-wahoo, ahi, or ulua—priced according to availability (several of the local radio stations carry MBC's "Fresh Catch" report several times a day). Drinks are quite special here: When was the last time you had a watermelon daiquiri?

Monterey Bay Canners serves lunch from 11am to 4pm, dinner from 4 to 11pm Sunday through Thursday, until midnight on Friday and Saturday; cocktails available from 11am to 2am all week. There are sister restaurants at 2335 Kalakaua Ave. and at Pearlridge Center.

Fans of the **Yum Yum Tree,** that delightful pie shop and restaurant at Kahala

Mall (see below), are thrilled to find another branch at Ward Centre. That makes it all the easier to stop in whenever the urge—maybe macadamia-nut or lemon-crunch or·English-toffee pie—becomes overwhelming to take home a whole pie, or just have a delicious slice here. The menu is the same as at Kahala, and the setting is charming, both inside and out, with the feeling of a big country house with a large porch, shady and cool, thanks to the big blue umbrellas. This Yum Yum Tree serves breakfast food from 7am to noon and again from 11pm to closing, lunch also from 11am to 5pm, dinner from 5pm to midnight (until 2am on weekends), and cocktails from 7am to 2am. As you travel around the island, you'll find Yum Yum Trees at Pali Palms, Mililani, and Pearlridge.

Ryan's Parkplace (tel. 523-9132), is a big, rambling, stunner of a room with highly polished wood floors, gleaming brass, lazily rotating ceiling fans, windows all around, myriad lush plants, and a shiny kitchen open to view. Ryan's is seriously committed to "foods for all moods"—and that means quality in everything from gourmet dishes to simple fare, from recipes that are low in sodium, fat, and cholesterol to sinfully rich creations for sybarites. "Unstructured dining" is the operative term here. So whether you're in the mood for a light snack or fancy dinner, you can get exactly what you want here. And that includes meat, chicken, and fish broiled with mesquite charcoal from Mexico; fish fresh from Hawaiian, mainland, and Alaskan waters; pasta made fresh daily; and desserts that range from low-cal Tofutti to chocolate-truffle pie. Check the list of daily specials, and tell your server of any special dietary needs; he'll be happy to oblige as much as possible. Prices, considering the high quality here, are quite reasonable. Consider, for example, dishes like mesquite grilled chicken with Thai peanut sauce or lemon pepper fettuccine with bay shrimp and fresh mushrooms—all between $7.95 and $12.95. We're partial to the Three-Salad Sampler, which includes Mediterranean chicken salad, Ryan's pea salad (fresh peas and bacon in a heavenly herb dressing), and the pasta salad with pesto, quite a meal at $8.95, as well as the hearty French-onion soup, and a tasty mesquite-broiled Cajun chicken, $10.75. Like everything else at Ryan's, the bar list is generous: A good selection of California wines is available by the bottle or by the glass. There are also temperature-controlled beer selections and a moderately priced bar list. Ryan's serves lunch from 11am to 5pm except on Sunday, and dinner from 5 to 11pm; the bar is open until 1:15am. Reservations are accepted.

Another star at Ward Centre is **Andrew's** (tel. 523-8677), perfect when you're ready for a slight splurge. This is gourmet Italian, and although the prices are not low, they are not as high as the excellence might warrant. Muted rose and browns from floor to ceiling produce a sedate effect, reinforced by the upholstered banquettes with dropped lamps, fabric-covered walls, and flowers on the tables. Lunch is à la carte, with your choice of a dozen pastas that range in price from the house cannelloni, filled with veal and spinach, at $9.75, to linguine filled with lobster, scallops, calamari, and shrimp, at $14.75. There are choices galore of fish and fowl in the same price range; beef and veal run a little higher. Daily specials, like spaghetti Putanesca, are $9.95.

Considering that complete dinner meals include antipasto, mixed-green salad, minestrone, ice cream or Italian rice, plus beverage along with your entree, the price range of $16.20 for the house cannelloni to $25 for lobster tails is not exorbitant. We chose à la carte at a recent dinner and found the cannelloni di mare (stuffed with seafood) at $13.95 a tasty and filling meal. Half a dozen other pasta choices go for around $9, and there are a few seafood and chicken dishes at about $10.50. Drinks are moderately priced. And skilled service contributes to a memorable experience.

Andrew's serves lunch Monday to Saturday from 11am to 3pm, and a Saturday brunch from 11am to 3pm. On Sunday, a regular lunch is served from 10am to 4pm, and there's a special brunch until 3pm. Dinner starts at 4pm nightly, and is served until 10pm Sunday to Tuesday, until 11pm Wednesday to Saturday.

Mexico is represented at Ward Centre by **Compadres** (tel. 523-1307), which gets a resounding *olé!* from us. We're not at all surprised that it was voted "Best Mexican Restaurant" in Hawaii by the *Honolulu* magazine poll, for several years in a row.

It's a big, very attractive place with comfortable rattan basket chairs and soft lights, and a young and energetic staff to serve you. The food is *muy bueno*, and the prices won't damage your budget. The same menu and prices are in effect all day long. The sandwiches, like the chicken and avocado at $7, are all served with thick-cut deep-fried potatoes and Mexican salad, but you'll probably want to sample such Mexican specialties as the various platillos, which include refried beans, Alfonso's rice and Mexican salad, all $7. Arroz con pollo at $10.95 and chicken mole at $10.45 are both good, and everybody loves the house specialty of fajitas—grilled, marinated meat or chicken, sliced thin and stuffed into warm tortillas with a great salsa, $9.95 and $10.95. As for the desserts, we can't resist the apple chimichanga—brandied apples in a flour tortilla, deep-fried and topped with vanilla ice cream or cheese, at $2.95. Compadres opens for breakfast at 7am, offering a wide assortment of omelets, plus chili rellenos, huevos Dos Ricardos, and much more. The complete menu is served from 11am until midnight daily. Always a special treat.

Downtown Honolulu

Jake's Downtown Restaurant, at 1126 Bishop St. (tel. 524-4616), is a tremendous favorite with people who work downtown. Don't let the lunchtime line scare you away; the turnover is quick, and the wait is never long. Jake's is a most attractive place of the red-brick, stained-glass, cozy booth, wood-paneled variety; the food is excellent and the service quick and courteous. Although the usual breakfast and lunch items are here in abundance, the stars are the wonderful buttermilk pancakes, blueberry or strawberry crêpes, macadamia-nut pancakes, blintzes with fruit compote and sour cream, and strawberry and blueberry waffles, served with hot fruit compote and sour cream, from $2.25 to $3.45. Plenty of omelets, too, and eggs Benedict served with home fries, at $6.50. There's homemade seafood chowder every day, as well as a variety of meat sandwiches, most under $6. Save some room for either the carrot cake or the deep-dish apple pie. Jake's is open from 6am to 8pm Monday through Friday, and 7am to 2pm on Saturday and Sunday. No dinner is served.

It's tiny. You might call it a "hole in the wall." But it's a giant pleaser for downtown weekday lunches. The **Red & White Café** is located at 1001 Bishop St., on the walk behind Bishop Square at Tamarind Park (tel. 531-0774). When you enter, you stop immediately at the hot-plate counter. There your order is filled in a jiffy and you're a half step from the cashier who packs it for comfortable picnic dining on nearby outdoor tables or on the stone sitting walls in the park. But here's the best news: Delectable dishes such as artichoke pasta salad, brown rice and vegetables, chicken with mushrooms, Thai chicken curry, linguine with clams, and vegetable lasagne are priced from only $3.90 to $4.25. A different specialty is featured each day, like Italian sausage fettuccine, chicken enchiladas, or spaghetti with meatballs. Soup of the day is $1.25. This is a health-minded place. Everything is prepared fresh daily; the rolls are whole grain, and no MSG is used. They open at 6:30am for continental breakfast and close at 4pm. Closed Saturdays and Sundays.

There's more to eat than just croissants at the **Croissanterie,** at 222 Merchant St. (tel. 533-3443), a charming, airy place with abundant potted palms and whirring ceiling fans. Sure, there are 36 different kinds of croissants served here, priced from $2.45 to $4.25, and including such innovations as the Gobbler's Enchantment (turkey and cream cheese) and our favorite, fresh strawberries and cream cheese topped with brown sugar; but they also have very good sandwiches, laden with sprouts and served on nine-grain bread, as well as deli sandwiches with potato salad or coleslaw, from $3.75 to $4.95, and good salads and quiches, too. To go with it, there are espresso, cappuccino, café mocha, and other coffees. Croissanterie is open from 6am to 9pm weekdays, to 4pm on Saturday. Closed Sunday.

For a quick, inexpensive and very good breakfast or lunch while shopping or sightseeing downtown, pop in at tiny **Donna's Diner** at 1148 Bishop St. (tel. 531-8660). You can tell it's good because of its popularity with the office and shop workers. Breakfast begins at $2.75 and includes coffee. Soups are a specialty and a meal in themselves: Portuguese bean soup is $4.50, pig's feet or oxtail soup is $4.95, wonton $3.12, and saimin $2.60. And generous plate lunches start at $3.25, burgers at $1.50. Open from 5:30am to 2:45pm, Monday through Friday only.

If you're sightseeing by car and want a lean, reasonable, fast-service restaurant where the food is above "fast service" average, try **Kenny's Coffee House,** a local favorite at the Kam Shopping Center, Likelike Hwy. and North School Street in Kahili (tel. 841-3733). How Kenny's manages to keep the prices so low is hard to figure out. Standard broiler items like steaks, chops, and chicken run from only $5.25 to $6.75, and most are accompanied by fruit cocktail, soup or salad, and roll and butter. The menu is the same all day, from 6am to 11pm, until 1am on Friday, Saturday, and Sunday. There's a dinner special each night, ranging from Swiss steak to seafood platter, roast pork, and roast beef—all from $5.95. Japanese meals, served from 5 to 11pm, featuring yakitori and teriyaki entrees, are $4.95 to $7.65. Kenny's is a bright, cherry place with high ceilings and floor-to-ceiling windows. The bright-green booths and yellow-and-orange color scheme reinforce the cheery mood. You'll be well fed and well pleased here.

If you prefer a picnic, try Kenny's take-out deli next door, where meat and chicken picnic trays are just $3.75, and the chicken isn't fried, but broasted. Tasty.

Restaurant Row

Restaurant Row, Honolulu's newest dining-shopping address, is alive and well and flourishing mightily at 500 Ala Moana Blvd., not far from downtown Honolulu. It's a high-tech, strikingly modern, neon environment, surely not your "old Hawaii," but an enjoyable contemporary urban playground. The best bet for budget dining here is **Rose City Diner,** (tel. 524-ROSE), a sister to the popular Los Angeles restaurant of the same name. This restaurant and soda fountain is pure '50s camp (it was purportedly started by "Rosie Cheeks," a local gal who went to the mainland in the '50s to make it big as a model but became the "Queen of the Diners" of New Jersey instead). It's complete with 1950s artifacts (including TV programs shown on a Motorola set of the period, miniature jukeboxes at each table playing old Harry Belafonte records), Nathan's hot dogs, egg creams, blueplate specials, meatballs and gravy, chicken pot pie, malted milk shakes, and nothing on the menu higher than $8, for chicken parmigiana. Bargains begin with the "2 + 2 + 2" breakfast: This Early Bird special, served from 7 to 11am, features two eggs, two pancakes, two pieces of bacon, and coffee for all of $2.22. Most plate dinners range from $5.27 to $8, and they include sensational lumpy mashed potatoes, with bits of onion and potato skin in the lumps! Another sensation is the chili sundae; it's served in a sundae glass and consists of layers of chili, sour cream, and shredded cheddar cheese topped with a cherry tomato; it's $2.98 and a definite conversation piece. Rosie's "sliders"—hamburger, tuna or chicken salad on miniature rolls, served in a basket with french fries—are fun for lunch: three slider burgers are $3.98. No liquor is served, so BYOB. Rose City Diner is always celebrating something, so you might wander into a Pineapple Upside-Down Cake Bakeoff, a Hula Hoop Competition, or the 1950s Hairstyling Exhibition. Stylish and fun. Open for all three meals, from 6am daily.

Our favorite Restaurant Row dining place—indeed, one of our favorites in all Honolulu—is a bit more expensive, but worth saving your dollars for: that's **Sunset Grill** (tel. 521-4409), a handsome 200-seat restaurant featuring grilled, rotisserie, wood-fire, and oven-roasted foods in a sophisticated indoor-outdoor setting. Blond woods, glass walls, and a large grill in the center of the restaurant set the mood for dining that is casual in style, but elegant where it counts in every detail of food preparation and service. Among the little touches that make a difference: parmesan cheese grated at the table for your onion soup, wines poured tableside, even if all you order is a glass. Have a drink—they're known for terrific martinis—and doodle on the place mats (crayons are provided) while you're waiting for your meal; the best place mat art is displayed on the walls up front, and artists win prizes!

If you're watching the budget, come for just a sandwich: their half-pound hamburger, typical of the grilled specialties here, sizzles over keawe logs, and is topped with grilled onions, peppers, and a choice of cheese, plus potato salad, a meal in itself at $7.95. But splurge a bit here, and try some of the appetizers and soups ($4.75 to $9.95); the Maui onion soup is a winner. Then there's skewers of sesame chicken or jumbo shrimp, and roasted garlic with goat cheese on sourdough bread—just to start. Make your main course a pasta, perhaps the roast chicken linguine with basil, olives, and a sun-dried tomato pesto ($10.95); or choose one of the excellent rotisserie dishes, which come with grilled fresh vegetables. From the charcoal grill, the baby back ribs (marinated in a secret sauce of shoyu and marmalade) are unlike any ribs you've tasted elsewhere; also tops are the fresh fish (from $12.95), the marinated breast of chicken with garlic and cilantro, $11.75, and a not-to-be-missed side order of garlic cheese bread using French sourdough. Desserts are splendid, too: bread pudding with whisky sauce, an elegant crème brûlée, or simply a fruit sherbet with strawberries. Perfection!

Sunset Grill is deservedly very popular; the downtown business crowd throngs the place at lunch, and people come from all around town for dinner, so do make reservations. On Friday and Saturday nights, it's a great place to come after a concert or the theater; then, it's open from 11pm to 1am for appetizers, salads, sandwiches, and desserts. The rest of the week, hours are 11am to 11pm.

Other Restaurant Row establishments include **Marie Callender,** a popular family-style chain (see the "Around the Island" section); **Studebaker's,** a nightclub in the style of the '50s and '60s, where "you bop 'til you drop"; and **Paradise Bakery and Cafe,** a local favorite for quiches, soups, salads, muffins, and great chocolate-chip cookies. The **Black Orchid,** the cornerstone of Restaurant Row, is its premier fine-dining gourmet restaurant. Since both Tom Selleck and Larry Manetti (of *Magnum, P.I.* fame) are part owners, it's a celebrity hangout, the place to see and be seen. While dinner is pricey, lunch can be managed for around $10 to $14; there's also excellent jazz here, and dancing to live music until 4am.

To get you to Restaurant Row with ease, the merchants here have set up a trolley service from Waikiki; you can be picked up Thursday through Sunday from 5:30 to 8:55pm from the Ilikai, Tapa Tower of the Hilton Hawaiian Village, Royal Hawaiian Shopping Center, Hyatt Regency Waikiki, and the Hawaiian Regent Hotel. Return trolleys run until 9:15pm. Cost is 50¢ each way. (To verify hours and service, ask any of the restaurants when you phone for reservations.)

At Keehi Lagoon

Few Honolulu residents and practically no tourists know about Keehi Lagoon. **La Mariana Restaurant & Bar,** 50 Sand Island Access Rd. (tel. 848-2800), is a well-kept secret, a hideaway for the boat owners of the La Mariana Sailing Club at Keehi Lagoon. The restaurant and the marina itself are owned by a feisty lady named Annette La Mariana Nahinu, who has been fighting to keep the area alive for over 40 years. The restaurant is ramshackle romantic, its furnishings—wooden tables, rattan chairs, glass balls, and fishing nets—reputedly salvaged from the old Don the Beachcomber restaurant. One dines here either indoors or on the shaded lanai, in full view of the boats. Nothing formal, nothing fancy here—just the way Hawaii used to be before the big money forces took over. The restaurant's Filipino chef is excellent (although the pork adobo appetizer is about the only concession to his ethnic origins), and specializes mostly in steak, seafood, and freshly caught fish. Prices are reasonable: island favorites like ahi or marlin, ulua or red snapper are all under $15; steaks run $10.50 to $14.50 at dinner. The price of entree includes fries or mashed potatoes or rice, salad, hot rolls and butter, and coffee or tea. Lunch is reasonable, too, with the emphasis on meaty sandwiches (burgers from $3.25, a steak sizzler on a bun at $5.50). La Mariana serves lunch weekdays from 10:30am to 2pm (to 2:30 weekends) and dinner from 6 to 9:30pm every day. You'll need to drive here (it's not far from the airport), and it's best to phone for precise directions.

In the University Area

The best place to eat at the University of Hawaii is at the **Campus Center,** close to University Avenue in the middle of the campus. Its huge, upstairs, newly renovated cafeteria serves breakfast and lunch from 7am to 2pm weekdays. Depending on the day, you may get lemon chicken, tasty seafood items, veal cutlets, or barbecue ribs. They also have fresh pizza, pasta, grilled items, and a variety of salads and desserts from $1.50 to $3.50. The lower level of the Campus Center is the Snack Bar, which features "local foods" such as loco moco, bentos, chili and rice, and plate lunches, from $1.50 to $2.75 (open from 9:30am to 3pm). Bakery items and gourmet salads can be purchased at Kampus Konfections, located in the convenience store called Kampus Korner (open 9am to 6:30pm).

Also pleasant is **Manoa Garden,** in Hemenway Hall, open from 10:30am to 8pm weekdays. It features deli sanqwiches to order and salad by the ounce. You can get a cold pitcher of beer here, and Thursdays and Fridays feature live outdoor entertainment. You can sit indoors or, if the sun is shining in Manoa Valley, try the lanai and throw some crumbs to the Brazilian cardinals, sparrows, and doves.

A popular destination in the Varsity Center is **Bubbies,** 1010 University Ave. (tel. 949-8984), a favorite after-theater spot. Keith Robbins, who hails from the East Coast and named the shop after his grandmother, serves wonderful homemade ice cream and desserts—in addition to delectable ice cream ($2.16 the scoop), you can have cheesecake or apple pie, or chocolate-chip or macadamia-nut cookies along with your coffee. Curtains at the window, fans overhead, plants, an old-fashioned pendulum time clock, and a photograph of "Bubbie" complete the scene. Open from noon to midnight, until 1am Friday and Saturday. Bubbie's ice cream is also served at some of Honolulu's finest restaurants.

The Buzz's restaurants have been popular with residents and visitors alike for as long as we can remember. Our favorite of these handsome places is **Buzz's Original Steak House,** just off University Avenue at 2535 Coyne St. (tel. 944-9781). The decor is art nouveau, with wood paneling, stained glass, and wonderful '30s light fixtures. Steak and seafood are the mainstays of Buzz's bill of fare, but they also have one of the best salad bars in town, at just $6.95. A perennial-dieter friend of ours swears by it. This is one place where we wouldn't want to pass up the pupus: sautéed mushrooms, artichoke surprise, escargots ($2.75 to $5.50). A good dinner choice is the kal-bi platter (marinated beef ribs, Korean-style), at $10.65. Other specialties on the low side of the menu include Buzz's beef kebabs at $9.95 and top sirloin (six ounces) at $9.95. All entrees come with bread, veggies, and that salad bar. And don't miss Buzz's incredible ice-cream pies, at $2.75 a serving. Buzz's in the university area is open Sunday to Thursday from 5 to 10pm, on Friday and Saturday to 10:30pm.

The longtime mecca for pizza lovers in this area is **Mama Mia,** at 1015 University Ave. in Puck's Alley (tel. 947-5233), and real "New York pizza" it is too, since the owner is a transplanted New Yorker. There's a pie for every taste (even a vegetarian pizza with whole-wheat crust—$9.89); terrific spaghetti and lasagne dinners for under $10; some really lusty and crusty hero sandwiches. They now have a full liquor license. The place stays open from 11am all the way to 2am, so it's fun to come here—and sit at the sidewalk café if you like—after the evening's entertainment. Occasionally there's entertainment here, too—perhaps a grown-up puppet show, or just music.

One of our favorite places for submarine sandwiches in these parts is **Mr. Sub,** 2600 S. King St. in Puck's Alley, a clean and cheery spot that is very, very popular. (At many a chic Honolulu cocktail party, the pupus turn out to be six-foot-long Mr. Subs!) All the subs are good, but our favorite is the no. 4 supersub—prosciutto, pressed ham, salami, cappicola, and cheese, covered (as are all the subs here) with lettuce, tomatoes, onions, and dressing, $2.25 for a half, $4.50 for a whole. The people here really work hard at maintaining quality, quantity, low prices, and superfast service! Open daily from 8am to 9pm.

At Kahala Mall

A big favorite in the lovely Kahala residential area is the **Yum Yum Tree Restaurant and Pie Shop** (tel 737-7938) in Kahala Mall This is such a pretty place, with seating both on the lanai and in the wood-and-stone inside room. Service is fast and friendly, and the food is good: We like the bacon-and-avocado sandwich with sprouts and tomatoes on granola whole wheat bread, $6.25; the salads; and the main dishes—mahimahi, sirloin, country fried chicken, and the like, served with soup or good salad (choice of dressing), fries or baked potato, roll, and butter—all $10.45 at dinner, closer to $6.45 at lunch. Best of all are the yummy pies for dessert, baked in their own kitchens; the pie display at center stage makes it difficult to resist taking a whole one back to your hotel. It's rumored that folks who stay at the posh Kahala Hilton Hotel a few blocks away like to come here now and then for a quick and inexpensive change of pace.

It's open for all three meals, starting at 7am with breakfast, until midnight daily. There's a newer Yum Yum Tree at Ward Centre (see above).

Manhattan-style delicatessens may be catching on in Hawaii. **Bernard's New York Deli** (tel. 732-DELI) is certainly getting kudos. Bernard's is kosher-style from chicken soup to apple strudel. New Yorkers will get homesick just reading the menu: half a broiled chicken with matzoh balls and carrots, stuffed cabbage rolls with potato pancakes and salad, two kosher-beef knockwursts with baked beans and salad are all $7.95, as is gefilte fish with borscht and matzoh. You might want to start your meal with a bowl of "homemade" chicken soup or cold schav or borscht with sour cream. Then perhaps on to a deli sandwich of corned beef or chopped liver, hot pastrami or kosher salami, most priced from $4.95 to $6.95. Any side dishes you're fancying, like potato latkes, potato knishes, stuffed derma? They're all available. So are blueberry or cheese blintzes with sour cream, delicious old-fashioned creamy rice pudding, and homemade cheesecake, with a choice of over 85 flavors.

Bernard's is a full-service restaurant with cane chairs, and checkerboard floors. It opens every day at 7am, and closes at 9pm Monday through Thursday, 11pm Friday and Saturday, and 8pm Sunday. Deli breakfasts are served daily until 11am.

For a bit of Mittel Europa in Kahala Mall, stop in at the **Patisserie** (tel. 735-4402), a bakery that also serves sandwiches and pastries at its sparkling counter and several little booths. Sandwiches, served on their home-baked breads (we like the country Swiss), with sprouts or lettuce, run to the likes of Black Forest ham, head cheese, roast beef, bratwurst, and pastrami; prices go from $3.40 to $4.50. And there's hot German potato salad, quiche Lorraine, and carrot salad, too. If you don't want anything quite so heavy, Black Forest cake, dobosh, and freshly baked pies should be just right. Open weekdays from 7am to 9pm, until 7pm on Saturday and 5pm Sunday. Check their shops, too, at the Edgewater and Outrigger West hotels in Waikiki, and the ones downtown, at 33 S. King St. and 700 Bishop St.

THE NATURAL LIFE

Enter **Down to Earth Natural Foods,** 2525 S. King St., just Ewa of University Avenue, go to the rear, and there you will find **The Natural Deli** (tel. 949-8188), a delightful spot where you can dine on "healthy, home-style vegetarian cooking at its best." Only natural ingredients are used; there are many dairy alternatives for vegans and those watching their cholesterol—and the food is delicious, as well! There's a changing parade of hot specials every day (you're invited to call and find out what's cooking for the day), and these might include almond vegetable tofu, chick peas à la king, nondairy lasagne, or shepherd's pie, from $4.25 to $5.75. Always on hand are tofu or tempeh burgers, a variety of veggie sandwiches like avocado or mock tuna ($2.50 each), hearty homemade soups, and a plentiful salad bar that goes for $3.19 a pound. There are plenty of cold deli items like tabbouleh, pesto pasta, burritos, and basmati salad to take out. Nearly a score of healthful desserts await your guilt-free enjoyment. What will it be? Banana cake, papaya-banana cobbler, pumpkin cream pie, or bread pudding? None costs more than $1.79. There's a counter, a few tables right there, and more seating upstairs. The Natural Deli is open every day from 10am to 9pm.

Wherever you see the name **Vim and Vigor Foods,** you can be sure you're getting very fresh, tasty natural food There are two Vim and Vigors in town. Their take-out and drink counter at Ala Moana Center keeps huge lunch crowds happy with luscious sandwiches like avocado, tuna, or egg combinations on whole-grain breads with sprouts, from $2.95 to $3.95. Plenty of honey ice creams, fruit smoothies, and the like, too. The Vim and Vigor at Kahala Mall has a small salad-sandwich bar in back of the health-food store that dishes out big portions of very tasty food, plus lots of home-baked cookies and pies. Don't miss their wonderful breads up at the front counter, especially the whole-wheat cinnamon-raisin bread.

See the "Restaurants in Waikiki" section for details on **Country Life Vegetarian Buffet**, 421 Nahua St., and **Ruffage Natural Foods**, 2443 Kuhio, in the Royal Grove Hotel, which also boasts a tidy little sushi bar.

DINING FOR ART

At the **Garden Café** of the Honolulu Academy of Arts, 900 S. Beretania (tel. 531-8865), the dining lanai is under the trees just outside one of the world's great art collections. The waitresses, the cashier, even the cooks are all volunteers, and all profits from your meal go to further the work of the academy. Lunch is served from 11:30am to 2pm Tuesday through Friday. Almost everything has a gourmet touch: The soups include chicken curry and crème mongole; you might get green bean-and-bacon salad (delicious), or green salad with sliced fresh mushrooms; as for sandwiches, it's turkey, ham, and roast beef. Lunch, including beverage, is $6; wine and beer are available. The desserts, $1.50 extra, include ice cream, guava sherbet, and special dessert bars. Only one menu is served each day. Reservations recommended.

Since there is usually a film or lecture at the academy at 7:30 Thursday nights, the volunteers also serve a Thursday supper at $8.50 (tax included) for a light meal of internationa cuisine. Wine and dessert are extra. Reservations are recommended.

Note: The Garden Café is open from a week after Labor Day until the Friday before Memorial Day; closed Christmas and Thanksgiving.

If you make a visit to the **Contemporary Museum**, 2411 Makiki Heights Dr. —and you should—you can also enjoy another artistic dining experience, at the **Contemporary Café** (tel. 523-3662). It's an attractive spot, with prints on the walls, some outside tables in the courtyard. The menu is sophisticated: You can graze on appetizers like smoked salmon carpaccio or moules à la crème (broiled New Zealand green-lipped mussels topped with a light saffron béchamel), on pastas and salads (the wilted spinach salad is a favorite), or on sandwiches like the ahi Caesar (the ahi poached in wine and tossed with Caesar dressing), from about $3.50 to $7.95. If all you want is an espresso or a cappuccino and a rich dessert, like the flourless chocolate roulade or the amaretto crème caramel, that's available, too. The Contemporary Café is open from noon to 3pm Sunday, closed Tuesday, and open all other days from 10:30am to 3:30pm. Since it's a small and very popular spot, reservations are "strongly recommended."

KIDDIE TREATS

So you're traveling with the kids? By all means, take any youngsters up to age 12 or so to **Showbiz Pizza Place** (tel. 373-2151), at the Aina Haina Shopping Center out on Kalanianaole Hwy., not far from the Kahala Mall. There's a big stage at the front of the dining room, and every so often the curtains part to reveal very cleverly designed, life-size mechanical-animal musicians and singers, such as Beach Bear, Mitzi Mouse, and Fatz the Gorilla. These ingenious creations appear most lifelike, and they "sing" and "play" instruments. There are also people in animal costumes who circulate in the dining room and visit with young diners. As if that weren't enough, there are myriad video games. This is a most popular place for local kids to celebrate birthdays. And the food isn't half bad. The pizzas—Super Combo (cheese, sausage, beef, pepperoni, etc.), Aloha Delight (cheese, ham, pineapple, toasted almonds), Vegetarian Favorite, and Taco Pizza sell for $9.95 small, $12.95 medium, and $16.45 large. There's a salad bar with a good variety of fixings, $3.49 for all-you-can-eat. You can even buy the kids a Showbiz Pizza T-shirt. Showbiz Pizza Place is open every day except Christmas.

SPLURGES

A dinner-only spot that combines a fine meal with an educational experience is the **Pottery Steak and Seafood Restaurant,** in the Waialae-Kahala area, at 3574 Waialae Ave. (tel. 735-5594). Not only is your meal served in unusual pottery—eating and drinking vessels fired in kilns right on the premises—but you can see the potters in action up front. And when you've finished your meal, you can buy the dishes and take them home! As you might expect, this attractive restaurant is decorated throughout with clay vessels that re-create some of the history and romance of early-world pottery. And the food is excellent. If you want to stay on the low side of the menu, have the Potter's Delight, ground New York sirloin, at $8.75. Like all the other entrees, it comes with a choice of soup or salad, rice or a baked potato with a variety of garnishes, vegetables, and loaves of garlic bread that continue to toast in their hot ceramic loaf-shape containers. Or splurge and order fresh fish of the day (quoted daily) or a variety of steaks from $12.75 up. We can recommend the Cornish game hen at $16.75, moist and tender and fired in its own clay vessel—you get to keep the pot. For dessert, go all out with the special potter's coffee, laced with rum, topped with whipped cream and served in a handsome mug. The Pottery is open from 5:30 to 10pm Tuesday through Sunday, and reservations are advisable.

The dining critic of the *Honolulu Star-Bulletin* has called **Alfred's European Restaurant** "one of the top five restaurants in the city." We couldn't agree more. A visit to chef/owner Alfred Vollenweider's gracious dining room on the 3rd floor of the Century Center, 1750 Kalakaua Ave., corner of Kapiolani (tel. 955-5353), is like visiting a fine restaurant on the continent where every detail is handled perfectly, from the china on the table to the attentive service by the waiters to the superb French-continental cuisine. Everything is prepared fresh, using only the best market ingredients. And nothing comes out of the kitchen until Alfred—who spends part of each evening walking around the restaurant in his tall chef's hat, checking on everything—makes sure that it is perfect. While a meal here is not inexpensive, neither is it overpriced by today's standards, and it offers top value for the dollar. Dinner starts with four or five salad-relish dishes prepared according to the season, plus a basket of European-style breads. Soup du jour follows that, and then it's your choice of such dishes as a flavorful coquilles St-Jacques au beurre blanc, grilled breast of duck, filet mignon aux champignons, live Maine lobster, or fresh fish taken from local waters and sautéed, steamed, or poached in a light champagne sauce. Prices range from about $15 to $26 for the complete meal. Desserts are extra but more than worth the price, especially for creations like the soufflé glacé Grand Marnier, or the unforgettable strawberries Romanoff, fresh strawberries marinated in liqueur and topped with Häagen-Dazs ice cream, served in a tall champagne glass. Wines are decently priced, because Alfred shops around for the best values and passes the savings on to his customers. Irish, Swiss, and other specialty coffees, English and herbal teas, plus brandies and cordials top off the meal. Lunch is also pleasant and well priced, from about $7 to $13 for egg dishes, salads, fresh fish, sandwiches, plus a daily chef's special that includes soup or salad, for $9.25.

Alfred's is open every day but Sunday, serving lunch Monday to Friday from 11am to 2pm, and dinner Tuesday to Saturday from 6 to 10pm. Reservations are advised. Validated parking.

A modest splurge and a modest distance from Waikiki—two blocks—is **Tripton's American Cafe** at 449 Kapahulu (tel. 737-3819). (It's one flight above the Chinese restaurant, Hee Hing; there's parking in the basement garage.) The owners, who ran restaurants in the Virgin Islands and, more recently, on Kauai, serve world-class cuisine at reasonable prices. Their liver pâté is more than just chopped liver: It is carefully blended with nutmeg, mace, parsley, and garlic, $5.50. The salmon mousse is highlighted with dillweed and cucumber, blended with sour cream. Create your own salad at your table by choosing five condiments and the dressing; your waiter then tosses it with romaine lettuce, tomatoes, cucumbers, and croutons. It comes with soup, is large enough to be a full meal, and costs $12.75; they call it "the biggest salad you've ever seen." Main dishes run from $12.75 to $18.75, with choices such as daily chicken specials, fresh catch of the day—broiled or sautéed—New York steak, and prime ribs. The decor is lovely—peach and green tones accented by tropical greenery, and two levels, which add privacy. A well-equipped bar adds spirit. Check the chalkboard for marvelous desserts of the day. Tripton's serves dinner only, from 5:30 to 10pm weekdays, to 11pm weekends.

FRENCH

At last, a medium-priced French restaurant par excellence in Honolulu! We're referring to **Le Guignol,** at 1614 Kalakaua Ave., between King Street and Kapiolani Boulevard (tel. 947-5525). This is a tiny place, reminiscent of a small dining room in a French boîte. It's owned by French chef Marcel Trigue and his wife, Madeleine. It is most pleasant, with its crisp tablecloths and paintings of French scenery; the food is very good and most reasonably priced. Appetizers are typically Gallic: pâté, escargots, crevettes Provencal, and some a bit different, like scampi flambé in Pernod with cream and garlic. These are priced from $4.95 to $5.95. The flavorful French-onion soup is $2.95. Entrees include Cornish game hen in a mustard sauce; rack of lamb béarnaise; sliced veal in a light, creamy mushroom sauce; shrimp with fresh basil sauce; and fresh fish-of-the-day. These are served with bread and butter, vegetable and potato, and range in price from $9.50 to $13.95. Finish your dinner with a light sherbet, caramel flan, or blueberries jubilee.

Le Guignol serves dinner only, from 5:30 to 10pm nightly.

HAWAIIAN

You'll probably have your first experience with Hawaiian food at a luau, and then you'll find the same dishes appearing again and again in Hawaiian restaurants and on the "plate lunch" menus of other restaurants all over town. We'll first tell you about the major Hawaiian food specialties, then give you some tips on a "poor man's luau," and finally show you where to find the budget-priced Hawaiian restaurants.

The Food and How to Eat It

You're already on speaking terms with poi. The other basic dishes are kalua pig (pig steamed in an underground oven, or imu), laulau (ti leaves stuffed with pork, salt fish, bananas, sweet potatoes, and taro shoots, and steamed), chicken luau (chicken cooked with coconut milk and taro or spinach leaves), sweet potatoes, pipikaula (jerked beef), and lomi-lomi salmon. The last is a triumph of linguistics over gastronomy: Lomi-lomi means massage, and this is salmon "massaged" with tomatoes and chopped onions, then marinated. Haupia (coconut pudding) and a piece of coconut cake are the usual desserts, along with fresh pineapple.

Food is served on paper plates, and the proper way to eat is with your fingers; plastic spoons are provided for the timid. The correct way to eat poi, by the way, is to dip one or two fingers in it (in the old days you could actually order "one-" or "two-finger" poi), scoop it up quickly, and attack. But nobody expects that of a malihini.

Budget-Restaurant Recommendations

Close to Waikiki, a very popular place to find ono Hawaiian food is **Ono Hawaiian Foods,** at 726 Kapahulu Ave. (tel. 737-2275). It's a little place, with about 10 tables, its walls covered with photos of popular local entertainers who are patrons. Try the kalua pig at $4.65, or the laulau plate at $4.95, or just go mad and have the combination kalua pig *and* laulau at $6.10. These and other plates come with pipikaula (Hawaiian beef jerky), lomi-lomi salmon, poi or rice, and haupia. The atmosphere here is very friendly; the place may be short on size, but it's definitely long on aloha. Open Monday through Saturday from 11am to 7:30pm.

Another spot close to Waikiki for good Hawaiian food is **Aloha Poi Bowl** at 2671 S. King St. in University Square (tel. 944-0798). There are only six booths and a few big white plastic-topped tables in a plain, storelike room, but the food is the star. In addition to those luau staples like laulau, lomi salmon, kalua pork, tripe or beef stew, and chicken long rice, which run from $2 to $3.50, there's always a daily special; the day we were there it was fried akule fish at $7. Combination orders run $4.25 to $6.65. Be sure to top off your meal with that coconut dessert called haupia, 80¢. Open daily, 10:30am to 9pm, Sunday, 3 to 8pm.

People's Café, 1310 Pali Hwy. (tel. 536-5789), is another favorite place for authentic, inexpensive Hawaiian food; the local office workers come here when they have a hangover and want some of that nice, soothing-to-the-tummy poi. Poi plate lunches go for about $7.40 to $8.80, and always include kalua pig and laulau. The prices are the same at lunch and dinner. A good place to remember for take-out orders; there's a $3.75 bento box. Open every day, from 10am to 7:30pm, Sunday from noon.

ITALIAN

Castagnola's Italian Restaurant, at Manoa Marketplace (tel. 988-2969), reminds us of the little trattorias one sees everywhere in Rome and Florence—even though, more likely than not, you will be served by a friendly Asian or Polynesian waiter. Decor is fresh and simple, the food terrific, and the prices reasonable. Complete meals, offered all day, can be ordered in a regular portion or for the light eater; this means that rigatoni ricotta, linguine marinara or with white clam sauce, and eggplant parmigiana are all $9.90 regular, $7 for the light eater. Similarly, veal—be it scaloppine, alla marsala, milanese, piccata, or parmigiana—is either $14.90 or $10.50. There are luncheon sandwiches under $5, and an individual pizza is just $2.80. Castagnola's is one of the few places in Honolulu where you can find cannoli, those flavorful ricotta-filled pastries. Try this, or chocolate gelato, spumoni, or zabaglione for dessert. Castagnola's is open Monday from 11:30am to 3pm, Tuesday through Saturday from 11:30am until 10pm. Closed Sunday.

Che Pasta, at 3571 Waialae Ave. (tel. 735-1777), is a charming Italian restaurant in the Kaimuki neighborhood; we found the food to be quite special and the service impeccable. The dining room is elegantly furnished, yet the ambience of the place is warm and friendly. Dinner can be quite reasonable here if you stick with the pastas, like the delicious saffron cannelloni ($10) or the linguine al pesto ($8). We sometimes come here and make a whole meal on the $5.75 antipasto. A flavorful house specialty is the Cacciatore Espresso, breast of chicken with tomato, mushroom, olives, onions, and garlic, $10.50. The lunch menu features a variety of salads, notably spinach, poached black tiger prawns, pasta salad, and Che Pasta's lovely antipasto, all priced between $5.50 and $7. Sandwiches too, plus some delicious pasta entrees like the fettuccine Alfredo, $7.95. It's a great temptation to overdo it on their wonderful fresh Italian bread (a new supply is whisked to your table as soon as your basket is empty), but be strong and save room for the gelato and sherbet, or the chocolate Grand Marnier cake. A *bellissimo* treat. Lunch is served from 11:30am until 2pm Tuesday to Friday; dinner hours are 5:30 to 10pm Tuesday to Sunday. Closed Monday.

Note: If you're in downtown Honolulu, you can enjoy similar cuisine at slightly lower prices at **Che Pasta, A Bar & Grill,** at 1001 Bishop St. at Bishop Square. The same philosophy and practice prevail here: "A fresh approach to Italian cuisine, using only the finest and freshest ingredients available." It's a busy, bustling business lunch spot, as well as an early evening jazz club.

Ambrosia Ristorante, 1192 Alakea St., corner of Beretania (tel. 522-1111), is a delightful new find in downtown Honolulu. It's especially festive at dinnertime, when the hurricane lamps on the tables are lit, and there's usually a strolling musician. Among the appetizers ($4.50 to $7.50), we like the sautéed clams with roasted tomatoes in herb-and-wine sauce. Huge salads, like the Mediterranean (romaine lettuce, roast breast of chicken, vegetables, and tomato sauce), run from $3.95 to $7.95. Fish, meat, and poultry entrees, equally generous in size, go from $10.95 to $12.50. Or, you can always rely on such pasta dishes as spaghetti with basil, $7.50; rigatoni Florentine, $8.95; fettuccine parmesan, $8.45; all the way up to the seafood pasta at $13. The luncheon crowd goes for the sandwiches with that continental touch, priced mostly at $6.95. The same dishes are served at both lunch, 11am to 2pm, and dinner, 5 to 10pm. Service is attentive; there's parking in the rear. Closed Sunday.

If you happen to be on Alakea Street and would like Italian food, but without the ambience and at a cheaper price, try **Ron's Place,** 801 Alakea, corner Queens St. (tel. 536-5354). Would you believe lasagne at $3.30 and specials like spaghetti and meatballs served with garlic bread at $3.80? This is an arcade take-out place, with tables just outside. We didn't promise tablecloths and roses! Open Monday through Friday 10am to 5pm.

JAPANESE

Japanese cuisine is well known in every big American city these days, but in Honolulu, it's an old, old story. With the vast number of Japanese-Americans who were born and live here and the vast number of Japanese who visit, Japanese restaurants and sushi bars are so numerous you might think you're in Tokyo instead of Honolulu, U.S.A. And the cuisine has so permeated the islands that you'll find Japanese dishes—beef hekka, shrimp tempura, saimin—on menus everywhere. Hekka is a kind of poor man's sukiyaki (a beef and vegetable stew), and tempura means anything deep-fried in batter. Saimin (known in Japan as *rahmen*), the seaweed-chicken-noodle soup that we mentioned earlier, is just the thing for the starvation budget; a large bowl, which will cost about $4 to $5, will do for a whole meal, and you can get it almost anywhere. You can even make it at home: instant saimin, direct from Japan, is sold in the food departments of most Japanese stores, like Shirokiya at Ala Moana. Speaking of Shirokiya, their second-floor gourmet-food department is a one-stop lesson in Japanese food, and they have marvelous take-out dishes you can eat on the spot, in their dining lanai, or back in your room.

Bento is a word you'll soon become familiar with in the islands; it means a Japanese-style box lunch. One of the places the local people favor for bentos is **Taniguchi Stores,** 2065 S. Beretania St. in the McCully area. The large bento, all of $2.75, includes rice, fish cakes, shoyu barbecued chicken, hasukantira (veggies), and pickled salad. For $1.75 you get a medium bento, with two kinds of rice balls seasoned with peas and seaweed, fish cakes, egg roll, veggies, and marinated squid. Open daily.

For a chance to sample authentic Japanese dishes for just pennies, try the **Oriental Snack Bar** at Woolworth's on Kalakaua Avenue in Waikiki or the one at the Ala Moana Shopping Center. Both are big hits with the office workers and shoppers. The prices vary minutely at the two: sushi selections are $1.80 to $7.95, a bowl of saimin is $4.50. The Kalakaua Avenue store has a sushi bar and bento lunches. We slightly favor the Ala Moana Woolworth's since, after filling up your paper plate, you can go out and sit in the pretty mall watching islanders mill about you as you nibble. Incidentally, two cone sushis (cold, marinated rice cakes) tucked in your bag make a tasty lunch-on-the-run.

When you dine in a regular Japanese restaurant, all you order is your main course; it will come served on a tray with several small dishes like pickled vegetables, soup, rice, and tea. Nobody will think you're a square if you ask for a fork, but why not live dangerously? By the end of your first Japanese meal, you'll get the hang of chopsticks, more or less.

Many of Hawaii's Japanese restaurants are pretty expensive affairs, complete with kimono-clad waitresses and lavish settings. We have a couple of favorites, however, where you can dine quite reasonably at lunch and pay an average of $10 to $14 for complete dinners.

First, we've always like **Suehiro,** at 1914 King St. (tel. 949-4584). Try to get one of their ozashiki or tatami rooms, where you sit on the floor and dine at a low lacquered table (you take off your shoes before you enter, of course); the setting will immediately put you in a tranquil mood, ready for a different kind of experience. You usually need a party of eight and a reservation for these rooms, but if a room happens to be open you may double up with other waiting guests. On one visit we teamed up with a big, charming family of Japanese-Americans, and had a family-style dinner at $13.50 per person that included a tasty miso soup (a clear broth made with soybean paste), namasu (pickled cucumber), sashimi, shrimp tempura, tenderloin filet and mixed sushi. All of this was served with several side vegetables, sauces, rice, dessert, and plenty of tea. It was a colorful and memorable experience. At the regular restaurant tables, you may order a similar dinner special for $25 for two people, and there are many entrees in the $7.50 to $12.95 range. There is an extensive sushi menu, and half-a-dozen special lunches from $6.25 to $7.50.

Note: You can also get a tasty Japanese box lunch here, for picnics and trips. Open 11am to 2pm and 5 to 9pm daily.

Kabuki Restaurant Kapiolani, 600 Kapiolani Blvd. (tel. 545-5995), is a very pretty restaurant—light-wood paneling, lots of mirrors, white stoneware dishes with blue flowers, an attractive little sushi bar—that offers a chance to sample many Japanese dishes at reasonable prices. Live Maine lobsters and live Dungeness crabs are available and prepared to your liking; also popular is the lobster sashimi. Hibachi dinners, cooked at your table for two or more people, include soup, rice, tsukemono, special sauces, and tea, along with main courses such as beef or chicken yakiniku, from $9.50; a tasty teishoku dinner with a main course of salmon, sashimi, and assorted vegetables, is $10.75. For lunch, the combination teishoku meal is $7.25; regular lunches are $6.15 to $8.50. And the sushi here is excellent. Lunch is served daily from 11am to 2pm, dinner Monday to Saturday from 5 to 9:30pm, Sunday from 5 to 9pm. The Sushi Counter is open daily from 11am to 2pm and from 5pm to midnight, Monday through Saturday, and Sunday from 5 to 10pm.

You can sit at a tempura bar, pretty much like a sushi bar, and watch the chef prepare tasty tidbits at **The Tempura House,** 1419 S. King St. (tel. 941-5919). Black vinyl chairs line the black vinyl bar. There are also tables for four in this long, narrow store converted into a restaurant. At lunch, prices start at $6 for chicken cutlet but rise quickly to $10.50 for sashimi (raw fish). Most of the authentic Japanese tempura, like the popular unagi (eel), are over $11, and go up to $14 for the combination seafood and vegetable tempura, all of which are very light and delicate tasting. Prices for the same items, larger portions, go up about $3 at dinner. Console yourself knowing that these dishes would cost four times as much in Japan. Lunch is served from 11am to 2pm, dinner from 5 to 10pm, Monday through Saturday. Closed Sunday. There is limited free parking in the rear; in the evening, street parking is plentiful.

For Japanese food with a local flavor, try **Irifune,** at 563 Kapahulu, close to Waikiki (tel. 737-1141). Although short on decor, it's long on good food, large portions, and low prices, which are the same at lunch and dinner. For example, it's only $6.50 for the Kushiyaki stick meal, which consists of miso soup; pickled vegetables; three skewers of barbecued chicken and veggies; a salad of lettuce, tomatoes, and chopped cabbage with a delicious house dressing; rice; and green tea. Have this with seafood at $7, or mixed seafood and chicken at $8. Irifune specialties include their chicken and seafood sukiyakis at $9, shrimp tempura at $6.50, and a variety of garlic creations, like garlic tofu, chicken or seafood with vegetables, at $6.50 and $8. Best of all, go with their fresh spicy garlic ahi, market priced. Unlike most Japanese restaurants, Irifune does serve dessert, and a delicious one at that: ice-cream crêpes, filled with seasonal fruit, $2.50.

Irifune is open every day except Monday, serving lunch from 11:30am to 1:30pm, dinner from 5 to 9:30pm.

On the way to Sea Life Park (TheBUS no. 57) or Hanauma Bay, you may want to stop at the Aina Haina Shopping Center on Kalanianaole Hwy., the home of **Otomi** (tel. 377-5700). From exterior to interior, from the classic decor to the exotic taste sensations, you'll think you're in Kyoto. Hanging Japanese lanterns, framed rice-paper collages, other folk-art touches, and waitresses in colorful happi coats add to the illusion. We often see Japanese visitors dining here at the polished-wood tables. Check the plastic replicas of dishes in the showcase before you enter—just like on the Ginza in Tokyo. Lunch dishes range from $3.50 for zaru soba, a Japanese noodle; to $7.95 for tempura sashimi, with dishes like pork tofu and beef sukiyaki in between. Dinner features a number of entrees like fried chicken, butterfish, miso or seafood platter, from $7.95 and up; more exotic dishes like shabu shabu for two go up to $24.75. You may want to take out a bento lunch of shrimp and seven other items, $3.75, and continue on your outing.

Otomi is open Tuesday to Sunday from 11am to 1:45pm for lunch, from 5 to 9:15pm for dinner, and in between these times, the cocktail bar and sushi bar are open. There's plenty of free parking.

CHINESE

Cities with large Chinese populations always have enough inexpensive restaurants to keep you going for some time, and Honolulu is no exception. It's especially good for budgeteers, since many of the restaurants are quite lavish and yet offer a number of surprisingly reasonable dishes. The problem here is choosing from an embarrassment of gourmet riches: Local friends each swear that their favorite is "the best." Remember that since most of Hawaii's Chinese came from the southern districts, most restaurants feature Cantonese dishes; but happily, the more subtle Mandarin cooking of the northern provinces and the fiery Szechuan cooking that's so popular on the mainland have found their way to several of our budget choices.

One of the most popular Chinese restaurants in town is **Yong Sing**, 1055 Alakea St. (tel. 531-1366). It's a huge place occupying all of a downtown building, and the vast dining room is nicely, if not elaborately, decorated in red and gold. There's a huge menu from which to choose, with many well-priced goodies. The last time we were here we had a succulent almond duck and chicken with oyster sauce, the house specialty. An excellent $19 dinner for two includes egg-flower soup, almond chicken, sweet-and-sour pork, beef broccoli, and fried rice. For something unusual, ask the waiter for a dim-sum lunch. This consists of many different varieties of Chinese dumplings: either steamed, baked, or fried, some filled with sweetmeats and served as main dishes; others, dainty pastries for dessert. Five or six of these and plenty of the free-flowing tea—and you've had a lovely, inexpensive treat. But be sure to get there between the hours of 11am and 2pm for the dumplings; they sell out fast. Yong Sing also has cocktails at reasonable prices, take-out orders anytime, and plenty of parking available. It's open from 7:30am until 9pm seven days a week.

We like everything about the new **Chan's Chinese Restaurant**, 2600 S. King St. (tel. 949-1188), from the sparkling clean and modern decor (pale pink and gray walls, white cloths and red napery, Chinese art and artifacts on the walls) to the cheerful service and that delicious food—at very reasonable prices. Owner Jennifer Chan blends an array of Mandarin, Szechuan, Shanghai, Cantonese, and Peking dishes: The Mandarin menu is tucked between the glass tabletop and the tablecloth, and offers slightly spicier fare, like the clams in wine sauce, at $6.95. If crab is in season, go for the lusty crab with black bean sauce, market priced. Or feast on a meal of tasy dim sum, offered from 9am to 2pm. If you'd like to try a Chinese breakfast, then join the locals who come here for their *jook*—that's rice soup, with a choice of chicken, seafood, meat, or fish: Most jooks are $3.50. For lunch or dinner, there are dozens of dishes under $6—like a chicken with black mushroom casserole, moo shu pork with pancakes, or roasted duck. Chan's is open daily from 9am to midnight. Parking in Puck's Alley is validated.

There are precious few northern Chinese restaurants in the islands, so praise be for **King Tsin**, 1110 McCully St. (tel. 946-3273), an attractive, pleasantly decorated place popular with both visitors and local folk. The food is reasonably priced, subtly flavored, and most fun to eat with a group, as we did the last time we were there. A Chinese friend had ordered for us over the phone, and our soup and appetizer were whisked to our table moments after we arrived. Our party of four began with pot stickers, small dumplings stuffed with pork, two orders at $3.50 each, and two orders of sizzling rice soup at $4.50 per order. For our main courses, we had moo shu pork, $6.50; dry-fried beef—super hot—at $5.95; King Tsin chicken, $5.95, a delicate combination of tender white meat of chicken and pea pods; braised bean curd, $4.95; and sweet-and-sour fish, an entire rock cod, complete with tail and head, smothered in sauce, around $12, depending on size. We all ate until we couldn't manage another bite—and still had a huge doggie bag to take home. Lunch prices are about 10% cheaper than dinner. With the exception of the aforementioned beef —about which the menu warns you—the food here is not overly spicy, as it can be at other northern Chinese restaurants. Open daily for lunch from 11am to 2pm and dinner from 5 to 9:30pm.

Vegetarians who love Chinese food swear by the **Yen King Restaurant** in the Kahala Mall Shopping Center, near the Kahala Hilton Hotel (tel. 732-5505)— there are at least 30 meatless dishes on the menu! So do lots of other folks who've discovered this attractive restaurant that specializes in the cuisines of Peking and Szechuan. There's a lot to choose from here (most dishes run $4.25 to $7.50), but two dishes that we never miss are their famous Singing Rice Soup (it "sings" when the crispy rice is added to the hot broth), and Chinaman's Hat, which consists of very light "pancakes" that you stuff and wrap at the table with a luscious filling of pork and vegetables. From then on, choose what you like: crackling chicken, lemon beef, sautéed clams—they're all good. So are the Peking-style dumplings and spring rolls among the appetizers. As for those vegetarian dishes, we found the lo hon chai vegetable dish delectable. Desserts at Chinese restaurants are usually unimaginative, but not here. If they're not too busy, they might make you their fried apple with honey: flaming apple cubes covered with a honey–maple syrup sauce are dipped into ice water right at your table. The result? A treat you won't forget. Everything on the regular menu is available for take-out, and take-outs during the dinner hours (4 to 9:30pm) are charged lunchtime (11am to 4pm) prices. Yen King has full bar service, and is open seven days a week.

When you pull up in front of **Yuen's Garden Seafood Restaurant,** 2140 S. King St. (tel. 944-9699), you are intrigued at what may lie behind the window curtains and inside the Chinese-scripted door. Once inside, seated in the red-backed chairs enjoying the Cantonese, Szechuan, and Mandarin dishes, you know that the real intrigue lies in the food. Despite the huge menu, it is the seafood that inspires most of the raves. Prawns can be bought by the pound at $18; a half-pound usually produces five large prawns. We like the fried prawns, served with radish and cilantro, at $7.95. Other good seafood choices, most in the $7 range, are scallops, clams with black bean sauce, sweet-and-sour shrimp, and sea bass filet. Also great are the hot-pot courses served in casseroles; there are five to choose from in the $6 range. We vote for the seafood combo and the roasted duck hot pot made with eggplant and plum sauce.

Yuen's Garden Seafood Restaurant is open daily from 10:30am to 9:30pm.

Still in the mood for seafood? **Imperial Seafood Palace,** 1010 University Ave. (tel. 944-8838) is a Hong Kong–style Chinese restaurant that features live seafood true to that tradition. Live lobsters, Dungeness crabs, prawns, and oysters are offered daily at going market prices. Dishes like sautéed seafood with vegetables, shrimps with cashew nuts, scallops with Chinese peas are all reasonably priced at $6.50. And most poultry and meat dishes are only $4 to $4.25. A deep rose carpet sets a rich aura of expectancy that is fully realized. Interesting Asian art adorns the walls. Imperial Seafood Palace is open daily from 10:30am to 2:30am.

Seafood is the specialty of the house at **Won Kee,** a popular spot in the Chinese Cultural Plaza (tel. 524-6877). The dining room is pleasant enough, decorated in rich burgundy and light pink with scenes on the wall that depict birds; the carpeting is thick and plushy, and wind chimes tinkle faintly. But the star attraction here is the food. The menu abounds with such fish and seafood delicacies as sautéed Dungeness crab with ginger and garlic sauce, $16; steamed island prawns and jumbo shrimp, $13.90 and $11.50; and a stir-fried lobster, $24 a pound. Delicious! Steamed island fish is highly recommended; at various times they have kumu, golden perch, sea bass, opakapaka, and other varieties, priced according to the current market value. On the low side of the menu ($8.50 to $10.50), you can feast on deep-fried crispy oysters, sweet-and-sour crispy fish filet, or seafood casserole. And if you'd rather not have fish or seafood, you'll be happy with dishes like sliced beef with seasonal vegetables, sweet-and-sour pork, golden crispy chicken. Won Kee serves lunch from 11:30am to 2:30pm and dinner from 5 to 10pm every day.

Rating high with the local Chinese community is **Maple Garden,** at 909

Isenberg St. (tel. 941-6641), a small, attractive dining room with Chinese decorations on the walls, wood paneling, and soft lights. The Szechuan dishes are so tasty and authentic that a doctor friend of ours from Taiwan says that he takes all of his visiting friends and relatives there. Mr. Robert Hsu, the owner, is constantly adding new delights to the menu. The house specialty is Szechuan smoky duck, crispy on the outside and tender on the inside, served with steamed buns—you tuck the meat into the buns. A very generous order (you'll probably need a doggie bag) is $6.95. If you really like the super-hot Szechuan-style cooking, you'll love the eggplant with hot garlic sauce or the pork with hot garlic sauce, $5.75 and $5.25; they're real eye-openers. (The eggplant recipe has received an award from the *Los Angeles Times*.) There are more than 75 entrees on the menu priced at $6.50 or less, including hard-to-find singing rice—actually it's more of a whistle—served either with pork and vegetables or with shrimp, $6.25 in either case. Lunch is from 11am to 2pm Monday through Saturday; dinner from 5:30 to 10pm every day. There's ample parking space; and you can phone for easy bus or auto directions from Waikiki.

Just about 10 minutes away from Waikiki, in the area of McCully and King streets, is the ever-popular **New Golden Duck,** 930 McCully St. (tel. 947-9755). It's a tremendous dining room furnished with red-leather booths and chairs, extremely popular with local Chinese families for big parties and receptions. Almost everything on the large and varied menu is under $7, with most items about $3.50 to $4.50. Some of our favorites include lemon chicken and shoyu chicken, shrimp with broccoli, beef with sweet-and-sour cabbage, shrimp vegetable noodle, and oyster roll. The portions are so generous and the food so good that you'll want to visit this one again and again. New Golden Duck opens at 10:30am daily and closes at 1:30am on Friday and Saturday, at 12:30am the rest of the week. From Waikiki, take TheBUS no. 2 to Kalakaua and King, transfer to a no. 1 going to Diamond Head on King Street (or walk) four blocks to McCully Street.

One of the most popular Chinese restaurants in Honolulu since 1963, and still going strong, is **Hee Hing,** at 449 Kapahulu Ave. (tel. 734-8474), not far from Waikiki in a Diamond Head direction, near the Honolulu Zoo. There's a good reason for this popularity: It's a handsome, spacious restaurant, with good-luck murals, paintings, and collages adorning the walls, plates brilliantly bordered with Chinese "Walls of Troy," and a superb Cantonese cuisine—worthy of the finest traditions of Chinese cooking. And the prices for these delicious, authentic Chinese treats are always reasonable. The menu is voluminous, so take a little time to study it, or ask the waiter for advice. Don't miss trying the dim sum here; they serve over 75 Hong Kong–style dim sum every day. The house specialty, exclusive to Hee Hing, is drunken prawns—live prawns, marinated in white wine, cooked tableside, priced seasonally. There's a vast variety of other live seafood dishes, too, as well as fresh fish prepared in a choice of five different styles. Or, you might decide to feast on one of the sizzling specialties—like sizzling chicken with black bean sauce, sizzling tenderloin of beef, sizzling pork chops with onions—from $7 to $7.95. Earthen-pot casserole dishes, $6.50 to $14.95, are a whole other way to go. Then there are taro-nest specialties, the usual chicken, pork, duck, and beef dishes, at least 16 vegetarian offerings, and a vast array of soup-style noodle dishes, rice soups, and more. Everything we've tried here has been excellent. For dessert, forgo the fortune cookies in favor of a seasonal fruit pudding or fried apple fritters. A great find. Hee Hing serves lunch from 10:30am to 2:30pm, then dinner to 9:30pm, every day.

The local Chinese population has been keeping the **On On Chinese Restaurant** at 909 Kapahulu Ave., just a mile outside Waikiki (tel. 735-4557), busy for a decade now. This is an intimate place with hanging greenery over each of the tables which line the walls on either side. Co-owner Faith Wong and her husband promise to respect all requests to avoid using MSG. They are especially proud of their specials such as lotus beefstew, $6.25, and chicken with black mushrooms, $6. You have something like 100 items to choose from, most in the $4.50 to $6.75 range, and that includes roast duck and many other favorites. It's open every day from 11am to 9pm, with the same menu in effect all day.

Do you like potstickers? That's one good reason for going to **Woodlands**

Potsticker Restaurant, 1289 S. King St. (tel. 526-2239), but not the only one. All the food here is especially good, and it's a local favorite. The Chinese-tiled ceiling and impressive Asian statuettes and art prepare you for a special experience. You may want to start with some of those potstickers: We like the pan-fried dumplings, the chicken with chives, and the onion cake, $3.50 to $4.95. Bird's Nest Soup—the real thing—with chicken is another impressive starter ($12.50), or try the crabmeat tofu soup, $7.95. Prawns, scallops, and steamed catch-of-the-day dominate the dozen seafood dishes, mostly in the $9-to-$19 category. Best bargains are some 30 special-ty chicken and duck choices, mostly $4.95 to $6.75, but watch out—some of these may be highly spiced. Woodlands Potsticker Restaurant is open daily, from 11am to 2pm for lunch, from 5 to 9pm for dinner. Parking in the rear.

Shoppers at Ward Warehouse have only to cross the road in the rear of the com-plex, and there's **The Chinese Chuckwagon** at 1020 Auahi St. (tel. 537-5208), in the Ala Moana Farmer's Market. We like to come on weekend nights, when there's a nine-course buffet meal for $11.95 adults, $7.95 children. The menu changes every week, but there are always at least 10 hot dishes: such as roast duck, sweet-and-sour fish, clams with ginger and garlic sauce, beef Szechuan, stuffed tofu, and chicken with vegetables. Soup, hot tea, and an almond-float dessert are also included. The buffet is available from 5:30 to 9pm weekends; table service is offered daily, and prices are moderate. This is a very plain place that looks like a luncheonette, but it has comfortable booths and a few tables.

BURMESE

You'd hardly expect to find several small, exotic-food stands inside the building on the ground floor of 801 Alakea St., near Richard Street. Exceptional among these is **Curry Place** (tel. 536-4667), featuring Burmese cooking, which you can either take out or eat right there if you can find an empty counter seat. Owner Linda Loo is originally from Burma, and the long route she took to get here is evidenced by the Indonesian, Szechuan, and Indian dishes on her steam table. Since one entree is $2.75, two $3.55, three $3.95, and four $4.25, you can afford to be adventuresome. Be sure to sample the lumpia, a vegetable stick, $1. Then take your pick among au-thentic Burmese and Indian curries, rices, and salads. Linda serves lunches only, 10:30am to 2:30pm, Monday to Friday.

FILIPINO

Filipino food, it is said, originated with Malay settlers, was spread by Chinese traders, stewed for 300 years of Spanish rule, and was finally hamburger-ized by the Americans. What has arrived in Honolulu is delicious, and you can find it at **Jo-Ni of Hawaii,** 1017A Kapahulu Ave. (tel. 735-8575), the only fine Filipino restaurant that we know of on Oahu. The windowed dining room is bright with a pink-and-cream decor and cane chairs made in the Philippines. A booklet menu awaits you on the white plastic-topped table. Your first decision is whether to select a festive main dish or a regional specialty. You needn't worry about prices, since both are inexpensive: festive dishes range from $5.75 to $9.95, regional specialties mostly from $3.95 to $5.95. At a recent meal, from the festive range we sampled langua—tender slices of ox tongue simmered in mushroom sauce, delicious! Beef flank rolled and stuffed with boiled eggs and sausage is another festive item. Among the regional specialties, you might try adobo Manila, a stew with pork and/or chicken in a vinegar, garlic, and soy sauce; or the more delicate hipon sa gatong bicol, shrimps simmered in co-conut milk, along with squash and long beans, $6.95. Choose a few side dishes like pickled vegetables, to act as dipping sauces.

Jo-Ni of Hawaii is open every day except Monday, from 11am to 2pm for lunch, 5 to 9pm for dinner.

INDIAN

The **India House,** at 2632 S. King St., near Puck's Alley (tel. 955-7552), is owned by Ram Arora, formerly the specialty chef at the elegant (and super-expensive) Third Floor Restaurant at the Hawaiian Regent Hotel. His own place, besides being very much more within our reach, is attractive, cool, and relaxing. Brass lamps and lush plants abound in the small dining room that accommodates perhaps a dozen tables. A sari-clad hostess will greet you, make you welcome and assist in ordering. Should you wish to try tandoori (clay oven) cooking, have the boti kebab, the fish tikka, or tandoori chicken, served with pullao (rice pilaf) and a wonderful naan bread, from $7.95 to $8.95. Combination dinners are perhaps a better buy, $12.50 to $16.95, and there are plentiful à la carte choices—curries, keema, chicken, shrimp, lamb, or vegetarian dishes, from $6.95 to $9. A particularly good dessert choice is the gulab jaman, a "dairy delicacy served in rosewater syrup." We'd call this one a thoroughly delightful dining experience. India House is open for dinner every day from 5 to 9:30pm.

THAI

Every now and then one discovers a place where the food is exotic and delicious, the staff cordial and attentive, the atmosphere warm and cozy, and the prices painless. Such a find is the **Mekong Restaurant,** a charming bit of Thailand at 1295 S. Beretania St. between Keeaumoku and Piikoi (tcl. 521-2025 or 523-0014), where a meal is a cultural experience. The small dining room sparkles with white-linen tablecloths and blue-linen napkins, posters on the wall, and a pretty latticed ceiling. An upstairs room is usually open. The voluminous menu will explain the basics of Thai cooking, but you'll do just as well to tell your waiter what you like and follow his suggestions. Thai cooking is a cross between East Indian and Chinese, and while it can be highly spicy, almost every dish can be ordered either mild, medium, or hot. Our waiter explained to us that the hottest—and most popular—dishes are Thai green curry (beef, pork, or chicken sautéed in green chile and curry in fresh coconut milk), $5.50; and Evil Jungle Prince (beef, pork, or chicken sautéed with hot spices with either hot or sweet basil leaves), $5.25. We chose, however, a number of mild dishes that were exquisitely spiced: not-to-be-missed spring rolls (you "sandwich" them at table in fresh lettuce and mint, top with a flavorful carrot-based sauce, and sprinkle with ground peanuts—incredible!), $5.50; a memorable chicken-ginger soup in a fresh coconut-milk base, $5.50; a dish of thin, crisp noodles with tiny bits of chicken, $4.95; water chestnuts fried rice, $5.25; and a shrimp curry at $7.25. (These are lunch prices; dinner items are up to $1.25 more.) Bring your own bottle if you want wine. Dessert was another unforgettable treat: tapioca pudding unlike any you've ever tasted, in a warm coconut milk; and half-ripe Thai apple-bananas, again cooked in coconut milk. Thai teas are just a little bit different, brewed with vanilla beans and served with condensed milk to make them quite sweet. Eating at Mekong is such a delight that you might be tempted to end your culinary wanderings right here. Open for lunch from 11am to 2pm Monday to Friday, and for dinner from 5:30 to 9pm every day.

So successful has the Mekong Restaurant been, that owner Keo Sananikone has gone ahead and opened four more temples of Thai cuisine, two of them nearby: **Mekong II,** at 1726 S. King St. (tel. 941-6184), which does serve beer and wine, and the grandest of them all, **Keo's Thai Cuisine,** at 625 Kapahulu (tel. 737-8240 or 737-9250). So spectacular, in fact, is the latter, that if you're going to have only one Thai meal, we suggest you pay more for the same items this one time and eat here, imbibing the beauty along with the luscious food. Keo has created what might be called a garden-jungle atmosphere: tiny lights strung into the plants, umbrellas over some of the tables, ceiling fans, statues, carvings, portraits on the wall, orchids everywhere—it's a stunner. Dinner only is served here, daily from 5:30. Reservations recommended at this celebrity hangout.

The newest outpost of the Keo empire are **Keo's at Ward Centre,** which we've told you about, above, and **Keo's at King Street.** At Ward Centre prices are the same as at Keo's Thai Cuisine, and the setting is similarly beautiful. The advantage for us is that this one is in a more convenient location, and it does serve lunch. Reservations: 533-0533. The King Street Keo's, 1486 S. King St., has an elegant setting, lower prices than the other Keo's, and serves dinner only, nightly from 5:30pm: Reservations: 947-9989.

Just a block mountainside from the Ala Moana Shopping Center is another Thai winner, **Siam Orchid,** 638B Keeaumoku St. (tel. 955-6161). The setting is charming: fans, Thai artwork on the wall, rattan chairs, pink cloths under glass, orchids on the tables, banquette seating. The menu is thoroughly authentic, reflecting the different styles of the various regions of the country. And prices are modest at both lunch and dinner. What to choose? There's a huge array of dishes, some hotter than others (ask your waiter), but you can't go wrong with appetizers like stuffed chicken wings or squid salad (most run $5.95 to $6.95). Or, begin your meal with a white-tofu or fresh-cabbage clear soup ($5.95 to $7.95 for soups), and choose from such entrees as fresh chile chicken, beef on a sizzling platter, pork with ginger-curry sauce, or Thai garlic shrimp. Most entrees run from $6.25 to $7.95, with the seafood dishes a few dollars higher. As in most Thai restaurants, there's a healthy list of specialties for vegetarians. Lunch is always a good buy, with half-a-dozen noodle specials around $5. Everything is prepared to order, and no MSG is used.

Siam Orchid is open every day except Sunday, serving lunch from 11am to 2pm, dinner from 5:30 to 9:30pm.

The King Street/Moiliili area, not far from Waikiki, has two Thai restaurants that the locals like. So do we. Both are small, neighborhood places with reasonable prices and very good food. **Chiang-Mai Thai Restaurant,** 2239 S. King St. (tel. 941-1151), has perhaps a dozen tables and some simple decor. It specializes in the food of northern Thailand, and calls itself the "home of sticky rice and exotic food." Yes, you can order the sticky rice (really mochi rice in a bamboo container), and the exotic foods might include anything on the long menu from golden-fried calamari with fresh lemon grass and spices among the appetizers and a creamy tofu soup to a shrimp pineapple curry, or hot and spicy clams, ginger beef, or cashew chicken. Appetizers and salads run from $3.95 to $6.95; main dishes, $4.95 to $6.95. Vegetarians have a full menu—almost two dozen dishes—from which to choose. Chiang-Mai serves lunch Monday to Friday from 11am to 2pm, and dinner nightly from 5:30 to 10pm.

Pataya Thai Restaurant, 1614 S. King St. (tel. 942-7979), is even smaller—minuscule, in fact—but its kitchen is powerful. This is the place to experiment with some unusual Thai dishes like Kuruma shrimp curry (shrimps and vegetables cooked in southern Thai style) or chicken sautéed in pepper sauce and basil. Or, stick to more familiar dishes such as "the original Evil Jungle Priest": It can be made with beef, chicken, or shrimp; the ingredients are sautéed in a very hot pepper sauce and coconut milk over a "hot, rocking flame"—not for the cautious appetite! Dishes range in price from $5.25 to $8.95. Vegetarians have about a dozen dishes of their own. Pataya Thai serves lunch Tuesday to Friday from 11am to 2pm, dinner weekdays from 5 to 9pm, weekends from 5 to 10pm.

KOREAN

So few cities in the world give you a chance to sample good Korean cuisine that you shouldn't pass up the opportunity in Honolulu. Koreans make up a relatively small part of the islands' population, but their culinary tradition has left its mark, especially in the ubiquitous kim chee—pickled cabbage seasoned with red-hot peppers. You'll find it in grocery stores, on menus everywhere in Honolulu, and even at the beach stands along Waikiki where they serve kim chee dogs. But the cuisine has much more to offer: barbecued meat dishes, hearty noodle soups, tasty meat dumplings, fish filets sautéed in spicy sauces, and daintily shredded vegetables are some of the other standbys. A few, but by no means all, of the dishes are served with fiery hot sauces; if you're not accustomed to that sort of thing, check with the waitress before you order.

Honolulu has only a handful of Korean restaurants, and the oldest and best of these, the **House of Park,** at 2671D S. King St. in Moiliili, on the way to the university (tel. 949-2679), is the kind of family-style place that gives you a real experience in nontourist dining. Small and tidy with white walls and flower arrangements—an attempt at decoration—it caters to local Korean and other Asian families (lots of cute keikis spill about), and a smattering of university students. There are a few booths and tables up front (at one, a man may be rolling dumplings for the soup), from which you can see the big open kitchen in the back. We love the combination of mon doo and kuk soo—hot noodle soup with Korean dumplings stuffed with beer, pork, and vegetables. The waitress once explained to us that this is "New Year's Soup, but so popular we make it every day." The house specialty is kal bi, barbecued short ribs, and it's excellent. Most dishes run $4 to $8. The plate lunch—barbecued meat, na mul (Korean-style vegetables and fish fried in an egg batter), and rice is a buy at $4.40. Kim chee and hot sauce come with all orders. While you're here, try the famed Korean ginseng tea. The restaurant closes each night at 9pm and all day Sunday. While you're in Moiliili, by the way, note that there are a number of similarly small, family-style Asian restaurants, with low prices and, we suspect, good food.

Ted's Drive-Inn, 2820 S. King St. (tel. 946-0364), is a small Korean lunch-counter operation that features, in their words, "Seoul food." Although the spelling differs here and there, the dishes are quite similar to those at the House of Park. You could have bul gogi (barbecued beef) at $3.75, or kal bi with mon doo (dumplings) at $4.75. Non-Korean offerings include beef-curry plates and a teri-beef burger. A *Honolulu Advertiser* survey rated Ted's as serving "among the top 10 best plate lunches in Honolulu."

You can be your own Korean chef at the **Cho Mark Restaurant,** 1679 Kapiolani Blvd. opposite the Kapiolani Theatre (tel. 944-4803), close to Waikiki. Gas cookers at the tables enable you to grill your own meat to your taste; then you wrap the meat and vegetables in large lettuce leaves, as they do in Thailand, and dip into an assortment of delicious sauces. A complete cook-it-yourself lunch or dinner is $10. You can also order already-cooked meals for about $11; courageous types may want to try beef intestines or octopus. Cho Mark is a small, intimate, mom-and-pop-type operation. No reservations.

Small, sparkly clean, and friendly pretty much sums up **O-Bok** in Manoa Marketplace, 2851 East Manoa Rd. (tel. 988-7702), a little Korean place that serves wonderful food at very moderate prices. All entrees here are served with na mul (vegetables), kim chee (best described as a fiery coleslaw), and rice. The most popular Korean specialty in Hawaii seems to be kal bi, tender barbecued short ribs. They are particularly good here, and priced at $6.75. Other very good dishes, priced from $4 to $6.45, are the barbecued chicken, the fish or meat jun (breaded with an egg batter), and the bi bim bap (mixed vegetables, beef, and fried egg on rice). Very tasty too are the mon doo (a kind of Korean wonton); try them in soup or fried, as a side dish. To explore several of these taste sensations, order one of the mixed plates: The special plate at $4.70 includes kal bi, barbecued chicken, mon doo, tae-ku (dried codfish), and na mul. The lunch plate (which you may also order at dinnertime), consists of barbecued beef, chicken, na mul, kim chee, and rice. Westerners tend to think of Korean food as being extremely spicy; in reality, it is only the kim chee that makes your eyes water. Open every day, except Monday, from 10am to 8pm.

MEXICAN

Does **El Burrito,** 550 Piikoi, near the corner of Kapiolani Blvd. (tel. 533-3457), offer the best value for Mexican food in town? Some of our readers say this is so. We can certainly say that their special plates give you more food for the money than you will find in many other Mexican establishments. Pollo con mole, for example, is plenty of chicken in a mole sauce, served with rice, beans, and two tortillas, only $6.50. Steak à la Mexicana and chili with beef, chicken, or pork boast the same accompaniments, big portions and $6.50 price. The same menu is on all day, which means you can have their namesake burrito ($2.75 to $4), deep-fried chimichangas, tostadas, and the like, anytime between 11am to 8pm Monday through Thursday, until 9pm Friday and Saturday. Closed Sunday. El Burrito won't charm you from the outside, but once seated you can easily imagine yourself in a cozy Mexican hideaway.

Authentic Mexican dishes cooked in the Aztec tradition would be baked in underground ovens. Since that's not quite feasible in a city like Honolulu, Mary and Louis Quintero do the next best thing at **Quintero Cuisine,** 2334 S. King St., adjacent to the Old Stadium Square shopping area (tel. 944-3882). A tasty example is carne al Arriero, steak cooked with garlic, onions, and peppers, $8.90. Pollo à la Mexicana, chicken fried with ranchero sauce, $7.25, is also good. We like the nachos among the appetizers and soups like the Fideo, a tomato-based broth with sautéed noodles and Mexican spices, $2.50. Lunch dishes run from $3.95 to $5.90, dinners from $7.75 to $9.25. This is a small and plain little restaurant, but the service is personal and homey. The same menu is available from 11am to 10pm Monday through Saturday, and from 4 to 10pm on Sunday.

RUSSIAN

A Russian snackbar in downtown Honolulu is a cultural anachronism, but we don't mind a bit. **Rada's Piroshki,** 1144–1146 Fort Street Mall, specializes in the piroshki—a delicate, flaky bun stuffed with beef, cheese, cabbage, mushrooms, whatever combination suits your fancy. Whenever we're downtown, we simply can't resist the chicken, mushrooms, and cheese piroshki, but the other combinations are also delicious. One big piroshki is $1.30. The chicken soup is also marvelous, and the Russian fried squid, $1 a bag, are . . . uh, different. Rada's is a family operation, and the people in charge make you feel welcome. But alas, they close at 6:30pm weekdays, 5:30pm Saturday, and are open only from 10am to 3pm Sunday. Warning: Piroshkis may be habit-forming.

VIETNAMESE

Vietnamese food is rare in Honolulu, with just a few restaurants offering this subtle cuisine, which combines a number of Asian and sometimes European influences. Local friends swear by Mark Fu, well known for his catering work and as chef of **Hale Vietnam,** 1140 12th Ave. in Kaimuki (tel. 735-7581). Chef Fu specializes in the cuisine of the Mekong Delta region and serves it in a casual setting of Southeast Asian art and tropical plants. Lunches run from $4 to $6.95 and include an appetizer of imperial rolls, crisp Southeast Asian delights wrapped in rice paper and filled with seafood, pork, and fresh herbs. You may choose to have them nonfried and they're just as good that way. The prices also include a hearty Vietnamese beef-noodle soup. Prices for the same items are a little higher at dinner. We like their Vietnamese vegetable dish at $7.95. A beef or spiced chicken dish is grilled at your table. Plan on spending between $10 to $12 for dinner, including entree and beverage. Unless you're an old hand at Asian food, ask that your dishes be done "mild" or "medium."

Hale Vietnam is open every day, serving lunch from 11am to 2:30pm, dinner from 5 to 9:30pm weekdays. On Saturday, Sunday, and holidays, it is open from 11am to 10pm.

Very popular in the Chinese Cultural Center, **Vietnam City Seafood,** 100 N. Beretania (tel. 599-5022), is a huge place that features a cocktail lounge and entertainment as well as authentic Vietnamese lunches and dinners. Prices are modest at both meals. At lunch, especially good buys are the long-rice dishes, which range from $3.75 (for shrimp and crabmeat) to $7 (for fresh prawns with shredded pork). You could have a duck curry with French bread at $4.95, but better call your shots—mild, medium, or hot on the curries. Be sure to have an appetizer at dinner: their sizzling barbecue taste tempters—beef satays and shrimp kebabs—are irresistible, even at $5 and $6. Vietnamese soups range from $4.75 to $5.50; fish and rice plates are $6.75. There are a number of dishes dating back to the French influence in Vietnam, but without those French names: beef fillet with beef cubes or breaded pork chops, both $5. And French coffees, too, plus lemon drinks and a variety of Vietnamese beverages.

Vietnam City Seafood serves lunch from 11am to 3pm, dinner from 5 to 9pm; cocktails and entertainment from 9pm to 2am.

In the downtown area, **Tay Do's Restaurant,** 1138 Fort Street Mall, corner Pauahi St. (tel. 531-8446), is the place of authentic Vietnamese cuisine. Most Vietnamese restaurants are small and bare bones, but this one is of moderate size, with ceiling spotlights and beige benches and tables. You can start with those lovely rice paper rolls—spring rolls, pork rolls, or shrimp rolls—then move on to the Vietnamese plate meals which offer 10 choices between $4.25 and $5.25. They are served not on plates but on platters, and they are huge. Our barbecued boneless chicken, on a bed of rice with lettuce, cucumber, and tomato slices, was very good. Of course, there are noodle dishes, soups, and steak choices. Almost everything is $4.25, with a few items at $5.25 and $6.95. Tay Do's Restaurant is open from 8:30am to 7pm Monday to Saturday, serving the same menu throughout the day. Closed Sunday.

Even closer to Waikiki, the **Diem Vietnamese Restaurant,** also known as the **Diem Coffee Shop & Restaurant,** 2633 S. King St., just a block Diamond Head of University Avenue (tel. 941-8657), is another good bet. This is a small, family-run eatery that is kept sparkling clean; its checkerboard floor is the dominant decorative theme. Spring rolls, roast shredded pork rolls, and other rice paper rolls make good appetizers, from $2.50 to $5.95. Special plates featuring chicken, catfish, or pork are $5 to $7; a few fancier Vietnamese dishes, like beef kebab and beef cooked in vinegar, are $6.50 and $7.95. If you prefer sandwiches, they'll put together a Vietnamese-style sandwich with a combination of several of the above items at only $3. Diem Vietnamese Restaurant is open weekdays from 9am to 9:30pm and on Saturday and Sunday from 10am to 9:30pm.

3. And Elsewhere on the Island

RESTAURANTS IN KAILUA

One of Honolulu's very finest restaurants is just a short drive across the Pali in pretty little Kailua town. It is **L'Auberge Swiss,** at 117 Hekili St. (tel. 263-4663). The owner, who is also the chef, is Alfred Mueller, formerly head chef for the Hilton Hawaiian Village. Only dinner is served at this charming place, Tuesday through Sunday from 6 to 10pm. The dining room very much resembles the little country inns one sees in Switzerland, Mueller's boyhood home. The food is superb and the service friendly; the dining room is presided over by Mrs. Mueller, who was born and raised in Hawaii. It's difficult to choose what to start with: there's country pâté, oysters Rockefeller, escargot bourguignonne, and the French-onion soup gratiné, which is sheer poetry! L'Auberge's specialties—which range from $13 to $16.50—are all magnificent: take your choice of the likes of chicken piccata albergo (boneless breast of chicken on pasta); weinerschnitzel; émincé de veau Zurichoise (tender pieces of veal in a rich cream sauce with mushrooms and Rösti potatoes; or scallops and shrimp sautéed in a delicate sauce, served with pasta. And then there's that great Swiss favorite, cheese fondue, with dinner salad, for at least two lucky people. Light Swiss dinners, such as bratwurst with Rösti potatoes, and the fresh pasta-of-the-day, are all about $8.50. Fondue is $9. Reservations are a must; kamaainas come from all corners of the island to dine here.

Cinnamon's, at 315 Uluniu St. (tel. 261-8724), is named in honor of a bear in a charming French children's story that was owner Bonnie Nam's favorite when she was a little girl. A big, plush replica of Cinnamon, sporting a crisp white baker's cap decorated with a red heart, waits to greet you just inside the front door. The restaurant is on the ground floor of an attractive neighborhood shopping plaza. It's so popular that on weekends they have to put extra tables out on the mall to accommodate everyone. The restaurant itself is small and cozy: four of the tables are under a pretty white gazebo. And the tab will be very reasonable. For lunch, we like the chicken-cashew salad, $5.95, and the grilled three-cheese deluxe sandwich, $3.95. Country quiches with salad, the garden vegetable platter, and burgers are all very popular, too. At dinnertime, pick one of the house specials and you'll have a delicious meal from $6.95 to $15.95, with such entrees as chicken fantasy, with broccoli hollandaise; kebabs of lamb, chicken, beef, pork, or fish; and broiled top sirloin. Most are accompanied by soup or salad; rice, fries, or baked beans; vegetables; and hot dinner rolls. On the à la carte dinner menu, the fiesta taco-grande salad and the chef's super salad (described as "a salad bar brought to your table") are fun, as are the roast pork with apple dressing, chicken cutlet with country gravy and vegetables, seafood crêpes Florentine, seafood platter, and fresh fish, all $6.50 to $13.95. Doors open at 7am for breakfast (freshly baked cinnamon rolls, coffee cake, croissants, muffins, cornbread, and pancakes) and do not close until 8:30pm Monday to Thursday, 9pm Friday and Saturday, 2pm Sunday.

Coffee fanatics have their own hangout in Kailua, a place called **Kailua and Cream,** 108 Hekili St. (tel. 262-9727). Sit down at one of the widely scattered tables—there's a feeling of living-room privacy here—and choose from among 20 to 30 types of coffee, a large selection of teas (herbal and regular), and a variety of pastries including a super banana cake: fresh, moist, and deliciously iced. Owner Ken takes pride in serving you coffee or tea just the way you like it, and prices are modest: pastries for 85¢ to $1.40, espresso for 95¢.

When we first saw Doug's, we exclaimed, "Gee, a deli!" That turned out to be its name. **Gee . . . A Deli!** is at 418-F Kuulei Rd., Kailua (tel. 261-4412), directly behind McDonald's. You'll know this is a New York–style deli right away: sandwiches can be served on onion roll or rye and are inches thick. (You could also have them on a sub roll.) There are all the usuals, including a very good beef bologna at $4.89, plus a dozen or more clubs and combos, bagels with cream and lox, too. Although this is an extremely popular place, service is fast and efficient. And there are five or six large tables, so you don't have to eat in the car. Hours are 10am to 6pm Monday to Saturday, 11am to 5pm Sunday.

There's another interesting place to eat in Kailua, should you happen to be out this way. That's the cafeteria of the **Castle Medical Center,** 640 Ulukahiki St., over the Pali at Waimanalo Junction. The hospital is run by Seventh Day Adventists, and everything served is vegetarian, delicious, and at old-fashioned prices. All the hot entrees—like stir-fry veggies with tofu or Creole patties—are $1.25; a salad-and-sandwich bar is available at 20¢ an ounce, so you can easily put together a very reasonable meal. Take the elevator or stairs down one flight as you enter the hospital and you'll see the cafeteria. It faces a rear garden and a beautiful view of the Pali. Meals are served to the public Sunday through Friday from 11am to 1:30pm and from 4:30 to 6:30pm. A la carte breakfast—waffles, eggs, fresh fruits, and beverage —is served between 6:30 and 9:30am weekdays.

AROUND THE ISLAND

The very cheapest way to eat on your round-the-island journeys is to bring your own picnic lunch, but there are also a few restaurants that make fine budget-wise refueling stops. The several shopping malls in Kaneohe offer a bonanza of inexpensive eateries. At the enclosed **Windward Mall,** for example, the standout restaurant is **Marie Callender's** (tel. 235-6655), a charming, airy spot, where $5.75 brings you a terrific pot-pie lunch. It's served in a ceramic casserole, has an all-vegetable crust, and is a meal in itself. Quiches, salads, and desserts are all fantastic here. If you head into the food court, similar to the one at Ala Moana Shopping Center, there are many more places to choose from. **Cinnabon,** for example, is a singular experience. Customers start lining up before opening time (10am) to buy these incredible cinnamon rolls, each measuring about 5 inches in diameter and about 3 inches high, topped with a mound of whipped cream. You can watch the team of bakers turn them out. People have been known to make a meal out of them, even if not exactly a balanced one. They're $1.79 each. Pizza fans have **Harpo's,** and brag of their fresh veggies on hand-rolled dough, and sausages, by a local maker. Two slices of their deep-dish–style pizzas, plus green salad and soda, will set you back $5.30 for pepperoni, $5.70 for vegetarian. If you've been to Ala Moana Center, you know that **Patti's Chinese Kitchen** is great. Now there's a Patti's here, too, and it's inexpensive and filling.

Still hungry? **The Taco Shop** features tacos at $1.49 and seafood enchiladas at $3.25; **Yummy Korea BBQ** offers barbecue chicken at $4.25, veggies and rice included. **Deli Express** creates a variety of sandwiches at $3.95, all with lettuce, tomatoes, alfalfa sprouts, and macaroni salad. **Little Tokyo** displays a score of items in plastic replicas to help you decide, like the fried mahimahi at $4.25. And don't forget the coffee shop on the second floor of **Liberty House,** where you can get vegetarian sandwiches at $3.55 and roast beef at $4.95, as well as hot plates like a health plate or honey-dipped chicken, both at $4.75. Windward Mall's opening and closing times vary with holidays, seasons, and days of the week.

A charming Thai restaurant might be just the place for a meal as you travel around the island. **Thao Phya Thai,** located in the Windward Shopping Center in Kaneohe (tel. 235-3555), offers authentic food, a garden atmosphere enlivened by Thai art, and a staff that radiates the Thai brand of warm aloha. We like to order their luscious vegetarian spring rolls as soon as we're seated, wrap them in lettuce, and dip them into a delicious sauce while we're making our menu decisions. Other appetizers include beef or chicken satays or fried tofu in a spicy peanut sauce or stuffed chicken wings, all from $4.75 to $5.75, and enough for two or three people. Curries excel because they are made with fresh coconut milk. Most main dishes run from $4.50 to $5, and nine beef entrees, including red curry beef with red chile and coconut milk, are all $5.45. *Warning:* If you're not ready for a three-alarm fire, order your dish "mild"; even that may still be hot for most Western tastes. There's a large selection of pork, poultry, seafood, and noodle dishes: try their "newspaper noodles." And don't miss the finale: tapioca in coconut milk or ice cream in syrup with palm seeds. Thao Phya Thai is open for lunch and dinner, serving the same menu at both, from 11am to 2pm and 5 to 9pm, every day except Sunday. *Aroy!*

For a meal in a splendid setting, turn mauka just past Kaneohe, and proceed about a mile toward the mountains and **The Chart House.** The Chart House chain had just taken over the old Haiku Gardens restaurant at the time of this writing, an old kamaiina favorite surrounded by two acres of gorgeous gardens and grounds that you will probably still be able to explore (see details in Chapter IX). Plans for lunch were not yet formulated, but dinners will be like those at other Chart Houses: delicious steak and seafood items priced from $13 to $20, with an all-you-can-eat salad bar and hot bread, in a stylish and sophisticated setting.

Further along, you'll find Swanzy Beach, a scenic picnic spot. If you haven't packed your own, stop in at **Kaaawa Country Kitchen,** across the street. It has some outdoor tables, plus lots of take-out items, like plate lunches of teriyaki beef or fried chicken, $3.95 to $4.75. It's next to the Kaaawa Post Office.

The **Texas Paniolo Café,** 53-146 Kamehameha Hwy., in Punaluu (tel. 237-8521), has a rustic, western appearance inside and out; it's a wooden-frame building with a front porch, and the interior walls resemble adobe. Country-western wails from the jukebox during the day; at night, there's live entertainment. You'll just love the stuffed rattlesnake on the walls! And if you're braver than we are, you can also have rattlesnake chili at $8.75, or a half-pound rattlesnake burger at $9.75, the menu notation states "in season or when available." If the rattlers are not available, however, there is plenty of other very tasty Tex-Mex food. Among the appetizers, we vote for the chili con queso—a crock of melted cheese, tomatoes, and green chiles with tostitos for dipping, $5.55. A half-pound bowl of beef chili with rice or beans and crackers is $5.50; a chiliburger or jalapeño burger with cheese is $6.25. Dessert offerings include such Texas treats as pecan pie. Open every day except Sunday from 11am to 11pm.

Kahuku is just about midpoint in your 'round-the-island journey, so a visit to the **Country Kitchen** (tel. 293-2414) in the tourist attraction called the Kahuku Sugar Mill might just be in order. As you wend your way past shop after gift shop, you come upon the giant machinery of the mill itself. Nestled to the left of it is a restaurant that contrasts sharply with the massive steam engine and pistons that once processed sugarcane: rich carpeting, antique lamps, wood paneling and wainscoting, polished-wood tables, and Victorian touches set the scene for dining at Country Kitchen, a local branch of Country Kitchens International of Minneapolis.

The menu is especially intriguing because all three meals can be eaten any time of the day, from 8am to 9pm, seven days a week. Breakfast choices average $4; lunches offer a selection of sandwiches from $4.50 to $6.50, like a Reuben smothered in french fries; and dinner includes hearty plate dinners from $6.25 to $10.25 (the latter for a 10-oz. steak). Favorite local dishes like Loco Moco, Hawaiian chopped steak, and Portuguese sausage are also available. Apple cherry or blueberry cobbler à la mode is the perfect dessert. A final word about their special "Old-Fashioned Calico Bean Soup." It's made with six kinds of beans and good enough to make the Country Kitchen famous.

Where can you get the best sandwich on the North Shore, maybe on all of Oahu? We'd cast our vote for **Kua 'Aina** (tel. 637-6067), a sparkling sandwichery across the street from the courthouse in Haleiwa. It's tiny, neat as a pin, with wooden tables, framed pictures of local scenes, a few tables on the porch. And the atmosphere is casual, with people coming in off the beach. We haven't stopped raving yet about the sandwiches we had on our last visit: mahimahi with melted cheese, Ortega pepper, lettuce, and tomato at $4.50, tuna and avocado ("the tastiest combo in the Pacific") at $3.85, and a great baconburger at $4.15. Sandwiches are hearty enough to be a whole meal, and are served on either a Kaiser roll, honey wheat-berry bread, or earth rye. Kua 'Aina is open daily from 11am to 9pm.

Haleiwa is, in fact, an ideal place to break for lunch, for this little town is surfers' headquarters, and when they come off those mighty waves, surfers have to eat. You can join them at several spots, in addition to Kua 'Aina. In the Haleiwa Shopping Plaza you can get tasty Mexican dishes at **Rosie's Cantina** (tel. 637-3538), an attractive, high-tech-looking spot, where à la carte dishes run about $2.25 to $5.95. Rosie's serves all three meals, features delicious tortas (hamburger or chicken with fries or beans on thick bread) and offers spectacular savings at its Wednesday night Taco Fiesta Buffets: from 5 to 7pm, it's all you can eat for $4.89 per person; the ante goes up to $5.69 per person between 7 and 9pm. On the other side of the shopping plaza, there's **Kiawe Q and Deli** (tel. 637-3502), a pleasant-looking spot with comfortable chairs, natural woods, plants, and Hawaiian music. If you like kiawe wood-smoked meats, you'll love their barbecued ribs, chicken, hot sandwiches, and burgers, modestly priced from $2.95 to $4.95. They also have smoked locally caught fish, homemade desserts, and freshly ground Hawaiian-roast coffee. Take-out available.

You can have a cozy lunch in an elegant setting at **Steamer's Restaurant & Bar** (tel. 637-5071), in the Haleiwa Shopping Plaza on Kam Hwy. It's a big, low-lit, wood-paneled place, with shiny brass accents and an enjoyable outdoor dining area. And the food lives up to the decor. The hearty seafood omelet is great at lunch, accompanied by rice or fries and blueberry or French crumb muffins (omelets run $5.45 to $6.45). A good variety of hot sandwiches, accompanied by salad and rice pilaf or fries, makes a satisfactory meal for $4.50 to $6.50. If you like tempura vegetables, Steamer's Tempura Delight Platter, $8.25, is one of the best. Dinners start at $10 and feature entrees like prime rib, scampi, and crab legs (all you can eat) for $14.95, and the fish of the day for $17.95. All entrees are accompanied by seafood chowder or house salad, Steamer's bread, rice pilaf, and fresh steamed vegetables. Steamer's is open from 11:30am to 9:30pm, seven days. The bar is busy until 2am.

Another wonderfully picturesque spot for lunch or dinner is **Jameson's by the Sea,** on the outskirts of Haleiwa at 62-450 Kam Hwy. (tel. 637-4336). Take in the harbor, the sunset, and great food and drink. Lunch is served downstairs in The Pub, and features hearty fish, seafood, and meat sandwiches ($5.95 to $8.50), some excellent shrimp, crab, and seafood Louie salads ($7.95 to $8.50), and a variety of interesting pupus. There are many well-priced daily lunch specials, including fresh fish. Dinner features seafood caught daily in local waters, from $14.95 to about $18.95. Open daily.

You can get a substantial, reasonably priced lunch in the big, garden-like dining rooms of **Helemano Plantation,** a five-acre complex in the midst of the pineapple fields on the outskirts of Wahiawa. Not only is Helemano Plantation an agricultural farm, growing fruits, vegetables, and flowers, it is also a vocational and educational center for many of Hawaii's retarded citizens. They work as trainees in the many areas of Helemano: in the farm, the restaurant, the gift shop, country store, or in the bakeshop. Its Country Inn restaurant is known for its excellent Chinese cuisine and reasonable prices. At least five hot entrees are available each day and these might include roast duck, teriyaki beef, Chinese spareribs, beef with broccoli, spicy eggplant, and many more. A mini-lunch plate will cost you $3.75, and a full all-you-can-eat buffet including salad bar is $7.50. You can also browse through the tempting display of freshly baked treats at the bakeshop, which includes island-style manapuas (steamed or baked buns stuffed with pork or chicken) as well as pineapple and coconut danish, and chocolate chip, peanut butter, and coconut drop cookies. Stop by for the free hula show and take time to browse through their "Best of the Best" collection of handcrafted gifts and souvenirs made by the handicapped and disadvantaged from all over the world.

To give yourself a very special treat at the end of your around-the-island journey, stop in for dinner at **Kemoo Farm,** 1718 Wilikina Dr. (tel. 621-8481), overlooking Lake Wilson in Wahiawa, holding forth in these parts for 72 years and still going strong. And no wonder: This is a place where the spirit of old Hawaii still lingers, with excellent food and drink, gracious service by caring waitresses, a gentle mood. The price of your entree includes a complete dinner, and that means a delicious homemade soup (the seafood chowder we sampled recently was thick with potatoes and chunks of shrimp, crab, and mahimahi), salad bar, fresh vegetables, potatoes, or rice. Prices are reasonable: fried chicken, teriyaki chicken thighs, sweet-and-sour pork, and sautéed filet of mahimahi are all on the low end of the menu, from $9 to $15. Add another $1.50 to the price of your meal and have Kemoo's pine-mint tea; they make it right here by marinating the pineapple in a simple syrup with fresh mint —quite wonderful.

Lunchtime offers some unusual salads (like Japanese somen), in addition to regular entrees and sandwiches, from about $6.50 to $10.50. Lunch is served daily from 11am to 2pm, dinner from 5 to 8:30pm, with the exception of Monday and Saturday. There's a $6.95 buffet lunch on Thursday. Sunday brunch is on from 11am to 3pm. Alas, Charles K. L. Davis, who used to preside over lunchtime shows on Wednesday and Sundays, is now singing his "naughty but nice" songs in other climes.

A WORD ABOUT SHAVE ICE

A unique treat that's loved by just about everyone in the islands is a phenomenon called shave ice. That's not "shaved" ice. When it's pointed out to them, mainland visitors often sneer. "Oh, we have that at home—we call them snow cones" (or ices, or slushes). It isn't any of those things, it's just wonderful Hawaiian shave ice. Half the fun of having it is watching the ice being shaved. You can have a "plain" shave ice—that's just the incredibly fine ice particles bathed in syrup—and there are all kinds of syrups. Strawberry is the most popular, but there's also vanilla, guava, lemon, cherry, orange, root beer, coconut, and combinations of the above, known as "rainbow." Or you can have ice cream on the bottom, or azuki beans (a sweet Japanese bean used in desserts); or throw caution to the winds and have ice cream *and* beans on the bottom. Shave ice is served in a cone-shaped paper cup, with both a straw and a spoon.

Shave-ice places abound, but after years of diligent sampling and research, we offer our favorites: **Matsumoto's Grocery,** at 66-087 Kam Hwy. in Haleiwa, across from the intersection of Emerson Street, is a family operation. On weekends the lines can be long, because the local people drive out from all over the island; it's a pleasant wait, everyone is friendly. Should the length of the line at Matsumoto's be too horrendous, walk a few doors toward the center of Haleiwa town on the same side of the highway to **Aoki's Shave Ice.** At both, prices vary slightly, from about 75¢ for a small plain shave ice to $1.25 for the large size with ice cream and beans. There's usually a 5¢ extra charge if you want rainbow—that's three or more flavors in a fetching striped motif.

The **Island Snow** shave-ice shops that you'll find scattered around the island, though not quaint, rural mom 'n' pop stores, dispense some very respectable shave ice in the usual flavors, plus some unusual ones—like pistachio—for $1.25 and up. They also have a variety of T-shirts, sweatshirts, visors, and other memorabilia.

Caution: Shave ice is definitely habit-forming.

4. The Night Scene

Contrary to what you'd expect, the night scene in Honolulu is not all hula girls in grass skirts and sentimental songs on the ukulele. Sure, there are palm trees and schmaltz aplenty, but there are also ultrasophisticated jazz groups, authentic Polynesian music and dances, songsters, psychics, comedians, discos, sing-alongs at the piano, and no dearth of gorgeous seaside gardens where you could easily while away a few years. We'll tell you about the free shows first, then take you on a tour of the "in" bars and cocktail lounges, and on to a rundown of what we consider the most exciting entertainment in town.

But you really don't need any planned entertainment to enjoy Waikiki at night. There's a great show going on wherever you look: You can observe the people, browse in the shops, catch the sounds of music almost anywhere you go. It's fun to watch the newcomers parade up and down Kalakaua Avenue, survey the scene at the big hotels, or take our favorite walk, the "scrounger's stroll."

THE SCROUNGER'S STROLL

Since the possibilities for standing at a small distance and watching shows other people are paying for (while they're enjoying drinks or food) are fairly extensive, you could start this little excursion almost anywhere in Waikiki. But we like to start at the **Poolside Polynesian Show** of the Sheraton Princess Kaiulani, where there's a delightful show on the outdoor stage every evening from 5:45 to 9:45. Join the crowd-watching for a while, then cross the street at the Diamond Head end of the Sheraton Moana Surfrider Hotel, where there's a paved path leading to the ocean. Follow it to the back of the hotel and onto the beach; here you can gaze at the floodlit shore and listen to the music drifting from the romantic Banyan Court, just behind you. You can even have a nighttime swim if you want to; no one will stop you (all the beaches are public property up to the high-water mark), or just meander barefoot along the sands Ewa until you come to the beach of the Royal Hawaiian Hotel. If you've timed your scrounger's stroll correctly, you'll arrive in time to watch from afar the show at the Royal's fancy Monarch Room; it's not exactly a ringside table, but it's fun.

Wander down the beach to the Outrigger Waikiki Hotel, where **The Luau** takes place Tuesday, Friday, and Sunday at 7pm. There'll be lots of people watching the show from the sand. Emcee Doug Mossman (formerly of *Hawaii Five-0*) usually acknowledges the scroungers; he calls them the "graduating class." Join the fun and see the $24.50 entertainment gratis.

BARFLY'S TOUR

If you'd like to watch the sunset in luxury, arrive early (about 6pm) at the cocktail lounge of **Reef's Pool Terrace Bar** for a front-row seat. Head mauka on Kalakaua Avenue and cross Koa Avenue to King's Village for a drink at an English pub, the **Rose and Crown.** Brews from the mother country, of course, plus an assortment of beers and cocktails, sing-along piano, darts, all sorts of special nights. Plus all-day happy hours. The **Lobby Bar** of the Hawaiian Regent Hotel is pleasant, and so is **The Library,** a contemporary wine bar and lounge overlooking the beach, where it's fun to meet people and discuss wines or relax over a drink. A big favorite with the Honolulu theater crowd is **South Seas Village** at 2112 Kalakaua Ave.; they come to hear John Saclausa at the piano bar, every evening except Sunday from 9pm until closing. John plays, people get up and sing, and everybody has a good time. Wine coolers are $2.50 in the evenings, $2 in the daytime.

Viewpoints

Waikiki is full of gorgeous rooms with a view, but for the most sensational of all, take the glass elevator (on the outside of the hotel; it's eerily exciting going up) to **Annabelle's** at the top of the Ilikai. This 30-story high, glass-walled aerie is to Honolulu what the Top of the Mark is to San Francisco: The place to see the million lights of the dazzling metropolis spread out before you. Before 9pm, standard drinks are $2; after 9pm they're $4. Dancing starts at 5pm with Big Band sounds and favorite oldies; from 9pm until closing at 4am, the sound is disco. Alas, there's a $4 cover (no cover for ladies on Wednesday). But even if you're not a drinker or a dancer, don't miss the ride up in the glass elevator, from which the view is also spectacular, and at least peek at the room. (Incidental note for parents looking for ways to amuse their kiddies: They love a ride in the glass elevator.) More about discos ahead.

Another thrilling view is to be had from **Windows of Hawaii Revolving Restaurant** atop the Ala Moana Office Building, a merry-go-round for sybarites. Twenty-three stories up, and affording an almost identical view to that of Annabelle's, the room revolves slowly, affording spectacular views of mountain, sea, and city. Cocktails are served all day. New England-style cuisine, with fish fresh from the fishing boats, is featured.

At the center of Waikiki is another glamorous revolving restaurant, the **Top of Waikiki**, in the Waikiki Business Plaza Building at 2270 Kalakaua Ave. The top tier of this gigantic wedding cake of a restaurant is the cocktail lounge, very glamorous by candlelight and starlight. Views of all of Waikiki are yours for the price of a drink: beer from $2.75, exotics from $4.50.

At the Sea

For one of the most majestic views in town, try the glorious **Hanohano Room** of the Sheraton-Waikiki; the panorama stretches all the way from Diamond Head to Pearl Harbor. Drinks are pricey: beers will cost you $3.75, imported beers are $4.50, and mai tais cost $5.75. There's entertainment and piano music nightly, from 9:30 on. No cover, no minimum.

If ever you've dreamed of picture-perfect Hawaii, treat yourself to sunset cocktails at **The House Without a Key,** the oceanside lounge at the recently rebuilt Halekulani Hotel. Here, under a century-old kiawe tree, you can watch the waves splash up on the breakfront, the sun sink into the ocean, and hear the music of a top island group, The Islanders (Sunday, Monday, Tuesday, Thursday, 5 to 8:30pm) and the Hiram Olsen Trio (Wednesday, Friday, Saturday, 5:30 to 8:30pm). Kanoe Miller, a former Miss Hawaii, does some beautiful dancing. Draft beers at $3.50, exotic drinks higher. A sunset cocktail pupu and light dinner menu is served from 5 to 9pm daily. Don't miss this one.

The Sheraton Moana Surfrider, one of the classic oceanfront hotels in Waikiki, is another neat place for a drink near the water's edge. Its **Beach Bar** offers mixed drinks from $4.75, beer from $3.50 domestics, $4.50 imports.

At some of the Waikiki hotels, the cocktail gardens overlook the lagoon—and one of our favorites is the **Tahitian Lanai** in the Waikikian Hotel (a superb example of modern Polynesian architecture; as you walk through to the garden, note the hotel's cavelike lobby with the roof of an ancient spirit house). A lively local crowd hangs out at the **Papeete Bar,** known for its sing-alongs, from 5pm to 1am. During the afternoon happy hour, it's $1.75 for standards and beer, and they have free pupus, too.

Another romantic spot we favor greatly is the **Hala Terrace** of the Kahala Hilton, a short drive from Waikiki. You can sip your drinks on the beachside patio and watch the surf roll in. At 8:30pm a cover descends for the Danny Kaleikini dinner show (more about that later).

Pupus and Happy Hours

Now we come to the more practical side of pub-crawling: how to drink at half the price and get enough free food for almost a meal at the same time. The trick here is to hit the bars during their happy hours (usually from 4 to 6pm but sometimes greatly extended), when they serve free pupus or lower their prices, or both. Note that these hours and prices are apt to change often, but these places always offer a good deal of one sort or another.

All-out winner in this department has to be **Studebaker's** (tel. 531-8444) in Restaurant Row at 500 Ala Moana, a lively, deafeningly noisy 1950s time-warp (complete with a bright red Studebaker, lots of neon, and a DJ spinning platters), which serves a *free* buffet along with your drinks weekdays from 4 to 8pm and Sunday from 6 to 9pm. There are always four hot entrees—they could be pepper steak, teriyaki chicken, or shrimp fettuccine, to name a few—plus seven salads, brown breads, and raw veggies with dip. Beer is $2.75 and $3.75, well drinks are $3 all day. "Happy Hour" simply refers to the patrons' delight in the free buffet. (*Note:* No one under the age of 23 is allowed in after 4pm and IDs are checked.) Dress code.

There's a generously long happy hour (11am to 8pm) at the **Crow's Nest**, located above the Jolly Roger at 2244 Kalakaua Ave. Several readers have written to praise this place for being "the friendliest and cheapest bar in Waikiki." Mai tais are just $2. No cover, no minimum, entertainment nightly from 8pm, and plenty of free peanuts (their shells cover the floor). . . . **Rose and Crown,** that jolly old English pub at King's Village, offers mai tais at $3, beer and standards from $1.50, and its 11am to 7pm happy hour. . . . All the way from 6am to 9pm, the **Waikiki Broiler** in the Waikiki Tower Hotel, 200 Lewers, brings out the mai tais and chi chis at low prices, $1.75 and $2.25. There's entertainment from 5 to 9pm. . . . Nothing skimpy about the happy hour at **Monterey Bay Canners Lounge** in the Outrigger Hotel. It runs from 7am to 7pm, and during all that time, mai tais are $1.50, daiquiris $3.25. As if that weren't enough, there's a double happy hour between 4 and 7pm, when all well drinks are $2.50. Oysters and clams on the half-shell are 85¢ each. And—you won't believe this—there's still a third happy hour, from 10:30pm to closing. That's when well drinks are $1.75, Irish coffee and chi chis are just $1.75. . . . Ever-popular mai tais are just $1.75 during the long (6am to 6pm) happy hour at the **Rigger** in the Outrigger Hotel, and from 6 to 10pm Bloody Marys are $1.85. There's a big-screen TV for sports events, entertainment nightly beginning at 9pm with no cover charge, and popcorn served free all day.

Marco Polo, on the fourth floor of the Waikiki Shopping Plaza, has happy hours, from 5 to 7pm. Different drinks are featured each day at low prices. . . . During the 3 to 6pm "Specials" time at the Mahina Lounge, at the Ramada Renaissance Ala Moana Hotel, regular drinks are $4, exotics are $5.

DISCO AND ROCK

The disco/rock scene is bigger, better, and noisier than ever in Honolulu. A recent look around revealed something like a dozen clubs packing them in, and more on the way (there is also a fairly high rate of turnover). Besides offering plenty of exercise, the local clubs are mostly inexpensive; usually, they have a modest cover charge or none at all, and just a few insist on a two-drink minimum and/or a fee. Live bands usually alternate with disco, and the action gets under way between 9 and 10pm in most clubs and only ends when everyone drops from exhaustion— anywhere between 2 and 4am.

One of the most popular disco spots and perhaps the biggest singles scene in town is **The Point After,** at the Hawaiian Regent Hotel (tel. 922-6611), with European decor, twin dance floors, and hi-tech video dancing that features popular rock tunes as well as "oldies but goodies." Cover is $5 for out-of-staters, $3 for Hawaii residents. . . . **Masquerade,** at the corner of Kalakaua and McCully (tel. 949-6337), boasts "the heaviest sound system in Hawaii." Cover is $3 under 21, $5 over. . . . **Wave Waikiki,** 1877 Kalakaua Ave. (tel. 941-0424), is Hawaii's biggest, brassiest live rock 'n' roll nightclub. It features a live band and light show every night, cocktails and dancing from 9pm to 4am. Cover is $5; you must be 21 or over. . . . In addition to its fancy name, **The Pink Cadillac,** 478 Ena Rd. (tel. 942-5282) has progressive and new wave dancing from 9pm to 2am nightly. The cover is only $5 if you're over 21; otherwise, a hefty $12 for those under 21. If all that dancing makes you hungry, try the **Surf Café,** located underneath the club, for hefty homemade burgers and things.

Photos of famous racers, car ads, drag race posters, auto seat booths, and a drive-in movie set make up the decor at **Hot Rod Dinin' & Dancin' at Discovery Bay,** 1778 Ala Moana Blvd., opposite the Ilikai Hotel (tel. 995-1956). Disco is on from 9pm to 2am, with DJs playing the classics of the '50s and '60s in the early evening, bringing it up to current hits by midnight. The dress code is the same as for dining anywhere: You must have something on. Cover is $5, but have a meal there anytime (low to moderate prices)—it's open 24 hours, seven days for dining—and get a free pass.

The Japanese have entered the disco scene in a big way with the recent opening of the $5 million **Maharaja Restaurant and Disco** at the Waikiki Trade Center, 2255 Kuhio Ave. (tel. 922-3030), reputed to have the best sound and light system in the islands. The theme is East Indian, the mood is opulent (mirrored ceilings, Italian marble), and the crowd is an international mix, which perhaps accounts for the stiff dress code—like, no jeans, T-shirts, or sneakers. (No formal wear, either, it should be added.) They play all types of music, including Top 40s. This is the first Maharaja Club outside of Japan, which has 100 such. Cover charge Sunday through Thursday is $5, Friday and Saturday $8. A restaurant serves a wide range of both Japanese and Western dishes at moderate prices. Open from 6pm to 2am daily.

The staff of colorfully costumed characters at **Bobby McGee's Conglomeration** in the Colony East Hotel (tel. 922-1282) really attracts the guests. It's a lively spot also known for good food. There's a live DJ, a great sound system, and dancing until 2am. . . . **Spats,** in the Hyatt Regency Hotel, is a handsome and immensely popular room where you're likely to run into (or bump into) a big crowd on weekends. . . . For dancing right at the beach, nothing can beat the **Shore Bird Beach Disco,** Waikiki's largest beachfront disco, with a laser light show, a 10-foot video screen, two DJs, and dancing nightly on two dance floors, from 9pm to 2am. . . . **Scruples,** in the Waikiki Marketplace at 2310 Kuhio Ave. (tel. 923-9530), is one of the town's hottest nightspots, with DJs spinning Top 40s hits every night from 8pm to 4am. . . . **The Black Orchid** in Restaurant Row is perhaps Honolulu's most sophisticated supper club. There's dancing from 10pm to 3:30am Tuesday through Saturday to groups like No Excuses, an up-tempo rock band; from 5:30 to 9pm, jazz singer Azure McCall is usually on hand.

There's a fancy feeling and dress code to match at **Rumours,** at the Ramada Renaissance Ala Moana Hotel (tel. 955-4811), completely redone now and with first-of-its-kind-in-Hawaii audio, video, and lighting. It features musical videos, a light show complete with special effects and four of the islands' best DJs. During the Thursday and Friday happy hours, they play music from the early '60s through the late '70s, which they call "The Big Chill." There's a cover charge nightly from 8pm.

The best dancing spot outside of Waikiki has to be the previously mentioned **Studebaker's** in Restaurant Row (tel. 526-9888), where not only can you "bop till you drop" but you are given sustenance while doing so. Pay your $1 cover charge, buy a few inexpensive drinks and enjoy the free buffet from 4 to 8pm. No one under 23 is allowed in after 4pm.

JUST DANCING

Remember the Big Band days of the '30s and '40s, when people actually did the fox-trot, the tango, and the waltz? Well, they still do, thanks to the Royal Hawaiian Hotel Monarch Room's Sunday afternoon Tea Dances. From 4:30 to 8pm, Del Courtney and the Royal Hawaiian Hotel Orchestra provide the sounds. You don't even need to order a drink; tea and coffee, as well as harder stuff, are available. Cover charge is $6 (tel. 923-7311).

JUST FOR LAUGHS

Comedy clubs are big everywhere these days, and Honolulu is no exception. The **Honolulu Comedy Club** at Top of the I in the Ilikai Hotel (tel. 922-5998 for reservations) features both local and mainland comedians in 90-minute performances held Tuesday, Wednesday, and Thursday at 9pm, Friday at 8 and 10pm, Saturday at 7, 9, and 11pm. Cost is $12 per person.

A CHOICE LUAU

Luaus are fun affairs—everyone arrives dressed in aloha shirts and muumuus, a great ceremony is made of taking the pig out of the imu (camera buffs have been known to go wild with joy at this part), there's lively Polynesian entertainment, and the mai tais flow freely.

Honolulu offers a number of luaus, but the one that's most consistently praised is the **Paradise Cove Luau,** which is actually more than a luau; it's a Hawaiian theme park as well, combining fun, education, and entertainment in an experience the whole family will enjoy. The festivities are held 27 miles from Waikiki, on a 12-acre beachfront site in the town of Ewa: nearby, Oahu's newest resort development is rising. Guests can wander through the village of thatched huts, learn ancient Hawaiian games and crafts, enjoy the spectacular sunset over the ocean, help pull in the fish in the nets during the hukilau, and watch a program of ancient and modern hula at the imu ceremony. Then it's a fabulous buffet meal and a spectacular Polynesian show: The fire dancer alone is worth the price of admission. Cost of the luau is $37.50 for adults, $31.50 for teenagers, and $20 for children 6 to 12; round-trip bus fare from Waikiki is $6. The luau is on every night of the week: phone 973-LUAU for reservations.

Note: At the time of this writing, Paradise Cove was undergoing a $5- to $10-million expansion program; when it's completed, it will include a market of Hawaiian handcrafts, a plantation village, a nursery, an arcade of shops replicating old downtown Honolulu, and a restaurant, waterfall, and pool, with bridge and walkways meandering throughout. It should all be in order by the end of 1991.

ACCENT ON ENTERTAINMENT

Let us be perfectly honest. To see the top nightclub shows in Hawaii, you're going to break your budget—and then some. When a big name is entertaining, the local clubs usually impose a cover charge plus a minimum of two drinks, which can swiftly add up to more than you'd think. On top of that, many of them prefer to accommodate their dinner guests only—and dinner at these places is usually in the $50-and-up bracket. However, for those times when you're willing to go all out, here's the information on the top names and places. Check the local tourist papers when you're in town for exact details; a top star might just happen to be on the mainland when you're in the islands, but somebody new and unknown might be making a smashing debut. Prices quoted here are subject to change.

We'd give up almost anything to catch a show by **The Brothers Cazimero,** featured entertainers at the Monarch Room of the Royal Hawaiian Hotel. They are beloved champions of authentic Hawaiian music and dance, and many of their songs, and the dances of their company, featuring the incredible Leina'ala, are truly from the heart of Hawaii. No need to spend $52.50 for the dinner show unless you want to, when the cocktail show is only $20.50. It's presented Tuesday through Saturday at 8:30pm and again on Friday and Saturday at 10:30pm. Local people say this late show is the best one of all, a time when Robert and Roland "let their hair down" for a mostly local crowd (we caught the late show on our last visit, and it was only $15.). If The Brothers aren't in town, don't fret: The Monarch Room will have another top artist, perhaps songstress Emma Veary. Reservations: 923-7311.

Note: If you're in town on May 1, which is "Lei Day" in Hawaii, don't miss **The Brothers Cazimero**'s annual concert at the Waikiki Shell. It's a fabulous production, and all of Honolulu comes dressed in their aloha finery. General admission is usually $12, reserved seats are around $15. Arrive early and bring a picnic supper.

Don Ho, who is probably Hawaii's best-known entertainer, seems to be permanently ensconced at the Hilton Hawaiian Village Dome Showroom. Don heads up an exciting Polynesian extravaganza, for which you'll have to pay $41.50 for adults, $28.50 for children, if you want dinner. It's still expensive—but more sensible—to come for the cocktail show, which will set you back only $24 for adults, $16 for children, and includes a tropical drink, tips, and taxes. Reservations: 949-4321, ext. 70105.

Again, try the cocktail show—it's yours for the price of two drinks plus an $8 cover—rather than spending $57 for the dinner show to see **Danny Kaleikini** at the Hala Terrace of the Kahala Hilton Hotel. Seating is at 8:45pm nightly except Sunday. Danny is undoubtedly one of the islands' top entertainers, a brilliant musician who dances, sings, plays a variety of instruments (including the nose flute), and watches over a talented company of Hawaiian entertainers. The show is deliberately low key and in excellent taste. Reservations: 734-2211.

Al Harrington, the "South Pacific Man," can always be counted on for an excellent show; he's an island favorite. You can catch him at the Polynesian Palace of the Reef Towers at $26 for adults, $16.45 for children at the cocktail shows, Sunday through Friday at 5:45 and 8:45pm. Should you want to dine, there's a sit-down dinner at 5pm, and a hot entree buffet at 8:30pm, each at $39 for adults, $20.80 for kids under 12. Reservations: 923-9861.

For more than 20 years, the show put on by the seven talented entertainers who call themselves the **Society of Seven** has been an island favorite. These young men, who can sing, act, play a variety of musical instruments, and even reprise Broadway musicals (we caught them recently in their mini-version of *Phantom of the Opera*), know how to keep an audience cheering. Music, imitations, comedy routines, rock music, oldies, and island favorites are all part of the act. It's held at the Outrigger Waikiki Main Showroom at 8:30 and 10:30pm nightly except Sunday (on Wednesdays, 8:30pm show only). Dinner will cost you $47 for adults, $27 for those under 12. Or, come for the cocktail show, which, at $25 for adults, $13.50 for children, includes tax, tip, and either two standard drinks or a cocktail. Students 13 to 20 years old may attend the cocktail show for $17. Reservations: 922-6408 or 923-0711.

The **New Generation** was known until recently as "The Bad Boys Club." This five some may be touring with "New Kids on the Block" when you visit, but if you can, catch their pop-rock act and you'll understand why they're Hawaii's newest big music story.

Another name to look for is Glen Maderos. He's a local boy who not only made good but *is* very good. Born on Kauai 20 years ago, he hit the top 10 with his first record "Nothing's Gonna Change My Love for You" in 1987. Glen has appeared on the *Tonight Show* and *Good Morning America.* You'll be lucky to catch him; hope he's not touring Europe when you arrive here.

There are several good Polynesian shows on the beach, but if you're just going to see one, make it **Sheraton's Spectacular Polynesian Revue** at the stunning Ainahu Showroom of the Princess Kaiulani Hotel. Although the tab is $44.50 for adults, $16 for children, the value is excellent: a 1½-hour long authentic Polynesian revue that pulls out all the stops (Fiji war chants, Samoan fire-knife dancers, Tahitian *aparimas,* and much more), an excellent prime rib buffet, and one drink. Or just have cocktails and see the show at $20.50 for adults, $14.25 for children. Reservations: 922-5811.

An engaging blend of live performance and "electronic wizardy," **Voyage—The Story of Hawaii,** relates the Hawaiian experience through music, dance, and story. Featured are the ancient Hawaiian hula, the pulsating Tahitian "tamure," the Chinese ribbon dance, and Japanese, Korean, and Filipino vignettes. The show, which is held in the Plaza Showroom of the Waikiki Shopping Plaza, 2250 Kalakaua Ave., has been praised for its award-winning cinematography and quadraphonic sound system. Show times are 6:45 and 8:30pm nightly. Tickets, $11 or $17, which include two drinks, can be purchased at the door (tel. 922-6600).

Although a lot of his material is local, **Frank De Lima,** who plays at the Peacock Room of the Queen Kapiolani Hotel, seems to be adored by both islanders and tourists alike (we're among the latter). Frank is a musical comedian rather than a standup comic, and he uses the guys in his back-up group (who are also very funny) in his zany song parodies and skits. Frank is not smutty, just crazy, so you can feel perfectly comfortable bringing older children. His show is on Wednesday through Sunday at 9:30pm, with a second show Fridays and Saturdays at 11:30pm. There is a two-drink minimum (beer and wine at $3, mixed drinks for $5.50), plus a $5 cover.

Note: Frank is highly visible these days—on TV, at benefit performances, at shopping-center promotions—so it's quite possible you can get to see him for free. Watch for him. He's great!

The Royal Hawaiian Hotel's Mai Tai Bar is oceanside, right out there on the sands of Waikiki. What a glorious spot, as the sun goes down, to hear Hawaiian music. **Keith and Carmen Haugen,** a highly admired duo, make their music from 5:30 to 8:30pm, Tuesday through Saturday evenings, and there is neither cover nor minimum. A great place to start your evening.

The lovely garden of the Sheraton Princess Kaiulani Hotel is the scene of a Polynesian show every evening from 5:45 to 9:45pm. You can order a few drinks, get some free pupus (no cover, no minimum), or just stand along the side (there are even chairs) and watch the entertainment, free.

On Friday evenings, when local people finish work, they like to head for the **Pau Hana Show** at the Hyatt Regency Hotel. So should you. Traditional Hawaiian music, dances, and songs are presented for the cost of a few drinks. No cover, no minimum. You can also stand by the giant waterfall and just watch.

Although there is no longer a show at the **Blue Dolphin Room,** a cozy place with a turn-of-the-century atmosphere, poolside at the Outrigger Hotel, it's still nice to come here, have a drink, and listen to the pianist, until 10pm. Beer is $2.25, mixed drinks from $2.50, exotics $4. All meals are served here, indoors and out, right beside the sands of Waikiki Beach. And don't tell anyone we told you, but it's possible to catch sight of The Luau from here (see above, under "Scrounger's Stroll"), on Tuesday, Friday, and Sunday nights at 7.

Again, you need only pay the price of the drinks when you go to hear Herb Ohta, who usually plays at the **Colony Lounge** of the Hyatt Regency Hotel. And go you should—Herb is a true virtuoso of the ukulele, and his touch is uncanny. He is often known, in fact, as Ohta-san, the suffix being one of respect.

Traditional Bavarian biergartens in Waikiki? Of course! Waikiki now has two of them. Newest is the **Bavarian Beer Garden** on the top floor of the Royal Hawaiian Shopping Center, which boasts Waikiki's biggest dance floor. There's ballroom dancing to live music from 6pm every day except Monday, a well-stocked bar, and inexpensive German food. No cover, no minimum. Long on the Waikiki scene is the **Hofbrau** in the International Market Place. Between the oom-pah-pah band's sets, the waitresses, in authentic costumes, dance polkas with the customers. Food and drinks are inexpensive, and there is no cover or minimum.

Michael W. Perry and Larry Price, Honolulu's top-rated morning-drive radio personalities, do their radio show live every Saturday from the **Hanohano Room** of the Sheraton Waikiki Hotel, beginning at 8am. They have lots of guest stars and give away prizes. Breakfast features eggs Benedict or blueberry pancakes on a large menu, and the tab is $12.95 and up per person. Reservations (tel. 922-4422) are a must.

READERS' RESTAURANT AND NIGHTLIFE SELECTIONS: "The lunch buffet at **Maiko**
at the Ilikai Hotel is a steal at $8.50, considering that they offer crab, sushi, sukiyaki, salad bar, dessert, and many other things, plus validated parking. It's a relaxing place to eat, where the tea and Japanese soup are brought to your table. No view to the outside, but you can step outside and be on the beach in a few footsteps. At dinner, the price is $15.95 Monday to Wednesday, and $16.95 Thursday to Sunday. . . . Don't forget **Smitty's** when you're in Kaneohe and you want to go to a really nice, comfortable, informal restaurant, but you don't want to spend much money. At Smitty's, most of your meals should be in the $4 to $7 range, with a few items higher. You'll sit there wondering how you can pay so little in such a nice restaurant. The menu has good variety for the whole family. And they sell pies to go. Smitty's is part of a very large Canadian chain. They're located makai of Sears in the Windward Shopping Center, across the street. . . . When you visit the botanical park in Wahiawa, be sure to eat at the **Seoul Inn** on California, near Kam Highway. The waitress brought in a tray of dishes—four spicy dishes of delicious vegetables, plus soup. Following that, she brought a huge plate of more vegetables, with about four scoops of rice and large portions of barbecue chicken and beef on top. All of this cost $3.75 including tax! You should ask for an extra plate and split it with a friend or two. So who says Hawaii is expensive!" (Mark Terry, Honolulu, HI).

"We found a gem of a restaurant by accident. We had missed the return trip on the Waikiki Trolley and knew we had an hour to kill. Directly across from the Trolley's Chinatown stop was a Vietnamese restaurant. Knowing nothing about Vietnamese food, we were very hesitant. Our meal turned out to be one of the very best that we had during our two-week vacation. The menu was imaginative. The food was truly fresh. Service was pleasant and speedy. And the bill was LOW. We recommend it highly and hope they stay in business a long time so that we may visit them on our next trip. **Pho Mai Vietnamese Restaurant,** 1029 Maunakea St., tel. 599-5244" (Beth and Jim Hutchinson, Ship Bottom, N.J. . . . "**John Dominis,** right on the waterfront at Kewalo Basin, is higher for dinner than our budget prices—scallops were $18—but EXCELLENT. If someone is going to splurge, this is the place to do it" (Sally Phillips, San Jose, Calif). [*Authors' Note:* John Dominis is at 43 Ahui St., tel. 523-0955.] . . . **Trellises Restaurant** at the Outrigger Prince Kuhio Hotel charges around $16 for its Friday night seafood buffet. It is excellent in every way, recommended for a 'Big Splurge' meal" (Lynda Lamb, Colo, S.C.).

"Here are some tips on inexpensive eating places I discovered on my last trip. **Central Union,** 1660 S. Beretania, has a nice lunch at their Union Station, Tuesday, Wednesday, and Thursday, 11am to 12:30pm, with a *suggested* donation of $2. The **Kapiolani Hospital Cafeteria,** Punahou Street, near Wilder Street, on the second floor, has good food. So does the **Aloha Cafeteria** at the University of Hawaii, on the first floor of Aloha tower, off Dole Street, almost opposite East/West Road. For nonstudents, there's a flat rate, inexpensive, and all you can eat" (Mrs. Dorothy Astman, Northport, N.Y.).

"When looking for nice-but-cheap restaurants, don't overlook the Kaimuki area just mauka of Diamond Head Center. These places are priced low for locals. At the **New Taste Restaurant** on Waialae Avenue, for example, you have your choice of lunch specials for under $3—large portions, too. At the **Kal Bi Korean Restaurant,** in an alley near 12th Avenue, under $5 may buy more than you can eat. And they serve very good food" (Mark Terry, Honolulu, HI). . . . "You always hear about luaus and that you just can't go to Hawaii and not attend one. We didn't and we have no regrets. We saw a better show at the Polynesian Cultural Center, ate authentic food at Trader Vics and avoided being herded around with 200 other people. At **Trader Vic's,** in the International Market Place, we both had great meals and the prices were not too bad. I had the Hawaiian platter, which was lomi-lomi salmon, poi, smoked pork, Maui onions, and pineapple. It was delicious and only cost about $12. Sure beats the price of a luau" (Carol Robinson, Lubbock, Tex.).

"I found a great spot in Kailua that I want to share with your readers. It is **Pizza Plus** at 130 Kailua Rd. in the Kailua Beach Center, two blocks from Kailua Beach. The owners are transplanted Massachusetts natives named Mark and Marie O'Leary. They serve up gourmet pizza by the slice or pie and have a fantastic chicken plate 'haole style' for under $5. Well worth a stop after a hard day of windsurfing or swimming at Kailua Beach" (Joe Riley, Brockton, Mass.).

"The **Denny's** restaurant next to Holiday Inn Waikiki was excellent. The restaurant is located on the second floor at the corner of Kalakaua and Kapahulu avenues and has 'outdoor' tables around the perimeter that overlook Waikiki Beach. They offer their 'Grand Slam' breakfast (eggs, pancakes, sausage, bacon) for only $3.95. What a terrific way to start a day!" (William Wessale, Houston, Tex.). . . . "I went back several times to the **Perry's Smorgy** at 2380 Kuhio Ave. for the breakfast buffet. What a feast for $4.20! Breakfast included fresh papaya and pineapple, grapefruit, bananas, stewed prunes, applesauce, bananas rolled in coconut, sausage, eggs, bacon, french toast, pancakes. A very mild ham was being sliced off the bone right in front of you. There was fresh Kona coffee, urns filled with orange juice and pineapple juice, three kinds of sodas, and three kinds of doughnuts. And the tropical decor was beautiful. The Perry's dinner I had at the Outrigger Waikiki, overlooking the ocean at sunset, was also great" (Marietta Chicorel, Sedona, Ariz.).

"Here's our personal 'Restaurant Review.' **Lewers Street Fish Company,** Outrigger Reef Towers, 247 Lewers St. Three stars. Very inexpensive, 'ono' food. We recommend the 'Beer Battered Mahi Mahi' and the 'Beer Battered Calamari.' Check *Spotlight Hawaii* for a discount coupon to make dinner even cheaper. . . . **Monterey Bay Canners,** Ward Warehouse: three stars! If you can afford just one splurge, consider MBC. Look for the board advertising the specials for the evening, $13 to $14. . . . **Orson's Chowderette** at the Ala Moana Mall: great for lunch. I recommend the calamari and fries. And the iced tea was delicious. . . . (Candy and Paul Erhard, Alexandria, Va.).

"The **Crouching Lion Inn,** just about five miles from the Polynesian Cultural Center, is one of the best restaurants in Windward Oahu. An imposing structure, the Inn was the actual residence of a Norwegian contractor and his large family who emigrated to Hawaii in 1912; the original hand-wrought iron fixtures add a charming quality to both the inside dining room (in which a fire blazes nightly in an enormous stone fireplace) and the outer dining room overlooking the bay. Among the menu specialties, I highly recommend the Slavonic Steak Continental, the Royal Hawaiian pork kebabs, the luscious chicken macadamia (boneless breast of chicken, dipped in a brandy and egg batter, deep fried, laced with a sweet-and-sour sauce. Most entrees are $13.25 to $18.35. Lunch is pleasant, too, and at both lunch and dinner, every table receives a freshly baked loaf of either white or whole wheat bread, warm from the oven. And don't miss their "mile high" coconut cream and other cream pies, each $2.75. Service is excellent, both pleasant and unobtrusive. I highly recommend The Crouching Lion as a first-class experience in leisurely dining in a beautiful setting, far removed from the hub of the city" (Jane James, Pearl City, HI).

"**Sizzler's** offers Senior Citizens a 20% discount on meals with the exception of advertised specials on Monday nights. Senior ages start at 55. Their salad bar is bigger and better than it was last year—and the food, too. . . . **Chuck's Cellar** in the Outrigger East Hotel has $5.95 Early Bird Specials from 5:30 to 6:30pm, which include very good thick soup, all-you-can-eat salad bar, and different entrees each night. A good variety salad bar and a good bargain." (Barbara and Ron LePage, Port Colborne, Ontario, Canada).

"I would like to recommend the **Bavarian Beer Garden** in the Royal Hawaiian Shopping Center. It is a restaurant with very inexpensive food, German style, ranging from about $9 to $14. The wine and beer are in the low-price range. Each evening there is a dance especially for older people who like to dance such dances as waltz, tango, fox-trot, and other dances of this type. In general, the establishment has an excellent atmosphere; it gives one the feeling of 'Gemutlichkeit' " (Ernst Schmidt, Calgary, Alberta, Canada).

"A restaurant we stumbled upon which caught our fancy was the **Islander Coffee Shop** in the Reef Towers Hotel on Lewers Street. The food was all appetizing, reasonable, and efficiently served. We enjoyed several meals there and found it a friendly place to meet and converse with people of many ethnic backgrounds. The management and waitressing crew were especially friendly to the customers. . . . Some of the best meals we had on Oahu were at **Woolworth's** near the International Market Place. For sandwiches and salads, you can't go wrong here" (James H. Cox, Middletown, Ky.).

"We made one great restaurant discovery which we would like to pass along. On our way to Hanauma Bay we discovered the **John Richards Restaurant** at Kokoa Marina in Hawaii Kai. We had a super buffet lunch for $6.95, including roast beef carved to order. Our table had a beautiful view of the harbor. The buffet lunch is served every day from 11am to 2:30pm" (Ted and Eileen Matthew, Santa Barbara, Calif.). . . . "We discovered a 'Big Splurge' restaurant which is so good that we ate there three times. It is **Kyo-Ya** at 2057 Kalakaua. Mostly Japanese eat there. The food is exquisite to look at and tastes wonderful. Portions are large, which is unusual for a Japanese restaurant" (Caryl Ritter, Dillon Beach, Calif.).

"One of the few high-quality fast-food eateries in Waikiki is the **Jack-in-the-Box** restaurant next door to the Waikiki Grand Hotel on Kapahulu. Here the customer can have his choice of window booth dining with views of the Honolulu Zoo across the street, sitting at one of the tables in back facing a pool and courtyard, or simply ordering 'to go.' Highly recommended, among the many fine budget offerings which include hamburgers, chicken, steak sandwiches, and shrimp, are the various Breakfast Crescents stuffed with combinations of bacon, eggs, ham, and cheeses, all around $2.50. This spot deserves recognition!" (Connie Tonken, Hartford, Conn.).

"**Kamaina Suite** at the Willows, 901 Hausten St., tel. 946-4808, was superb. It charges a fixed price for each person, and wine and drinks are extra. The price is $42.50. With tax and tip, it's virtually impossible to get out for under $100—but it's worth it. In fact, this restaurant may well be worth the trip to Hawaii, all by itself. We will definitely return to Oahu if only to experience Kamaina Suite again" (Barbara Bazemore and Dave Butenhof, Hudson, N.M.).

"One item we really couldn't do without is a collapsible cooler. We took two guided tours; lunch was not included in either. So when everyone else was crammed into snack bars and restaurants, we sat on the beach at Pat's on the North Shore of Oahu and on the Volcano Rim in Haleakala National Park on Maui. Several people commented that they thought we had a great idea. Even bologna sandwiches were great under those conditions!" (Cindy and Alan Horwitz, Marlboro, Mass.).

"We recently visited Waimea Falls and found ourselves past lunchtime and hungry. A lengthy search for a decent place to eat produced only a couple of 'greasy spoons' and two places we walked out on (a rarity for us) when we saw the ridiculous prices on their menus. Then we found a gem—**Rosie's Cantina** in the Haleiwa Shopping Center, right at the highway. The mental image created by the name was quickly dispelled when we went inside and found a light, airy, spotlessly clean café with attractive decor. The menu was surprisingly varied and prices were modest. Best of all, the food was absolutely to-notch" (Walter and Pat Rector, Penn Valley, Calif.).

"The **Super Chef** is a restaurant at 2424 Koa Ave., right behind the Hyatt Regency Hotel and next to King's Village (tel. 926-7199). The owner is Raymond Chou, who also owns the Won Kee Restaurants in the Aloha Surf Hotel and downtown Honolulu. At the time of our visit, Super Chef was running two-for-one dinners. We had a choice of rack of lamb or steak at $16 for two. They also had a lobster and filet mignon dinner at $12.50 per person, with complimentary hors d'oeuvres. This place has a nice atmosphere. From many of its tables, you can watch the chef working at this grill. . . . The **Waikiki Beachcomber Hotel** at 2300 Kalakaua Ave., serves a very nice prime-rib buffet for only $10.95 before 6pm, in an attractive dining room. A chicken dish, mahimahi, and salad bar are also included. . . . Visiting Elks may enjoy good food in a very pleasant atmosphere at the **Honolulu Elks Club** at 2933 Kalakaua Ave. (tel. 923-5722) on the no. 2 bus line. Their buffets are excellent and prices are reasonable. The atmosphere is great. Some of the *Magnum P.I.* TV shows were filmed here" (Dr. John Lopresti, Jr., Bricktown, N.J.).

"We stayed at the **Turtle Bay Hilton** which is a wonderful hotel. For lunch one day we had their buffet. The selections were varied and delicious, and especially nice was their scrumptious dessert bar with out-of-this-world cakes and tarts. . . . We also stopped at a little restaurant called **D'Amicos** in Sunset Beach. The façade was not very impressive, but the pizza was very good and they make the most delicious homemade ice-cream cookie sandwiches. It's worth a stop for this special treat" (Eloise Weissbach, Hauppauge, N.Y.). . . . "For coupons and bargains intended for Honolulu residents—not us tourists—pick up the *Sunday Star Bulletin and Advertiser*. You will find coupons that do not appear in the throwaways at the corner of every Waikiki street. . . . Singles may feel alone on a sunset sail, but not on the **Leahi Catamaran Sunset Mai Tai Sail**. The green-sailed catamaran is docked at the Sheraton Waikiki Hotel, and leaves at 5pm every day for a 1½-hour sail. Drink as many mai tais as you want. I stopped counting after *ten*. There's live music on board, a hostess, and the captain even had pupus the night I sailed. The price: around $22. During the day, there are one-hour sails, without drinks, for $12. . . . For a late-night date with an ocean view, try the lounge on the upper lobby of the **Outrigger**. Sit at a table for two on the lanai, overlooking the beach, and order a $10 drink for two, served with two very long straws. It will make you feel warm, tingly, and tipsy" (Robert Pray, Los Angeles, Calif.).

"Even though we stayed at the Hilton, we kept our food budget very low with no problem, eating very well indeed. To do this, you have to buy groceries for breakfast, and sometimes a light lunch, in your room. We are not big eaters in the morning, so we just bought muffins, sweet rolls, cereal, fruit, milk and orange juice. From home we brought coffee, packets of sugar, paper bowls and plates, and plastic utensils. **The Pâtisserie**, in the Edgewater Hotel on Beach Walk, sells muffins, rolls, and bread at half price when they are one day old. These keep very well for three or four days. Also, **King's Bakery** on Hobron Lane has excellent bran muffins and delicious Hawaiian sweet bread that keep very well for days" (Karen and Joan Polsen, Halifax, Nova Scotia, Canada).

"One of the highlights of our stay was the **Windjammer Cruise**. It consists of a 2½-hour sail, from 5:15 to 7:45pm, aboard the *Rella Mae,* Hawaii's largest sailing vessel. The price of $45 per person includes transportation from major Waikiki hotels to the *Rella Mae* and back, open bar, a delicious, seated dinner, terrific revue dinner show, and dancing to an exciting live band. We were amazed at how well organized the whole operation was and how gracious, helpful, and cheerful all the crew were. It was a real fun trip from beginning to end. We highly recommend the Windjammer Cruises, 2222 Kalakaua Ave., Suite 600, Honolulu, HI 96815 (tel. 922-1200 or toll free 800/367-5000)" (Mr. and Mrs. Norm Johnson, Ontario, Calif.). [*Authors' Note:* Windjammer Cruises also offers a moonlight cruise from 8 to 10 nightly that can be bought as a dinner-and-cocktail sail or a cocktail sail only. Tickets are $45 per person for dinner and cocktails, or $25 for cocktails only. Prices do not include tax.] . . . "Be careful with outdoor buffets in the hot weather. They seem to be worth the money in terms of quality, but we got food poisoning at one of the 'better hotel' buffets" (Pat Connor, Arlington, Mass.).

"We saved **The Willows,** 901 Hausten St., for our last night in the islands and what a perfect choice. It was expensive—$50 with wine, tax, tip, etc., but worth every cent of it. The atmosphere outside is incredible; the three-piece ensemble playing 'Hawaii City Lights' reduced me to tears. The food was superior, as was the service; all in all, a must" (Sheila Pritchett, Villanova, Pa.). [*Authors' Note:* The Willows is one of the islands' most gracious "old Hawaii" restaurants, situated on a beautiful pond amid the garden surroundings. Try it for a big-splurge meal; at dinner, most à la carte entrees are in the $15 to $25 range; a complete dinner is around $30. Call 946-4808 for reservations.]

"For great decor with your meals, try the Chinese and Japanese restaurants in Waikiki;

they are all authentic. We were warned against going into the Chinatown area at night because of the thefts. Please inform your readers that it is not a safe place after dark" (Barbara Smith, Winnipeg, Manitoba, Canada).

"Our hint: We took from home silverware, paring knife, can opener, two-cup coffee pot, and the makings for morning coffee. Every one of our hotel rooms had a small refrigerator. We bought orange juice, papaya, danish, whatever, and had breakfast on our lanai each morning before leaving. Many days we stopped in the grocery store and got sandwich fixings, canned iced tea, and fruit, and had a picnic on the beach. We not only saved money, but time as well. Many days we saw the tourists lined up at the coffee shops trying to have breakfast before catching a tour bus" (Mary Lou and Davie Bregitzer, Cleveland, Ohio). . . . "When you cannot get a hotel with a kitchenette, take along the following equipment, which will fit right in with your clothes in the suitcase: a four-cup percolator or hotpot; an eight-inch electric frying pan; one pancake turner; one sharp paring knife; plastic or stainless-steel cutlery; coffee mugs; a plastic pot scraper; paper plates; two or more plastic margarine dishes to use for soup, cereal, salad, or dessert dishes; salt and pepper shakers. With these utensils I cooked up some really adequate meals. The little frying pan holds four eggs at a time, and if you cut bacon strips in two, you can fry up a good panful. Two small steaks can be cooked, and then add and cook some frozen vegetables in a bit of water, and you have a meal in a dish. The little hot pot is for beverages as well as instant soup or porridge. One night I cooked an exotic creamed shrimp and hot rice dish by buying frozen 'boil in a bag' food. The extra plastic trays used for the meat become service trays, etc. It is a challenge to cook up imaginative meals and it can be done!" (Mrs. Margaret Springett, Moose Jaw, Saskatchewan, Canada). . . . "If you're going to be doing some cooking, save your pill bottles, remove the prescription labels, and fill them with all the spices you will need (salt, garlic salt, pepper, etc.), and label the containers. These take very little room and won't break" (Mrs. I. Hodgeman, Bloomington, Minn.).

"For readers who may be staying in or near the downtown area, here are some suggestions. **McDonald's** serves Portuguese sausage with rice and eggs for breakfast at the Fort Street Mall branch, as well as the usual choices. You can walk across the street to **Woolworth's** and get baked goods or a wide variety of prepared ethnic foods. Try the bread pudding at Woolworth's if they have it that day. Sit on the bench on the mall and watch the little birds circle you, watching for food" (Mark Terry, Alameda, Calif.).

"Here are some ideas that have worked beautifully on our Hawaii trips and have saved us well over $100 on breakfasts alone. (1) Buy a small beer cooler, put in a few cubes of ice, and you have a refrigerator you can use in your room, or take with you on day trips, to keep your milk, butter, sandwich meat, etc., fresh and sweet. It can be easily carried from one island to another, too. (2) On King Street in Honolulu, **King's Bakery** makes a Hawaiian sweet bread that has the unique quality of not drying out even after being cut. The taste is delicious, something like a sweet roll, and it will keep fresh in your room for days. (3) In the islands, orange juice comes in a quart glass 'milk' bottle. Fill this almost full of cold water, put in a few spoonfuls of instant coffee, insert one of those pigtail immersion heaters (made for heating liquid in a cup and available in most variety stores), using a clothes pin to stop it from going too far down, plug in, and voilá!—a quart of excellent coffee in about five minutes" (Sheldon Myers, Berkeley, Calif.).

TRANSPORTATION WITHIN HONOLULU

FROM BUSES TO CARS TO RICKSHAWS

In the chapters immediately following we'll discuss the sightseeing and activities of Honolulu and its suburbs. In this chapter, we deal with the cheapest ways to get to those activities and see those sights.

So many people think it's difficult to get around the islands that they succumb in advance to those package deals that wrap up your whole vacation in advance: transportation, hotels, sightseeing from the limousine window, all for one flat—and unnecessarily high—fee. And even if they've already discovered the do-it-yourself trick of staying at budget hotels and eating at low-cost restaurants, panic strikes when it comes to sightseeing—and how else to "do" Honolulu unless someone takes you by the hand on a guided tour?

Tours are okay, of course, pleasant and useful if you have only a day or two and want to pack in as many sights as you can. And you may want to take one (or else rent a car) when you circle the island of Oahu (see "Guided Tours," below). But for sightseeing in Honolulu, at your own pace, there's a method that's much cheaper, and much more fun—

THE BUSES

We refer, of course, to the MTL buses (known as TheBUS) owned by the city and county of Honolulu and operated under contract by the private firm of MTL, Inc. MTL has routes all over the island, which gives you a chance to mingle with the island's nontourist population. (You'll really feel like a kamaaina when someone asks you how to get to a certain place!) The friendliness of the Hawaiian drivers, too, will be quite an experience, especially if you come from an overcrowded city on the mainland where every passenger is a potential enemy. In a bus dispute some years ago, the drivers figured out a novel way to show their dissatisfaction with the company: they just refused to collect fares from the passengers!

But don't count on that. You'll pay 60¢ for a ride on TheBUS. Exact change in coins is required. Children pay 25¢. Free transfers, which can extend your ride considerably in one direction, must be requested when you board and pay your fare.

Bus schedules are not, unfortunately, available on the buses themselves, but if you have any questions about how to get where, simply call TheBUS information number at 531-1611. Keep in mind that the buses you will take from Waikiki to Ala Moana Shopping Center or to downtown Honolulu must be boarded on Kuhio Avenue.

Note: Senior citizens (65 or over) may ride free on the buses at all times. Appropriate proof of age (driver's license, birth certificate, passport, or baptismal certificate with seal), is required, and a temporary bus pass will be issued within 15 minutes. Apply at the MTL office, 725 Kapiolani Blvd.

If you're staying in Honolulu and doing extensive bus riding for any length of time, it may pay for you to buy a monthly pass. They cost $15 for adults, $7.50 for youths up to high school age (generally considered 19 or younger). Bus passes may be purchased any time during the month. They are available at TheBUSPass Office at 725 Kapiolani, at the Manoa Campus Center of the University of Hawaii, at Foodland and Emjay supermarkets, Satellite City Halls, and at Pioneer Savings Bank. All purchases must be made in cash: checks or credit cards are not accepted. Fares are subject to change.

RENTING A CAR

This alternative to the buses is more expensive, of course, but it may or may not be necessary, depending on what you plan to do in Honolulu. If you're going to stay mostly in Waikiki and perhaps venture forth to downtown Honolulu, forget it: The costs of renting and parking will not justify the expense; you can do better by sticking to buses and an occasional taxi here and there. (Save your money for renting cars on the neighbor islands where they are essential.) If, however, you want to spend time on the windward side of Oahu, or tour the entire island, a car is a must. But do remember that the bottom line on car rentals is not always what it appears to be. There has, in fact, been a great deal of complaint from consumer groups who are hoping to force the industry to include all mandatory charges in their basic advertised fees; many car rental companies oppose the plan. Thus, the budget-wise car renter must be on the alert for hidden charges (delivery, drop-off, extra charges for drivers under 25, for example, and most especially, for insurance coverage). Since Hawaii is a no-fault state, if you do not have insurance you are required to handle any damages you might incur before you leave the state. However, you may be able to avoid the cost of collision-damage wavers (anywhere from $10 to $12 per day), which the companies are eager to sell you, if your company back home provides rental-car coverage. Your policy should include personal liability, property damage, fire, theft, and collision (usually a $100 deductible, although many companies have much higher deductibles). Your company should also be able to provide fast claim service in the islands. It would be a good idea to obtain the name of your company's local claim representative in Hawaii before you come; bring along your policy or identification card if you plan to do that. And check with your credit card company to see if it provides rental-car coverage: gold cards issued by the leading companies usually do the trick.

If you do decide to rent, you'll have your choice of just about any type of vehicle, foreign or domestic, from the numerous U-drive agencies in town. The most inexpensive cars are usually those with manual shifts; if you want an automatic shift, you'll have to pay several dollars more. Prices are also higher for standard-size cars. And rates are always higher—as much as $5 or $10—in the busy winter season than in summer. As for the car-rental agencies themselves, they are very much in competition for your business, and since rates are constantly changing and new attractive deals are offered all the time, a little comparison shopping at the time of your arrival will pay big dividends. We'll give you the names of the top budget companies and their rates as of this writing, and we'll pass on the warning they gave to us: "Rates are subject to change at any time without notice." Most of the companies offer flat rates with unlimited free mileage.

All-Island Rentals

If you're going to visit several of the major islands, the easiest way to rent your cars is to make one telephone call to a company that provides service on all of them. We've had excellent cars and service from **Dollar Rent-A-Car** of Hawaii, one of the major companies in Hawaii, with locations on the *six* major islands—including Molokai and Lanai (it is the only company on Lanai). There are half a dozen offices in Waikiki alone (one is at 333 Royal Hawaiian Ave., tel. 926-4254); there are another half a dozen on Maui Their range goes from economy cars like GEO on up to full size sedans, Jeeps, convertibles, and Cadillac luxury sedans. For their compact cars with standard transmission, it's $30 daily, $150 weekly; compact deluxe automatics go for $35 daily, $200 weekly. They will rent to drivers under 25 at an extra charge of $5 per day, with a major credit card. Free "Adventures in Dining" coupons are often available. The local reservations number is 944-1544. For toll-free reservations from the U.S., phone 800/367-7398.

Give **Alamo Rent-A-Car** a call and find out if they're offering one of their "Sun Sale" specials if you're traveling in the winter. They often offer a good deal on an economy two-door Metro; last year it was $20 per day, $114 per week. Regular rates are about $27.99 per day, $97.99 per week for an air-conditioned, automatic, economy car, all with unlimited free mileage. Alamo is in Honolulu, Waikiki, Maui, Hilo, Kona, and Lihue (cars at airport terminals in neighbor islands, courtesy bus in Honolulu). Call Alamo toll-free at 800/327-9633, 24 hours a day. Certain restrictions apply, including age and credit card requirements. Rates do not include gas, tax, or a nominal under-25 surcharge.

With a fleet of over 7,000 cars, **Budget Rent-A-Car,** the well-known mainland and international car-rental agency, offers a vehicle for every taste and pocketbook. Since rates fluctuate so much, Budget does not care to quote them, but they are always competitive. Free coupon books chock-full of free admission to Hawaii's major visitor attractions, free meals, and free gifts are given to all renters. There are offices at 2379 Kuhio Ave. in Waikiki, plus many Waikiki branches (tel. 922-3600). There are locations at Honolulu and neighbor-island airports, and also on Maui, Kauai, Molokai, and the Big Island. For reservations, call toll free 800/527-7000, or write Budget Rent-A-Car of Hawaii, Central Reservations, P.O. Box 15188, Honolulu, HI 96830-0188.

Friendly service and good deals are available at **Tropical Rent-A-Car Systems,** 550 Paiea St. (tel. 836-1041). They offer flat rates only (no mileage charges), economy stick shift (no air-conditioning) from $24.95 per day, $89 per week. Air-conditioned compacts are $29.95 per day, $119 per week. They also have station wagons. Tropical has offices on all the neighbor islands, and rents to drivers 21 (with a major credit card) to 70 only, and not to campers. Tropical has two offices in Waikiki (call 949-2002) and a toll-free reservation number: 800/367-5140. Rates are subject to change.

National Car Rental of Hawaii, 3080 Nimitz Hwy. (tel. 836-2665), has convenient locations at the airports on Oahu, Hawaii, Kauai, and Maui, and offers competitive unlimited-mileage rates for all types of cars, including convertibles, sports cars, and vans. The toll-free number is 800/CAR-RENT.

Thrifty Car Rental has locations on Oahu, Maui, and Kauai (but not on Hawaii). They have direct-line courtesy phones at all baggage-claim areas. Usually, standard compacts rent for $23 daily, $129 weekly. New models, no mileage charge. Call 833-0046 in Honolulu for reservations, or write to them at 3039 Ualena St., Honolulu, HI 96819.

United Car Rental, 234 Beachwalk (tel. 922-4605), rents cars on three major islands (it is right at the airports at Maui, Kauai, and Kona) and offers attractive rates on its fleet of late-model cars, from compacts to Cadillacs, vans, and Jeeps. Compact standards are $18.95 daily (sometimes they will go lower), $113.70 weekly; automatic compacts are $21.95 daily, $131.70 weekly.

Avis Rent-A-Car, Honolulu International Airport (tel. 834-5564), serves all five major islands, and offers a special for seven days of driving an automatic Dodge or similar car on a combination of two or more islands—about $199 a week. For toll-free reservations, phone 800/831-8000.

Hertz Rent-A-Car, 233 Keawe St., Room 625 (tel. 836-2511), features an All-Island touring rate that covers seven days or more on any combination of the four major islands. Days do not have to be consecutive and there is no mileage charge. The seven-day rate starts at $149 for a stick-shift car, or $25.99 for one day. Daily rates offer free unlimited mileage. For toll-free reservations and information, call 800/654-3131; in Honolulu, 836-2511. Hertz has offices at airports and hotels on all the major islands. You are advised to reserve at least a day in advance. A major credit card is required.

Honolulu Only Bargains

If you don't mind not driving the newest models, you'll be able to save a few dollars at **Maxi Experienced Cars,** 413 Seaside Ave., Honolulu, HI 96815 (tel. 923-7381). Their fleet has had a bit of experience—cars are a few years old—but they rent them from just $13 per day and $80 per week. Most of these are automatics. Convertibles and Jeeps are also available.

Waikiki Rent A Car, 224 McCully, Honolulu, HI 96815 (tel. 946-2181) has a full line of cars available and often offers special deals, like a compact automatic for $22 per day on a three-day-minimum basis; **Honolulu Rent-A-Car,** 1856 Kalakaua Ave., Honolulu, HI 96815 (tel. 942-7187), makes a similar offer: $17 a day, on a three-day-minimum basis, for a Toyota shift or automatic. There is also a full line of other cars at higher rates.

General Notes

It's a good idea to have a major credit card if you're going to rent a car in Hawaii. Otherwise, you will have to pay cash in advance, or at least a deposit, or leave an unsigned check with a personal signature.

If you're under 21, you're out of luck here when it comes to renting a car. Hawaii state law prohibits anyone under 18 from driving with an out-of-state license (even though islanders can get licenses at 15!). There used to be one or two agencies that would rent to drivers 18 to 20, but as of this writing, there are none that we know of. There may be special stipulations for 21- to 24-year-olds, like paying a surcharge and having a major credit card. When you reach 25, you can just show your license, fill out the papers, and drive away.

A further tip: In general, it's cheaper to pick up a car at the airport than to have it delivered to your hotel and picked up when you're finished with it. And airport pickup, of course, avoids the costs of cabs or bus coming into town.

RENTING CAMPERS AND TRAILERS

We're sorry to have to report this, but as of this writing, there is no place on all the major islands of Hawaii where one can rent a camper or a trailer. The last of its kind, Travel/Camp in Hilo, is just a memory now; its owner has gone into the bed & breakfast business. If any new companies open, we will let you know about them in our next edition.

WAIKIKI TROLLEY

It's cheaper than your own car, more expensive than TheBUS. But the new Waikiki Trolley service presents an entertaining alternative means for getting around the busiest tourist areas. **E Noa Tours** runs two quaint-looking motorized trolleys that recall the spirit of turn-of-the-century Honolulu. From 9am to 4:20pm, they ply the route between the Royal Hawaiian Shopping Center and Dole Cannery Square, making stops at Chinatown, Iolani Palace, and 13 other fascinating places, the driver all the while pointing out places of interest and presenting a painless lesson in Hawaiian history. If you buy a $10 all-day pass ($7 for children), you can hop on and off as much as you like. Phone 526-0012 for routes and schedules.

BIKING AROUND

Honolulu, like big cities everywhere, has become very cycle conscious. Bicycles used to be available for rental at a number of locations, but lately most of the hotels and rental agencies (like Hertz) have stopped renting them because of the high equipment-mortality rate. "We kept finding them in the ocean," said one supplier. But we did find *one* place where they can still be rented: **Aloha Funway Rentals,** at 2025 Kalakaua Ave. (tel. 942-9696), offers them from $10 to $13 per 24-hour day; they also have Mopeds and cars as well as snorkel equipment and boogie boards.

RICKSHAWS

Here's a novel—if not exactly inexpensive—way to sightsee: hire a rickshaw. Although pedicabs were a common sight in Waikiki for several years, in 1988 they were banned from the main arteries; however, they are still managing to stay in business on the side streets. Each pedicab driver is an independent contractor and may charge passengers as he pleases. The ones we talked with asked $10 for 15 minutes, but they love to haggle and, if business is slow (as it often is due to the large proliferation of pedicabs), you can ride for much less. Just be sure that you and the driver agree on price and distance before you hop in. The young people who sit on the bicycle seats and pedal you around, incidentally, all appear to be in excellent physical condition, tanned and healthy—unlike their counterparts in Asia.

TAXIS

Good news! It's now very easy to get a cab in Waikiki. Simply step out into any major thoroughfare, lift your hand to signal, and within five minutes, you'll undoubtedly be on your way. Although they are not cheap (the first flip of the meter is usually $1.40), taxis are useful for emergencies and for short trips, and could be practical if a few of you are traveling together. If you want to call a cab in advance, your hotel desk can usually get one for you, or you can call any of the numerous companies listed in the telephone book.

Here are the telephone numbers of a few taxi companies:

Charley's Taxi—531-1333
Aloha State Cab—847-3566
Sida of Hawaii—836-0011

GUIDED TOURS

If you're traveling alone, you'll have to invest about $25 (maybe more) for a guided tour around the island of Oahu. But if there are at least two of you, renting a car slices the per-person expense considerably. Even more cheaply, you can travel almost all the way around the island of Oahu for a mere $1.20 in bus fare (details in Chapter VIII). And economics aside, we believe there is no travel thrill like that of a do-it-yourself exploration of a new part of the world, where you make your own discoveries at your own pace, free to follow the intriguing bypaths that don't always appear on a planned itinerary. Best of all, you can throw your lunch and bathing suit in the back seat for a picnic or swim whenever you feel like it.

ADVICE FOR DRIVERS

A few words about driving in Honolulu. Many of the major thoroughfares of Honolulu are now one-way streets, which helps the flow of traffic, but often makes it seem that you are driving miles out of your way to reach a specific destination; downtown Honolulu is an especially confusing place to drive in. You may want to keep in mind that in this area Beretania Street is Ewa, King Street is Diamond Head, Pensacola traffic now heads makai (to the sea), and Piikoi cars go in a mauka (to the mountains) direction. In Waikiki, Kalakaua traffic is Diamond Head most of the way, with a short stretch downtown running in both directions; Kuhio Avenue is two-way and the Ala Wai Boulevard is Ewa.

Those painted white arrows on the various lanes are not to be ignored. They indicate in what directions you are permitted to drive from each lane: right only, left only, left and straight ahead, or right and straight ahead. It's legal to make right turns when the light is red at most intersections—but not all—so read the signs first. And if you come across a sign reading "We appreciate your kokua," it's not an invitation to pay a toll. Kokua means cooperation in Hawaiian.

Parking for the night can be a problem in the Waikiki area, where you may find yourself driving around and around the block. *Tip:* Ala Wai Boulevard, along the canal, is less crowded than other main thoroughfares (but cars must be off one side of the street by 6am). In the downtown area, there are both municipal and private parking lots. Street meters charge only 1¢ per minute; in some busy locations the meters allow no more than 12 to 24 minutes. Read each meter carefully.

Mainland driving licenses may be used until expiration date. After that you'll need a Hawaiian license, obtainable from the Department of Motor Vehicles, for those 15 and older.

READERS' TRANSPORTATION TIPS: "You must shop around for car rentals. I called various car rental companies, using their 800 numbers. I asked for the very best deal and ended up paying a low weekly fee for an Alamo car with air conditioning, AM-FM radio and automatic transmission. It even pays to call back the same place a second time, and after they quote a price, always ask: 'Is this your best deal?' Often they will then quote a 'spring special' or some such" (G. Vaughan Parker, Santa Barbara, Calif.). . . . "In general, if you're not going much beyond Honolulu, I think driving in Oahu is more trouble than it's worth. There is an apparent maniacal hatred for U-turns in Honolulu. If you make a mistake (and signs were not always as clear or as numerous as I would have liked, some of the freeways divide quite unexpectedly), you can go for miles before finding any way to turn around, and any way you do find is likely to be circuitous" (Lisa Yount, Richmond Annex, Calif.). . . . "Please remind people to lock rental cars even if leaving them just to take a picture. We met several people who stopped just to see a particularly scenic view and came back in less than five minutes to find coolers, cameras, whatever gone" (Sandy Abramovich, Thomaston, Conn.).

"If a person is going to visit some of the attractions and/or plans to eat even one meal at other than the Jack-in-the-Box, and intends to rent a car for a drive to points around the island, rent the car before seeing the attractions. The freebies and discounts that come with many of the car rentals add up to some real savings. In other words, don't do something like taking a dinner cruise on a catamaran at full price and then learn you could have gone for free or at a substantial savings with a coupon that comes with a car rental" (The Ed Glassner Family, Kent, Ohio). . . . "Several of those places that advertise 'used cars' to rent for $7 to $9 a day are using false advertising—telling us that they don't have any of those types of cars in now and that they expect one in three weeks or so—a come-on!" (Paula Fisk, Greenwood, Ind.). . . . "If you're renting from an agency that gives out free coupons, note that you can only use your coupons while you are renting the car. You must show your car keys and/or your contract when you try to use a coupon. I don't really know if the free coupons are worth it. It might be cheaper to rent from an agency without coupons" (Carl and Debbie Adams, St. Louis, Mo.). . . . "I thought you might like to tell your readers about Budget's coupons for people who rent cars in Hawaii. I was delighted to get coupons for free meals and free souvenirs on each of the islands I visited. As a single traveler, I was especially delighted to find that there were no 'Buy one, get one free' or 'Two for the price of one' coupons. It's the first time I've ever encountered 'One-free!' " (M.L. Siero, Stockton, Calif.).

"Don't rent those cars that have a brand name 'Rental Car' on them. They are red flags for car thieves. Warn the pedestrians: Hawaiian drivers do not give right of way to pedestrians, even in a crosswalk! Tell the readers to cross only with the light or only when no cars are approaching. Most Hawaiian drivers do not stop for pedestrians in the street, they go *around* them, which can be very scary—the cars sometimes miss you only by inches" (M.B., Mililani, HI).

"I rented cars on all the islands except Lanai, and found parking at hotels and motels was quite limited in some cases. Fortunately, I always managed to get a spot. It would be wise to check that a hotel has parking available if you plan to rent a car. Also, be aware that some of the hotels, particularly in Honolulu, charge for parking" (Jane Kenney, Kingston, N.H.). . . . "If you're parking your car in Waikiki, try Fort DeRussy's huge parking lot (it's free) or the side streets near Kapiolani Park" (Jack Nakamoto, Ottawa, Ontario, Canada).

"We never had any hassles this time over refusing to purchase insurance at the car-rental agencies, as we did on our earlier trip to Hawaii. At one of the large car-rental agencies, we politely refused air conditioning and automatic transmission on every island (we rented four different cars), but that was thrown in at no extra charge! We wondered if they actually had any cars without these as standard features" (James H. Cox, Middletown, Kentucky).

"When you arrive at the airports in Hawaii and have already reserved a car, don't call the car agency trying to speed things along before you've retrieved your luggage. They ask if you've gotten your bags yet. If you haven't, they'll tell you to get them and then call back. Only then will they send their airport pickup bus to get you" (Norman Saulnier, S. Ashburnham, Mass.).

"Suggestions to drivers: You can be tagged for even one or two miles over the speed limit.

Watch parking directions carefully. We parked in a driveway, in the evening, that had a closed fence around a vacant lot and obviously wasn't being used for anything that year—and received a ticket. Also, watch the meters: around Fisherman's Wharf, for example, they *do not* stop at 6pm" (Sheila Pritchett, Villanova, Pa.).

"It was interesting to take TheBUS to the New Windward Mall in Kaneohe (take no. 56 'Kailua—Kaneohe' or no. 52 'Kaneohe—Kailua'). The mall has a Liberty House (with lunch specials), Penney's, Sears, etc., and is enclosed. The bus route over the Pali and Kaneohe Bay on no. 56 is scenic" (Marge O'Harra, Portland, Ore.). . . . "Your experience with public buses on Oahu may vary considerably. At certain times of the day, your bus may be packed with people and go jolting down rough streets (and the seats are *hard*). Some of the drivers have a union attitude. But you can see a lot of territory on bus rides, and avoid the hassle of looking for scarce parking spots at your destination. Parking is often *very* scarce in Honolulu, even by San Francisco standards" (Mark Terry, Honolulu, HI). . . . "We found TheBUS quite difficult in Honolulu—usually crowded, slow, and uncomfortable, as well as hard to determine schedules. However, the guide from a local paper helped" (Melvin H. Boyce, Corte Madera, Calif.).

"TheBUS was the best transportation and *cheapest* way to get anywhere on the island compared to rather expensive tours" (Joan Fuggi, Wallingford, Conn.). . . . "You are absolutely right about TheBUS. We could have gotten along without a car for a few more days by using TheBUS. It's easy to catch onto the routes as plenty of free information is available, and for price, TheBUS has to be one of the last bargains left on earth" (Robert and Jean Carroll, Helena, Mont.).

VI

SHOPPING IN HONOLULU

1. SHOPS IN WAIKIKI
2. ALA MOANA CENTER
3. AROUND TOWN

Muumuus and macadamia nuts, koa woods and calabashes, tapas and tiki figures—these suggest the exotic items for which you'll shop in the islands. Although Hawaii is not one of the great bargain shopping areas of the world (no free-port prices or favorable money exchange for dollar-bearing Americans), it still offers a fascinating assortment of things Polynesian, Asian, and American for the inveterate browser and souvenir hunter. We'll skip the expensive items—jewelry, objets d'art, Asian brocades and silk, elegant resort wear and stick to the good buys for the shopper who wants quality and low prices, which is where you, the $60-a-day'er, come in. Although many stores have upgraded their merchandise and are concentrating on higher ticket items with which to entice those hordes of affluent Japanese tourists, there are still plenty of good buys left for the rest of us.

1. Shops in Waikiki

Much of your island shopping can be done right in Waikiki: along Kalakaua Avenue and in the hotel gift shops, and at the International Market Place, Kuhio Mall, King's Village, Royal Hawaiian Shopping Center, the Atrium Shops at Hemmeter Center, and the Waikiki Shopping Plaza. First we'll cover Waikiki in general, listing our recommendations by type of merchandise. Then we'll head for the special shopping areas and see what's up.

HAWAIIAN WEAR
Begin on Kalakaua Avenue if you're looking for island muumuus, aloha shirts, which we've suggested you plan to buy here, in our earlier section on packing. Countless shops carry these items, but be sure to take a look at the reliable Waikiki branch of Honolulu's major department store—**Liberty House**—where there are extremely attractive selections of clothing for men and women, and children, too. There's nothing provincial about Liberty House; they have everything from swimsuits for baby at $6, up to designer sportswear separates at $300 and more. There are so many stores, on Kalakaua and in the hotels and shopping centers, that you could spend days and days just going from one to another. A store we like very much is **Casa D'Bella II** at 2352 Kalakaua. They carry some stylish designs from New York and California as well as local resort wear. And they have a good collection of fashion

shell jewelry, too. **Island Fashions** at 2520 Kalakaua can always be counted on for generous discounts on both muumuus and aloha shirts (a well-dressed friend of ours claims he gets his entire shirt wardrobe here, never paying more than $15!). They have five other stores in Honolulu, and outlets on Maui, Kauai, and the Big Island as well. The manufacturers of Hawaiian clothing we like best include **Malihini of Hawaii, Bete, Sun Babies, Princess Kaiulani, Tori Richards, Hilda** (women's clothing), and **Kahala and Cook Street** (better men's apparel); you'll find these brands all over town. Note, too, that most of the specialty shops will make up muumuus for Mother, aloha shirts for Dad, and junior versions of both for the kiddies in matching fabrics, and will also make clothes to your special size. (We should tell you that locals consider this very "touristy.") Many will make bikinis to order, or at least allow you to match the top of one to the bottom of another. Made-to-measure work usually takes just a day or two and in most cases and costs no more than ready-made garments.

Prices for Hawaiian clothes are pretty standard everywhere: better muumuus average $40 to $50 short, $70 to $80 and way up, long. To realize substantial savings on aloha wear, your best bets are three places outside of Waikiki we'll tell you about later: Hilo Hattie's Fashion Center, Island Muumuu Works, and Muumuu Factory.

VINTAGE ALOHA SHIRTS

You know, of course, that antique aloha shirts—those from the 1930s, 1940s, and 1950s—for some inexplicable reason, have become high fashion on the mainland. Why show biz celebrities and socialites are willing to pay up to anywhere from $100 to $1,000 for rayon shirts that have been hanging in somebody's closet for 30 or 40 years is a "puzzlement" to us, but the demand is there, and those shirts that do make their way into places like **Bailey's Antique Clothes & Thrift Shop** at 758 Kapahulu St. (tel. 734-7628), are snatched up quickly by folks like Robin Williams and Tom Selleck and Steven Spielberg, to drop just a few names. Bailey's is a fascinating store, however (it also stocks other early island wear from various cultures), and well worth a look; if you can't afford one of the pricey items, note that they have over 1,000 shirts in the $5 to $10 range, 1,200 shirts from $10 to $20, and something like 300 shirts from the 1950s, which range from $20 to $125. Approximately 300 "silky" rayon shirts from the 1940s command prices of from $100 to $1,000. Another shop, **Kula Bay,** with branches at the Royal Hawaiian Hotel and the Hilton Hawaiian Village, has done some clever work taking authentic prints from shirts of the 1930s, 1940s, and early 1950s, having them painted on long-staple cotton in more muted colors, and turning out handsome, very well tailored aloha shirts for about $80. For photos of the originals, and a history of the aloha shirt, read the book called *The Hawaiian Shirt,* by H. Thomas Steel, published by Abbeville Press, and available at many local bookstores.

SOUVENIRS AND SMALL PRESENTS

Scads of Honolulu tourists swear by the low prices at the **ABC Discount Stores.** There are literally dozens of ABC stores in Waikiki, sometimes two to a block! You can usually expect to save 20% to 25% here on small items, sometimes more. Hawaiian perfumes and macadamia nuts are always a bargain at ABC stores. Most are open seven days a week, from 7:30am to midnight. Most ABCs also have drugs, cosmetics, grocery sections, gift packages ready for mailing, deli, fresh produce, and liquor, and usually the lowest prices anywhere on Hawaiian scenic postcards.

A number of other stores cut the regular prices on standard items—perfumes, cosmetics, souvenirs—and you'll find quite a few of these shops on Kalakaua in the area just Diamond Head of Uluniu Avenue, up toward the Queen Kapiolani Hotel. You can also count on good buys at **Holiday Mart,** which you'll read about ahead. **Woolworth's,** in the Bank of Hawaii Building on Kalakaua, now charges more for some standard souvenir items than ABC and some of the other shops, but their discount on jade, coral, opal, and 14-karat gold items is good. (It's nice to know that they'll mail your gifts and souvenirs home for you.) **Long's Drugstore** in Ala Moana is another excellent source for small items; their values are consistently tops.

What to buy? Hawaiian perfumes make delightful small presents. Royal Hawaiian is the leading brand name for island fragrances—pikake, ginger, orchid, plumeria—all of them sweetly floral and worlds away from the sophistication of Paris. Gift packages complete with artificial orchids begin around $5; higher-priced perfumes have a real orchid right in the bottle.

As for jewelry, black coral, mined in the waters off Maui, is handsome in small tree shapes and in numerous other pins and pendants. An exquisite pink coral called angelskin has also been found off Maui waters. Blue coral is the "look" with jeans and casual tops. Crystals are popular here, as they are everywhere. You'll see all of these, in abundance, at jewelry stores all over the islands.

You can buy Hawaiian delicacies—such exotic tastes as guava jelly, coconut syrup, passion-fruit ambrosia, Kona coffee, macadamia nuts—at almost any grocery store, but should you want to send a package home, the best and most reasonably priced places are Long's Drugs, ABC Discount, and the **Waikiki A-1 Superette.**

T-shirts, practically a uniform in Hawaii, make fun presents for almost everybody on your list; they're in every store, at every price. **Crazy Shirts,** which, like the ABC Discount Stores, seems to be on almost every block in Waikiki, can be counted on for witty designs, good fabrics, and prices of around $18 for Ts, around $40 for sweatshirts. For information on Crazy Shirts' factory outlet stores, see ahead under "T-Shirt Secrets."

Eelskin is another very big item for presents. Almost every eelskin store claims that it sells "wholesale." Reputedly the country's largest wholesaler, **Leather of the Sea,** in the Waikiki Shopping Plaza, 2250 Kalakaua Ave., fourth floor, has many good buys. Also in the same shopping center, **Ali Baba** and **Eelskin Elegance** offer good values. You should be able to pick up a wallet for $20 or less.

INTERNATIONAL MARKET PLACE

The oldest and most colorful shopping area in Waikiki, this place is still fun, despite the fact that there are now so many booths and tourists that it sometimes reminds us of rush hour in the New York subway. And prices are apt to be a mite higher on the same items than they are in the department stores or at Ala Moana Center, although they might come down considerably if you're willing to do a bit of bargaining (it doesn't always work, but it could be worth a try). And do note that comparison shopping pays off here; one booth might be selling T-shirts for $12, another one around the corner for $8 or $9. Informal, semi-open shops set around a giant banyan tree and interspersed among tropical plantings stay open until 11 at night, giving you plenty of time for al fresco browsing. Directly behind it, with an entrance on Kuhio Avenue, is Kuhio Mall, with more of the same. An entertaining scene, especially in the cool of evening.

Unfortunately, few of the shops here now carry genuine Hawaiian and Polynesian craft items like lauhala hats, carvings from native woods, or tapa cloth. What you will find are scads of places selling jewelry (everything from plastic to shell to ivory, coral, and lapis), candles, T-shirts, beach cover-ups, and resort wear. Many stands all called **The Pearl Factory** sell pearls in the oyster. Shops and kiosks come and go with great rapidity, so our best advice is simply to roam where fancy leads you. It might be fun to get a laser shirt: Two young men named Gregory and Michael stand in the center of the Market Place with their trained scarlet and blue-and-gold macaws; They'll take a picture of you with the birds, and/or in Polynesian costumes, and turn them into T-shirts (printed by a laser process), postcards, place mats, and the like. Great fun! Also fun are Doctor Doo-Wop's Artificial Tatoos, which features swim-proof tatoos; and Fingernail Fashions, where you can have a design painted on your nails that will last for months. As for more serious art, at the rear of the Market Place, one flight up, is **Art of Paradise,** an attractive gallery featuring arts and crafts by local artists. Note the hand-marbled silk scarves and the raw-silk clothing as well as fine arts.

Let's hope it doesn't happen, but one of the sites being considered for Hawaii's proposed giant convention center is the International Market Place. If approved, the Market Place will be just a memory within a short time.

AT KUHIO MALL

Kuhio Mall is directly behind the International Market Place, and, at first glance, looks exactly like it. But there's something unique here, and it's up a flight of stairs and called **The Craft Court.** Here, in delightful contrast to all the mass-produced goods sold everywhere, is an artisans' working gallery, where everything is made by hand. You deal directly with the craftsmen, who can often be seen making jewelry, throwing pots, sewing and painting on garments, and giving demonstrations of lauhala weaving and the like. One of our favorite booths here is called **Rags to Riches:** Sandra Akina does some fascinating jewelry of acrylic clay with shells, in a price range for about $18 to $40. We also like her "Surf and Sand Drops"—these hand-blown glass ornaments are $10 as Christmas baubles, $20 mounted on koa-wood boxes. . . . Maggie Mintz is responsible for the lovely hand-painted clothes at **Fringe Works,** Glen Okuma for handsome baskets woven from the leaf of a coconut palm, using lost Hawaiian weaving techniques (from $10; a coconut-weave hat is $25). . . . **Hawaiian Flowers and Plants** has dried, plastic, and silk flora, as well as certified plants and cut flowers ready for the mainland. They also feature butterflies mounted, framed, and treated as works of art; Allan Hsu paints them by hand on T-shirts ($25). You'll always find something special here, like boat models artfully made from rolled newspaper (Polynesian canoes begin at $8) or tapa cloth done by a craftswoman from Tonga. Don't miss **The Crafts Court** if you really want to see what Hawaii's talented craftspeople are doing.

Down on the street level at Kuhio Mall, the best bargain outlet is **Swimsuit Warehouse,** which offers sizeable savings in name-brand swimsuits for women. The going price was $23.95 for bikinis $26.95 for one-piece suits at the time of our last visit. This wholesale operation offers suits for serious swimmers and suits for everybody else, in every style from bikini to skirt, high and low cuts, with special sections for larger women. Junior sizes run 5 to 13, missy sizes 8 to 22. No decor to speak of, just racks of great suits! Other locations can be found in both the Royal Hawaiian Shopping Center and the Waikiki Shopping Plaza and at 343 Saratoga Rd. . . . Look for a shop called **Y.K.K.,** which can create some unusual gift items for you. They'll take your picture and put it on a T-shirt, a calendar, a poster, a plastic button, or whatever. Prices are reasonable.

The classiest shop downstairs at Kuhio Mall is **Island Logo,** which features designer T-shirts that bear the legend "It's always summer in Hawaii." T-shirts, tanks, sweatshirts, and the like feature logos highlighting polo, tennis, snorkeling, canoeing, and yachting, all very tasteful, at about $13 for Ts, $23 for sweatshirts.

Free Polynesian shows are held every night at 7 and 8.

ROYAL HAWAIIAN SHOPPING CENTER

Across Kalakaua from the International Market Place is one of Waikiki's newer shopping centers, and in many respects its most sophisticated. "An oasis of green in Waikiki" is what the builders promised when ground was broken several years ago, and despite the outcry against the lavish use of concrete, it's pretty much what they've delivered. Occupying three city blocks along Kalakaua Avenue and fronting the entrance to the Royal Hawaiian and Sheraton Waikiki Hotels, this stunning 6½-acre, 120-store complex is indeed graced with flowers and trees, ferns and shrubbery, and hundreds of trailing vines and Hawaiian plants. A high level of taste is evident in the shops, restaurants, and a huge variety of daily programs—Polynesian minishows, classes in coconut frond weaving, playing the ukulele, dancing the hula, stringing leis, learning Chinese wok cooking or Hawaiian quilting—as well as special events—enough to keep the visitor busy and happy for a long time. Unfortunately for us, the trend here is toward more and more upscale marketing: On the ground floor, Japanese visitors wait in line to get into designer shops like Lancel, Chanel, and Louis Vuitton. On the second and third floors, **McInerny**

Galleria, which replaced the outstanding China Friendship Store, features a series of pricey boutiques—Armani, Hermès, Valentino, and more of that like. However, the budget shopper can still do pretty well here: at several outright discount stores like McInerny's Bargain Attic where sportswear is sold for no more than 75% of its original prices (we've seen $48 bikinis for $25, $27 women's knit shorts for $13.49) and **Swimsuit Warehouse** (all bikinis, $23.95, all one-piece suits, $26.95); at lower-priced apparel shops like Hilo Hattie and Ritz; as well as at several unique spots where merchandise is outstanding, and prices are fair.

In this category, then, be sure to visit **The Little Hawaiian Craft Shop** on the third floor where a fantastic assortment of unusual finished jewelry sits alongside buckets and barrels of raw materials, the same kinds that were used by the ancient Hawaiians. This is a workshop for craftspeople using natural island materials in both traditional and contemporary styles. Replicas of museum pieces sit among $4.50 hand-carved tikis and buckets of 50¢ shells. They have some wonderful hard-to-find sandalwood necklaces—fragrant, lovely, and well priced, from about $18. Almost everything here is handmade in Hawaii. Great ideas for presents include kukui nut rings at $5 (many kukui rings, pendants, and necklaces), Hawaiian exotic wood key chains at $3.50 each, coconut shell necklaces at $10. They also have a small booth on the main floor, where they sell that very popular 14-karat-gold Hawaiian heirloom jewelry, engraved with your own name. The goldsmith promises a completed product in 24 to 48 hours.

The shop also includes an outstanding wood gallery that shows local woodworkers of the calibre of Pai Pai, known for his woodcarved replicas of Hawaiian and Pacific images, along with stone replicas by Salote. Only island woods—among them koa, mango, Norfolk pine, milo, macadamia, ohio lehus, and keawe—are used. Prices range from $3.50 to $3,000. Collectors will want to note the traditional and contemporary handcrafts from the islands of the Pacific—Fiji, New Guinea, Tonga, the Solomons, Micronesia, Polynesia, Melanesia—with an ever-changing kaleidoscope of spirit figures, tapas, weavings, war clubs, drums, masks, spears. The owners make frequent trips to these areas to find these treasures. Well worth a look. If you need any custom jewelry work done, try their Jeweler's Work Bench.

Ready to treat yourself to something special? Stop in and visit Marlo Shima who runs **Boutique Marlo** on the second floor, Building A. Using only silk, cotton, and other natural fabrics, dying them in the subtlest and softest of colors, Marlo creates women's clothing of great beauty. Although dresses go from about $80 to $200, you can find many modestly priced scarves, necklaces, fabric bags, and the like, with the same high standards of quality and beauty. We also like the stylish women's clothing at the **Accessory Tree** on the third floor, especially their handsome batik jackets for around $85. Treat your keikis to some cute clothing at **Sunshine Kids,** also on the third floor.

Between Buildings B and C is the **Royal Bridge,** with a scattering of carts and kiosks. Of interest to collectors of those vintage Hawaiian shirts is **Paradise Antiques,** which sells shirts from the 1930s and 1940s—not exactly cheap at about $395, but worth having a look at.

Although Asian storekeepers sell it in Honolulu, the ginseng available ta **Ginseng King** is grown in Wisconsin. Stop in at their store, learn about the therapeutic effects of the centuries-old root, and perhaps buy a few tea bags (35¢ each), or a large bunch of the root itself ($25) to be used in making ginseng chicken soup.

If you've bought too much on your shopping rounds and are wondering how to get it all home, visit **GBC** on the second floor. They'll do professional packing, wrapping, and shipping, or sell the materials—corrugated boxes, mailing tubes, sealing tapes, etc.—that you need to do it yourself. United Parcel Service is available here, and there's a U.S. post office just next door.

Where can you eat here? We've already told you about **The Great Wok of China, Spaghetti! Spaghetti!,** and the **Bavarian Beer Garden** in Chapter IV: There's also **Naniwa-ya,** which has an old-fashioned Japanese inn setting for popular Japanese food; a **Teppan Steak House;** and, for moderately priced Japanese meals, **Daruma,** where you can check the plastic replicas of the dishes in the window.

Free entertainment, lectures, and demonstrations go on all the time; check the local papers for details. The Royal Hawaiian Shopping Center is open from 9am to 10pm Monday through Saturday, until 9pm on Sunday.

KING'S VILLAGE

It's supposed to look like a 19th-century European town, with its cobblestone streets and old-fashioned architecture, but King's Village is very much a part of modern Honolulu. Behind the gates at the corner of Koa and Kaiulani avenues (across the street from the Hyatt Regency Waikiki, at Hemmeter Center) is a cozy bazaar that contains a variety of shops, several restaurants, and an open market—all done up in a style that recalls the 19th-century monarchy period of Hawaiian history, when royal palaces were built in Honolulu, and Hawaiian kings and queens journeyed to London to be presented at the court of Queen Victoria.

The shops, however, are not so much European as the typical Honolulu-international mix, with lots of Asian and Polynesian crafts, plus plenty of Hawaiian resort wear and souvenirs. All are small and in good taste; King's Village is a commercial venture, certainly, but there's no commercial ugliness about it. We think you'll enjoy browsing here.

Prices at King's Village go from just a little to quite a lot. **Harriet's Custom Made and Ready to Wear,** for one, has held the line on inflation for many a year: ready-to-wear garments begin at $22 for muumuus, $18 for aloha shirts. For custom work, prices begin around $60 and $90 up for muumuus, depending on fabric, size, and style. This is one of the few stores in Waikiki where you can buy fabric by the yard. (We've had excellent comments from readers over the years on the quality and care of their workmanship.) And Harriet has some of the best prices on T-shirts anywhere—really nice all-cotton ones for just $9. A further example of the savings possible: We spotted long beads here for $4.40 that were $6 at a specialty store around the corner; T-shirt clasps that we had seen on Maui for $5 were just $1.50 here. . . . In the area called Bishop Court, **Space Creations** has a wide variety of merchandise; we spotted leather goods, Balinese wood carvings, cuff links, and tie tacks made of shiny U.S. dimes for $21. . . . **Kitamura's** of Kyoto is an outstanding shop here. Collectors come to purchase their Japanese antique dolls, including an extensive collection of samurai dolls. Admire these and the magnificent wedding kimonos from $125 and way up; then content yourself with a T-shirt with a Japanese print—perhaps a Kabuki scene or a samurai portrait—for $12.95. Their unisex cotton yukattas are good buys at $40. . . . You can take home a good wooden tiki for about $45, courtesy of **Hime,** an intriguing wood-carving shop, which has many lower priced items as well, like a collection of whaling figurines. . . . **The Royal Peddler** can always be depended upon for quality brass gifts with a nautical theme, plus the likes of handcrafted music boxes from Italy, scrimshaw, and collectible dolls and clowns. . . . **Casa Tesoro** has lovely things from the Philippines like dresses, tops, linen bags, and children's clothing. We admired their paisley bags, which begin at $18.95.

If you're a fan of European sports cars, don't miss **Euro Motor Emporium,** a "dream car" boutique, chock-full of sports car accessories—at least you could get a cap to go with your Jaguar, Mercedes, or Ferrari.

There's a large branch of the ever-popular **Crazy Shirts** here: We love the Kliban cat designs.

Talk about antique jewelry! How would you like to wear jewels that are at least a million years old? Pendants made of shark's teeth sell for just $3.50 to $5 at **The Fossil Shop,** which also carries minerals, crystals, shells, and handmade boxes in addition to fossils and jewelry. A perfect sandstone ball, formed 180 to 225 million years ago, its color and design induced by a mineral spring containing iron oxides, was found in Utah, and sells here for a mere $25.

Kids will love the dollhouse miniatures at **Village Miniatures,** the Mickey Mouse clothing and toys at **Gift Doll.** And we were thrilled to see dresses and aloha shirts by Malihini—hard to find elsewhere—very well priced at **Judy House** on the top floor. They carry several other lines as well. . . . Some of the little booths on that floor sell those "silky" necklaces from Korea that have become rather hard to find. They run about $5 for three or four, depending on the vendor. . . . Beautiful haku leis (head leis) made of silk and dried flowers can be found at **High Ling Flowers** for $25. Put them on a straw hat for a smashing effect. You can also have your picture put on a plate here for $8. Linda Chen, a prominent floral designer and teacher of flower arrangement, is responsible for the creations here.

King's Village has a number of fast-food outlets and restaurants, including **Sweet Memories** near the fountain up top. It offers goodies such as macadamia iced coffee, pies and cakes, cappuccino and espresso. And it's always good fun to stop by for a drink or a meal (steak and mushroom pie, ploughman's plate) at a new old-English pub, **The Rose & Crown.** Happy hour features neat munchies and continues from 11am to 6:30pm. There are sing-alongs at the piano every night. **Bangkok Orchid** is popular for Thai food, **Odoriki** for Japanese.

There's more to do at King's Village than shop and eat. There are the King's Village Honor Guards to watch, so waxlike that they should be at Madame Tussaud's. The changing-of-the-guard ceremony takes place every night at 6:15. There are often free shows; watch the papers for specific times. Open daily from 9am to 11pm.

THE ATRIUM SHOPS AT HEMMETER CENTER

Towering 44 stories above Kalakaua Avenue between Kaiulani and Uluniu avenues, the multimillion-dollar Hemmeter Center, topped by the very posh and expensive Hyatt Regency Hotel, houses a beautiful and elegant shopping complex. You may do more sightseeing than actual shopping here, but see it you must. The shops surround the central courtyard in three tiers; a spectacular waterfall splashes from the third tier into a crystal pool in the courtyard below. The center part of the courtyard is open at the top, a massive metal sculpture hovers above, and beyond that is the sky. At night the courtyard is lit by massive polished brass lampposts. Combined with the brick-red ceramic-tile floor, it all creates an effect that is at once modern Hawaii and Hawaiian monarchy, each style complementing the other superbly. Sweeping staircases lead to the two upper tiers of shops, as do unobtrusive escalators.

As for the shops, they are a quality collection, and many, like Gucci and Jindo Fur Salon, are in line with the pricey atmosphere of this place. But there are several others for the budget-wise, like **Swim Inn, Nani Fashions II,** and **Hawaii Fashions. . . . The Royal Peddler** is known for gifts in depth, including handsome chess sets and nautical curios. . . . **Cotton Cargo** has some great togs for women. . . . Upscale resort clothes for women and a Mickey Mouse line for children can be found at **Annie's Fashions. . . . Tarbo** is stocked with stylish jewelry, some of it using native materials. . . . **Cal-Oahu** is a worthwhile source for really good shoes, plus lightweight luggage, hats, and bags. . . . Mickey Mouse shirts and paraphernalia can be found at **Yokahama Okadaya. . . .** Pick your favorite gems; there are plenty of sources to choose from: **The Coral Grotto, House of Opal, House of Jade,** and **Jewels of Hawaii** are all here. . . . There's lots of fancy footwork to be seen at **Islander Thongs.** There are now 70 shops on three floors.

A variety of free events takes place here every afternoon, from fashion shows to classes and demonstrations to special entertainment; check the local papers for exact details. The Atrium shops are open daily, from 9am to 11pm.

WAIKIKI SHOPPING PLAZA

The first impression one gets on seeing the enclosed Waikiki Shopping Plaza, 2250 Kalakaua Ave., corner of Seaside, is that it more properly belongs in New York or San Francisco or some sophisticated European city. Shops like Courrèges, Bally of Switzerland, and **Hunting World** have little to do with the islands. But as you ascend the escalators to the four shopping floors, it gets better and more versatile, with more of an island flavor. The traffic-stopper here is the five-story fountain by island designer Bruce Hopper, a wondrous, half-million-dollar creation with lights that change colors, and fascinating Plexiglass spheres and bubbles that make the waters dance. There's a different point of interest at each level, creating new surprises as you ride the escalators.

First, however, let us pose a question: How's your Japanese? If it's not up to snuff (ours isn't), fully half of the stores, their names, and merchandise descriptions will be unintelligible to you. Sticking to English, however, you can still browse around and find a few shops offering good bargains. On the first floor, as you enter from Kalakaua Avenue, is the enormous, two-level **Advantage Hawaii,** which offers good prices on a huge variety of souvenirs, food, aloha wear, and more. We recently spotted Aloha Teddy Bears, on sale for $9. . . . Check the racks at **Villa Roma,** a high-fashion shop for women (they often run clearances on sports items), and also ogle the pretties at their other shop, **Chocolates for Breakfast,** with delectable designer women's clothing. . . . Stock up on some reading matter at **Waldenbooks,** which has a very large selection. . . . Art lovers will enjoy the **Art Forum Gallery,** which also has branches in Tokyo, Osaka, and Los Angeles. . . . All bikinis were $23.95, all one-piece suits were $26.95 at this branch of the **Swimsuit Warehouse.** . . . The owner of the **Hawaii Cloisonee Factory** makes some nice jewelry, fashion artifacts not available anywhere else in the U.S., and not expensive.

Eelskin, in case you hadn't noticed, is that leather from the sea that is extremely popular in Hawaii, and "wholesale outlets" abound: one of the best of these, **Ali Baba Imports,** is right here. Among the huge display of merchandise, we saw well-made eelskin wallets from about $18 to $40, handbags for around $60. We even saw eelskin jewelry—bracelets for $4, necklaces for $10. Note that Ali Baba has another store at the Waikiki Business Plaza, Suite 201, 2270 Kalakaua Ave., and a toll-free ordering number: 800/222-7785. You might also check and comparison-shop several other eelskin stores at the plaza, like **Leather from the Sea** (see above) and *Eelskin Elegance,* where we made some excellent purchases on our last trip.

While most of the shops at the Waikiki Shopping Plaza are not budget-oriented, the basement restaurants certainly are, with a bevy of fast-food counters offering varied ethnic foods. **Marco Polo,** on the fourth floor, has reasonable prices (See "Restaurants," Chapter IV). And in the fourth-floor showroom, nightly at 6:15 and 7:45pm, there's "Voyage," a multi-media extravaganza, describing a tale of Hawaii in music and dance. Shops are open 9am to 9pm daily.

MILITARIA UNLIMITED

Once part of the Fort DeRussy Museum, **The Military Shop of Hawaii,** 1921 Kalakaua Ave., may well be the largest store of its kind in the country. Insignia, military patches from all the services, military models, camouflage clothing, and accessories are all for sale. And there's a large selection of military books as well. For those interested in such things, a fascinating spot. Open every day except Sundays and Christmas, 9am to 6pm (tel. 942-3414).

BEATING THE HIGH PRICE OF POI—FOOD SHOPPING

If you're going to do any cooking in your kitchenette apartment, you're also going to be shocked when you do your first shopping for groceries. Food costs in Honolulu are substantially higher than in big cities on the mainland (almost one-third more, in some cases), and if you pick up your groceries in the hotel shops, sometimes much more than that. (We were stunned recently to have to pay almost $1 more on a quart of grapefruit juice in a hotel shop than it cost in a nearby supermarket.) The hotel shops are a convenience, and we're glad to have them, but if you're going to do any serious shopping, you're far better off taking your rented car and heading for the supermarkets. The big Honolulu chains are **Star, Times, Safeway,** and **Foodland** (and **Emjay's,** a subsidiary of Foodland). There are several of each of these, with addresses in the phonebook. **Gem** on Ward Avenue, and **Holiday Mart,** 801 Kaheka St. (two blocks mauka of the Ala Moana Shopping Center), also offer low prices. In Waikiki, the best food prices (albeit on limited selections) are at the **ABC Discount Stores.**

Natural foods are generally not inexpensive, so we were delighted to find "healthy food at prices that don't make you sick" at **Down to Earth Natural Foods,**

2525 S. King St. (tel. 947-7678), near University Avenue. *Honolulu* magazine has rated this friendly place as the best overall natural-food store in Honolulu. As big as a supermarket, Down to Earth has dozens of bins of grains and beans, a large refrigerator case of organically grown fruits and vegetables, and a Natural Medicine Center that features, among other items, Chinese herbs, including ginseng and "dragon eggs." All products, including vitamin and mineral supplements, are totally vegetarian. Open from 7am to 10pm Monday to Saturday, until 9pm on Sunday. Also on the premises is a natural fast-food restaurant called **Natural Deli,** which observes the same hours.

Just down the block, at 2357 S. Beretania St., is **Kokua Co-op Natural Foods and Grocery,** where you can find a full line of natural foods and organic produce. They have fresh sandwiches, cold drinks, and a wide variety of snacks and gourmet vegetarian deli items. Open daily. Phone 941-1922 for more information.

Terrific baked goods—freshly baked whole-grain breads (oatmeal, raisin, cinnamon, sprouted wheat), pies, and cakes—are the main reason for tracking down one of the popular **Vim and Vigor** stores; you can find them at Ala Moana Center, Kahala Mall, Pearlridge Shopping Center, and elsewhere in Oahu. They also have good prices on an extensive selection of dried fruits, nut butters, fresh produce, and many other natural and organic items. Their snack bars are great, too.

If you'd like to shop for produce, fish, and meat with the local people, be sure to visit the **Ala Moana Farmer's Market** (a block in from the Ala Moana–Ward intersection at Auahi Street), where the atmosphere is pungent and the prices low. It's a great place to get acquainted with local Hawaiian foods and taste sensations. The long, low building is lined with a number of stalls, some with ready-to-eat items. Here you can sample poi, raw fish, and other delicacies such as ogo, palu, and tako. In case you're not feeling all that adventurous, you can settle for a 12-ounce can of New Zealand corned beef or imu kalua pig, both cooked and ready for your own private luau. At **Haili's Hawaiian Foods,** in business since 1867, we saw one-day and two-day poi and even sour poi, all quite difficult to find.

It's also good fun—and good value—to attend one of the **People's Open Markets,** sponsored by the city of Honolulu. Farmers bring their produce to various spots on different days. The market closest to Waikiki takes place on Wednesdays, from 9:45 to 10:45am, at Paki Playground; you'll find it on an outdoor basketball court behind the fire station on Kapahulu Ave., mauka of the Honolulu Zoo.

Get yourself downtown to **King's Bakery** at 1936 S. King St. (tel. 941-5211), which makes an incredibly delicious sweet bread that they will package and airmail to the folks back home. A charge of $13.05 covers the shipping box, two loaves, and postage. Boxes of six and twelve are also available. You can sometimes find these breads sold at the airport, just before you reach the gate to board your plane.

SHOPPING FOR SURFERS

If you're really serious about surfing, or learning to surf, let us point you in the direction of **Local Motion** at 1714 Kapiolani Blvd., near the Ala Moana Shopping Center (tel. 955-SURF). Any surfer will tell you that in order to learn to surf safely and joyously you need good instruction and a well-constructed board. Many of those for rent at beach stands are outdated, hence the need for a source like Local Motion. You can rent a board for $20 for the first day and $15 for every day thereafter. By the week, it's $75. And they also sell snappy sports and leisure clothes. Local Motion is also at the Windward Mall in Kaneohe and at Koko Marina in Hawaii Kai and at the Pearl Kai Shopping Center in Pearl City.

2. Ala Moana Center

Honolulu's fabulous modern shopping center (the largest open-air mall in the world), just across the Ala Moana Beach from Waikiki, is an example of island architecture at its best. Landscaped with trees, flowers, fountains, and a meandering stream down its Central Mall, which is graced with large works of sculpture, Ala Moana Center is always packed with enough island families to make it worth seeing for that reason alone. But the stores are, of course, the main attraction—more than 150 of them, an international bazaar full of intriguing wares. We'll mention just a few, but shopping buffs will come back here many, many times. (From Waikiki, take TheBUS no. 8; it runs on Kuhio Avenue every few minutes.) The center is only 10 minutes away.

One of Hawaii's biggest department stores, **Sears Roebuck,** is here, with the usual mainland amenities and the unusual Hawaiian specialties—like orchid plants (Sears will ship to the mainland and guarantees live delivery), and a tremendous selection of muumuus and island clothing at very reasonable prices. **J.C. Penney** is known for fashion and for excellent value in all departments, as is **Watumull's.** The flagship store of **Liberty House** is here, and most striking it is, its eaves decorated with Hawaiian tapas. Count on top-quality goods in all departments.

We always enjoy browsing around the large Japanese department store **Shirokiya,** which has everything from state-of-the-art stereo to kids' T-shirts that glow in the dark, with a wonderful array of fashion, cosmetics, china, housewares, furniture, and fine arts in between. Its gourmet-food department, on the 2nd floor, is worth a trip in itself. There are dozens of booths and counters here where delicious food is being cooked, baked, and/or sold; at one booth, two young women create Ogura An, divine little filled pancakes; at another, they're turning out Okinawa doughnuts; still more booths offer freshly roasted chestnuts, tasty manapuas, and, of course, a vast array of wonderful sushi and other traditional Japanese fare. You can assemble a meal for yourself out of these offerings, pay at the cash register, and then either take them home or to a little dining lanai to savor on the spot. Most days, from 3:30 to 8pm, there's an evening buffet and sushi bar, priced according to what you eat.

Shirokiya is also a good place to find unusual and inexpensive gift items. Check the luggage accessories counter in particular: handsome coasters with designs of Ukiyoe prints or antique kimonos make marvelous small presents for around $5. Fashion note: Shirokiya also carries socks, with a space for the big toes: You wear these *tabis* with your *zoris,* of course.

There are also dozens of small shops in the center, reflecting just about every interest and taste. **Summer's Place** is a lovely gift shop full of precious stuff, notably scrimshaw, dollhouse miniatures, wind chimes, and unusual greeting cards. They have another shop at Pearlridge Center. . . . **Paniolo Trading** has clothes and accessories for the equestrian (paniolo means "cowboy" in Hawaiian). . . . **Ethel's** has some stylish women's lines, including Liz Claiborne Petites. . . . And **Benetton** brings the Italian sense of style here in vibrantly colored sportswear. **Banana Republic** is a must if you're going on safari, going on a trip, or just want to look stylish. These are not bargain stores, but everything is of great quality for the price.

Quality is also the word at **Elephant Walk,** which has lovely hand-painted shirts, prints, Hawaiian dolls, jewelry, and wood chimes, among other treasures. The level of taste here is consistently high. . . . Fashion is foremost at **Mosaic** and at **Villa Roma. Chocolates for Breakfast** has the sort of elegant clothing for women that never goes out of fashion. . . . Bold, unusual designs grace the sportswear for women at **Defense d'Afficher,** whose shops originate in Paris. . . . Only linen, cotton, and other natural fabrics are used to create the stylish fashions at **Alexia.** . . . Need something neat for the beach, the boat, or the bar? **Latitudes** is the place. . . . Lots of good trinkets and small presents can be found at both **Ala Moana Gifts** and **Products of Hawaii.** At the latter, we saw wind chimes, prints, pot holders, candy, coffee, and many gift items, all at good prices.

Prides of New Zealand seems a bit incongruous in hot Hawaii, selling woolen sweaters, sheepskin rugs, and sheepskin car seats, but the people here swear that sheepskin is cool. . . . Stop in at **Musashiya** for wonderful patterns and fabrics, or pick up a surfboard at lively **Hawaiian Island Creations. . . . Tahiti Imports** takes

Tahitian prints of their own design and makes them into muumuus, aloha shirts, bikinis, and pareaus. They also sell their exquisite hand-printed fabrics by the yard.

The Sharper Image, the catalog store to end all catalog stores, is a fabulous playground for adults, so even if you have to push along the aisles with the crowds, don't miss it. Come in and try their exercise bikes, the self-massage table or massage chair (soothing after a hard day's shopping), and scads of other curiosities.

We picked up several gifts on our last trip from **The Compleat Kitchen and More.** A company called What a Melon creates charming designs of Hawaiian flowers and fruits with a motto reading "Grown in Hawaii," and puts them on pot holders, aprons, towels, and more. We love their Manoa Lettuce Bag, with instructions in pidgin: "Mo bettah den da plastic from da supermarket." Agreed. . . . **Island Shells** has lots of stunning jewelry, shell and wood chimes, shell roses, and the like, and prices are always fair. And their shell flower arrangements are beautiful. . . . It's fun to go fly a kite in Honolulu, and the place to get your equipment is at **High Performance Kites,** right near the centerstage. Many of their kites come from one of our favorite places on Molokai, the Big Wind Kite Factory. . . . Also near the centerstage, and in a sense the "heart" of the shopping center, is the **Honolulu Book Store,** with superb selections in every category, especially Hawaiiana, and newspapers that may—or may not—make you nostalgic for home, like the *Los Angeles Times, San Francisco Chronicle, New York Times,* and *Wall Street Journal.*

Need some decorating ideas? Striking posters, many with an Eastern motif, begin around $30 at the **Art Board.** . . . Many fine prints and posters can be found at **Art Avenue.** . . . **Otsuka Galleries** specializes in Asian art. . . . **Iida's** is crammed with colorful Japanese giftware and decorations.

Feet getting to you? The **Slipper House** is a good place to replace whatever worn-out sandals you're trudging around in. They claim to have the widest selection of casual footwear in the state, with over 400 styles of made-in-Hawaii sandals, including hard-to-find golf slippers with cleats, for $22. They also have hard-to-find cotton *tabis* for $11.50, and a wide array of lightweight totes and carrying bags. . . . Best known for traditional men's and boy's wear, beautifully made and well priced, **Reyn's** also features good-looking women's clothes. Many shops on Oahu and the neighbor islands as well. . . . For over 25 years, **Irene's Hawaiian Gifts** has been a favorite with residents and visitors alike for unique island gifts. Their specialty is unusual carvings from native woods and collectors' items, like Hawaiian dolls, bells, birds, and sea life, made locally and sold at good prices. . . . Candles in the shape of Hawaiian tikis and pineapples make novel presents. You'll find them at the **Hale Kukui Makai Candle Shop.** . . . Check in at the big **Vim and Vigor Health Food Store** for excellent selections of honey, nut butters, whole grains, organic foods, superb home-baked goods that should not be missed, and other healthies. . . . Stop in, too, at the **Crackseed Center,** if you want to know what Hawaiian youngsters clamor for (crackseeds, originally a Chinese confection, are a cross between seeds and candies—very sticky, very tasty).

Coffee-lovers should definitely pay a visit to **Gloria Jean's Coffee Bean,** where coffees from all over the world (not just Kona coffee) are featured. They're available by the cup and by the package. And the aromas are irresistible. . . . Chocaholics, too, will find the temptations at Ala Moana hard to resist, like the chocolates at **Ed and Don's** and **See's Candies.** And forget we ever told you about **Mrs. Field's Chocolate Chippery,** which turns out warm and moist cookies studded with chips, sold individually, or by the pound at around $7 to $8.

The newest addition to Ala Moana is **Palm Boulevard,** which is being called the Rodeo Drive of Honolulu. Budgeteers won't find much to buy here, but it's always fun to browse at the likes of Alion, Chanel, Polo/Ralph Lauren, Georg Jensen Silver, Gucci, Jaeger, and Adrienne Vittadini, to drop just a few names.

One of the most intriguing stores at Ala Moana is the **Foodland Supermarket.** It's like an international food fair, reflecting the cultures that make up Hawaii—and the rest of the world. You walk along seemingly endless aisles of exotic foods: fresh-frozen coconut milk, packages of weird-looking Japanese dried fish, health foods, tortillas, English biscuits, French cheese, you name it—if it's edible, this place has got it. The salad bar includes kim chee, lomi-lomi salmon, and fresh poi, so create your own lunch. You can, in addition, pick up some okolehao, Hawaii's potent ti-root drink, in the large liquor department. If life has become boring in that little kitchenette of yours, don't miss a visit here. There's also an inexpensive souvenir section.

For more bargains in souvenirs and small items at Ala Moana, it's trusty old **ABC Discount Stores, Long's,** and **Woolworth's.** Check out the weekly specials at the latter; we recently saw a $6.79 bag of Lion Brand Coffee selling for $5.29.

The best bargains at Ala Moana are available when the stores take to the sidewalks—the ground-floor level, that is—displaying racks and racks of clothing for very low prices.

Remember the center, too, for free entertainment during local holidays and at special ethnic celebrations; you may catch a Japanese or Philippine dance group, a Hawaiian show, or some of the island's top nightclub entertainers. For years now, the **Young People's Hula Show,** presented every Sunday at 9:30am on the centerstage, has been a Honolulu institution. Don't miss it. A more-or-less continuous program of local events and entertainment takes place on the centerstage.

Should you wish to make a contribution to various Hawaiian charities and educational organizations, you can do so easily. A kiosk on the street level called **Worthies** sells T-shirts of various attractive designs created by Clarence Lee, all bearing the legend "Ala Moana Center Hawaii." The cost is $12, and proceeds go to benefit charities. A worthy idea.

RESTAURANTS AT ALA MOANA

Ala Moana Center has always been one of the best locales in town for inexpensive dining. And the 850-seat, glass-enclosed dining court called Makai Market, on the makai (sea) side of the center, makes the possibilities for entertaining eating here better than ever. We'll begin at the market, then move on to some other center choices.

At Makai Market

Makai Market is served by a score of self-service specialty kitchens. Name your desire—Hawaiian, Italian, New York deli, seafood, Japanese, Chinese, health food—the food is here and you can put together a meal for around $3 to $4 at lunch, $5 to $6 at dinner. You serve yourself, then take your food to the pretty tables under the bright buntings overhead. A Hawaiian trio plays here Friday from 5:30 to 7:30pm. You can start with a drink from the center bar with its "Let's Make a Daiquiri" neon sign; daiquiris, piña coladas, and other favorites are about $3 to $4, and there are smoothies and nonalcoholic cocktails as well.

Take a look around and see what you might like. **Thirst Aid Station** has "Remedies and Prescriptions" that include sodas, smoothies, yogurt, and soup (62¢ to $2.21). . . . **Tsuruya Noodle Soup** dishes up bowls of hot soba or udon, from $3.25 to $5.15. . . . at **Sbarro Pizza,** folks line up for the calzone, under $3.50, and for specials like baked ziti Sicilian style and garden salad, $4.49.

Panda Express has Mandarin dishes on one side, Szechuan on the other. On the Mandarin side, try the spicy chicken with peanuts at $2.95, or go Szechuan with roast duck at $3.25. . . . There's no way you can miss **Hawaiian Poi Bowl,** which dishes out food from a bright-red lunchwagon. There's a teri-chicken plate and a poi-bowl combo, from $3.25 to $4.95.

Yummy **Korean BBQ** has full-meal combo plates at $4.95, lunch or dinner. . . . **The Aloha Grill Bar** has its own bar seats on which to enjoy their budget deluxe burgers at $1.25. . . . At **La Cocina,** jumbo burritos served with beans and rice are $3.95, with other Mexican combo dishes up to $4.95. . . . Pasta and pizza in the traditional way are featured at **Sbarro;** ziti, calzone, spaghetti, lasagne, and tortellini primavera are all served with garlic rolls at prices from $4 to $5.

Looking for light food? Try the **Kitchen Garden,** which offers croissant sandwiches and salads, plus baked potatoes, plain and fancy; both quiche and chili go for

$4.50. . . . For a cholesterol feast, however, we might suggest **Kiawe-Q-Ribs,** where you can get kiawe-wood-smoked pork, beef brisket, ham, chicken, or turkey to take out at $4.25 to $5.95 a pound or to eat on a hot French roll at $3.95; and **La Rotisserie,** which offers a fried-food buffet including seafood, beef Burgundy, and mahimahi in ginger butter from $4 to $5—as well as a delicious seafood salad for $5.99.

For years before Makai Market opened, **Patti's Chinese Kitchen** and **Lyn's Delicatessen** were bywords among visitors and locals alike. Now they've moved into the market and they are still mighty crowd pleasers. Patti's is famous for its plate lunches; for a choice of any two items, the price is $3.25, $4.20 for three items, $4.95 for four. These might include Peking-style roast duck, beef with broccoli, shrimp roll, shoyu chicken, sweet-and-sour fish, crispy almond duck, and on and on, ad delicious infinitum. Considering that these dishes are not cooked to order, they are still tasty and certainly a lusty bargain meal. As for Lyn's, it's long been one of the best kosher-style delis in town, known for thick corned beef and pastrami sandwiches ($3 to $3.70), lox and bagels, fragrant and garlicky hot dogs, plus plate lunches, and very special buys on steak dinners.

Want more? **Orson's Chowderette** is a small version of the popular Orson's in Ward Warehouse. Finger foods like fish nuggets and clam strips are $2.15; chowder —New England, Manhattan, or seafood—$2; salads like shrimp and crab, $4.15 to $5.25; and burgers of mahimahi, shrimp, or oysters, $2.35 to $2.85. . . . You can sample Thai food—plate lunches from $2.79 to $4.55, spring rolls $1.89—at **Little Cafe Siam.** No MSG here!. . . . **Wingo** is fine when you crave fried chicken; it's served on a jumbo plate for $3.99.

Makai Market is open weekdays from 9:30am to 9pm, Saturdays from 9:30am to 5pm, and Sundays from 10am to 5pm. It occupies a half acre of space, serves 13,000 meals a day, and employs over 500 people—who obviously don't starve.

Ala Moana Restaurants Outside Makai Market

Should you feel the need for something a little more in the peace-and-quiet department, where you might sit down with friends in a comfortable atmosphere and enjoy a leisurely, reasonably priced meal, try **Bella's Coffee House** (tel. 955-7891), where you can relax in turquoise-and-pink booths under cooling ceiling fans. Lunch is satisfying, with such dishes as mahimahi at $5.40, chopped sirloin at $4.90, and interesting combos at $6 to $7.50. Sandwiches, as low as $3.10, are served with soup and your choice of french fries or macaroni; we recently sampled a good cream-of-broccoli soup and a mahimahi sandwich for under $6. At dinner, the menu remains basically the same, but prices go up about $1 and dessert is included. There are several well-priced specials each day.

For an all-American meal, there's **Peppermill** (tel. 946-4044), a few doors away. It's cafeteria style with pleasant seating: tables are wood, chairs reed, tiled floors beige. Lamps add a colonial touch. The roast beef sandwich, $3.95, is very popular. Homemade soup and salad are served with a freshly baked half-loaf of bread at $3.75. A half avocado filled with chicken mango or shrimp is $5.50. Hot daily specials like half of a roasted chicken; authentic Indian curry; homemade meat loaf, served with a starch and hot vegetables, are in the $5.50 to $7.50 bracket. All entrees include soup or salad. We found the portions liberal and a cut above standard fast food.

There must be plenty of natural-food enthusiasts in Honolulu; they mob the wonderful take-out counter at **Vim and Vigor** every lunchtime. Vegetarian sandwiches like tofu burger, veggie burger, and nut-and-mushroom burger, around $3.95 are popular; so, too, are sandwiches like turkey breast, bacon, lettuce, and tomato, and roasted pork, as well as tostadas, burritos, and plate lunches like brown rice and veggies, $4.25. Try one of their cooling smoothies, or fruit drinks made to order from fresh island fruits, in the middle of a hot Honolulu afternoon. Too bad there's no seating area, but there are benches outside. If you like unusual breads, take home a loaf of whole-wheat sweet bread, sprouted wheat, or carrot-onion!

On that same rear level, you can join local Japanese families having dinner, from

4 to 9pm, at **Wong's Okazu-ya.** That's when they prepare such Japanese specialties as shoyu butter fish with tofu and vegetables, sukiyaki, and combination tempura plates, from about $4.75 to $7.50. Meals include soup, tsukemono, rice, and tea. The rest of the day, from 8am to 4pm, they'll fix you up with a hearty bowl of wonton min, saimin, or special ramen for $3.05 to $3.80. In addition, you can choose your own plate lunch from their delicatessen, which has over 50 items, including sushi, chow mein, fried rice, and teriyaki. The average plate lunch costs $4 to $5.

VITAL STATISTICS

Most Ala Moana Center establishments stay open seven days a week, opening at 9:30am Monday through Saturday, at 10am on Sunday. They close at 9pm Monday through Friday, at 5:30pm on Saturday, and at 5pm on Sunday. From Kalakaua Avenue in Waikiki, you can take TheBUS no. 8 and you'll be at Ala Moana (barring traffic) in about 10 minutes. Parking areas are numerous—and they even have coconut palms coming through the concrete! If you should have any trouble finding a parking space, however, you can get valet service at peak shopping times and on holidays. Just drive up on the mall (or second) level, and around to the ocean side. Smack in the middle, midway between Sears and Liberty House, you will find the service. The cost is $2, plus tip.

JUST OUTSIDE ALA MOANA CENTER

There's a very special crafts shop across the road and one block mauka of Ala Moana Center. **Creative Fibers** at 450 Piikoi St. is a find. It carries everything from needles and thread to glamorous batik jackets from Bali. Exotic cottons from Asia and Europe are stacked next to pareaus, under $6 a yard. There are *molas* from Central America, Indian spreads, and other unusual fabrics. You'll find beads and trinkets and jewelry, Turkish hand-weaves, silk scarves, marvelous indigo cotton fabric designed by Escher of Holland and inspired by themes from Java. Kits for making fabric nursery-rhyme books are $6, and a delight. Closed Sundays.

---

3. Around Town

WARD WAREHOUSE

One of the most eye-catching of Honolulu's shopping centers is Ward Warehouse, located on Ward Avenue between Auahi Street and Ala Moana, across from Fisherman's Wharf. More than 65 shops and restaurants occupy the handsome two-story structures fashioned out of great rough-hewn planks, and there seems to be a higher-than-usual level of taste and selectivity here. Many are decorator shops of interest primarily to residents, but there is an equal number to delight the visitor.

A dazzling showplace for handcrafts is the **Artist Guild,** a gallery and outlet for many local craftspersons: You'll see beautiful ceramics, leaded glass, fine furniture made of local hardwoods, flower pillows, jewelry, modern and traditional metal sculpture, and soft sculpture. Note the Old Hawaiian prints (from $12), and lovely notepapers, too. . . . You'll find art posters from Hawaii—and just about everywhere else—at the **Art Board,** which shows Luigi Fumigalli, among other popular local artists. Note their collection of original photographs, and T-shirts bearing designs by such leading artists as Robert Lyn Nelson and Dean Howell. . . . Fine art posters, art reproductions, and original prints may also be found at **Frame Shack.** Nicely matted small prints begin at $4. . . . If you're in town for a while and want to learn the fine art of making artificial flowers, stop in at **The Extra Dimension,** which sells beautiful flowers and gift items and represents the Miyuki Art Flower Studio of Hawaii. All the flowers are made of different fabrics and are quite handsome.

The most striking women's clothing at Ward Warehouse might well be the fashions found at **Mamo Howell, Inc.,** a store new to the center. Mamo Howell was a well-known island hula dancer and later became a Christian Dior model in Paris. She's turned her artistic flair to designing, and the results are stunning muumuus long and short; their inspiration comes mostly from Hawaiian-quilt motifs. Her designs are unmistakable once you've seen them—and you'll see them on the best-dressed women in town. Dresses are out of our price range (they go upward of $135), but quite affordable and also lovely are an array of small items using similar patterns, especially the quilted and unquilted tote bags, lined with nylon, $25 to $35. Mamo does charming children's clothing, too.

Kinnari has been a longtime favorite at Ward Warehouse, for unusual women's clothing. Here Yupin, a lissome Thai lady, designs creative dresses, skirts, and blouses; a touch of appliqué floral design, patchwork or hand-embroidery sets each apart from the others. Considering the quality and the fact that minor alterations are included in the price of the garment, prices of $95 and up are understandable.

Pomegranates in the Sun has established a loyal following of fashion-conscious women in the few years that it's been here. It features local artists and designers inspired by the Hawaiian atmosphere. There are many one-of-a-kind items. Although prices are not generally inexpensive, we saw delightful cotton sundresses at $55, tops at $30 and $40, designer umbrellas from Australia at $28.

Birkenstock Footprints deserves your attention: It's the place to get those ugly-looking, marvelous-feeling, naturally contoured Birkenstock sandals that give you a "barefoot on the beach" sensation even on hard surfaces. They're for men, women, and kids of all ages, and the average price is about $75 for adults, $56 for children. With your feet all nice and comfy, you're ready to continue your explorations of Ward Warehouse. You may want to pick up some Christmas ornaments from **Kris Kringle's Den,** or some gorgeous fans among the Chinese arts and crafts at **Heavenly Lotus.** . . . Note the lovely jewelry, handmade crafts from around the world, shell mirrors and feather leis at **Ono Gallery,** the potpourris, sachets, and lacy and frilly things for bed and bath at **Private World.**

The **Executive Chef** is for the compulsive cook; we saw wineglasses, cookie molds, French copperware, and other kitchen joys, at good prices. One of their niftiest items is the Vacu-Vin, a wine resealing system for home use, $20. And if that isn't enough, they'll sell you a home version of the Cruvinet for $200. You could also settle for a foil cutter for wine bottles for just $6.95.

Next door to Executive Chef is a new shop run by the same management, **Bath and Butler,** which features bath and travel accessories as well as unique personal care items. You could get a Hawaiian print umbrella for $35, maybe a witty item like a sponge in the shape of a sneaker for $14.50. . . . Every kind of athletic shoe and then some is available at **Runners Route Plus.** . . . and **Island Sunspot** is the place for swimwear for men and women.

Conscientious Honolulu mommies shop **Child's Play** for creative play and learning materials, educational toys, and books. An excellent selection. . . . They collect dollhouse miniatures in the gigantic dollhouse that is **My Favorite Things.** . . . And moms-in-waiting, or those who've already delivered, find **In Bloom** just what they've been looking for: attractive maternity and baby clothes under one roof. As soon as baby gets older, they graduate to **In Bloom the Next Generation,** which has charming clothing, furniture, and gifts for children from age 2 up. . . . Children of all ages, and men and women, too, love the line of "Native clothing," all made from pure hand-woven cotton and hand-printed in original designs, at **The Native Company.**

Imported women's clothing, much of it from Bali, can be found on the first floor of **Imports International.** Walk up one flight to see their collection of baskets, wicker, rattan, paintings, wood carvings, sheepskin, silver jewelry, cloisonné, and more. . . . Silk flowers and plants blossom realistically at **Greenhouse Magic;** it's hard to tell their orchid and hibiscus plants from the real thing. Lovely silk leis are $6.95. . . . Quality gift items—inlaid music boxes, scrimshaw, Italian porcelain antiques and collectibles—are easy to find at **Traditions.** . . . Need a book or a tape, a newspaper or greeting card? **Waldenbooks** has a large branch here, and they'll order any book for you, at no extra charge.

End your excursion, perhaps, at the **Coffee Works,** a charming shop that purveys all manner of imported coffees, teas, and chocolates, as well as some very attractive vessels from which to sip them. Coffee makers too. Happiness is a slice of carrot cake and a cup of café Vienna, at their adjoining café whose specialties are roast beef, turkey, tuna, or veggie sandwiches, served with lettuce, tomatoes, bell peppers, and cheese, quite a mouthful for $5.25.

We've told you about the **Chowder House** for a quick seafood meal, the **Old Spaghetti Factory** for pasta in a fabulous setting, and **Dynasty II** for a Chinese buffet lunch, and **Restaurant Benkai** for some fabulous Japanese buffet meals. **Stuart Anderson's Cattle Company** is locally famous for well-priced prime ribs and chicken dinners, served in an upbeat setting with a great view of Kewalo Boat Basin. For light snacks, choose among the fast-food stands (seating in a central courtyard) at the **Food Express** (everything from burgers to saimin to health-food salads), or visit **Harpo's** for pizza. There are outside tables on the lower level.

Look for **The Art Cove** at Ward Warehouse. Since a different local artist is featured each day, you get a chance to meet and talk with the artist, perhaps buy some of his or her work at studio—not gallery—prices.

Ward Warehouse's Amphitheatre hosts a variety of events and entertainment, from tea dances to flower shops to bon dances and then some. Shopping hours are 10am to 9pm Monday through Friday, until 5pm on Saturday, and from 11am to 4pm on Sunday. Restaurants stay open until late in the evening. From Waikiki, take TheBUS no. 8 (except those marked "Waikiki Beach and Hotels") from Kuhio Avenue, or Kalia Road. It's about a 15-minute ride from Waikiki.

WARD CENTRE

Down the road a block, at 1200 Ala Moana Blvd., Ward Centre is a worthy follow-up to Ward Warehouse, another sophisticated collection of boutiques and restaurants, all with a high level of charm and taste. The emphasis is on small, very expensive boutiques, so we usually find ourselves coming here to eat at some of our favorite restaurants—**Compadres, Crêpe Fever, Mocha Java, Keo's at Ward Centre, Andrew's, Monterey Bay Canners, Ryan's Parkplace,** and **Big Ed's Deli** (see Chapter III, "Honolulu: Restaurants") and doing a lot of just looking, thanks, at the pricey shops. But it is fun to explore **Sedona,** "Your New Age Resource," a delightful store whose cactus in the window and crystals, jewelry and such are reminiscent of that new age town in Arizona. Check for news of the latest metaphysical happenings, perhaps pick up some Tinkerbells—"spherical meditation bells used to summon the nature spirits." Anytime after noon you can get a psychic reading here: $15 for 10 minutes, $25 for 20. . . .

Small women should definitely have a look at **Size Me Petite,** a shop with stylish collections. . . . If you want a really classy hat, **Honolulu Hat Company** is the place. No need now to make a special trip to their original store on S. King Street; the new branch at Ward Centre carries a huge selection of Panama hats (from $25), lauhala headgear (from $45) and hand-stitched feather hatbands, too. A very special store. . . . **Ross Sutherland,** one of the oldest quality-menswear stores in Honolulu, has a new branch here.

Peony Arts is stocked with fragrances, potpourris, and other accessories for bed, bath, and table. You might pick up a lacy handkerchief, an embroidered apron, or some bits of fragrance, like English soap leaves. For a unique and inexpensive gift, get some vaporizing oil to put on a lamp, imported from England, at $3.50 to $10. . . . You can pick up attractive women's shoes, handbags, and sportswear at **The Shop for Pappagallo.** . . . Art lovers will want to spend time at Ward Centre's two galleries: **Images International,** which shows some of Hawaii's top local artists and also has Asian prints that begin around $40; and **Art A La Carte,** a cooperative venture featuring the work of a dozen local artists who take turns "sitting" the gallery and often work right here. Unframed works begin at $25, matted cards at $10.

Of course, you'll want to stop by **Mary Catherine's** for "an extraordinary bakery experience"; this European-style bakery uses only fresh and natural ingredients, avoids additives and imitation flavors, and produces divine breads (brioches, baguettes, challah, a very popular French sourdough multigrain), as well as even more divine cakes and pastries on the order of chocolate-mousse cake or guava or passion-mandarin cake. If you just can't wait to sample the goodies, repair to the tables a few steps up, in the rear. . . . While your taste buds are thus activated, saunter over to **R. Field Wine Co.** at the opposite end of Ward Centre: in addition to fine wines, it stocks the likes of dried morels imported from France, smoked butterfish, Beluga caviar, top-of-the-line pastas and cheeses flown in from Europe, plus the remarkable Clearbrook preserves. . . . Satisfying your sweet tooth, you can get the fabulous Crêpe Dentelle milk chocolate, Irish cream, strawberry, or cappuccino cordials, divine Kona coffee beans or macadamia-nut popcorn among other goodies at **Honolulu Chocolate Company,** which also sells Valrhona—considered the world's finest chocolates. Watch out for the prices on this, however. We saw a chocolate bar for $5.75!

Ready for a bit of a splurge? Have an unforgettable lunch or dinner at **Il Fresco;** it's one of the best Northern Italian–Cajun style restaurants anywhere, and their goat-cheese specialties and pasta dishes are extraordinary. Top-rated!

To reach Ward Centre, again take TheBUS no. 8 from Waikiki, a 15-minute ride.

DESIGNER DISCOUNTS

Just opposite Ward Centre, at 1112 Auahi St., is a shop known to few tourists; but **The Ultimate You** (tel. 523-3888), which might be called the "Bergdorf Goodman of the consignment shops," is very well known indeed to Hawaii's most fashion-conscious women. This is where they come for new and next-to-new high fashion at surprisingly low prices. Owner Kelsey Sears has contacts with socialites and celebrities in the islands, in California, and in Europe; when they get slightly bored with their designer duds after wearing or two (or when they've compulsively bought five-of-a-kind sweaters and never worn them), they send them to Sears, who resells them for anywhere from 50% to 90% off retail price. She insists that everything be in "pristine condition." Half of the store consists of brand-new merchandise, much of it from European designers, that is also heavily discounted. Obviously, the stock here changes daily, so you never can tell what you will find, but it's worth a look-see. Some examples: A $3,000 Gucci alligator handbag sold for $495; a $600 Yves St. Laurent skirt for $90; brand new, $150 Hermès scarves for $29; and $300 garments worn once or twice for $80 or $90. A $100 dress could go for as little as $49, a $75 silk blouse for as little as $25. "Every day minimiracles happen here," Sears says.

Since the shop deals with the island's best-known celebrities, we asked the inevitable question. No, there has been no sign of Imelda Marcos's shoes.

The Ultimate You is open from 11am to 6pm, Monday through Saturday.

Before you leave the area, stop in at **Private Collections,** a few doors away at 1108 Auahi St. (tel. 528-1822). Brigiha Bennett and Gwen Nagata, who used to work at The Ultimate You, have opened a charming little store selling unique jewelry and crystals, with an emphasis on silver jewelry. Prices begin at just a dollar, and go way up for the finest gemstones.

DOWNTOWN HONOLULU

Downtown is where the local people do a lot of their shopping, and we'll let you in on a kamaaina secret known to very few tourists. Head for 1 N. King St., where **Liberty House's Penthouse** is located. Discounted merchandise from all the Liberty House stores around town is brought here, and the initial reduction is a whopping 50%. On top of that, the price is automatically dropped another 35% on the first Monday of each succeeding month. Most of the items consist of women's and children's clothing, but occasionally you'll see men's aloha shirts and other menswear, as well. On a recent shopping foray we found $100 handbags at $50; $150 dresses at $75, and $30 aloha shirts at $15. Enough said? At their clearing-house, you can also get towels, sheets, pots and pans, and gift items at 50% off. This is one of those places where on some days you'll find nothing suitable, on other days you'll strike it rich!

The rest of Liberty House and the other Fort Street stores have merchandise similar to what you find in their Waikiki and Ala Moana branches, but perhaps a shade more citified, since they cater mostly to a local trade. It's fun to come here during the lunch hour, when local people are shopping, eating lunch on the many stone benches and seats that dot this fountained area, and watching their kids play in the sand. Traffic is closed off, creating one long window-shopping promenade. If you're hungry, stop off at any of the restaurants or fast-food stands mentioned in Chapter III (**Rada's Piroshki** is at 1144–1146 Fort Street Mall).

If garment factories appeal to you, there's one you can be taken to, free and with extras thrown in. The **Hilo Hattie Fashion Center,** at 700 Nimitz Hwy., offers something like 40,000 Hawaiian fashions to browse through, all for sale at factory prices, plus free refreshments, free alterations, a lei greeting, and even a free bus trip to its doors. (They'll also take you to the Dole Pineapple Cannery.) And the **Crazy Shirts Factory Outlet,** 1095 Dillingham Blvd., is just a block away. Phone 537-2926, or check the tourist papers to find out where you can pick up the Fashion Center Fun Bus; or simply take TheBUS no. 8, marked "Airport," from Waikiki or Ala Moana.

Anyone who likes stuffed bears will be delighted with a **Bear in Mind,** 1171 S. King St. (tel. 521-2284), at the corner of Piikoi. Owners Al and Amy stock hundreds of collectible bears, from Steiff all the way down to little travel bears you can carry in your pocket, as well as anything you can think of in bear-related items, such as stationery, erasers, pencils, T-shirts, rubber stamps, or notepads. Open weekdays from 10am to 5:30pm, Saturday only until 3:30pm.

Speaking of bears, would you believe house calls by teddy bears? **Bearmania in Hawaii** runs a "bear mobile" that will come to your hotel with hundreds of teddy bears to choose from, ranging from $5 to $150, as well as stickers and novelties from 50¢ and up. They also invite you to mail your bear to Hawaii; they'll put it on the "Bear Trail to Paradise" and send it back to you with photos of your bear in various Hawaiian scenes. Phone 395-BEAR and ask for Yvonne Bear Becker. You read both her name and number correctly. Or write her at 777 Kapiolani Blvd., #2007, Honolulu, HI 96813.

THE CHINATOWN LEI SELLERS

When local people need to buy leis, they usually head for Chinatown—and so should you. Although leis are sold all over town, especially at the airport and on the ocean side of Kalakaua Avenue, the best prices and finest quality can usually be found among the Chinatown lei sellers. There are several stores on Maunakea Street; some of our favorites are **Cindy's Lei Shoppe** at no. 1034, **Violet's** at no. 1165, **Jenny's Lei Stand** at no. 1151, **Lin's** at no. 1017. **Lita's Leis** is around the corner at 59 N. Beretania St., and **Aloha** is at the corner of Puuahi. Local friends advise that Cindy and Lita both make beautiful haku head leis that dry splendidly and can be worn for a long time. Cindy's carries the largest selection of flower leis in the state, and all six make up orchid, plumeria, double carnation, and other leis, at prices ranging from $3 to $8 and up, depending on the season and the availability of flowers. Should you want to send leis to your friends back home—a lovely but no longer inexpensive gift—the price, by Express Mail, will be about $27 and up. We also like the flowers—and the low prices—at **Chiyo's,** located inside and at the front of the Thrifty Drugstore at 3610 Waialae Ave. in the Waialae-Kahala area. You can shop by phone (tel. 734-6337 or 737-5055), and be assured that your order will be well and speedily taken care of. They'll bill you later.

If you'll see your friends within a day or two of your arrival, it's cheaper to carry flowers with you. Better still, give your friends the flower leis your Hawaiian friends will doubtless drape around your neck as they bid you aloha—if you can bear to part with them.

Buyers beware: The most expensive times to buy leis are May Day, the graduation season (end of May), and New Year's; that's when $3 vanda leis can suddenly become $12!

MAUNAKEA MARKETPLACE

Under construction at press time, the Maunakea Marketplace should be open by the time you read this. With street frontage on Hotel, Pauahi, and Maunakea streets, it is in the heart of Honolulu's revitalized historic Chinatown. It contains an open market, retail shops, restaurants, and an interior courtyard able to accommodate a thousand people for cultural events and local entertainment. Covering an acre, this is the largest retail-shopping complex in downtown Honolulu. Full details in our next edition.

FOR RENT

If you need to rent something while you're in Honolulu—maybe a TV set or a radio, a stroller, even wheelchairs or crutches, we have a terrific place to recommend: **Dyan's Rental.** Their rates are low, they deliver to your hotel cheerfully and promptly, and they're very nice to do business with. Just call them at 531-5207, and a delivery person will emerge from their huge downtown warehouse with exactly what you need.

Rent-A-Center is good to know about should you need VCRs, video cameras, FAX machines, typewriters, word processors, and other electronic paraphernalia. Call them at 947-9933.

BARGAIN HUNTERS' HEAVENS

A mecca for penny-pinchers, **Holiday Mart** is in a residential neighborhood at 801 Kaheka St. (two blocks mauka of the Ala Moana Shopping Center). It's a huge discount store, jammed with local people busy buying everything from groceries to books to toys to toasters, all at fat discounts. Buys are especially good if you watch for specials in Hawaiian wear for men, women, and keikis. While you're here, stock up on groceries and booze—the prices are excellent, much better than in the smaller stores at the beach. If it's time for lunch, you can join the crowd at the outside Chinese cafeteria deli, which has a good take-out department, as well as some 20 items on the steam table. Holiday Mart is open every day from 8am to midnight, until 10pm on Sunday.

Visit the factory store of **Blair's,** at 404-A Ward Ave., for good buys in seconds of their fine monkeypod, koa, and other wood carvings, known for many years for excellent quality. Some of these factory store items may have small flaws, but they can be repaired, and the savings are huge. (Many of our readers have been happy with their purchases here.)

FLEA MARKETS

Dauntless shoppers who enjoy flea markets have two to choose from in Honolulu. The **Aloha Flea Market,** at Aloha Stadium, is the biggest, with some 1,000 booths to browse through. It's on every Wednesday, Saturday, and Sunday from 6am to 3pm. You can get there by TheBUS no. 20 from Waikiki to Aloha Stadium, or, to go in style, take the private Aloha Flea Market Shuttle Bus, which takes you there and back in an air-conditioned coach with a large baggage section for your purchases. The $6 fare includes admission. The **Kam Super Swap Meet** is held at the Kam Drive-In, across from Pearlridge Center every day of the week, beginning at 6am. Wednesday is considered the busiest day. Take TheBUS no. 20 from Waikiki. Admission to both flea markets is under $1.

T-SHIRT SECRETS

You'll see **Crazy Shirt** stores all over the Hawaiian Islands—everybody loves their clever designs and sayings. They make great presents, too, so if you want to buy a lot of them, you can save a bundle by going to one of their two outlet stores in Honolulu. One of the stores is at 4410 Lawehane (adjacent to Costco, near Pearl Harbor). The other was in the process of moving at the time of this writing, so look it up in the phone book or ask information. At both, you can get discontinued styles, factory seconds, and display merchandise for 50% off retail prices; they frequently have special closeouts, which knock the prices down even further—to as much as 75% to 85% off retail. Neat!

WHOLESALE HEIRLOOM JEWELRY

Greg Reeser is an extremely talented young man who wholesales Hawaiian Heirloom Jewelry to the public. His company, **Precious Metals Hawaii**, 1600 Kapiolani Blvd., Suite 616 (tel. 955-6657), is not only the largest manufacturer of such jewelry in the state, but also aims to have the best prices as well: these begin at $36 for a solid gold pendant enameled with either your name in Hawaiian or with initials. When the last Hawaiian queen, Liliuokalani, attended Queen Victoria's jubilee, she was given a gift of a bracelet that inspired this style of jewelry so popular in Hawaii today. When a return gift was brought to the current queen of England, Greg Reeser was chosen as its designer. In addition to bracelets, he created special rings, pendants, rope chains, and earrings. Hours are Monday through Friday from 9am to 5pm, Saturday to 4pm.

MUUMUU MADNESS

Saving money on muumuus is great fun: Why pay $70 or $80 or more for a muumuu is a department store or fancy resort shop when you can pay about half if you know where to look? In addition to **Hilo Hattie** (see above), we have some special bargain favorites. **Island Muumuu Works**, 660 Ala Moana and at Dole Cannery Square, sells Hilda of Hawaii muumuus at just one price: $43. They also have pretty head or hat leis made of silk flowers and leaves, which go for about $30. Aloha shirts are $20.50. Open Monday through Saturday from 9am to 5 or 6pm. There are also stores at Maui Mall in Kahului, Maui, and at Dickenson Square in Lahaina, Maui.

Princess Kaiulani, the manufacturer who first started using the pretty small-figured calico prints in pastel colors, opens its attractive factory showroom at 1222 Kaumaulii St. (tel. 847-4806) to the public Monday through Saturday from 9am to 5pm. You won't see the models currently in such stores as Liberty House and the better specialty shops, but you will find equally lovely ones with slightly different fabrications. This manufacturer's long muumuus start at about $150 retail; you can find some beauties here for $65 and up. We saw some divine jumpsuits for $45 last time we visited; they would have been about $75 retail. Princess Kaiulani's dresses are ultra-feminine, with eyelet or lace or ruffles; the fabrics are top quality.

Muumuu Factory to You—you'll see that name on several stores in Honolulu: in Waikiki, there's one at 2520 Kalakaua Ave. in the Diamond Head part of town, another one in the Wailana Hotel at 1860 Ala Moana Blvd. Nothing fancy in the way of decor here, just racks of aloha wear for men, women, and children, but the styles are acceptable and the prices are very good. Most garments are mixtures of cotton and polyester, although some are 100% cotton. We saw long dresses from $25 and up, short ones from $21 and up, men's aloha shirts from $17.

RESORT WEAR

Stunning savings—as much as 40% to 70% off regular retail prices—make the 20-minute-or-so drive out to **Malia: The Factory Outlet**, at 2200 Dillingham Blvd., eminently worthwhile. Malia does contemporary resort fashion—jackets, big shirts, cotton sweaters, skirts, dresses. On a recent visit we walked away with a beautiful $64 silk sweater for $15 (they were selling at two for $25). We've never seen muumuus here, but Malia does carry men's cotton aloha shirts in exclusive prints, $38 elsewhere, only $25 to $28 here. Malia's selections change constantly and are better some days than others, but typical examples would include $76 dresses for $56, $28 shorts for $15, $35 T-shirts for just $10. Great fun, good buys. Open Monday to Saturday from 9am to 5:30pm, Sunday from 11am to 4pm.

AT THE ZOO

The Honolulu Zoo has a gift shop called the **Zootique**, filled with toys, books, kites, apparel, jewelry, and novelties with bird and animal themes. Our special favorites are the T-shirts made especially for the zoo with sayings like "Lion on the Grass at Honolulu Zoo" or "See You Later, Alligator," with appropriate line drawings underneath. Perhaps you'll walk away with some pop-up books, a stuffed animal or two, and some souvenirs sporting the zoo's logo. The Zootique is open from 8:30am to 4pm every day (except Christmas and New Year's), and all proceeds go to the Honolulu Zoo Hui, a nonprofit organization of friends of the zoo who raise funds for zoo improvements and educational programs.

KAHALA MALL

Still haven't had enough of shopping malls? Hop into your U-drive, go up Kapahulu to Lunalillo Freeway East, exit at Waialae, and you'll find yourself at Kahala Mall, part of the big Waialae Kahala Shopping Complex that the local folks love. Kahala Mall is an enclosed shopping center, with a main lobby like that of a hotel—carpeted and decorated with a beautiful fountain and plantings. Stretching out in various directions from the lobby are a bevy of interesting stores. Since Kahala Mall has lately expanded from a popular neighborhood center into a "world-class shopping center," there's a great deal to see here. At some of the boutiques, it will be "just looking, thanks," but there are still many places of interest to the dollar wise shopper.

Worth a special trip is **Following Sea,** a shop-gallery that represents the work of some 350 professional craft artists from 40 states, and sponsors outstanding monthly exhibitions. Everything is unique, and the inventory changes constantly. Prices range from a little to a lot, but there is a fine selection of ceramics, woodwork, and jewelry in the $30 to $60 range. Their most popular items are hand-blown oil lamps, from $20. On a recent visit we saw koa, a native Hawaiian hardwood, beautifully crafted into notebook covers, chimes, jewel chests, and unique boxes from $25 to $300; plus exquisite leaded-glass boxes each with a beautiful seashell set into the top, from $53 to $75. Following Sea is working with local craftspeople to develop new and unique items. Save this place for gifts for some special person—or for yourself.

Cotton Cargo bursts at the seams with lovely, pricey clothes—mostly from Mexico and India. . . . Both custom-made and ready-to-wear couture clothing, plus accessories and jewelry, draw the cognoscenti to **Jeffrey Barr.** . . . **Cielo** also excels in the couture look for fashion-conscious women; **Altillo** has the tops in European men's clothing. In a more familiar, popular-priced range, there's **The Gap, Benetton,** and the ubiquitous **Crazy Shirts.**

Alion features the type of très chic clothing for milady that you see in *Vogue* and *Elle.* . . . **Koala Blue,** of which Aussie pop singing star Olivia Newton-John is a part-owner, deals in things Australian—stuffed kangaroos and koalas (toy ones!), T-shirts, caps, and kangaroo jigsaw puzzles, also an Aussie Milk Bar, where you can get coffee and ice-cream treats. . . . **B Cool** abounds in wild T-shirts, stickers, rubber stamps, toys, ceramic masks, baubles, bangles, beads, and the like. . . . One of our favorite shops, **Something Special,** is here, with its beautiful gifts, cards, English toiletries, Cane Haul Road and Raj T-shirts (delightful), Hawaiian-designed silk-screened Ts, toys, and all sorts of enchanting pretties. . . . We like the selection of beautiful stationery, cards, desk accessories, bookmarks, and calendars at **The Paperie.** . . . You can choose upbeat houseware gifts at **The Compleat Kitchen . . . .** and **Jennie's Garden** has a good selection of leis, cut flowers, arrangements, and quality houseplants.

Top off your shopping excursion with a snack or a meal at the **Yum-Yum Tree,** a restaurant enormously popular with the neighborhood people for its well-priced food, deft service, and friendly atmosphere. Be sure to try a slice of their incredibly good pies—strawberry cheese and English toffee are among the choices; you'll want to take a whole pie home with you. Or, enjoy a delicious northern Chinese meal at **Yen King,** one of the best such restaurants in these parts. **California Pizza Kitchen** is stylish with both table and counter seatings in a smart black-and-white room. Its pastas and pizzas—wood-fired with a variety of unusual toppings like Thai chicken or Cajun or vegetarian goat cheese—are light years ahead of the ordinary. Other popular island restaurants represented here include **Bernard's New York Deli, Patti's Chinese Kitchen,** and **Chuck's Steak House.**

NEAR THE BISHOP MUSEUM

Nake'u Awai, at 1613 Houghtailing St., is a bit out of the way—unless you combine it with a visit to the Bishop Museum—but it is worth a trip if you like the unusual in fabrics and design. Joel Nake'u Awai is a young Hawaiian designer whose beautiful silk-screened fabrics are a blend of the traditional and the contemporary in Hawaiian art. After he designs and executes the textiles, he has them whipped up into long skirts, shirts, muumuus, bags, and sundresses. While not cheap, the prices are certainly competitive with those of the better department stores and specialty shops; and the designs are exclusive. We also saw some very good-looking T-shirts with Hawaiian designs for $12 and up, and an interesting array of locally crafted items—lauhala fans, floppy-brimmed hats, gift cards, woven bags, and books of Hawaii—for $4.16 and up. Inquire about his fashion shows. If you can catch one of them you're in for a treat. They're as imaginative as the clothes and include appearances by guest luminaries. The shop is open only until 3:30pm weekdays, until 2pm on Saturday; closed Sunday.

PEARLRIDGE SHOPPING CENTER

Out in Aiea, about a half-hour drive from Waikiki, is Pearlridge Shopping Center, a multimillion-dollar complex that is a big favorite with the local people. Pearlridge boasts 170 stores, 16 theaters, and three "phases". It's built on opposite sides of an 11-acre watercress farm. Shoppers travel between Phase I and Phase II in Hawaii's only monorail train. From your perch in the monorail, you'll enjoy a panoramic view of Pearl Harbor. Across the street, Pearlridge Phase III houses several more shops, theaters, and an office complex. Kids will enjoy Pearlridge and so will grownups; it's a good place to keep in mind for a rainy-day family excursion.

As at most of the shopping centers catering to the local trade, familiar names such as **Liberty House, Sears, J.C. Penney, Long's Drugs,** and **Woolworth's** dominate the scene. **Shirokiya** shows the Japanese influence, with many captivating art objects from Asia. For those who must have the very latest in fashions, Pearlridge is an embarrassment of riches. For women, **Contempo Casuals, Pepperkorn, Casual Corner,** and **Rosebuds** are just a few to tempt the shopper. For the latest in men's fashions, **Coda, Jeans West, Oak Tree, Cozmos,** and **Kramers** have it all. Other popular stores include **Taj Clubhouse, Benetton, Curious Porpoise,** and **Sam Goody.**

Point your kids in the direction of **Playwell** and they'll be happy: It's jammed with just about every imaginable kind of toy. **Fernandez Fun Factory's Flagship** in Pearlridge Phase II must surely be one of the world's fanciest "penny arcades," featuring the newest and most elaborate electronic games.

Hungry? Pearlridge has two food courts that "bring the world to you": **Zen's Korean Barb-B-Que, Elena's Filipino Foods, Greek Connection, Tsuruya Noodle Shop,** and **Taco El Paso** suggest the possibilities. Free-standing restaurants include **Sizzler's Steakhouse, Denny's, Bravo, Monterey Bay Canners, Anna Miller's Coffee Shop,** and the newest restaurant, **Banditos,** which prides itself on Hawaiian Nu-Mex cuisine.

Official store hours at Pearlridge are from 10am to 9pm Monday through Saturday and from 10am to 5pm on Sunday. You can easily squeeze your visit to Pearlridge into your trip to Pearl Harbor or Makaha. If you're driving to Pearl Harbor on Kam Highway, you see it on your right just after you reach Pearl Harbor's entrance to the U.S.S. Arizona Memorial. If you're driving out the H-I Freeway, take the Aiea exit. When driving out the Lunalilo Freeway from downtown, you'll see Pearlridge on the freeway directory signs. By bus, Take TheBUS no. 20 from Waikiki to Pearlridge. *Note:* You can combine your visit to Pearlridge with one to the **Kam Super Swap Meet** (see above), which is held at the Kam Drive-In, across from the shopping center, every day of the week, beginning at 6am.

READERS' SHOPPING SUGGESTIONS: "Parents with teenagers may want to purchase a **Hard Rock Café** shirt for the teenagers back home. The café is located at 1837 Kapiolani Blvd.

Sweatshirts are $20, T-shirts are $15. . . . Pareaus (long dresses that can be wrapped and worn in many ways) are available at airport gift shops for $15. . . . Also at the airport: Don't purchase leis inside the airport. A short walk will take you to the lei stands outside where you can get nice leis for as little as $2. . . . I have been a psoriasis sufferer off and on for 30 years. I bought some Kukui Nut Oil and it has been great for my skin. It's $8 for four ounces. Write or call The Hawaiian Kukui Nut Co., P.O. Box 685, Waialua, Oahu, HI 96791, at 637-5620 or toll free at 800/367-6010. Mail orders are available. This oil is used to soften dry skin, ease tiny lines, soothe sunburn, rashes, and windburn. Early Hawaiians first discovered the plump, mellow nuts of their native kukui trees contained a pure, clear oil with amazing ability to protect their skin against the rigors of everyday life. For centuries, the Hawaiians kept this natural phenomenon a secret!" (Judie Carbaugh, Sykesville, MD.) [*Authors' Note:* Agreed. We too find kukui nut oil extraordinary. It can be purchased at many shops in Waikiki and at the factory store in Waialua.]

"A very inexpensive, not well-known (yet!), import-export, wholesale place, but open to the public, is **Betty's,** on the fifth floor of the Waikiki Shopping Plaza on Kalakaua Avenue; take the escalator. I got wooden necklaces of parrots, zebras, whales, giraffes for $1, and matching earring sets for 50¢. They have many other items, and expensive ones, too. The people who *sell* at Aloha Stadium Flea Market *buy* here." (Mrs. Dorothy Astman, Northport, N.Y.).

"Anyone who shops at the Aloha Stadium Flea Market should try on any clothes they wish to buy. I bought two shorts I thought would fit—the small was a bit snug, but the medium size was way too tight! Your suggestion on shopping at Goodwill paid off. I bought some aloha shirts, 100% rayon for $2.25 each" (Tracy White, Madison, Wisc.). . . . "We found the local ABC stores and Long's at Ala Moana almost indispensable. A special 'thank you' should go to **Exotics Hawaii,** a flower shop in the Royal Hawaiian Shopping Center. The owners were helpful in picking out flowers and seeds for us to take home. They answered questions on the ease of growing orchids as well as what type of pot would be best for growing plumeria" (Candy and Paul Erhard, Alexandria, Va.). . . . "Because Honolulu was our first stop, we were reluctant to shop there, afraid we would see something we liked better later on. This was a mistake. Honolulu was definitely cheaper on most souvenir items. My daughter found lovely shell bracelets for her friends in the posh Royal Hawaiian Shopping Center for 50¢. The same bracelets were $1.50 in Maui. The same was true for other items of jewelry and T-shirts. Also, most vendors in the International Market Place rapidly came down from their original prices when we hesitated. Bargaining seemed to be an acceptable way to do business" (Frances S. Kielt, West Hartford, Conn.). . . . "Warn your readers about the way they can get taken by some of the saleswomen in the gift shops. They would quote a price on an unmarked item, then up the price at the sale. We thought we all heard wrong until we compared stories in the car!" (Clareana Berched, Medford, Mass.). . . . "Tell people to buy the straw beach mats for 89¢ or 99¢ at the drugstores. I've seen them sold for $3 at the beach" (Karen J. Sinnreich, New Brunswick, N.J.). . . . "The Mission Houses Museum Shop in Honolulu had a wonderful selection of interesting items, all reasonably priced. I was able to buy most of my gifts in that one place. In contrast, I found gift items at the Polynesian Cultural Center to be overpriced" (Nancy E. Sephton, Berkeley, Calif.).

"For a sampling of different Japanese treats, visit **Shirokiya Department Store** in Ala Moana Shopping Center. Half of the second floor is devoted to Japanese food, and they sometimes have free samples. The foods are quite exotic, so I would recommend it for the adventuresome. . . . Aloha shirts are 'in' now on the mainland, so for the benefit of readers who want a good selection, here's what I found. I shopped for hours in Waikiki and came up with little I liked. The stores I visited all seemed to have limited selections. But guess which store had the best selection I saw on the island? **Sears** at Ala Moana Center! They had some of the finest makers and the shirts were attractively displayed. I brought eight home for Christmas gifts" (Eric Shuman, Topeka, Kans.).

"**The University of Hawaii Bookstore** is a delightful place to shop for take-home goodies: They have a wide variety of sweatshirts, jackets, caps, track bags, etc., all with the U.H. logo, plus lots of stationery, cards, etc." (Brenda English, Fox Creek, Alberta, Canada). . . . "Buy postcards at **ABC** stores for the best buy. We were able to purchase 10 for 90¢. Don't forget to bring stamps from home, as you lose money on those small stamp machines. . . . "We found the best buy for cans of macadamia nuts to be at **Hilo Hattie's.** . . . Instead of buying the pearls at the stands for $5 each, look for the oysters in a can, at three for $5 at some places. These pearls are very nice, and the equivalent of what you can get at the International Market Place" (Ricky A. Blum, Los Angeles, Calif.).

"After taking the free bus tour to Hilo Hattie's Fashion Center at 440 Kuwili St., we noticed the **Salvation Army** store. We asked if they minded if we walked over there after visiting their factory, and they said, 'Of course not, just come back anytime for the free bus trip back to Waikiki.' I found three muumuus and three Hawaiian shirts for $20. Wow—what a good deal, and fun to boot!" (Mark and Kay Irwin, Phoenix, Ariz.). . . . "If you can cook, see if you can find uncooked macadamia nuts and roast them yourself: 12 ounces cost me $4, considerably cheaper than 5 ounces for $2 in a can. They are unsalted, and will keep in a refrigerator or freezer. Occasionally there are sales on macadamia nuts at the **Macadamia Nut Factory** stores on Kalakaua that even beat the prices at Long's Drug Store and other comparable places. I purchased six 5-ounce cans of whole nuts for $10.95" (Barbara Karchin, Naperville, Ill.). . . . "We found the shopping center to be well planned, very modern, and quite expensive. We discovered that the **Swap Meet** at Aloha Stadium was a bargain-hunter's paradise. So very many new items, never before used, with prices sometimes at only one-fifth the cost of what the downtown shopping centers were asking. It was open each Saturday and Sunday from 6am to 3pm" (Jerald R. Borgie, San Diego, Calif.). . . . "We received many, many bargains at the **Aloha Stadium Swap Meet:** for example, Hanes T-shirts going in Waikiki for $8 and up, three shirts for $10; hanging shell mobiles for as little as $3, baseball hats for $2, and many other souvenir items we found throughout the island at much higher prices" (Phyllis M. DiChiara, Yonkers, N.Y.). [*Authors' Note:* At any swap meet, you can get great bargains, but remember—you can also get taken! We've compared prices on the same item, and found as much as a $6 difference, below or above the regular retail price. Careful shopping is in order.]

"There is a U.S. Post Office in the **Royal Hawaiian Shopping Center,** also an ABC store. We found it convenient to purchase a six-can box of macadamia nuts in packages all ready for mailing, then go right up to the post office. Mail service to the mainland is very good, and we didn't have to carry the packages home and mail them later" (Pearl B. Weber, Brick Township, N.J.). . . . "The **Bishop Museum** is always a 'must' on our list, but I want especially to recommend the museum bookstore and gift shop. It really is the only place to buy good books on Hawaii, beyond the picture books that have nice color pictures and price tags and little else, which one finds everywhere. Two special purchases: *A Hawaiian Reader,* edited by A. Grove Day and Carl Stroven. This little paperback gem is a collection of short chapters by 30 different authors, including Mark Twain and Robert Louis Stevenson, organized chronologically and 'providing an informal history of Hawaii' in a most enjoyable way. It features diaries and first-hand accounts in particular ($4.95). Also special is a little pamphlet entitled *Current Facts and Figures About Hawaiians* by George S. Kanahele. This is a little book of statistics that was a real mind- and eye-opener for us. The information is a bit depressing, but explains a lot of what the observant tourist must notice about daily life in the islands. The chapters are: population, land, health, education, crime, business and employment, income, welfare, voter registration, and Hawaiian agencies" (John and Anne Duffield, Costa Mesa, Calif.). [*Authors' Note: A Hawaiian Reader* has long been one of our favorites (see the Introduction). We have also found an excellent selection of books on Hawaii at the **Honolulu Book Store** at Ala Moana Center.]

"I recently began a series of allergy shots and, to continue their effectiveness, decided to take my serum along. My physician suggested contacting one of the Kaiser hospitals. I did so and had my weekly shots in the outpatient section each week. It was low cost and very accommodating to me" (Mary M. McAndrew, Farmington, Minn.).

"If you are buying liquor, note that it is cheaper at the **ABC** stores than at liquor or wine stores. For example, Tia Maria was more than $1 cheaper at ABC, and prices were also lower on certain wines" (Karen and Joan Polsen, Halifax, Nova Scotia, Canada). . . . "We found an absolute treasure on Kuhio Avenue near Kuhiolani called the **Food Pantry.** Prices there were the cheapest we found anywhere for food and drinks (hard and soft!), sometimes nearly a dollar cheaper than at the ABCs. They have a rather small selection of souvenir and gift items, but these too are cheaper than elsewhere" (Michael C. Healy, Victoria, Australia). . . . "If you are visiting someone in the U.S. Navy, you can shop at the **Exchange** on Oahu if you bring your returning plane tickets with you (this proves that you're not a resident). The prices in the Exchange are reasonable, and the quality of the merchandise is higher than in many 'tourist' stores" (Debbie Tait, Burlington, Mass.).

"The seven **Goodwill** stores on Oahu are great places to find good, 'gently used' muumuus from such stores as Liberty House, McInerny, Watumull, etc. They have a large selection, all dry-cleaned, for $7.95, sometimes less on sale. . . . I stopped in a **Salvation Army** store one day, and enjoyed it so much I went back. It was very clean and neat, and they had a big selection of muumuus, priced from $1.55 and up, about $10 for lovely Eastern brocades! I bought many, some just for the materials, others to wear. One day, I got five long muumuus! They also have bathing suits for 89¢ and up, and monkeypod from 49¢. [*Authors'*

Note: There are seven Salvation Army stores on the island.] . . . "I also liked the Thrift Shop at the **University of Hawaii** for books, Hawaiian clothes, jewelry, household items. It was open only Tuesday, Wednesday, and Thursday, so check before going (also closed during the month of August). The thrift shop at **Central Union Church** on Beretania, near Kalakaua, is one of the best. It's large, bright, clean, and well stocked with nice items at reasonable priced. Open Wednesday 9am to 3pm and Saturday 9am to noon. . . . I found another thrift shop, the **Laniolu Good Samaritan Thrift Shop,** 333 Lewers St., open Monday, Wednesday, and Friday 9am to noon. It is in the Lutheran Senior Retirement Center, and profits go to the Center" (Mrs. Dorothy Astman, Northport, N.Y.). [*Authors' Note:* Another excellent thrift shop is **St. Andrew's Economy Shop** at St. Andrew's Cathedral, downtown at Beretania and Queen Emma streets, open Monday, Wednesday, and Friday from 9:30am to 4pm, Saturday until 1pm, tel. 536-5939. The **Punahou Thrift Shop,** run by the famed Punahou School, also offers good values, and is open Monday, Wednesday, and Friday from 9am to 2pm, tel. 944-5848. Hours can change at these shops, so be sure to phone before you go.]

"My husband and I both wear large sizes, and we have never enjoyed shopping anywhere as much as we did in Honolulu. We could walk into almost any store and find racks of attractive things to fit us" (Mrs. Norman Cohen, Swampscott, Mass.). . . . "We purchased a lovely ukulele from **Kamaka Hawaii, Inc.,** 550 South St., where factory seconds are priced $200 to $300, when available. [*Authors' Note:* Visitors are welcome to visit their small factory, where they hire predominately handicapped workers and train them as craftspeople.] . . . Shopping at the Japanese department store at Ala Moana Center is a must if you are a short person—my wife found racks and racks of size 5 dresses; the average Japanese being short, it follows. However, when shopping, we had to watch ourselves when it came to style. Many things that were conservative there are considered wild by mainland standards" (William D. Devlin, San Francisco, Calif.). . . . "There is so much to photograph that one can easily run out of film. In spite of our good stock of film, we had to buy more. We strongly recommend **Long's Drugstore** in the Ala Moana Center, where we found the best bargains in town. Long's price on both the film and the processing was lower compared to others, resulting in a net savings of $1.25 per film. Slide films were also cheaper than elsewhere. An excellent place for this kind of shopping" (B. K. Mehra, Mississauga, Ontario, Canada). . . . "The view of Pearl Harbor from the monorail at Pearlridge is great. My two-year-old nephew really loves it. He thinks 'Pearlridge' and 'monorail' are synonyms" (Florence Klemm, Colorado Springs, Colo.). . . . "We found the shops and the people at **Ward Warehouse** gave the most unusual selections and friendliest service of anywhere we've traveled" (Mrs. Eric Jones, St-Eustache, Québec, Canada).

VII

HONOLULU ON THE HOUSE

1. SOMETHING FOR EVERYBODY
2. ETHNIC HAWAII

The fantastic bargain of Honolulu is the enormous amount of entertainment and activities—free or at low prices—that are available to the visitor. Few communities in the world share their activities so wholeheartedly with the newcomer.

Part of the reason for this, of course, stems from Hawaii's real need to attract tourists—for tourism is one of its largest industries. But commercial motivations aside, there's enough genuine aloha to go a long way—and to give you so much to do that it becomes hard to decide what to sample and what to pass up!

There are three vital areas where the action takes place; they surround each other like concentric circles.

First, there's Waikiki, the heart of the tourist scene. Some people never leave it and feel they've had a marvelous vacation. Just beyond that is the big, exciting world of Honolulu, one of the great cities (the 12th largest in the United States, in fact). And beyond that, Windward Oahu and the joys of country life and rural beauty. We think you ought to try some of the doings in all three areas—as much as you have taste and inclination for.

The activities described below will give you the broad, overall picture. For up-to-the-minute, day-by-day news of what's going on, consult the *Waikiki Beach Press, Guide to Oahu, This Week on Oahu, Spotlight Oahua, Paradise News,* or *Key,* free publications found in most hotel lobbies, on Kalakaua Avenue, and elsewhere. (These papers also carry many bargain discount coupons, which could add up to considerable savings on shopping, restaurants, car rentals, and the like. Be sure to check them out.) The "Aloha" section of the *Sunday Star Bulletin & Advertiser* provides a run-down of events for the coming week. *Oahu Drive Guide,* available at the offices of the U-drive companies, has plenty of information, plus excellent driving maps. Finally, you can pay a visit to the Information Office of the **Hawaii Visitors Bureau,** on the eighth floor of 2270 Kalakaua Ave. (tel. 923-1811); they also have a booth at the Royal Hawaiian Shopping Center. Innumerable brochures highlight current activities.

1. Something for Everybody

ON THE BEACH
The best place, of course, to get your basic training for a Hawaiian vacation is on **Waikiki Beach,** that fabled stretch of sand that curves from the Ala Wai Canal to the

shadow of Diamond Head. Stretched out among other bodies in various states of pose and repose, you can calmly watch the frantic traffic out in the breakers where the surfboard and outrigger-canoe crowds are busy trying to run each other down. The blue Pacific, the coconut palms, the trade winds—everything around you induces a lotus-land lethargy that has caused more than one vacationer to tear up his return ticket home ($60-a-day'ers, naturally, should cash theirs in). The best part about all this is that it's absolutely free; there's no need to stay at any of the lush seaside cara-vansaries to use the beach. All of the beach area is public property, up to the highwater mark, even though some of the big hotels do rope off special areas for their guests. Swim in front of the hotels if you like, but you'll have just as much fun at **Fort DeRussy Beach,** near the Ewa end of the beach (a good bet for families, but you can't buy anything at the snack bar unless you have a military card), and at **Kuhio Beach Park,** one of the best natural beaches in Waikiki and headquarters for the surf-ing and bikini crowd. The beach has been considerably widened, and now it's better than ever. However, we should warn you that there is at least one 22-foot-deep hole in the midst of otherwise knee-high (for an adult) water, and there is no way such anomalies in the ocean floor can be corrected—fill them in one day and they'll be back the next. Parents of small children and nonswimmers should exercise caution here. In fact, the director of water safety for the city and county of Honolulu sug-gests that visitors always check with the lifeguard on duty at a beach before swimming.

Kuhio Beach begins Diamond Head of the Sheraton Moana Surfrider Hotel, at Uluniu Avenue. Incidentally, it is named for Prince Jonah Kuhio, who once lived on the site. He was the last titular prince of Hawaii, a hereditary high chief and for 10 consecutive terms the territory's delegate in Congress. We like the name the Hawai-ians gave him: Ke Alii Makaainana, the People's Prince.

If you'd like to learn to surf, try the concessions at Kuhio Beach, or in front of the Sheraton Waikiki, Sheraton Moana Surfrider, or Hilton Hawaiian Village Ho-tels, or inquire at the recreation desk of any large hotel. A beach boy will teach you (and one or two others) for just about whatever the traffic will bear ($20 per hour is a usual fee). You've got to be a strong swimmer. According to the experts, you'll need three months to become a real surfer, but if you're reasonably well coordinated, you should be able to learn enough to have some fun in a day or two. If you're not, don't torture yourself. Take a ride in an outrigger canoe instead. With six or seven others in the canoe, you paddle out to deep water, wait for a good wave, and then, just as the surfer does, ride its crest back to shore. It's a thrilling experience, slightly strenuous, but with little possibility of broken bones.

Looking for a beach far from the maddening crowd (well, as far as you can get)? Take the bus going to Diamond Head on Kalakaua Avenue (on the Makai side) to **Queen's Surf,** just across from Kapiolani Park, a lovely beach area frequented most-ly by local families (and, at the Diamond Head end, mostly by the island's gay population). There's a snackbar here, plus locker rooms, showers, and picnic tables. Another good family beach, practically surfless, is the one at **Ala Moana Park.** And if you drive out to the marina behind the Hotel Ilikai, all the way to the left, you'll find a delightful beach between the Hilton Hawaiian Village and the marina. It's kind of an "in" spot for kamaainas, but tourists don't seem to know about it. There's also plenty of space for free parking here (a rarity in Waikiki).

Want to see how the other half lives, and have a swim, too? It used to be possible to visit the elegant Kahala Hilton Hotel via the hotel's shuttle bus, which makes fre-quent trips between Kahala and Waikiki. Now, however, that service is reserved for hotel guests only, so either drive, or take local transportation: (take TheBUS no. 1 on S. King Street, then transfer on the corner of Waialae and Koko Head and take TheBUS no. 14 to the corner of Puueo Street and Kahala Avenue; turn left and walk a few blocks to the hotel). The drive to Kahala (head Diamond Head on Kalakaua past Kapiolani Park, which leads to Diamond Head Road, which runs into Kahala Avenue), takes you along a lush tropical route spilling over with trees and flowers, past millionaires' villas (many of the newer houses belong to Japanese millionaires), to the Kahala Hilton Hotel in the residential section of Kahala. The hotel's architects and decorators have done a masterful job of translating the old Hawaiian motifs in a contemporary setting; the splendid round rugs in the lobby are an example. You can stroll around the lovely grounds and watch the mini porpoise show in the lagoon near the swimming pool. Feeding times are at 11am and 2 and 4pm, daily. If you get hungry, there's the **Hala Terrace** surfside for food and drink, and the **Plumeria Café,** a courtyard café, for sandwiches, ice cream, snacks, and full meals. After you've explored the grounds, you're off for a swim at **Waialae Beach Park** next door (a bit rocky, however), reached by walking in a Ewa direction from the Kahala sands. If you're driving, parking charges are modest.

SERIOUS SURFING

The best surfing area in these parts is known as the **Cliffs,** and it's at the base of Diamond Head. In surfers' language, the waves here are high-performance, nonhollow walls (no tube rides), and are usually 2 to 6 feet high. They can be some of the most beautiful peaks in Hawaiian waters. Combine them with the views of Diamond Head and you've got a surfer's paradise. The Cliffs is immediately past the lighthouse on Diamond Head Road, just past Waikiki. There is parking on the road and a paved trail to the beach below. Showers are available. We'd consider this one for experienced surfers only, but the watching is also great.

SNORKELING

Once you start traveling around the island, there are literally dozens of beaches, one more beautiful than the next. One of the nearest of these beaches, and an ideal one for snorkeling, is **Hanauma Bay** (you can rent snorkeling equipment at many places in Waikiki, and other snorkelers are always willing to help beginners). And you don't need your own car to get to Hanauma Bay; simply board the Hanauma Bay Shuttle, operated by TheBUS. It runs from Waikiki to Hanauma Bay every half hour from 8:45am to 1pm, and can be boarded at the Ala Moana Hotel, the Ilikai Hotel, or at any city bus stop. It returns every hour on the hour from noon to 4:30pm. Or, try one of the private companies like **Polynesian Swim 'n' Snorkel,** which will pick you up at your Waikiki hotel, provide a snorkel mask and fins, give you instructions, and take you to and from Hanauma Bay, all for a cost of $4.95. Phone 523-1023 for information. For more details on Hanauma Bay, see Chapter IX, "Around Oahu," and the Readers' Suggestions, ahead.)

Note: Serious snorkelers and scuba divers who will be touring the neighbor islands may wish to write for a copy of "Dive and Snorkel Guide," published by Destination Hawaii, a nonprofit association. Over 40 locations, about 10 on each island, are mapped and described. Send $2 (includes postage and handling) to UH/ SGES, 1000 Pope Rd., MSB 205, Honolulu, HI 96822.

HIKING

If you'd like to discover what those mountains are actually like across the Ala Wai, the **Hawaiian Trail and Mountain Club** will take you on a hike along one of the numerous beautiful trails around Honolulu, where you'll feel far removed from both city and beach. You pack your own lunch and drinking water on these hikes, which usually start from the Iolani Palace grounds at either 8am on Sunday or 9am on Saturday. The hiking fee is $1, plus a modest charge if you plan to carpool to the hiking site. Visitors are made welcome and usually make up about half the population of the group. For a packet of valuable information about hiking and camping in Hawaii, as well as a schedule of upcoming hikes, send a legal-size stamped, self-addressed envelope plus $1.25 to P.O. Box 2238, Honolulu, HI 96804. If all you want is the schedule, just send the envelope and omit the $1.25. Or, you can check the schedule printed in the "Today" section of the *Honolulu Star Bulletin.* For information, phone 534-5515 or 488-1161. . . . If you'd like to go hiking with the local branch of the Sierra Club, write to Sierra Club, Hawaii Chapter, P.O. Box 2577, Honolulu, HI or phone them at 538-6616.

For books, topographical and other maps, and information on camping, hiking, bicycling, and outdoor activities in Hawaii, contact **Hawaii Geographic Maps & Books,** P.O. Box 1698, Honolulu, HI 96806 to request their free brochures and lists. Their publication, *Hawaii Parklands,* with 100 color photographs, is impressive. It sells for $25 hardcover, $15 softcover, plus $3 postage and handling. The Hawaiian Trail and Mountain Club recommends two books: *Hawaii's Best Hiking Trails* by Robert Smith (Wilderness Press, 1982, $11.95) and *Hawaiian Hiking Trails* by Craig Chisolm (Fernglen Press, 1985, $9.95). Both contain detailed camping and hiking information on all the islands.

TENNIS, GOLF, AND OTHER SPORTS

Tennis in Honolulu? Certainly. It's free at 26 public courts. Pick up the brochure called "Golf and Tennis in Hawaii" at the Hawaii Visitors Bureau for complete listings. The **Ilikai Hotel** has a lot of tennis action: six specially surfaced courts, ball machines, a full-time tennis pro, private lessons, daily clinics. Hours are 7am to 6pm, and the fee is $9 per hour singles, $12 doubles. The pro shop rents racquets and does overnight stringing. They'll even help you find suitable partners (tel. 949-3811). . . . There are 14 public golf courses on Oahu, most with relatively low greens fees. The nearest one to Waikiki is the 18-hole **Ala Wai Golf Course** at 404 Kapahulu Ave. Reservations are taken by phone (tel. 296-4653) one week in advance starting at 6:30am. All reservations are usually given out by 7am. Huge lines of local people start to form before dawn to take advantage of any cancellations. Ala Wai is reputedly the busiest golf course in the world, with over 500 persons playing daily. Visitor rates are $18 weekdays, $20 weekends. Cart rental is $11; club rental, $10. With a car, you can drive to Hawaii Kai and the **Hawaii Kai Golf Course,** 8902 Kalanianaole Hwy., in about 20 minutes. It has an 18-hole par-3 course, an 18-hole championship course, and a driving range. Rates for the par-3 are $18; for the championship, $60. There's a restaurant on the premises. Phone 395-2358 for information and reservations. If you're planning a drive out to the North Shore, you can take advantage of the little-known (to visitors) **Kahuku Municipal Golf Course,** which has the benefit of an ocean view and very low greens fees—for islanders. Out-of-state rates have recently been upped to $14 for 9 holes, $18 for 18 holes on weekdays, and $14 and $20 on weekends. The 2,725-yard course is usually not crowded, except occasionally on weekends. Note that there is neither pro shop nor restaurant here. Tee times are required only on weekend mornings. For information, phone 293-5842. For a listing of golf courses elsewhere on Oahu, see again, "Golf and Tennis in Hawaii," available from the HVB. . . . **Kapiolani Park,** is certainly one of the world's most active recreational areas. It has archery and golf driving ranges, fields for soccer, rugby, and softball, courts for tennis and volleyball, a jogger's circuit training course, and lots more. For details, call the Department of Parks and Recreation headquarters at 523-4631 (they can also give you information on swimming lessons). . . . Oahu also has loads of facilities for riding, waterskiing, skin diving, plain and fancy fishing, even birdwatching. (Look for listings of Audubon Society programs in the daily papers.) The Hawaii Visitors Bureau can direct you to the right places. . . . You can even go glider riding, out at Dillingham Airfield on the North Shore, using the facilities of the **Honolulu Soaring Club.** You can get instruction in doing it yourself or go for a joy ride on a sailplane ($60 for two passengers, $40 for one). Look Ma, no engines! Phone Bill at 677-3404 for information. Rates are subject to change. No reservations are required, and things glide along here seven days a week, 10:30am to 5:30pm. Bring your camera.

We realize that you probably didn't come to Hawaii to go ice skating, but if that's your pleasure, Honolulu has a beautiful rink: the **Ice Palace Chalet.** Located in Stadium Mall, across from Aloha Stadium and Castle Park, this place has really caught on with the local folk. Admission is $5 for adults, $4.50 for students; the admission price includes rental of skates. The rink is open daily; phone 487-9921 for public skating hours. Don't fret if you forget to pack warm hats, mittens, and gloves; there's a little shop here that will sell them to you.

SUBMARINE ADVENTURES

Although it's not inexpensive, a dive aboard the submarine *Atlantis* is such a special experience that we'd consider it a highly worthwhile splurge. The sub descends to a depth of 100 feet in the waters off Waikiki, treating passengers to views of coral reef and brightly colored reef fish that normally only scuba divers can see. One of a growing fleet of such high-tech subs (there's another one in Kona on the Big Island, several more in the Caribbean and Guam), the *Atlantis* is totally equipped for safety and comfort, is fully air-conditioned, and maintains normal atmospheric pressure—no chance of getting the bends. You will, however, get a thrill as you peer out of the portholes and view the eerie world beneath the waves. Cost is $67 for adults, $33.50 for children. The adventure begins at the Alii Tower of the Hilton Hawaiian Village, where a catamaran takes you to the dive site, then back for an enjoyable sail along the Waikiki coast. Dives begin daily at 8am; allow about two hours for the entire trip. Reserve in advance by phoning 522-1710.

FITNESS, HAWAIIAN STYLE

There's no need to let up on your fitness program just because you're on vacation. If you like to do your daily routines out on the beach, join the free exercise class every day except Sunday from 9 to 10:30am at the beach at Fort DeRussy. . . . Jogging is big in Honolulu, as it is just about everywhere else. You can join those getting in shape for the **Honolulu Marathon** (it's held the first or second weekend in December) at a free Marathon Clinic, every Sunday at 7:30am at the bandstand in Kapiolani Park. . . . If you're in town in mid-February, grab your sneakers and join some 30,000 other participants in the 8.2-mile **Great Aloha Run/Walk,** the largest running event in the islands, and the fourth-largest run in the United States. There's an entrance fee of $14; proceeds go to charity. Phone 735-6092 or write to Great Aloha Run/Walk, 710 Palekaua St., Honolulu, HI 96816. . . . **World Gym,** 1701 Ala Wai Blvd. (tel. 942-8171), stays open 24 hours a day to accommodate those who want to work out with weights, Universal machines, and Nautilus equipment.

After all this exertion, you may be in need of a massage. The **Honolulu School of Massage** at 1123 11th Ave. in Kaimuki (right behind Diamond Head) is a reputable, state-licensed organization that offers low-cost massages by apprentice massage therapists at a cost of $17 for a half hour, $30 for an hour. For a licensed massage therapist, costs are higher. And, oh yes, massage helps relieve jet lag, too. Phone 733-0000 for an appointment. The school is accessible by TheBUS no. 14, no. 1, and no. 3. (Fees subject to change.)

SPECTATOR SPORTS—THE SURFING SCENE

Some visitors to Hawaii find that watching others exert themselves is the most fun of all—and this usually means gazing at the surfers on Waikiki Beach or at the Cliffs (see above). It's an incredible and never-ending show, especially enjoyable if you've brought your binoculars. If you'd like a closer view, try to catch one of the surfing movies that are shown frequently in the summer at places like the **Waikiki Shell** and **McKinley Auditorium.** They're instructive and thrilling, and much more dramatic than watching the scene from afar at the beach.

Surfing, by the way, was the favorite sport of Hawaiian royalty and originally had religious connotations. In the early part of this century, Jack London, among others, helped revive the sport, and today it's an absolute passion with every able-bodied islander, far surpassing the interest of the mainlander in, say, baseball or skiing. Of course, many mainlanders move to Hawaii for the lure of the surf. (A T-shirt we saw on our last trip proclaimed, "Work is for those who can't surf.") Radio weather reports always include a report on the latest surfing conditions. A special phone (tel. 836-1952) also gives the latest reports. And the proudest possession of any Hawaiian teenager is, naturally, his or her surfboard.

Other island spectator sports that you might like: football, baseball, motorcycling, high school basketball, soccer, wrestling, truck and tractor pulls, mud bogs at **Aloha Stadium,** basketball, karate, wrestling, boxing, and Japanese sumo wrestling at **Neal S. Blaisdell Center Arena.** World-class polo is played each Sunday during polo season (early March through August) at **Hawaii Polo Club** at the Mokuleia Polo Grounds in Mokuleia, one of the three polo fields in the world located on a beach. The first of two matches begins at 2pm, but gates open at 11am for some pretty fancy tailgate picnics. Admission is $5 per person; children under 12 get in free. Last year the English, Australian, Boston, South American, Mexican, Japanese, German, and celebrity teams were invited to play with the local club. For more information, phone 637-7656 (637-POLO).

THE HULA AND OTHER ETHNIC DANCES

Just as you expected, everyone in Hawaii does the hula except the lame (being old or blind is no hindrance). Island youngsters learn the hula just as mainland children take ballet or tap lessons. Social directors and hotel instructors patiently instruct the malihinis, and wherever you look there's a hula show under way. All this is fun, and some of it is good dancing, but much of it is a bastardization of a noble and beautiful dance, Hawaii's most visible contribution to the arts.

The original hula dances were sacred, performed in honor of the goddess Laka (who supposedly entertained her sister, the volcano goddess Pele, with the first hula). Laka's devotees lived under a strict system of kapus (taboos), studying the hulas as well as the chants and meles, by which the myths of the race were transmitted from one generation to another. In the whaling days, some of the hulas became a bawdy entertainment for the sailors, and the good missionary fathers, who would have found dancing sinful on any account, naturally forbade it. But the hula managed to survive. Today the styles of hula range from the most serious to the most amusing, from the ancient and sacred to the modern hapa-haole and comic.

Happily, there's been a great revival of interest in serious hula lately, and if you're lucky you may get to see outstanding dancing at some of the better nightclub shows (the Brothers Cazimero at the Monarch Room of the Royal Hawaiian Hotel, for one) or at concert presentations. True devotees of hula should visit the islands during the month of April. That's when the **Merrie Monarch Festival** is held in Hilo, on the Big Island of Hawaii, a week-long virtual Olympics of hula, with dancers from all the various hula halaus (schools) of the islands competing in both ancient and modern hulas. You probably won't be able to get tickets to the events themselves (they are usually sold out by the preceding Christmas), but they are fully covered on television and are a true joy to watch. On a recent trip, we sat enthralled for nights in a row viewing the competition and the judging—as did just about everyone else on the islands.

One of the most delightful hula shows, in our opinion, is the **Young People's Hula Show,** presented every Sunday morning at 9:30 on the centerstage at the Ala Moana Shopping Center. The children, all students of Ka'ipolani Butterworth, ranging in age from about 3 to the teens, are talented nonprofessionals, bursting with charm and aloha. It's all free and more enjoyable than many an expensive nightclub show. (Their video, "Hawaii's Children in Dance," could be a memorable gift.)

Look for notices in the papers of concerts presented by **Dances We Dance,** an educational and performing organization that sponsors both ethnic and modern dance concerts throughout the state. On one trip we were lucky enough to catch a concert by The Ladies of Na Pualei O Likolehua, as part of a special season of Hawaiian dance. Performances are usually held in State-of-the-art Mamiya Theatre at St. Louis Center for the Arts, on the St. Louis–Chaminade campus, 3140 Waialae Ave. To see a noncommercial dance presentation by a respected hulu halau like this one is a very special experience.

You'll note, by the way, that hula dancers—who can just as well be men as women—tell the story with their hands while their feet keep up a steady rhythmic pattern. They often use instruments to help them: The smooth stones or pebbles that they click together, that sound like castanets, are known as ili ili. The seed-filled gourd that sounds like a South American maraca is known as the uli uli. The hollow gourds are called ipus. Pui li, splintered bamboo sticks, produce a rattling sound, and kalaau are hard wooden sticks struck together to make a noise like that of a xylophone.

According to the experts, probably the best ethnic dancing of the Pacific Islands is that done by the dance group at the **Polynesian Cultural Center,** which we'll tell you about in Chapter IX. They often do free minishows at the Royal Hawaiian Shopping Center. Watch for outstanding programs of Japanese, Korean, and other Asian dances at the University of Hawaii.

DO-IT-YOURSELF DANCING

You too can do the hula! Hula-dancing lessons are given everywhere—at the Ys, at the university, and at any number of private dance studios. Free classes are sometimes given at hotels and shopping centers, but since the times of these lessons change with the seasons, it's best to consult the local tourist papers. Lessons in Hawaiian dance are given at the **Bishop Museum Atheron Halau,** 1525 Bernice St. (tel. 847-3511), at 1pm Monday through Saturday and on the first Sunday of the month, free when you pay general museum admission of $4.75 adults, $2.50 for those 6 to 17. . . . Free hula classes are usually given Monday, Wednesday, and Friday at the **Royal Hawaiian Shopping Center,** Building C, third floor, at 10:30am. (You'll also find free classes here in the Hawaiian language, ukulele, coconut weaving, and lei-making, every morning from 9:30am on, phone 922-0588.)

MUSIC

Classical music lovers have no cause for complaint in Honolulu. Western concert artists of the stature of Emanuel Ax stop here en route to the Far East or on round-the-world tours; Japanese soloists and orchestras pay frequent visits. You might catch opera companies and the like from China. You can enjoy subscription concerts by the **Honolulu Symphony,** which performs under the baton of its music director, Donald Johanos, and famous guest conductors. Soloists include internationally acclaimed virtuosos, and programs include choral works and appearances by the San Francisco Ballet. Pops concerts and the Starlight Festival in the Waikiki Shell are among the most widely attended symphony events, as are the annual presentations of *Nutcracker* and *Messiah*. Associate conductor Henry Miyamura conducts the very popular Youth Concerts, Youth Opera, and the annual Keikis' (Children's) Concert at the Waikiki Shell, where guest stars have included Big Bird.

Try to attend a performance of the **Hawaii Opera Theater,** which holds a yearly Opera Festival in February and March, featuring internationally acclaimed opera stars complemented by Hawaii's finest singers, a locally trained chorus, and the Honolulu Symphony. This year's season, the company's 31st, features Verdi's *Aida,* Mozart's *The Marriage of Figaro,* and Bernstein's *Candide*. And the islands' most gifted young musicians play with the Hawaii **Youth Symphony,** which performs during the school year.

If you enjoy chamber music, you'll want to hear the excellent **Hawaii Chamber Orchestra**. From October through April, concerts are held once a month, and each concert is presented twice. Friday night performances are held at 8pm at Waiokeola Church across from Kahala Mall, and repeat performances take place the following Sunday at 4pm at St. Peter's Church in downtown Honolulu. Dates can be checked through the papers or by calling 734-0397. Tickets are $8; $6 for seniors, students, and military.

The **Hawaii Chamber Jazz Players** strut their stuff in July and August. Programs of traditional and improvisational jazz in the true folk tradition are held on Friday nights at a location not yet set at the time of this writing, check local papers. Tickets are $8; $6 for seniors, students, and military, and can be purchased at the door. For information or reservations, phone 734-0397.

THEATER

Hawaiian theater, long of the tired-businessman, light-entertainment school, is getting more mature and more varied all the time. Very popular here is the **Honolu-**

lu Community Theater, an able group that presents a year-round program of current Broadway shows, revivals, and musicals old and new. It's been going strong since 1915! Performances are held in the Ruger Theater on the slopes of Diamond Head. Tickets range from $11 to $18.75. For information, call 734-0274.

Now in its 22nd season, the Manoa Valley Theater (formerly the Hawaii Performing Arts Company) provides an intimate setting for a broad spectrum of the theatrical offerings. Their 150-seat Manoa Valley Theater at 2833 E. Manoa Rd. brings the lights up 42 weeks of the year on a variety of productions ranging from the Bard to Broadway, from classics to musical comedy. Tickets range from $12 to $15, depending on the production and the night of the week. Call 988-6131 for dates and availability of seats.

Up at the John F. Kennedy Theater, the University of Hawaii's outstanding Department of Drama and Theater presents the great classics of Asia and the West—Shakespeare, Kabuki, and modern plays, as well as ballet and modern dance. Besides the eight or so major productions staged each year, they present at least six shows produced by Kumu Kahua, a theater group that performs plays written by Hawaiian residents. For information on tickets and productions, call 948-7655.

At the Mid-Pacific Institute, just mauka of the University of Hawaii, artists-in-residence have formed a group called Starving Artists Theatre Company. They produce a full season of avant-garde and new plays, both local and international. These new kids on the block provide an excellent showcase for new artists and playwrights. Productions are held in the auditorium of the institute's Kawaiahae Building. Performances are usually held Thursday through Sunday, with tickets going for around $10, $2 less for students and seniors. For information on tickets, phone 942-1942.

Should you find yourself on the windward side of the island, you might stop in to see an offering by the Windward Theater Guild, a good local company. Performances are held in the Windward Community College in Kaneohe; tickets are $8 for adults, $7 for all others; and you call 262-0104 for information and reservations. Also outside of Honolulu, Broadway theatrical productions and name entertainment shows, some of them free, are presented at Schofield Barracks and Fort Shafter. Call 655-9081 or 438-2831 for information and reservations.

The easiest way to find out what's playing when you're in town is to call the theater hotline sponsored by the Hawaii State Theatre Council. It's a 24-hour information line on all plays and musicals currently showing on Oahu, providing dates, places, and numbers to call for reservation information. Phone 988-3255 any time of day or night.

HO'OPONOPONO

The early Hawaiians were very practical psychologists, and some of their ancient practices are gaining the attention of psychologists and educators today. If you'd like to learn some of the secrets of that ancient wisdom, updated for today's world, try to catch one of the free evening lectures on Ho'oponopono (the art of problem-solving and stress release), given by Morrnah Simeona and her staff at The Foundation of I (Freedom of the Cosmos), 2153 N. King St., Suite 303. A native Hawaiian, Morrnah is renowned throughout the islands as Kahuna Lapa'au, a healer, herbalist, and authority on the Hawaiian teachings; she has been named a "Living Treasure of Hawaii." Among her colleagues is psychologist Stanley Hew Len, Ph.D. We attended one of these free lectures and a Ho'oponopono workshop (for which there is a fee) on a recent trip and found it fascinating. For information, phone 842-3750.

CHANOYU: THE JAPANESE TEA CEREMONY

As refreshing as a quick trip to Japan, the twice-weekly demonstrations of the Japanese tea ceremony held at 245 Saratoga Rd. (near Fort DeRussy) offer a fascinating look at the ancient "Way of Tea." Sponsored by the Urasenke Foundation of Hawaii, a nonprofit group whose goal is "to find friendship in a bowl of tea," the demonstrations are held every Wednesday and Friday (excluding holidays) from

10am to noon: donations are welcomed. Seated in a formal Japanese tatami room in a garden setting, guests are introduced to the proper customs for the preparation and partaking of tea, and are served a sweet and powdered green tea from exquisite "tea bowls." You may ask questions and take pictures if you wish. A must for lovers of Asian culture.

Monthly Tea Gatherings are also held. For information, phone 923-3059.

THE STUDENT LIFE

Here's a tip that can save you scads of dollars. The **University of Hawaii at Manoa** sponsors a number of low-cost activities for the benefit of its students. But nonstudents may join in the fun and savings simply by paying an activity fee that covers a six-week summer session. Inquire at Campus Center, Room 212, on the Manoa Campus of the University of Hawaii.

FREE SHOWS

There are quite a few of these, and most of them are worth your time. If you're in town on a Friday, don't miss the Tribute to King David Kalakaua at the **Hilton Hawaiian Village;** it's an imaginative re-creation of the period of Hawaiian monarchy in the late 19th century. Things get under way at 6:30pm with a march to the hotel's porte cochere, where the Hawaiian anthem is sung; from then on it's a torchlight ceremony, Hawaiian music, and hula dancing at 7; fireworks at 8; plus more entertainment until 10pm (tel. 949-4321 for details).

The same Hilton Hawaiian Village is also the place to catch dancers and musicians from the Polynesian Cultural Center who perform on the **Village Green** every Tuesday from 3 to 6pm. A different Polynesian culture is highlighted each month (tel. 847-8200) for information. . . . Every evening between 5:30 and 9, the lovely poolside terrace at the **Sheraton Princess Kaiulani Hotel** is the scene of a free show featuring songs and dances of Polynesia. Have a drink or not, as you like (tel. 922-5811). . . . Although it was free for years, the **Kodak Hula Show,** a venerable Waikiki institution, now has an admission charge of $2.50 for adults (children under 12 are still free). Even without the benefit of a light meter, you should enjoy this lively production of authentic music and dance by talented artists. Naturally, it's nirvana for photographers. There is special seating for the disabled. The show is held at the Waikiki Shell in Kapiolani Park, on Tuesday, Wednesday, and Thursday at 10am. Get here early for a good seat, because even with bleachers that seat 4,000 people, it's always crowded. (For free Hilo Hattie bus transportation, call 537-2926.)

Everybody loves the **Young People's Hula Show** at the Ala Moana Shopping Center (details above). And from mid-June through August, free Hawaiian entertainment is also scheduled at 2pm on Tuesday and Thursday at Ala Moana. . . . Check the papers for dates of free entertainment at Pearlridge Shopping Center. . . . Kuhio Mall presents a free hula show every night at 7 and 8. . . . Don't miss the free show at the beach in front of the **Reef Hotel** every Sunday, from 8 to 9:30 or 10pm. Lots of bright amateurs get into the act. . . . Free concerts and cultural shows are given in the Great Hall of the **Hyatt Regency Waikiki,** often at noon or 5pm, but since the schedule varies greatly, you should check with the Hyatt Hostess Desk (tel. 922-9292) for exact times. . . . Hawaiian music and dance performances are presented at the **Atherton Halau** of the Bishop Museum, Monday through Saturday at 1pm.

Free concerts are generally held Sunday afternoons at 1 at the **Kapiolani Park Bandstand.** Entertainment includes Polynesian revues, ukulele clubs, visiting mainland troupes, jazz and rock musicians, and usually the famed Royal Hawaiian Band. Call 926-4030 for more information. . . . You can nearly always be sure to catch the Royal Hawaiian Band at its Friday noontime concerts at the **Iolani Palace bandstand.** These lunchtime concerts are very popular with the local people who work nearby; bring a lunch and have a listen. . . . Or join the local crowd on Friday at noon for **The Mayor's Aloha Friday Music Break,** held at Tamarind Park, at the corner of Bishop and King streets (tel. 527-5666) . . . On Wednesday evenings during June, July, and August, you can see "The Wildest Show in Town" at the

Honolulu Zoo. The zoo stays open until 7:30pm, and there's a show at 6pm on the stage in the main courtyard. Most families bring a picnic supper to eat during the show. We've seen the Honolulu City Ballet, a troupe of Scottish bagpipers (many of them Japanese and Hawaiian!) in full regalia, the Honolulu Boys' Choir, puppet shows, kabuki theater, and a New Orleans jazz group. . . . The Waikiki-Kapahulu branch of the **Hawaii State Library** system, 400 Kapahulu, offers varied programs for adults and weekly story hours for 4- and 5-year-olds. It's also pleasant to just sit and read in the bougainvillea-shaded lanai at this library in a coconut grove at the foot of Diamond Head. The building itself is an architectural gem, built of sandstone, wood, and glass, with koa furniture. Visitors are also welcome to borrow books, free of charge. . . . There's free entertainment galore at the **Royal Hawaiian Shopping Center.** You can usually count on a minishow presented by the Polynesian Cultural Center, on Tuesday, Thursday, and Saturday between 10am and noon in the Fountain Courtyard. For news of special programs, check the local papers.

There is now a **Mayor's Performance Hotline** (527-5666) to inform you about cultural activities and performances. You'll hear a recording that describes activities planned for the current month at Honolulu Hale (City Hall), Iolani Palace, Kapiolani Park Bandstand, and at Tamarind Park (on Bishop Street). The service, operated by the Mayor's Office of Culture and the Arts, also announces any last-minute cancellations.

If you happen to be in town when one of the major cruise ships puts into Honolulu Harbor, you can enjoy one of the best free shows of all: **Boat Day.** The festive celebration of old has been revived, and once again bands play and hula girls dance as passenger ships arrive or depart. Cruise ships are serenaded by the Royal Hawaiian Band at the piers served by the Aloha Tower at the foot of Bishop Street, always at 9am. For information on Boat Days, phone Theo H. Davis & Co., Marine Department, 540-0400. Unfortunately, this happens only several times a year; but maybe you'll be lucky enough to catch it.

THE ART SCENE

A lot of good artists are coming out of Hawaii—young people with a mixture of backgrounds whose work shows multiple influences. Perhaps because of the natural beauty that surrounds them, their paintings tend to be more representational here than in other art centers, but ways of seeing are as modern as they are in Paris or New York. Not a few have married Eastern atmosphere with Western techniques, another example of the fortuitous cross-fertilization that goes on in every area of Hawaiian life.

With the opening of the **Contemporary Museum at the Spalding Estate,** 2411 Makiki Heights Drive (tel. 526-1322), Honolulu has become the art center of the Pacific. The lovely old 1920s mansion in a magnificent garden setting overlooking the city and the sea has been transformed into a series of state-of-the-art galleries, housing exhibits focusing on 40 years of art in Hawaii. Local artists like Jean Charlot and Madge Tennant are represented, as are such internationally known stars as the late Andy Warhol. A permanent pavilion houses David Hockney's stage set from the Metropolitan Opera production of *L'Enfant et Les Sortilèges,* complete with a stereo sound system playing the Ravel opera that inspired this major work. Docent tours are available. Galleries, art, gardens, all vie for attention. The gardens alone, a series of exquisite terraces meandering down to a stream bed, falls, and pools, are worth the trip. The gardens were designed by a Japanese landscape artist as a place where one might meditate and experience harmony, so each vista has its stone seat for contemplation. There's also an attractive gift shop with artist-designed T-shirts, jewelry, cards, and the like, and **The Contemporary Café,** an indoor-outdoor eating spot with sophisticated cuisine and moderate prices. The Contemporary Art Museum is open from 10am to 4pm daily; closed Tuesdays. Well worth the admission price of $3 for adults, $1 through age 14. Even better, on Thursdays admission is free.

New galleries are opening all over town. You'll want to visit **Arts of Paradise** on the second floor of the International Market Place. Artist owned, it features work in all media of Hawaii's top professional artists. Call about free demonstrations and talks by participating artists in the Gallery Theatre (tel. 924-2787). . . . Older Waikiki galleries include the distinguished **Royal Gallery** in the Royal Hawaiian Hotel (tel. 922-8818). . . . Then there's **Images International of Hawaii,** with galleries at Ala Moana Shopping Center, Palm Blvd. (tel. 926-5081), **Otsuka Gallerie** (tel. 947-5081), and **Ward Centre Pavilion** (tel. 583-6755). Galleries feature internationally acclaimed artists: Hisashi Otsuka, Caroline Young, Tatsuo Ito, Raymond Page, Gary Hostallero, and Dario. . . . Also worth your attention at Ward Centre is **Art À La Carte** (tel. 536-3351), an artists' co-op featuring ceramics as well as paintings.

Downtown, the impressive **Honolulu Advertiser Gallery** on the first floor of the News Building at 605 Kapiolani Blvd. (tel. 526-1322) continues to be a showcase for local and mainland artists despite its new galleries at the Contemporary Museum (see above). . . . **The Gallery** at Pauahi Tower in Bishop Square always has an outstanding show running. . . . For the past 19 years, **Territorial Savings and Loan Association** has been presenting exhibitions by Hawaii's artists as a public service (no commission is taken) at its Downtown Office Gallery, Ground Floor, Financial Plaza of the Pacific, corner of Bishop and Merchant streets. Exhibits are open Monday through Thursday from 8am to 3:30pm, and Friday to 6pm, every month except December (tel. 523-0211). . . . The **AMFAC Plaza Exhibition Room** at AMFAC Center, Fort Street Mall and Queen Street, has interesting group exhibitions of contemporary paintings, crafts, sculpture, and photography, as well as cultural and historical presentations. Exhibitions change monthly. Open 9am to 5pm weekdays, closed Saturday and Sunday. . . . On Saturday and Sunday, local artists exhibit and sell their work on the zoo fence near Kapiolani Park—a sort of twice-a-week Greenwich Village Art Show.

Something of an artistic renaissance is going on in Chinatown these days. Old buildings have been refurbished, there is new construction, and a small artistic colony continues to grow. At last count, there were a dozen galleries here, including **Pegge Hopper** at her own gallery, 1164 Nuuanu Ave. (tel. 524-1164); the **Gateway Gallery,** 1050 Nuuanu Ave. (tel. 599-1559), owned by and presenting local artists; and **Waterfall Gallery,** 1600 Nuuanu Ave. (tel. 521-6863), which often mounts photographic exhibits by its talented owner, William Waterfall, among other shows. Pen-and-ink artist Ramsay has her own gallery at 1128 Smith St. and also owns the adjacent **Gallery Café,** where it's fun to drop in for drinks, tropical nonalcoholic beverages, snacks, pupus, and moderately priced dinners, too. Around the corner at 1 Nuuanu are two upbeat galleries: **The Gateway,** featuring fine arts and collage jewelry; and **Art Space,** which handles fine arts and accessories, and showcases performing arts as well.

As you drive around the island, you'll have a chance to visit several worthwhile galleries. **Ko'Olau Gallery,** located on the second floor of the Windward Mall Shopping Center in Kaneohe, is a co-op gallery, staffed by the artists themselves, showing a variety of locally produced artworks in many media. You can say hello to the gallery artists daily from 9:30am to 9pm. . . . Also in Kaneohe, serious lovers of art and beauty must not miss a visit to **Hart, Tagami & Powell Gallery and Gardens,** 45-754 Lamaula Rd., where painters Hiroshi Tagami and Michael Powell open their gallery and tranquil Japanese gardens to visitors on Saturday, Sunday, and Monday, from around 10am to 3:30pm. An appointment is necessary: phone 239-8146. . . . **The Fettig Art Gallery,** 666-051 Kam Hwy., in Haleiwa (tel. 637-4933) has always been a good spot to see works by local artists and craftspeople.

Art is, in fact, everywhere in Honolulu; the builders of large public facilities are becoming more and more art-conscious, and you will find monumental pieces of sculpture, some outstanding, such as a Henry Moore in Tamarind Park at Bishop and King streets downtown, some less distinguished, in such places as the Ala Moana Shopping Center, Hemmeter Center, Royal Hawaiian Center, the Waikiki Shopping Plaza, the University of Hawaii, the state capitol, and at Sea Life Park in Windward Oahu. The fountain sculptures at Ala Moana are particularly worth a look.

To see some excellent works by Hawaii's talented craftspeople (and perhaps to pick up some distinctive small presents), pop into some of our favorite places. **Following Sea,** at the Kahala Mall Shopping Center, 4211 Waialae Ave. (tel. 734-4425), is a visual experience. It presents the works of many American craftspeople in ceramics, glass, jewelry, fiber, and woodwork. Each piece is more glorious than the next. Many island artists are represented. . . . A high level of taste and artistry is evident in the works found at **Artist Guild** at Ward Warehouse. . . . Quality crafts have come to the heart of Waikiki: The **Crafts Court** at Kuhio Mall is an artisans' working gallery, featuring handcrafted jewelry, pottery, weavings, ceramics, clothing, painting, and more.

Keep an eye out for these artists: Randy Hokushin in pottery; Bumpei Akaji in welded sculpture; Jewel Lafferty and Jeanne Robertson in watercolors; Louis Pohl in mixed media; Shirley Hasenwager and Dodie Warren in prints and drawings; Lola Stone in acrylics; David Lee in oils; Connie Hennings-Chilton for Polynesian portraits; Francis Haar, photographer; and Wong Ching, contemporary Chinese art. This is but a partial list of the talented Hawaiian artists whose works are increasingly being recognized outside the islands. Incidentally, Hawaiian art is considered a good investment and is being scooped up by mainlanders.

The Art Establishment

Hawaii has her art establishment, of course, names that are known in art circles everywhere. Perhaps the greatest of these was the muralist Jean Charlot, who, along with Orozco, Siqueiros, and Rivera, brought the art of the mural to revolutionary heights in Mexico in the '20s and '30s. Charlot, who moved to the islands in 1949, contributed much to Hawaii's art world. Other prominent figures include painters/muralists Herbert Kawainui Kane and Juliette May Fraser; painters such as Pegge Hopper known for glorious Polynesian portraits; Robert Lyn Neson, who does extraordinary marine paintings; Guy Buffet (a Frenchman who paints the Hawaiian scene with remarkable élan), Reuben Tam, wood carver Ron Kent, Ben Norris, Tadashi Sato, Kenneth Bushnell, and Edward Stasack (also known for sculpture). John Kelly, who died some years ago in his 80s, was Hawaii's master printmaker; his colored etchings of the Polynesians are considered the best of their kind ever done.

A great lady of the arts in Hawaii was Madge Tennent, who came to Hawaii at the turn of the century via South Africa and Paris and broke away from the academy and its conventions to record on canvas her massive portraits of the Hawaiian people. You can visit her gallery, the **Tennent Art Foundation,** at 203 Prospect St., from 10am to noon Tuesday through Saturday, 2 to 4pm on Sunday, or by special appointment: call Elaine Tennent at 531-1987. Closed Monday. Celebrations in 1989 marked the 100th anniversary of her birth.

Don't leave Hawaii without a visit to the **Honolulu Academy of Arts,** 900 S. Beretania St., where you'll see the work of island artists and much more. The academy is one of the most beautiful art museums in the world; it offers a look at the best of both Eastern and Western art. The physical plant is ideal for viewing art, divided as it is into a series of small galleries that open into tranquil courtyards; the Chinese garden, in particular, is exquisite. There's a superb collection of Asian art—a magnificent sculpture of Kwan Yin, the Chinese goddess of mercy, Chinese scrolls and carvings, Korean ceramics, Japanese screens—as well as a good representation of Western masters, including works of Picasso, Braque, Monet, and Van Gogh. Note also the Kress Collection of Italian Renaissance painting. Stop in the bookshop for prints and other distinctive gift items, and perhaps have a meal at the lovely **Garden Café** (lunch is served from 11:30am to 2pm Tuesday through Friday). The museum is open Tuesday to Saturday from 10am to 4:30pm, on Sunday from 1 to 5pm. Supper is served in the Garden Café on Thursday evening at 6:30; reservations recommended (tel. 531-8865).

Admission to the academy is free. Locked lockers are provided free of charge for visitors' parcels. The academy is about a 15-minute ride from Waikiki on TheBUS no. 2. Closed Monday.

MISCELLANEOUS ACTIVITIES

The **Honolulu Senior Citizens Club** welcomes newcomers to its social and recreational activities every Wednesday from 9am to 2pm at the Ala Wai Clubhouse. There's bridge, canasta, and checkers. Membership is only $5 a year, and it's certainly worth that to go on some of the club's regular outings—sightseeing tours, picnics, etc. These usually start from the Ala Wai Clubhouse (on the other side of the Ala Wai Canal) on Wednesday mornings, under the auspices of the city recreation department. For more information on other activities for senior citizens, contact the **Hawaii State Senior Center** (tel. 847-1322). . . . Visitors are welcome at the **Siddha Meditation Honolulu Center,** 1925 Makiki St. (tel. 942-8887). Free evening programs of chanting and meditation are held every Wednesday and Saturday at 7:30pm. Newcomers to Siddha meditation should come at 7pm for a brief orientation. The center is up in the hills, in a beautiful residential area of Honolulu. Phone for information. . . . There's a group for just about every interest in Honolulu, from barbershop-quartet singers to coin collectors, and they all extend their aloha to the visitor. Check the papers for news of their meetings. Bridge buffs will find duplicate bridge games at local hotels practically every night of the week. Meetings of mainland fraternal organizations take place constantly.

SERVICES FOR THE DISABLED

Disabled people are made very welcome in Hawaii: There are more than 2,000 ramped curbs on Oahu alone, hotels provide special facilities, and tour companies provide many services. Helpful brochures are available for each island. For details, send a legal-size, self-addressed, stamped envelope for each brochure desired (Oahu, Maui, Kauai, Big Island of Hawaii). Each brochure lists accessibility features of Hawaii's major hotels, shopping malls, beach parks, and sightseeing and visitor attractions. Write to the **Commission on Persons with Disabilities,** 5 Waterfront Plaza, Suite 210, 500 Ala Moana Blvd., Honolulu, HI 96813.

Handicabs of the Pacific, P.O. Box 22428, Honolulu, HI 96813 (tel. 524-3866), provides special transportation facilities for the disabled: wheelchair taxi service and a variety of tours, including luaus, cruises, and sightseeing journeys.

MEDICAL SERVICES

We hope it won't happen, but should you need medical assistance while you're in Honolulu, you have several good possibilities. The **Straub Clinic and Hospital,** one of Hawaii's best-known medical centers, now has a Waikiki satellite: The Straub Walk-In Health Center, on the third floor of the Royal Hawaiian Shopping Center. The clinic is open Monday through Friday from 8:30am to 5:30pm, and no appointment is necessary. For information, phone 926-4777. . . . Prominent Queen's Medical Center also has a Waikiki affiliate: **Queen's Health Care Center,** 1778 Ala Moana Blvd., in the Discovery Bay Shopping Center. The clinic is open from 8am until 10pm daily, and no appointment is needed. For information, phone 943-1111. If you are staying in Waikiki, your taxi fare to the Waikiki clinic and back to your hotel will be deducted from your bill; see any hotel desk for a taxi slip. . . . Should you require a house call—or hotel call—contact **Doctors on Call** (DOC). They're on duty every day, 24 hours a day, and a phone call to 926-4777 will bring them to your hotel room promptly; the charge is $85 (office visits, $45). DOC also maintains 24-hour-a-day walk-in clinics at the Hyatt Regency Hotel (Diamond Head Tower, 4th floor, tel. 926-4777), the Outrigger Reef Towers Hotel (room 242, tel. 926-0664), and at the Hawaiian Regent Hotel, (Kuhio Tower, 2nd floor, tel. 923-3666). No appointments are necessary. . . . Of course, in a medical emergency, you can always call 911 and get an ambulance, or go to the emergency department of the Queen's Medical Center, 1301 Punchbowl St. (tel. 547-4311). All of these facilities work with most insurance plans. . . . If you have medical questions but you're not sure you need a doctor, you can call **Ask-A-Nurse,** a 24-hour health-care information and physician referral service sponsored by Queen's and Castle Medical Centers. Dial 533-NURS for assistance. From the outer islands, phone 1/800-342-5901. Hearing impaired: 523-9609. . . . In a dental emergency you'll get good care at reasonable cost at the **Hawaii Family Dental Center,** at Sears in the Ala Moana Shopping Center. Phone 944-0011 for information.

FREE AND LOW-COST CLASSES

The **Waikiki Community Center,** 310 Paoakalani Ave. (tel. 923-1802), offers a wide variety of classes in art, hula, mah jong, shiatsu, tap dancing, and more. Nonmembers usually pay $1 per class; members, who pay $15 a year and receive a calendar and newsletter, pay 50¢. . . . If you'd like to learn to make feather or flower leis, do Hawaiian quilting or lau hala (fiber) plaiting, attend one of the demonstrations of traditional Hawaiian folk crafts, held Monday through Saturday, from 9am to 2:30pm at the **Atherton Halau of the Bishop Museum.** Cost is $5 plus materials. We have enthusiastic reports each year on these delightful classes. For information, phone 847-3511. . . . Free classes in hula, fresh-flower lei making, and Hawaiian ti-leaf hula-skirt making, as well as displays of the art of Hawaiian quilt making, are featured in the Great Hall of the **Hyatt Regency Waikiki** at various times. Specific information is available by calling 923-1234. . . . You can learn how to slice a pineapple, make a flower lei, weave a coconut frond, and lots more, in the huge array of classes presented at the **Royal Hawaiian Shopping Center.** Consult the local papers for schedules. . . . Honolulu's **Department of Parks and Recreation** has an extensive recreation program for adults, teenagers, and children. Visitors are welcome to participate in classes (of up to 10 sessions). Events are announced in the local papers. . . . If you're staying in town for a month or two, you may want to sign up for one of the short-term, low-cost, noncredit classes at the **University of Hawaii at Manoa** (see "Sightseeing in Honolulu," Chapter VIII). On the agenda one summer: Kundalini yoga, batik, folk guitar, occult numerology, belly dancing —and then some!

FREE AND LOW-COST FACTORY TOURS

Free refreshments and more than 40,000 fashions to select from at factory prices are available at **Hilo Hattie Fashion Center,** 700 Nimitz. Call them at 537-2926 and they'll tell you where their free bus will pick you up in Waikiki. . . . Jewelry from the bottom of the sea is the subject of the tour run by **The Hawaii Jewelry Design Center** at 1520 Liona St. This is the home of Maui Divers of Hawaii, who were the first to mine black coral more than 30 years ago; now their creations include a variety of corals, as well as other precious stones, in 14-karat-gold settings. The half-hour tour, given daily from 9am to 3pm, includes a film and a walk through the manufacturing center where you may watch artisans at work, followed by a visit to the sales room. Admission is $3. Phone 949-6729 for reservations and directions. . . . To see how many Hawaiian gift items—hula skirts, dolls, shell jewelry, ornaments, kitchen accessories, etc.—are made, you can take a free tour of **Lanakila Crafts** at 1809 Bachelot St., Monday to Friday (except holidays) from 8am to 3:30pm. Lanakila is a private nonprofit organization that provides vocational training and employment placement services for severely handicapped adults. Their products are sold in the finest gift stores in Hawaii. They are also available in their Gift Shop. Call 531-0555 for information and to arrange tours. . . . If you're driving around the island, you may want to take time to stop off in Waialua, not far from Haleiwa, to visit the **Hawaii Kukui Nut Company** at 66-935 Kaukonahua Rd. (tel. 637-5620). Here you can see raw kukui nuts being processed into beautiful jewelry (kukui-nut leis were once reserved only for Hawaiian royalty), and you'll also get a chance to sample pure Kukui Nut Oil, a remarkable ancient beauty secret. Factory specials at the gift shop and free samples are available. Tours are held daily from 9am to 5pm. . . . And don't forget the **Dole Cannery** tour, which we describe in full in Chapter VIII. Admission is $5.

CALL HOME

Five dollars doesn't buy a great deal in Hawaii these days, but it can buy you a 10-minute phone call back to the mainland, or a series of phone calls for up to 10 minutes. Here's how it works: You go to one of **Phone Line Hawaii's** Waikiki telecom centers at either the International Market Place, 2330 Kalakaua, or the Discovery Bay Center, 1778 Ala Moana Blvd., where the cards are on sale, every day from 8:30am to 11pm. Then you use your card from any telephone, either in a phone booth or your hotel room, and you eliminate the charges that hotels levy on operator-assisted calls. Cards for calling Canada cost $12, and overseas cards are also available.

WALKING TOURS

The people at **Kapiolani Community College** would like to take you for a walk. In the course of their popular two-and-a-half-hour walking tours, which leave from various points downtown, you can visit with "Ghosts of Old Honolulu," attend "Galas of Old Honolulu," and relive the events of the 1893 "revolution" that almost toppled the Hawaiian monarchy. Costumed historic role-players take part. Cost is $5 for adults, $2 for children and students. Make reservations by calling 734-9211. Tours are usually listed in the *Waikiki Beach Press*. . . . The **Mission Houses Museum** presents a walking tour of "Historic Downtown Honolulu" every Monday and Friday morning at 9:30. The cost of $7 also includes admission to the museum (tel. 531-0481 for reservations). . . . **Auntie Malia Solomon,** the well-known Hawaiiana expert, leads a free walk to places of historical interest in Waikiki, every Tuesday and Wednesday at 10:30am from the Hyatt Regency Museum, on the second floor of the hotel, behind the waterfall. Wear comfortable shoes, for it's about a two-mile, two-hour trek. For more information, phone 923-1234, ext. 6410.

HAWAIIAN WEDDINGS

What could be nicer than getting married in Hawaii? You can get married and honeymoon in the same place, and the cost need not be exorbitant. The idea has become so appealing that thousands of visitors are now seeking out Hawaiian weddings in offbeat settings—perhaps on the beach, on top of a mountain, aboard a catamaran, in a lighthouse—even in a church. For help in planning a Hawaiian wedding, you can contact several private services, suggested by the Hawaii Visitors Bureau. **Aloha Wedding Planners** offers a variety of picturesque locations and takes care of every detail, from the ministers to the photographers. Rhona and Eleanor, the wedding coordinators in charge, are both incurably romantic and decidedly practical; they avow that their service is "always first class, even if your budget is strictly economy." Write them at 1031 Auahi St., 2nd floor, Honolulu, HI 96814 (tel. 523-144). . . . **SOL-Hawaii** (that's for "Sounds of Love") offers weddings in the great outdoors as well as in more intimate settings, and also on the neighbor islands. They can be reached at P.O. Box 8494, Honolulu, HI 96830-0494 (tel. 734-5441) or by calling their toll-free number, 800/262-1885. . . . Rainbows are considered a good omen when they appear on the day of a wedding. **Rainbow Connection** does not guarantee one, but they do guarantee to coordinate your entire Hawaiian wedding at a hotel or at one of their beautiful sites—even on a yacht at sea. From standing in as witnesses to arranging video coverage, they take care of every detail. Prices run from $195 to $795—for a wedding on a 44-foot yacht, it's $395, and if you want to spend the night on the yacht alone and cook your own champagne breakfast in the morning, that's another $195. Write Rev. Barry D. McLean at 45-995 Wailele Rd., #73, Kaneohe, HI 96744, or phone him at 247-0754. . . . **Waimea Falls Park** is one of Hawaii's most popular locations for weddings in paradise. The experienced staff can make all of the necessary arrangements for the perfect ceremony and reception, including minister, flowers, music, limousine, champagne, and more. Custom wedding packages are available with a wide range of prices suitable for any budget. Contact the Wedding Department, Waimea Falls Park, 59-864 Kamehameha Hwy., Haleiwa, HI 96712 (tel. 638-8511).

Planning to marry in Maui? **A Hawaiian Wedding Experience** began by specializing in West Maui weddings, but it became so popular that it has expanded its services to the other major islands as well. They've been pioneers in planning romantic weddings for islanders as well as visitors for many years, offering everything from sunrise ceremonies on the slopes of Haleakala to sunset weddings at the beach, weddings on horseback in the mountains or lavish Royal Hawaiian Wedding Luaus. Write to Kalani Kinimaka, who runs this family operation at A Hawaiian Wedding Experience, Central Reservations, P.O. Box 8670, Honolulu, HI 96830-8670, or phone 926-6689 for wedding information on Maui, Kona, Kauai, and Waikiki.

On the Big Island, a sunset wedding at the lush **Kona Village Resort** would be pure heaven: P.O. Box 1299, Kaupulehua-Kona, HI 96745 (toll-free 800/367-5290). . . . **The Mauna Lani Bay Hotel,** one of the most beautiful in the islands, offers a Wedding in Paradise, for around $2,000 per couple, that includes the ceremony and all details, plus a three-night stay in a room overlooking the sea. Phone 800/356-6652 for details. . . . Guests of the glamorous Kona Surf Resort on the Big Island can be married at the hotel's **Kona Royal Chapel.** For information on wedding and honeymoon packages, write Kona Surf Resort & Country Club, 78-128 Ehukai St., Kailua-Kona, HI 96740, or phone toll free, 800/367-8011.

On Kauai, **Coco Palms Resort** has been a favorite wedding and honeymoon spot for years, with its private wedding chapel nestled amid a lush, 45-acre coconut grove. They'll do everything from selecting the minister, music, and flowers, to providing a Hawaiian conch-shell blower: P.O. Box 631, Lihue, Kauai, HI 96766 (tel. toll free 800/42-MARRY). . . . The luxurious new mega-resort, **The Westin Kauai** at Kauai Lagoons, also offers some spectacular wedding ideas—like being married on a 40-acre lagoon overlooking the water at its Chapel by the Sea. The wedding couple is driven to the chapel in a horse-drawn carriage. Call the hotel's wedding consultant at 245-5050 for information. . . . Kauai's restored-plantation estate of the '30s, **Kilohana,** is also the site of numerous weddings; they can be held indoors in an elegant living room overlooking the gardens, in the gardens themselves, or even in a turn-of-the-century carriage riding through the plantation's grounds. Write to wedding coordinator Shelley Powell at Kilohana, P.O. Box 3121, Lihue, Kauai, HI 96766.

---

2. Ethnic Hawaii

Now we come to perhaps the most colorful aspect of the Hawaiian scene—the life of its various cultural groups. For us, this is what most makes Hawaii a marvelous place to visit. All the ethnic festivals and celebrations are exciting; just take in whatever is going on when you're there. Some people even plan their trips to the islands around the festival calendar; we wouldn't go that far, but we would advise you never to miss a festival that's going on when you're there—it might be the best part of your trip.

THE FESTIVAL CALENDAR

Here are the ethnic events, plus other events of interest, that take place only on certain dates. We've set them forth in roughly chronological order.

New Year's Eve. Celebrations are much like those on the mainland, except that the firecrackers are noisier (Asian style), costume balls are held at the leading hotels, and purification ceremonies are performed at Buddhist temples, to which visitors are welcome. January 1 is open house among island Japanese families.

Narcissus Festival. For three weeks before and five days after the Chinese New Year (which usually falls in the first week of February), the community blows its collective top in a running series of lantern parades, fashion and flower shows, banquets, house-and-garden tours, the crowning of the Narcissus Queen, and dancing in the streets.

Cherry Blossom Festival. A Japanese cultural and trade show, this is held in February or March, complete with a queen, pageant, and a coronation ball, plus demonstrations of tea ceremonies, flower arranging, and more.

Japanese Girls' Day. Japanese girls are presented with dolls on the first March 3 after their birth and every March 3 thereafter. In accordance with this delightful custom, public displays of dolls—usually costumed in the dress of a royal court—can be found in windows of the big Japanese department stores.

Prince Kuhio Day, March 26. Hawaii's beloved "people's prince" and first delegate to Congress is honored with impressive ceremonies first at Iolani Palace and later at his tomb at the Royal Mausoleum. At Kuhio Beach in Waikiki, the site of his home, a memorial tablet is decorated with leis. Hawaiian societies hold special programs and events.

Merrie Monarch Festival, April. This all-island competition between Hawaii's best hula halaus (schools) is held yearly on the Big Island of Hawaii, is sold out months in advance, and is enthusiastically watched on TV by just about every man, woman, and child in the state of Hawaii. Wonderful!

Lei Day. On May 1, everybody wears a lei, and there are contests for the most beautiful leis (judging at Kapiolani Park) and a wonderful Lei Day concert at the Waikiki Shell usually by the Cazimero Brothers, in the evening. Tickets are around $13 for general admission. Come early, bring a picnic supper and a blanket, and join Hawaii's people for a joyous event. (We know visitors who plan their entire trip around this event—they wouldn't dream of missing it!)

Japanese Boys' Day. You needn't be Japanese to have your family fly a brightly colored paper-and-fabric carp in your honor. Many island families have taken up the custom; watch for the flying fish each year on May 5.

Kamehameha Day, June 11. This is a state holiday (many offices will be closed) and one of the biggest celebrations of them all; there are parades and festivities all over the islands.

Japan Festival in Hawaii, June 13 to 15. One of the newer annual events in Honolulu, it includes a Bon Dance Festival (see below), a Tabishibai of the samurai period, a Japanese folk-dance show, and, of course, a parade.

Bon Odori Festival, late July. One of the most colorful events in the islands, these traditional dances are done to welcome the arrival of departed souls in Paradise. The dances are usually sponsored by Japanese temples whose members practice their steps for months. Watch the local papers for dates.

Aloha Week, mid-September to mid-October. Take the celebrations of all the ethnic groups, roll them into one, and you'll get some idea of Aloha Week—or Aloha Weeks, as they should more properly be called, since this is a movable festival, taking place on different islands in a more-or-less progressive order. The Asian, Polynesian, and Western groups all get together for this hoolaulea (gathering for a celebration), each vying to demonstrate the warmth and beauty of the wonderful Hawaiian aloha. The eight-day-long spree features music and dance events, demonstrations of ancient arts and crafts, a beautiful orchid show, water sports, an enormous flower parade, pageants, the crowning of both a king and a queen, and even a Molokai-to-Oahu Canoe Race (terminating at the Hilton Hawaiian Village Beach). This is a great time to come to the islands. Check with the Hawaii Visitors Bureau for the exact dates of Aloha Week celebrations; as stated, they vary from island to island.

Bodhi Day. On the nearest Sunday to December 7, the enlightenment of Buddha is commemorated with religious observances in the Buddhist temples and with Japanese dance programs and ceremonies elsewhere.

Princess Bernice Pauahi Bishop's Birthday. Hawaiian societies and schools state a moving expression of remembrance for the beloved princess at the Royal Mausoleum on December 19.

Christmas. What could be nicer than a Polynesian Christmas? There aren't any chimneys, so Santa might arrive in an outrigger canoe or on a surfboard. He might —it's not as bad as it sounds—be wearing a hula skirt. Carols are sung to ukulele accompaniment. If you happen to be in Lahaina during the Christmas season, you'll see two imaginative coral Christmas trees. Elsewhere, Christmas lights are hung on everything from evergreens to bamboo. There are special programs for the children at the Honolulu Academy of Arts. The stores are jammed, just as they are on the mainland, but surprisingly, a view of the bustling crowds (thronging the mall at Ala

Moana Center, for example) is one of the prettiest of holiday pictures. The Christmas greeting: "Mele Kalikimaka!"

READERS' ACTIVITIES SUGGESTIONS: "A fish auction is held every Monday through Saturday at 5:30am at **United Fishing Agency,** 117 Ahui St. We went about 7am and saw fish we didn't know existed, such as a 114-pound moon fish. This auction was far bigger than others we've seen and the people were more than happy to answer our questions. . . . Rent an underwater camera for $10 to $12, including a 24-exposure roll of film, from almost any scuba or snorkel shop, and you will get more comments on these pictures than on any others of your trip" (Kenneth Kendall, Omaha, Nebr.).

"Getting married in Hawaii? For rules and regulations write to the State Health Department, 1250 Punchbowl St., Honolulu, HI 96813, tel. 548-5862. Permits must be obtained for weddings in state parks. Contact State Parks Division, P.O. Box 621, Honolulu, HI 96809, or tel. 548-7455. For weddings in national parks, write Superintendent, Haleakala National Park, P.O. Box 369, Makawao, HI 96768, tel. 572-9306; or, Superintendent, Hawaii Volcanoes National Park, HI 96718, tel. 967-7311. . . . For a complete listing of cultural and sports events, six months at a time, send for a copy of He Kukini, Hawaii Visitors Bureau, 2270 Kalakaua Ave., Honolulu, HI 96815, tel. 923-1811" (Judie Carbaugh, Sykesville, Md).

"While we were in Honolulu I had the misfortune to break a tooth and had some difficulty in finding a dentist. The Travel Desk at our hotel suggested the *Yellow Pages* (utterly confusing), and we also went to the Queens Medical Center in Waikiki without success. In the end we went to the Hawaii Visitors Bureau at Ala Moana, where we were told about the **Hawaii Family Dental Center** at Sears Ala Moana (tel. 944-0011). There were a number of doctors there and I was able to obtain emergency treatment the same afternoon, at very reasonable cost. Charming people, too" (Joanne Ledward, Bournemouth, England). . . . "There are a lot of barbershops in Honolulu's Chinatown with haircuts at $3 to $4, several at $3 for senior citizens. Not being a senior citizen, I had a haircut at $3.50. So who says Honolulu is *expensive?* Shop and ye shall find" (Mark Terry, Honolulu, HI).

"The free bus ride to Hilo Hattie's was entertaining as well as informative. Although my sister had rented a car, we took the bus to Hilo Hattie's and had a great time singing and learning all kinds of things from our bus driver. The **Polynesian Cultural Center** was wonderful, and the Navy's free tour of **Pearl Harbor** cannot be surpassed" (Sandra Munson, Birmingham, Ala.). . . . "For an all-day outing, we arrive at the suburban bus stop at Ala Moana at about 9am and board bus no. 52 to ride around the island. We get off at Turtle Bay Resort for a very lovely lunch, and after that we walk around. If the surf is up, there is nothing more exciting than to watch the waves rolling in. Then we take bus no. 57 back home. This is a two-hour ride each way and it is really a complete circle-island ride—and a very lovely one, too. We take this trip every year" (Mrs. Mildred Hodgeman, Bloomington, Minn.).

"The best thing about a Hawaiian vacation is the Hawaiian people. Everyone is always ready to answer your questions with a smile. The tour guides and bus drivers are always singing or making you laugh. We came home thoroughly refreshed from this trip! Even with the hustle-bustle in parts of Waikiki, we enjoyed every minute of our vacation" (Margaret A. Pyzik, Naperville, Ill.).

"Tourists who are needlework enthusiasts should know that they can learn Hawaiian quilting at the **Bishop Museum** on Monday and Friday from 9am to 2:30pm. Lei making and other crafts are featured other days. For $5, you receive personal instruction for the entire day! Kits containing everything you need to complete a quilted pillow are around $25. The class is held in the Atherton Halau building on the museum grounds. The ambience is strictly "hang loose," with sides of the building open to the sunny breezes and the museum's musical presentation taking place at 1pm on the stage in the same room. You can come and go if you wish to see the museum exhibits or the planetarium show. The day I was there happened to be the teacher's 70th birthday: In honor of the occasion, she was wearing several fresh-flower leis and also did a hula dance as part of the musical presentation. At noon an array of Asian foods ranging from lobster to who-knows-what was brought on and the 15-or-so quilters enjoyed a delicious birthday lunch! On the days she is not teaching at Bishop Museum, 'Aunt Debbie' Kakalia demonstrates quilting at a shopping center" (Janet Bryan, Stockbridge, GA.). [*Authors' Note:* Evening classes are also held in feather-lei making. For information, call 848-4109.]

"On Sunday we went to the worship service sponsored by **Waikiki Beach Chaplaincy** on the shore outside the Hilton Hawaiian Village hotel. It ran from about 10:30am to noon and included a good deal of music and a sermon. People were there in every form of dress and undress imaginable—perhaps 300 to 400 persons. The services have been conducted there since 1970. We decided that it was one of the best services we had ever attended. Certainly God could be worshiped in this way in this beautiful place, and it was fitting to pause and thank Him for His gifts to us, including the particular one of being in Hawaii" (Jim Cox, Middletown, Ky.).

"Even if you do little else, be sure to go **snorkeling at Hanauma Bay.** We took an early trip, from 9 to 12:30; the next day we realized that we probably wouldn't have been able to walk if we had spent the whole day. One word of advice: If you decide to rent a camera for underwater pictures (a lot of fun), check with a score of camera shops first. We rented ours from the snorkeling outfit, but it did cost $20 to rent the camera, complete with 27-exposure film. Be advised that you cannot change the film in the camera if you rent from the snorkeling firm. It would have been better to rent in town and get two cameras with film for about the same price" (Candy and Paul Erkard, Alexandria, Virg.).

"For those who wish to try the **snorkeling at Hanauma Bay,** we recommend a very early start. When we arrived, the beach was relatively quiet, but by the time we were ready to leave, it was practically standing room only" (Judy and Geoff Horner, Abbotsford, B.C., Canada). . . . "It is our opinion that Hanauma Bay is not really a place to stop for a swim, but a wonderful place to snorkel *or* see fish without snorkeling gear. No one was swimming: Mobs of people were sunning themselves, snorkeling, or just standing in the water feeding the fish that are all around. To get the most enjoyment from the place, the reader should know ahead of time to bring food—particularly frozen peas—to feed the fish. We wish we had" (Marjorie Diamond, Tiburon, Calif.). . . . "As a first-time visitor to Hawaii, I truly enjoyed the **snorkeling at Hanauma Bay.** A bit of advice for anyone who is considering bringing food for those beautiful fish. First, an investment in some Ziploc bags. They keep the food, especially bread, from getting soggy and falling apart. The best food that I have found is frozen peas" (Lynn Dalton, Stony Point, N.Y.). . . . "Our son had a lot of fun swimming at Hanauma Bay in the clear water. A professional scuba-diver told him to feed cheese to the tropical fish and it worked great, better than bread. The cheese that comes in a tube and squeezes out is the best" (Ingo Platzer, Omaha, Nebr.).

"Do you get the idea that we love Hawaii? TRUE!! We go, rent a car, take the paper and read it all, even do the Word-a-Day puzzle! We go to thrift shops, local activities such as festivals and concerts, attend a church, walk miles in the warm evening air and the equally warm days, watch for the TRULY Hawaiian music events, bring home the TRULY Hawaiian records and tapes, and weep and laugh with the people as they strive to maintain a wonderful culture" (Virginia R. Horn, no address given).

"For the second time we were privileged to view the annual **orchid show at Neal Blaisdell Center** around the middle of October, and we highly recommend it for those with an interest in flowers. Cacti and anthuriums are also on display and have been judged. The picture-taking opportunities are endless, and chatting with growers and other visitors was an extra for us. Attending right after lunch, midweek, was less crowded than at other times. . . . We always check the Honolulu paper immediately after arrival to find out what is on display at the Academy of Art. We were able to view an antique Portuguese quilt show one time; another time, it was Japanese screens. The permanent collection is always good to see, and the building itself is charming. And it's a quick trip by bus from Waikiki" (Elizabeth Greer, El Cerrito, Calif.).

"Persons wishing to take noncredit courses should inquire at the **University of Hawaii at Manoa,** College of Continuing Education, 2530 Dole St., Honolulu, HI 96822, for course information, schedules, and fees. They will mail a copy of their brochure about a month before the classes are scheduled. One would not have to be in Honolulu for a long stay to take advantage of some of these courses; some are one-day seminars" (Dian Presmanes, Atlanta, Ga.). . . . "We each bought an inflatable raft for $4.99, and loved going way out where the waves were breaking: It took practically no room to bring the rafts home. We felt sorry for the people who bought beach mats; many had to hand-carry them on the plane because they were too wide to fit into suitcases" (Carl and Debbie Adams, St. Louis, Mo.). . . . "Do not carry extra money to the beach—leave your wallet with a friend, or put your money and keys in a **waterproof wallet** that you can wear swimming. Thieves seem to love Waikiki Beach" (Nancy Grant, South Easton, Mass.). . . . "Please advise your readers against **cashing traveler's checks** in banks. There is a minimum fee of $2 for this service. If the check is cashed in a store, restaurant, or hotel, no fee is charged" (Marian Ruggiero, Brooklyn, N.Y.).

"For the more active visitor interested in hiking, phone or write the **Hawaii Geographic Society,** P.O. Box 1698, Honolulu, HI 96806 (tel. 538-3952), for maps and advice on hiking or camping on Oahu or other islands. . . . An excellent hike to the top of Diamond Head is conducted by **The Clean Air Team**, every Saturday morning at 9am. You cover three miles each way in two hours. The cost is $3, but worth it, and can be hiked by anybody as the people are split into groups of fast, medium, and slow walkers, each with a leader. A must! For information, phone 944-0804" (Jim Drouin, Edmonton, Alberta, Canada).

"For those planning to be in Honolulu for Christmas, we would recommend attending **Christmas Eve services** at historic **Kawaiahao Church** in downtown Honolulu. The beautiful Christmas music is sung in both Hawaiian and English, giving the visitor a chance to sing along, and feel the island blend of cultures" (Mrs. John O'Harra, Portland, Ore.). . . . "We enjoyed being in Waikiki for May 1st, **Lei Day.** There were lei-making exhibits all over and a contest at the park, where we saw the very impressive coronation ceremony of the Lei Day Queen and also a large craft show with many beautiful things, some very reasonable" (Kay Loesch, Cordova, Alaska).

"Sharks are occasionally seen offshore, sometimes only 100 yards off the beach, but newspaper reports indicate that only five persons have been killed by sharks in Hawaiian waters in the past 85 years. Drowning is fairly common, though. It seemed that at least five were drowned every week or so. Visitors should be impressed with the extreme hazards of swimming in the surf in winter and even in just sitting on rocks where the occasional extra-large wave can sweep you off" (Jack and Ruth Phillips, Summerland, B.C., Canada).

"The beach at **Kailua** is great for children. There are good waves without dangerous undertow. . . . **Ala Moana Beach Park** is much more desirable for children than Waikiki. The water is shallow and there are no rocks or coral" (Kim Andrews, Lincoln, Nebr.). . . . "Please check local papers the day you arrive. We did not do so and missed a beach fair on the one afternoon that we did not have rain when we were in Honolulu." (John Ruble, Hillsboro, Ohio). . . . "I would like to suggest that Hawaiian malihinis turn on their AM radios to 1420, **KCCN,** the only radio station playing strictly Hawaiian music. This immediately sets them ir the mood for the Hawaiian experience" (Diane Miyazaki, Wahiawa, HI).

"The **Hyatt Regency Waikiki** continues to provide great free entertainment. Check the tourist papers. On New Year's Eve in their Great Hall we danced to big-band entertainment with hundreds of balloons sailing down at midnight, vendors with Maui potato chips, pretzels, and other inexpensive treats—a very pleasant evening. Speaking of New Year's Eve, Waikiki was much quieter, with new fireworks regulations and great supervision by HPD. . . . The best fun is still free, wading in the warm surf at midnight in December while friends at home are shoveling snow" (Mrs. John O'Harra, Portland, Ore.).

"Those interested in other murals of Jean Charlot should stop off at the **Leeward Community College** exit and look at the mural painted in the lobby of the theater there. I think it's one of his best so far. You can see the fresco from the upper-level glass doors. . . . Check with the **State Department of Land and Natural Resources** for hiking maps, or check with the **Sierra Club** for information on local trails. To me, you haven't seen Hawaii until you have hiked up the mountains, eaten the wild fruits, and seen the magnificent tropical plants along the way. There is hardly any mountain trail where you will not find guava when it is in season. . . . The **State Foundation on Culture and Arts** can give you a schedule of what's happening culturally for the month. Some things are free" (Shirley Gerum, Haleiwa, HI). . . . "The **Prince of Peace Lutheran Church** is an interesting attraction on Waikiki Beach; it's on the 12th—top—floor of 33 Lewers, and is referred to as 'the church with a view from the pew' and that is certainly true" (Jerald R. Borgie, San Diego, Calif.).

"I have a suggestion for vacationers who would like to make a very reasonable trip. My mother took two very interesting but not difficult courses at the **University of Hawaii,** one on the geography of Hawaii, the other on the botany of Hawaii. Both courses enhanced our trip very much. My mother is a teacher, and with these credits she moved up, one notch in her income bracket, about $1,000! Also, for the time she was in school (about two months), the trip was deductible from her taxes!" (Bonny Warner, Mt. Baldy, Calif.). . . . "In winter and spring, watch for the fairs and carnivals held at local schools such as **Punahou, McKinley High, Iolani,** or the **University of Hawaii.** They have lots of local color, good ethnic foods (great Portuguese malasadas), interesting white elephant and antique booths, carnival midway areas, etc. They are usually free and are fun to attend. There are sometimes local fund-raising events at the **Blaisdell Center** or on the large stage at **Kapiolani Park,** at which the name Hawaiian entertainers, like Don Ho or Danny Kaleikini, appear, and these events cost little—much cheaper than going to see the same performers at a nightclub. We saw an excellent show with some of the best island talent and Don Ho as emcee at the park, in a benefit for Life of the Land, the local ecology group" (Mrs. Joseph G. Astman, Levittown, N.Y.).

"I found the **Hawaii Trail and Mountain Club's Sunday walks** one of the most enjoyable parts of my vacation, introducing me to wild country that I should certainly not have seen on my own. An easy walk within Honolulu may be worth a mention. By getting prior permission from the National Guard in Diamond Head (open 8am to 4pm Monday to Friday), we walked to the top of Diamond Head Crater, an easy 35-minute walk, although the last part involves a steep iron ladder, and needs a flashlight. Worth doing for fantastic views and orientation" (David Brokensha, Santa Barbara, Calif.).

"**Fort DeRussy Beach** is extra nice because of the grass and trees and benches. True, it is primarily for the armed forces, but just walk up the beach and you can stay there all day. We watch the papers closely and always attend native celebrations and gatherings; sometimes news of one is passed on to us by a native. Enjoy them as an honored guest; you will be richly rewarded" (Mrs. S. R. Kranek, Brocksville, Ohio).

VIII

SIGHTSEEING IN HONOLULU

1. DOWNTOWN HONOLULU

2. PUNCHBOWL, LOWER TANTALUS, AND NUUANU

3. UNIVERSITY OF HAWAII AT MANOA, EAST-WEST CENTER, AND MANOA VALLEY

4. BISHOP MUSEUM AND DOLE CANNERY SQUARE

5. PEARL HARBOR

6. PARADISE PARK AND LYON ARBORETUM

7. A WAIKIKI CHECKLIST

Now we come to the serious center of any trip to a new place—seeing the basic sights. If you want to know what makes the 50th state tick, you must explore the city of Honolulu. And if you really want to experience the sights and sounds and feel of a city, the best way to do it is to get out and walk. Happily, it's also the cheapest way and the most fun.

Commercial tours are expensive and can only skim the highlights. We think the city merits more attention. The local buses of the MTL, a good pair of walking shoes, and the instructions that follow will get you to all the major places. And more important, you can go at your own pace, devoting the most time to what most interests you—and you alone.

These itineraries have been set up as basic touchstones for seeing Honolulu. Improvise at your pleasure. Take two days to do a one-day trip, and spend the other half of each day at the beach if that's what suits you. We've set forth seven different tours of Honolulu and vicinity, only one of which (the trip to Pearl Harbor) will involve more than $1.20 in transportation costs. In following our directions, please remember once again that makai means to the sea, mauka is to the mountains. Diamond Head is in the direction of Diamond Head crater, and Ewa is away from Diamond Head.

If you have any questions about what bus goes where, phone MTL at 531-1611 for information. You may phone anytime between 5:30am and 10pm—and the people here are really knowledgeable and friendly. If you're at Ala Moana Center, you can use the no-cost direct telephones to MTL, which are located at the bus stops on the north and south sides of the center. You should also note that traffic on Kalakaua Avenue, Waikiki's main thoroughfare, goes Diamond Head most of the way. All buses running from Waikiki downtown should be boarded on Kuhio Avenue. Remember that bus fare is 60¢ (exact change in coins required), and that senior citizens can use the buses free at all times by showing a bus pass. (You must apply for a senior citizen bus pass in person, at 725 Kapiolani Blvd., with documented proof that you are 65 years of age or older. You will then have your picture taken with a special camera and receive your temporary bus pass within 15 minutes. Information: 531-7066. Oh yes, they call it The BUS.

WAIKIKI TROLLEY

Here's a way to make your sightseeing a bit more comfortable without breaking the bank: hop aboard the Waikiki Trolley. For a cost of $10 per day for adults, $5 for children, you can travel between the Royal Hawaiian Shopping Center and Dole Cannery Square, making stops en route at Ala Moana Center, the Hilton Hawaiian Village, the Ramada Renaissance Ala Moana Hotel, the Honolulu Academy of Arts, Ward Warehouse and Fisherman's Wharf, Ward Centre, the state capitol and Iolani Palace, the Mission Houses Museum and the King Kamehameha Statue, Chinatown, the Hawaii Maritime Center, Restaurant Row and the Hilo Hattie Factory. You can stay on for the entire two-hour, narrated trip or hop on and off whenever you like and continue on another trolley. Recalling Honolulu's turn-of-the-century streetcars, these jaunty red motorized trolleys with an old-fashioned look (etched-glass windows, polished brass rails, hand-carved oak interiors) stop each hour at the locations listed above. As you study the trips outlined below, you'll be able to see when and where the trolley can take you to some destinations. Phone 526-0112 or check local papers for exact routes and schedules. For more information, phone 599-2561.

1. Downtown Honolulu

Plan to spend at least a full day on this trip, which covers the major sights of the city: the Honolulu Academy of Arts, the Mission Houses, Kawaiahao Church, civic center including the state capitol, Aloha Tower, the *Falls of Clyde,* the financial and shopping districts, Chinatown, and the downtown Japanese neighborhood. It's a long trip, but once you've done it, you'll have seen the heart of Honolulu. If you prefer, break the trip up into a two- or even three-day jaunt.

THE ACADEMY OF ARTS

Your first destination is the Honolulu Academy of Arts, which you reach by taking TheBUS no. 2 in Waikiki right to the academy at the corner of Ward and Beretania (that's how the early Hawaiians pronounced Britain), and you'll spot the low, pretty building of the academy. Magnificent art treasures await within. (See "The Art Scene," Chapter VII, for details). Open Tuesday through Saturday from 10am to 4:30pm, and from 2 to 5pm. Closed Monday and major holidays. Admission is free.

NEAL S. BLAISDELL CENTER

Now retrace your steps back across Thomas Square to King Street; coming into view is the dazzling Neal S. Blaisdell Center ("NBC" to the locals), a giant $1.25-million complex with an arena, a concert theater, and a convention hall. There are no official tours of the building, but apply at the administration office if you are seriously interested in seeing it; they will have someone show you around. Don't forget to ask for a schedule of coming events while you're there; some big names in the entertainment world may be appearing. The arena, which can seat up to 8,800, has seen such recent stars as Lionel Richie and Whitney Houston. Home court of the University of Hawaii Rainbows, the center is the scene of many sporting events, from boxing and wrestling to gymnastics, tennis, and basketball. Family entertainment includes the Ice Capades and the circus. The Concert Theater, home of the Honolulu Symphony, hosts ballet, opera, modern dance, national touring-theater shows, and many other specials: noted pianist John Browning was presented here recently. The exhibition hall has numerous displays and trade exhibits presenting many items unique to the islands. Since this is Hawaii, all is landscaped in a tropical setting with lovely gardens and a lagoon, a perfect natural backdrop to this modern-day marvel.

Note to Parents: Kids will enjoy feeding the tame ducks and geese that live in the ponds on the grounds. They are lovingly cared for by the staff of the city auditoriums, but are always happy for a handout! You often see local keikis and their moms feeding them loaves of day-old bread.

THE MISSION HOUSES

Now we go back to the Hawaii of old. Cross Ward Avenue on the Ewa side of the center, then turn left on King Street and walk Ewa three short blocks to King and Kawaiahao streets. There you will come across the Mission Houses Museum, three 19th-century buildings that will give you a tremendous insight into the lives of the missionaries in Hawaii—and the unlikely intermingling of New England and Polynesia. One of the houses, the home of missionary families, was built of ready-cut lumber that was shipped around Cape Horn from New England; a second, made of coral, houses a replica of the first printing press in the islands, which produced a Hawaiian spelling book in 1822; the third, also of coral, was the warehouse and home of the mission's first business agent.

A huge renovation and restoration project has been completed here, and the museum is more attractive than ever. Restored to the period 1821–1860, the Frame House includes furnished parlors, bedrooms, kitchens, and cellar, a collection of original missionary furniture and other personal artifacts documenting the lives of the families who lived and worked here. This house makes possible the study of a life-style and set of cultural values that had a profound influence on Hawaii's history. A new gallery in the 1831 Chamberlain House holds changing exhibits.

If possible, plan your visit for a Saturday. That's when history goes live at the museum as costumed players portray the missionaries in a program entitled, "Honolulu 1831." (Admission fee is the same as during the week.)

The Mission Houses are open Tuesday to Saturday 9am to 4pm; Sunday noon to 4pm; closed Monday. Admission, which includes a 45-minute guided tour, is $3.50 for adults, $1 for children 6 to 16, free for children under 6. Be sure to pick up a copy of the Mission Houses' 75¢ booklet guiding you through "Historic Downtown Honolulu"; it's very helpful. Also note that a guided walking tour of that area leaves the Mission Houses Museum Monday and Friday morning at 9:30. The fee, including museum admission, is $7, $2 for children 6 through 16. Reservations are advised (tel. 531-0481). If you happen to be in town in June for the Kamehameha Day celebration, don't miss the Fancy Fair on the grounds; about 50 booths are set up to sell local handcrafts, plus refreshing things to eat and drink.

KAWAIAHAO CHURCH

Outside the Mission Houses Museum, turn left and cross Kawaiahao Street to Kawaiahao Church. Inside, the tall, feathered kahilis signify at once that this is royal ground. You're standing in the Westminster Abbey of Hawaii, the scene of pomp and ceremony, coronations, and celebrations since its dedication in 1841. On March 12, 1959, the day Hawaii achieved statehood, the old coral church was filled with ecstatic islanders ringing its bell noisily and giving thanks for the fulfillment of a dream long denied. The next day, the Rev. Abraham Akaka linked the spirit of aloha with the spirit of Christianity in a sermon that has since become a classic in the writings of Hawaii. Note the vestibule memorial plaques to Hawaiian royalty and to the Rev. Hiram Bingham, the missionary who designed the church. Note, too, the outstanding collection of portraits of the Hawaiian alii by artist Patric. If you have time, come back on a Sunday morning at 10:30 when you'll hear a Hawaiian-English service and some beautiful Hawaiian singing. You can visit the church from 9am to 3pm weekdays, on Saturday from 9am to noon. Group tours can be taken during the week by appointment.

Behind the church, and seven to eight years older than it, is an adobe school-house, one of the oldest school buildings in the state.

CIVIC CENTER AND IOLANI PALACE

On the sidewalk outside the church, walk across King Street to the neo-Spanish city hall, or **Honolulu Hale.** Just Diamond Head of Honolulu Hale are two very attractive New England–style red-brick buildings with white trim. These house such city and country departments as municipal reference and records. Continuing in a Diamond Head direction, on the expanse of rolling lawn between these build-ings and the towering gray-stone monolith beyond, you'll see a highly controversial piece of art acquired by the city and country at a cost of $120,000. Created by famed Japanese-Hungarian sculptor Isamu Noguchi, this sculpture is entitled **Sky Gate.** It consists of four pieces of what is apparently a gigantic stove pipe, painted flat black and welded together. Three of the pieces are supporting "legs" for the fourth—forming a sort of eccentric quadrangle—which rests atop them. One is meant to stand on the concrete walk beneath the quadrangle and look at the sky through it. This acquisition created a veritable storm of controversy and was the subject of thou-sands of letters to the editors of Honolulu's two daily newspapers. You'll either love it or hate it!

The aforementioned gray-stone monolith is the **Honolulu Municipal Building,** 650 S. King St., which houses the departments of transportation, buildings, and public works, and much more. Like *Sky Gate,* this building was greeted with some-thing less than unmitigated joy by Honolulu's citizenry, many of whom feel that its architecture is out of keeping with the rest of the civic center, which consists of low-rise structures. When you stand in front of the municipal building by the flagpoles, the very attractive gray building with the terracotta roof that you see is the **Hawaii Newspaper Agency,** which houses the two daily newspapers. Many consider it one of the loveliest monarchy-style buildings in the city. Walk through the municipal building and out the other side, cross the little park area, and on the other side of Beretania Street you'll see the **Board of Water Supply,** a lovely pale-green building with a beautiful lawn and fountain.

Now retrace your steps in an Ewa direction, this time along Beretania Street; the beautiful new building you see across from the rear of Honolulu Hale is **Kalanimoku** (Ship of Heaven), a state office building. It houses the state depart-ments of land and natural resources, fish and game, and forestry, among others. The building has a cool, wonderfully open design, and at night, softly colored lights filter through the cut-out designs at its top. It is gorgeously landscaped with plantings of natal plums, giant zinnias, lau'e fern, various species of palms, and bright Shasta dai-sies.

The Punchbowl side of Kalanimoku is directly across from the **state capitol.** It's time to take a look now at this magnificent structure, completed in 1969 at the cost of $25 million. The open-air roof sweeps skyward like the peak of a volcano, reflecting pools signify an ocean environment, and Hawaiian materials and motifs have been used tastefully throughout. If the state senate and house of representatives are in session, you're invited to come in and see politics in action in the 50th state. You are also invited to visit, browse, and "experience" the offices of Hawaii's gover-nor and lieutenant-governor during regular working hours (8am to 4:30pm, Monday through Friday); Hawaii is one of the few states that allows the public to visit its executive office without an appointment or on official business. Be sure that you at least see the building; it is a glorious architectural achievement. Note, too, Marisol's controversial statue of Father Damien, and other works of art in front of the building, facing Beretania Street. Just outside the makai side of the building are two relatively new works: a replica of the Liberty Bell and a statue of Hawaii's last reigning monarch, Queen Liliuokalani.

After viewing the state capitol, go back the same way you came in. Walk makai and you are at the central building of the **Hawaii State Library.** It's a Greco-Roman

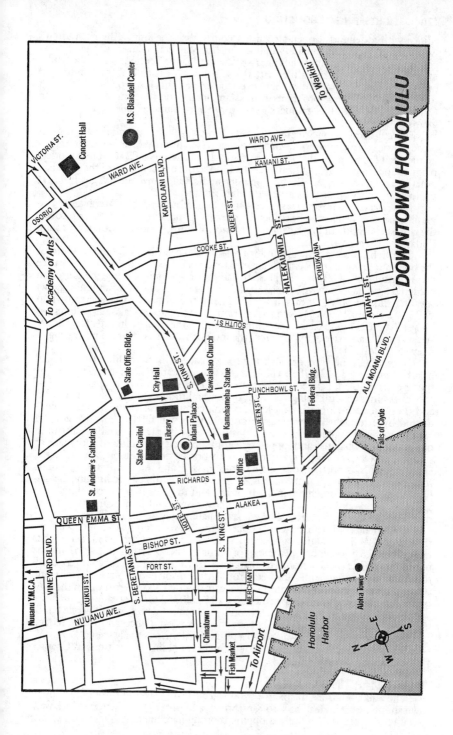

DOWNTOWN HONOLULU

edifice with a delightful open-air garden court. Visit the Edna Allyn Children's Room to see Hawaiian legend murals by Juliette May Fraser, and take in the other paintings hung throughout the library; those by Madge Tennent are of particular interest. Library hours may differ with the season but are usually from 9am to 8pm on Tuesday and Thursday, until 5pm every other day, but closed on Sunday. Don't forget to ask about free programs at the state library and other public libraries on Oahu. They include films, puppet shows, story hours, music recitals, and ethnic programs.

Directly across King Street is the **State Judiciary Building,** and right outside it is the famous statue of **King Kamehameha,** dressed in a royal feathered cape and a helmet that looks curiously Grecian. A symbol of Hawaii (you'll see it in countless pictures and on postcards), this larger-than-life statue of the unifier of the islands is not a great work of art, but it's appropriately heroic. On Kamehameha Day, June 11, the local citizenry decks the statue with huge leis.

Just Ewa of the library you'll see a streamlined building, the **Archives of Hawaii.** Inside are invaluable documents, journals, photographs, and other records, the largest collection of Hawaiiana in existence. Visiting hours are Monday through Friday from 8am to 4:30pm.

The archives are on the grounds of **Iolani Palace,** which is Diamond Head of the building, at King and Richards streets. Take a good look at the only royal palace on American soil. Until 1969 the state capitol, it was built during the glittering golden era of Hawaii by King Kalakaua and his queen, Kapiolani. But it housed its royal tenants for only 11 years, from 1882 until the monarchy was overthrown in 1893 by a group of haoles linked to American sugar interests. Kalakaua's successor, his sister, Queen Liliuokalani, spent nine months in the royal bedroom under house arrest after the abortive coup to restore the monarchy. (She is known for her song of farewell, "Aloha Oe.")

Now, after nine years of work and for a total cost of $7 million (the original palace came in for $343,595 in 1882), a massive restoration has been completed by the Friends of Iolani Palace, and the Hawaiian flag flies over it once again. Some of the furnishings are still being restored, but several rooms are ready for the public, and the American-Florentine building is eminently worth seeing. Tours are conducted by extremely knowledgeable docents who will fill you in on plenty of Hawaiian history as they show you the throne room with the king's tabu stick (made of a 17-foot narwhal tusk and topped by a gold sphere, it was endowed with mana or spiritual power); the king's quarters, with his books, dressing table, and desk; the entry hall with its portraits of the alii of old Hawaii; and the dining room with its royal portraits of European monarchs. While it becomes difficult to imagine the daily life of a royal household in such quiet, almost ghostlike surroundings, the splendid woods and carvings, the gleaming bannisters and shining mirrors, the remarkable plaster reliefs on the ceilings, have a hauntingly beautiful effect.

The Friends of Iolani Palace conduct 45-minute tours every 15 minutes until 2:15pm. Wednesday through Saturday. Reservations are requested, and tickets not claimed 15 minutes before the start of a tour will be sold to anyone who happens to be waiting for a cancellation. The charge is $4 for adults and $1 for children ages 5 to 12 (children under 5 not admitted). You'll have to don enormous khaki "airplane slippers" over your shoes to protect the delicate wooden floors. We thought the tour overly long, but worthwhile nonetheless. Call 522-0832 for reservations.

Look Ewa across King Street and you'll see a beautiful pink Spanish-style building with palm-tree sentinels; it houses the U.S. Post Office and other federal agencies. Where else but Hawaii could a post office look positively scenic?

Ready for lunch? Check our "Downtown Honolulu" suggestions in Chapter IV for some good restaurants.

HAWAII MARITIME CENTER

The walk to the next major attraction—a big one—takes us through the downtown shopping area. Head back to King Street, and turn right for a three-block walk to the Fort Street Mall, a lively shopping thoroughfare lined with fast-food stands and throngs of local people. You'll find Liberty House here, one of Hawaii's leading department stores, as well as a big, fascinating Woolworth's, with plenty of souvenirs. If you walk four blocks makai on Fort Street, you'll come to the **Aloha Tower** at Pier 9 on the waterfront. The tower, open 8am to 9pm daily, provides a good cool view of the harbor and city in all directions, and it's a fine spot for nighttime photography of harbor lights and the downtown area. Aloha Tower is actually one of the five components of the Hawaii Maritime Center: the others include **Pier 7** itself, the *Hokule'a* (that's the Hawaiian double-hulled canoe, which is a replica of the one in which the first Hawaiians are believed to have sailed from the Society Islands, using no instruments or charts—only stars, planets, and ocean signs), when she is in port, and the *Falls of Clyde,* the only four-masted, four-rigged sailing ship still in existence.

The newest of these components—and the crowning glory of the Hawaii Maritime Center—is the stunning, $6-million **Kalakaua Boathouse,** named after King David Kalakaua (the "Merry Monarch"). He was devoted to water sports, and his late-19th-century boathouse—of which the new structure is reminiscent in design—stood very close to this location. There's plenty to see here, so plan *at least* an hour to take it all in. The center, tastefully designed and brilliantly executed, traces the maritime history of Hawaii from ancient times to the present. On the first floor, note such authentic artifacts as 18th-century feather capes and stone idols, and suspended from the ceiling, giant canoes that once voyaged across the Pacific. On the second floor, you'll want to linger at such displays as the 1850s Ship Chandelry—a full-scale, walk-in diorama of H. Hackfeld & Co., the all-purpose whaler's store that later became Hawaii's leading department store, Liberty House! Dioramas and exhibits of the famed Matson Line luxury ships of the 1930s and 1940s recall the languorous, romantic mood of early Hawaiian tourism. Audio/visual exhibits—like the one showing scenes from the 1922 silent film on whaling, *Down to the Sea in Ships*—abound. You'll want to climb the nine (short) flights to the Widow's Walk to see a glorious view of Honolulu Harbor. And stop in at the gift shop, too, for $10 Boat Day posters, T-shirts decorated with old prints, *Falls of Clyde* aloha shirts, shark teeth pendants and the like.

Kids will enjoy everything here, and especially a visit to the *Good Ship Lollipop,* a replica of a ship's deck, where they can steer, furl the sails, shoot the water cannon, and even climb into the crow's nest. After your visit here, let everybody relax with a slightly splurgy meal or snack at the lovely Coaster's Restaurant, behind the center and right out there facing Honolulu Harbor. Food is sophisticated and upbeat, and the setting cannot be topped.

The Hawaii Maritime Center is open every day from 9:30am to 5pm. Admission of $6 for adults, $3 for those 6 to 17 (free under 6), also includes entrance to *The Falls of Clyde.* For information, phone 536-6373 or 532-1717.

If you're feeling really flush, come back some evening for a two-hour sunset or twilight cruise aboard the four-masted, square-sailed *Rella Mae* of **Windjammer Cruises.** Costs are around $45 for the dinner show, $35 for the cocktail show; guests have a choice of seeing a Polynesian revue or "Comedy Club at Sea." Various package deals with popular Waikiki restaurants and clubs are available, and some of these also include admission to Hawaii Maritime Center. Information: 922-1200.

HAWAII'S WALL STREET

After you emerge from the Maritime Center, walk across Ala Moana Boulevard to see some of the newer buildings of the State Civic Center Mall. These are the $37-million **Prince Jonah Kuhio Kalanianaole Federal Building** and **U.S. Courthouse,** two unusual low-lying structures with terraced roofs in the style of Nebuchadrezzar's Hanging Gardens of Babylon. (They are situated makai of the civic center; the state capitol is mauka, and Iolani Palace is in the middle). Two outdoor sculptures here have also caused quite a stir, mostly of the favorable variety. In the courtyard, George Rickey, known for his kinetic and moving sculptures, has fashioned the 31-foot-tall *Two Open Angles Eccentric,* and that's just what they are—two huge stainless-steel open and transparent frames that slice through the air but never collide as they frame buildings and sky. In the plaza is Peter Voulkos's 25-foot-

long and 6-foot-tall bronze called *Barking Sands,* composed of serpentine and geo-
metric forms. Be your own art critic and give your verdict. Some lovely fiberworks by
Ruthadell Anderson and Sharyn Amii Mills can be seen in the lobby and on the
fourth floor of the courthouse.

Two blocks mauka of the federal building is Merchant Street—the Wall Street
of Hawaii—where the "Big Five," the great financial powers of the islands, have
their offices (money and the sea are always closely linked in seaport cities around the
world). You'll see the handsome offices of Castle and Cooke, Ltd., Davies Pacific
Center, Dillingham Transportation, Amfac Center (at Merchant and Bishop), and
the almost-Asian decor of the Alexander and Baldwin, Ltd., building. (The Ltd. appearing after all these names is a remnant of the days when British influence was
strong in the islands; so is the Union Jack, which coexists with the American Stars
and Stripes in the Hawaiian flag.)

Now, retrace your steps, and walk mauka on Bishop Street four blocks to Hotel
Street; turn left here and walk Ewa five short blocks to Maunakea Street. On the Ewa
corner you'll see the pagodalike headquarters of Wo Fat, and you'll know you're in
Chinatown.

THE ASIAN NEIGHBORHOODS

Now we leave money, power, and the affairs of state for a look at Asian Hawaii.
Chinatown begins at Maunakea Street (walk left), with its jumble of shops laden
with crafts, herbs, and Chinese groceries. Many new merchants, from Vietnam,
Thailand, and other parts of Southeast Asia, have also set up shop here, making the
area more fascinating and exotic than ever. You can shop in the markets for salted
eggs, dried octopus, and blocks of Chinese brown sugar (reputedly delicious),
among a mélange of strange products. There are several Chinese acupuncturists and
Hong Kong herb doctors here (the local people swear by them), should you feel the
need. It's fun to poke around on your own, but if you want something organized,
two tours are available. If you're free on a Tuesday morning, make arrangements for
the three-hour **Chinese Chamber of Commerce tour,** which includes visits to
shops and two temples. The price is $4 (optional lunch, $5). The tour leaves at
9:30am from Chinese Chamber of Commerce headquarters at 42 N. King St. (tel.
533-3181 or 533-6967). The **Hawaii Heritage Center,** at 1128 Smith St., second
floor, has a tour on Wednesday and Friday (except holidays), from 9:30am to
12:30pm. Cost is $4 per person. For information and reservations, phone 521-
2749. If you're on your own and it's time for lunch, join the local folks at any of the
plain little restaurants in the neighborhood, or at venerable **Wo Fat,** where a window
table will give you a good view of the goings-on below. On a recent excursion, we
stopped in at a nondescript little sandwich shop on 150 N. King St. called **Ba-Le;**
there we snacked on Vietnamese dem-sem and pastries and a cool glass of gotu kola
herb juice: novel, and not bad! Ba-Le is very popular among the locals, especially for
its sandwiches—chicken, ham, meatballs, and the like—served on their own homemade French bread, piled high with carrots, cilantro, and pickled turnip, for around
$3.

The **Chinese Cultural Plaza** itself—which occupies the block bounded by
Beretania, Maunakea, Kukui, and River streets—somehow never really took off as a
major cultural-shopping area, and often seems half-deserted. This is not one of our
favorite shopping centers, since many of the goods seem to be overpriced. We do,
however, like **Dragon Gate Bookstore,** with dragon puppets, books, and calendars
(in Chinese, of course); and **Excellent Gems** and **Bin Ching,** both of which do jewelry repairing and carry pearls and jades. There are several enjoyable restaurants here,
including **Vietnam City Seafood** and **Won Kee,** which we've told you about in
Chapter IV. You might stop in at the **Exhibit Hall** to see the current show.

As you wander through Chinatown's little streets, you'll notice that Old Chinatown is giving way to several new buildings, a park, and continued upgrading of
historic older buildings such as the **Hawaii Theatre** on Bethel Street, which has recently been restored to its original 20s' art deco ambience. It's hosted everything
from beauty pageants and band concerts to the Hawaii International Film Festival,

even political functions. There are now about a dozen art galleries in the neighborhood, including that of the renowned pen-and-ink artist **Ramsay** at 1128 Smith St., **Pegge Hopper** at her own gallery at 1164 Nuuanu St. (her works are seen all over the islands), and **William Waterfall,** 1160a Nuuanu St., among others. Most of these galleries are open weekdays from 10am to 4pm, until 1pm Saturday, and closed Sunday.

The biggest new development in Chinatown is the gigantic Maunakea Marketplace, which should be open by the time you read this. It's in the heart of Chinatown, fronting on Hotel, Pauahi, and Maunakea streets, and will contain shops and restaurants galore, as well as an open market, and a 1,000-seat interior courtyard for major cultural events and local entertainment.

On to Japan. Walk three blocks mauka from King Street until you come to Beretania Street. Turn left and walk Ewa a block or two to the Nuuanu Stream, where the ambience is slightly Southeast Asian. Across the street on Beretania, half a block Ewa, is the modern Town Inn facing Aala Park. Much of the old Japanese neighborhood—scrubby little saimin stands and pool halls, fish and grocery stores under quaint Asian roofs—has been torn down to make way for new construction. Here's where you'll find the **Kukui Market Place,** with its distinctive blue roof and a pretty courtyard to rest in.

Keep going now, for the best is yet to come. A few blocks mauka on River Street, on the other side of Vineyard Boulevard, is a green-roofed Taoist temple. Slip off your shoes and walk inside for a face-to-face contact with Eastern religion. Joss sticks and incense burn at the altar, food offerings calm the ancestral spirits, and the U.S.A. seems far, far away. This is the **Kwan Yin Temple.** (There's another statue of Kwan Yin—far more splendid, we think—in the Honolulu Academy of Art.)

---

2. Punchbowl, Lower Tantalus, and Nuuanu

Here's a compact tour that's typical of the variegated texture of Hawaii: a U.S. military cemetery, a summer home for Hawaiian royalty, some beautiful residential districts, the resting place of the Hawaiian nobility, two Buddhist temples, and one of the most exciting botanical gardens in the world.

To take this half-day ramble, start with TheBUS no. 2 on Kuhio Avenue heading for town (request a transfer). Get off at Alapai Street and walk a quarter of a block left, where you can pick up the TheBUS no. 15 ("Pacific Heights"). This leaves every hour on the half hour, so time your trip carefully. Get off at Puowaina Drive and walk for 10 minutes to your first destination, the **National Memorial Cemetery of the Pacific** in Punchbowl Crater. Buried inside the crater of an extinct volcano (which had, with prophetic irony, been named the Hill of Sacrifice by the ancient Hawaiians) are some 26,000 American servicemen who perished in the Pacific during World War II, the Korean War, and the Vietnam War. Astronaut Ellison Onizuko is buried here. Also listed here are the names of all Pacific war service people who have been recorded as missing or lost or buried at sea. (Visiting next of kin of any service person reported as missing during World War II, Korea, and Vietnam are urged to visit the administration office for information regarding grave locations.)

Parents from all over the mainland and from the islands come to Punchbowl on pilgrimages. The endless rows of gravestones of young people form a sobering sight, an awesome monument to the futility of war. When you've had enough, walk for another 10 minutes to the lookout at the crater's rim for a sweeping panorama of Honolulu just below. Punchbowl is open to the public every day from 8am to 5:30pm September 30 to March 1, until 6:30pm the rest of the year.

Walking back to the bus stop, get TheBUS no. 15 again and continue on it for a grand ride through the residential district of Pacific Heights. At the end of the line, another breathtaking view of the city and the Pacific awaits. When you pay for the return trip, get a transfer and leave the bus at Pauoa Road, along which you walk right two blocks to Nuuanu Avenue and TheBUS no. 4R ("Nuuanu-Dowsett"). This bus will take you through damp, lush **Nuuanu Valley,** glorious in scenery and island history (here Kamehameha won the battle that gave him control of Oahu). Unfortunately, there's no bus to the Nuuanu Pali with its magnificent view of Windward Oahu.

The first stop on this leg of the trip is the white-frame mansion on the left side, the **Queen Emma Summer Palace.** Emma and her consort, King Kamehameha IV, called this Victorian country retreat of theirs Hanaiakamalama, and it is faithfully maintained as a museum by the Daughters of Hawaii. Hawaiiana mingles comfortably with the 19th-century European furnishings of which Hawaiian royalty was so fond. Stop in at the gift shop for Hawaiian books, notepapers, postcards, and other tasteful items. The museum is open daily from 9am to 4pm. Admission is $4, $1 for ages 12 to 18, 50¢ for under-12s; there are conducted tours through the rooms for all visitors.

Ride on the same bus farther down Nuuanu Avenue, past the brightly colored Chinese Consulate to the **Royal Mausoleum,** on the right. Here's where the last of the Hawaiian alii, the Kamehameha and Kalakaua dynasties, and others of royal blood are buried. You can browse around from 8am to 4:30pm weekdays. Closed weekends and most holidays except for Kuhio Day (March 26) and Kamehameha Day (June 11).

Resuming your makai trip on TheBUS no. 4, ride down to the **Soto Mission of Hawaii,** a Zen Buddhist temple, at 1708 Nuuanu Ave., between School and Kuakini streets; just look for its severe central tower and eight smaller octagonal ones (these represent Buddha's Path of Life). The interior is as ornate and Japanese as the exterior is austere, somewhat Indian. Walk in and have a look. They'll be happy to answer any questions. Free. Call 537-9409.

Leaving the temple, walk mauka to Kuakini Street, then turn right one block to Pali Highway, and right again for half a block to the **Honpa Hongwanji Mission Temple** on Pali Highway; this is the cathedral of the Jodo Shin Buddhist sect in Hawaii.

Now retrace your steps to Nuuanu Avenue and walk makai two blocks to Vineyard Boulevard. Turn right and you'll find the entrance to **Foster Botanic Garden** about one block away at 180 N. Vineyard Blvd. This is a marvelously cool oasis on a hot day and one of the most impressive botanical collections to be found anywhere. There are 15 acres of rare trees, flowers, plants, and unusual species of vegetation, many of them brought from Asia. Orchids bloom throughout the year. Here you can measure the minuteness of man against a tree 20 times taller than you are, and ogle such rare specimens as the cannonball tree, the bombax, and the sunshine tree. On the grounds is a C-shaped granite monument, presented in 1960 to Honolulu by its sister city of Hiroshima, from which most of the first Japanese immigrants came to work the island plantations. A free, self-guided-tour brochure is available at the reception office. There are also free guided tours, on Monday, Tuesday, and Wednesday. All tours begin at 1pm, and reservations are necessary (tel. 533-3214). Foster Garden is open daily, 9am to 4pm. Admission is $1 for adults.

For the return, walk back to Nuuanu Avenue below School Street, board TheBUS no. 4 bus to Hotel and Bethel streets, where you will transfer to TheBUS no. 2 back to Waikiki.

3. University of Hawaii at Manoa, East-West Center, and Manoa Valley

Here's your chance to see what all those students are doing when they're not on the beach at Waikiki. Just as they do, take TheBus marked Route 4 that runs from the corner of Kapahulu and Kalakaua right to the university campus. From here you can meander around the beautiful grounds of the university, one of the most relaxed institutions of higher learning we've seen anywhere. Nobody thinks it's unusual for that fellow in the library pouring over the card catalog to be barefoot, so why should you?

Although many of Hawaii's socially conscious families still send their children off to mainland colleges (in the old days it was the Punahou-Yale route), the island's own university is the goal of thousands of other youngsters. Established in 1907 as a small agricultural and mechanical arts college, the university has grown into an important center for the study of tropical agriculture, marine biology, geophysics, astronomy, linguistics, and other fields. Its student body of more than 21,000 reflects the multiracial composition of the population of Hawaii. In addition, students come from all 50 states (about 2,000 per year) and more than 60 foreign countries (some 1,200 each year).

The **East-West Center,** a separate institution at the Manoa campus, is particularly worth your attention. A meeting place of Eastern and Occidental cultures, it brings students, professionals, and research scholars here from Asia, the Pacific islands, and the mainland United States in an exciting exchange of ideas. All students have been given awards that send them first to the University of Hawaii and later out on field work—in the mainland United States for the Asians, in Asia or the Pacific for the Americans. Later, most of the Asians will go back home to teach or work in government posts, and most of the Americans too will go to live and work in Asia.

Walk over to see the starkly simple East-West Center buildings, a masterful architectural blending of Eastern and Western styles. Free tours leave Wednesday at 1:30pm from the Friends Lounge on the Garden Level of **Thomas Jefferson Hall,** but it's easy enough to walk around by yourself. The lounge area of Jefferson must certainly be one of the most interesting student centers in the world. Where else might you pick up copies of *Thailand Illustrated, The Wall Street Journal,* and *Social Casework,* all from one rack? Asian and other art exhibitions are frequently held in the lounge art gallery.

Walk now to the rear of Jefferson for a peaceful moment at the lyrical Japanese garden, with its waterfalls, stone ornaments, lanterns, and flashing carp. And be sure to see the **John Fitzgerald Kennedy Theater,** one of the best equipped in the world for staging both Western and Eastern dramas. It's the official home of the university's drama department, and a technological center that draws theater people from both sides of the Pacific to study, teach, and produce plays. Naturally, this is a great boon for the Honolulu theater-going community; a typical season might include productions of a Japanese Kabuki classic, Shakespeare, and a contemporary Broadway comedy. An authentic Beijing opera was recently staged here—in English.

You'll want to tour the rest of the University of Hawaii campus, too. Stop in at the University Relations office in Hawaii Hall, room 2, to get maps and directions for a self-guided tour. You'll find plenty to see, especially if you're interested in art—the university definitely is: there are two art galleries, and frescoes, sculptures, and works in other media are seen everywhere, from the **Campus Center** to the systems administration center, **Bachman Hall.** Begin on the first floor of that building with Jean Charlot's impressive two-story fresco depicting old and new Hawaii. At **Bilger Hall** are four more murals of old Hawaii, done by leading artists: Juliette May Fraser, Richard Lucier, David Asherman, Sueko Kimura. Artist Murray Turnbull is represented by a stained-glass window in **Keller Hall** and in a series of murals in the **Music Building.** A ceramic work graces one entrance to the Campus Center.

Students of modern architecture will want to see the **Biomedical Sciences Buildings,** designed by Edward Durell Stone.

Nature-lovers can have a treat here, too, trying to identify the 560 or so varieties of tropical plants and trees that bloom all over campus. If you need help, check the **University Relations Office** at Hawaii Hall for a map showing names and locations. We'll give you a start: The tree on the side of Hawaii Hall, which looks as if it has large sausages dangling from it, is a native of West Africa, where the oddly shaped fruits are used externally for medical purposes. Here, however, they're just decorative.

Take a gander at the bulletin board in the Campus Center, the student union. You may pick up a tip on a plane ticket to Los Angeles, or someone with a room to share. Need a haircut? The barbershop at **Hemenway Hall** has women barbers; haircuts for both men and women are always a good buy.

Want to take a summer course? The university enrolls over 17,000 summer students in some 500 courses. Get into Hawaii's social and cultural mix with, perhaps, some Asian studies courses in history, languages, literature, etc. For a physical view of the islands, try Botany 105 (ethnobotany), Geography 368 (geography of the islands), or Oceanography 201. For a catalog and details, write in advance to the Summer Session Office, 101 Krauss Hall, 2500 Dole St., Honolulu, HI 96822.

The university's noncredit summer courses are also intriguing. How about sailing, stained-glass craft, Ikebana (Japanese flower arranging), hula, ESP, and self-hypnosis—for starters?

Lush **Manoa Valley,** in which the university is located, is one of the most beautiful residential areas in Honolulu and well worth an exploratory trip. You can see its flowering streets and graceful old homes from TheBUS no. 6, which you board on University Avenue, back where you entered the campus. The ride up East Manoa Road to Woodlawn will take you past an interesting Chinese cemetery (marked with a big Chinese gate) at the intersection of Akaka Place, where there are often food offerings on the graves.

Taking the same bus back (on the opposite side of the road) toward the university, get off at the intersection of Manoa Road and Oahu Avenue. If you walk a little way to the right on Oahu Avenue, you'll discover the beautiful tropical garden that house the **Waioli Tea Room,** a famous Honolulu restaurant operated by the Salvation Army for many years, which has closed as a commercial restaurant but reopened as a conference center. The gardens are still open to the public. If a wedding ceremony is not going on, you can visit the Little Chapel on the grounds, designed for the children of Waioli. It's rumored that Robert Louis Stevenson courted the muse in the little grass shack now rebuilt as the Robert Louis Stevenson Memorial Grass House.

4. Bishop Museum and Dole Cannery Square

Today's trip takes you to one of the Pacific's most important museums and then on to observe one of Hawaii's major industries in action. It takes half a day.

To reach your first destination, the **Bishop Museum** at 1525 Bernice St. (tel. 847-3511), board TheBUS no. 2 "School–Middle Street" and ride it all the way past the center of town to School and Kapalama streets, where you get off and walk one block makai on Kapalama, then turn right on Bernice Street. The museum complex entrance is at midblock. Inside its stone walls (which look more like those of a fortress than a museum) is a world center for the study of the Pacific—its peoples, culture, history, artifacts. Most fascinating for visitors is the Hawaiian Hall, where special exhibits illustrate particular aspects of early Hawaiian culture. Note the collection of priceless feather cloaks; one uses half a million feathers from the rare mamo bird (each bird produced only a few feathers, so the kings built up feather treasuries—which were among the prime spoils of war). Other exhibits re-create the way of life of the Hawaiians, showing the outrigger canoes, a model heiau, weapons, wooden calabashes; trace the history of the Hawaiian monarchy; explore the marine and plant life of the Pacific. All this, plus the fascinating exhibits of ethnographic art, make for a rewarding visit, worth as much time as you can give it. You can have an inexpensive snack at the Museum Lanai Restaurant. Stop in too at Shop Pacifica for Hawaiian gifts, a cut above the usual, including books on Hawaiian and other Pacific cultures, hand crafted feather leis and native koa-wood boxes and bowls, reproductions of Polynesian artifacts, and rare and unique jewelry of the Pacific. The museum is open from 9am to 5pm Monday through Saturday and the first Sunday of each month; closed Christmas Day. Admission is $5.95, $4.95 for those 6 to 17 years old, and includes a show at the adjacent Atherton Halau and entrance to Kilolani Planetarium. For a Visitors Information recording, call 848-4129.

Note: If you're interested in studying **Hawaiian crafts,** you've come to the right place. Classes are held Monday to Saturday from 9am to 2:30pm, at a nominal charge (usually $5, plus a materials cost). It's quilting Monday and Friday; fresh-flower lei-making Tuesday and Wednesday; Iauhala weaving Saturday; feather leis Thursday. Classes are held in the Atherton Halau (phone 847-3511 for schedules), also the site of special events, which are usually held on weekends. Inquire, too, about field trips and special programs.

Sharing the museum grounds is **Kilolani Planetarium,** a great spot for anyone interested in space exploration and astronomy. The planetarium has the only observatory in the islands available to the public; it is open after the fascinating evening sky shows on Friday and Saturday at 7pm. Shows are also held weekdays at 11am and 2pm. Admission is $3 or is included with museum general admission at $5.95. Call 848-4136 for recorded program information.

After leaving the Bishop Museum grounds, you can face the modern industrial world again at the **Dole Pineapple Cannery.** To get there from the museum, board TheBUS no. 2 at School and Kalihi streets, disembark at Hotel and River streets, and transfer to TheBUS no. 19 on the opposite side of the street (make sure it reads "Airport-Hickam").

If you're coming direct from Waikiki, take TheBUS no. 19 (Airport-Hickam), or, better still, the "Pineapple Transit;" it makes pickups at major stops in Waikiki every few minutes and takes you to **Cannery Square** for a charge of 50¢, one way. These trips are widely advertised in the local tourist papers, but a caveat should be issued here: The 50¢ fare covers only transportation and admission to Cannery Square, which features a shopping mall, a restaurant, and some historical displays. Entrance to the actual tour of the Dole Cannery costs $5—and that is usually not mentioned in the advertisements. Our personal feeling is that the trip, in a neat little air-conditioned bus, is a good bargain (it actually makes for a pleasant little sightseeing tour), but if you're watching your pennies and if there are several of you in your family or group, the $5 admission fee is a factor to consider.

The visit to the world's largest fruit cannery begins in the Dole Theatre with a multimedia show and proceeds to the walk-through tour of the cannery itself; tours are held whether or not the cannery is actually in operation (overhead video displays explain the operations each step of the way). The sheer size and efficiency of the operation is impressive. You'll see thousands and thousands of pineapples bobbing along on huge conveyor belts, looking oddly like lambs for the slaughter. There's an amazing machine (the Ginaca) that can peel and core 100 pineapples in 60 seconds! And there are rows of workers checking and sorting the fruit before it goes into the cans; during the height of the summer harvest season, when the cannery operates at peak capacity, many of these workers will be high school and college students earning next year's tuition. That silly-looking pineapple on top of the building, by the way, is not filled with pineapple juice; it's the water tower.

When you come to the end of the tour you're given free juice and a bit of pineapple. After that, you may want to stop for a snack or do some shopping at Cannery Square. We were delighted to find **Island Muumuu Works** on the second floor; this wholesale outlet for Hilda of Hawaii, where all first-quality muumuus are just $43, has long been one of our favorite Maui shops (there's another Honolulu location at 660 Ala Moana Blvd.). Also of interest is **The Logo Shop,** featuring T-shirts, visors, and assorted paraphernalia bearing the Dole logo; **The Dole Marketplace** for pineapples to ship home, and **Island Accents,** which has some interesting jewelry and wood carvings. **Good Vibrations** has novelties to take home as memorabilia, **Island Gems** shows costume jewelry at reasonable prices, and **Pearl Factory** is one of those ubiquitous places where you buy an oyster and gamble on the pearl you'll find inside.

Now, if you've brought the kids with you, don't leave Cannery Square without paying a visit to the **Hawaii Children's Museum of Art, Science and Technology at Cannery Square.** This new museum is so enthralling, in fact, that it's worth an excursion in its own right. It's a state-of-the-art learning center, where everything is designed to give the child a hands-on experience in science, technology, the arts, and Hawaiian culture. Five main parts all revolve around "You"; in "Fantastic You," you can see a skeleton that peels its skin to reveal its insides. You can stand in front of a mirror and see yourself riding a bicycle. You can look into a huge mouth to see what teeth look like. In "Wonderful World," you can push a button and know the weather anywhere. There are also technology, arts, and culture exhibits—all involving "You." The museum is open Tuesday through Friday from 9am to 1pm, and on weekends from 10am to 4pm. Admission is $5 for adults, $3 for children ages 2 to 17 (tel. 522-0400).

Cannery Square is open every day from 9am to 5pm. The last cannery tour begins at 4pm. For information, phone 531-8855.

To return to Waikiki, simply hop on the Pineapple Transit bus.

---

5. Pearl Harbor

Anyone who remembers—or has heard about—December 7, 1941, should not leave the Hawaiian Islands without seeing Pearl Harbor. The cheapest way to get there is by TheBUS; bus no. 20 goes right from Waikiki to Pearl City. From Ala Moana Center, you can take no. 50, 51, or 52. The trip should take about an hour. Ask the driver to let you off at the **U.S.S. Arizona Memorial.** You can also take private bus service direct to the Arizona Memorial via the Arizona Memorial Shuttle Bus, $6 round trip (tel. 926-4747).

The $4.2-million visitor center, administered by the National Park Service, provides an ideal starting point for your trip to the U.S.S. Arizona Memorial. Its museum contains exhibits related to the events surrounding the attack on Pearl Harbor by the Japanese on December 7, 1941. Step up to the information desk, where you will be given a tour number, and find out approximately when your shuttle boat will leave. Because the crowds can be enormous—up to 5,000 on very heavy days—you may have to wait for two hours or more, unless you arrive before 8am, when the wait should be a bit less, although it may still be more than an hour. While you're waiting, you can study a detailed mural of the *Arizona* or check out the books in the bookshop. When your number is called, you enter the theater to see a 20-minute film, and then are ferried on a navy boat to the U.S.S. Arizona Memorial. Tours operate daily from 8am to 3pm and are free.

Dedicated in 1962, the memorial is a covered white-concrete bridge rising starkly above the hull of the battleship *Arizona,* victim of a direct hit on the day that bombs fell on Hawaii, and the tomb of over 1,000 American servicemen (some 2,403 in all were killed that day). It has recently been named a National Historic Landmark. The outlines of the ship shimmer just below the water, and, as if warning that the story is not yet finished, oil slicks still rise from the rusting hulk. Like Punchbowl Cemetery, it is an eloquent witness to the fury and folly of war. A big experience.

Note: If the weather is stormy, call the Arizona Memorial at 422-0561 to find out if the boats will be operating. Children under 45 inches in height are not permitted on the shuttle boats, but they are permitted at the visitor center and in the theater; those 6 to 10 must be accompanied by an adult; bathing suits and bare feet are taboo.

If you have time, you can take a short walk from the Arizona Memorial to visit **Bowfin Park,** where the U.S.S. *Bowfin,* a World War II submarine launched one year after the attack on Pearl Harbor, is moored. Next to the submarine is the new **Bowfin Museum,** with fascinating submarine memorabilia and a gift shop. You can look through periscopes at a new structure built over the submarine's conning tower. A memorial honors submariners lost during World War II. Admission is $6 for adults ($1 for military personnel with ID), $1 for children 6 to 12. Open every day, from 8am to 4:30pm. Information: 423-1341.

6. Paradise Park and Lyon Arboretum

Paradise Park, a showcase for exotic birds that was a longtime favorite for families traveling with children, was planning to close for renovation as we went to press. Although plans were indefinite as to details of the $5 million makeover and as to when the park would reopen, it is quite likely that the 14-acre park set in a tropical rain forest will include a flock of life-size dinosaurs by Dination. Adults and kids will be able to participate in hands-on experiences at the Discovery Center, and will enter the grounds through the Imaginarium, a depiction of the world 150 million years ago. Watch the local papers for details when you arrive. There will probably be free shuttle buses making the trip from major Waikiki hotels: call 988-2141 for information. Public transportation can get you here within 45 minutes from Waikiki; take TheBUS no. 8 to Ala Moana, then TheBUS no. 5 with the sign reading "Paradise Park." You can continue on to Lyon Arboretum after your trip to Paradise Park, or make it a separate excursion: in either case, the last stop of the bus is Paradise Park, and you must then walk approximately 15 minutes to reach the arboretum.

The most exciting focus at Paradise Park is birds—mostly from South America and Africa (Hawaiian birds can be found in the Honolulu Zoo). You'll see rare birds as they are found in their natural habitats, in lush jungle and forest settings of great beauty. As you arrive, you'll descend into a mammoth cage with a circular walkway and all the parrots and macaws come up to you for a handout. Scheduled shows held at the Kamehameha Amphitheater offer birds that play poker, ride bikes across a tightrope, and do other amazingly human things. There is also a trained-duck show ("Animal Quackers") on the grounds, special shows at various times featuring different ethnic entertainment (the park's theme is a multicultural one), and children's entertainment. You can also take the marvelous jungle trails (don't miss the grove of Asian bamboos), see demonstrations of Hawaiian arts and crafts, gawk at and photograph what seem like millions of orchids, trees, flowers, and plants. And you're sure to enjoy the "Dancing Waters" show. Plan on 3 ½ to 4 hours to enjoy it all.

Henri's Hawaii Restaurant overlooking the grounds is a beauty, and prices are not overly expensive. Or you can fill up on hot dogs, soft drinks, and ice cream at the modestly priced snack bar. Admission to Paradise Park is $7.50 for adults, $6.50 for juniors 13 to 17, and $3.75 for children 4 to 12. It is open daily, except Christmas Day, from 10am to 5pm.

Few tourists know about **Lyon Arboretum,** 3860 Manoa Rd. (tel. 988-7378), but Honolulu residents certainly do. It's prized as one of the most beautiful nature spots in Honolulu, an important research facility for the University of Hawaii, and an educational center where one can take short courses in such subjects as flower arrangement, bonsai, island cookery, orchid-growing, and much more. You're welcome to visit on your own, admiring the beautiful gardens lush with orchids, camelias, gardenias, ginger, coffee, and many native plants. If you're in town at the right time, however, call ahead to reserve one of the free guided tours held each month, on the first Friday and third Wednesday (at 1pm) and on the third Saturday (at 10am). Do visit the gift and book store which has items of high quality: handmade cards, books on horticulture and Hawaiian history, kukui leaf T-shirts, implements for use in Hawaiian crafts, even a curry powder by Ranjit Cooray, quite famous in these parts. Admission to Lyon Arboretum is a bargain indeed: a donation of $1 is all that is necessary.

7. A Waikiki Checklist

We're not going to map out any formal tour of the Waikiki area, since you'll be spending so much of your time here anyway. We'll simply remind you of some of the attractions you can see more or less anytime, before or after a swim at the beach.

The big hotels are great, of course, for strolling in and out of in the evening (see Chapter IV). While you're at it, check out the sleek modernity of the **Ilikai,** and the new **Honolulu Prince Hotel,** the tastefully Polynesian architecture of the **Waikikian,** the graceful airs of the newly restored **Sheraton Moana Surfrider,** the old-world splendor of the **Royal Hawaiian.** The **Hawaiian Regent** is done in beautiful taste, with its open-air lobby surrounding a central court aglow with a fountain and two lagoons. Walk up two flights of stairs to the pool and the Ocean Terrace, and you'll be rewarded with one of the most beautiful open daytime views in Waikiki. The hotel seemingly juts out right over the beach (even though it's across the street), and the glorious colors of ocean and sky surround you wherever you look. The famed **Halekulani Hotel,** the last of the low-rise, Hawaiian-style cottage hotels on the beach, has been totally rebuilt. The $100-million project has preserved the main two-story structure as an indoor-outdoor dining area and added five interconnecting high-rise buildings. It's luxury all the way here, in the first world-class hotel to be built in this area in 25 years. The **Hilton Hawaiian Village,** which has recently undergone a major, $80-million upscaling, represents Henry J. Kaiser's first contribution to Hawaii (he sold it to Hilton some years back and moved on to even bigger projects). It's a fascinating cornball beach city of its own, with 20 acres of tropical gardens, an artificial lagoon, a vast array of indoor and outdoor bars and restaurants, six pools, a beautiful beachfront, a dazzling array of shops, even its own post office. Walk around for a few minutes and you'll view a cross-section of Hawaii's visitors—anybody from a gaggle of Shriners on one side to a group of blushing young Japanese couples on another.

Near the Hilton is the **Fort DeRussy Military Reservation,** a great low-cost recreation area for the military on a prime strip of Waikiki Beach. The beach is open to the public, and many claim it's the best in Waikiki. There is no public parking. (The 15-story Hale Koa Hotel here offers attractive, well-priced rooms to active and retired military, dependents, and widows of retired personnel.) You may want to stop in for a quick visit to the **U.S. Army Museum** in Fort DeRussy Park, which contains military memorabilia dating from ancient Hawaiian warfare to the present. It is housed in Battery Randolph, built in 1909 as a key installation in the defense of Honolulu and Pearl Harbor. On the upper deck, the **Corps of Engineers Pacific Regional Visitors Center** graphically shows how the corps works with the civilian community in managing water resources in an island environment. The museum is open Tuesday through Sunday from 10am to 4:30pm, admission free (tel. 438-2821).

You will, of course, want to spend a lot of time shopping and browsing at the **International Market Place, King's Village,** the **Waikiki Shopping Plaza,** and the **Royal Hawaiian Shopping Center** (details in Chapter VI). Check the local tourist papers for news of free entertainment and events.

Of course you'll have to see **Hemmeter Center,** a stunning architectural landmark encompassing the super-luxurious Hyatt Regency Waikiki Hotel, plus a shopping center, restaurants, and cocktail lounges. The entire area is dramatically landscaped, with tropical foliage, trees and plantings, huge sculptures, many-storied waterfalls, flowing lagoons, picturesque kiosks, and Polynesian objets d'art. It's on Kalakaua, between Uluniu and Kaiulani avenues.

On a more serious note, you may wish to stop in at the **Damien Museum,** 130 Ohua St., corner of Kalakaua Ave., behind St. Augustine's Catholic Church (tel. 923-2690). The small museum presents a moving account of the work that Father Damien de Veuster did with the victims of leprosy on the island of Molokai. The museum contains prayer books used by Father Damien in his ministry, as well as his personal items. A continuously running video, recounting Damien's story, is narrated by Terence Knapp, a local actor who has portrayed Father Damien in award-winning performances on stage and on TV. He fittingly honors one of Hawaii's heroes. The Damien Museum is open Monday to Friday, 9am to 3pm, Saturday from 9am to noon, closed Sundays and holidays. Free (donations accepted).

There are more than a few things to see at the Diamond Head end of Waikiki, up near Kapiolani Park. Past Kuhio Beach, at Kapahulu Avenue, the **Honolulu Zoo** looms up on your left (the entrance is at 151 Kapahulu Ave.). It's noted for its collection of native Hawaiian and other tropical birds, displayed in various bird-jungle habitats. There's also an elephant given to the children of Hawaii by Indira Gandhi; a Bengal tiger; a lion; and three adorable Himalayan sun bears. With Diamond Head providing the background, plenty of trees and flowers (including a giant banyan and date palms), white doves, and keikis tumbling about, it's one of the most charming zoos anywhere. At the moment, it's undergoing a multimillion-dollar renovation: Phase I, "The African Savannah," is now under way. You may be able to catch the elephant show: call the zoo at 971-7171 for schedules, which change frequently. The zoo is open every day (except Christmas and New Year's Days) from 8:30am to 4pm. During June, July, and August, the zoo stays open until 7:30 on Wednesday evenings, with free entertainment starting at 6pm at the stage under the earpod tree, just behind the flamingos. Take a picnic supper and join the fun. Local artists hang their work on the fence outside on Saturday, Sunday, and Wednesday. Be sure to stop in at Zootique, the charming gift shop (described in Chapter VI). Admission to the zoo is $3 for adults, free for children 12 and below.

From here on, Kalakaua Avenue is a regal, although narrow, tree-lined drive. And a little farther on, where Kalakaua meets Monsarrat Avenue, **Kapiolani Park** begins (those are the Koolau Mountains in the background). The 220 acres of the park have facilities for just about everything from soccer to rugby to picnicking; also archery, a golf driving range, and tennis. The Royal Hawaiian Band plays frequently in the bandstand, and major musical events take place in the Waikiki Shell. For a particularly beautiful view, note Diamond Head framed in the cascading waters of the splendid Louise C. Dillingham Fountain.

Bordering the ocean on the right is a stretch of wide, palm-dotted grass lawn with a fringe of sand to let you know you're still at the beach. Swimming here is excellent, since the surf is quite mild; it's a big favorite with local families. **Kapiolani Beach Park,** with locker room, rest rooms, picnic tables, and snack bar, is just ahead.

The **Waikiki Aquarium** is also up here, just past the beach, and it's a lot of fun. Here's your chance to see, among other sea creatures like giant calms and sharks, the *lauwiliwilinukunukuoioi;* if you can't pronounce it, just ask for the long-nosed butterfly fish. An outdoor display, **Edge of the Reef,** is a simulated living reef environment that includes hundreds of colorful fish, live coral, and a tidal surge. The aquarium is open daily 9am to 5pm (closed Thanksgiving and Christmas). Admission is free for children 16 and under; an admission donation of $2.50 is asked of all adults, to help feed the fish and fund educational programs. Stop in to see their attractive gift shop, the Natural Selection. Everything in it, from T-shirts with fish designs, books, posters, cards, linen, and home accessories—relates to the ocean and its life-forms. They have a good selection of children's toys and books, too.

Now it's time to rest your feet—and see something new—by hopping aboard TheBUS no. 14 going Diamond Head on Kalakaua Avenue. The bus will take you through the lovely **Waialae-Kahala** area and **Kaimuki** suburbs, and up the mountain to **Maunalani Heights.** From there, you can look straight down into **Diamond Head Crater.** Koko Head on the left, Waikiki slightly to your right. For your return trip, change to TheBUS no. 2, and you'll be back in Waikiki. Or if you prefer, stay on the no. 14 and ride up to **St. Louis Heights** for a magnificent panorama of Honolulu. A forest of beautiful Norfolk pines with picnic tables and a splendid view of Manoa Valley awaits you here at the **Waahila Ridge State Recreation Area.**

Note: If you're making this little trip on wheels, you can actually drive right inside Diamond Head Crater—the only drive-in crater on Oahu, except for Punchbowl. Here's how you do it. Follow Kalakaua until it circles left, just past the Colony Surf Hotel; then make your first right to Diamond Head Road. Come up Diamond Head Road, past the lighthouse on the right. Take your first left before the triangular park; you are now entering the Fort Ruger area. Watch for the Diamond Head Crater sign on the left and follow the road to the left. Go through the tunnel, and you're in Diamond Head State Monument. Hiking trails go up to the rim of the crater. The area looks quite undramatic, but where else, but in Hawaii, can you drive into a volcano!

TOURS FOR THE DISABLED

Handicabs of the Pacific offers special tours for handicapped passengers, in specially equipped vans than can handle six wheelchairs. Typical city tours cost $40 per person. For information, phone 524-3866.

READERS' SIGHTSEEING SUGGESTIONS: "I think the thing that impressed me as much as anything else was riding the buses of Honolulu and Waikiki, listening to so many varied foreign languages, and smiling into those beautiful, colorful faces, and receiving courtesy and warm smiles back. That's surely the way to get around to attractions on the windward side of Oahu, and at 60¢, how can you do it more cheaply? Plus—without extra cost, you get so much of the literal color of the islands as you listen, look, and perhaps share with someone else. It's magnificent. While many tourists have discovered this fun way to get around, we were amazed that thousands more had not. We took the bus to Pearl Harbor, to Punchbowl Cemetery, to the airport when going on a one-day excursion to Molokai, to Ala Moana Shopping Center, and to other sites in and around Honolulu. Delightful!" (James H. Cox, Middletown, Ky.).

"Perhaps you could suggest that people lock their cars, especially when stopping at scenic spots. This was the first thing my family in Hawaii warned us about, as there has been a lot of trouble with tourists' cars being robbed while they viewed the sights. One time when we were at the Blow Hole, we heard a police officer stop a couple and ask the woman if she had left her purse in the open car. When she said 'yes,' he politely but firmly told her to go back to get it, and lock the car. He also said, 'You people are careless, then you come to us and expect us to do something about it when your things are stolen' " (Mrs. Joseph Astman, Levittown, N.Y.). . . . "Please advise all visitors to do their sightseeing on their own. Bus sightseeing trips consisted of a few 10-minute stops at scenic points and too many long stops at tourist traps, always trying to sell something. Also, they *all* seem to arrive at a point at the same time, dumping hundreds of tourists together trying to see the same sight in the same 10-minute time limit, and generally raising havoc" (John C. Schmid, Line Lexington, Pa.).

"Be sure to visit **Lyon Arboretum** in Honolulu. Take Manoa Road past Paradise Park. It's free, with labeled trees and flowers. We saw orchids in trees, heard the birds sing, had benches to sit on, and even saw a rainbow" (Jo Anne Ruby, Salem, Oreg.).

"Unless someone is an avid, strong hiker, I suggest passing up the trail to Manoa Falls. The trail will take half an hour to an hour going up, and is filled with rocks and roots and slippery spots. It is a difficult trail with many opportunities to twist an ankle or fall and break something. If you get hurt on that trail, who is going to carry you out? You can see plenty of Hawaiian jungle, cultivated and uncultivated, just by visiting the nearby **Lyon Arboretum,** which is free. And the trails are much better" (Mark Terry, Alameda, Calif.).

AROUND OAHU

You haven't really seen Hawaii until you've left the urban sprawl of Waikiki and Honolulu and traveled to the other side of the mountains for a look at Windward Oahu. And what a look that is! There are jagged cliffs and coral beaches; Stone Age ruins and tropical suburbs; a vast military concentration; backwoods country towns sleeping in the sun; endless stretches of breadfruit, banana, papaya, hibiscus, lauhala, coconut palms—the glorious vegetation of the tropics so ubiquitous as to be completely taken for granted. And best of all, some of the most intriguing sightseeing attractions in the 50th state are here: Sea Life Park, the Byodo-In Temple, and the Polynesian Cultural Center.

Not one advertising billboard defaces the landscape; they're kapu in Hawaii. The only signs you will see are those of the Hawaii Visitors Bureau's red-and-yellow warrior pointing to the places of interest. There are dozens of spots for beachcombing and picnicking, so pack your bathing suit and lunch. If you get an early start, you can certainly make this trip in one day, but there's so much to see that two would be much more comfortable. We'll provide a basic itinerary around which you can plan your time.

TRANSPORTATION

You can see a good part of the island by sticking to public transportation. TheBUS no. 55 "Circle Island," which leaves Ala Moana Center at 5 and 35 minutes after the hour, from 6:05am on, daily, will enable you to see many island points of interest: the big surf at Haleiwa, Sunset Beach and the North Shore, the Polynesian Cultural Center, to name some. (The cost will be at least $1.20, with no transfers; you'll have to pay 60¢ every time you reboard the bus.) Many of our readers make this trip and praise it highly. But since it is a commuter service, not a sightseeing bus, and would take you many, many hours, we personally believe it's not the most efficient way to go. We therefore recommend that you part ways with the public transportation system and rent a car. If you're traveling alone or don't want to drive, you can, of course, take any of the standard around-the-island sightseeing tours. (We've had excellent reports, over the years, on those offered by **E Noa Tours**—tel. 941-6608; for a report, see the Readers' Suggestions at the end of this chapter.) For two or more it's far cheaper to rent a car for the day (total costs should come to about $30), and the really akamai way to do it is to find three or four other people and split the expenses down to practically nothing. But the main thing is to make the trip, whatever way you decide. *If you're driving, remember to lock your car doors and take your valuables with you when you get out to look at the sights.*

A NOTE ON OUR MAPS

The maps in this book are for the purpose of general orientation. When doing any extensive driving, we suggest you follow a more detailed road map. We have personally found the maps in *Drive Guide to Oahu,* free from any car-rental company, to be excellent.

ON YOUR WAY OUT OF TOWN

You start at Waikiki, driving Diamond Head on Kalakaua Avenue past Kapiolani Park; this will lead you into Diamond Head Road, which runs into Kahala Avenue past the sumptuous residential area of Black Point. Sculptor Kate Kelly's monument to Amelia Earhart is just past the Diamond Head Lighthouse. On your right, a paved trail leads to the cliffs, where you can watch some fancy surfing. At the end of Kahala Avenue, where it hits the Waialae Golf Course, turn left on Kealaolu Avenue; follow this road to Kalanianaole Highway (Rte. 72); the entrance will be on the right. Before you turn, you come to **Waialae Beach Park,** with modern facilities, covered pavilions, and wide, wide beaches, right next door to the prestigious Waialae Country Club. The swimming here, however, is not too good, since there are many rocks in the water. Next door is the splendid Kahala Hilton Hotel; you might want to have a look at the lovely grounds.

Just before you reach Koko Head, you'll pass the entrance to Henry Kaiser's once-controversial **Hawaii Kai**—a 6,000-acre, $350-million housing development that's a small city in itself. You can drive in for your own tour of inspection. (A resident advises us that there is a beautiful view at the top of the hill past the Hawaii Kai Golf Course overlooking the ocean and the south end of Windward Oahu.) While you're in this area, you may want to stop in at **Waterfront Village,** a charming small shopping complex perched right out on the waters of Koko Marina, and tied in by walks and a shared parking lot with the much larger Hawaii Kai shopping center.

Koko Head and **Koko Crater,** now coming into view ahead, are reminders that Oahu, like all the Hawaiian Islands, is a volcanic mountain spewed out of the Pacific. During Oahu's last eruption (volcanologists say it happened at least 10,000 years ago), these craters and the one that houses **Hanauma Bay** were born. One side of Koko Head has been washed away into the sea and the result is an idyllic beach, one of the most popular in the islands. Since the placid turquoise waters cover a cove in the purple coral reef, it is a perfect place for beginning and advanced snorkelers. (Rent snorkels in Waikiki or bring your own; none are available here.) Hanauma Bay is now a marine reserve, and so gentle have the fish become that parrot fish, bird wrasses, and others will eat bread from a swimmer's hand. There are dressing facilities, and camping, barbecue, and picnic areas. Although the beach is a very long walk from the parking area, the driver can drive all the way down to the beach, discharge his passengers, and then drive up to park. Or all of you can take a train from the parking lot to the beach for a small fee. *Be sure to lock your car and remove any valuables!* Needless to say, the islanders love this place, and the only problem is that you've almost always got to share it with quite a lot of them. (Before you begin this stretch, see "The Pali and Makiki Heights," below.)

1. The Seaside Drive

For the next few miles, you'll be driving along one of the most impressive stretches of rocky coastline in the islands. The black lava cliffs hurtle down to the sea to meet a surging purple Pacific, all set against a brilliant blue-green background of sky, trees, and flowers. Park the car at any of the designated areas, or at the popular **Blow Hole,** where the water geysers up through an underwater vent. (The areas before the Blow Hole are just as pretty, much less crowded.) With the wind in your hair and the surf crashing below, you'll feel light years away from the trivialities of civilization. Just beyond the Blow Hole is **Sandy Beach;** beyond that is **Makapuu,** where people are actually surfing on those horrendous waves. These two beaches are strictly for the experts; beginners had better watch from the sand. More important, this is the site of a big Hawaiian sightseeing attractions—Sea Life Park.

SEA LIFE PARK

There's plenty of entertainment, education, and fun here for the whole family. First, there's a show in the Hawaii Ocean Theater, a live training session in which porpoises and penguins show off their agility and brains. Shows alternate with those in the Whaler's Cove, which re-creates Hawaii's early whaling history in a narrated pageant. There's a ⅝-inch scale replica of the whaling ship *Essex*. At the 300,000-gallon Hawaiian Reef Tank exhibit, you may descend three fathoms below the surface for a skindiver's-eye view of a typical offshore coral reef, full of brilliantly colored marine creatures, some 3,000 of them. Dangerous hammerhead sharks are just inches away—on the other side of the glass. You'll want to see the Kohole Kai Sea Lion Show and visit the sea lion feeding pool: You may feed the splashy animals fish, and try your luck at coaxing them to do a trick or two.

In addition, you'll want to visit the Bird Sanctuary, which shows species of marine birds seldom seen by the public (the red-footed booby, masked booby, and albatross, among others); visit the Penguin Habitat and the 1,500-gallon Touch Pool, where you can touch starfish, sting rays, and more. Stop in, too, at the Hawaiian Monk Seal Care Center and the Pacific Whaling Museum, which houses the largest collection of whaling artifacts—scrimshaw, harpoons, rope work—in the Pacific. You can pick up T-shirts, ceramic art, stuffed animals, marine jewelry, and the like at the Sea Chest gift shop.

Admission to Sea Life Park is $12.95 for adults, $8.50 for juniors 7 to 12, and $4.50 for children 4 to 6; free for children under 4. The park is open daily from 9:30am to 5pm, Friday until 10pm; on Friday, a Hawaiian show is included in regular park admission. For more information, phone 259-7933 or the Waikiki office at 923-1531. Note that several tour companies run excursions to Sea Life Park several times a day, making Waikiki hotel pickups. MTL buses also make hourly runs to the park (call 531-1611 for information).

ON TO HEEIA

Continuing north on Hwy. 72 now, you'll soon see Rabbit Island, where the water turns turquoise. The inland view along this coast is also spectacular, thanks to the towering **Koolau Mountains;** their corrugated slopes (an example of the forces of erosion at work on volcanoes) provide a nice balance to the restless sea on your right.

Just past Sea Life Park, you'll find **Waimanalo Beach Park,** which many island families consider the best beach on Oahu: pleasant surf, grassy knolls, picnic tables, the works. You may want to come back here for a long stay. For now, drive on for a few more miles and you'll come upon what was long considered one of Oahu's most magnificent beaches by the few people lucky enough to enjoy it—the military. This is **Bellows Beach Park,** nestled against the mountains, a 46-acre strip of fine sand, lively but not dangerous surf, and wooded picnic groves of palm and pine. After long years, Bellows has been opened to the public, but on weekends only, from Friday noon to midnight Sunday; and on federal and state holidays. There are public bathhouses. (It's a favorite spot for tent and trailer camping; permits from the Recreation Department, City and County of Honolulu.) Bellows is a perfect place for a picnic lunch (bring your own, as there's nothing to buy), or a swim. The only danger (aside from an occasional Portuguese man-of-war) is that you may be tempted to spend the whole day and forget about your exploring. Keep going, for the best is yet to come.

A SIDE TRIP TO KAILUA

At this point in the journey, it's possible to make a little side trip to Kailua, one of Honolulu's most pleasant suburbs, by staying on Hwy. 72 until it intersects with Hwy. 61, then turning right on 61 until you reach Kailua, a few miles down the road. The reason for this trip is the beach: Kailua Beach Park, and especially Lanikai, are absolutely beautiful, with gentle waves, white sand, and much smaller crowds than you see at Waikiki. We always feel this is what Waikiki must have been like in the old, pretourist days. There are several attractive restaurants in Kailua, too, like L'Auberge and Cinnamon's, which we've told you about in Chapter IV.

And should it be a weekend and you're in the mood for a hike, you should know about **Ho'Omaluhia Botanical Park** in Kaneohe, at the end of Luluku Road. Here, at the foot of the Koolau Mountains, are pleasant hiking trails, a Hawaiian garden, a lake, and much more. At the center, you'll find a small art gallery and exhibit hall. There are escorted walks on weekends: Saturday 10am to 12:30pm, 3 ½ miles; Sunday, 1 to 2pm, 2 miles. Groups under 20 can be accommodated, but both individuals and groups should phone in advance to make reservations for these hikes (tel. 235-6636). Be sure to wear proper footwear and bring an umbrella as it often showers, rainy season or not. Open daily.

Haiku Gardens

On Hwy. 83, you might want to stop and stretch a bit at a lovely area called Haiku Gardens. For years, Haiku Gardens Restaurant occupied this lovely kamaaina estate. At the time of this writing, it was being turned into an exciting Chart House Restaurant. Plans were to keep the gardens open to the public free, during daylight hours. A lily pond dominates all, and from it, trails lead off to, among other things, a lovely grove of golden bamboo from Java, Hawaiian grass huts, a palm grove, a bird sanctuary, fragrant plantings of ginger and anthurium, and exotic fish ponds. To reach the gardens, turn left off the highway at Haiku Road and proceed mauka about a mile. Closed Mondays.

BYODO-IN TEMPLE

For devotees of Eastern culture, we know of no more rewarding spot in the islands than the Byodo-In Temple in the Valley of the Temples, which should be your next destination. It's about two miles from Haiku Road, and you can reach it by driving back to Kahekili Highway from Haiku Gardens and proceeding north. (If you haven't stopped at Haiku Gardens, continue on Kamehameha Hwy. to Pineapple Hill, proceed to the intersection, then turn left the way you came onto Kahekili Hwy,; you'll come to Valley of the Temples in about half a mile.) An exact replica of the venerable Byodo-In, reputed to be the most beautiful temple in Uji, Japan, this temple was constructed at a cost of $2.6 million and dedicated on June 7, 1968, almost 100 years to the day after the first Japanese immigrants arrived in Hawaii. The temple sits in a magnificently landscaped classical Japanese garden fragrant with pine, plum, and bamboo. Inside, you can gaze at the intricately carved screens, and panels, and pay obeisance to the magnificent gold carving of Amida, the Buddha of the Western Paradise. Many of the Buddhist faithful in the islands come here, of course, but a visit is every bit as much an aesthetic as a spiritual experience. While you're meditating, turn the kids loose in the gardens, supply them with a package of fish food (thoughtfully sold in a tiny teahouse gift store), and let them feed the flashing carp in the two-acre reflecting lake. The shop also imports religious items and other Japanese gifts from Kyoto. Have a look. Admission is $1.50 for adults, 75¢ for children.

On Saturday, Sunday, and Monday, from 10am to 3:30pm, art lovers who have made an appointment in advance by phoning 239-8146 can stop now to see the exquisite **Hart, Tagami & Powell Gallery and Gardens,** a combination art gallery, aviary, and Japanese garden that is the home and studio of two of Hawaii's leading painters, Hiroshi Tagami and Michael Powell. It is just a few miles from Valley of the Temples: When you call for an appointment, ask for specific directions. A visit here is a rare privilege, an extraordinary entry into a world of beauty.

Just two miles past the Valley of the Temples, you'll come to one of Oahu's newer visitor's attractions: **Senator Fong's Plantation and Gardens.** Former U.S. Senator Hiram Fong has opened his magnificent 725-acre estate to the public; visi-

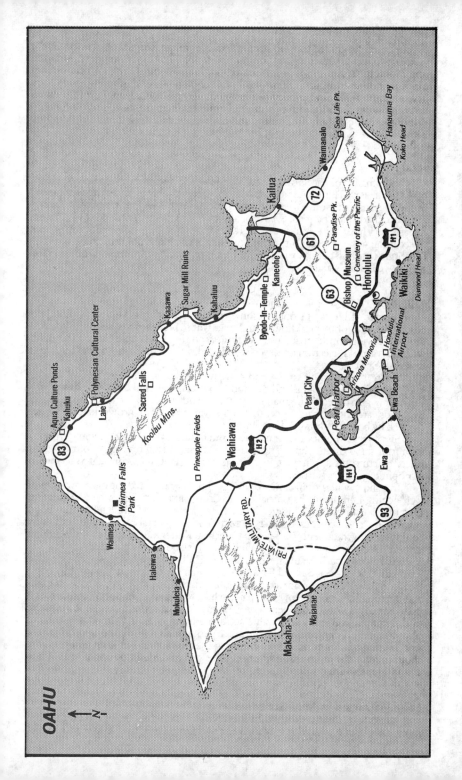

tors are taken on guided tours in open-air trams through five gardens named for the various presidents under whom Fong served in his 17 years in Congress. After the tour, you can stop at the Visitors Center, perhaps have lunch or take a class in lei-making or other Hawaiian crafts. Check out the **Banana Patch** gift shop, too: They have some one-of-a-kind jewelry pieces and designer Hawaiian apparel. Plan on an hour or so for this delightful excursion. Admission is $6.50 for adults, $3 for children 5 to 12. Open daily, from 10am to 4pm; the last tram tour departs at 3pm (tel. 239-6775).

Heeia

For a change of pace now, get back on Hwy. 83 and retrace your way to Heeia, on Kaneohe Bay. This is a good place to stop, stretch your legs, and switch to another mode of transportation. Glass-bottom boats at **Heeia Kea Pier** take you on a nar-rated excursion at a charge of $7.50 for adults, $3.50 for children under 12. Cruises depart every hour daily. Make advance reservations by calling 239-9955. Also, check to see if the water is clear that day; if not, there's not much point in going out. The **Deli Snack and Gift Shop,** right on the pier, offers local-style plate lunches (around $4), as well as the usual snacks.

THE ROAD TO LAIE

Outside of Heeia, it's one awesome view after another as you weave along the coast, past acres of tropical flowers and trees whose branches frequently arch across the whole width of the road. You can't miss spotting **Pineapple Hut** on the right, which has a good selection of carved wood, shells, macramé planters, and the like at reasonable prices.

You're now coming to the end of Kaneohe Bay, and the next HVB marker you'll see will point to an island that looks like its name, **Mokoli'i** (little lizard); it's sometimes also called Chinaman's Hat. On the other side of the road, tangled over by weeds, are the ruins of a century-old sugar mill. Cane grown here was once shipped by boat to "distant" Honolulu.

Just over two miles past the large garment factory building on your left, look for a fruit stand on the right. The only indication is a sign reading "Cold Coconut Juice." Here you can purchase local fruits grown right in this area, at Waikane. In our opinion, they're the best.

In a short while you'll come to a rocky cliff that reminded the old Hawaiians of a crouching lion, hence its official name: **Crouching Lion.** The scenic **Crouching Lion Inn** is just in front. This area is fine for a picnic; **Kaawa Beach Park** has good swimming, and so does **Swanzy Beach Park,** just before Punaluu and fully equipped with the amenities. The next beach, at **Kahana Bay,** is safe for swimming inshore, but there are no dressing facilities, and the bottom is muddy.

As you approach Hauula, you'll see the HVB marker pointing to a side road leading to the 87-foot **Sacred Falls.** Even though the trail is lined with impressive trees and flowers, our considered advice is to pass this one up; in order to see the falls and the mountain pool below, you have to hike for about an hour on a rather rough path. But that's not the problem: Over the past few years, there have been a number of drownings, robberies, and tragic accidents here; locals definitely consider this place bad news. Coming up now, the beach park at Hauula is well equipped with the usual bathing facilities, and the swimming is safe inshore. But keep going; you're about to reach the picturesque village of Laie, one of the high points of your Wind-ward Oahu sojourn.

Laie: Polynesia in Miniature

Laie is Salt Lake City with palm trees. No slouches at missionary work, the Mor-mons arrived in Hawaii not long after the first Protestants; over 100 years ago they founded a large colony of Hawaiian and Samoan brethren of The Church of Jesus Christ of Latter-Day Saints, whose descendants still live here.

In 1919 the Mormons established a Hawaiian Temple, the first Mormon house of worship outside the mainland; in 1955 the Brigham Young University–Hawaii Campus, a fully accredited liberal arts institution; and in 1963, the **Polynesian Cultural Center,** a loving re-creation of Polynesia in miniature. On beautifully landscaped grounds, seven authentic Polynesian villages—Tahitian, Marquesan, Samoan, Maori, Tongan, Fijian, and of course, Hawaiian—have been built, peopled with islanders who demonstrate the ancient crafts of making tapa (barkcloth), pounding taro roots into poi (a Hawaiian food staple), weaving baskets of lauhala, wood carving, and the like. All this is part of the church's effort to revitalize the ancient Polynesian cultures by giving them a dramatic showcase and, at the same time, to provide job opportunities for Polynesian young people who need to work their way through school.

A visit here is an absorbing excursion into a long-ago, far-away culture. You'll find such curiosities as a splendidly carved Maori war canoe, all 50 feet of it carved from a single log (it took two years to make—in ancient times, it would have taken 20); a native queen's house; Tongan grass huts lined with tapa; and Samoan sleeping quarters for a high chief. Most striking of all, perhaps, is the Maoris' sacred house of learning, with its carved and woven inside panels. The *veddy* British accent of the Maori guides, dressed in island costumes, may come as a bit of a shock until you remember that they are New Zealanders, Commonwealth subjects. As you make your way around, either on foot or by tram or canoe, you'll find that they are the other guides who explain their traditions with such deep feelings are the most impressive aspects of the cultural center.

Various events are scheduled throughout the day, like the "Pageant of the Long Canoes." The stellar entertainment here is a spectacular production of Polynesian dancing and singing called *This Is Polynesia*. It's just a trifle showbiz (colored waters, tricky lighting), but the performers—people brought from Polynesia to man the villages, or students at B.Y.U. Hawaii—are quite good, and some of them, such as the Fijian men in their traditional war dances, do probably the best ethnic dancing in the islands.

To see everything at the Polynesian Cultural Center, including *This Is Polynesia,* you will have to pay $38.95 for adults, $19.95 for children 5 to 11; this includes the all-you-can-eat Gateway Buffet (sweet-and-sour ribs, island fish, and more). For an extra $6, you can have the Alii Luau dinner (traditional favorites like kalua pig, lomi-lomi salmon, poi, teriyaki chicken, etc.). Although these prices make it a splurge for us, considering that it encompasses your daytime activity plus dinner and a show, the value is good. For the dinner-show package alone, prices are $34.95 adult, $14.95 children. And for everything *except* the dinner and show—that is, admission to the seven villages and all daytime activities—the charge is $24.95 adults, $9.95 children. *Note:* It is suggested that visitors arrive no later than 2pm to enjoy the full experience. If you're staying for the evening, you may want to plan this as a special excursion, rather than as part of an all-day, around-the-island trip.

Visitors can pick up tickets at the center's ticket office on the ground floor of the Royal Hawaiian Shopping Center, Building C. While you're there, check the schedule; there are often miniperformances on Tuesday, Thursday, and Saturday morning, 9:30 to 11:30am. You can also book round-trip motorcoach transportation at about $9 per adult.

The Polynesian Cultural Center is open Monday through Saturday; closed Sunday, Thanksgiving, Christmas, and New Year's Day. For further information, call the box office at 293-3333 or toll free 800/367-7060, or the Waikiki ticket office at 923-1861. If you are driving directly to Laie from Honolulu, take the Pali Hwy. and turn north on Kamehameha Hwy.

While you're here, you'll also want to see the **Hawaiian Temple;** it stands back from the road on high ground, above a pond, an illuminated fountain, and at the head of a long avenue of royal palms. Best approach for a Taj Mahal–like vista is to leave the highway at Halelaa Boulevard. A complimentary Historical Laie Tour is available. You'll tour the Mormon Temple, Brigham Young University–Hawaii, and the Laie community on a re-created 1903 Hawaiian streetcar. By the way, not all the students here are Mormons; the school is open to others, provided they take the pledge not to smoke or drink, and "to live good Christian lives."

Laie Beach used to be the scene of the Mormon hukilaus, once considered one of the island's top visitor attractions. The ocean at **Laie-Maloo** is safe for inshore swimming, although the beach is not a public park and has no dressing facilities.

You won't want to leave Laie without a drive out to **Laie Point** (the turn-off is just past the entrance to the cultural center), where you get a dramatic view of the rugged coastline. Walk out over the porous lava rock as far as you can go safely for the best view of all. Some old Hawaii hands swear it's the best view in the islands. Sunset devotees shouldn't miss this one.

THE HALFWAY POINT—KAHUKU, KUILIMA, SUNSET BEACH, AND HALEIWA

Now the road runs inland through sugar country, starting with the village of Kahuku, the halfway point of your trip. The old **Kahuku Sugar Mill** has reopened, and while it no longer offers the excellent guided tour it once did, it's still worthwhile to make a stop here, perhaps to eat at the delightful **Country Kitchen Restaurant** (see Chapter IV, "Honolulu Restaurants"), or to take a self-guided free minitour of the first room of the old mill. The awesome machinery is color-coded so you can tell the electrical system from the steam, water, or bargasse (fiber) system. Follow the arrows so as to view the process in order. You may take this tour any day between 10am and 6pm. In the building behind are some vendors' stalls offering the same sort of jewelry and T-shirts that you can get all over Waikiki—and far more economically at the local swap meets!

Back in the car, keep an eye out for the roadside stands; in summer, you can get home-grown watermelon here—the best on the island. And you can also get fabulous shrimp here in Kahuku at **Amorient Aquafarm,** where we always stop off for a luscious snack. Amorient Aquafarm is a 175-acre diversified shrimp and fish farm; they grow a variety of prawns and other seafood in one-acre ponds that are visible from the highway. Their stand, open every day from 10am to 5:30pm, offers freshly cooked shrimp tempura ($6.75 for a dozen pieces), shrimp cocktail ($3.95) or shrimp cooked tails ($10.50 per lb.). Feast at a roadside table or in your car.

The road reaches the shore again at Kuilima, where you might want to have a look at the sumptuous Turtle Bay Hilton and Country Club, one of the most beautiful resorts in the islands. The scenery is spectacular here, especially the view at the swimming pool, perched atop a cliff overlooking the ocean on two sides as the waves pound in. (If it's time for lunch, you might want to try the 11am to 2:30pm "minideli" buffet for about $11.50 in the scenic Bay View Lounge. There is a charge for parking here, but the fee can be validated at lunch.)

Back to the car again for a drive along **Sunset Beach,** with its huge breakers crashing in at your right. It's safe for summer swimming, but in winter it's a wild, windy stretch, exciting to walk along; better still, you may be lucky enough to see some spectacular surfing here, for this is Oahu's North Shore, currently *the* place for the surfing set. Traffic may be jammed for miles, from here to Haleiwa, if there's an important surfing contest going on. If you're wondering whether you should try it yourself, be advised that the surfing areas range from pretty dangerous to very dangerous to one that's called "Banzai Pipeline" (remember the wartime suicide cry of the Japanese?). **Waimea Bay,** just below Sunset, has the distinction of having Hawaii's biggest waves, sometimes crashing in as high as 30 feet. However, in the summer months Waimea Bay is tranquil, the waves are gentle, and swimming here is close to perfection.

While the surfers are tempting fate, you can survey a more primitive form of human sacrifice (and this time we're serious) by turning left on Pupukea Road (it's one of the few paved roads here, and you should note that it's opposite a fire station and next to a market). As soon as the road begins its ascent up the hill, take your first right and continue on up to **Puu O Mahuka Heaiu.** Here, on a bluff overlooking Waimea Bay (another view-collector's spot), are the ruins of a temple where human sacrifice was practiced. When Captain Vancouver put in at Waimea Bay in 1792, three of his men were captured and offered to the bloodthirsty gods. Today all is tranquil here, and the faithful still come, offering bundles of ti leaves in homage.

For a refreshing change of pace, head back to nature now at **Waimea Falls Park,** opposite Waimea Bay Beach Park, a botanical Eden nestled in a lush, 1,800-acre historic Hawaiian valley. There's a lot to do here: You can watch world-class cliff divers plunge 60 feet into the waterfall pool, or see the park's resident hula troupe, dressed in authentic costumes, perform beautiful ancient (kahiko) hula. At the Hawaiian Games Site, you can play the sports of old Hawaii, such as ulu maika (lawn bowling), o'o ihe (spear throwing), or konane (Hawaiian checkers). You can wander through more than 30 botanical gardens that showcase some of the world's most exotic and rare plants, or explore numerous trails that wind their way through the park. Hop onto the narrated minibus to the waterfall, then join knowledgeable park guides for walking tours through the gardens and historical sites. At the kauhale kahiko (ancient Hawaiian living site), step into old Hawaii and experience the way Hawaiians were thought to have once lived.

You can also enjoy a relaxed picnic in the grassy meadow or a sumptuous lunch at the all new **Pikake Pavilion,** a spacious open-air dining center overlooking the mouth of the valley. Grab a quick island snack or cold drink at one of several snack bars within the valley, or browse through **Charlie's Country Store** for island gifts and mementos.

Twice each month, the park offers romantic evening strolls to the waterfall and back by the light of the full moon. A donation of $5 per family directly benefits the Waimea Arboretum Foundation, a nonprofit scientific and educational organization dedicated to protecting Hawaii's rare and endangered plants.

Waimea Falls Park is also one of Hawaii's most popular wedding locations; couples can exchange vows in a lush, secluded garden or next to a gorgeous waterfall. For more information on planning such a special event, contact the park's **Wedding Department** at 59–864 Kamehameha Hwy., Haleiwa, HI 96712.

Admission is $11.95 for adults, $6.50 for juniors ages 7 to 12, and $2.25 for children 4 to 6. Waimea Falls Park is open daily including holidays from 10am to 5:30pm. For more information, call 638-8511 or 923-8448.

Pupukea Beach Park in this area has good swimming and outstanding snorkeling in the summer months. A few miles farther along, at **Haleiwa Beach Park** on Waialua Bay, you'll find the last swimming spot before you strike into the heart of Oahu. It's a fine family-type place—lawns, play areas, pergolas, dressing rooms, showers, fishing, camping, and picnicking area.

The Youth Scene at Sunset Beach and Haleiwa

If you're seriously interested—or even slightly—in the youth culture, you'll be welcome among the inhabitants of Sunset Beach and Haleiwa, an area that attracts a number of young people who want to live close to nature and the big surf. They're not putting on a show for sightseers or tourists, just quietly doing their thing—and an attractive thing it is. Haleiwa is like a very tiny version of Cape Cod's Provincetown, with its distinctively artsy atmosphere, small gift shops, art galleries, and boutiques. Hand-painted dresses and original designs, most of them made in the area, are offered by Inge Jausel at **Oogenesis Boutique** at 66–249 Kam Hwy. Japanese-inspired designs grace tops, pants ensembles, and simple dresses that can be worn belted or unbelted. Prices are reasonable. Under the "Inge Hawaii" label, these garments are now being sold in mainland stores. Inge's other store, **Rix,** 66–145 Kam Hwy., offers contemporary designs in fashion. . . . **Deeni's Boutique** at 66–079 Kam Hwy. in Haleiwa specializes in swimwear, T-shirts, and sportswear, with some of the lowest prices and best selections in town. . . . Art lovers will want to browse the galleries, especially places like **Pacific Island Arts** in the North Shore Marketplace, 66–250 Kam Hwy., which offers a chance to see honored island artists at work. . . . The **Wyland Gallery,** 66–150 Kam Hwy. specializes in the work of noted marine artist Wyland (everything from originals to posters), and also shows photographs, wood sculptures, and more. . . . Have a look, too, at the **Fettig Art Gallery,** 66–051 Kam Hwy., an important outlet for the local painters and potters. Handcrafted pottery, locally made candles and sculpture, as well as paintings, are well priced.

Hungry? You've come to the right town. Some of our favorite North Shore restaurants are here (see Chapter IV), like **Kua'Aina** for super sandwiches, **Steamer's** for local fish and seafood in a glamorous setting, and **Jameson's by the Sea,** open to beautiful views and breezes as it overlooks Haleiwa Harbor. Wherever you eat, skip dessert and drive over to **Matsumoto's Grocery** at 66–087 Kam Hwy. in Haleiwa (across from the intersection of Emerson Street) for the ultimate shave-ice experience. Local people drive out from all over the island to queue up here, while no fewer than four girls form an "assembly line" to shave and season the ice. We won't swear that you'll really love shave ice with ice cream and azuki beans on the bottom, but can you say you really know Hawaii unless you've tried it? Matsumoto's also sells nifty T-shirts, caps, and sweatshirts with their logo in pretty colors—great souvenirs. Aoki's, just down the road, is an alternative if the lines are just too long.

Since Sunset Beach is a spiritually attuned community, it abounds in centers for yoga, Zen, and other such disciplines; the people at any of the shops can give you information on any groups that may interest you. This area is a world apart from the urban crush of Honolulu, the tourist scene at Waikiki, and the rat race everywhere. Try to schedule your visit in time for the fantastic sunset, which turns the horizon to a brilliant blazing red.

THE RETURN TRIP

At the intersection of Hwy. 82 (Kamehameha Hwy.), turn left and follow it as it climbs to **Leilehua Plateau.** Here the tall sugarcane gives way to seemingly endless miles of pineapple—dark green and golden against the red earth. It's the largest pineapple area in the world. Just as you're beginning to feel like the Ancient Mariner (you can't pick any), you'll find the **Dole Pineapple Pavilion,** just north of Wahiawa, where you can buy a whole "pine" or get a half-dozen delicious spears, fresher than any you've ever tasted. The custom here is to sprinkle a little unrefined Hawaiian salt on the pineapple; it helps cut the acidity. You can also shop for Hawaiian souvenirs here and order fresh pineapple packs delivered to the airport for your flight back home. Dole does not conduct tours through the fields, but many operations are visible from the highway. In case you're curious, the variety of pineapple grown here is called sweet cayenne.

In the midst of these Wahiawa pineapple fields, one mile past the pineapple hut, is the Del Monte Corporation's **Pineapple Variety Garden,** right at the junction of Hwys. 82 and 809. It's small, but well worth a brief stop to see a huge variety of species and pineapple plants from all over the world—Asia, Africa, South America, and various small islands. Just ignore the tremendous spiders that build their webs among the plants; they're nonaggressive and totally harmless—to people and pineapples.

Next stop is for the history-anthropology buffs: a Stone Age spot where the royal chieftesses of Hawaii gave birth. Just before **Wahiawa,** watch on the right for a dirt road leading into a clump of eucalyptus trees in a pineapple field on the Kaukonahau Gulch—the **Place of the Sacred Birthstone.** The large flat stone protruding several feet above the ground was a primitive delivery table; legend had it that a son delivered on this stone would be born with honor.

Just before you reach Wahiawa, still in the pineapple fields, you may want to stop and stretch your legs at a five-acre, working vegetable and flower farm called **Helemano Plantation,** which serves a tasty and inexpensive buffet lunch at around $7.50 between 11am and 2:30pm (see Chapter IV, "Honolulu Restaurants"). However, if it's past lunchtime, you can still browse at the gift shop, get some fresh produce at the country store, visit the bakery, or even join a lei-making class. Helemano Plantation provides many retarded people with training and vocational opportunities, and is a division of Hawaii's admirable Opportunities for the Retarded, Inc.

Now take Hwy. 99 into Wahiawa, a town that serves as a center for personnel stationed at **Schofield Barracks** (where James Jones met his muse) and **Wheeler's Field**. It's also a huge pineapple depot. The bright spot here is **Kemoo Farm,** a restaurant overlooking Lake Wilson that's been a big favorite with the kamaainas since 1927. Besides the very good food (see a complete review in Chapter IV), Kemoo Farm sells some attractive gift items in its country store lobby. In this area you may also want to visit the **Schofield Museum,** with its military and historical documents (open daily until 4pm), and the **Wahiawa Botanical Garden,** at 1396 California Ave. (east of the highway), 1,000 feet high, where you can wander through four lovely acres of rare trees, ferns and shrubs, many orchid plants, and a Hawaiian garden. Don't forget your camera. Admission is free.

You'll pass through more sugar fields as you drive along the now-four-lane Kamehameha Hwy. (Hwy. 99) or the new Interstate Highway H-2. From here on, it's fast sailing home. At the intersection with Hwy. 90, take that road to the left; it will take you past Pearl Harbor (you might visit the U.S.S. Arizona Memorial if you have the time; see Chapter VIII for details) and the Honolulu Airport. At Middle Street, turn right onto Hwy. 92 (Nimitz Hwy.), which will take you past the harbor; take Ala Moana and Kalakaua into Waikiki.

But before you settle into your hotel, consider the following two other points of interest, which you could take in at the start or at the end of your trip—or save them for another day.

2. The Pali and Makiki Heights

The only major attraction you haven't seen on this trip is the view from the **Nuuanu Pali,** a glorious panorama of Windward Oahu from the top of a jagged cliff. It's a historic spot, too, because it was here that Kamehameha the Great vanquished the Oahuans in a fierce battle in 1795. Thousands of the defeated fell to their deaths on the rocks below. (You could start the round-the-island trip via the Pali, but you'd miss the scenery in the Koko Head area, which we find more appealing.). You can see the Pali by turning left off Nimitz Hwy. in downtown Honolulu onto Nuuanu Avenue (or Bishop Street, which runs into Pali Hwy.), which you follow until it hits Pali Hwy., and on to the Pali.

Just before you reach the Pali, however, you might want to stop at one of the island's newer points of interest. If you drive about a mile up the Pali and turn left at Jack Lane, you come upon the beautiful **Tendai Mission of Hawaii** and its enormously impressive 25-foot statue of Senju Kannon, the Thousand-Armed Goddess of Mercy. The Tendai sect of Mahayana Buddhism ended 1,200 years of confining its worship halls to Japan when it opened the Hawaii mission in November 1973. You're welcome to inspec the grounds and building any day during regular activity hours. (There are no specific times of opening or closing.) Occasionally, you'll see local groups using the facilities for flower-arranging, tea ceremonies, and handcraft exhibits.

Another spectacular view that we think you shouldn't miss is the one from **Makiki Heights.** In a way, we like it better than the Pali, since this is a top-of-the-world view, completely unobstructed. Here's how to get there: from Waikiki, take Kalakaua Avenue until it ends at South Beretania Street; go past Makiki to Keeaumoku Street, turn right, go across Hwy. 1 and turn right on Wilder. Go one block, then make a left on Makiki, which runs into Round Top Drive, then Tantalus Drive, and up, up, up. The road, which is excellent all the way, goes through the Round Top Forest Reserve. Stop at **Puu Ualakka State Park** (open from 7am to 6:45pm daily) and have a look at the glorious view from Round Top. Back in the car, continue in the same direction you were going; you'll end up just about where you started, having come full circle.

3. Tips for Tourists

SWIMMING

Don't attempt to swim at any beach that is not also a public park; dressing-room facilities will give you a clue. Although dangerous areas are usually posted, the signs may be missing, or you may not see them. The following beaches on this drive are *unsafe* because of undertow or heavy surf: Koko Head Beach, Waimea Beach and Sunset Beach on the North Shore (in winter), and Light House Beach at Makapuu. Never swim where there is a steep beach, a rocky shoreline, or large waves. Never turn your back to the ocean. In case of trouble, call the police at 911 or dial zero.

CAMPING

If you want to join the local families camping on some of the beaches (besides the beauty, a really cheap way to cut overnight costs), obtain a permit from the Department of Parks and Recreation on the first floor of the Honolulu Municipal Building, 650 S. King St. Call 523-4525 for details, plus a list of the parks that have facilities: water, toilets, sometimes sinks and barbecue stoves. Note that all city-beach park campgrounds are closed to camping every Wednesday and Thursday. There is no charge for camping permits.

READERS' SUGGESTIONS IN WINDWARD OAHU: "We highly recommend upgrading the **Polynesian Cultural Center tour** to an Ambassador tour. We paid extra for this, but we got a guided tour by one of the Brigham Young University students for the day, kukui nut leis, special seating for the evening buffet, seating within the first five rows for the evening show, plus the intermission dessert of mango sherbet. We wished that we had had even a few more hours to spend here. The evening show is thrilling, the buffet food was some of the best we had during our whole vacation, and the student performers are all eager to please" (Margaret A. Pyzik, Naperville, Ill.). . . . "Please let your readers know that at the P.C.C. it is best to follow the crowds. We thought we'd be smart and avoid the crowds, but it turned out that we missed almost every exhibition because we arrived at the wrong times" (Carol Robinson, Lubbock, Tex.).

"Mention should be made about the hazards of camping in certain areas overnight. People come here expecting 'Paradise' and find that violence is the same all over. Many bad incidents have occurred to overnight tourist campers in the Waianae and Waimanalo areas. These two areas have many local people of low economic station who know tourists have money and are easy marks. Local folks don't even camp alone on the beaches in these two areas. A warning should be given" (Alton Rogers, Honolulu, HI.). [*Authors' Note:* Local friends report the Waianea area is still dangerous for tourists, but that Waimanalo is safe during the daytime.]

"Rather than take one of the big tours, where there are so many people and the whole experience is so impersonal, I strongly recommend that people take the small 8- to 11-person tours. I went with **E Noa Tours** (tel. 599-2561) on an around-the-island tour and it was the best day I spent in Hawaii. Since the cost is $49 including lunch and snorkeling lessons, it's not cheaper than renting a car, but I would not have learned as much as I did about the Hawaiians, their land, culture, and values. Not only that, but when you get on the bus, the driver asks if there are any places in particular you would like to see, so you don't miss a thing. There were eight of us on our tour, and in that full day of traveling I made some beautiful friends. The driver knew so much about everything—there wasn't much he couldn't answer—and he had us constantly rolling with laughter. The tour is complete with snorkeling at Hanauma Bay and a multitude of sights" (Kristin Fry, Calgary, Alberta, Canada). [*Authors' Note:* E Noa also offers other excellent tours: A City Tour at $16, Pearl Harbor $22, Diamond Head $21, and Polynesian Cultural Center $63.]

"When reaching Wahiawa on their 'round-the-island' trip, people should take time to drive around the winding roads of this 'island city'—it is surrounded by lakes and streams—and they'll discover lovely homes and camera-worthy mountain settings. It's no longer a dreary-looking place: It has several new 'sparkling' businesses and the run-down buildings on California Street have been torn down for a housing project for older Hawaiians. There's a big Long's Drugstore shopping complex" (Capt. A. Plant, Wahiawa, HI). . . . "Pass up the hike to **Sacred Falls**, Hauula, unless you're a vigorous and determined hiker. Even experienced hikers cannot reach Sacred Falls in an hour's hike. The trail has been neglected and jungle has leaned over the path; one must duck under and climb over trees. The path is indeed rough, rocky, and usually muddy. Plan an hour and a half up, an hour back. . . . At Punaluu there's **Kahana State Park.** An excellent trail starts up the mountain toward the Koolau range. It quickly becomes pitted with mudholes, but is still a good foot trail and gives a good opportunity to see Hawaiian mountain jungle. There are a few papaya and banana plantings, and some oldtime-style Hawaiian dwellings. An hour's hike brings one to a freshwater swimming hole; it is possible to cross a dam here for an extended hike. Allow half an hour to return to Kam Hwy. A permit to hike is required, but may be obtained, free, at Kahana Park Headquarters. Open 7am to 6:45pm." (David Moore, Phoenix, Ariz.). . . . "On our first full day in Hawaii, six of our party rented a full-size, air-conditioned Lincoln and used your book as a guide. The highlight of the day was our lunch stop in a little town named **Wahiawa,** and the name of the restaurant was **Kemoo Farm.** It was a great, relaxing spot, overlooking a small lake, with a pineapple field beyond. The food was superb. If you like fresh pineapple, what a spot! Pineapple on the salad bar and large wedges of pineapple in the iced tea. We just had to let you know how much we enjoyed Kemoo Farm" (Richard and Angie Ager, Hyattsville, Md.).

"At **Sunset Beach,** beside the waves, which *did* reach 30 feet, we joined in with beach-combers who were sifting puka shells in the sand. We stayed here for about half an hour sifting the sand through our fingers and found several dozen beautiful shells" (Dave Kaiser, Fort Lauderdale, Fla.). [*Authors' Note:* A word of caution: Shell-hunters should never turn their back to the ocean when the surf is high; more than one person has been swept out to sea by a high wave.]

"Here's why I liked **Mahaka Beach:** First, it was the only place where we discovered great tidepools. They were teeming with aquatic life of every possible variety (visit when the tide is out). Second, the snorkeling was wonderful. Be sure to wear sneakers when walking over the tidepools or snorkeling because there are thousands of spiny urchins on the sea floor. And third, the Hawaiians we met on the beach were as friendly as anyone we met in Hawaii. One fine lady even showed us how to find the best shells, and invited us to her home to take boxes of them home with us! I would recommend placing your beach mat and belongings close to where others are; we felt quite safe there. It was also April, so the ocean was quiet" (Eric Schuman, Topeka, Kans.).

"Your readers should know about the park at **Kualoa,** near Chinaman's Hat. It is marked on the makai side of the road just past Kualoa Ranch. Take the first turn right after you pass the gates. Soon you will reach one of the most respected places: this is where the Hokule's was launched, just because of this. Be sure to take a look" (Mrs. Clarence Gaber, Kailua, HI). [*Authors' Note:* Swimming is poor here, but it's a beautiful park, a place where island families like to camp.]. . . . "Please caution people not to leave any valuables in their car, even if it's locked. There must be many other seasoned travelers accustomed to traveling the continental United States and stopping at overlooks with all their luggage, cameras, etc., in the cars and having no one disturb their property. We started our circle tour and got to the lookout just beyond Hanauma Bay and went over the fence to take pictures. We were gone five minutes at the most. When we returned, the car's lock mechanism had been removed and all camera equipment, the tape recorder, binoculars, and purse were gone. At Koko Marina, the police told us there are people who make their living doing this, so they are very quick" (Linda Loreny, Toledo, Ohio).

X

TO THE NEIGHBOR ISLANDS

POLYNESIA WITH PLUMBING

Too many tourists start and end their Hawaiian holidays in Honolulu—and think they've seen Hawaii. Yes—and no. They've seen the one major city and the major resort area, but far more awaits: a Hawaii at once more gentle and more savage, where the old gods still have powers. To see the desolate moonscapes of the volcanoes and Hawaiian cowboys riding the range, to see beaches so remote and pristine as to make Waikiki seem like Times Square, and to visit South Seas villages just coming into the modern age, you'll have to venture to the three other important Hawaiian Islands: the Garden Island of **Kauai**, the Big Island of **Hawaii**, and the Valley Isle of **Maui**. You may also want to visit **Molokai**, which remains much as it was 50 years ago; it is also the home of Kalaupapa, the settlement for the treatment of Hansen's disease, leprosy. The island of **Lanai** is almost wholly given over to growing pineapples; resort development has just begun here and is slated for a super-luxury market. You may want to splurge on one of the sailing-ship cruises out of Lahaina, Maui, that spend the day there for about $125. Going to the neighbor islands requires a little effort for the budget traveler, but we strongly urge you to try.

THE MONEY FACTOR

Most people do it the easy way, by simply taking one of the various package tours around the islands. A flat fee, paid in advance, covers your plane fare, hotels, meals, sightseeing. There is nothing wrong, of course, with this method except that it's expensive, even when you go as an economy tourist. We think you can do much better on your own. Besides, on a tour you've got to go where you're taken—in a group—thus missing all the fun of discovering the off-the-beaten-pathways that appeal to *you!*

Another alternative is to "flightsee" the islands from the air, landing briefly for meals and hurried sightseeing, and returning the same night; theoretically, you've "seen" five islands, but that's just a once-over lightly, about as satisfying as those European jaunts that take you to seven countries in six days. And the one day costs about $175 to boot!

The best way to see the neighbor islands is on your own; and doing that will cost you just a little more than you've been spending in Honolulu. You should be able to stay within a reasonable budget here. You can almost always find a good hotel room from $50 to $80 (you should, of course, be traveling with a companion); there are plenty of restaurants where you can get well-priced meals; and the supply of kitchenette-condo apartments, where you save money by doing your own cooking is enormous.

A money-saving plan is to check the special car-hotel deals that the major airlines—Aloha and Hawaiian—often make in conjunction with the leading car-rental companies and some of the island hotel chains. If the airlines are sold out on any of these special programs, try a local travel agency; they'll often be able to help you.

You can also save money on hotels and condos, by joining **Club Costa,** details on which are given in Chapter III, "Honolulu Hotels."

Your major expense on the outer islands will be transportation. Only one city on one island—Hilo, on the island of Hawaii—has anything resembling a public transportation system, and even that is not very extensive. (Buses do cross the island east to west and back.) There is also bus service in Lihue, Kauai, and in the Lahaina-Kaanapali and Kihei areas of Maui, but none of the buses run for any great distances. So unless you want to stay put, you have only two choices: taking expensive sightseeing tours or renting your own car. The latter is not cheap either, especially on days when you must pile on a lot of mileage, driving from one end of an island to another. If you're a couple or a family, your car costs per person will naturally be fairly low. In any case, you won't be sorry you made the trip.

WHICH TO CHOOSE

Each of the three major neighbor islands is fascinating and important to visit, and we strongly recommend that you make the circuit tour. (We suggest Molokai and Lanai as added attractions, after you've seen the others.) If you decide to go to only one island, read carefully the chapters ahead on the sights of Maui, Hawaii, and Kauai before you make your decision. Each has its special fascinations. **Maui** has become the most popular of the neighbor islands, especially appealing to an affluent condo crowd; it has some of the best golf courses in the state of Hawaii. Its great natural wonder, and its chief claim to fame is Haleakala, the largest dormant volcano in the world, with a moonlike crater that you can explore on foot or horseback. The popular, picturesque old whaling town of Lahaina, remote and lovely Hana, and a succession of golden beaches are strong lures. The Big Island of **Hawaii** is the most varied, geographically, of the islands, almost like a small continent in miniature. It has few beaches (except in the Kona area), but it has the islands' second-biggest city (Hilo), the volcanic wonderlands of Mauna Kea and Mauna Loa (Volcanoes National Park is a must on any itinerary), and a cattle ranch big enough to belong to Texas. **Kauai** is perhaps not as well known as it should be; it is still refreshingly rural, small, beautiful, and easily assimilated. Waimea Canyon, a smaller version of the Grand Canyon, is its principal natural attraction. It also has a string of unforgettable beaches (you've seen them as Bali H'ai in the movie version of *South Pacific* and as Matlock Island in the television production of *The Thornbirds*). For advice on itineraries, see suggestions on inter-island travel in Chapter I.

CAMPING ON THE NEIGHBOR ISLANDS

Camping is popular on all the outer islands (as well as on Oahu, of course), and throughout these pages you will find various references to camping. Unfortunately, as of this writing, there is no place where one can rent a camper. Of course, you can bring your own equipment (see the Readers' Suggestions ahead for some interesting tips), but note that permits in advance are required. Check with the offices of the Hawaii Visitors Bureau (you can write them in advance; their addresses are given in the Introduction) to find out where to get permits for each island. And note references to various special camping grounds and cabins in the pages ahead. Note too, alas, that camping, especially tent camping, is no longer as safe as it used to be.

BICYCLING ON THE NEIGHBOR ISLANDS

We've had excellent reports on a bicycle touring service that promises fascinating adventures on the islands of Hawaii, Maui, and Kauai. Ron Reilly and his associates are all dedicated cyclists who gave up professional careers in other fields to work at what they really enjoy. And what they really enjoy is taking people off the beaten tourist track, to show them the beauty, the fun, the challenge and excitement of cycling around Hawaii's neighbor islands. Although there are reputable mainland companies that also offer bicycle tours of the islands, none are based in Hawaii, nor can share the insights, understanding, and local experience that these people have. Trips are exceptionally well planned; they do the work, and the participants have the fun. Six-day, five-night cycling tours—Maui Magic, Kauai Keepsake, and Hawaii Highlights—cost approximately $785 per tour based on double occupancy, and include all accommodations, meals, maps, a support van, and the guidance of two experienced leaders. This does not include your bicycle rental or your airfare to the islands. For information, write to **Island Bicycle Adventures,** 569A Kapahulu Ave., Honolulu, HI 96815 (tel. 955-6789 or toll free 800/233-2226).

AND KEEP IN MIND

Driving distances on the neighbor islands can be great, particularly on the Big Island of Hawaii, and you may have trouble finding gas stations, especially ones open on Sunday: keep the tank full. Be sure to check your U-drive carefully before going on a long trip, and get a phone number where you can reach the agency at night in case of problems. Remember, too, to ask the agency for some good road maps indicating distances, and don't hesitate to ask questions and directions before you take off.

Also, even though it's easier than it used to be to find inexpensive places to eat as you scoot around the islands because of the rise of fast-food outlets, it can be a long drive between meals. It's always a good idea to throw a few sandwiches and some fruit in your beach bag, along with the suntan lotion and the road maps.

A NOTE ON PACKAGE TOURS

If you do decide on a package deal, remember that there are all kinds, sizes, and shapes. The most expensive ones park you at the luxury hotels and take you sightseeing in private limousines; the cheapest put you up in standard hotels, take you sightseeing in motor coaches, and may not provide meals. If they don't you have a chance to shop around for inexpensive restaurants, which will charge much less than what the tour companies figure on as the cost of three meals. Do some careful studying and comparing before you sign up for one. Here, to aid in that task, are some of the major travel companies that offer tours to the outer islands:

Island Holidays Tours, 2255 Kuhio Ave., Honolulu, HI 96830–0519 (tel. 945-6000).

Hawaiian Holidays Tours, 2222 Kalakaua Ave., Honolulu, HI 96815 (tel. 926-9200).

American Express, 2222 Kalakaua Ave., Honolulu, HI 96815 (tel. 942-2666 or 800/241-1700).

Trade Wind Tours of Hawaii, 150 Kauilani Ave., (P.O. Box 2198), Honolulu, HI 96815 (tel. 923-2071).

Akamai Tours, 2270 Kalakaua Ave., Honolulu, HI 96815 (tel. 922-4685 or 800/922-6485).

Pleasant Hawaiian Holidays, 270 Lewers St., Honolulu, HI 96815 (tel. 926-1833).

READERS' SUGGESTIONS ON SEEING THE NEIGHBOR ISLANDS: "We were one week on each of the islands of Kauai and Maui, and four days on Oahu. We took our tent, air mattresses, and sleeping bags in two duffle bags; the sleeping bags were unnecessary, and next time we will take a washable blanket sewn into a bag, across the bottom and part way up the open side. Our other necessities were carried in two small army knapsacks and my shoulder bag. . . . Since our accommodation costs—camping permits and $10 for a cabin at Hana—totaled less than $25 for the entire time on the islands, we could well afford to rent a car and travel as much as time would permit. So we saw a great deal more of each island than anyone on a tour. . . . **Camping** there is quite a different experience from what we are used to in Canada.

On the islands, you have to use a small stove that uses fuel or charcoal, and since the fuel for the little stoves cannot be taken on the plane you have to refuel on each island; the driftwood and coconut husks you can gather are usually too damp to burn. Charcoal takes a long time to be ready. Personally, we were seldom at camp during the day other than for breakfast, so we just tucked any burnable garbage in a bag and picked up any odd sticks we came across in our travels. This was sufficient to boil a couple of cups of water for coffee or a cup of instant soup. Some camps have fireplaces, but if there was no cooking facility, we would just make a ring of three or four beer cans—no lack of them, either!—and put our small cook-whatever-you-are-having-in-the-skillet over the small fire built between the cans; it worked very well. . . . I am 55 years of age and my husband past 60, so we were usually the oldest campers around, and what a fine, respectful, yes, even admiring attitude did we receive from everyone we met. By the time we reached Oahu I was feeling so much a part of the scene that I found myself feeling sorry for those tourists on the buses!" (Mr. and Mrs. C. G. Huffman, Saskatoon, Saskatchewan, Canada). [*Authors' Note:* Bravo!]

"Seeing **Lanai** is like reliving the life of the ancient Hawaiians. Many ancient sites have remained unidentified to protect their preservation. It's best to rent a Jeep—about $60 a day but worth it—because most of the sites are along dirt roads (Make reservations a few weeks in advance by phoning 565-6952). After you've seen Shipwreck Beach, the Kahe'a Heiau and Petroglyphs, and the Ho'Okio Battlegrounds (get James A. Bier's map in the bookstores), you're ready for swimming and snorkeling at Manele Bay, which, is, in my opinion, the most beautiful beach in Hawaii. You are sure to enjoy Lanai. This is one place that will always keep its Hawaiian charm, as long as modern civilization doesn't overtake it. Even if the things that you see most are pineapples, you'll remember what the Hawaiian spirit is like for the rest of your life" (Liam Kernell, Honolulu, HI).

"If you wait until you get to Hawaii to book your trips to the other islands you can take advantage of the overnighter packages available, which include round-trip airfare for two and a room and rental car for two nights, for low fees, from **Roberts of Hawaii.** You have to be in the islands to make these reservations" (Kenneth Kendall, Omaha, Nebr.). [*Authors' Note:* There are many deals like this that can only be booked from Hawaii, since the companies are usually forbidden from advertising them outside the islands; they are mainly for kamaainas. It's wise to check these out when you are in the islands.]

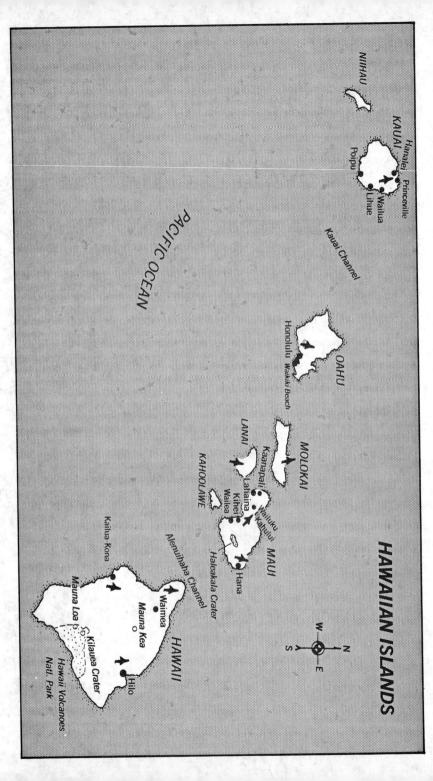

XI

THE ISLAND OF KAUAI

1. ISLAND HOTELS
2. ISLAND RESTAURANTS
3. THE NIGHT SCENE

About 15 jet minutes out of Honolulu and 110 miles to the west, your plane lands you in a tropical Switzerland. This is Kauai, the northernmost and oldest of the major Hawaiian islands, one of the lushest tropical spots on earth.

Kauai (pronounced correctly Kah-*wah*-ee, lazily Kah-*why*) is the oldest Hawaiian island in both geologic and historic time. The fantastic verdure of its cliffs and canyons was formed over millions of years of volcanic growth and collapse, by the endless workings of streams and ocean waves on its bleak cinders and craters (contrast these with the newly formed volcanoes on the island of Hawaii for an idea of the awesome powers of nature). In island lore, Kauai was the original home of Pele, the goddess of fire and volcanoes, before she moved southward. It was also the homeland of a race of pre-Polynesians, whose origins are anybody's guess—including anthropologists'. Some believe they were the survivors of the lost continent of Lemuria. In legend they're called Menehunes, South Sea leprechauns who stood about two feet tall, worked only in darkness, and accomplished formidable engineering feats in the space of a night's work.

The first Polynesian settlers chose Kauai, too, landing at the mouth of the Wailua River somewhere between A.D. 500 and 900. They crossed the Pacific in outrigger canoes in a voyage of many months, probably from the Society Islands. Other Polynesians came later, but time stood still on Kauai and the rest of the Hawaiian Islands until 1778, when Captain Cook arrived at Waimea and the modern history of Hawaii began.

So much for history. Geographically, Kauai is a small island, about 32 miles in diameter. Its central mountain receives an average of 500 inches of rainfall a year, making it one of the wettest spots on earth, which accounts for the lushness of the surrounding landscape. You can see all the important things in Kauai in three days—but the longer you stay, the luckier you are.

ARRIVAL

Your plane lands at the sleek new $36-million Richard A. Kawakami Terminal, the third busiest in the state. From here to Lihue town, or whatever your destination, you'll have to either drive in your own rented car or take a cab.

U-DRIVES

For information on the major budget U-drive companies—offering excellent flat-rate packages on all the islands—see Chapter V. If, however, you haven't done so, or prefer a time-plus-mileage deal, simply walk up to any of the car-rental agencies just across the road from the airport. We drove a car from **Sunshine of Hawaii** (tel. 245-9541) on our last trip and were pleased, with both the car and the courteous service. And it's especially nice that the cars are right at the airport. Rates, which are subject to change, begin at $20.95 daily for a compact standard without air conditioning, $109 weekly. For an automatic four-door with air conditioning, the price is $25.95 and $139. You can call them toll free at 800/367-2977. . . . **Rent-A-Wreck of Kauai** (tel. 245-4755) rents used and new vehicles starting from $18.95 and up. Call the toll-free number, 800/254-4755, for reservations. . . . If you'd like to drive around Kauai in a Jeep CJ-7 or Wrangler, contact **Adventures Four Wheel Drive, Inc.,** 3148 Oihana St. (tel. 246-1144) which claims to have the lowest daily and weekly rates for four-wheel drive vehicles on Kauai. Prices are around $60 a day, $315 a week. They also offer Jeep tours and four-wheel drive instruction. Their toll-free number is 800/356-1207.

If you're staying at a hotel or condo in the Poipu area, **Westside U-Drive,** which services this area exclusively, is a good bet. They offer free front-door delivery and pick-up of all cars, and reasonable rates, beginning at $22.95 for a compact standard, $24.95 for a compact automatic, during the slow season. Their number is 332-8644.

Remember that in busy tourist seasons, prices may go up considerably, and advance reservations are always advisable.

---

1. Island Hotels

IN LIHUE

The tiny town of Lihue is the most centrally located place to stay in Kauai, since it's the starting point for your eastern and western tours of the island. Lihue is the county seat and the center of Kauai's government, commerce, and culture. It's also home to the gigantic new luxury resort, the Westin Kauai. There's only one budget accommodation in the center of town we think visitors will find suitable: that's **Motel Lani,** at Rice Street where it meets Kalena (tel. 245-2965), a pleasant place patronized by both Hawaiians and tourists. The 10 small but modern rooms rent from $25 to $30, single or double; from $32 to $35 triple. All have a small refrigerator. There's an extra charge of $10 per person for any number over three, with rollaway cots provided. Rates are subject to change without notice. Two nights' deposit required. Janet Naumu suggests that you reserve in advance by writing to P.O. Box 1836, Lihue, Kauai, HI 96766.

AT NAWILIWILI HARBOR

Two miles down the road from the center of town, at Nawiliwi Harbor, just across the road from Kalapaki Beach and a stone's throw from all the activity of the Westin Kauai, sits one of Kauai's top budget choices. An older hotel has been taken over by new owners, renovated from top to bottom, and spruced up with white paint and green trim, and has reemerged as the sparkling **Garden Island Inn,** 3445 Wilcox Rd., Lihue, Kauai, HI 96766 (tel. 245-7227). Owners Steven and Susan Layne have done a terrific job in transforming the 21-room, two-story hotel, from the lovely gardens and miniature waterfalls cascading into several koi pools on the outside, to the bright, cheerful rooms within, all with ocean views, and some with private lanais. Rooms are light and sunny, with textured ceilings, rattan furniture and floral spreads, ceiling fans, tropical flowers, and original watercolors. Each room features a wet bar with refrigerator, color cable TV, and coffeemaker complete with complimentary Kona coffee. Bedding is either one queen-size bed or two twin beds: The bathrooms have showers but no tubs. And the rates are excellent for rooms of this quality: from $45 a night double on the ground floor, $55 a night on the second floor, for rooms with private lanais. Family rooms are $55 to $65. A suite with four beds and a living room could house a family of four at $65 a night; it has its own microwave oven and a larger refrigerator. A suite with a three-sided private lanai, a queen-size sofabed in the living room and a queen-size bed in the bedroom, plus a complete kitchen, is $75 to $95 a night. You can make yourself comfortably at home at the Garden Island Inn, pick oranges and papayas from the trees, and be at beautiful Kalapaki Beach, one of our favorites in the islands, in about a minute. For information and reservations, phone Steve and Susan toll free at 800/648-0154.

COCONUT PLANTATION

Nine miles out of town, near where the Wailua River meets the ocean, is the site of the Coconut Plantation complex of hotels in Wailua. These are more expensive than the ones in the Lihue area since they are situated directly on the ocean, but here on the windward side of the island the surf is rougher (and the weather apt to be rainier) than on the leeward side. If you have a car, it's no problem, since it's a short drive to the splendid beaches of leeward Poipu. If you don't have a car, however, and want ocean swimming, we recommend choosing a hotel in Poipu (see ahead).

In this area—which has the advantage of beautiful scenery, the Coconut Plantation Market Place, and lots of good restaurants—a good-value choice is the attractive and informal **Kauai Sands Hotel,** part of the hospitable chain of Sand & Seaside Hotels, even though recent renovations have brought prices up. Both the dining room and bar look right out onto the beach, and there are two swimming pools. The rooms are nicely done in greens and blues borrowed from the ocean hues; they are all carpeted and air-conditioned. During the winter season (mid-December to the beginning of April) single or double, standard rooms with two double beds are $69; superiors are $74; deluxe are $80; with kitchenette, $87. It's a good idea to take the room-and-car-rental package here; you can have the use of a Budget Rent-A-Car for rates of $77, $86, $91, and $97. During the summer season, all room rates go down about $12.

Another good way to save dollars here is to patronize the hotel's dining room, Al and Don's, which serves dinner entrees between $7 and $12, and features "fresh catch of the day" nightly. The cocktail lounge offers good prices from 5:30 to 10pm. For reservations, write to Kauai Sands Hotel, 2222 Kalakaua Ave., no. 714, Honolulu, HI 96815; or phone toll free 800/367-7000.

Aston's Kaha Lani condominium complex is located behind the Kauai Resort Hotel, and just adjacent to the beautiful Wailua Golf Course, on the beach at Wailua Bay. It's great for those who want to swim in the ocean or pool, snorkel, play tennis (there is one court, lit for night play), or golf. Kaha Lani means "Heavenly Place" in Hawaiian, and the resort is aptly named. Each unit is privately owned, so the decor is different in each. We've seen several units and found them all—well, heavenly. Each has a full kitchen with dishwasher, color TV, a lanai, telephone, ceiling fans, and clock-radios. There are one-, two-, and three-bedroom apartments set in two- or three-story buildings. During the summer season (April 16 to December 21), the one-bedroom suites are $117, $134, or $145, depending on whether they are garden, ocean view, or ocean front, for up to four persons. The two-bedroom, two-bath apartments are $149, $166, and $177, for up to six persons. The three-bedroom, two-bath accommodations—all ocean view—are $230 a day for up to eight people. In peak season, add $30 more in all categories. Disabled-accessible rooms are available. Across the road is Coco Palms Resort with its three fine restaurants, and just down the road Coconut Plantation beckons—if you can tear yourself away from this little corner of heaven.

For reservations, phone toll free 800/367-5124, or write to Kaha Lani, 4460 Nehe Rd., Lihue, Kauai, HI 96766.

It's not easy to get an apartment at **Mokihana of Kauai,** 796 Kuhio Hwy., in the Coconut Plantation area (tel. 822-3971) in the busy winter months; that's when this handsome condominium complex is usually chock full of owners. But during

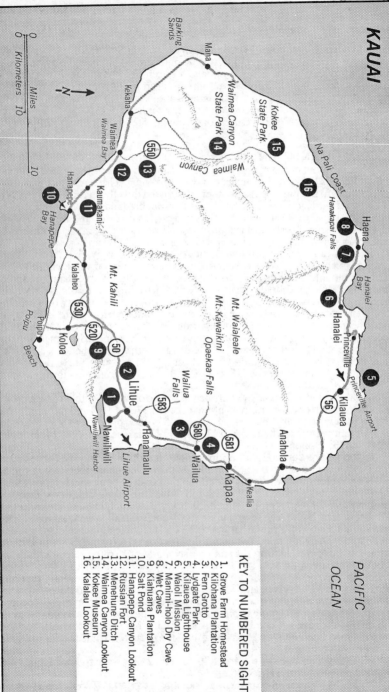

KAUAI

KEY TO NUMBERED SIGHTS:

1. Grove Farm Homestead
2. Kilohana Plantation
3. Fern Grotto
4. Lydgate Park
5. Kilauea Lighthouse
6. Waioli Mission
7. Manini-holo Dry Cave
8. Wet Caves
9. Kiahuana Plantation
10. Salt Pond
11. Hanapepe Canyon Lookout
12. Russian Fort
13. Menehune Ditch
14. Waimea Canyon Lookout
15. Kokee Museum
16. Kalalau Lookout

PACIFIC
OCEAN

the summer season, May through September, it's possible to get a rental. The 80 studio apartments are nicely furnished with limited kitchen facilities (refrigerator, hot plate, and electric frying pan), bath and/or shower; they're right on the oceanfront and two miles away from a championship golf course. Mokihana also boats an 18-hole, par-36 putting green, shuffleboard, a large swimming pool, and a barbecue area. And the original Bull Shed Restaurant, a superb steakhouse right on the waterfront, is here. Apartments rent for a low $45 per night, single or double. For triple occupancy, it's $50. Readers who've managed to wangle a place here have sent good reports. For information, contact Hawaii Kailani, 119 N. Commercial, Suite 1400, Bellingham, WA 98225 (tel. 206/676-1434).

KAPAA

Farther up Hwy. 56 you'll hit the area of Kappa, which boasts the cute little **Hotel Coral Reef** (tel. 822-4481), right on the ocean and close to everything. You could even make do without a car here, because within minimal walking distance is a pretty good public swimming beach, a freshwater swimming pool, a tennis court, a library, and a laundromat—and several great little budget restaurants. The hotel has a stretch of white, sandy beach, and there is good swimming and snorkeling in the deep water between the reefs. There are two wings here, and while the older wing offers decent accommodations for $35 a night double, they are not particularly cheerful. But the newer, oceanfront wing, is a winner. These are spacious rooms looking out on the beach just 50 yards away; they have private lanais and small refrigerators, large glass sliding doors and louvered windows to catch the prevailing trade winds, and either double or twin beds. The ground-floor rooms have brown terrazzo-tile floors; the upper units are carpeted. These rooms are $69 per day, single or double. Children under 12 years old stay free with their parents if they use existing beds; there is an $8 charge for a rollaway bed or crib. Room-and-car packages are available. For reservations, phone toll free, 800/843-4659, or write to Iron Mike & the Princess, Inc., 1516 Kuhio Hwy., Kapaa, Kauai, HI 96746.

One of our favorite places to stay on Kauai is the comfortable and very attractive **Kapaa Sands**, 380 Papaloa Road, Kapaa, Kauai, HI 96746 (tel. 822-4901). It's just a few minutes' walk from Coconut Plantation, yet there's a secluded feeling at this friendly hostelry right on the beach. The pretty, two-story green buildings house studios and two-bedroom apartments. All rooms have color TV and ceiling or floor fans. Studios, with lanais and separate, fully equipped kitchens, go for $69 garden with ocean view, $79 oceanfront. The two-bedroom units are charming duplex apartments (two bedrooms and full bath upstairs, sofa bed and half-bath downstairs), each with two lanais, that go for $89 garden with ocean view, $99 oceanfront. Minimum stay is three days in summer, seven days in winter. (Expect a rate change soon here.) Incidentally, the gracious and friendly manager, Mrs. Harriet Kaholokula, is the mother of two members of the very popular island cabaret and recording group, Na Kaholokula. Write for reservations to the address above, or phone toll free, 800/222-4901.

For a touch of luxury in Kapaa at a very good price, **Kapaa Shores**, 4-0900 Kuhio Hwy., may be just the ticket. This 81-unit condominium complex (of which 20 units are available for rental) is right at the beach, and each and every apartment has a varying degree of view of the ocean, garden, or pool. They are beautifully furnished, many in avocado-and-white decorative schemes, with full electric kitchens, and patio furniture to make dining on your lanai a treat. To help you prepare your meal, the kitchen is fully equipped, and includes a frost-free refrigerator, automatic dishwasher, and garbage disposal. The one-bedroom apartments can sleep up to four people, in a queen-size bed in the bedroom and a queen-size sofa in the living room. Six people can be cozy in the two-bedroom apartments, which are duplexes with vaulted ceilings; they have a queen-size bed in one of the bedrooms, two twins in the other, and a queen-size sleeper sofa in the living room. During the low season, April 16 to December 15, one-bedroom apartments with partial ocean view run $45 to $75 a day, depending on the length of stay: two-bedroom apartments with partial ocean view are $60 to $95. One-bedroom, ocean-view apartments are $53 to $83, two-bedroom, ocean-view apartments are $68 to $103. During high season, December 16 to April 15, one-bedroom apartments with partial ocean views are $55 to $90, two-bedroom apartments with partial ocean views are $75 to $110. One-bedroom, ocean-view apartments are $63 to $98, two-bedroom, ocean-view apartments are $83 to $118. Pluses include the tennis court, 40-foot swimming pool, sunbathing decks, and barbecue area. For reservations call toll free 800/854-8843 outside of California and Canada; Canada 800/824-8968; California 800/472-8449; or write Hawaiian Apartment Leasing Enterprises, 479 Ocean Ave., #8, Laguna Beach, CA 92651. The local phone is 822-3055.

If you're looking for a very relaxed, very casual bed-and-breakfast in this area, **Kay Barker's Bed & Breakfast** might be just the place. This is a spacious home on the slopes of the Sleeping Giant mountain, about a 10-minute drive from Hwy. 56; its back deck runs the length of the house (80 feet) and looks out over peaceful gardens and pasture land. Guests have access to the deck, a large living room and dining room, a separate TV room, a refrigerator for storing snacks, and a washer-dryer. They're welcome to use ice chests, beach mats, boogie boards, and the like. There are several rooms to choose from. The Plumeria Room (king-size or twin beds) and the Orchid Room (king-size bed only) both have private bathrooms with shower, and look out over the front garden; they rent for $30 single, $40 double. The Ginger Room, "the honeymooners' favorite," is larger, has wicker furniture, and a private bath with tub and shower, and overlooks the back garden and pasture lands of Mt. Waialeale; it has its own private entrance. Rates are $40 single, $50 double. A cottage suite called Hibiscus sits by itself in the back garden; it has large rooms, a king-size bed, TV, a sitting room with wet bar, refrigerator and microwave, and a private lanai from which to catch the great views: It's an excellent bargain at $50 single, $60 double. George Barker, who runs the place, whips up good breakfasts (they might include fresh fruits and juices, beverages, banana-nut muffins, french toast, or whatever), and makes everyone feel comfortable. Families with children are welcome. Smoking and "social drinking" are acceptable. For reservations, write to George Barker, P.O. Box 740, Kapaa, Kauai, HI 96746, or phone 822-3073.

Note: If this place is full, George may be able to put you in touch with other B&Bs in the area.

NEAR POIPU BEACH

In the other direction from Lihue, 12 miles south, stretches the idyllic Poipu Beach area, dry and sunny, where the surf crashes a Mediterranean blue-green on palm-fringed, white-sand beaches. Of course, this area is more expensive than Lihue, but you are right at the beach, and a glorious one it is—in our opinion, the best on Kauai. An old favorite here is the **Garden Isle Cottages,** a group of private cottages set in Hawaiian flower gardens, offering island ambience and scattered within a two-block area along the Poipu coast. The hospitable owners, Sharon and Robert Flynn (Bob is an artist), work hard at preserving the feeling of old Hawaii in all of their cottages by using batiks, ethnic fabrics and furniture, and Bob's paintings and sculpture. There are TVs in all the cottages, and a central phone in the garden. Hale Melia, across the lane from a small sunning beach and gentle lagoon for floating and snorkeling, has three accommodations: two studios, each with bath and lanai; the smaller is $46 to $50, and the larger runs $50 to $55, double. You'll be in heaven if you can land the apartment which has a very large living/dining room with an open-beamed lahala ceiling, kitchen, and bath, surrounding an enclosed tropical garden patio that you will probably never want to leave. It rents for $75 to $85 double.

Then there are the Sea Cliff Cottages, whose unique location—perched on a cliff over Koloa Landing, where the Waikomo Stream meets the ocean—gives them an ambience that can be described only as idyllic. You can watch the sun come up over the water from your lanai. They are beautifully furnished with a spacious living/dining room, kitchenette, one bedroom, bath, plus washer-dryer, and rent for $85 to $95 double. A new deluxe accommodation consists of a one-bedroom apartment with living room, dining room, and kitchen, plus a lanai on the ocean and a patio in a tropical garden, it's $107 to $115 double; with two bedrooms and two baths, suitable for up to four persons, it's $140 to $150. A studio apartment with lanai on the ocean, with toaster, coffeepot, and refrigerator, is $68 to $76 double.

Hale Waipahu, located on the highest point in Poipu at Poipu Crater, affords a 360-degree view of mountains, ocean, sunrises, and sunsets. Your own private "lap pool" overlooks the Poipu coast. Charming wood shutters, open-beamed ceiling, and wicker furniture in the living room, latticed dining room, full kitchen and bath, and one bedroom: It all goes for $107 to $115 double per night. An extra bedroom/bath suite is $60 to $65 double.

The office of Garden Isle Cottages is located in Robert Flynn's gallery and is open only from 9am to noon. Good restaurants are nearby, but remember that you'll need a car to get around here. Write to Garden Isle Cottages, 2666 Puuholu Rd., Koloa, Kauai, HI 96756 (tel. 742-6717).

When people are traveling they need a friend. And Den and Dee Wilson, the amiable owner/managers of the **Prince Kuhio Condominiums,** 5160 Lawai Rd., have such a talent for friendship that staying with them gives one of the feelings of coming home. And it's a good place to come home to! The nicely furnished apartments here overlook either Prince Kuhio Park and the ocean on one side or a lovely pool in a garden setting on the other; there's a beach known for good snorkeling right across the road, and there are good swimming beaches nearby (the one we like best is the front of the Hotel Sheraton). The famed Beach House Restaurant is a few steps away. A variety of studios and apartments are offered. From December 15 to April 15, studios are $64 double daily; one-bedroom apartments for four are $79 and $89; the rest of the year, studios are $54, one-bedrooms are $69 and $79. All the units are fully equipped for housekeeping with kitchen and comfortable living space; all have private lanai and cable TV. Two handsome new two-bedroom penthouse units are now available for $149 in winter, $95 in summer. There is no maid service unless requested upon arrival. The central barbecue is a popular spot, and this is the kind of place where it's easy to make friends. Contact Prince Kuhio Rentals, P.O. Box 1060, Koloa, Kauai, HI 96756; the toll-free reservation number is 800/722-1409. The local phone is 742-1409.

Just across from Prince Kuhio is another large condominium complex, the 74-unit, 13-year-old **Kuhio Shores.** The big attraction here is its location on the waterfront: one side of the building faces ocean waves, another a more peaceful harbor; every room has a water view. The units have very large living rooms and fully equipped kitchens with dishwashers and garbage disposals, and are very pleasantly furnished. The one-bedroom units rent for $90; the two-bedroom/two-bath apartments run from $110 to $125. There is a four-day minimum stay. For information, write to R & R Realty & Rentals, R R 1, Box 70, Koloa, Kauai, HI 96756; or phone toll free 800/367-8022. Inquire about their other vacation rentals, too.

Many people dream of moving to an island, having a lovely home of their own, and renting out a handful of cottages in their garden. Hans and Sylvia Zeevat (he is Dutch, she is Dutch-Indonesian), who came to Hawaii from Holland, have realized that dream on Kauai, and the result is four wonderful, reasonably priced accommodations for those lucky enough to get into the **Koloa Landing Cottages,** 2704B Hoonani Rd., Koloa, Kauai, HI 96756. The Zeevats are exceptional hosts (see the Readers' Selections, ahead, for several personal comments), and they delight in treating their guests like family: They ply them with fresh fruit from their own trees, give them tips on where to snorkel and what to feed the fish. ("This is just a family operation, nothing fancy," says Sylvia.) They have two cottages and two studios: spacious and tastefully decorated, they have open-beamed ceilings, ceiling fans, cross-ventilation, well-equipped kitchens (blenders, dishwashers, microwave ovens, mixers, etc.), cable TVs, and—hard to find in Poipu—telephones with their own private numbers! Guests like to barbecue out in the garden; restaurants and good swimming beaches are all within walking or very short driving distances. Each cottage has two bedrooms (queen-size beds), two baths, and a lovely living room; they rent for $70 for one or two persons, $85 for three or four, $10 each for up to two more people. The studios are $50 for one or two people (one of the studios has no steps, so would be convenient for a disabled person). A minimum stay of four days is required. Since so many guests book again for the next year when they leave, reserve as far in advance as possible. Write to the previous address, or phone Sylvia Zeevat at 742-1470.

If your idea of bliss is a hammock strung between two coconut palms and overlooking the pounding surf, then you might want to get one of the five rooms at **Gloria's Spouting Horn Bed & Breakfast,** 4464 Lawai Beach Rd., Koloa, Kauai, HI 96756 (tel. 742-6995). It's located on an idyllic rocky coastline within sight and sound of the surf and the famed Spouting Horn saltwater geyser, and the hammock is right out there, behind the house. The house is charmingly furnished with American oak and English-walnut antiques; there's a Baldwin piano, TV, and VCR in the living room; most guest rooms have queen-size beds, private lanais, and private bath. All but one have a view of the ocean. One oceanfront accommodation catering to honeymooners is The Tea House; it overlooks a koi pond and features a private bath with Japanese-style soaking tub (for two!). Continental breakfast consists of a papaya boat filled with fresh, locally grown fruit, juices and beverages, and home-baked pastry or muffin. Rates vary from about $50 to $90 for the different units. No children under 14, no pets, and smoking only on the lanai. Write Gloria at the address above, or phone her at 742-6995.

Evie Warner and Al Davis, the very nice people who run the statewide Hawaii Bed & Breakfast Service we've told you about several times in this book, have built some very attractive vacation-rental units behind their house on their own tropical acre of land, just up the road from Poipu Beach Park, one of the best places to swim in this area. This is **Poipu Plantation,** 1792 Pe'e Rd., Koloa, Kauai, HI 96756 (tel. 742-7038 or 822-7771), which consists of nine good-size units, all of them attractively furnished, done in tropical decor, with ceiling fans, excellent modern kitchens, phones, and TVs. Washers and dryers are outside. Three one-bedroom units on the garden level go for $65 to $70 a night for two, $10 for each additional person. The one-bedrooms with "peek-a-boo" ocean view are $70 to $75, those with full ocean view, $75 to $80. There are also several duplexes, luxury accommodations with two bedrooms, two baths, even marble floors in the bathrooms. These rent at $80 to $85 for two, $100 to $105 for four. There's a gazebo out in the garden, which is quite lovely, with its apple trees, blossoming plumerias, bougainvillea, and gardenias. Evie and Al are friendly hosts and see to it that everybody is well cared for. Write to the previous address, or phone toll free 800/733-1632.

The **Stouffer Poipu Beach Hotel,** blessed with a perfect location right on the beach, has long been one of our favorite places on Kauai. Rates have jumped quite a bit here in the past, but if you want an on-the-beach resort hotel, this is still a fine choice. Standard rooms are $90; single or double, and since all the rooms in this hotel are exactly the same, the only thing that determines the difference between a $115, $130, or $160 room is its location; garden, ocean-view, or beachfront. But the rooms are all good, spacious, nicely furnished, with private lanais, a huge dressing area, and best of all, a compact little kitchenette unit that makes fixing breakfast or a quick meal a breeze. The three buildings surround the pool, whirlpool and grassy area, and the dining room is right in the middle of it all. There are six tennis courts, with a pro shop next door. The neighboring property, Stouffer Waiohai Beach Resort, is an exquisite resort hotel, all of whose guest services you can use, including the Waiohai Athletic Club (gym, Jacuzzi, sauna, massage, etc.). Write Stouffer Kauai Reservations, 2251 Poipu Rd., Koloa, Kauai, HI 96756, or phone toll free 800/426-4122. The local phone is 742-1681.

We'd have to call the **Poipu Bed & Breakfast Inn,** 2720 Hoonani Rd., Koloa, Kauai, HI 96756 (tel. 742-1146) one of the most beautiful bed-and-breakfast establishments in the islands. Proprietress Dottie Cichon, an artist herself and a collector of art, has lovingly renovated and restored a 1933 plantation house, filled it with carousel horses and pine antiques, ornate white Victorian wicker furniture, handcrafts, and tropical splashes of color everywhere. Rooms are luxury all the way: Each has its own private bath (with either a whirlpool tub and separate shower or a tub-shower combination), refrigerator, remote-control color TV, and AM-FM clock radio. Continental breakfasts—fruits, juices, muffins, pastries, beverages—

are served in the morning out on the lanai or in the splendid "great room"; later on, the "great room" is the scene for afternoon tea and for evening popcorn-and-movie gatherings. (Incidentally, while most such places provide breakfast *and* bed, this is the only one we know that will provide breakfast *in* bed—if you ask.) Tennis and pool privileges at the nearby Kiahuna Tennis Club are included in the price of all rooms. And numerous beaches are just around the bend. Four rooms are available in the main house: the White Ginger Room with a queen-size bed, $75; the Kahili Mountain Rose Room, with either two twin beds or a king-size bed, $90; the Bougainvillea Room, with king-size bed and whirlpool tub, $110; and the Pink Plumeria Room, the most spacious, with a western king-size bed and whirlpool tub, $125. These rates are for double occupancy: It's $5 less for single occupancy, $15 more for each extra child or adult in the same room, and $10 more for stays of just one night.

Although they are largely beyond our budget, Dottie also has a number of cottages for rent nearby and in Kalaheo; these range from a $100-a-night Mandarin Garden Studio to a super-luxury oceanfront two-bedroom, two-bath condominium at nearby Whaler's Cove for $225. All are furnished in exquisite taste; some are as large as a complete home and could comfortably suit a family for a long stay. For further information and reservations, phone toll free 800/552-0095.

Halemanu Guest Ranch is one of the most unusual bed-and-breakfasts we've seen on Kauai. It's just a few miles up a country road from Koloa town, yet once you reach the house, you feel as if you're in another country, and hundreds of miles from everything. The sense of peace is almost palpable. The house overlooks the Waita Reservoir and the ocean far below; the only sounds you hear are those of birds (Halemanu means "house of birds"). The house was built in the mid-1800s, up in the mountains in Kokee, and was the home of the Knudsen's, a well-known Kauai seafaring family. In 1987, Vladimir Knudsen, now in his 80s, and his wife Karna, moved the house to this new location, kept most of the original mission oak furniture and the old family mementos, and turned it into a bed-and-breakfast operation. Staying here is almost like living in one of those old mission house museums one sees in the islands! It's by no means plush; it is rustic, yet comfortable and clean. There are no TVs, but each room does have a private bath. Manager Margaret Prescott, her husband Clint, and their children live on the property, and each morning Margaret leaves breakfast—fruit and juice, English muffins, toast, coffee and tea, for the guests. There's an old-fashioned, homey living room, and separate sleeping quarters which consist of the Honeymoon Suite and Grandma's Room, each $100 a night, Grandpa's Cottage and Sinclair's Cottage at $75, and a cabin with twin beds at $40. For information, write Halemanu Guest Ranch, P.O. Box 729, Koloa, Kauai, HI 96756, or phone 742-1288.

If you are really into the great outdoors—but not enough to backpack it and sleep under the stars—**Kahili Mountain Park** might be the place for you. Seven miles from Poipu Beach, the park is off Hwy. 50 west, just beyond the 7-mile marker. Mount Kahili rises majestically behind the little cabins and cabinettes nestled near a small swimmable and fishable (bass) lake. The park is operated by the Seventh Day Adventist Church; their school is on the premises. The less expensive of the two types of accommodations, the cabinettes, go for $20 double, $4 for an extra person. They are grouped in a circle around the bathroom-and-shower buildings. They each have one room, with a small dining lanai where there's a small refrigerator, a two-burner hot plate, and a sink. Cookware is furnished. Cabins, consisting of either one large room or two small ones, have a bathroom with a sink and toilet; there's a private shower outside each cabin. They also have a full-size refrigerator, as well as the two-burner stove and sink and go for $35 double, $4 for an extra person. All of the accommodations have screened windows with outside canvas awnings that can be pulled up for protection against wind and rain. Linens are furnished. These facilities are very plain and rustic. There is a laundry room on the premises, as well as a basketball court. Peace and beauty are the main attractions here. Prepayment in full is required for all reservations; a minimum stay is two days. For reservations, write Kahili Mountain Park, P.O. Box 298, Koloa, Kauai, HI 96756 (tel. 742-9921).

For those who prefer to be away from the tourist scene, yet close enough to enjoy its advantages, **Classic Vacation Cottages,** in the tiny country town of Kalaheo, would be a fortuitous and budget-wise choice. The three self-contained cottages on a hillside are set in a garden adjacent to the custom-built home of Richard and Wynnis Grow. The Grows have decorated them handsomely, with stained leaded windows, well-equipped kitchens, a living room and porch, and a double bed in the bedroom. They all have TVs and daily linen service. The one-bedrooms rent for $55 a night with ocean view, $55 a night garden view; the garden studio is $45; a third person in any of the units is $10. Guests are welcome to use the hot tub, Jacuzzi, and outdoor barbecue. Kukuiolono Golf Course is a 5-minute drive away, and Poipu Beach about 10 minutes; tennis courts and a park for jogging are nearby. For reservations, write Richard and Wynnis Grow, Classic Cottages, 2687 Onu Place, P.O. Box 901, Kalaheo, Kauai, HI 96741 or phone 332-9201.

PRINCEVILLE AND HANALEI

Think of Princeville, on the north shore of Kauai, and you think of luxury living, of championship golf and tennis amid a green sweep of mountains and valleys. You don't think of budget accommodations here, but we did find a few needles in the haystack. Lowest prices in Princeville are at two condominium resorts run by Hawaiian Islands Resorts. At **Pali Ke Kua,** a two-story condominium complex overlooking the ocean from a point high on the cliffs, you could actually rent a bedroom and bath for $55 a night from April 1 to December 20, for $65 the rest of the year. It's not advertised, but it can be done by closing off one of the bedrooms in the two-bedroom units. The one- and two-bedroom apartments are expensively furnished in modern decor, boast full kitchens with washer-dryers; they go for $95 mountain view, $105 ocean view, and $125 oceanfront in summer; for $105, $115, and $140 in winter. Two-bedroom apartments are $110, $120, and $140 in summer; $120, $130, and $160 in winter. An extra person is charged $10 a day, $60 a week. The units at **Hale Moi,** just across the way, which overlooks the Robert Trent Jones Golf Course, are less expensive. During low season, a hotel room with refrigerator and bath is $55; a studio with full kitchen and bath is $75; and a 1½ bedroom suite, with full kitchen and two baths, is $100 (for up to four). During the winter season, add $10 to all these rates. For reservations at both these condos, you can write to Hawaiian Island Resorts, P.O. Box 212, Honolulu, HI 96810, or call toll free 800/367-7042. Kauai addresses are Pail Ke Kua, P.O. Box 899, Princeville-Hanalei, Kauai, HI 96714 (tel. 826-9066); Hale Moi, P.O. Box 1185, Princeville-Hanalei, Kauai, HI 96714 (tel. 826-9602).

The Cliffs at Princeville is the largest condo complex in the area (220 units). Set amid graceful lawns and gardens, and perched atop cliffs overlooking the ocean far below, it offers as much of peace and privacy, sports or excitement, as one would wish. On the grounds are four tennis courts, a putting green, a large pool area with Jacuzzi, and a recreation pavilion complete with a huge fireplace, wet bar, and an indoor whirlpool bath and sauna. All of the suites are perfect little one-bedroom, two-bath houses, fully carpeted, beautifully and individually furnished in bamboo and oak, with oak doors, completely equipped kitchen, and cable TV. All have been decorated in excellent taste. These suites can be divided to provide the following possible combinations: a one-bedroom, two-bath unit with garden view for one to four people at $110 ($15 more for ocean view); and a one-bedroom-with-loft, two-bath unit for one to four people at $145 garden view ($20 more for ocean view).

Again, the Princeville Makai Golf Course, designed by Robert Trent Jones, is right at hand; the sandy beach at Hanalei is about a five-minute drive; and opportunities for horseback riding, surfing, windsurfing, scuba-diving, and much more are all close by. For reservations, call 826-6219, or write to Box 1005, Hanalei, HI 96714.

Hale Ho'o Maha (House of Rest) on the North Shore of Kauai, perched on the cliffs in Princeville at Hanalei, is an ideally suited bed-and-breakfast home. This single-story, private residence boasts of windows all around for magnificent views of mountains, ocean, and golf course. You are five minutes from fine sand-bottom beaches, rivers, waterfalls, and riding stables. A short walk will take you to a natural saltwater swimming hole enclosed by lava rocks; waves break over one side and create a bubble-bath effect—private and lush. The home has two large bedrooms. The Pineapple Room has a 7-foot round bed, private full bath, and private entrance off the lanai. The Mango Room has a double bed, cable TV, and shared bath. Guests have full-kitchen privileges and use of the bogie boards, beach mats, gas grill, washer-dryer, and cable TV. Your host and hostess, Kirby and Toby Searles, share their home in its entirety. A continental breakfast is served on the lanai each morning. Smoking and social drinking are acceptable. Rates are $65 a night for the Pineapple Room, single or double; $50 per night for the Mango Room, single or double. Write to Kirby B. Guyer-Searles, P.O. Box 422, Kilauea, HI 96754, or phone 826-1130.

A block from the beach at Hanalei, the **Hanalei Bay Inn** is a find. Manager Ed Gardien, who used to manage the Big Sur Inn in California, brings a relaxed feeling to this little cottage colony that looks as if nothing has changed much since the '60s. Nothing has. The four units here, all separate, each have a simply equipped kitchenette, and either twins or a queen-size bed. In back of the units is a spacious garden that boasts banana, papaya, mango, and avocado trees; guests are welcome to step outside and pick their breakfast. Cottages rent for $55 a day for one or two people, $50 a day if you stay for three days or more (tax included). Ed lives in a large house on the property, and rents out the small back bedroom as a bed-and-breakfast accommodation for $45 single, $55 double per night. He'll lend you ice chests, head rests for the beach, assorted snorkeling equipment. The atmosphere is casual and companionable—which makes this a nice place to depressurize yourself from civilization for a bit. Write to Hanalei Bay Inn, P.O. Box 122, Hanalei, Kauai, HI 96714, or phone Ed Gardien at 826-9333.

A CAMP AT HAENA

Hikers, backpackers, campers, take note: If you're about to hike the Na Pali trail and need a place to relax and get a good night's sleep before or after, the YMCA of Kauai has a perfect solution for you. **Camp Naue** is located right on the beach at Haena, in an idyllic setting under the ironwood and kumani trees. Two bunkhouses situated on the crest of the beach are divided into four separate areas, each with 10 to 12 bunk beds; the facilities are coed, but there are separate baths for men and women, and hot showers. Bring your own sleeping bag, as the camp does not provide linens or towels. There's a covered beachfront pavilion, a campfire area with picnic tables, and one of the island's best beaches—in summer—for swimming, snorkeling, and surfing (in winter, the ocean is very rough here). There is no refrigeration (the kitchen is for group use only), and if you need food supplies, it's best to stock up on them in Hanalei. You can also stop in at **Hanalei Camping and Backpacking** in Ching Young Village to rent tents, sleeping bags, backpacks—whatever you'll need for your expedition or your stay at camp. The cost of a bed is $10 a night indoors; tenters, with their own tents, pay $8 for one person, $5 for an additional person. Camp Naue is primarily given over to large groups, but often has space for walk-in visitors. They do not take reservations, but if you call their Lihue office at 246-9090 not more than two weeks in advance, they'll advise you of the likelihood of getting space here. On weekends, you can call the caretaker at the camp at 826-6419. Or, write to YMCA of Kauai, P.O. Box 1786, Lihue, Kauai, HI 96766. The camp is just a mile and a half from the trailhead at Kalakau.

KOKEE

Forty-five miles away from Lihue, in Kokee State Park (just beyond Waimea Canyon), you'll find **Kokee Lodge**, 3,600 feet up in bracing mountain air. The cabins are owned by the state but operated by a private firm, and the prices are low—a practice we'd like to see imitated all over Hawaii. This is a place only for those who have enough time to really linger in Kauai (on a two- or three-day trip a stay would be impractical, since the time and cost of driving to the other sights of the island would outweigh the savings here). The cabins vary in size from one large room, which sleeps three, to two-bedroom units that will accommodate seven. Cabins rent for $35 and $45 per night. The cabins are rustic, furnished with refrigerators, stoves, hot showers, basic eating and cooking utensils, blankets, linens, and pillows. You can buy a pile of wood and make a fire in the wood stove when the night air gets nippy in this cooler northern Kauai that seems a world away from beaches and coconut palms.

Daytime activities at Kokee include driving or hiking on gorgeous trails and swimming in hidden freshwater pools. You can also hunt boar and wild goat, fish for trout in the nearby mountain streams, or just laze in the sun. Kokee Lodge Restaurant serves breakfast, lunch, and snacks daily from 8:30am to 5:30pm, dinners from 6 to 9pm only on Friday and Saturday. The restaurant provides take-out orders and snacks for outdoor picnics, and for those wishing to cook, there's a simple grocery store on the premises. (Bring your own supplies, however, if you're planning on cooking anything fancy.) There's also a cocktail lounge and a gift shop. For reservations: Kokee Lodge, P.O. Box 819, Waimea, Kauai, HI 96796 (tel. 335-6061). Management advises making early reservations, since holiday weekends are very popular here, and so is the trout-fishing season in August and September.

A BED AND BREAKFAST RESERVATION SERVICE

Bed & Breakfast Hawaii, the largest reservation service in the islands, is headquartered right here in Kauai. Not only do they have a wide range of carefully inspected accommodations all over the state, they also work with Dollar Rent-A-Car to provide lower prices on car rentals for their guests. Write for a free brochure to Bed & Breakfast Hawaii, P.O. Box 449, Kapaa, HI 96746 (tel. 822-7771). For $8.50 you receive a directory of homes and apartments with rooms for rent called *B&B Goes Hawaiian.* Or call them toll free at 800/657-7832. FAX: 822-2723.

---

2. Island Restaurants

IN LIHUE AND ENVIRONS

Lihue has some excellent budget restaurants frequented mostly by the local people, and you'll be glad you joined them. One of the best is the **Lihue Barbecue Inn** on Kress Street (tel. 245-2921), where the cuisine is Japanese, American, and Chinese—and very good, too. There's a bar and lounge off to one side of the restaurant. You'll know why the Barbecue Inn has been going strong for some 50 years now when you have a look at the prices: a typical dinner menu lists 32 complete dinners—and that includes soup or fresh-fruit cup, tossed green salad, vegetable, beverages, and dessert, accompanying such main courses as shrimp tempura, baked mahimahi, broiled teriyaki pork chops, corned beef brisket with cabbage, chow mein chicken with spare ribs—for $12.95 and under! (Complete meals start at just $5.95.) Fresh fish is served whenever it's available. Complete lunches are even cheaper; we counted 32 of them for $6.95 and under! These often include seafood platter, Chinese chicken salad, mahimahi sandwich, or teriyaki chicken. The menu changes daily, but whatever you have here will most likely be good—especially the freshly made pies (can you believe 75¢?) and the homemade bread. Do try their frozen chi-chis—among the best on the island. One of the most appealing inexpensive restaurants in Lihue, the Barbecue is patronized by family groups; and over the years we have had consistent letters of praise from our readers about it. It's open from 7:30am to 1:30pm and 4:30 to 8:30pm; closed Sunday.

Another place that's long been popular with the locals is the **Tip Top Café,** in shiny air-conditioned quarters at 3173 Akahi St., just north of the Lihue Shopping Center. It's a family-style restaurant, the prices are modest, and while the food is not of gourmet quality, it's dependable. Service is apt to be on the slow side. We often have breakfast here (pancakes are served all day, and the macadamia-nut ones, $3, are delicious). There's a Chinese plate lunch for $4.50, and lunch entrees like pork chops are also $4.50. Dinner entrees such as teriyaki pork, breaded fish filet, and ground-round steaks with eggs average $6.50, and that includes soup, salad or potato salad, rice or potatoes, and coffee. The Chinese combination-plate dinner is $6.50. Prices are subject to change. This is a good place to remember if you need a box lunch for an all-day excursion; either American- or Asian-style take-out lunches are available at $3.75. Pick up some homemade jams from the gift department. The Tip Top Bakery is famous for its macadamia-nut cookies and Portuguese sweet bread, baked fresh daily. The Tip Top stays open from 6:45am until 8:30pm daily (tel. 245-2343 or 245-2333).

The **Hamamura Saimin Stand,** 2956 Kress St. (tel. 245-3271) is a beloved Kauai institution. Locals have sung its praises and gobbled up its saimin for as long as anybody can remember. It's a very simple spot, a trifle weather-beaten on the outside; inside are two long rectangular counters with stools. Slide onto one, order anything on the small menu, and you're in for a great taste treat as well as one of the cheapest meals on Kauai. We like to have the saimin special at $3.65—that's a large bowl of saimin topped with vegetables, eggs, and wontons—filling and delicious. Order a stick of tender barbecued chicken or beef, too (80¢), and finish up with their lilikoi chiffon pie at $1.05. All in all, quite a meal for $5.50. Hamamura Saimin is open almost always, from 10am to 2am Monday through Thursday, until 4am Friday and Saturday, and from 10am to midnight Sunday.

Another local place where you can eat a delicious meal for around $5 is **Kun-Ja,** 5252 Rice St., corner of Hardy (tel. 245-8792). It's a simple spot, tidy, with just a few decorations, and owner Kun-Ja Woo greets you with a smile, takes your order, and prepares your meal. She does all the usual Korean dishes like *mun doo kook so* (dumpling and noodle soup), *kalbi* (broiled short ribs), and *pul koki* (barbecued beef), plus a few specialties of her own like a hot-and-spicy kim chee soup. Prices run from $3.50 to $5.75, the latter for Kun-Ja's Special—that's barbecued beef, chicken and pork—a nice little meal in itself, since it's served with soup, and several little dishes of mixed vegetables, sprouts, and rice. Should you want to have dinner here, come early as the restaurant often closes at 8pm. Open Monday through Saturday, from 9:30am.

It's not only local people who frequent the **Dairy Queen Kauai** at 4302 Rice St. (tel. 245-2141); many visitors and condo dwellers have discovered it hits the spot for an inexpensive meal. The same menu, used all day, lists something like 15 or 16 daily specials in the $2.95 to $3.95 range. That might include breaded fish filet, stir-fry chicken broccoli with noodles, or a half-pound mushroom burger. Regular entrees, $3.50 to $4.95, include a roast beef platter, teriyaki steak, sautéed mahimahi, butterfish, and a seafood platter. And they also have burritos, tacos, chili, saimin, salads, and several sub sandwiches, including a vegetarian one. The little dining room adjacent to the counter and take-out area has red-plastic booths, bamboo screens, plants—it's not bad. Dairy Queen serves daily from 7am to 10pm.

At the junction of Kuhio Highway and Rice Street, just across the highway from the Lihue Shopping Center, at 3-3257 Kuhio Hwy. (tel. 246-9112), you'll find the very popular Kauai branch of **Subway Salads and Sandwiches.** If you recall what we told you about them in the Honolulu restaurant chapter, you know that they are sparkling clean, little counter establishments with just a few tables that dispense great sub sandwiches at remarkable prices. They bake their own whole-wheat and white bread daily. Sandwiches come in two sizes: 12 inch and 6 inch. The 12-inch size ranges in price from $2.59 for veggie to $6.99 for seafood and crab; most are priced between $3 and $4. Six-inchers range from $2.59 to $4.89. Choices include meatball, pastrami, ham, roast beef, tuna, steak, and cheese, and combinations of the above. Garnishes—have them all if you like—are black olives, cheese, onions, lettuce, tomato, dill pickles, green peppers, oil, and vinegar. One of our local friends has tried them all, but always seems to come back to the meatball with everything! Any sandwich may be ordered as a salad, with the same garnishes. Subway also bakes its own cookies, such as chocolate-chip macadamia nut, for 79¢. Open Friday and Saturday 10am to 2am, Sunday to Thursday, 10am to midnight.

Dining at the fabulous Westin Kauai luxury resort is going to be expensive, no matter which way you cut it, but you're certainly going to want to see this amazing place, so you might consider a meal at the very informal **Cook's at the Beach** (tel

245-5050), the closest thing to a family restaurant this jet-set resort has to offer. One side is completely open to the 26,000-square-foot swimming pool with its multiple waterfalls and immense marble animal statuary. Cook's is attractively decorated in an outdoorsy mood, with abundant greenery and lazy ceiling fans helping the trade winds along. For breakfast, the french toast made with Portuguese sweet bread is a popular choice. The lunch menu features an array of salads and sandwiches, priced from $3.95 to $9.95. As the sun begins to set and strains of Hawaiian music begin to drift through Cook's at the Beach, you might want to try Hot Rock Cuisine, a new and healthful concept in dining in which you grill your own dish—maybe chicken fajitas or a seafood combination—on a pure natural rock heated to 500°. The dinner menu also features fresh pastas, sizzling platters, fresh island fish, and other local favorites priced from $9.95. Cook's at the Beach is open daily, from early morning until late in the evening.

It's so pleasant to have a meal at **The Terrace** restaurant at the Westin Kauai (tel. 245-5050), since this open-air spot looks out serenely over the swimming pool at the Spa to the Haupu mountains beyond. And one can feel virtuous while dining on light spa cuisine, all of it beautifully prepared, very tasty, and decently priced. Entrees such as grilled chicken breast with lemon dill linguine or Cobb salad are under $10. Most sandwiches and salads are under $8; we like the curried tuna salad with mango chutney and the fresh mahimahi sandwich with Maui onions. Every Friday between 11am and 2pm there's an authentic "Aloha Friday" menu with all the traditional dishes. It's also fun to drop by just for a healthy smoothie such as The Breakpoint: that's strawberry, guava juice, milk, and lehua honey with a cinnamon stick, $4.50. The Terrace is located in the Kauai Lagoons Golf and Racquet Club, is very casual (swim or tennis togs OK), and serves only breakfast and lunch.

In front of the Westin Kauai, at Kalapaki Beach, is a new restaurant that's a mighty crowd pleaser: **Duke's Canoe Club** (246-9599). The restaurant surrounds a waterfall, with tables interspersed among the rocks below, and overlooking the sands of Kalapaki Beach. Original mementos of the career of Duke Kahanamoku are everywhere; huge outrigger canoes are on the ceiling. It's actually two restaurants in one: upstairs is the more expensive Duke's Dinner House, featuring seafood, steaks, and ribs, and downstairs is Duke's Kau Kau Grill, a beachside café and lounge with a breezy air. Best prices for us budgeteers are downstairs: You could have Hawaiian local plates—BBQ chicken or ribs, fresh fish, teriyaki beef kebab or stir-fry chicken cashew, all served with "two scoop" rice or fries and "one scoop" macaroni salad or baked beans, from $8.95 to $9.95. Burgers and sandwiches begin at $5.95 and are served with Maui chips: There are a few salads and neat pupus like saimin, sashimi, and calamari rings. Vegetarian dishes are available. Upstairs, the values are still good: several fresh fish dinners under $16, smoked ribs and chicken under $15, top sirloin at $14.95, and the spa-cuisine–style ginger chicken at $12.95. Most entrees include a tossed green salad, a basket of freshly baked banana-macadamia nut muffins and dinner rolls, and steamed vegetable rice. Wherever you sit, don't miss the frozen mai tais (they're blended with passion-fruit sherbet) or desserts like Kimo's original hula pie.

Both levels are open daily: Duke's Dinner House from 5 to 10pm, Duke's Kau Kau Grill from 4 to 11pm.

Casa Italiana, at 2989 Haleko Rd., across from the Lihue Shopping Center (tel. 245-9586), serves up *delizioso* Italian cuisine in a comfortable setting furnished with outdoor chairs and tables, soft lighting, and lots of wrought iron. It's a dinner-only place, nightly except Sunday, from 5:30 to 10pm. You can dine quite reasonably by sticking to one of the pasta dinners, which include a trip to the salad bar and the chef's sublime garlic and pepper breads. Fresh pasta is prepared daily on the premises. Your meal of spaghetti or ravioli, with such accompaniments as red or white clam sauce, Italian or Portuguese sausage, meatballs, olives, or shrimp marinara, will cost from $8.95 to $12.95. Or, go for a variety of chicken or veal specialties, from $14.95 to $19.95. Spumoni and a bit of cappuccino will top off your meal nicely. Reservations recommended.

The local people rave about **Kauai Chop Suey** at Pacific Ocean Plaza (tel. 245-8790). Our favorite local couple loves this place, and takes all their visiting friends to dinner here. Despite its unimaginative name, it serves superior food, all in the Cantonese style. There are about 75 items on the menu, at least 50 of them under $6, so the budgeteer cannot go wrong here. There's something for everyone: roast duck, egg foo yong, squid with vegetables, shrimp with broccoli, lemon chicken, stuffed tofu, sweet pork, or char sui (an island favorite), and much more. And the soups—seaweed, scallop, abalone—are quite special. The place is large and comfortable, decorated in typical Chinese style. Large parties are seated at round tables with revolving "Lazy Susan" centerpieces, the better to sample all the delicacies. Kauai Chop Suey serves lunch Tuesday to Saturday from 11am to 2pm; dinner, Tuesday to Sunday from 4:30 to 9pm. Closed Monday.

The **Eggbert's: Kauai's Family Specialty Restaurant** is a long name for a friendly little restaurant at 4483 Rice St., in the Haleko Shops. It's an attractive place, with wooden partitions, ferns, flowers, and ceiling fans to keep the trade winds moving. The day starts here at 7am with a variety of terrific omelets from $3.50 to $6.45 (two eggs), $5 to $7.95 (three eggs), and great banana hot cakes. Also excellent: five varieties of eggs Benedict (half orders, $4.95 to $5.65; full orders, $7.25 to $8.75). Their handmade hollandaise is quite special. Lounge service begins at 7am; their Bloody Marys are very popular, and drinks are reasonably priced. All breakfast items are served all day, but lunch dishes are added on at 11am. That's when you can have soups, salads, sandwiches, and burgers, from $3.95 to $6.75. Dinner is sometimes on, sometimes off: call to see if it is being served, as reservations are advised. Open daily.

The tiny **Restaurant Kiibo** at 2991 Umi St. (tel. 245-2650) is a comfortable, nicely furnished place where the food is outstanding. The pretty little sushi bar up front gives way to a small dining room with 10 or so tables. Japanese lanterns supply the soft lighting, and examples of Japanese folk art adorn the walls. Two of us had a lovely dinner here for under $25. Our meals included a flavorful miso soup, rice, tsukemono (pickled salad), and tea. We enjoyed our $9 chicken sukiyaki and $7.50 beef teriyaki to the accompaniment of soft Japanese music in the background. Other good choices include the tempura, which are sold à la carte at $1.50 each—a large platter of shrimp, vegetable, and seafood tempura should run about $11—and the donburi, huge bowls of rice topped with sukiyaki or teriyaki or something equally interesting, from $7 to $9. A child's dinner is available at $5.25. Lunch offers similar dishes at lower prices. Chances are good that you'll be the only haoles at the Kiibo; it's a local favorite, off the usual tourist beat. Lunch from 11am to 1:30pm, dinner from 5:30 to 9pm. Closed Sunday and holidays.

Kukui Grove

Kauai's multimillion-dollar shopping center, **Kukui Grove,** just outside Lihue on Hwy. 50 toward Poipu Beach, has several attractive eating possibilities for us. Our favorite is not a traditional restaurant at all, but a café area in the midst of Stone's Gallery called **Stone's Espresso Café.** Freshly roasted coffee is sold by the pound, and its fragrant aroma makes everything you eat here taste wonderful. In addition to a variety of coffees, espressos, cappuccinos, herbal teas, and coffee specialty drinks, you can get soups, bagels, dessert, quiche, and wonderful homemade cookies. A lovely place for a sophisticated snack. Open most days from 9:30am to 6pm, to 9pm Friday and Sunday from 10am to 5pm. Call 245-6564 for take-out orders.

Probably the most popular specialty restaurant here is **Rosita's Mexican Restaurant** (tel. 245-8561), in an attractive indoor-outdoor setting: many plants, stained-glass lanterns, ceiling fans, stucco walls, cozy booths. You can dine leisurely here, at lunch and dinner, on Mexican and American favorites and sometimes a combination of both, like the hamburger ortega and hamburger ranchera lunch specials at $5.25. Combination plates run $5.35 to $8.25. Their seafood chimichanga is good at $6.95, and so is the arroz con pollo at $8.95. Dishes tend to be highly spiced. Don't pass up Rosita's famous margaritas—when was the last time you had a *banana* margarita? Friendly owners Rosita and Rick Shaw keep this lively place open seven days a week, from 11am to 10pm. Where else can you go between 2 and 4:30pm?

The **Kukui Nut Tree Inn** (tel. 245-7005) is a family restaurant, serving all three meals in a summerhouse atmosphere. Latticework arching over the booths and on the ceiling makes this nicer than your average coffee shop. The food is American with island touches, and prices are quite reasonable. The day starts at 7:30am with omelets and pancakes, plus local foods like taro cake or a Japanese breakfast—the traditional Asahi or the contemporary Fuji—$4.75 and $4.25. Lunch features some 15 entrees from $4.75 to $8.25—and that includes the likes of the mahi tempura and teri combo, honey-stung fried chicken, grilled beef liver with onions and bacon. Entrees are served with hot vegetables and a starch; they are preceded by soup or fruit cocktail, and accompanied by garden greens and rolls with butter. Especially popular are such salads as vegetarian chef, tofu, and Moloaa papaya with turkey salad, all served with unique dressings made locally: papaya seed, passion fruit with herbs, luau (Hawaiian French), and Maui onion dressing. At dinner, the bill goes up about 70¢, but dessert is included. With prices like these, it's no wonder this place is always crowded. There are also special menus for keikis and kupunas (under 12 and over 65). Drinks are available. The kitchen closes at 8pm, except on Friday (9pm) and Sunday (3pm).

Snacking possibilities at Kukui Grove include **Joni-Hana** for hot lunches and sushi to go; **Family Kitchen,** which feeds a local crowd with hearty breakfasts, $3.85 plate lunches, sandwiches, burgers, saimin, and sushi, in a pleasant self-serve, sit-down setting; **J.V. Snack Bar** for Filipino plate lunches; and **Ed & Don's,** known around the islands for good sandwiches and ice creams.

At Kilohana Plantation

One of the nicest restaurants to open in Kauai in many a tropical moon is **Gaylord's,** at Kilohana, the legendary plantation estate of the 1930s that has been lovingly restored and is open to the public. Gaylord's (tel. 245-9593) is a courtyard restaurant open to a manicured green lawn around which tables are arranged on three sides. The restaurant is done in whites, pinks, and greens, with soft-cushioned chairs, white tablecloths, pink napkins, fresh flowers on every table. Dinner at Gaylord's *is* pricey (entrees from $15.95 to $21.95), but at lunchtime you can have a first-class dining experience for a modest tab—and many agree that the food is better at lunchtime. We like both Gaylord's Papaya Runneth Over, island papaya stuffed with delicate bay shrimp (or salmon or chicken) salad, at $7.95; and the bay shrimp and avocado sandwich on homemade bread, with a choice of soup or salad, fries or rice, $7.95. Burgers run $5.95 to $6.95. There is often a vegetarian selection of the day which can't be beat for freshness, since many of the greens are grown right in Kilohana's acres. Homemade desserts like Kilohana mud pie, French silk, and double chocolate mousse are special. Lunch is served Monday to Saturday from 11am to 3:30pm; Sunday brunch, with a special menu (cheese blintzes, eggs Benedict, croissant sandwiches and the like, $8.95 to $9.95), is on from 10am to 3pm. There's a light supper menu from 5 to 6:30pm, and dinner is on from 5 to 9pm, with special selections for children under 10 every night at $9.95. Reservations are usually not needed at lunch, but essential at dinner.

Hanamaulu

It's well worth making a short trip from Lihue (about two miles north on Hwy. 56) to dine at the **Hanamaulu Restaurant and Tea House.** It's an attractive place, and the Japanese garden is really something to see, beautifully landscaped with stone pagodas, pebbled paths, and a pond filled with flashing carp. We suggest you call a day in advance and reserve one of the charming ozashiki, or tea-house, rooms; you take off your shoes, sit on the floor at a long, low table, and the shoji screens are opened to face the lighted garden. (You may be able to get one of the rooms without reservations, but it's best to call ahead; tel. 245-2511.) The food here is excellent and inexpensive; the Chinese and Japanese plate lunches at about $6.50 are good buys.

You'll get soup, fried chicken or shrimp, chop suey, spareribs, rice, and tea on the Chinese menu; miso soup, pork tofu or teriyaki steak, takuwan, rice, and tea on the Japanese. For dinner, the special plates start at $7, entrees like chicken sukiyaki go for $6, and you can feast on a veritable Eastern banquet for about $13 per person. An excellent sushi bar and Robatayaki are attractions here. The Miyaki family are cordial hosts. The restaurant is open from 11am to 1pm and from 5 to 9pm. Closed Monday.

The Planter's, at the mile-two sign in Hanamaulu, is a nice, dim, cool place with a big lanai where you may eat if you choose. In addition to a variety of burgers and sandwiches ($4.25 to $5.50), lunch features such entrees as catch of the day, teri chicken, a deep-fried shrimp platter, and kiawe-broiled New York steak, served with salad or homemade soup, rice or fries, plus vegetables, all for $7.95. You can't go wrong at dinner either, since, on the low side of the menu are such entrees as roast chicken, chicken teriyaki, and fettuccine florentine, $9.95 and $11.95, served with salad with homemade dressing (blue cheese and buttermilk dill are tasty), home-made soup, rice or noodles romano, and fresh homemade bread. Prime rib au jus, broiled over kiawe, is a good buy at $13.95. And children's meals are available for $7.50. The Planter's serves lunch Monday to Friday from 11am to 3pm, dinner every day from 5 to 9:45pm. Happy Hour is 2 to 5pm.

RESTAURANTS ON THE EASTERN AND NORTHERN ROUTE

This is the most populous part of the island, with many budget restaurants.

In Wailua and Kapaa

Exquisite is the word for the dining experience at **Restaurant Kintaro,** 4-370 Kuhio Hwy., between Coco Palms and Coconut Plantation (tel. 822-3341), a sparkling bright restaurant, authentically Japanese down to the prettily wrapped chopsticks on the table. The rather bland exterior does not even suggest the harmonious Japanese scene inside: kites and kimonos on the walls, blond woods, shoji screens, a long sushi bar from which the chefs turn out tender marvels. Have a seat, read the menu, sip a glass of saké or a cocktail while you're reading, and you'll be pleasantly surprised: several complete dinners run from $11.95 to $14.50 and include a variety of delicious small dishes. First you are served chilled buckwheat noodles in a flavorful sauce, presented on a *zora,* a wooden box with bamboo top. Next, also served on traditional wooden platters, arrive miso soup, rice, Japanese pickled vegetables, and your main course—it could be the delicious chicken yakitori (boneless broiled chicken, onion, bell pepper, and teriyaki sauce and salad) or salmon yaki, which we sampled. Or it could be a tasty tempura combination. Kintaro is justifiably proud of its teppan cuisine, including steak, shrimp, lobster, and fresh island fish with scallops, from $15.95 to $26.95. Be sure to have the green-tea ice cream for dessert. A pot of green tea accompanies your meal. There are various sushi and sashimi combinations for appetizers or for those who wish to eat at the sushi bar. Kintaro serves dinner only, Monday to Saturday from 5:30 to 9:30pm.

A favorite of steak and seafood lovers, the **Bull Shed,** 796 Kuhio Hwy., just north of Coconut Plantation, behind the Mokihana of Kauai condos (tel. 822-3791), is a Kauai tradition. The atmosphere is great: a large, airy, wooden-frame building overlooking the ocean, so close to it that waves wash up against the sea wall. If you're watching the budget or your waistline, you can make do with visits to the superb salad bar (salad bar alone is $6.95). Or splurge on some of the specialties; entrees, which run from $10.95 to $18.95, include prime rib, garlic tenderloin, yakitori, shrimp and scallops, a variety of Hawaiian fishes, and more; and all entrees include steamed rice and a trip to that salad bar. Open from 3:30pm daily for cocktails; dinner is served every night from 5:30 to 10pm. Reservations are not accepted and it's apt to be crowded, so get there early; prime ribs, the house favorite for which many people make a special trip, can run out early on.

The **Wailua Marina Restaurant** at Wailua River State Park (tel. 822-4311) has long been one of the most popular restaurants on Kauai, offering good food, good prices, and a very special setting. You can dine riverside and catch the breezes on their open lanai, or indoors in the huge dining room with its slanted ceilings, murals, stuffed fish, and turtle shells on the wall. How they manage to serve almost 20 dishes from $7.25 to $13.95—and they include seafood curry, shrimp and petite sirloin, stuffed prawns with crabmeat, and sirloin steak—is a mystery to us, especially since every meal includes delicious hot rolls with butter and a green salad with a choice of dressing (the blue cheese is excellent), plus vegetables and a starch for that same low price. Our baked stuffed chicken cooked in plum sauce with a mini-lobster salad was quite good, and so was the house special of baked stuffed pork chops. Another 9 or 10 entrees, including seafood specialties like Alaskan snow crab claws and petite filet steak, range from $11.75 to $19.25. Homemade pies cost $1.50. Lunch offers more excellent bargains, like corned beef and cabbage at $4.95, a pineapple boat with fresh fruit at $4.50, and filet of mahimahi at $6.25. Most sandwiches are under $5. Dinner is served from 5 to 9pm daily, lunch from 11am to 2pm, and breakfast from 8:30 to 11am. Free transportation from Wailua-area hotels in the evenings only. A find.

If you're in the mood for a treat now, stop and have lunch with the rich at the glorious **Coco Palms Resort.** Lunch is an extravagant buffet with several hot entrees —usually including chicken and roast beef—and many, many choices of vegetables, potatoes, salads, breads, yummy desserts, and fresh fruits. The price is $11. And it's so nice to sit in the lovely open dining room overlooking the palms and the lagoon, where their famous torch-lighting ceremony is held nightly at 7:30pm. Lunch is served from 11am to 2pm. Be sure to walk around the beautiful grounds and browse through their shops. Reservations: 822-4921.

If you're making this trip on a Sunday, even better: Coco Palms' Sunday Champagne Brunch is one of the best on the island. It features a huge seafood buffet including island favorites like fresh shrimp, sashimi, octopus, and lomi-lomi salmon; an omelet bar; eggs Benedict; and outrageous desserts. Price is $17.50, and it's on from 10am to 2pm.

If you've been to Honolulu, you know the great value and dining to be had at the **Perry's Smorgy Restaurants:** now there's a Perry's in Kauai, at the Kauai Beach Boy Hotel (tel. 822-3111), in a glorious location overlooking the water. The dining room, which has both chairs and tables and booths, is enormous; the buffet tables are laden with goodies; and the price is always right. Breakfast, served from 7 to 10:30pm, is a bonanza at $3.95; it features all you want of fresh fruits, juices, smoked ham and sausage, eggs, hotcakes, french toast, pastries, and wonderful Kona coffee. At lunch, 11am to 2:30pm, your tab of $5.45 entitles you to unlimited fried chicken, mahimahi, beef stew, spaghetti, and garlic bread, plus plentiful helpings from the Orchid salad bar. Dinner, 5 to 9pm, is $7.95; and for that price you get hand-carved round of beef, golden fried shrimp, mahimahi almondine, southern-style chicken, spaghetti, and garlic bread, plus the salad bar. All meals include beverage; lunch and dinner also include dessert. Tax is included in the quoted prices. A super family choice.

If you've developed a taste for real Hawaiian food, you can satisfy it in plain surroundings at the **Aloha Diner** in the Waipouli Complex, 4-971 Kuhio Hwy. (tel. 822-3851). Best bets are the lunch specials from $5.10 to $6, including kalua pig or laulau, lomi-lomi salmon, rice or poi; and the more elaborate dinner specials from $7.50 to $9.50—including kalua pig or laulau, lomi-lomi salmon, chicken lau, poi or rice, and haupia (coconut pudding). A la carte entrees, from $3 to $4.25, include beef stew, squid lau, and other favorites. Several readers have praised this one. Open Monday to Saturday from 10:30am to 9pm; closed Sunday.

The little town of Kapaa offers a bonanza of budget restaurants, all on or near the main street, Hwy. 56. An old standby here is **Kountry Kitchen** (tel. 822-3511), a dressed-up diner with carpets, Tiffany-type lamps, gingham curtains at the windows, and a flavor of olden times. The flavor of the food is pretty good, too: You can have complete dinners like fresh local fish, all-vegetable quiche, baked ham, country beef ribs, sesame shrimp, or broiled mahimahi from $8.25 to $10.95, and your entree is accompanied by vegetable soup or salad, vegetables, rice or potatoes, and a loaf of home-baked bread. Beer and wine are available at dinner, which is from 5 to

9:30pm. Lunch, served from 11am to 2:30pm, runs to sandwiches, super burgers, and dishes like fried chicken, grilled mahimahi, chef's salad, and roast beef, from about $6 to $7. Many people consider Kountry Kitchen to offer the best breakfasts in this part of the island, so don't be surprised if you see people lining up for it. Breakfast, served from 6am to 2pm, offers crispy hash browns, a big favorite with all omelets and egg orders on the complete breakfast. The omelet bar is very popular, especially the build-your-own combination, since such unusual omelet ingredients as hamburger, tuna, raisins, and kim chee are all ready and waiting. And the coffee is great, too.

King and I, 4–901 Kuhio Hwy. (tel. 822-1642) is everybody's "great little restaurant" find. Yes, it features Thai cuisine. It's a small, family-run establishment, with crisp white tablecloths, nice paintings on the wall, greenery, orchids, Thai sculpture—a gentle atmosphere. The family grows all their own herbs and spices. The food is exceptionally good, and the prices are easy to take: most dishes go from $4.95 to $8.95. Start with one of the appetizers like the spring rolls or chicken wings, then have a soup (we like the Siam chicken-coconut soup) and a main dish, like the garlic shrimp, the Siam eggplant with chicken, or one of the curries—like yellow curry with shrimp. (Watch out, though: those curries can be hot, unless you tell your server you'd like them mild.) Vegetarians have 10 good dishes to call their own. Now for dessert: how about banana with coconut milk, followed by Thai iced coffee with milk? Super! The King and I serves dinner nightly from 5 to 9pm, and lunch on Monday, Tuesday, Thursday, and Friday, from 11am to 2pm.

For a splurge meal worth every cent, indulge yourself with dinner at **A Pacific Café,** at Kauai Village on Kuhio Hwy. (tel. 822-0013), the new restaurant that's created a stir in island food circles. A Pacific Café is the creation of executive chef/owner Jean-Marie Josselin, who's garnered awards for creative cooking in Paris, on the mainland, and here in Hawaii, where he was formerly executive chef at the Coco Palms Hotel. Josselin has created a stylish restaurant that boasts Asian art and decor, native Hawaiian woods and plants, an open kitchen with rotisserie and a wood-burning grill and wok, so guests can watch the chefs create their magic. And magic it is—Josselin creates extraordinarily good ethnic dishes of the Pacific Rim, using a blend of Asian and European culinary techniques. Since the menu changes constantly to take advantage of the freshest local fish, game, and locally grown vegetables, there's no telling what you may encounter on a specific night, but here are some samples of his signature dishes. Among the appetizers, $3.95 to $11.50, you might have smoked chicken lumpia with a curried lime dip, or deep-fried sashimi with a wana sauce, or potato skins with smoked marlin and sour cream. For salads and soups, $2.75 to $3.50, how about a sizzling squid salad with a sesame lime dressing, or lemon soup with barbecued chicken and steamed wontons. It's easy to make a meal on two or three such appetizers, soups, and salads. From the wood-burning grill comes such entrees, served with vegetables and a choice of rices, as stir-fried Hawaiian lobster with Japanese eggplant and cashews, grilled rack of lamb with a plum tamarind sauce, or grilled Hawaiian aku with a papaya black-bean relish: most entrees go from about $16.75 and up (some are market priced). Do save some room for dessert, preferably the platter of assorted miniature pastries baked fresh every day.

A Pacific Café serves dinner only, daily from 5:30 to 9:30pm, and Sunday brunch from 10:30am to 2pm. Lunch is a possibility for the future. Reservations advised.

"Ono" means "delicious" in Hawaiian, and that's what to expect—delicious food for the whole family—at **Ono-Family Restaurant,** 4–1292 Kuhio Hwy. in old Kapaa town (tel. 822-1710). Pewter plates and fancy cookware hang on the wood-paneled walls; ceiling fans create a pleasant breeze: European and Early American antiques and paintings add to the charm of this warm and inviting place. This is a family-owned operation, and it shows in the care and attention that the Geralds and the Smiths lavish on their guests, especially senior citizens and children; many come back year after year because of that warm welcome. Omelets are featured at breakfast, and so are Canterbury eggs (grilled English muffins topped with turkey, ham, veggies, eggs, and cheese), at $5.55, and quite a way to start the day. From 11am to 4pm, after which the restaurant closes, you can get "Special Delights" from $4.55 to $7.95 (their $4.75 fish sandwich, with vegetables, sprouts, and cheddar cheese on grilled Branola bread is a meal in itself); super burgers from $3.65 to $5.35; and, for the health conscious, a variety of buffalo burgers, which have 70% less fat and 50% less cholesterol than beef and taste just fine—they're $5.25 to $6.75. Be sure to try their Portuguese bean soup; it's an island classic. A variety of fresh fish meals are served daily, along with chicken and beef dishes; the price of entree, from $9.95 to $11.95, includes Portuguese bean soup or tossed salad, rice pilaf or fries, fresh sautéed vegetables, and molasses rye bread from the famous Jacques Bakery. There's a special menu for children. Open daily from 7am to 9pm.

Good food, solid drinks, and an ongoing beach-party atmosphere are the things that make **Jimmy's Grill** at 4–1354 Kuhio Hwy., (tel. 822-7000) in the heart of Kapaa, so popular. Jimmy's is ensconced in a large, two-story building with open air and balcony dining upstairs. The downstairs bar, with its sandy floor and beachy decor, is a fun place to pop into just for a drink and some of their wonderful pupus —nachos, guacamole, sashimi, teri beef ($3.75 to $4.75), and amazing potato skins ($6.95 up). If you want a bigger meal, climb the fire-engine-red staircase to the large dining room; the entire street side of the building is open, and a table here gives you a fine vantage point on busy Kapaa. There are delicious salads, burgers, chicken, hot pastrami, and fresh-fish sandwiches, all around $6 to $8.50. The specialties of the house—barbecue beef ribs, St. Louis–style pork ribs, spicy chicken, New York steak, fresh fish, and homemade pasta—are served up in generous portions and priced from about $9 to $18. Jimmy's is open every day from 11am to 11pm; "Groovy Hour" is on from 4 to 6pm.

Another neat denizen of Kapaa's "restaurant row" is **Makai**, a very pretty tropical, laid-back little place in a house across from the beach at 4–1421 Kuhio Hwy. (tel. 822-3955). Mediterranean-style cooking is their specialty, and although it is moderately priced, it is exquisitely prepared and presented—quite out of the ordinary for a small eatery on one of the neighbor islands. Can you imagine a ham, pineapple, and Monterey Jack cheese omelet for breakfast? You can have one here for around $5, among other breakfast delights, including homemade blueberry muffins, croissants, and giant waffles. Sandwiches, such as fresh catch and tuna salad (made with fresh ahi), are excellent, as are the luncheon plates, in the $6 to $7 range. Salad fans will flip for Makai's chicken macadamia-nut salad. And there are pita sandwiches in the Greek manner—with marinated beef, chicken, lamb, and feta cheese —aplenty. We like to begin dinner here with their Mediterranean Dip Combination (hummus, baba ghanoush, and so on). Entrees include ginger chicken pork medallions with baked apple, spit-roasted game hen, New York steak, and grilled prawns —all served with sweet onion soup or garden salad, and your choice of rice, pasta, or vegetable. Prices range from $9.50 to about $15. Last time, we opted for mahimahi baked in phyllo served with an exquisite lemon butter sauce. You can end your meal with a wonderful chocolate mousse or macadamia-nut cream pie or, in season, Key lime pie. And try the Greek wines, too. Open daily from 7:30am to 2pm and from 6 to 10pm.

We've always liked **Norberto's El Café**, even when it inhabited much more modest quarters in the Roxy Theatre building; now that it's moved to a new home at 1375 Kuhio Hwy. (tel. 822-3362), we like it even better. The attractive, two-level dining room is nicely decorated in Mexican style, and the food is as tasty as ever. Norberto's always cooks with very fresh ingredients, does not use lard or any other animal fats (so vegetarians can feel comfortable here), and offers excellent value. Don't worry about breaking the budget, as complete dinners range from $8.95 to $11.95, and that includes soup, vegetables, refried beans, Spanish rice; there's plenty of chips and hot salsa on the table to go with your margaritas or beer. The steak or chicken fajitas are just about our favorites, but olés, too, for the rellenos Tampico and the nifty Mex-Mix Plate: that's a chicken chimichanga, a chicken taquito and an enchilada with Spanish rice and beans, all for $10.95. All dishes can be served vegetarian style if you ask. If you have any room left, top your meal off with a piece of rum cake or chocolate-cream pie, homemade and delicious. A good family choice, Norberto's serves dinner only, from 5:30 to 9pm daily.

Tropical Taco, in the Kapaa Shopping Center (tel. 822-3622), is another popular Mexican eatery in these parts. Although most of the action here seems to be centered in the cantina—they're big on margaritas, Mexican beers, and batidos (tropical-fruit smoothies)—the adjoining café with its serapes on the wall, Mexican decor, serves very good, fresh food (again, no lard or animal fats used, and everything can be made up for vegetarians), at very reasonable prices. In addition to the usual Mexican dishes they have some inventions of their own, like fish tacos, a Baja California specialty: fresh fish is beer-battered, then deep fried and served on a tortilla topped with cilantro, fresh cabbage, tomatoes, and homemade salsa—$5.95 and great fun. Their Outrageous Burritos, $5.95, is, well, outrageous; and their Fat Jacks, deep-fried and filled with chicken or beef, $6.95, are also tasty ($7.95 with fish). The café part of the operation is open from 11am to 9:30pm, or later, and the cantina from 11am to closing.

You know you can't go wrong at a **Zippy's** anywhere in Hawaii; the one at 4-919 Kuhio Hwy. in Waipouli, mountain side of the road, is no exception to the rule. Burgers start at $2, taco salad is $5.75, Zippy's special chili with rice (ono!) is $2.95 for a large bowl. A variety of plate lunches, like beef teriyaki, breaded veal cutlet, fried chicken, etc., with rice and salad, go from $5.25 to $6.55. Best of all—Zippy's is always open!

Sizzler Restaurant on Hwy. 56, opposite Kinipopo Shopping Village, is one of the most popular budget restaurants in Kauai. Unlike some others in the Sizzler chain, this is not a self-service operation. Instead, you place your order at the counter and pay for it as soon as you come in, then you sit back at your table while the waiter brings you your food and serves you coffee. The best feature is the fresh-fruit and salad bar combined with the pasta and tostada bar, with luscious papayas and avocados grown a few trees away, delicious pastas, protein salads, breads, rolls, and sweets. You could easily make a complete meal of this alone: it's $6.99 for all you can eat. However, most people do opt for the meat and fish dishes; their steak, as always is excellent, and only $8.99. Fresh fish is featured every day, $6.89 at lunch, $11.99 at dinner, and it could be any of the local game fish, like mahi, ono, ulua, ahi, or yellowfin tuna. Breakfast is another bargain meal; $4.99 for eggs Benedict or omelets, $2.69 for french toast. And there are great drink specialties, too, like mai tais, chi chis, and daiquiris, from $1.79 to $3.69. Sizzler is open from 6am to 10pm Sunday to Thursday, until 11pm Friday and Saturday. No need to make a reservation—just come, with a big appetite. Perfect for families.

At Coconut Plantation

It's hard to decide what's more fun, shopping or eating at the Coconut Plantation Market Place, but there are temptations aplenty in both areas. There's an international assortment of restaurants and snack bars here, and most are in the budget range . . . See the people at **Don's Deli & Picnic Basket** if you need a picnic lunch. They'll custom-make it for you, with meats, cheeses, salads, breads, and ice-cold drinks, and give you directions to secluded beaches as well. They also have good sandwiches to eat right there. Sandwiches average $3.79; picnic baskets for two are $12.95, and packed in unique local boxes. . . . **Taco Dude** is a bright new spot for Mexican food. Pink chairs, white counters set the scene for tasty items like burritos, $4.50; tacos, $1.75; quesdadillas, $3.25; and a taco salad at $4.25. . . . **Island Chicken** has more than just delicious fried chicken (two pieces for $2.25), accompanied by onion rings, biscuits, potato salad, and the like; it also makes beautiful salads of fresh local fruits, and fruit whips, too, for $2.60. They do great picnic lunches for two or more people. . . . **The Fish Hut** has tasty goodies galore: They feature fresh charbroiled fish—ahi, mahimahi, ono, and more—in sandwiches from $4.50, and as dinners from $6.50. And they also have Old English–style fish 'n' chips. . . . Pizza is available by the slice ($1.75) at **Bella Rosa Pizza,** and so are meatballs ($4.95), lasagne ($6.95), and calzones ($4.50). . . . Burgers at $2.65, hot dogs at $2, beer and wine coolers can be had on the porch at **Sweet George's Lanai,** a steakhouse. . . . **The Banyan Café** has teri-burgers at $2.75, plate lunches from $4.50 to $5.25. . . . **Café Espresso** is a fun stop for fresh Kona coffee or cappuccino ($1.75) or espresso ($1.45), plus cinnamon rolls, muffins, hot bagels with cream cheese, and more. . . . And **Tradewinds,** a South Seas bar, has all the atmosphere its name suggests and is especially relaxing during the 4 to 6pm happy hour. . . . At the rear of the Market Place is **Buzz's Steak and Lobster,** which often features an all-you-can-eat sandwich and salad bar at lunch, between 11am and 2:30pm, for $6.75.

The **Jolly Roger** restaurant (tel. 822-3451), adjacent to the Coconut Plantation Market Place, is always busy, and with good reason. It's part of a family of restaurants in the islands that offer consistently good food and service. There's everything you ever wanted for breakfast, including the heavenly Mac-Waple, a golden-brown waffle smothered with spicy cinnamon apples and macadamia nuts, about $3.45. Lunch features salads, sandwiches, burgers, and specialties like a stuffed quesadilla, fettuccine Alfredo, grilled mahimahi, or a Monte Cristo sandwich, from $6.25 to $7.75. And for dinner, choose from the complete meals, such as smothered chicken; mahimahi; a delightful seafood combination platter; chicken Polynesian, with a fragrant sweet-and-sour sauce, all accompanied by soup or salad, hot vegetables, and a starch. Or the paniolo, a charbroiled sirloin steak smothered with fresh sautéed mushrooms, bell peppers, and onions. Nothing costs more than $11.95. Check the local tourist papers for discount coupons; you might be able to get the likes of two steak teriyaki dinners for $14.95. There's entertainment every night and a prolonged happy hour, from 11am to 7pm. Jolly Roger is open daily, serving breakfast from 6:30am to noon, lunch from 11am to 5pm, dinner from 5 to 10pm, cocktails till 2am.

You're in no danger of missing the **Kapaa Fish and Chowder House** on Kuhio Hwy., just past the Coconut Market Place (tel. 822-7488). It's the only building in the area—and probably on the island—with a boat on its roof. Yes, there it sits, cargo nets hanging down over the roof's edge; the interior decor is nautical as well. Ask to be seated in the garden room in the back; it's the nicest part of the restaurant. A lively and fun-loving crowd fills this place every night. Food is generally very good, although sometimes a bit uneven. There's plenty to choose from: seafood, catch of the day, steaks, prime ribs, and a few Cajun specialties. There are wonderful chowders, of course, New England or Manhattan clam chowder and Kapaa fish chowder, $3.50 a pot. Most entrees run about $13.75 to $18.95; you can stay on the low side of the menu with calamari, shrimp scampi, chicken divan, and seafood fettuccine. Along with your entree, choose a starch plus fresh vegetable of the day and freshly baked rolls. For dessert, it's super-rich cheesecake and "gourmet mud pies" to end all mud pies, $3.75. Open for dinner only, from 5:30pm to closing every day.

RESTAURANTS ON THE WESTERN AND SOUTHERN ROUTE

You should have no problem dining on your trip around the southern and western end of the island, for there are several excellent choices. Not all, however, are in the budget category.

Old Koloa Town

If you don't like the way your food is done at the **Koloa Broiler** (tel. 742-9122), on Koloa Road in Old Koloa Town, a few miles from Poipu Beach, you have no one but yourself to blame. This cute little place is one of those broil-it-yourself affairs—and that way, they really manage to keep the prices down. You can choose from top sirloin, marinated beef kebab, mahimahi, barbecue chicken, beef burger, from $6.25 to $10.50 (fresh fish is sometimes available at market price); and with your entree comes salad bar, baked beans, rice, and sourdough bread. Lunch offers the same choices, but the burger is $4.75. The only dessert on the menu is macadamia-nut ice cream, so you may want to skip the dessert here and walk over to the Koloa Ice House (see below) for mud pie. Koloa Broiler is a lively, fun kind of place, simply decorated (try to get a seat out on the lanai), with a jolly bar, a neat list of exotic drinks, and lots of local people enjoying their meals. You will, too. Koloa Broiler is open from 11am to 10pm every day.

The **Koloa Ice House** (tel. 742-6063), two blocks away from Koloa Broiler and across the street from the U.S. Post Office, is housed in a green wooden historic building and has just a few tables and booths inside, but it's also fun to sit at any of the eight tables in the garden lanai. You can get a good variety of deli and veggie sandwiches here, as well as a mahimahi sandwich, quiches, nachos, bagels and cream cheese, burritos, homemade soup, veggie burgers, and the like (most items run between $4 and $5). On our last visit we tried the mahimahi burger and the tofu veggie burger on an onion roll, each $4.33 and real fillers, stuffed with heaps of lettuce, sprouts, tomatoes, and onions, with a pickle on the side. They're famous for their Volcano Mud Pie—a cookie-crust ice-cream pie at $4—and a number of other sweet treats. Everything here is available for take-out. Open from 9:30am to 9:30pm daily.

Everything about **Mango's Tropical Restaurant and Bar** (tel. 742-7377), in the same block, is tropical: its "warm weather cuisine," the palm trees and hanging plants, the wallpaper with its lush fern motif, even the quaint old fishermen's bar suspended from the ceiling—everything, that is, except the bar, which is a genuine antique imported from old Philadelphia. The pretty, candlelit dining room with its knotty-pine paneling opens onto the courtyard of Old Koloa Town. While on the one hand Mango's is a lively, casual drinking scene, on the other it's fast becoming a popular family restaurant with a wide menu at good prices—and a choice of whether you want to eat light or heavy. Breakfast, served from 7 to 10am, offers hearty fill-'er-uppers, like three-egg omelets, eggs Benedict, even breakfast quesadillas (flour tortillas with cheese, eggs, salsa, and sausage, served with hash browns), from $5.95 to $7.75. Lunch is a good time to try lighter items, like the Oriental chicken salad, the papaya stuffed with bay shrimp salad, or the Sun Lover's Veggie Sandwich —avocado, tomato, cucumber, sprouts, etc., on sourdough bread: from $4.95 to $9.95. Dinner entrees include Hawaiian chicken (broiled), Polynesian crispy chicken (deep-fried), mahimahi, baby back ribs, and a beef-and-vegetable kebab. Entrees are accompanied by salad with a delicious homemade dressing, rice, vegetable garnish, and hot rolls. For dessert, try their famous mud pie or cheesecake or maybe mango sherbet. Mango's is open daily from 7am to 10pm, with a happy hour from 3 to 5:30pm.

If you like deep-dish pizza, you'll be well pleased with the tasty pies at **Fez's Pizza** in Old Koloa Town. Call ahead (tel. 742-9096) and they'll have your choice ready to take out. Or you can eat at the little garden lanai. Medium pizzas are $7.75 with one topping, $8.75 with two, $9.75 with three; you can also have pizza bread (lunch only), made on a French roll, for $4.25; plus delicious meatball, pastrami and cheese, and vegetarian sandwiches, for $5.25; with pastas from $6.25 to $6.75. Choose from 20 varieties of beer, wine, or soda, to go with your meal. The menu is largely the same at lunch and dinner.

Taqueria Norteños (tel. 742-7222), next to the Kukuila Store in Koloa, is a tiny taco bar that packs a mighty wallop. Owner Ed Sills, former chef at the prestigious Plantation Garden Restaurant, and his wife, Morgan, have been running their own place for several years now, turning out excellent food and keeping the prices low. Now they've opened a dining room in the former gift shop next door, decorated it attractively, and piped in Mexican music. You pick up your food at the counter and carry it to your table. This way, they can still keep the prices low. You should be able to get a good meal here for under $6. They often do regional specialties such as posole (pork and hominy stew) and enchiladas of various sorts. When you want some good Mexican munchies, pop in for tacos, $1.65 to $2.05; burritos, $2.05 to $3; tostados, $2.05 to $2.85; nachos, $2.05. Taqueria Nortenos is open from 11am to 11pm every day except Wednesday, when they close at 5:30pm. The dining room closes at 9pm. Call them in advance and they'll pack you a nice picnic for the beach.

Poipu, Kalaheo, and Hanapepe

For a splurge meal in Poipu, the **Beach House Restaurant** on Spouting Horn Road (tel. 742-7575) is a glamorous choice. Nestled right on the sand, it's an idyllic spot, perhaps the best around for viewing the sunset, the surfers, maybe an occasional whale or two in winter, or just waves crashing on the beach beneath the stars. Decorated in elegant, understated modern lines, adorned with many flowers, the restaurant has 22 fabulous window tables. These are on a first-come, first-served basis, with a reservation. Wherever you sit, though, you'll enjoy gracious service and excellent food. Fresh fish and seafood are the specialties of the house, and when they say "fresh" they really mean it: The restaurant is often the first stop for local fishermen docking at Kukuliulu Harbor. Broiled ahi and sautéed opakapaka are excellent at $19.50; king crab legs at $29.50 is a house specialty; and there are at least 22 "mambo combos"—partnerings of fish, seafood, and steak, from $18.50 to $28.50. Dinners are accompanied by salad, rice or fries, and home-baked muffins. Start your meal with the malihini pupu platter so two of you can sample sashimi, deep-fried South Pacific sea rolls, zucchini sticks, and more ($8.50), and end with any of the blended ice-cream and liqueur drinks. There's a good list of French and California wines, and several pleasing house wines at $2.50 the glass. In short, a place to relax, celebrate, throw cares and calories to the winds. The Beach House serves dinner only, from 5:30 to 10pm (bar open from 4:30pm). Reservations are requested to assure the best tables.

Brennecke's Beach Broiler, on the second (and top) floor of the building across from Poipu Beach Park (tel. 742-7588), likes to proclaim that it's "Right on the beach . . . right on the price." What could be a better combination? The aim here is to provide quality food at a reasonable price, and the happy crowds attest to its success. Decorated with window boxes blooming with bright flowers and the names of island fish spelled out in big white letters on the wall above the kitchen, this is a most attractive place. A variety of original tropical drinks—with or without liquor—might get the meal off to a good start. The menu offers plenty of possibilities, so choose anything from a sandwich, salad, or pupus at lunch, to the same plus entrees at dinner. The Beach burger, fresh fish, and French dip-au-jus sandwiches served with nachos are excellent, $6.50 to $8.50. On the low side of the dinner menu, summer chicken, skewered with vegetables and basted with either tropical teriyaki, barbecue, or garlic butter is $13.50; durum-wheat pasta, cooked al dente with butter and vegetables in the lightest of cream sauces, is $10.95; the same pasta with fresh clams is $13.95. And fresh island fish, kiawe-broiled and served with pasta primavera, is $18.50. All entrees include a choice of delicious clam chowder, or a light salad, garlic bread, and pasta primavera. Several keiki dinners go from $3.95 to $8.95. Brennecke's is open every day, serving lunch from 11:30am to 2pm, late lunches and appetizers from 2 to 4pm, dinner from 4 to 10:30pm. During the Sunshine Happy Hour, 2 to 4pm, most drinks are reduced in price, and mai tais are $2.50. Browse in their mini-deli for some island foods that you might want to bring back to your apartment, plus beach and gift items.

The flamingos are made of neon at **Cantina Flamingo,** 2301 Nalo Rd. (tel. 742-9505), not real as they are in Mexico. But the food is authentic Mexican and absolutely terrific—and there's nothing on the menu at higher than $10. No wonder this place is always packed! But don't despair; a short wait (they do not accept reservations) gives you a seat at a bountiful Mexican table. There's an airy feeling to this attractive restaurant, with its open-beamed ceiling, plants, sombreros, a wall of brick, even two large aquariums in which Black African Belly piranhas survey the scene. Of course you'll want to start your meal with margaritas—they come in nine different fresh-fruit flavors—but the plain is just fine with us. Proceed to appetizers like the cheesy quesadillas ($5.25) or the sopa de albóndigas, a tomato-vegetable–based broth with spicy baked meatballs ($2.25). You can't go wrong with any of the main dishes: We can personally tell you that the seafood fajitas (a cantina specialty), the arroz con pollo, the flautas Kauai (stuffed with chicken, shrimp, broccoli, and cheese, then puffed fried), were all super (each was $9.95). Deep-fried ice cream is nifty, too, especially since it's made with Lappert's macadamia-nut ice cream. A meal at Cantina Flamingo is an experience one wants to repeat—as soon as possible.

To reach the restaurant, take your first left past Brennecke's Beach. Cantina Flamingo is open every day from 3:30 to 9:30pm. Nachos are free during Mexican Munchie Time, from 3:30 to 5:30pm.

We think you'll agree that **Keoki's Paradise,** at the entrance to the Kiahuna Shopping Village on Poipu Road (tel. 742-7534), is aptly named. Open and airy, it overlooks a gem like lagoon. Soda-fountain chairs at the bar are painted cheerful reds; the bar, with its own roof, looks like a little Polynesian palapa. The bar and the seafood and taco bar open at 4:30pm and close at midnight; dinner is served nightly from 5:30 to 10pm. All dinners are accompanied by tossed green salad with house dressing, a basket of freshly baked muffins and French rolls, and steamed herb rice. There are plenty of selections in the $9.95 to $13.95 range, like filet of mahimahi, top sirloin, New York–steak sandwich, Polynesian chicken, Koloa pork ribs, and low-cholesterol "spa cuisine" ginger chicken. Seafood selections and prime rib are higher. It's fun to start with the Fisherman's Chowder (ono!) at $1.95, and sample the side dish of onions and mushrooms, $3.95. In a Mexican mood? A variety of appetizers and entrees, from guacamole to steak fajitas, go from $2.50 to $8.95 in the lounge. Keoki's Paradise claims that its Hula Pie is "what the sailors swam to shore for." The idyllic setting and the friendly ambience here are sure to make you want to linger . . . and linger. Keoki's Paradise, by the way, is run by the same talented management that runs some other neat restaurants—Duke's Canoe Club and Sharkey's in Kauai, and, on Maui, Kimo's, Leilani's, Kapalua Bar and Grill, and Chico's.

The Plantation Gardens Restaurant at Kiahuna Plantation has long been one of Kauai's most gracious fine dining spots—with fine dining prices to match. So it's great to know that the same management also runs the **Tropical Garden Café at Plantation Gardens** (tel. 742-1695), where you can have tropical drinks, pupus, salads, sandwiches, and inexpensive entrees in a charming indoor-outdoor setting, overlooking the gardens of Kiahuna Plantation. Seated on your white wicker chair, relax with a frozen fruit daiquiri or some such, maybe have one of their famous crab-stuffed mushrooms and Maui-onion pupus, and order up a filling salad like the Chinese wonton chicken salad ($8.95), or a charbroiled fish sandwich ($7.95), or one of the entrees such as charbroiled Hawaiian chicken, prime rib, shrimp tempura, or petite top sirloin, from $7.95 to $10.95. Fresh fish of the day, caught in nearby waters, is $10.95. There's a special dessert each day, or go with the house favorite, naughty hula pie—a macadamia-nut ice-cream pie topped with chocolate fudge and whipped cream. The café menu is offered from 5 to 10pm daily, and it's considered one of the best deals in the Poipu area.

Pizza Bella in the Kiahuna Shopping Village is much more than your average "pizza parlor." It has an attractive layout—black-and-white tile floors, white wicker chairs, greenery, ceiling fans, even a few outside tables. Here you can dine on 8-inch, California-style gourmet pizzas—topped with homemade sauce and four cheeses; or with barbecued chicken and cilantro; or perhaps with a mélange of seafood or with smoked salmon or Cajun-style seafood—from $7.95 to $8.75. Less modern tastes might go for the old-fashioned pies, $2.25 a slice, $9 for a medium, 12-inch pizza. Then you have regular lasagne and veggie lasagne, $6.95 and $5.95 each; pasta marinara with or without meatballs, $4 and $5.75; and a variety of hot and cold sandwiches. There's wine, beer, and a nice atmosphere. Since Pizza Bella is open every day, from 11:30am to 10pm, keep it in mind for lunch or a light dinner if you're staying in the neighborhood. They deliver in the Poipu area: tel. 742-9571.

Just as pizza is elevated to special status at Kiahuna Shopping Village, so, too, is the lowly hot dog. Thanks to Chef Tyler Barnes, who is in charge at **Paradise Hot Dogs,** visitors to this little counter-with-tables can now get the only old-fashioned German franks on Kauai. Barnes, who gets the veal-and-pork franks (low in fats, nitrates, and salt) from a German sausage factory on the West Coast, steams them in a beer-and-water mixture in the traditional way. He calls this one The Plain Paradise ($2.95). But he also does more elaborate things, like topping his foot-long dogs with pineapple and teriyaki sauce, or with Swiss-cheese fondue in white wine, or with mango chutney and grated coconut. For nonmeat-eaters, there's a turkey frank, charbroiled mahimahi filet dog. (The Sea Dog) and charbroiled eggplant with miso sauce (The Rising Sun). Take your dog, fries, homemade chili, and whatever, sit down at one of the two or three outdoor tables, out front or in the little garden area off to the side, and rest your feet before you continue your shopping. Open from 10am to 9pm Monday to Saturday, Sunday from 11am to 6pm; phone 742-7667 for take-out orders.

About 40 years ago, Gwen Hamabata's parents and her grandmother started a simple little restaurant in Hanapepe and called it the **Green Garden** (tel. 335-5422). It's doubled and redoubled its size many times over in those years, and today it's one of the most charming local spots around, with the kind of flavor and tradition that can come only from a family business where everybody cares. Gwen and her mother, Sue, are the "working bosses," who make sure that all the guests, whether they be the faithful locals or the scores of visitors, enjoy their modestly priced and delicious Asian, American, and Hawaiian food. We were told that in the aftermath of Hurricane Iwa in 1982, when much of the island had no electricity, Green Garden, which had its own generator, fed everyone in the neighborhood nonstop—and refused to accept payment! You'll feel as if you're sitting in the middle of a greenhouse, with orchids on the tables, plants surrounding you everywhere, an entire screened wall facing a garden, bamboo chairs, and white walls. For a real treat, do as the locals do: have a family-style Asian meal. Just tell them what you like and what you want to spend, and they'll create a meal for you. Highlights might be the luscious barbecued chicken, shrimp wontons, vegetable-stuffed eggrolls, tempura aki, shrimp omelets, and scallops with noodles. Reserve this meal at least half an hour in advance.

More simply, you can make a lunch of one of their sandwich specials (we especially like their fresh fish on toast with tomato, onions, and lettuce) for about $5 and under, which are served with a good tossed salad, french fries, and either tea or coffee, iced or hot. Lunch entrees, which include sweet-and-sour spareribs, a seafood special and Korean-style boneless barbecue chicken run from $5.50 to $6.50 and have the same accompaniments as the sandwich lunches. Dinner is a complete meal, featuring similar entrees from $6 to $8, all accompanied by homemade soup or fruit cup, tossed salad, a starch, vegetables and rolls, and tea or coffee. Fresh fish of the day goes for about $11, and kiawe broiler specials like filet mignon at $13 and the East West Special (charbroiled petite teriyaki steak and shrimp tempura) at $7.50, are also well priced. And whatever you do, be sure to save room for Sue's homemade pies, $1.50. We'll vote for the macadamia nut and lilikoi, but then again, the chocolate-cream pie is divine, too! Open from 7am to 2pm and from 5 to 9pm. Note that if a tour bus happens to disgorge its hungry passengers here, things can get a bit hectic. Better to come on the late side of the lunch hour.

Note: At the time of our last visit, Gwen Hamabata, long a community leader and political activist, had just been appointed assistant mayor of the County of Kauai!

Brick Oven Pizza, on the main road in Kalaheo, is just about everybody's favorite pizza place in Kauai; it's been around for years, makes delicious "pizza with the homemade touch," and stays open until 11pm, so you can stop here just about any time hunger pangs strike as you're driving this road. It's a cozy restaurant with red-and-white gingham tablecloths in true pizzeria fashion. Home-baked pies with delicious crust, either whole-wheat or white, start at $6.20 for a 10-inch plain cheese pie, and go all the way up to $19.40 for a 15-inch pizza-with-almost-everything combo. In addition to pizza, there's a vegetarian sandwich with cheese, mushrooms, olives, squash, etc., for $3.95, and a Hot Super Sandwich with Canadian bacon, salami, and a variety of cheeses and vegetables, for $4.30. A spicy Portuguese smoked-sausage sandwich is $4.45. Green salads are available, and so are wine and beer. Open 11am to 11pm, every day except Monday (tel. 332-8561 for pizza to go).

In Princeville and Hanalei

Chuck's Steak House (tel. 826-6211) is rightfully one of the most popular places at the Princeville Mirage Shopping Center. An attractive porch, plants, ceiling fans, dark walls, secluded booths, paintings, and antiques everywhere set a cozy scene. Lunch is fun here, with daily specials from $3.95 to $8.95. There's a salad bar, too, $5.95. Dinner features steaks and prime rib from about $13.50 to $19.25, seafood, and fresh-fish specials, from $14.25 to $19.95. All meals include salad bar, hot bread and butter, and steamed rice pilaf; the salad bar is available on its own for $8.25. For dessert, hesitate not: The mud pie is wonderful. Chuck's is also known for great tropical drinks and fine wines. Chuck's serves lunch from 11:30am to 2:30pm weekdays only, dinner every day from 6 to 10pm. Cocktails are served on weekdays from 11:30am to 11:30pm, on weekends beginning at 5pm.

Where can you find a good-size concentration of the employees of the Princeville Mirage Shopping Center come lunch- or snacktime? One of the two places: either in **Café Zelo's** (tel. 826-9700) or in their offices pigging out on their take-out goodies. We're not surprised: Café Zelo's serves three tasty meals a day, and prices are quite modest. At breakfast, for example, you could have fruit-filled pancakes topped with whipped cream for $4.25. At lunch, you can sample Zelo's specialties: lox and bagel, the real thing, at $6.75; a super spinach lasagne at $6.50, or sizzling fajitas served with warm tortillas at $6.95. Chicken Acapulco, charbroiled chicken breast topped with melted cheddar, salsa, and avocado is another tasty specialty at $6.95, and all of these (except the lox and bagel) are on the dinner menu as well. Tasty salads—Caesar, Mediterranean, Cajun chicken, and Chinese chicken—as well as burgers are served up at both meals, and delicious pastas and fresh fish, market priced, at dinner. This is a pretty tile-and-woody spot, with a counter and tables out on a small lanai. They bake their own French bread, yummy cookies, and pies daily.

The **Ching Young Village Shopping Center** in Hamalei has a few possibilities for budget eating. **Foong Wong** is a large, simple restaurant, rather sparsely decorated, but with good, if somewhat bland, Cantonese food: plate lunches run about $5.95, and dishes like Szechuan beef, curry chicken, eggplant with garlic sauce are all under $7. . . . **Papagayo Azul** in the old Ching Young building is a little Mexican eatery at which you order at the service window and take your food somewhere to feast upon. Tacos are $2.25; burritos, $3.95; burrito Papagayo (with everything!), $4.95. They even have charbroiled chicken, $4.50 for a half . . . The **Village Snack and Bakery Shop** has plate lunches like fried chicken and teriyaki beef for $4.95, and is also a popular spot for breakfast, which runs from $2.15 to $4.25. The best treats here are the home-baked pies: guava, lilikoi, chiffon, lemon–cream cheese, at $1.50 a slice. Box lunches are $4.95, with a salad and drink. . . . You can get your pizzas on a homemade whole-wheat crust with sesame seeds at **Pizza Hanalei,** which really works at making a good pie; they use fresh vegetable toppings and herbs picked from their own garden. It's $1.60 for a slice, $5.85 for a small pie, or try their unusual pizzaritto: that's cheese, vegetables, meats, and spices rolled up into a pizza shell and eaten like a burrito, $3.95. Delivery in the area: tel. 826-9494.

The **Hanalei Shell House,** on the main street in Hanalei, is a small restaurant that's long been popular with the locals. It's been in the same family for years, and now the younger generation—Steve and Linda—have taken over and spruced it up so that it looks quite good, with wooden tables, ceiling fans, plenty of greens. The bar up front is always lively. They serve breakfast from 8 to 11am, with several specials, like $3.50 for three eggs, hash browns, toast or muffin. Lunch features half-pound burgers, from $4.50 to $5.95, omelets and quesadillas, from $5 to $6.95. The dinner menu always includes fresh, locally caught fish, sautéed or broiled, market-priced; blackened fish Cajun style was $16.95. Exotic tropical cocktails are available all day, seven days a week, from 8am until 11pm. Dinner is served until 11pm, later than any other place in the area.

Hanalei also has a couple of food stands that are fine for quick snacking. On Saturday and Sunday from 11am to 4pm, you'll find Roger Kennedy and his **Tropical Taco,** a green truck next to the Hanalei River at the parking lot of the Dolphin Restaurant, where he dishes up gourmet-quality, all-organic burritos, tacos, and the like, all including beans, meat, lettuce, salsa, cheese, and sour cream (vegetarian combos, too), a complete lunch for around $3 to $5. Take your food over to the shady riverbank just a few steps away and enjoy your picnic Mexicana.

At Kokee

If you're going to go up to Waimea Canyon—and, of course, you should—it's nice to know that you can now tie your visit in with a meal at Kokee Lodge (tel. 335-6061) in Kokee State Park, which has spruced up its dining room and greatly expanded its hours. It now serves breakfast and lunch daily; dinner Friday and Saturday nights. We were thrilled to learn that Sherrie Orr, who used to run the late, lamented Sherrie's White Flower Inn in Honolulu, has now become resident manager at Kokee and is adding her own unique natural-food specialties to the menu. This is a simple, rustic dining room with views of mountain and meadow, quite pleasant, where you can get fresh fruit and the usual egg and meat dishes at breakfast, served from 8:30 to 11:30am. Lunch, 11:30am to 3:30pm, is the time for green salad, a fruit bowl, burgers ($4.95 to $5.25), Portuguese bean soup, the local "soul food" ($3.95), or a daily modestly priced special. Dinner is served weekends from 6 to 9pm, so after you've watched the sun go down over the canyon, you can relax with a drink and order such dishes as boneless Cornish game hen, kal-bi ribs, teriyaki steak, filet of mahimahi, or vegetarian fettuccine, from $10.25 to $11.95. Any time of the day you can enjoy their homemade hot cornbread, quite delicious, served with Kauai honey, $2.50. We love their desserts—lilikoi-chiffon and French Silk pie, plus whatever special they've baked that day. They serve Lappert's coffee (the best), herb as well as regular tea, and cocktails, beer, and wine, too.

Undoubtedly, you'll see the magnificent moa (chickens) of Kokee on the grounds of the lodge. These are jungle fowl, descendants of birds carried to Hawaii centuries ago by the Polynesians in their outrigger canoes. The brightly plumed chickens, protected by the state, survive only here, in the mountains of Kauai; those on the other islands were destroyed by mongeese, which, somehow, never got to Kauai.

---

3. The Night Scene

IN AND AROUND LIHUE

Imagine a disco where the noise level is downright bearable! You can find it at the **Westin Kauai,** whose glamorous, five-level **Paddling Club** disco is so thickly, plushly carpeted that one can really enjoy the music, and dance to the latest videos on Kauai's biggest video screen. Mixed drinks should be about $4. . . . It won't cost you a thing to catch the torchlighting ceremony at the Westin Kauai's Kalapaki Beach. It's held every evening at dusk, as a double-hulled canoe is paddled to shore, Hawaiian dances and chants are performed and tales of old Hawaii are told. The torches are lit, and then the evening's festivities can begin. . . . Down the road from the Westin Kauai, at Nawiliwili Harbor where the luxury cruise liners dock, is **Club Jetty,** out there on the wharf for many years. There's early dinner music from 6 to 9pm, and then it's live-band entertainment and disco sounds Monday through Saturday with DJ Aunt Betty and bands imported from Honolulu and the mainland. Beer is $2 to $2.50, mixed drinks are $2 and up. No cover charge.

Looking for the cheapest drinks on Kauai? **Hap's Hideaway** on Ewalu Street in Lihue town (tel. 245-3473) claims to have them starting with 12-oz. draft beer for $1.25. They also have over 750 songs on the jukebox with Top 40s, '50s, and country and western music, a happy hour that stretches from opening at 1pm to closing time at 2am, a Montana accent, and not even a trace of Polynesian atmosphere.

The best cantina in this area is **Rosita's** at Kukui Grove Center, a popular bar and lounge, where you can admire the artwork, listen to local entertainers, and sip Rosita's "world-famous margaritas." You can have them by the pitcherful for $7.50, or by the glass at $3.50 (fruit margaritas are $3.75). Come by during the 4:30 to 6:30pm happy hour when there are specials, plus music. Entertainment on Thursday and Friday nights. The bar is open daily from 11am to 11pm or midnight.

Watch the papers for news of free shows put on at the **Kukui Grove Center.** They often take place on Friday nights or Saturday mornings, right in the mall. These shows by local entertainers are sometimes every bit as good as those at the high-priced clubs.

EAST KAUAI

You must see the **Coco Palms Hotel** at night. Five miles out of town on Wailua Bay, it's on the site of an ancient coconut grove and lagoon, where Hawaiian royalty once lived. Flaming torches cast eerie shadows on the water, there's much blowing of conch shells and other ritualistic goings-on, with an effect that reassures the visiting movie stars here that they've never left the set. Come around sunset time for a drink or just to stand and watch the impressive and very moving torch-lighting ceremony—a Kauai must.

Come back to Coco Palms around 9pm, and you can watch the Larry Rivera Polynesian Show Tuesday through Saturday. Dinner will be a bit above our budget (most entrees around $15 to $20, including soup or salad) but you get a chance to sample the award-winning talents of Executive Chef James Balanay. A nominal cover charge is added at show time.

The **Sheraton Coconut Beach Hotel** is a leader in entertainment on the island. You can usually find a trio like Kathy, Bill, and Les playing music to dance to—including Latin, oldies, and Top 40s hits—on Thursday, Friday, and Saturday, from 8 to 11pm, at its Cook's Landing Lounge. And the Sheraton's luau is on every night at 6:45, with a cost of $43 for adults, $26 for children 2 to 12, $20.50 for the show only (no food). Phone 822-3455, ext. 651, for reservations.

Leilani's Polynesian Revue, held Monday, Wednesday, and Friday at 7pm at the **Aston Kauai Resort,** features a charming group of local youngsters. Admission to the show alone is $10; it's also included with the price of the $16.50 prime rib buffet, served between 6 and 8:30pm. Information: 245-3931.

Probably the longest happy hour—let's call is a "Happy Day"—takes place at the **Jolly Roger.** From 11am to 7pm every day, standard drinks are available at special prices. Dancing begins around 8pm, when entertainers like Jim Striegel take the stand with music ranging from Hawaiian contemporary to pop.

AT POIPU BEACH

This side of the island is a bit quieter after the sun sets. Undoubtedly the liveliest place is the **Poipu Beach Hotel,** whose Poipu Beach Café offers dancing and entertainment every night of the week, as well a happy hour with complimentary pupus from 5 to 7pm, and a Sunday Jam Session from 5 to 10pm (tel. 742-1681 for information). . . . It's lovely to walk down to the beach here at night and along the waterfront to the neighboring **Stouffer Waiohai Beach Resort.** You can have a drink at the Terrace Bar, catch the sounds of Wally and Polei, who usually perform Tuesday through Saturday from 6 to 10pm; enjoy the view; and perhaps decide to come back here for a meal the next night (their salad bar is one of the best around and their Sunday champagne brunch is renowned far and wide). . . . There's dancing and entertainment nightly at the **Drum Lounge of the Sheraton Kauai,** overlooking the ocean. Groups like ESP Sound Machine (Monday and Tuesday) and Magic (the rest of the week) are often on hand. And if you're in Kauai on a Wednesday or a Sunday, you'll enjoy the **Sheraton's Poipu by Sunset Show,** whose headliners are the Na Kaholokula group. Brothers Robbie and Kimo are respected artists and present a fascinating program of contemporary and traditional Hawaiian songs. Hula artist Puamohala and five hula dancers provide the dancing. There's a three-hour open bar from 6 to 9pm, dinner at 7, showtime at 8; price is $42 for adults, $24 for children (as yet, no cocktail show here, which would be nice). Phone 742-1661 for reservations. . . . The setting for drinks is pure tropical magic at **Plantation Gardens Restaurant,** once the gracious home of a plantation manager. . . . Remember **Flamingo Cantina** around the Mexican Munchie hour, 3 to 5:30pm, when the nachos are free. . . . There's always a lively group hanging out in the bar/lounge at **Brennecke's Beach Broiler.**

THE PRINCEVILLE-HANALEI AREA

Tahiti Nui, on Hwy. 56, just before Aku Road and a stone's throw from Hanalei Shell House, has been the place for local color for many years. Sometimes it's incredibly busy, other times rather quiet, but always with a group of locals hanging out at the bar. The place has been done up with pareau fabric, Tahitian wood carvings on the walls, bamboo, and a thatched ceiling. The atmosphere is super-friendly. Some years ago, Jackie Onassis liked it so much that she came here two nights in a row and stayed until closing. There's entertainment in the lounge every night, and on Sunday and Monday you'll find country-western music. But the best entertainment here is impromptu; local entertainers often come in and sing, and owner Auntie Louise Marston, a bubbly Tahitian, can usually be persuaded to sing and do the hula. All this, and reasonable prices for drinks, too. Louise serves dinner, too, with a limited menu ($11 to $17) including items like chicken curry with fresh papaya or pineapple, smoked ribs, or catch of the day, served with rice, bread, and salad. There's a delightful luau Wednesday and Friday nights, for around $32 for adults, $16 for children. Reservations are a must (tel. 826-6277). This show is so popular that people even call from the mainland for reservations!

Fortune is fickle. We're told that the really "in" crowd in Kauai now hangs out at **Charo's,** a beautiful restaurant and bar on the beach near the Colony Resort in Haena. Haena is about a 15-minute drive from Hanalei, along many winding roads and narrow, one-vehicle-only bridges, so we suggest a "designated driver" if you're going out here to eat, drink, and make merry.

Jazz buffs have a treat in the Princeville area at the **Happy Talk Lounge** at the Hanalei Bay Resort. On Wednesday, Friday, and Saturday from 5:30 to 9:30pm, they can hear Michele and Michaelle performing jazz standards with Richard Simon on acoustic bass; on Sunday afternoon from 2:30 to 5:30pm, they can bring their own instruments and join in on the liveliest jam session on Kauai! Phone 826-6522.

Note: Check local papers and/or phone for information before you attend any of these: performers and times change frequently.

READERS' SELECTIONS ON KAUAI: "When I walked into my one-bedroom apartment at the Prince Kuhio Condominiums, I felt as if at last I'd come home—in fact, I had a real tough time leaving when my vacation was over. Each night I fell asleep listening to the wash of the ocean waves and the rustle of palm fronds, then woke up to a symphony of birds, brilliant sunrises, and ribbons of rainbows. My apartment was clean—no tobacco-smoke odor—beautifully furnished and had everything I could possibly have needed. Prince Kuhio is quiet, centrally located, and I found that it's respected by the locals. . . . **The King and I** is a local favorite and for good reason. The food is wonderful, and the prices are low. Being a vegetarian, I was pleased to find a nice selection to choose from. It certainly is a local treasure, well worth a visit. Just remember, if you're not used to Thai food—order mild!" (Jennifer Hickman, Angwin, Calif.) [*Authors' Note:* See text for details.]

"On Kauai, we stayed at the **Garden Isle Cottages** near Poipu Beach, in their Sea cliff Cottages overlooking the water, and found them to be everything you said, and then more. From there we went to the Sheraton Moana Surfrider on Waikiki Beach, the Hyatt Regency Waikoloa on Hawaii, and the Volcano House at Volcanoes National Park. Without question, our favorite place was the Garden Isle Cottages" (David C. Kent, Dallas, Tex.). . . . "During our week on Kauai your book was especially helpful. For instance, we ate a meal at the **Lihue Barbecue Inn.** I must admit that at first I was a little hesitant, because the restaurant is not particularly impressive from the outside. However, inside it was everything you said it would be: friendly service, good food, generous portions, and reasonable prices. We followed your advice and toured the Westin Kauai. What a place! We had lunch at the Inn on the Cliffs, a truly memorable afternoon" (Robert T. Germaux, Monroeville, Penn.). [*Authors' Note:* See text for details.]

"**Dani's Restaurant** in Lihue was a delight. Not the usual tourist fare. Rice was served with breakfast steak and eggs for $4. Coffee always there. Friendly, folksy people" (Jon and Andy McCormick, Port Allierni, British Columbia, Canada). [*Authors' Note:* Dani's is at 4201 Rice St.]. . . . "Be sure to go for dessert at the **Plantation Gardens Café** in Poipu. Go at night when the flowering lily pads along the entrance walkway are open (nocturnal) and the pond is loaded with frogs. The 'Naughty Hula Pie' is outstanding and well worth $3.50. And, of course, their Moir Gardens are outstanding—the cactus are breathtaking. . . . Not far from Banana Joe's, just on the south side of Kilauea, is a wonderful fruit stand, next to the Waldorf School. The smoothies were the *best* we had, the atmosphere was very special" (Jack and Peggy West, Portland, Ore.).

"At the **Poipu Shores Condominium,** our townhouse at cliff's edge was wonderful. The waves crashed continually on the rocks below and we enjoyed watching the sea turtles and dolphins. This was the best-equipped vacation home we have ever stayed in. The pool, also at the edge of the cliff, was perfect, and we were only a short five-minute walk from the public beach. Four of us shared this deluxe, two-bedroom, two-bath townhouse for $140 per night. There is also a bar on the premises. The toll-free number is 800/657-7959. . . . We also had a very lovely condo at the secluded **Hanalei Colony Resort.** It was spacious, well equipped, and had lovely grounds right on the beach. Swimming, however, was difficult because of the rocks in the water. We did have a nice pool, whirlpool, and barbecue area. It is 10 minutes past Hanalei, the road that crosses eight one-lane bridges on the way. Our ocean-view apartment was well worth the $110 a night and could sleep four. Fresh bananas from the grounds were always available in the office. . . . Toll-free number is 800/367-8047, ext. 148. . . . **The Hanalei Dolphin Restaurant** was one of the better restaurants on this island, if not the best. It has a nice atmosphere and excellent food and service. The homemade bread was wonderful, as were all the entrees. . . . At the Poipu Beach area, the Kiahuna Golf Club is a nice place for breakfast and lunch. The restaurant is all open with a lovely view of the fairways and greens. The food was good and reasonable. . . . There were several **Kauai Kitchens** on the island. They are not fancy and very local. They are clean, reasonable, and have some interesting local foods to try" (Martha Farwell, Illinois City, Ill.).

"Our two-bedroom, two-bathroom (yes, with marble floors in kitchen and bathrooms) apartment at **Poipu Plantation** was fantastic! It was huge and well equipped, with a deck that surrounded it on three sides. We had the bottom half of their duplex for $80 a day for the two of us. They also have a quad-plex and a triplex. . . . We *loved* Lappert's ice cream, especially chocolate macadamia nut in one of the fresh, made-on-the-premises waffle cones—they're huge!—which were often available dipped halfway in semi-sweet chocolate. We were *so* disappointed to get to the Big Island and discover *no* Lappert's!" (Cheryl Reese and Becky Gardner, New Richmond, Wisc.) [*Authors' Note:* See text for details on Poipu Plantation.]. . . . "**Coco Palms** is everything you say it is. We stayed there and loved it. The night show in the Lagoon Dining Room is excellent for nondrinkers, because you can order a wonderful, nonalcoholic fruit drink called a "Smoothie". . . . **Lihue Barbecue Inn** was great, and **Denmar's Pancakes and Mexican Restaurant** served one of the best breakfasts we've ever had" (Linda Lamb, Cole, S.C.).

"**Kauai Chop Suey** had fantastic food. If we had had time to pick a place to eat at a second time, this would have been it. Shrimp and fresh pea pods that were out of this world. We ate family style, trying several dishes, and it was all excellent—fried rice that was full of shrimp, chop suey, cashew chicken, and sweet-and-sour pork. Prices are great, too; it was the most reasonably priced place we ate at all week [*Authors' Note:* see text for details.] . . . We had champagne brunch at **Prince Bill's Restaurant,** on the 12th floor of the main building at Westin Kauai Lagoons. The price was $18 each, but for your big splurge of the trip, it's worth it! The view is awe-inspiring and the food was exceptionally good. A wide variety of foods and super service. We were treated like royalty. Even if a person is not staying at the resort, it's a must just to visit. Check the tourist publications for a half-price coupon for a carriage ride around the grounds, and take the boat around the lagoon to see exotic wildlife" (Mr. and Mrs. Steve Benner, Nevada, MO.). . . . "I am writing primarily to recommend a Korean restaurant at the corner of Rice and Hardy streets in Lihue. **Kun Ja's**—my mouth waters just writing the name! The barbecued chicken is so succulent and at only $5.75 came with soup and four or five little dishes of odds and ends (bean sprouts, salad, etc., etc.). We also tried the mahimahi and the barbecued beef—equally delicious and all really good-sized helpings." (Mary Dalton, Abbotsford, B.C., Canada). [*Authors' Note:* See text for details.]

"We ate at the new **Perry's Smorgy** in the Kauai Beach Boy Hotel twice, once for dinner at $7.95 each and once for breakfast at $3.95 each. The food was delicious, selections were all cooked just right, and there was enough variety to satisfy anyone's palate. We even got ice-cream sundaes with the dinner meal. The atmosphere was relaxing, open air, and the place was kept immaculately clean. We would recommend Perry's as one of the best places to eat on Kauai for the money, and the mai tais there were the best of all we had on the islands" (Margaret Z. Pyzik, Naperville, Ill.).

"We returned with pleasure to the **Green Garden Restaurant** after a visit to Waimea

Canyon and had a rewarding experience. I went ahead to get a table while my husband parked, and in so doing he locked our one car key inside. The hostess heard of the problem from me, and while he was trying unsuccessfully to reach AAA, she urged me to get him to 'enjoy his lunch, and one of our boys will open it for you.' And so he did, in about two minutes. Obviously, Green Garden will remain a favorite, and the lilikoi pie is as delicious as ever" [*Authors' Note:* We had exactly the same experience once at Green Garden; those people seem unphased by any problem.] . . . We stayed two weeks at the **Kauai Sands** in a very large room with a quite modest, but certainly adequate kitchenette. With the rental car included, we considered it a very good buy and will undoubtedly return. The room had recently been refurnished; the grounds are well kept; and the personnel helpful and friendly" (Elizabeth Greer, El Cerrito, Calif.).

"The **Islander on the Beach Hotel** on the grounds of Coconut Plantation was delightful, although the rates are not quite budget. There are no phones in the rooms, no elevators in the three-story building, no bar or restaurant, but the Jolly Roger Restaurant is next door, and their prices are moderate, they have a nice atmosphere, and the waitresses are friendly" (Mrs. Marilyn Wade, Bainbridge Island, Wash.). . . . "Your best dinner bargain in the vicinity of Coconut Plantation is **Al & Don's Oceanfront Restaurant** in the Kauai Sands Hotel. The ambience is Polynesian and guests receive personalized service. The menu features a surprisingly extensive variety of dishes for a budget hotel: ham steak Hawaiian, chicken Oriental, mahimahi scampi, beef Hawaiian, leg of New Zealand lamb, gulf shrimp, sirloin, or calamari steak, from about $7.25 to $12.95. And, the price of each entree includes soup or tossed salad, bread, french fries, whipped potatoes or rice, and dessert" (Connie Tonken, Hartford, Conn.). . . . "All the main restaurants in Hanalei are overpriced, so we ate at a sort of diner called **The Black Pot Luau Hut.** Large portions of delicious food, either Chinese or American, are served. The teribacon burger was wonderful. Still a bit steep, but prices were better than at other Hanalei eateries. A lot of locals come here" (Maggie L. Berry, Hayes, Va.).

"We spent eight weeks on Kauai. The two of us together spent about $64 a day on accommodations, meals, car rental, inter-island air fare, sightseeing, entertainment, etc.—in short, everything except the bus and air fares from here to Honolulu and return. . . . **Rent-a-Jeep** in Lihue also has some older cars, '82 Datsuns, for example, with a reasonable monthly rate, including insurance. Some rust, dents, torn upholstery, and missing parts, but they run reasonably well and no one would suspect you of being a visitor, so there would be little likelihood of a break-in. We rented for two months. . . . **Star Market,** in the Kukui Grove Shopping Center, Lihue, carries a great variety of fresh and frozen and precooked meats and fish, including octopus and lau lau—pork and fish wrapped in taro and ti leaves and steamed. . . . The Seventh Day Adventist Church, which runs Kahili Mountain Park, also has a summer camp in **Kokee State Park,** consisting of several cabins, one of which has a kitchenette. We rented it for $7 double for six days while we hiked the many trails in the park and in Waimea Canyon" (Jack and Ruth Phillips, Summerland, B.C., Canada). [*Authors' Note:* See text for details on Kahili Mountain Park.] . . . "We stayed at Kokee State Park for several nights. Having camped there in October 1980 in a pick-up camper, we were surprised to find January was more than nippy —and downright cold at night. Fortunately, we had opted for a cabin this trip, and the fireplace was really essential in the evenings. This was a minor complaint on an otherwise great stay—we even got used to those roosters" (John and Eleanor Vick, Longmont, Calif.).

"We were fortunate enough to rent an apartment at the **Prince Kuhio** for three nights with Den and Dee Wilson, a most accommodating and charming couple. Our apartment was a dream spot and made it most difficult to leave when we moved on to Oahu. We cannot recommend the Prince Kuhio and the Wilsons highly enough!" (Helen Dyan, Elmwood, Conn.). [*Authors' Note:* Our sentiments exactly.]

"The **Koloa Landing Cottages** in Poipu turned out to be the most pleasant place we've ever stayed at in the islands. They are well decorated, sparkling clean, and roomy. The Zeevats —Hans and Sylvia—made sure we saw some unusual sights. They even led us in their truck. Sylvia shared all the fruits grown on their grounds (bananas, limes, lemons, mangoes, etc.). Tell your readers not to miss an experience far removed from the big hotel scene, but close enough to check it out" (Gretchen and Ron Cowan, Huntington Beach, Calif.). . . . "I stayed at the Koloa Landing Cottages and had a great experience. The husband-and-wife owners are extremely helpful and friendly. Hans gave me an informative guided tour of Koloa and Poipu Beach, including a snorkeling lesson. This kind of human touch is something lacking in the mass tourism scene that is Hawaii, despite the great friendliness of most individual Hawaiians" (J. Dennis Harcketts, Falls Church, VA.). [*Authors' Note:* See the text for details.]

"For anyone heading to Kauai after the initial shock of Waikiki, we highly recommend staying in the **Kapaa** area, rather than Lihue-Poipu Beach or Princeville-Hanalei. While Kapaa lacks magnificent beaches, there is good swimming and secluded beaches are accessible down cane-haul roads. Kapaa's location allows easy driving to all Kauai's major attractions; and while there is only one large tourist complex in the area (Coconut Plantation), small shopping plazas dot Hwy. 56. A number of moderately priced restaurants with excellent food are right in town or nearby—Ono Family, Kintaro's, and Kountry Kitchen, just to name a few. But Kapaa's greatest asset is its people, whose open friendliness is a much better reflection of Hawaii than the glitter of Honolulu" (Robbie and Alan Kolman, Rensselaerville, N.Y.).

"We stayed at **Polihale State Park** and **Kokee State Park.** One needs permits to camp at any state park. On Kauai, the permits are issued at the state building in Lihue, or one can write to Division of State Parks, P.O. Box 1671, Lihue, HI 96761. Rangers checked our permits. To stay at **County Campgrounds,** go to the county building in Lihue. If it is after 5pm, one goes to the police station. The county permits are $3 per person per night; the state permits are free, but the office is closed by 3:30pm. As for restaurants, I recommend **Denmar's Pancakes** in Lihue (good, cheap breakfasts) and **Tahiti Nui** in Hanalei" (Rebecca Kurtz, Anchorage, Alaska). . . . "Few car-rental agencies are willing to rent to **campers.** Vandalism is scaring the companies off. When applying for a permit, campers should ask how many others are currently camping at each spot, and which have indicated plans to remain there for a bit. There is safety in numbers: don't camp alone" (Frank and Joyce Terwilliger, Swarthmore, Pa.).

"At the **Tip Top Bakery**—which we agree is marvelous!—try 'pipi kaula' with your eggs or pancakes. It is Hawaiian smoked beef, sort of halfway between beef jerky and smoked ham and very lean. . . . You can eat Hawaiian food by going to the local markets, which are generally considerably cheaper than markets in the tourist areas, especially on Kauai. You can get take-out lau lau, lomi-lomi salmon, and, of course, poi. Many exotic Japanese delicacies are readily available, plus more standard things like saimin noodles plus dishes that are very cheap" (Ernest Callenbach, Berkeley, Calif.). . . . "We were delighted with the courteous, efficient service and fine facilities at the **Poipu Beach Hotel,** but swimmers should be warned that the beautiful lagoon at their beach is filled with treacherous rocks and razor-sharp coral just a few feet from the shoreline; three of us received nasty cuts" (Bob and Doris Ryan, Grand Island, N.Y.).

SEEING KAUAI

Count on at least three days to see Kauai. After Lihue, the first two should be devoted to separate all-day trips, which between them circle the island: (a) an eastern and northern trip all the way to Hanea and the Na Pali cliffs, and (b) a southern and western trip, whose high points are Waimea Canyon and the magnificent end-of-the-road climax, Kalalau Lookout. To skip either would be unthinkable. The remaining third day is for side excursions, swimming, and going back to all the idyllic little spots you discovered on the first two trips. Even with three there's hardly enough time.

1. Lihue

Starting place for your adventures is Lihue, once a sleepy plantation village that is beginning to look startlingly modern, what with shopping centers, supermarkets, megaresorts, and the like. We think a visit to the **Kauai Museum,** 4428 Rice St., adjacent to the shopping center and across from the post office, is well worth your while. Stop in first at the Wilcox Building to examine the changing art, heritage, and cultural exhibits of both Asia and Hawaii. The **Museum Shop** here is one of our favorites, with its fine collections of South Pacific handcrafts, tapas, baskets, rare Niihau shell leis, Hawaiian books, prints, koa calabashes and other wooden ware. The Rice Building, entered through a covered paved walkway and courtyard, contains the permanent exhibit, "The Story of Kauai," an ecological and geological history complete with photographs, dioramas, and an exciting video. Be sure to see the Plantation Gallery, a permanent showcase for a collection of splendid Hawaiian quilts, plus koa furniture, china, etc. The museum is open from 9am to 4:30pm Monday through Friday until 1pm on Saturday; closed Sunday. Admission is $3 for adults; children under 18 are free when accompanied by an adult.

A few blocks away from the museum, on Hardy Street, stands the **Lihue Public Library,** a handsome contemporary building, where the latest audiovisual aids, including closed-circuit television, are available. Note Jerome Wallace's impressive abstract batik mural measuring 10 feet high and 27 feet long. Library hours vary with the season but are usually 8am to 4:30pm, plus some evening hours. Ask about their free programs, which include films, art shows, story hours, and ethnic programs.

At 3016 Umi St., Suite 207, on the second floor of the Lihue Plaza, is the head-quarters of the **Hawaii Visitors Bureau** (tel. 245-3971), with information on just about everything, including tips on where to play tennis and golf, deep-sea fishing charters, helicopter tours, boat tours, and kayaking and glider flights. Information on hiking, camping, fishing, and hunting is available at the Department of Land & Natural Resources, 3060 Eiwa St. (tel. 245-4444).

ON THE BEACH

If you follow Hwy. H-50 a mile toward the sea from Lihue up until its junction with 51, you'll come to the deep-water port of **Nawiliwili** (where the wiliwili trees once grew), Kauai's largest harbor and the site of a bulk-sugar plant that looks out on **Kalapaki Beach** across the bay. Although it adjoins the grounds of the luxurious Westin Kauai, this is the town beach, and you are welcome to use it. The surf, similar to that at Waikiki, is fairly gentle, with enough long rollers to make surfing or outrigger canoe rides great fun.

AT THE RESORT

Seldom does a resort become a sightseeing attraction in itself, but the newly completed $380-million **Westin Kauai** breaks just about every preconception of what a resort is. Everybody on Kauai has an opinion about it: some think it's too grandiose for a small Hawaiian island and would look better in, say, Las Vegas; others think it's just what the jet set ordered. Certainly you should see it, and plan several hours or even a day to take in its many wonders, natural and artificial. The megaresort to end all megaresorts, the Westin Kauai is built on an 800-acre spread of land at Kalapaki Beach called Kauai Lagoons, a network of artificial lagoons and in-land waterways that connects the hotel buildings to such features as 16 restaurants, two golf courses designed by Jack Nicklaus, seven tennis courts and a stadium, a European health spa, and six islands, which serve as habitats for exotic wildlife. Best of all, you needn't stay here to play here. You can come to dine, to shop, to see the massive reproductions of Asian art treasures, to stroll around the 21-acre reflecting pool with its white-marble statuary reminiscent of Versailles, or to have a drink by the side of the largest swimming pool in Hawaii with its own fountains and water-falls. Or, come visit the spa: Here you can get a facial or a massage, a fitness evaluation, work out on Universal equipment, or take a class in jazz or aerobic danc-ing. (Phone 246-5062 for information and appointments before you come and to find out which facilities are open to nonhotel guests and see Chapter XVIII on Alter-native Travel for more details.)

Here's how you go about your visit. No cars are allowed on the property, so park yours at the visitor parking lot and make your way to the visitor center. Here you can purchase a $2 *hapawalu* (a Hawaiian-style coin redeemable at shops or res-taurants), and then hop either a 35-passenger Venetian mahogany launch or a canopied outrigger canoe to visit the wildlife habitats. If you take the launch, the cost is $6 for adults, $3 for children. However, you may want to spend the $14 for adults, $6 for children it takes to get an outrigger canoe; only your party will be aboard, and the tour goes into greater depth. Whichever tour you take serves as an introduction not only to the wildlife islands (kangaroo island, zebra island, gazelle island, bird island, monkey island, and flamingo island), but to the resort as well: You'll see all of it. You'll pass by the resort's on-the-water wedding chapel, which surely must be the world's most romantic setting in which to tie the knot: The bride arrives in a white, horse-drawn carriage, the groom in a black limousine.

You may also want to take a carriage ride since the Westin Kauai has the world's largest working draft-horse operation: magnificent Clydesdales, Belgians, and Per-cherons will transport you through eight miles of carriage paths that meander through the grounds. Carriages carry up to four guests, and a half-hour ride is $21; stable tours and lagoon tours are available at $46 and $42 per carriage. (Check the tourist papers; sometimes discounts are offered on carriage rides.)

If you're feeling hungry, or thirsty, you've come to the right place: there are restaurants and lounges galore, offering ultimate luxury to casual elegance. Best bets for budget watchers, as we've told you in the preceding chapter, are **Cook's at the Beach, The Terrace,** and **Duke's Canoe Club.** But if you're feeling very splurgy indeed, then you have some delightful options. For lovers of Japanese food, **Tempura Gardens** is an experience: Kyoto-style cuisine is served in a setting of Japanese gardens, complete with waterfall, koi fish pools, and sculptured statuary. Although a meal here will cost you at least $28, rest assured that Japanese guests consider it a veritable bargain, since the same meal in Japan would run into three figures! **Prince Bill** has become very popular for its top-of-the-tower location affording commanding views of the oceans and mountains: steak and seafood are featured. And its Sunday Brunch is an extraordinary treat. **Inn on the Cliffs** highlights fresh local seafood and pasta—and a 200-degree ocean view. For the ultimate in *haute cuisine*, in a glorious setting, there's **The Masters,** considered one of Hawaii's best French restaurants. And, lest we forget, Kalapaki Beach, the heart of this glorious complex, is open to everybody and one of the nicest places to swim in all Hawaii.

Just in case you were curious, paying guests at the Westin Kauai spend $185 to $385 a night for a room, $400 to $1,500 for a suite.

LIHUE SHOPPING

Pint-sized Lihue now has the largest of all neighbor-island shopping malls, the $25-million **Kukui Grove Center.** Since it's just four miles from the airport on Hwy. 50 (headed toward Poipu), it makes a logical first stop in town to stock up on food and vacation needs. **Star Market** has everything from boogie boards to gourmet take-out foods. At **Sears** you can shop for the whole family, rent a car, survey a good selection of Hawaiian wear and island souvenirs. Such other trusty island familiars as **Long's, Woolworth's, Liberty House, Waldenbooks,** and **J.C. Penney** are here. One of our favorite stops is **Stone's Gallery,** which shows a large selection of indigenous arts and crafts of Hawaii, plus tasteful graphics, ceramics, jewelry, and other fine crafts, most by local artisans. If you're lucky, you may catch one of their frequent exhibitions and shows; the public is always invited to the openings, and there is usually "local-style" entertainment as well. This might be the place for you to buy a print by Pegge Hopper (her portraits of Hawaiian women with haunting faces and abstracted bodies are very popular in the islands; prices start at $15 and run into the hundreds), or a hand-painted T-shirt for $25, or a variety of posters that begin at $10, unframed. Gaze at the magnificent art-to-wear creations, like Hisako Barrow's dresses stitched from pieces of antique kimonos ($135 to $300), maybe pick up an original design T-shirt by Kauai artists, from $15 to $25. Note, too, the woven baskets, the tapa cloth, the photos of Old Hawaii by Boone Morrison. In the center of the store is **Stone's Espresso Café,** with wonderful teas and coffees to take home or sip in the store along with light meals and heavenly pastries (see Chapter XI).

See You in China is another of our favorite Kukui Grove boutiques. This gallery and gift shop specializes in hand-painted clothing, most of it in cotton, rayon, or silk. Cloisonné jewelry, 14-karat gold pieces, and hand-painted ceramic beads are part of an exciting jewelry collection. And there are totes, tiles, ceramics, and other crafts by local artists that would make fine gifts. . . . **Guava Lane** shows many small boutiques under one roof. The most interesting is Art Lines, which features artful jewelry, a large crystal collection, decorative sculptures; it's surrounded by shops with names like Fashion Spree, Resort, and X-Pec.

In addition to attractive kitchenware for the condo crowd, **Great Gourmet** has some terrific food to take home and eat: deli sandwiches, cheeses, pâtés, wines, coffee and teas, plus bread and rolls fresh from its own bakery (which smells wonderful!). Try the fresh cinnamon rolls and the macadamia-nut rolls baked daily. They're great!

Sally's Creations has created some coral fashion rings and earrings, averaging about $10. . . . **Crickets** sells beautiful, lacy, feminine lingerie plus leisure clothing for ladies. And they do very pretty giftwrapping, free. . . . Women's fashions can be found at **Deja Vu.** . . . **Coral Grotto** shows exquisite jewelry, plus artful coral sculpture by Coralie, from $18. . . . You'll find artful Asian imports at **House of Teak**

and Gifts, cute cards, stuffed animals, and American-style whimsey at **Jenai's Hall-mark Shop.** . . . And **General Nutrition Center** runs many specials and is a good place to replenish your vitamin supply—as well as get some fruit or vegetable juice.

The **Kukui Nut Tree Inn** for family-style meals and **Rosita's Mexican Restaurant** for spicy south-of-the-border fare are the big restaurant draws here, but there are about half-a-dozen good snack shops, too (see preceding chapter). Free entertainment is often presented on the mall stage; check the local papers for details. Kukui Grove Center is open weekdays from 9:30am to 5:30pm, on Friday night until 9pm, on Sunday from 10am to 4pm.

Physical fitness buffs take note: You don't have to miss your daily workout while you're in Kauai. Next door to the shopping center, at 4370 Kukui Grove St. (tel. 245-7877), is the **Kauai Athletic Club,** where guests may indulge in aerobic classes, weight lifting, racquetball, lap swimming, etc., to their heart's content, at fees of $12 per day. It's a beautiful, classy club, and the instructors are excellent. Massage and skin care are available. It has reciprocal privileges with many health clubs, maybe yours. (Up on the north shore, the same people run the **Hanalei Athletic Club** in the Princeville Golf Clubhouse, which has an excellent pool, Nautilus equipment, weights, aerobics, and massage.) Open until 10pm weekdays, 6pm weekends. *Note:* **The Spa** at the Westin Kauai (see above, "At the Resort") also has many excellent facilities and services.

Lihue Bargains

Always a good budget stop for resort fashions in Lihue is the big **Hilo Hattie's Fashion Center** at 3252 Kuhio Hwy. Phone them at 245-3404 and they'll take you out to the factory, where you can buy men's aloha shirts from $13.99, women's short muumuus from $13.99, plus souvenirs, macadamia-nut candies, and the like, all at excellent prices. There are always great specials here.

THE OLD HOMESTEAD

A visit to the **Grove Farm Homestead** takes a little advance planning, either by mail or by phoning 245-3202 for reservations. But it's worth the effort, as this is a trip backward in time, to the days of the old Hawaiian sugar plantations. Grove Farm Homestead has been lovingly preserved and still has a lived-in look. The plantation was founded by George N. Wilcox, the son of teachers who arrived with the fifth company of the American Board of Missions sent to Hawaii in the 1830s. (Part of Wilcox's original sugar plantation is now the site of Kukui Grove Center; see above.) His niece, Miss Mabel Wilcox, who was born and lived at the homestead all her life, left her estate as a living museum. The homestead tour is leisurely, with stops for light refreshments along the way in the big kitchen. The old homes are lovely, furnished with antiques, Oriental rugs, and handsome koa-wood furniture; there is an abundance of books, and sheet music is open on the piano. You'll visit the very different servants' quarters, too. Tours are held only on Monday, Wednesday, and Thursday, last about two hours, and get under way at 10am and 1pm. The cost is $3, but may be going up soon. Phone at least a week in advance, or write (reservations are accepted up to three months in advance) to Grove Farm Homestead, P.O. Box 1631, Lihue, Kauai, HI 96766.

KILOHANA PLANTATION

Gaylord Park Wilcox, the nephew of the founder of Grove Farm Plantation, built his own dream house back in 1935 and called it "Kilohana," which, in Hawaiian, means "not to be surpassed." The Wilcox family lived at the estate for 35 years, during which time it was the setting for much of the cultural and social life of upper-class Kauai. The house was closed in 1970, went through a short incarnation as a school, and has now been painstakingly restored to look just as it did in the 1930s, with many of its actual furnishings and artifacts. Now it is a combination historical house-museum and shopping bazaar, with boutiques taking over the old children's nursery, the family bedrooms, the library, the cloakrooms, and the restored guest cottages on the estate grounds. There is a variety of things you can do at Kilohana, like taking a 20-minute, horse-drawn carriage ride ($7), a guided tour, or a walk through the extensive grounds with their manicured lawns and gardens. But what you may want to do is browse and shop. There's a beautiful collection of shops, none of them inexpensive, but all offering quality in accordance with Kilohana's standard of excellence.

Before you begin your shopping, stop in to have a look at the foyer of the main house, where you'll see two enormous monkeypod calabashes—reputedly the largest in the state of Hawaii. In the olden days, Hawaiian kings stored their feather quilts in such calabashes: later, missionary women used them as "trunks" for patchwork quilts. These, however, are replicas, made to be used in the movie *Hawaii*.

In the house, be sure to see the shop called **Island Memories;** it boasts museum-quality replicas and one-of-a-kind island crafts. You'll find a few authentic Hawaiian quilts, quilting kits, artifacts from New Guinea, Balinese masks, aloha chimes with lovely tones, and stylish Art-Deco posters from the 1930s, re-creating old advertisements: one advises, for example, "Fly to the South Sea Isle via Pan Am." They're $30, unframed, and would look great on those walls back home. . . . **Kilohana Galleries** is noted for its collection of work by Hawaiian artists. Check out its **Artisan's Room,** too, for fine crafts—and it's **Hawaiian Collection Room** for rare Niihau shell leis, wood carvings, and a good sampling of scrimshaw. . . . You can get Kilohana Plantation T-shirts, polo shirts, hats, and tote bags—along with a nice array of hand-painted shirts and skirts—at **Cane Field Clothing Company.** . . . . Note the shells and nautical objects, the fine coral jewelry, at **Sea Reflections.** . . . Folk art from Japan, gift items, antiques, and kimonos represent the Japanese mood at Kilohana at **Half Moon Trading Company.**

On the estate grounds is a clutch of charming little shops. **Stone's at Kilohana,** in the A. S. Wilcox 1910 Guest Cottage, specializes in arts and crafts from all over the Pacific—including Tonga, Samoa, New Guinea, and Fiji. You'll see traditional handwork, wood bowls, hand-screened aloha shirts, ritual and ceremonial items, Hawaiian photographs by such artists as Boone Morrison, Pegge Hopper prints, jewelry, pottery, and sculpture. This is a sister shop to **Stone's at Kukui Grove** (see above). Next stop might be **Kauai Certified Tropicals,** which specializes in tropical flowering plants and foliage, already certified for shipping. They have coconuts which you can address and mail back home.

You can have a picnic at Kilohana or an excellent meal at the charming courtyard restaurant, Gaylord's (see preceding chapter).

Kilohana Plantation is located on Hwy. 50, two miles southwest of Lihue, headed toward Poipu. It's on the other side of the road and very close to Kukui Grove Shopping Center. Open daily from 9am. For information, phone 245-7818.

THE SPORTING LIFE

There are plenty of opportunities on Kauai for hiking, fishing, camping, golf, water sports, and such for those who have the time to stay and enjoy them. Check with the Hawaii Visitors Bureau, or write to them at P.O. Box 507, Lihue, HI 96766. Hiking information is available at the Department of Land and Natural Resources, in the state building in Lihue. For State Forest Reserve trail information, write to the District Forester, Division of Forestry and Wildlife, P.O. Box 1671, Lihue, HI 96766; for state park information, write to the Park Superintendent, Division of State Parks, P.O. Box 1671, Lihue, HI 96766.

---

2. The Eastern and Northern Route

Now you're ready for one of the big trips, an excursion around the glorious north and east shores of Kauai. Highway 56, which starts at Kuhio Hwy. in Lihue town, takes you the entire length of the tour. The distance is 40 miles each way, and it will take you a full day.

KAPAIA AND HANAMAULU

After you've gone a few miles out of town at Kapaia, you'll find a turnoff to the left to **Wailua Falls,** about four miles inland. Watch for the white fence on the right of the road and listen for the sound of rushing water; soon you'll see the HVB marker. After you've seen the falls, don't be tempted to drive further; turn around here and drive back.

Look now, on the left as you're driving to Wailua on Kuhio Hwy. (Hwy. 56), for a quaint store called the **Kapaia Stitchery,** especially appealing in that many things in it are made by hand. Owner Julie Yukimura makes items like dresses, muumuus, pareaus, and aloha shirts, which she sells at low prices. Or, you may select your own fabrics (Hawaiian print fabrics start at about $6 a yard for cotton) and have clothing custom made. Julie also asks local craftspeople, especially senior citizens, to make things up for her; we found lovely Hawaiian applique skirts and long muumuus made exclusively for the shop. Most exciting of all are the patchwork coverlets made of Hawaiian fabrics by four local grandmothers: prices are about $75 to $85 and would be at least twice as much anywhere else. Much sought-after traditional Hawaiian quilts ($2,000 to $3,000) are also in good supply. Hawaiian quilting cushions can be made to order ($80 to $90 for an excellent piece of work). And do-it-yourselfers can find Hawaiian-quilt pillow kits and hand-painted needlepoint designs of local flowers and themes. Small children on your gift list will be enchanted with the soft sculpture fairy-tale dolls; some are reversible like Cinderella and the fairy godmother, which turns into the wicked stepmother; some depict Hansel and Gretel's house or Goldilocks and the Three Bears; all are around $22 to $28. There's always something new and interesting here; it's always worth a stop.

WAILUA

Continuing on Hwy. 56, you'll soon come to the mouth of the **Wailua River** and one of the most historic areas in Hawaii. Here, where the Polynesians first landed, were once seven heiaus, or temple sites, by the sacred (wailua) waters. Just before you get there, you'll come to **Lydgate Park,** on the right, a grassy picnic area directly on the water, in which are the remains of an ancient "City of Refuge." You'll get a better idea of what a City of Refuge actually looked like when you see the restored one at Kona on the Big Island. But the concept here was precisely the same. In the days when the Hawaiians still carried on their polytheistic nature worship, life was bound by a rigid system of kapus, or taboos, violations of which were punishable by death. But if an offender, or a prisoner of war, could run or swim to a City of Refuge, he could be purified and was then allowed to go free. Not too much of the City of Refuge remains, but if you wade out into the river you may discover some ancient carvings on the rocks, once part of the heiau. More practically, **Lydgate Park Beach** is one of the best beaches on Kauai for children. Two natural "pools," created by rocks, make it safe for them to swim and play in the ocean. The snorkeling is lovely, there are stripies and butterfly fish feeding on the rock, the water is clean and clear, and the sand is white. There are restrooms, showers, and barbecue pits near the beach. Alas, there have been reports of vandalism here.

A relatively new Hawaiian ghost story got started out here. It seems that the old jail across from the Wailua Golf Course (now replaced by a new facility) may have been haunted. Local people tell us that it was once a burial ground and, before that, a battleground. Whatever the reason, the building shook, the lights went on and off by themselves, and strange mumblings were sometimes heard from the top floor. The police really did not like to draw duty there. Seems that once one of Lihue's finest was so shaken up in the middle of the night that he took all the prisoners, put them in his car, and took them to the police station in Lihue!

The Wailua, one of the two navigable rivers in Hawaii, is also the place where you can rent a tour boat for an idyllic three-mile trip to the fantastically beautiful **Fern Grotto**—an enormous fern-fronted cave under a gentle cascade of water, unapproachable any other way. Personally, we'd love to take this trip in our own private craft and, instead of being "entertained," spend the time contemplating the rare tropical trees and flowers that line the bank and pondering about the old Kauai alii whose bones still lie undiscovered in the secret burial caves of the cliffs above. But the tour boats are well run, the captains are entertaining, and the musicians' singing of the "Hawaiian Wedding Song" in the natural amphitheater of the Fern Grotto is a unique experience.

The cost of the 1½-hour boat trips is $9.38 (children, 4 to 12 half price), and both **Waialeale Boat Tours** and **Smith Motor Boat Service** make the cruises. Their phone numbers are 822-4908 and 822-3467, and you should phone in advance to make a reservation.

You may want to make a little excursion now to visit **Smith's Tropical Paradise,** a 22½-acre botanical garden that features a Japanese garden, a replica of Easter Island, huge tiki heads, a tropical fruit garden, and a small Polynesian village. Adults pay $4, children $2. This is also the site of an excellent luau and Polynesian show; you can see the show alone for around $12, enjoy the whole shebang for about $45. For reservations, call 822-4654 or 822-9599.

At this point on Hwy. 56, a side road called the **King's Highway** (named after the kings who had to be carried uphill in a litter, lest their sacred feet touch the ground) leads to the restored heiau, **Holo-Holo-Ku.** It's so serene here now that it's hard to realize that this was once a site for human sacrifice—where bloodthirsty deeds were done to calm the ancient gods.

Now you move on from Hawaiiana to observe some of the history of the Japanese settlers in Hawaii, recorded in a quaint cemetery just up the wooden stairs to the right of the heiau. If you continue driving along the King's Highway, you'll pass a rice field and soon, **Poliahu Heiau,** now a park that affords you a splendid view of the Wailua River. Next is **Opaekaa Falls,** plunging down from a high cliff (the name, quaintly, means rolling shrimp). At the top of the falls, nestled in a lush green valley is the **Kamokila Hawaiian Village,** where an ancient settlement has been restored. A guided tour here ($5 adults, $1.50 children) is an excellent way to gain an experience of premissionary Hawaii. Knowledgeable guides will show you the Oracle Tower (where villagers left gifts for the gods), the warriors' houses, the men's and women's eating houses, the medicine house (landscaped with Hawaiian medicinal plants), the chief's house, living house, sleeping house, and birthing house (in which are actual ancient Hawaiian birthing stones found in the area). You'll see craft and salt-making demonstrations, watch a demonstration of Hawaiian games and then be invited to participate in them. There are taro and banana patches, and a group of friendly pua'a—Hawaiian wild pigs of the type brought to the islands by the very first Hawaiians. A visitor is sure to come away with quite a respectable knowledge of the traditional ways of the Hawaiian people.

A shuttle boat now takes visitors from the highway to the village at a cost of $8, including the tour of the village.

Komokila Hawaiian Village is open Monday through Saturday from 9am to 4pm. For pickup from nearby hotels (for over four people), phone 822-1192.

When you retrace your path to Hwy. 56, you'll see a little group of buildings on the right, across from the Coco Palms; it's the site of **Rehabilitation Unlimited Kauai,** which showcases the last coconut factory in the Hawaiian chain.

At some point you're going to want to visit **Coco Palms,** perhaps for its splendid evening torch-lighting ceremony. Have a look at some of the attractive shops here; they are more reasonably priced than you might expect. The **Chapel in the Palms,** scene of many a Hawaiian wedding, was originally built by Columbia Pictures for the movie *Sadie Thompson,* starring Rita Hayworth, which was filmed here on the grounds.

On the ocean side of the road, at 4-370 Kuhio Hwy., is **Restaurant Kintaro,** where shoppers should make a stop even if they're not planning to eat. In an annex to the restaurant is **D.S. Collection,** a gallery-shop showing paintings, ceramics, glass, and other works by local artists, as well as some handsome imports from Japan:

ivory, celadon, kokeshi dolls, saké, and tea sets. Many good gift ideas here, and prices begin modestly.

THE MARKET PLACE AT COCONUT PLANTATION

Back on the highway now, continue toward the Coconut Plantation hotels and there, near the Islander Inn and the Kauai Beach Boy, you'll find the Market Place at Coconut Plantation. It's a handsome setup, with concrete planked walkways, country decor, flowers and shrubs everywhere, and enough diverting shops (over 70 at last count) to keep you busy for an hour or two. We have a few special favorites, like **Waves of One Sea,** with such international gifts as lacquer boxes from Thailand, ironwood pine baskets from Hawaii, Fukagawa porcelains from Japan, Russian stone carvings, and Kauai's largest selection of Pacific-island fans. Jewelry handmade of peacock and pheasant feathers begins at $20 for earrings; chokers start at $48. Note the handmade collector's dolls, from $19, and the charming Margaret Leach storyboard prints. . . . **Plantation Stitchery** specializes in needlepoints and patterns, and has a few dresses, too. . . . **Tahiti Imports** sells beautiful clothing and hand-screened fabrics at very reasonable prices. . . . **Ye Olde Ship Store** is the place for maritime art, antiques, and a fabulous collection of scrimshaw, the largest on Kauai. All the work is done on antique-fossilized ivory, which is becoming rarer all the time, and some distinctive pieces like those shown here now have high-investment potential. If you're looking for something simpler, you might pick up some antique brass ship keys (ca. 1875 to 1925) from Hawaiian and other Pacific ships, which would make neat little gifts—under $5.

Be sure to visit the exquisite **Kahn Gallery,** where a consistently high level of taste is evident in the selection of paintings, woodcuts, watercolors, pottery, and crafts by Hawaiian artists. Pegge Hopper, George Sumner, Guy Buffet, Roy Tabora, and Jan Parker are among their stars. The originals and limited-edition prints by these artists are shown here; posters of their work, among those of other artists, can be found at **Island Images,** on the other side of the Market Place. Small paintings to carry home and limited-edition prints could start low, although most are in the several-hundred dollar range. Look for another Kahn Gallery at the new Anchor Cove shopping center in Nawiliwili.

Isle Style lives up to its name with above-average crafts, accessories, jewelry (like titanium bracelets and earrings), stained-glass mirrors, hand-painted T-shirts by local artists, geckos copper or stuffed, and genuine shell jewelry boxes. . . . **The Dragon Fly** has a unique look for Hawaiian clothing—beautiful pastel shades of 100% cotton, hand-embroidered women's casual clothing. Prices range from $25 and styles include sundresses, jumpsuits, and baby wear in the same soft, feminine colors.

Melanesian/Polynesian Connection is an interesting new store here; it carries carvings, masks, wooden bowls from various Pacific countries; a hand-carved sandalwood pen starts at just $5. . . . **Elephant Walk** can always be counted on for beautiful gift items: wind chimes, oil lamps, dolls, shell flowers, and the like. . . . **Port of Kauai** is a maritime gallery with a lot of class: ships in bottles; authentic scrimshaw jewelry; and handsome paintings, originals and graphics, by Robert Lyn Nelson are featured. . . . You can get scrimshaw, 14-karat-gold charms, and Niihau-shell necklaces, which begin at $35 (and go way up!) at **Kauai Gold. . . .** Nuts, candies, and beautiful inexpensive flower leis at **Nutcracker Sweet;** freshly made chocolates at the **Rocky Mountain Chocolate Factory;** and T-shirts with great designs at **Crazy Shirts**—the gecko Ts are taking Kauai by storm.

Beautiful jewelry is not inexpensive at **Hudson & Co.,** but they often make special purchases and pass the savings on to the customer: We saw some fresh-water rice-pearl necklaces from China at $55. . . . **Coral Grotto** abounds in all kinds of coral, including beautiful black; necklaces start at around $25 and go up from there. . . . The **Whalers' General Store** is one of those very useful sundry shops, with everything from macadamia-nut brittle to liquor, sandals, shell souvenirs, and drugstore items. . . . Many kinds of coffees are for sale at **Café Espresso,** including chocolate-macadamia nut and decaffeinated Hawaiian Kona. While you're there, have a cappuccino, or a homemade Belgian waffle with fresh strawberries or blueberries, whipped cream, and macadamia nuts. (These folks are definitely not thinking about calories.) Fudge, too.

If you'd like to fly a kite on a Kauai beach, the people at **High as a Kite** have some beauties for you, which begin at $7 and go up to around $175 (some can be used for decorative art). "Kite dude" Kyle teaches people how to fly them. . . . Huggable plush animals, made on Kauai, are store exclusives. . . . Men's aloha shirts by Reyn Spooner cannot be beat; they have the best patterns. This local outpost of **Reyn's** also has women's shirts, muumuus, and other sportswear. . . . We saw some elegant muumuus for kids, as well as many other lovelies, at **Happy Kauaiian**—which also has special selections for queen-sizes, petites, and sells fabrics too. . . . **Coco Resorts Shop** has great things for the whole family. . . . And **Just You and Me, Kid** specializes in tasteful things for the kids: Hawaiian toys, games, souvenirs, dolls, and books, plus a good selection of Hawaiian T-shirts and aloha wear.

The kids will get a kick out of playing with the heavy equipment from the defunct **Kilauea Sugar Mill** that has been transformed into sculptural fountains they can control. When they tire of that, they may enjoy running to the top of the high wooden tower to see the beautiful view. And they'll be delighted with the children's hula show presented by the local hula schools every Thursday, Friday, and Saturday at 4pm. Be sure to check the calendars of events posted at each entrance for additional free daily activities.

Hungry? No problem. The marketplace abounds in snack bars and restaurants offering inexpensive meals (see the preceding chapter). And if you want to catch a first-run movie, **Plantation Cinema I and II** are right there. The marketplace is open seven days a week, from 9am to 9pm, with free entertainment daily.

KAPAA AND KEALIA

From Hwy. 56, back on the northern drive, you'll soon see a remarkable formation on the left as you enter Kapaa, the **Sleeping Giant**—the subject of another Menehune tall tale. The old fellow, so the story goes, was a kind of Gulliver whom the South Sea Lilliputians inadvertently killed.

On the opposite side of the road, opposite Foodland, look for a little store shaped like a Samoan house and called **Marta's Boat**. Marta Curry, who has five young children of her own, understands the needs of mothers and children and has stocked her place with items both pretty and practical, much of it handmade. Her specialty is 100% cotton (or silk or rayon; she will not carry blends) aloha clothing for children. Cotton T-shirts and infant sets hand painted by local artists are especially lovely. She also has a good selection of educational toys, many of which are good for the long plane ride home. Moms should have a look at the clothing racks for them; we saw some lovely pareaus, hand made in Honolulu in small quantities, which you won't see duplicated elsewhere. Next door is a natural-foods store run by her husband, Ambrose Curry; pick up a cooling bottled fruit drink here, or stock up if you need anything, for it's one of the few-and-far-between health-food shops on the island.

Next stop might well be a visit to the new **Kauai Village Museum & Gift Shop;** look for it in the clock-tower building of the Kauai Village Market, a short stroll from the big Pay-N-Save store. It is a special project of **Aloha International,** a nonprofit group founded by Dr. Serge Kahili King, dedicated to "Peace Through Aloha." The museum/store is a major part of the fund-raising program for a world peace center being built on Kauai. The museum and its mini-theater, showing videos, are free to the public. The gift shop is a delight, with many made-in-Hawaii arts and crafts, especially native wood products; volcanic glass, native olivine, and kukui-nut jewelry; books on Hawaiian shamanism and Hawaiiana; Hawaiian music, videos, maps; fine-art cards, prints, and posters; potted native trees and plants; and novel gift items. Children's Hawaiian story and activity books, toys, and games are also featured as part of the attempt to preserve and pass on the essence of Hawaiian culture. Prices are reasonable, and all profits go to foster these worthy goals. (If you would like more information on Aloha International, write to them at P.O. Box 665, Kilauea, HI 96754.)

Farm Fresh Fruit Stand, on the mauka side of the road at 4–1345 Kuhio Hwy., is well worth a stop if you want to pick up some pineapples, papayas, mangoes, or other local fruit to take back to your room with you. Or send it home: they are the island's largest pineapple shipper. Try a cold coconut, or maybe an exotic fruit like an atemoya, whose taste might be described as a combination of strawberries and bananas. And on Monday and Friday they receive supplies of the famous Jacques of Kauai breads—the garlic-and-pepper loaf is among the most popular.

Hee-Fat Marketplace, at 4–1354 Kuhio Hwy. in the heart of Kapaa, has a number of small shops. The one that's taking off mightily right now is called **Hot Rocket Clothing.** Owner Jay Schneider stocks exclusive T-shirts (most are $15) and sweatshirts (most are $45) which are hand painted and silk-screened here. Some of the more striking designs include "Marilyn Monroe," "Andy," and "Hot Gecko, Hawaii." Lots of hip clothing for men and women, jewelry, accessories, and more.

Jacqueline Sibthorpe, the artist behind **Art to Wear Kauai,** at 1435 Kuhio Hwy., in the Kauai Village Shopping Center, does beautiful work, hand painting on cotton and silk in tropical colors. Dresses start at about $65, bags at about $40; vibrant tops are $24. And the muumuus made of hand-batiked fabrics from Bali, machine-washable, are an excellent buy at $65. There's a neat collection of jewelry, too. The main shop is for women; just opposite it is another shop for men and children. Well worth a stop.

Some of the most beautiful fish in Polynesian waters live in the rocks and reefs around Kauai. The friendly, professional staff at **Sea Sage,** a dive shop at 4–1378 Kuhio Hwy., in Kapaa, can make the introductions for you, via various snorkeling and scuba-diving excursions. They'll rent you snorkeling equipment at $10 for 24 hours, and they run a "snorkel picnic" for $50. A half-day introduction to scuba-diving is $85, including all equipment. There are many other excursions for more experienced snorkelers and scuba-divers, and a full line of snorkeling and scuba equipment is for sale or rent. Reservations should be made in advance: call them at 822-3841 for details.

Continuing on, now, turn half a mile up the hill just before the bridge over Kealia Stream and you'll come to **St. Catherine's Catholic Church,** which boasts murals by leading Hawaiian artists: Jean Charlot, Juliette May Fraser, and Tseng Yu Ho.

Beyond Kealia, watch for the turnoff to **Anahola Beach** for a glimpse of one of those golden, jewel-like beaches that ring the island.

KILAUEA

Just in case you didn't know, Kilauea is the "Undisputed Guava Capital of the World." To make you aware of that fact—and to tell you everything about guava you ever wanted to know but were afraid to ask—**Guava Kai Plantation** has recently opened its doors to the public. (As you're driving on Hwy. 56, you'll notice its sign off to the left; open daily, 9am to 5pm, tel. 828-1925.) Four hundred and eighty acres of guava orchards are under commercial cultivation here; you can glimpse the orchards, see the processing plant do its stuff, visit the gift shop, and get free samples of guava juice and the fruit itself. You might also want to stop into their restaurant to have a sandwich and sample the likes of guava muffins, guava-glazed cinnamon rolls, guava sherbet, guava chiffon cake, and more. After this sweet interlude, get back on the road and on to the lighthouse.

The first church you'll see as you drive into Kilauea town, **Christ Memorial Episcopal Church,** has only-in-Hawaii architecture. It's made of lava rock. Its windows, executed in England, are of the finest design and construction. On the other side of the road you'll soon see **St. Sylvester's Catholic Church** in Kilauea—something new in church architecture. This octagonal "church-in-the-round," constructed of lava and wood, has a beautiful, open feeling. You'll recognize the work of Jean Charlot again, this time in the fresco paintings of the stations of the cross.

Now follow the road for two more miles to **Kilauea Lighthouse** (turn right into Kilauea to Lighthouse Road, which becomes Kilauea Point National Wildlife Refuge). Kilauea Lighthouse, high on a bluff that drops sharply to the sea on three sides, affords a magnificent view of the northern coastline of the island. Birds drift effortlessly in the wind like paper kites sent up by schoolboys; below, the turquoise sea smashes against the black lava cliffs. The historic lighthouse was built in 1913, has an 8-foot-high clam-shaped lens, but is no longer operative (a small light, 30 feet north of the old structure, is the present Kilauea light). The old U.S. Coast Guard Lighthouse Station has been taken over by the U.S. Fish and Wildlife Service. Birdlovers will have a field day here, as the area is frequented by such unique Pacific-sea birds as the red-footed booby, the wedge-tailed shearwater, the white-tailed and red-tailed tropic bird, and the Laysan albatross. Whales, spinner dolphins, and Pacific-sea green turtles are also seen in the area. Docents at the visitor center next door to the lighthouse can answer questions and point out current wildlife activity. Check out the bookstore with its books on Hawaiian natural history. The Kilauea Point Refuge is open daily except Saturday, from noon to 4pm.

On the way to Kilauea Lighthouse, **Kong Lung Center** makes a good stop for shopping, stretching, having a bite. The buildings are turn-of-the-century plantation, and the atmosphere is charming. The Kong Lung Company is Kauai's oldest plantation general store (1881) and it's very special, stocked with beautiful antiques, tasteful craft items (we spotted handsome African baskets and made-on-Kauai ceramics on our last visit), home accessories, and imaginative gift items. It has perhaps the best collection of muummuus on Kauai, plus batiks and clothing from all over the Pacific. Also in this little enclave is an excellent gardenlike Italian restaurant called **Casa de Amici,** where you can have a very pleasant lunch: Italian sub sandwiches that are a meal in themselves from $5 to $7, salads in the same price range, and fabulous rich desserts (daily except Sunday, 11am to 3pm). For a more inexpensive snack type of meal, step up to the counter at **Lighthouse Snacks** for quesadillas, veggie burritos, hot dogs, smoothies, ice cream, even shave ice. The **Lighthouse Farmer's Market** in the complex also offers good sandwiches, soups, and hot dishes of the day—plus fine wines and plenty of fresh island fruit. There is also the **Kahale Kai Trading Company,** which specializes in Asian art—kimonos, fans, paintings—and also carries attractive cards made on Kauai. Around the bend is a bakery with an unusual name: **The Bread Also Rises,** known locally for its pastries and foccacio, a tasty Italian bread. (Another famous Kauai bakery, Jacques, is at Oka Road in Kilauea town; rye molasses bread is a favorite.)

There's one more stop of interest in Kilauea, and that's the **Hawaiian Art Museum and Bookstore** at 2488 Kolo Rd., another project of Aloha International. It's similar to the gift shop at Kauai Village Museum and Gift Shop in Kapaa which we've already told you about, so check out either one, or both. It features work by local artists, one of the best selections of Hawaiian music in the islands, a picture book section for kids, and many books on Hawaiian culture, myth, and philosophy that are used in libraries and schools; many cannot be found elsewhere. Ask about the meetings held here on Wednesday nights by some of the leaders of Aloha International.

Continue, now, past **Kalihiwai Bay,** whose sleepy little village was twice destroyed by tidal waves, in 1946 and 1957, a reminder that the much-celebrated mildness of Hawaii is a sometime thing; the violence of nature (or is it the old gods?) is always here, a sleeping beast that can spring to life at any moment.

HANALEI

The glorious views continue. Keep watching for the lookout at **Hanalei Valley,** where you will be treated to one of the special sights of the islands. The floor of Hanalei Valley, which you see below, is almost Asian, with neatly terraced taro patches and the silvery Hanalei River snaking through the dark greens of the mountains. (A sunset visit here is spectacular; plan it for a later trip if you have time.) You may want to drive through the luxury resort development of **Princeville, at Hanalei** —surely a sportsman's idea of paradise—and perhaps have lunch here at **Chuck's**

Steakhouse or **Zelo's Deli.** Back on the road, you'll soon come to **Hanalei Beach,** one of the most imposing beaches in the islands, but swimming is safe only in summer months and only at the old boat pier at the river mouth. In winter, beware of high surf and undertow. To get to the beach, turn right at St. William's Catholic Church (another Jean Charlot mural is inside). There's a public pavilion, dressing rooms, and picnic facilities; your fellow bathers will include many local families.

In Hanalei Valley itself, history buffs will want to note the old **Waioli Mission.** The original church, built in 1841, is now used as a community center. More interesting, we think, is the old **Mission House,** restored in 1921 and full of fascinating furniture, books, and mementos of 19th-century Hawaii. On Tuesday, Thursday, or Saturday, between 9am and 3pm, you can take an absorbing guided tour here, for which there is no admission charge, although donations are welcomed. Plan on 30 to 40 minutes for this excellent tour. For groups of 10 to 20 persons, however, advance reservations are required and can be made by calling Barnes Riznik at 245-3202 or writing to P.O. Box 1631, Lihue, Kauai, HI 96766.

We loved the funky old Ching Young General Store that had sat in the middle of Hanalei town forever, so we looked upon its demise and the construction of the **Ching Young Village Shopping Center** with mixed emotions. The old-time aura is gone, certainly, but this is a pleasant and practical place with a few shops that are worth your time. The most tasteful of these, for us, is **On the Road to Hanalei,** which shows arts and crafts from all over—Bali, China, and many other places, as well as Hawaii. We saw beautiful tie-dyed pareaus, from $25 to $35, tie-dyed shawls at $75, books, and posters by Hawaiian artists. The gallery section of the store shows original masks from Africa and Indonesia, baskets and tapa cloth from the South Pacific, as well as handmade koa furniture. Note their collection of tasteful jewelry, too. . . . **Kauai Bay** has lots of sportswear, hand-painted silk dresses, lingerie, and totes with Pegge Hopper prints, from about $35. . . . **Spinning Dolphin** creates custom T-shirts, silk-screened while you watch. . . . **Jen's Jewelry and Gift Shop** features Asian carvings, fans, and the like . . . and **Hanalei Backpacking** can set you up for outdoor adventures. . . . Take a little time to browse through the **Native Hawaiian Cultural Center,** a cluster of small shops selling Hawaiian arts and crafts. **Keoni's,** for one, has beautiful haku lei baskets, lots of tie dyes, sarongs, and Hawaiian quilted pillows, all very tasteful. Craft demonstrations and shows are often held here. Have a look, too, at **Hale Lea Museum,** a small display of Hawaiian historical artifacts.

If you need some fresh produce, vitamins, or natural sandwiches, stop in at **Health and Natural Foods.** . . . **Pua & Kawika's Place** can provide you with fresh flowers. . . . Other practical resources at Ching Young Village include a Big Save Market; a Chinese restaurant, **Foong Wong;** and several fast-food operations (see Chapter XI).

Cross the road, now, and visit Hanalei's newest attraction: the **Old Hanalei School.** Built in 1926, this actually was an old school; it is on the National Register of Historic Places as architecturally significant; its design became a standard throughout Hawaii for school buildings. Carol and Gaylord Wilcox, of the prominent Kauai family who also restored Kilohana Plantation, saved the old building, moved it four blocks from its original site, and have lovingly restored it, keeping its significant architectural details intact throughout. At the time of our last visit, several shops were already in place, and a restaurant was preparing to open. Among the shops, **Tropical Tantrum** is a winner, with hand-painted women's clothing by artists Lauri Johns and Parker Price, a brother-and-sister team from Texas. They also show works by other island artists; prices begin around $59 and go up. (Across the street is their beachwear store called Little Grass Shack.) **Island Images** shows first-rate prints, posters, and the like; and **Hanalei Surf** is for the big waves set. As for the restaurant, **Hanalei Gourmet and Wine Bar** promises to be nifty, with a deli on one side for cold sandwiches, a sit-down café on the other. There'll be a wine-and-cheese shop, a wine bar with over 700 bottles, and a menu that will offer antipasto, Italian deli sandwiches, Reubens, "Shrimp Boils" at dinner, and much more. Picnic baskets will be available for those hiking the Na Pali Coast. It will be open every day, beginning with continental breakfast starting at 7am, until 10pm. Undoubtedly, this will be one of the most popular spots in Hanalei.

Our favorite shop in this area is called **Ola's,** and it's right next door to the Dolphin Restaurant in Hanalei. This is a serenely tasteful environment, a showcase for American craftspeople—in wood, glass, ceramic, metal, fiber, and mixed media. We love the whimsical hand-blown glass paperweights by John Simpson of Massachusetts, from $45; the wooden bowls by Jack Straka of the Big Island, from $70; and the hand-painted pewter pins by The Tin Woodsman, from $13. There are many boxes from all over the world. And many delights for children, too—toys, books, whimsy. A wonderful spot.

Lumahai Beach is next, and you'll recognize it immediately from pictures appearing in dozens of books, postcards, and magazines. It's probably the most widely photographed beach on the island, and deserves its fame: golden sand, a long tongue of black-lava rock stretching to the sea, a background of unearthly blue-green mountain. If the surf is not high, swimming will be safe here. It's a little difficult to find the entrance to the trail down to the beach (not indicated by any signs), but once you do it's easy to get down. If the surf is up, admire the view and move on.

HAENA

Beyond this point stretches the Haena region, where the shoreline gets dreamier by the mile. You can swim anywhere along here with the local people, but be very careful of surf and undertow in the winter months. Many people consider **Haena Beach Park** one of the best beaches on the island (although we personally prefer to swim at Ke'e, described below), and you won't go wrong swimming, camping, or picnicking here. Haena is what you always imagined the South Seas would be like—golden curving beaches, coconut palms, and lush foliage, jagged cliffs tumbling down to the sea. Is it any surprise that this spot was chosen as Bali Ha'i for the movie *South Pacific?*

On this drive through the Haena region, watch on the left side of the road for the **Manimi-holo Dry Cave,** which was supposedly dug by the Menehunes to capture an evil spirit that had stolen some fish. This is the area from which the Menehunes were also said to have left Hawaii. A short distance from here, up a small rise, is the first of two **Wet Caves,** the **Waikapalae;** about 200 yards further is the second, the **Waikanaloa.** For once, the Menehunes were not responsible—the caves were reputedly dug by Pele in a search for fire. Finding fresh water instead, she left in disgust. It's reported that you can swim in these pools (the old Hawaiians used to jump off the ledges into them), but we think you'll do better to wait for the end of the road a few hundred yards ahead and an out-of-this-world beach, **Ke'e.** This is one of those gentle, perfect beaches that's almost impossible to tear yourself away from. As you loll on the sand under the towering mountains, listening to the Pacific, which has quieted down to a ripple beside you, it's not hard to picture this spot when it was the site of a most sacred temple of Laka, the goddess of the hula. Nearby are the remains of a heiau that guarded the sacred hula halau, to which novitiates came from all over the islands to study the dances, meles, and religious traditions of their people. From the cliffs above, specially trained men would throw burning torches into the sea (possibly in connection with temple rites). To your left are the cliffs of the **Na Pali Coast** and the end of your auto trip.

NA PALI COAST ADVENTURES

If you'd like to see the spectacularly beautiful Na Pali Coast in detail, however, you have three alternatives: by foot, by boat, and by helicopter. For the first, see the Readers' Suggestions, ahead, for tips on hiking around the cliffs. Of the many boat trips offered, three are quite special. **Captain Zodiac Raft Expeditions** take small groups out in boats similar to those used for shooting the rapids on the Colorado River. (The trip is usually smooth and gentle, but can be as wet and wild as the Colorado River on occasion; a licensed Coast Guard captain is in command.) A full day's expedition costs $95; camper drop-offs are $60 one way to Kalalau, $110 round trip leaving from Hanalei. Morning and afternoon excursions are $75 and $65. For information and reservations, contact Captain Zodiac, P.O. Box 456, Hanalei, HI 96714 (tel. 826-9371 or, toll free 800/422-7824).

If "easy adventure" is more your style, take one of the cruises offered by the **Na Pali Coast Cruise Line.** The 130-foot-long *Na Pali Queen* carries about 40 to 50 people along the Na Pali Coast in comfort and style, provides time for swimming and snorkeling from the aft swimming platform, and serves one meal, either lunch or dinner. Small groups can take off for rafting trips into the sea caves. Cost is about $85 for a full day's trip. For information and reservations, contact Na Pali Coast Cruise Line, 4402 Wailo Rd., Kauai, HI 96705 (tel. 822-5113).

Helicopter trips are perhaps the most exciting way of all to see Kauai and to experience the grandeur of its remote and isolated areas. These are not inexpensive (figure roughly $2 a minute), with prices starting around $100 and going up to $200 per person for trips over Waimea Canyon and the Na Pali Coast, into the wilderness areas of Kauai, often swooping down the canyon walls to make stops at pristine beaches. Early-morning and sunset flights can be the most beautiful of all. A number of companies are now offering tours, and competition can be fierce. Local friends have been praising the trips run by **Menehune Helicopter Tours** (tel. 245-7705), one of the newer companies. **Will Squyres** is one of the veteran helicopter tour operators with thousands of flying miles under his belt (tel. 245-7541). **Jack Harter** (tel. 245-3774) was the first of the Kauai helicopter pilots and still very highly rates. **Papillon Helicopters** is the largest in the state (tel. 826-6591); **Kauai Helicopters** (tel. 245-7403), **Island Helicopters Kauai** (tel. 245-8588), and **South Seas Helicopters** (tel. 245-7781) are all highly reputable. **Ohana Helicopters** (tel. 245-3996), one of the newer companies, is doing a nice job: Chief pilot-owner Bogart Kealoha and his staff were all born and raised in the islands. **Niihau Helicopters** (tel. 335-3500) is the only one with a license to fly over Niihau, the "forbidden island"; its inflight narration concerns that island's history. Photographers are advised to bring plenty of film and a wide-angled lens if possible.

---

3. The Southern and Western Route

This tour is about as long as the northern one and requires another full day. Since the high point is Waimea Canyon, you might check with the forest ranger on duty before leaving (tel. 335-5871) to find out if there's fog over the canyon; if so, it might be preferable to save this trip for another day, if you have one. You may want a sweater, by the way, for the slightly cooler (but not at all unpleasant) 4,000-foot altitude of the Kokee region.

OLD KOLOA TOWN

Most of this drive is along Hwy. 50. Starting from Lihue, note the town of Puhi on your left (where you'll see a mountain formation called "Queen Victoria's Profile").

Continue driving until you see Hwy. 52 on your left, which leads you through a spectacular arch of towering eucalyptus trees (popularly called the "Tree Tunnel") and into the little town of **Koloa.** Hawaii's first sugar plantation town, Koloa was established in 1835 and continued through most of the 19th century as a busy seaport and home to a thriving sugar mill. The old plantation town has been restored, and now Old Koloa Town is an attractive collection of shops and restaurants, plus a few historic sites like the **Koloa Hotel,** a five-room inn built in 1898 for traveling salesmen from Honolulu, and its authentically restored ofuro, or Japanese bathhouse. Note the huge monkeypod tree planted in 1925; it stretches halfway across the road. Shops here are worth a little browsing, and you can do that until 9 every night. Perhaps the most appealing of the lot is the **Indo-Pacific Trading Post,** with an eclectic collection of fine arts and gifts, much of it from Hawaii, Asia, the South Pacific, and the Indonesian Archipelago. Owners Bob and Sutji Gunter make frequent trips to find their treasures; we spotted aboriginal sand paintings from

Australia at $88, hand-carved wooden flowers from Bali for just a few dollars, batik pareaus at $30, and great men's shirts from $50. At a smaller shop in the complex called **Nona-Koloa,** they carry jewelry, clothing, batik, lace, and the like, which they've collected from India, Tahiti, and Thailand. . . . **Island Images Fine Arts Prints** is an outpost of the distinguished Kahan Gallery at the Market Place at Coconut Plantation and Anchor Cove. Most prints start around $30, limited-edition graphic prints and seriographs by some of Hawaii's leading artists—names like George Sumner, Roy Tabora, and Pegge Hopper—begin at $300. . . . **Ralston Gallery of Fine Art** handles originals by Hawaiian artists such as Dane Clark, Frederick Kenknight, and Christian Riese Lassen. . . . Looking for a bathing suit? You'll do well at many shops here, especially **Swim Inn and Snazzy Rags.** . . . We found great black tote bags with Kauai prints for $30 at **Sgt. Leisure Resort Patrol.** . . . **Koloa Town Country Store** seems to have a little bit of everything, including macadamia nuts at low prices. . . . **Koloa Town Discount Mart** is the place for take-out snacks and drinks, beach towels, postcards, muumuus, aloha shirts, Tom Selleck posters, all "kine" stuff. . . . **Koloa Klothing** for men has good selections and fair prices. . . . **Paradise Shades** not only has tons of sunglasses, but some neat straw hats as well. **Tots, Teens 'N' Toes** dispenses just what you'd expect—things for kids and teenagers, cute hand-screened T-shirts for babies, and plenty of sandals for men and women, too. . . . In the courtyard, check out **Pendragon,** which has netsukes, Niihau leis, a custom collection of jewelry, plus some clothing, cards, and other items. . . . About the only place in Koloa town that hasn't been restored to the nines is **Sueko's,** an old mom-and-pop-type grocery and sundries shop. Good prices here for Lappert's coffee and macadamia nuts, too. Just behind and attached to Sueko's is a snack bar where you can get sandwiches and local-style plate lunches from about $3 to $3.50.

Lappert's ice-cream fans should know they can get their fix at **Lappert's Cream;** the day we were there, flavors included blueberry cheesecake, egg nog, pistachio almond, apple strudel, and more. (For the best prices on Lappert's, see ahead, under Hanapepe and Waimea.)

Some of the most enjoyable shopping on Kauai takes place here in Koloa, at the **Koloa Ball Park,** every Monday at noon—and other days at other island locales. It's called the **Sunshine Market,** similar to the Green Markets and Farmer's Markets in other states and cities. Local vegetable and fruit growers truck in their produce fresh from their farms, and so do local flower growers and other vendors: The result is a shopping bonanza for anybody who likes to eat! Come early, because everything is snatched up in about an hour, as prices are incredibly low. Island papayas, bananas, lettuces, tomatoes, sprouts, you-name-it, are sold at a fraction of supermarket prices; we saw key limes at 10¢ each, a lovely bunch of flowers for $2. There are usually a few trucks selling coconuts for about $1; the vendors will husk and crack them for you right there; you can drink the milk and take the rest of the coconut home, or eat it all.

In addition to the Monday at noon market at Koloa Ball Park, there's one on Wednesday at 3pm at the Kapaa Ball Park, on Thursday from 4 to 6pm, in Hanapepe at the First United Church of Christ, on Friday at 3pm, in Lihue at the Vidinha Stadium; and on Saturday in Kilauea at the Puu Lani Produce fruit stand. For more information on Sunshine Markets, phone 826-9288.

POIPU BEACH

With its glorious dry climate, golden sandy beaches, and breathtakingly beautiful surf, this is one of the choice areas of Kauai. From Old Koloa Town, Poipu Road leads you right into the heart of the area. Your first stop here might be at a place rich in both Hawaiian history and horticultural splendor, **Moir Gardens at Kiahuna Plantation.** As for the history, it was supposedly on this site that Laka, goddess of the hula and sister of Pele, goddess of the volcanoes, trained her initiates. For whatever it's worth, the vibrations are very good, and the gardens are spectacular; many of the monstrous cactus plants look like something out of Middle Earth. There is no charge to walk around the gardens, and there are sometimes tours leaving from the registration desk of the resort. You can walk from here onto the beautiful grounds of the Sheraton Kauai Hotel. To reach the gardens, drive roughly 14 miles from Lihue on Hwy. 50; then take Hwy. 52 to the Gardens at Kiahuna Plantation.

If you're not surfeited by shopping yet, by all means, drive in to see **Kiahuna Shopping Village** (right off Poipu Road, opposite Kiahuna Plantation), a tasteful selection of island stores, none of them cheap, but all high in quality. One of our favorites is **Tideline Gallery,** always filled with artistic gift ideas. They have the largest collection of volcanic-glass jewelry on Kauai: handsome earrings start at $19, necklaces go from $19 to $115. Batik paintings, marine sculptures, rare coral jewelry are all special here. **Elephant Walk** has so many beautiful things. Just to give you an idea: kaleidoscopes, African wood musical instruments, hand-painted clothing, exquisite koa-wood furniture by Martin and MacArthur. We love the Made in Paradise Magic Island Girls—hula dancer dolls, at $39. Note the line of jewelry made of niobium, a rare metal of intense hues, by Holly Yash. Earrings, bracelets, necklaces, go from $16 to $195. For a modestly priced gift, get a shirt-holder shell for just $8. . . . **Tutu's Toy House** has darling things for your keikis; we saw tiny happi coats, dresses, Hawaiian dolls, even clothing for teddy bears. . . . Marine art by such painters as Robert Lyn Nelson, ivory scrimshaw by Peter Kinney and Robert Sickles, complement a collection of marine antiquities and artifacts at **The Ship Store Gallery.** . . . Julia Pinkham of Kauai is responsible for all the hand-painted lovelies at **South Pacific Collection**—dresses, jackets, T-shirts, accessories. Great tote bags go for $43. . . . **Skids** is a neat shop, featuring classy sandals for every season. You'll find those Hawaiian golf thongs here, as well as Aqua Socks at $35—essential for walking on sharp coral reefs. They also have nice totes and woven bags from China, around $23. . . . **Tropical Shirts** has just that—myriad original silk-screened T-shirts, some with tropical flowers. All are hand-screened and embroidered on Kauai.

Even if you can't afford $300 or $400 for a feather collar, you must, at least, see the work of the island artist called **Bobbi** at **Jewels of Kauai.** Art to wear is Bobbi's stock-in-trade, and her fiber-art workshop in Honolulu is considered one of the best anywhere. She fashions extraordinary collars made of feathers, shells, and other natural materials; somehow, when you put them on, you imagine yourself as a royal princess. They are modeled after royal Hawaiian robes and capes, and have a bit of an Egyptian feeling. Collars without feathers begin at $100. (We're putting these on our "must have" list as soon as we win the lottery.)

Feeling hungry? **Keoki's Paradise,** one of our favorite Kauai restaurants, is right here, and so is **Pizza Bella,** for a light Italian meal, and **Paradise Hot Dogs** (see preceding chapter). You can also satisfy the hungries with frozen yogurt from **Zack's,** something sweet from Garden Isle Bakery, or a delicious scoop of ice cream from **Shipwreck Ice Cream.**

Kiahuna Shopping Village is open from 9am to 9pm Monday through Saturday, until 6pm Sunday. Children from a local hula halau are featured performers in a free show presented here Thursday at 5:30pm.

Now it's time to stop for a swim. **Poipu Beach,** which you'll reach soon after turning left past Plantation Gardens, is one of the best swimming beaches on the island. Youngsters can swim in a shallow little pool; there's rolling surf further out, and a picnic area and pavilion here, too. But please be warned: It is very, very easy to cut your feet on the rocks and coral here; we've seen it happen innumerable times. Please wear foot coverings to be safe. Another word of advice: Don't spend the *entire* day here, as there's plenty to see coming up ahead.

KAYAKING OUT OF POIPU

If you've got a morning or an afternoon to spare, here's a neat adventure. Check in at **Outfitters Kauai** right at the Kiahuna Shopping Village (call 742-9667 ahead of time to make a reservation), and prepare yourself for a great day of kayaking, snorkeling, bodysurfing, even whale watching in season. No previous kayaking experience is necessary; Rick Haviland, who runs these popular expeditions, provides an introductory kayaking lesson for beginners. All of you paddle close to Spouting Horn (see below), then off to a secluded white-sand beach for snorkeling (equipment provided) in an area rich in marine life (giant sea turtles, spinner dolphins, and flying fish abound), kayak surfing, bodysurfing, or just plain beachcombing. Cost is $44 for the three-hour excursion, which gets under way daily at 7:45am and 1:30pm. All you need is your swimsuit and a towel. Outfitters Kauai also offers a one-day ocean adventure paddling along a coastal wilderness on the southeast coast of Kauai in the shadow of 2,000-foot cliffs, at a cost of $95, including lunch; and one- and two-day expeditions along the Na Pali coast. They also rent mountain bikes for personal exploring. (See Chapter XVIII, "Alternative and Special-Interest Travel," for more details.)

WHALE WATCHING

Kauai waters host not only swimmers and surfers and snorkelers, they also host hundreds of humpback whales who migrate here every winter (December through March) from Alaskan and Arctic waters, seeking warm climes in which to mate and breed. How do you get to see these nonpaying guests? Easy! You take one of the whale-watching cruises that have become so popular in Kauai and Maui in recent years. One of the best is run by **Pacific Safari,** which takes no more than 26 passengers at a time aboard their ocean-certified 36-foot yacht, with glass panels providing panoramic views of the underwater world, for a two-hour whale-sighting cruise at $42 per person. Underwater hydrophones are linked to a 10-speaker stereo sound system, so it's quite possible that you'll get to hear the whales singing! Bring those cameras, of course, plus comfortable clothes, and motion-sickness preventives for those who may need them. The same company also offers a Sunset Safari, which gives you a chance to watch live sharks in their native habitat—as well as a glorious sunset. Other cruises are constantly being added. Most cruises depart from Kukuiula Harbor in this area. Pacific Safari's reservation office is in Old Koloa Town, or you may phone them at 742-7033; for advance reservations from the mainland, phone toll free 800/633-4533.

GEYSERS AND GARDENS

Trace your way back now to the fork in the road and this time take the other branch, the one on the right. Continuing past Kuhio Park (on the site of the birthplace of Prince Kuhio), you come to Kukuiula Small Boat Harbor, more familiarly known as **Sampan Harbor.** Be sure to walk out on the wharf for an absolutely gorgeous view; about a mile ahead to the right is **Spouting Horn,** where the water spurts up through several holes in the lava rock, and to your left is an uncannily blue-green Pacific hurtling itself against the black rocks. When you can tear yourself away, have a look at the vendors selling jewelry outside the parking lot; quality is high, prices consistently among the lowest in the islands. A great place to take care of a lot of gift shopping.

Which eelskin wholesale house is the most wholesale? Hard to say, because such outfits abound in the islands (especially in Honolulu). Certainly, one of the biggest and best is **Lee Sand's Wholesale Eelskin Warehouse** at the Hawaiian Trading Post, which you can find right outside of Lawai, on Koloa Road, where Hwy. 50 meets Hwy. 530. Sands, who claims to be the original importer of eelskin from Asia, sells to major eelskin distributors throughout the country and to such prestigious stores as Bloomingdale's in New York, where you can be certain the prices are much higher than what you find here. We saw lovely handbags from about $60. It is said that eelskin is 150% stronger than leather and becomes softer and more supple with use. (It's the kind of bag you just can't wear out.) As if eelskin were not exotic enough, this warehouse also sells accessories made of lizard, sea snake (snakeskin sneakers were $67), and (ugh!) chicken feet. Novelty items like wooden postcards and jewelry are also sold here.

Just outside Lee Sand's is a cute little hut called **Mustard's Last Stand,** where you're free to add not only mustard, but guacamole, sauerkraut, salsa, chili, fresh mushrooms, and three kinds of cheese to any hot dogs, sausages, or hamburgers you may buy there. They also have Lappert's ice cream. If you've got the kids in tow, they may want to take time out from touring for a game of miniature golf at **Geckoland,** a course with a Kauai theme. Open daily from 9am to 7pm.

Just outside of Kalaheo, watch for enchanting **Kukui-O-Lono Park**. The entrance is through a majestic stone gate, just south of Kalaheo. The name means light of the god Lono; at one time Kukui-oil torches here provided a beacon for fishermen at sea. Now the place is a public 9-hole golf course (greens fees are $5 for the whole day) and a small park, where you can see a Stone Age Hawaiian exhibit and a charming Japanese garden. There are birds everywhere.

You'll have to make reservations and pay $15 to tour the **National Tropical Botanical Garden** in Lawai, but nature lovers and photographers will find it eminently worthwhile. The 186-acre garden adjoins 100 acres of Allerton Gardens, a private estate. Tours lasting 2½ to 3 hours covering the National Tropical Botanical Garden and the entire Allerton Estate are given Monday through Friday at 9am and 1pm. Tours covering the botanical garden and part of the Allerton Estate are given Saturday at 9am and 1 pm and Sunday at 1pm. To reserve an escorted tour, which is limited to 12 people, phone the visitor center at 332-7361, or write to Reservations Secretary, P.O. Box 340, Lawai, Kauai, HI 96765. Whether you take a tour or not, you might want to stop by the Museum and Gift Shop, with its living botanical displays, walking tour of the visitor center plants, and native Hawaiian and tropical plants, open Monday through Saturday from 7:30am to 4pm. Tea and coffee are always available at the gift shop. (To drive there, take Hwy. 530 from Koloa and turn left on Hailima Road. Follow Hailima Road to the end, past the dead-end sign to the visitor center.)

HANAPEPE AND WAIMEA

Another of the wondrous scenic views of Hawaii awaits you as you approach the town of Hanapepe. Stop at the overlook for a glorious vista of **Hanapepe Valley** below, where rice shoots, guava trees, and taro patches cover the fertile floor. Waimea Canyon is off in the distance to the left. Hanapepe, where you ought to stop for lunch at the **Green Garden** (see Chapter XI), is quaint, with old wooden, balconied Chinese shops and an air not unlike that of an Old West town. Just past the Green Garden is a shrine, hallowed among those devoted to great ice cream. This is the factory-outlet store for **Lappert's Ice Cream.** Lappert's has created a bit of a sensation since it was introduced in Kauai a few years ago by Walter Lappert, who hails from Austria. It's found in all the best restaurants, and its flavors—passion fruit, mango, coconut macadamia-nut fudge, Kauai Pie, fresh-fruit sorbets, praline, pecan 'n' cream, Kona coffee, just to hint at the possibilities—are without peer. Sugar-free and fat-free flavors are also available. There are two reasons for getting your ice cream here. One, they have the best selection of flavors on the island; and two, since this is the factory outlet, they always have a scoop-of-the-day special for just 75¢ (as opposed to their regular price of $1.44 for a single scoop, $2.31 for a double). Even those who normally don't care much about ice cream become converts after the first swallow.

Just past Hanapepe, turn left at the "Hanapepe Refuse Transfer Station" sign. Go ³⁄₁₀ mile and turn right at the HVB marker, and you'll find yourself at **Salt Pond,** where the calendar seems to have stopped. It looks like a marsh dotted with strange covered walls, and it is here that salt is mined and dried (some of the drying beds in operation date back to the 17th century) as the Hawaiians have been doing it for centuries. You may be lucky and arrive while they are working; members of a local *hui* collect the crystals during the summer months. Then you can head for **Salt Pond Pavilion,** a great swimming and picnicking beach, with safe, calm water. This beach is a good place to recoup your strength for the next big series of sensations coming up at Waimea Canyon.

But first you arrive at the town of **Waimea,** which, like Wailua, is steeped in history. A favorite deep-water harbor in the olden days, it was the center of government before the coming of the white man, and the place where old Captain Cook decided to come ashore. Whalers and trading ships put in here for provisions on their long voyages in the Pacific. It was also here that the first missionaries landed on Kauai, in 1820. And it was on this site that an employee of the Russian Fur Company, Dr. Anton Scheffer, built a fort and equipped himself with a Hawaiian retinue, promising Chief Kaumualii help in defeating Kamehameha. The latter got wind of the scheme and gave Kaumualii orders to get his foreign ally out of Hawaii—which he did, pronto. But the ruins of the old fort, a stone wall mostly hidden by weeds, are still here; an HVB marker points the way on your left, before you come to the Waimea River. The fort may one day be restored—already restrooms and parking facilities have been built, and some of the old stonework is now visible. Until then, however, there's not much else to see here; the interest is mostly historical.

After you've passed the **Captain Cook Monument** and just before the police station, look for the turnoff to the **Menehune Ditch.** Follow the river about 1¼ miles, past some Japanese shops, a Buddhist temple, taro patches, rice paddies, and tiny houses; when you come to a narrow bridge swinging across the river, stop and look for a stone wall protruding above the road for a few feet on the left side. This is all that remains visible of the Menehune Ditch, a remarkable engineering accomplishment that brought water to the neighboring fields several miles down from the mountain. The curious stonecutting here has convinced anthropologists that some pre-Polynesian race created the aqueduct. Who else but the Menehunes? They did the whole thing in one night and were rewarded by the pleased citizens of Waimea with a fantastic feast of shrimp, their favorite food. They later made so much noise celebrating that they woke the birds on Oahu, a hundred miles away. While you're busy creating some legends of your own, you might see some Hawaiian Huck Finns, placidly floating down the river on rafts made of logs tied together, little bothered by either Menehunes or tourists.

The main highway now continues beyond **Kekaha** to the arid countryside around **Mana,** and beyond that to some enormous sand dunes known as the **Barking Sands.** The Kauaians swear they say "woof" when you slide down them, but that's pretty hard to prove. The U.S. Navy has now closed the area, so take the shorter drive to the canyon; you turn off the highway just past Waimea to Hwy. H-550. (A possible side trip at this point could be to **Polihale State Park;** just continue on Hwy. 50, past Mana. Polihale Beach is surely one of the most spectacular beaches in Hawaii, with awesome cliffs and sparkling white sand, but swimming here is treacherous. For sunbathing, walking, and a picnic, though, it's fine.)

WAIMEA CANYON

Now the road starts going up, through forests of eucalyptus, silver oak, and koa; soon you'll see the white ohia trees with their red blossoms of lehua (you'll see lehua again when you visit Volcanoes National Park in Hawaii). On you go, to the first lookout, Waimea Canyon Lookout. Park your car and prepare yourself for one of the most spectacular views in all Hawaii. You're standing now at the top of a 3,657-foot gorge, about a mile wide and 10 miles long. Millions of years ago this was the scene of a tremendous geologic fault, a great crack in the dome of the island; erosion, streams, and ocean waves cut the cliffs into jagged shapes whose colors change with the sun and the clouds—blue and green in the morning, melting into vermilion, copper, and gold as the sun moves across it and finally sets. The gorge is comparable to the Grand Canyon, smaller than its Arizona sister, but sometimes outdoing her in the violent rainbow of its colors.

Now the road continues another eight miles, and you're at Kokee State Park, very different from anything you've seen on Kauai. You're in the midst of bracing mountain country now, with wonderful hiking trails, freshwater streams for trout fishing (rainbow-trout season is each August and September) and swimming, wild fruit to pick in season, wild pigs and goats to hunt. The forest ranger here will give you details on trails. You can relax for a few minutes at the **Kokee Museum,** right next to the **Kokee Lodge Restaurant** and **Kokee Cabins** (once again, see Chapter XI), where you could spend a long, blissful holiday.

From here it's just four miles for a spectacular climax to this trip, the view from the **Kalalau Lookout.** Driving the winding road for these last few miles, you will pass the Kokee tracking station, now world famous for its part in the success of the Apollo II mission to the moon. It was from this site that a laser beam was flashed to reflectors that Neil Armstrong had set up on the lunar surface. At Kalalau, the thick tropical forest suddenly drops 4,000 feet down to the breathtakingly blue sea beyond, where it melts imperceptibly into the horizon. Below, on the knife like ridges, are the remnants of irrigation ditches, taro patches, and signs of careful cultivation that have been long since abandoned to the elements. Read Jack London's story, "Koolau the Leper" (in *A Hawaiian Reader*), for a fictional rendering of the indomitable Koolau, who hid in the ridges here and single-handedly held off the Hawaii National Guard in its attempt to get him to the leper colony at Molokai. His heroic wife crossed the dizzyingly narrow ridges hundreds of times in five years to bring food to her husband and son until they both died of the fearful disease and left her to return to her people alone.

This marks the end of your trip; depending on whether you want an early or late view of Waimea Canyon, you might schedule some of the other sights for the return trip. Another possibility is to drive directly to the canyon, arriving there in the morning, to avoid having your views obstructed by clouds, which sometimes form in the afternoon. Then plan your other events—perhaps lunch at the Green Garden, a swim at Poipu Beach—for the return trip in the afternoon.

READERS' SIGHTSEEING AND SHOPPING SELECTIONS: "The Rosetta Stone at

1596 Kuhio Hwy. in Kapaa is a very nice small metaphysical store with everything from incense to jewelry to dream pillows, along with a good selection of books. . . . There is a Hindu monastery outside of Kapaa which has in its possession an Earthkeeper Crystal, which is only 39 inches high and weighs 700 lbs. The public can view it in a Sunday morning ceremony at the monastery, along with their beautiful grounds overlooking a canyon and lake where ancient Hawaiian queens once bathed. They plan to build a much larger Iravian temple at a nearby site to house the crystal; daily services are held at this site. . . . At Waimea Canyon, one can take a moderate hike to Waipoo Falls to view ancient petroglyphs carved on cliffs. We also saw carved figures on the Na Pali Cliffs on one of the cruises up that coast. It amazes me that my travel agent thought there wasn't any archaeology on Hawaii!" (Dorene Carrel, Clearwater, Fla.). [*Authors' Note:* For information on the Earthkeeper Crystal, the Iravian temple, and when the public can visit, phone 822-3012, or write to The Church of San Marga, P.O. Box 1030, Kapaa, HI 96746].

"Please be sure to stop at the **Farmer's Market** in Kilauea, just to the right of Casa de Amici restaurant. It has excellent selections, particularly of health-food-type staples. They have a wonderful crisp bread, locally made, of whole-wheat flour, sesame seeds, and salt. And when I asked if cream cheese were the appropriate spread, I was taken to a refrigerated case with lovely locally made things such as herbed cream cheese. They even packaged my purchases in ice! They make wonderful-looking sandwiches to go. Great selection" (Jack and Peggy West, Portland, Ore.). . . . "Remind readers that when they book helicopter tours in advance, there could be a problem should the weather be inclement on the day of the flight. It is usually up to the pilot whether or not to fly. They could wind up flying on a drizzly, gray day with a low cloud cover, or risk being charged anyway. Check the local weather reports before booking, or try getting on a flight last minute, without a reservation, to avoid this situation" (Koanne G. Schmidt, Newark, Del.).

"Our best excursion in Kauai was a raft ride up the Na Pali coast. We urge readers to go on this excursion with **Raft Riders** (tel. 822-7759). . . . Raft Riders is owned and operated by Captain Mark. The groups are smaller and Captain Mark gives you really personalized service and will gladly accommodate any request within reason. He charges the same price ($70) as his larger competitors, but also supplies an underwater camera for the snorkeling portion of the trip. We really appreciated the personalized service that can only be given in a small, one-man operation" (Sally and Ben Marzouk, Great Neck, N.Y.).

"Our teenagers loved their 30-foot scuba dive with **Fathom Five Divers** (tel. 742-6991). This is a dive for those wondering if they want to go deeper and need to take more lessons to certify. They were very helpful people, patient and kind. The $60 each includes three hours of instruction, diving, and all equipment and transportation. . . . **Kalapaki Beach** rental provides instruction and equipment for $55 for three hours of sailboard lessons. Two lessons and you can become certified in this sport. . . . **Captain Andy's Sunset Cruise** (tel. 822-7833) was lovely; the cruise lasts two hours, and during the last half hour, you are served pupus and soft drinks as you watch the sun sink. The trimaran holds about 12 passengers, $35 each, children under 12 less. Our teenagers sat at the very front of the boat and got their faces full of salt water and loved it. Captain Andy also does half-day sails for snorkeling and whale and dolphin watching. . . . We enjoyed Waimea Canyon more from a newly discovered trail than from the designated tourist area. About 1½ miles beyond the entrance to Waimea Canyon State Park, there's a small parking area at the start of the Kukui Trail, which drops in switchbacks down the west wall of Waimea Canyon and ends at the Waimea River (a drop of over 2,000 feet in 2½ miles). At the start of the Kukui Trail, the Iliau Loop Trail is an easy ¼-mile nature walk. Plants are identified. You can see Waialeale Falls from this point. Exceptional picture taking material" (Mr. and Mrs. Steven Benner, Nevada, Mo.).

"During our stay on Kauai we met some really nice people who took us to the top of **Sleeping Giant.** Take a jug of water, camera, and a snack and leave early in the morning. The site at the top is beautiful. You hike past waterfalls, through large pine forests that make you think of the North Woods. This is an easy hike; we were a party of all ages, 6 to 65. Go to the intersection at Coco Palms and ask for directions. Even some of the locals don't know about this. . . . Hike up to **Kokee** and pick plums in season around mid-July; spend a day at the **Kauai Museum** and talk to the curator. . . . The **Flea Market** is a must. Did we get bargains? Island clothing for our luaus, shirts for $1, decorations to bring back, flowers, fantastic buys, and wonderful people" (Clyde, Barbara, Jeff, and Laura Quid, Schaumburg, Ill.).

"The **Kukuiula Store (Jimmy's)** on the road between Koloa and Poipu, was really great, not only for groceries, but also for liquor, which was cheaper than at City Liquor on Rice Street in Lihue. . . . The tour at **National Tropical Botanical Gardens** was superb; we became Associate Members" (Carl and Norma Pelzel, Orleans, Vt.). . . . "Based on personal experience, I would recommend that visitors to the outer islands take along a spare pair of glasses. I lost mine in the surf of Kauai, and was disappointed to find that no one on the island grinds lenses. I had to settle for a very expensive pair of contacts instead. . . . The small boats which take you on a tour of the Na Pali coast are very rough; my wife got very seasick on a boat that seats six to eight. For a more comfortable ride, take the larger tour boats. . . . While the **Fern Grotto boat trip** is ultra-touristy, the grounds surrounding it at **Smith's Tropical Paradise** are well worth walking around in. The park is immaculate, and there are many gorgeous tropical plants. Their evening show, similar to the one at the Polynesian Cultural Center on Oahu, is also very well done" (Neil Holman, Buffalo Grove, Ill.).

"Those **Hilo Hattie** people are really helpful. For cosmetic reasons my wife needed a bathing suit with a high front which was almost impossible to find. I mentioned this to one of the store managers and she had one especially made for her. I also noticed that they now have lower prices in their factory showrooms" (Robert L. Fgerstad, Minneapolis, Minn.). . . . "The **D.S. Collection,** next to Restaurant Kintaro, houses some exquisite works of native artists in pottery, jewelry, and paintings. We priced some of the same lithographs in Princeville and found them to be significantly higher. They also have some fine imported Asian porcelains. This place is definitely worth a splurge—after all, all that money one saves on lodgings has to be spent somewhere! We purchased a beautiful Japanese woodblock print for $32 and an original watercolor, matted and framed in koa wood for $65" (Jan and Mike Cobb, Buffalo Grove, Ill.).

"We found some of the best and easiest snorkeling on Kauai was at **Lydgate Beach Park** at the mouth of the Wailua River. The park has a sandy-bottom swimming area entirely enclosed by an artificial rock reef that is home for a great variety of colorful reef fish, including large parrot fish, all of which will eat bread from your hand. Because of the reef, there are no waves" (Jack and Ruth Phillips, Summerland, B.C., Canada). . . . "I bought a kite at one of the fancy gift shops and then found the exact kite for sale at the **Ben Franklin** store in Eleele for $9.95! Many of the items offered at the fancy tourist shops can be had for much less at **Long's** or **Pay 'N' Save"** (M.H.C., Lawaii, HI.). . . . "Readers should check on possible cancellations if they do not have reservations for the **Grove Farm Homestead Tour.** We were called a day after our inquiry" (John and Eleanor Vick, Longmont, Colo.).

"We would like to recommend the **Will Squyres helicopter ride.** Will Squyres was very good, quite calming, professional, and gave an interesting talk with anecdotes. His staff was pleasant, too. What a ride! Inside Mt. Waialeale!" (Susan Cassel, Hastings-on-Hudson, N.Y.). . . . "Our helicopter flight to Waimea Canyon with **Papillon Helicopters** was a fabulous experience, well worth the price. They were playing Bach at full volume on the headsets as we swooped in and out of the canyon. Unforgettable!" (Bob Harrison and Hal Goodstein, Provincetown, Mass.). . . . "The best **snorkeling** we've ever seen—including the Caribbean—was in the little bay directly in front of the Poipu Beach Hotel. The water is a little wavy here, but if you go out in the morning, it is manageable. The fish are absolutely unbelievable. . . . There is a little market of **jewelry vendors** by the Spouting Horn near Poipu Beach almost every day. We picked up some gorgeous coral and shell necklaces of good quality at three for $5!" (Susan and Terry Young, Crystal Lake, Ill.). . . . "The **Kauai Museum** in Lihue was wonderful. We stopped to take a 'quick' look around and left three hours later—and could have stayed longer" (Bart and Lynda Esterly, Capistrano Beach, Calif.).

"We recommend the **Kukuiolono Golf Course** at Kalaheo as the best and cheapest golfing anywhere on the islands. And the scenery is beautiful, too" (Ken and Dolores Dugan, Boise, Idaho). . . . "Do arrive early at **Waimea Canyon**. At 8:30am on a Saturday I shared the glorious view with only a family of mountain goats. It was a peaceful and very special moment of my vacation. At noon, when I passed the viewing point on my way out of the area, I counted eight buses in the parking lot! . . . Do take the **Fern Grotto Cruise** in the late afternoon. It's less crowded and more relaxing" (Paulette Getschman, Cudahy, Wis.).

"A **note of caution** to travelers: Our camera bag with camera equipment was stolen from our car, even though it was locked, while we watched the free Polynesian show at the Market Place at Coconut Plantation, which is held on Thursday, Friday, and Saturday afternoons between 4 and 5pm. Local police advise that all equipment—even in car trunks—can be a target for theft, since most people enjoy the show and thieves know they won't be returning to their car at that time" (Karolyn Fairbanks, Oroville, Calif.).

"**Yoneji's** on Rice Street in Lihue is a local grocery store that carries a little bit of everything and is favored by the locals—not your usual tourist shop, and a place for good buys. . . . Church bazaars not only offer good food at very reasonable prices, but they also present the visitor with an excellent opportunity to mingle with the local people. Plants, fruits, and fresh vegetables were for sale and there was also a rummage sale" (Louise Alberti, Modesto, Calif.).

"After having lived on Kauai almost two years and made a wide acquaintance among the local population, I feel qualified to tell others how to achieve a rewarding stay on the island—much more rewarding than the sterile, 'prepackaged' entertainments offered to tourists. Plan to stay a minimum of two weeks, and find a hotel that caters to the local people. Next day, explore. You can do this without a car, for a while. Find people with similar interests. Do you like to fish? Check with people at Lihue Fishing Supply. Whatever your interests are, there are people here who will enjoy sharing them with you. Photography? Hiking? See the people at the Forest Service in the state building. Ask questions. Be courteous, friendly. Talk to people—and learn to listen and to understand their slightly different way of speech. Away from Lihue there are 'mom-and-pop'–style grocery stores. Go there in preference to supermarkets. Learn to wear local-style clothes and especially footwear . . . island people are very easy to get acquainted with. Eye contact, a smile, and almost any attempt to make conversation will suffice to start an acquaintance" (David C. Moore, Phoenix, Ariz.).

"For those who are doing a substantial amount of cooking, we suggest shopping at the **Kukuiula Store** (*Jimmy's,* to the locals), located on the road between Koloa and Poipu. We comparison-shopped over a several-week period at stores in Lihue and Koloa and found the Kukuiula Store the lowest overall." (Robin and Bert Brumett, Seattle, Wash.). . . . "**Wailua Falls** in Kauai—near the Fern Grotto area—are the falls you see at the beginning of the 'Fantasy Island' television show. Also, some of it was filmed at Coco Palms, on their beautiful grounds in the coconut grove. . . . The torchlight ceremony at Coco Palms is still the best one to see" (Mrs. Elliot Gray, Cerritos, Calif.).

"We found the best **snorkeling** on Kauai was at the west end of the **Poipu Beach Hotel,** about 15 feet offshore, in 2 or 3 feet of water. Ke'e Beach was not nearly as good" (Betty and Bud Eldon, Los Altos, Calif.). . . . "Poipu Beach is excellent for snorkeling—and bad for serious ocean swimming because of the volcanic rock on the ocean floor close in. It's easy to bruise and cut yourself because it is shallow for quite a way out" (Jack and Doris Toussaint, no address given). . . . "Please warn people of the coral and rock on the ocean floor of Poipu Beach in front of the Sheraton Hotel. It's very hard to see and several people cut themselves. Fins are a necessity" (Beth and Chris Baines, Chicago, Ill.). . . . "We were somewhat disappointed in the bird life until we got to **Kokee Camp.** We stayed overnight in one of the cabins, had a very active morning bird walk—this was the best birding area we saw—and spent a very informative afternoon in the museum there" (Linda Adair Wasson).

"If readers decide to hike on the Kalalau Trail, beware of theft in cars left there. My gas tank had been drained when I got back and I knew of people whose windows had been smashed. . . . Campers and backpackers should be sure to bring all supplies; there are few camping supply stores in Kauai. Campers should be warned that Kauai's camping permits must be purchased in Lihue. I strongly recommend taking a look at the campgrounds before getting a permit" (Linda Haering, Santa Rosa, Calif.). [*Authors' Note:* There have been recent reports of vandalism and rowdyism at Kauai campgrounds.]

"We have just returned from an extensive trip to Kauai and we implore you to inform your readers of the dangers of the **Haena-Kalalau** 11-mile trail. Despite the fact that we are experienced hikers, in good shape, and had thoroughly read all available material on the trail, we were not prepared for some of the narrow ledges along the cliffs. In three or four places between Hanakoa Shack and Kalalau Valley, the trail narrows to one or two feet with a sheer drop of over 1,000 feet to the rocks below. Children and hikers who are not in the best of shape should not venture past Hanakoa. Locals told us that some hikers had been killed along the trail, but we did not confirm this. A good, safe, round-trip hike would be from Haena to Hanakoa Stream (just past Hanakoa Shack). This can be done in one day. Hanakoa Stream runs rapidly, and it is a good place to fill your canteen and cool your feet. Along the 11-mile trail, there are only three places to camp: Hanakapiai Beach, 2 miles in; Hanakoa Shack area, 6 miles in; and Kalalau Beach, 11 miles in. The Hanakoa Shack area is hot, humid, and loaded with mosquitoes. The entire trail takes at least 7 hours, and more like 10 hours if you rest along the way. Hikers should not be on the trail after dark" (Bob Rose, Ted Januszewski, and Reed Snyder, Oxon Hill, Md.). . . . "We spent two days making day hikes along the **Na Pali Cliffs** trail. It is a fairly easy foot trail extending 11 miles along this most magnificent coastline. Of course, it isn't necessary or even advisable to go the full 11 miles; a 2-mile walk to spectacular **Hanakapiai Beach** is really quite negotiable for all but the lame and infirm, providing they have stout footgear. This means heavy-soled tennis or deck shoes or 'desert' boots, and socks. The trail is not difficult, but it is rocky, and slippery in spots. A word of warning about the beaches along the trail. Those who are very modest or upset by nudity should be forewarned: the mode of dress at these beaches is undress. Hanakapiai has a marvelous stream flowing right into the ocean at the beach, so after a swim in the invigorating surf, one can rinse off in cool, fresh water. It is also a good idea to bring a canteen or a cup as the walker will get thirsty. There are a number of little springs that are safe to drink from along the way, but we wouldn't drink from the larger streams without using Halazone tablets" (Joann Leonard, Los Angeles, Calif.). . . . "The **Kalalau Trail** on the Na Pali coast is only for people who are fit and like to hike. We hiked only as far as Hanakapiai Beach. My suggestion: Get a sturdy walking stick or cane when you start out. At the very beginning of the trail, previous hikers had left their sticks as a courtesy" (Thomas M. Nickel, San Diego, Calif.).

"I have read several books on the **Kalalau Trail**, so was unprepared for the conditions of the first two miles to Hanakapiai Beach. It is rated as a hardy family hike, with good shoes recommended. My husband and I are in our 30s and in good shape. We wore proper clothes and hiking boots, and carried our camera and a snack in a fanny pack to free our hands and keep things dry. It had rained for at least four days previous to our hike, off and on, and that may have been part of the problem, but I understand rain is the norm there, so maybe not. Most of the last mile to the beach was downhill on a wet, clayey, bare trail. I have never been on anything that slippery. I am not exaggerating when I say it was like walking on ball bearings. We saw people dressed in street shoes and thongs, people carrying videocamera equipment in large metal suitcases, and people with four- and six-year-old children. Under *no* circumstances should they have been on the trail, at least in wet conditions. For us it meant totally muddy clothes, legs, and boots, and an occasional bruise. For them it could have meant injury or worse. Please stress to your readers that although the first two miles of the Kalalau Trail are probably easy when dry, they are treacherous when wet. Even if the trail is dry, it is necessary to cross Hanakapiai Stream to get to the beach. On the day we went, that meant jumping precariously from wet rock to wet rock and scaling a muddy steep hillock on the other side, which is okay for unencumbered adults, but not for small children or adults carrying videocameras or wearing street shoes. . . . Consider buying a **videotape** of Kauai, especially if you're not taking a helicopter trip. There's a choice of formats, and prices run from $39 to $50. Some of the Waldenbooks, like the one at Kukui Grove Shopping Center, play the tapes so you can decide. It's a marvelous keepsake, even more realistic than pictures or slides" (Maggie L. Berry, Hayes, Va.).

"On the north shore of Kauai, from the end of the road at Ke'e Beach, we hiked the two miles into **Hanakapiai Beach** (one hour and 20 minutes each way). A very rough, muddy, and precipitous trail. And when we arrived there—only huge boulders and pounding waves, no sand at all. They say the sand is only there in the summertime. . . . We tried tent camping, but it wasn't very much fun because of the rain, the risk of theft, and the long, dark evenings. Also, a rented car is usually essential because the campgrounds are far from grocery stores. The city/county parks generally were vandalized and offered very poor camping. The few state parks were much better; well equipped and maintained: **Malakahana** on Oahu near Laie and **Polihale** on the west side of Kauai were particularly beautiful. The last five miles to Polihale is through a muddy cane-haul road. . . . We were glad we took sweaters and rain jackets. During December, January, and February we needed them quite often, especially when it rained at an altitude of 4,000 feet. I could have used a pair of leather hiking boots on some of the rocky, muddy trails. It was 41° Fahrenheit one night at Kokee State Park" (Jack and Ruth Phillips, Summerland, B.C., Canada). . . . "While driving to Kokee, I picked up a young man with a tight necklace who said that 'he lives in the wild part of Kauai,' which he reached by a two-day hike from Kokee Camps. He gets supplies by boat. I asked him if he owned land there, but he said the land didn't belong to anyone. I asked him why he lives there. He said, 'Because it's like the Garden of Eden, with fruits and flowers'" (Mark Terry, Honolulu, HI.).

"We drove on from Kalalau Lookout for about one mile of paved road to the **Puu O'Kila Lookout,** about a third around the canyon rim, from where the view of the ocean far below is completely different. The trail to **Pihea,** along with four other trails, starts from here" (Mrs. Parker Hollingsworth, Pacific Grove, Calif.). . . . "Definitely drive beyond Kalalau Lookout to the **Puu O'Kila Lookout.** This was the most spectacular view of our trip. The beauty and silence of the Na Pali Cliffs and coast from this point cannot be described—as we reached the lookout, a rainbow was forming over the cliffs! There's a narrow ridge trail that lets you see the cliffs from many angles—it was easy to walk, but muddy in spots" (Debra J. Tait, Burlington, Mass.).

"Polihale Beach is not good for swimming, but it's a marvelous picnic-sketching-walking beach. There are long vistas of white sand, cliffs coming down to the ocean, fire pits, picnic pavilions—and no one there. Camping is allowed farther on. Go past Kekaha on Hwy. 50; when 50 goes left at the intersection, turn right on the narrow, paved road. Turn left at the HVB marker that reads 'Polihale Sacred Springs,' and follow the dirt road through the sugarcane field five miles to the beach" (Mrs. J. C. Chognard, Menlo Park, Calif.). . . . **Polihale Beach Park** was gorgeous—just enough people to feel safe. We didn't know what we would find at the end of that long, dusty road, but it was *definitely* worth the drive" (Cheryl Reese and Becky Gardner, New Richmond, Wisc.).

THE ISLAND OF HAWAII

1. HILO
2. BETWEEN HILO AND KONA
3. KAILUA-KONA

Ever hear of a tropical island with black beaches, snow-capped mountains, cedar forests, and one of the largest cattle ranches in the world? This is **Hawaii,** twice as large as all the other Hawaiian Islands combined (4,030 square miles), the orchid capital of America, and the residence of Pele, the goddess of volcanoes, who still stages some spectacular eruptions every couple of years. Islanders invariably refer to it as the Big Island, although it is sometimes called the Orchid Island or the Volcano Island; all the names are appropriate, and all suggest part of the fascination of this astonishing continent in miniature. To know the 50th state, you must know the island of Hawaii.

Like all the neighbor islands, the Big Island is more expensive for the budget tourist than Oahu; nevertheless, you should be able to stay fairly close to your $60-a-day budget. Your car rental—unless it's split up three or four ways—is your biggest expense here, for driving distances are sizable, especially from one side of the island to the other (about 100 miles).

Hawaii is about 200 miles southeast of Honolulu, and either Hawaiian or Aloha Airlines will take you to **Hilo** on the east or to **Kailua-Kona** on the west in roughly half an hour. You can also fly directly to or from Kona from the West Coast. Which city should you choose as your first stop? We've done it both ways, and our considered opinion is that it doesn't make a particle of difference. Let your itinerary and the airline schedules—the ease with which you can make connections to the next island on your agenda—be the determining factor. Hilo, the only real city on the island and the second largest in our 50th state, is the takeoff point for the imposing Volcanoes National Park and the lava-scarred Puna area. Hilo has been experiencing a slump as of late, but it still has its own gentle charm. Kona is fishing and the beach. From either you can drive across the island and see all the sights. We prefer to stay in one hotel in Hilo and one in Kona, but it's possible to make one side of the island your base if you don't mind long drives (please limit your driving to daytime hours for safety!). Read up on the hotels, restaurants, and nightlife in each area in this chapter, the particular sights in the next, and you'll know just where you want to stay and for how long.

U-DRIVES

Most agencies on the Big Island offer a flat rate with unlimited mileage—you buy the gas. You have your choice of the trusty and popular inter-island outfits like **Alamo, Dollar, Budget,** etc., whose main offices are all in Honolulu (see Chapter V,

"Transportation Within Honolulu," for details), or local agencies like **Phillip's U-Drive** (tel. in Hilo, 935-1936; in Kona, 329-1730), whose rates can begin at $19.95 for small cars, $29.95 for larger ones. **Sunshine of Hawaii Rent-A-Car Systems,** (tel. in Hilo, 935-1108; in Kona, 329-2926), offers standard compacts at $20.95 daily, four-door compact automatics with air conditioning for $25.95. Rates are slightly lower in summer. They also have a toll-free number: 800/367-2977. Advance reservations are a good idea (a must in peak seasons); other times you may be able to get your best deal by careful on-the-spot shopping.

One of your biggest expenses if you're driving from Hilo to Kona or vice versa will be the drop charge; it is usually a hefty $45 from Hilo to Kona or $30 from Kona to Hilo. The cheapest way to avoid it is to take the county bus which crosses the island for a cost of $6 (see details, below), then rent a car in Kona if necessary. That way, however, you might miss the sightseeing en route.

1. Hilo

ARRIVAL IN HILO

You'll know why it's called the Orchid Island as soon as you arrive at General Lyman Field: rain may be helping those orchids to grow. But don't despair; it's just a "Hawaiian blessing" and probably won't last long. Nobody in Hilo lets a little drizzle interfere with comings and goings. (In winter an occasional rainstorm will hit this part of the island harder than any other.) There's no public transportation into town, so pick up your car or get a cab (about $4) to take you to your hotel.

BUSES

For all practical purposes, you're going to need a car in Hilo, even though there is a city bus system. It's limited; however, the **Hele-On** bus does make two trips a day around town, one early in the morning, one in midafternoon. You can ask for the bus schedule at your hotel or call the Mass Transportation Agency (MTA) at 935-8241. Within both the Hilo and Kona areas, **Dial-A-Ride Transportation Service** is available weekdays from 7am to 3pm. This service, which includes accommodations for disabled and nonambulatory persons, provides "curb to curb" transportation service other than the fixed route and schedule service; it must be requested one day in advance. For information and reservations, call 961-3148 in Hilo, or 323-2085 in Kona.

MTA also provides island-wide public transportation bus service with buses operating Monday through Saturday, and fares ranging from 75¢ to $6 per ride. Bus routes connect Hilo with Kailua-Kona, Waimea, Honokaa, Pahoa, and Volcanoes National Park, among others. Again, call MTA at 935-8241. Bus schedules are sometimes available at the **State Visitor Information booths** in the airport, and usually at the **Hawaii Visitors Bureau** in the Hilo Plaza Building, Suite 104, 180 Kinoole St. (tel. 961-5797). Mrs. Lei Branco is the helpful lady to contact.

HOTELS IN HILO

Every now and then you come across a little hotel where you know you could comfortably settle down for a long, long time. Such a place is the **Dolphin Bay Hotel,** at 333 Iliahi St., Hilo, HI 96720 (tel. 935-1466), in a quiet residential neighborhood of Hilo, that's just a four-block walk to town. The 18-studio unit meanders in and out of a lush tropical garden resplendent with papayas, breadfruits, bananas, and the like; you are invited to step right outside your room and pick your breakfast! The rooms are modern, quite large, and nicely furnished, with full kitchens and large tub-shower combinations in the bathrooms. The standard studios, which rent for $31 single, $42 twin, sleep one or two comfortably. The superior studios, usually with a twin and queen-size bed (plus a built-in Roman-style tub!), are larger and can easily sleep three; these are $42 single, $53 double. There's also a marvelous honeymoon room with an open-beamed ceiling and a large lanai for $53; and some really spacious one- and two-bedroom apartments, perfect for families, are $63 for the one-bedroom, $74 for the two-bedroom, $8 for each extra person. Favorable weekly rates are available. Since the hotel is near Hilo Bay, a cooling breeze keeps the units comfortable all year long. Manager John Alexander dispenses the same kind of warmth and hospitality that have made this one of our best island finds over the years. He and his staff will map out tours, arrange trips, and advise on the best restaurants. Write or phone in advance if you can, since the guests who come back each year—many from Canada and the Midwest—keep this place hopping. Lots of readers' hurrahs for this one, even though there is no pool (see the Readers' Selections, ahead).

The **Hilo Seaside Hotel** (formerly the Hilo Hukilau Hotel; tel. 935-0821), near Hilo Bay, has long been a pleasant place to stay. The local branch of the kamaaina-owned Sand & Seaside Hotels (there are others in Kona, Kauai, and Maui) has attractive rooms (most with air conditioning) with lanais, TVs, and phones—rooms that overlook either the freshwater swimming pool, a fish pond, or lush tropical gardens. The hotel has been attractively renovated, and now the lobby is decorated with contemporary tiles and Oriental hardwood floors. Wood fenceposts, Polynesian murals, and tikis permit you to forget the mainland. There's a dining room and cocktail lounge. Singles and doubles are $58 superior, $61 deluxe. An additional person is charged $12. A hotel-and-car package for two persons goes for $73 superior, $77 deluxe, and includes hotel room and a Budget Rent-A-Car. The toll-free phone to Hawaii is 800/367-7000, or write to Sand & Seaside Hotels, 2222 Kalakaua Ave., Suite 714, Honolulu, HI 96815.

Uncle Billy's Hilo Bay Hotel, right on the ocean at 87 Banyan Dr. (tel. 935-0861), is a happy place, owned and operated by a Hawaiian family. It's run on "Hawaiian time" and the pace is leisurely; you can feel that pleasant Polynesian paralysis setting in the moment you step into the South Seas lobby, with fishnets and tapa-covered walls to remind you where you are. All rooms have air conditioning and cable television plus private lanai. The higher-priced rooms are huge: two double beds look lost in the room. During the summer season, from April 1 to December 15, standard rooms are $59, single or double; superiors are $64; deluxe $69; and oceanfront $74. A studio suite with kitchen is $69. Room, car, and continental-breakfast packages for two are available for $74 standard, $79 superior, $84 deluxe, $89 oceanfront; studio suites with kitchen, $84; prices go up $10 in·winter. Most rooms face a tropical garden that leads to a path to the swimming pool, next to the ocean on Hilo Bay. Uncle Billy's Fish & Steak Restaurant, right in the hotel, is a fun place for food and entertainment (see ahead). For toll-free reservations, call 800/367-5102 direct to Hawaii, or write to 87 Banyan Dr., Hilo, HI 96720.

Worlds away from the pleasantly hokey tourist world of Banyan Drive is the **Hilo Hotel,** at 142 Kinoole St., Hilo, HI 96720 (tel. 961-3733), a business-person's hotel in the center of town. The outside is very pleasant, with lava-rock walls, a large swimming pool, spacious gardens, and the excellent Fuji Restaurant for Japanese food and drinks, where the locals like to gather. The hotel rooms, all of which have a refrigerator, telephone, and a bath with stall shower, are clean and adequate, but nothing fancy. The price is right, though: standard rooms are $32 single or double, deluxe rooms, with TV are $39. Complimentary continental breakfast is served every morning from 7 to 10am. The hotel is very proud of its newer Niolopa Wing, which offers extraordinary value for a family; there are six very large (800 to 900 square feet) two-bedroom apartments, fully furnished, equipped with TV, all utilities and three telephones per unit, all for the price of $68 for up to four guests. Inquire about their room-and-car packages. Free continental breakfast is available, and there is plenty of parking space. The Hilo Hotel is the kind of place where you might find the members of a neighbor island high school baseball team spending

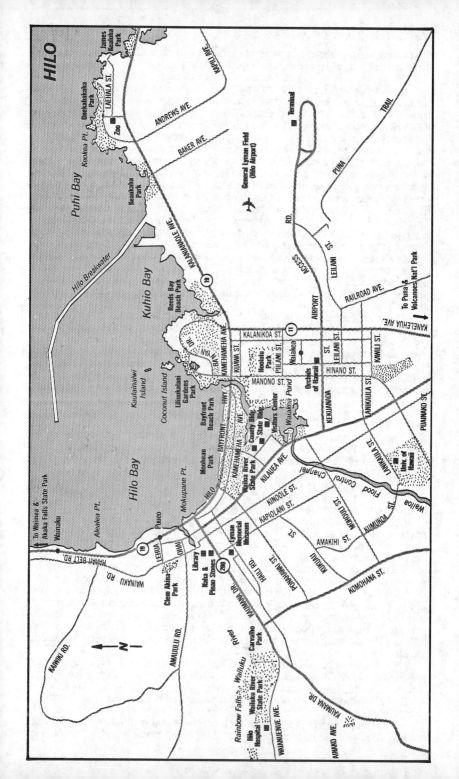

their vacation. At night, it's so pleasant to sit on the rocking chairs on the porch and listen to the tranquil Japanese music piped into the lobby.

When the lush, luxurious Sheraton Waiakea Village Hotel closed a few years ago, there was some question as to what would happen to the property. The result has been good news for the budget tourist. Half of the original 10 buildings, containing 149 studios and one-bedroom units, has been turned into the **Waiakea Villas Hotel,** 400 Hualani St., Hilo, HI 96720 (tel. 961-2841). The other half is long-term apartment rentals (at least one month). These handsome Polynesian-style buildings are set amidst 14½ acres of meandering waterways and lagoons in a giant tropical garden. If the hotel had better service and the grounds were better maintained, we'd be happier, but this is still excellent value in a lovely setting. Rooms, which are very large, are furnished in the island style, and private lanais all overlook either garden or waterways. Each room (except the standard) has a kitchenette (refrigerator, stove, burners, but no small appliances), color TV, and air conditioning. There's a swimming pool and tennis court on the grounds, as well as two restaurants: John Michael's for American food and Miyo for authentic Japanese cooking in a scenic setting. Rates for a standard studio, with a king-size bed or two double beds is $40; a superior studio with a king or two double beds and kitchenette is $50; a deluxe, large studio with king-size bed is $60; a one-bedroom suite is $80; and a honeymoon suite is $125. There is a charge of $5 for a phone; $9 for each additional person; $5 for a crib; no charge for children under 11 if no additional bed is required.

The cheapest lodgings in Hilo? They can be found at the **Lanikai Hotel,** 100 Puueo St., Hilo, HI 96720 (tel. 935-5556), which is not exactly the kind of place you'd write home about, but is acceptable. Of the 34 rooms, some have microwave ovens and refrigerators; none have TVs or phones; many share a bath with two or three other rooms. Singles go from $20 to $25 a night, doubles from $28 to $35; weekly rates are $95 single, $120 double; monthly, $275 single, $340 double. The setting is very pretty, a short walk from town, and the rooms look out on a pleasant, grassy slope.

BED & BREAKFAST RESERVATION SERVICES

The Big Island is rich in bed-and-breakfast accommodations, and more are cropping up all the time. We'll tell you about many of these as we travel to specific locations, but right now you should know about **My Island,** P.O. Box 100, Volcano, HI 96785. My Island was created by Gordon Morse (who used to run Holo Holo Campers) and his wife, Joann. When Morse closed the camper business a few years ago and thought he might retire, he started renting out a few rooms in his century-old Connecticut-style farmhouse in Volcano. One guest led to another and soon the Morses added three more rooms, two neighboring houses became annexes, and still the calls came. That's how My Island came into being; it now offers rentals in 19 houses, plus an all-island reservation system. Here's how it works: You call the Morses (the whole family is in the business) on their hotline—967-7710 or 967-7216—any time between 6am and 10pm Hawaiian time, and tell them what your wishes are. Morse likes to urge people to really move around the Big Island, experiencing the different climates and atmospheres of the various districts, from Hilo to Puna to Volcano, from Kailua to Waimea to Honokaa, and then some. Accommodations range from "nice mom-and-pop houses" to a splendid plantation-manager's estate with a pool and solarium set amid acres of jungle. Prices range from $25 to $45 single, $20 to $65 double, depending on location and what Morse calls "the jazziness of the place." FAX: 967-7110.

Barbara Campbell, who for 20 years was director of sales and marketing at the prestigious Kona Village Resort, retired recently and has turned her talents to setting up the Big Island's newest B&B reservation service called "Hawaii's Best B&Bs." She handles only upscale B&B lodgings, each home selected for its distinctive personality, attention to details, and the warm hospitality offered by its host. Her selections range from the most traditional host-home rooms to splendid private country cottages. Eventually, her service will cover all major islands. Daily rates go from $65 to $120 double; weekly rates, usually at 10% discount, are available at most properties. For more information about these hidden gems, write Barbara Campbell, P.O. Box 563, Kamuela, HI 96743. For reservations, phone toll free 800/262-4550.

Bed & Breakfast Hawaii, an all-island reservation system, also has many locations on the Big Island. Rates start at $30 single, $40 double. Write to Bed & Breakfast Hawaii, P.O. Box 449, Kapaa, Kauai, HI 96746, enclose $8.50 for a copy of their directory of homes and apartments called *B&B Goes Hawaiian.* You may call them toll free at 800/733-1632. The local phone is 822-7771. FAX: 822-2723.

BED AND BREAKFAST IN THE HILO AREA

You'll be warmly welcomed and made to feel right at home at **Hale Kai,** Evonne Bjornen's bed-and-breakfast place at 111 Honalii Pali, Hilo, HI 96720 (tel. 935-6330). And what a home it is, a superb double-decker house with an entire wall of glass overlooking Hilo Bay and the island's best surfing spot, Honalii Surfing Beach. Guests have use of the magnificent living room looking out over the waterfront, and just beyond it, a pool with Jacuzzi and comfy lounge chairs. Downstairs are three bedrooms plus a family room; they are beautifully furnished with either a king- or queen-size bed, each with its own bath and color cable TV. There's a lovely room upstairs with a queen-size bed, and, for special occasions—weddings, anniversaries, and such—Mrs. Bjornen will rent her master suite, with its own sitting room, sunken tub, king-size bed, atrium, and giant screen TV. That room is $95 a night; the others are $65 to $70. Minimum stay is two nights. Ms. Bjornen, a friendly woman who truly enjoys having guests in her home, likes to whip up fabulous breakfasts, and often puts her telescope out on the porch so that guests can watch the volcano when it's in action! Staying here would be like being on a lovely retreat—you may forget to go out and explore Hilo. Of this place, readers Brenda and Darrell Baker of Silver Springs, Maryland, wrote us: "We were welcomed like old friends at Evonne Bjornen's B&B. Her home was absolutely beautiful, and the breakfasts were the best we had on our vacation. We would highly recommend Evonne's great hospitality and lovely home to your readers."

Four miles north of Hilo, on Hwy. 19, **Our Place–Papaikou's B&B,** would make another charming place to stay close to Hilo town. Sharon Miller, a former Rolfer, and Ouida Taherne, M.D., both gave up busy life-styles in California and Mississippi to move to Hilo and set up a guesthouse here. They've found a lovely cedar-paneled home overlooking a stream, set amidst lush tropical vegetation. The "Great Room," splendid with its cathedral ceiling, has a library, fireplace, grand piano, and cable TV-VCR—all of which guests are invited to enjoy. Four rooms share a common lanai that looks out over Kupuu Stream. Two doubles rent for $45; a loft goes for $50; and a master bedroom with private bath is $55. Miller and Taherne are excellent cooks (they do complete breakfasts) and are friendly, helpful hosts—and their prices are right. Call them at 964-5250 or write to them at P.O. Box 469, Papaikou, HI 96781.

RESTAURANTS IN HILO

Hilo doesn't have much in the way of sophisticated bistros, so when one does open, it's likely to get raves. That's what's happened with **Lehua's Bay City Bar & Grill** at 11 Waianuenue Ave. in the downtown area (tel. 935-8055), the kind of place you'd expect to find in, say, San Francisco rather than sleepy little Hilo. But there it is, attractively decorated in subdued tones of grays, with plantings in the center of the room, mobiles hanging on the ceiling, and a big bar up front, from which flow some of the best margaritas in town. Owners Mark Himmel and Larry Johnson describe their cuisine as "East meets West with an island flair"—and that's just what it is. Most everything is homemade; only the freshest ingredients are used, seasonings and sauces are imaginative, and since many dishes are marinated and charbroiled, it's possible to eat food that's light as well as delicious. And prices are reasonable. There are some wonderful appetizers at dinner, like charbroiled prawns marinated in lime juice and served with a dill cucumber sauce, the chicken yakitori on skewers, and the summer rolls—charbroiled chicken wrapped in lettuce and mint leaves, in the Thai style, $1.50 to $5.25. Homemade soups are a good bet, as are the salads and burgers; a charbroiled chicken burger is a house specialty at $6.75. All entrees are accompanied by delicious charbroiled garlic toast, a garden salad (the creamy garlic dressing is very good), a hot vegetable and a choice of fries, baked potato, or white rice. They include barbecue ribs, charbroiled chicken, mixed grill (charbroiled prawns and chicken with papaya salsa and paniolo ribs), catch of the day, and porterhouse steak, from $9.95 to about $14.95. Spinach lasagne, $8.50, and the sauté medley of fresh vegetables, $7.95, will keep the vegetarians in the crowd contented.

Lunch offers similar entrees at lower prices, $6.25 to $12.95, soup-and-sandwich specials of the day, burgers, a very popular chicken with papaya salad, and the hearty Bay City Saimin; it's the classic noodle dish, but topped with charbroiled chicken, shrimp and fresh vegetables, $6.95. Desserts are homemade and super: Save some room for either the White Russian mousse or the chocolate banana cake, $2.95 and $3.50. On Friday and Saturday nights, Lehua's turns into a lively spot for Hawaiian entertainment, which continues late, usually until about 2am.

Lehua's Bay City Bar & Grill is open every day except Sunday, serving food continuously, lunch from 11am to 5pm, dinner from 5 to 10pm.

One of our favorite Hilo eateries is **Kay's,** 684 Kilauea Ave. (tel. 969-1776), which serves just about the best barbecued chicken we've ever tasted, anywhere. Local friends put us on to this large, Korean-style family restaurant, full of local color: screaming babies, people reading the newspapers, Formica tables, orange-leather booths. But never mind. The atmosphere is friendly, the staff is charming, and the food is ridiculously inexpensive, and so good that you'll want to come back more than once. The house specialty is the Korean crispy fried chicken, which we found a bit heavy; but go with the barbecued chicken—it's boned, flattened, marinated in a very light shoyu sauce in the Korean manner, and simply delicious. All dinners include hot rice, miso soup, vegetable of the day, and four kinds of kim chee. You can order your meal either small or large (we found small to be adequate). One choice— of Korean barbecued beef, kal bi, barbecued chicken, fried fish, shoyu pork, etc.—is $4.95 small, $5.95 for a full order; two choices are $5.95 and $6.95; three choices, $6.95 and $7.95. Don't be misled by the sign reading "Kay's Lunch Counter"; Kay now serves dinner, too, thank heavens. Breakfast and lunch are on from 5am to 2pm; then dinner, from 5 to 9pm. Kay's is open every day except Monday.

For a true taste of Japan, the place to go is the **Nihon Cultural Center,** 123 Lihiwai St. (tel. 969-1133), overlooking Hilo Bay and lovely Liliuokalani Gardens. The Nihon Restaurant houses an art gallery, a traditional tea room, an auditorium for cultural events, and at the heart of it all, a restaurant where traditional Japanese chefs ply their art. Of course there is a sushi bar—the menu describes these dainty morsels of fish and rice as "health foods"—and a dining room for regular Japanese meals. Sashimi, tempura, and tonkatsu lunches start at $4.50. Lunch specials are $6.75 and include a choice of two items and accompaniments. Dinners run from $5 to $14 and include the traditional sukiyaki. Complete combination dinners feature tempura, sashimi, and beef teriyaki. Traditional Japanese soup, pickled vegetables, and rice accompany the meals. Of course there's saké or Japanese beer to wash down your meal, and homemade green-tea ice cream for dessert. Lunch is served from 11am to 2pm, dinner from 5 to 9pm; the sushi bar is open from 11am to 2pm and 5 to 9pm. Closed Sunday. Reservations are advised.

You can relax in a very pretty setting at the **K.K. Tel Restaurant,** 1550 Kamehameha Hwy., between Hilo and the airport (tel. 961-3791). **K.K.** stands for the late K. Kobata, who was Japanese, and the food is mostly Japanese, with some American specialties. Lunch is an especially good buy; our favorites are the complete Japanese ozen lunches, served on a lacquered tray. With your main course at $6.50 to $7.25 —perhaps tonkatsu or beef teriyaki—come miso soup, rice, pickled vegetables, mukozuke, raw fish or salad, and tea. Seafood salads, sandwiches, and noodle dishes are also available. Dinners are a bit more expensive but still a good buy: Beef sukiyaki on the Japanese menu is about $9. American-style seafood and steak dishes start at around $8. If there are at least six of you, call for reservations to sit in one of the pretty ozashiki rooms; from here you'll see the authentic Japanese rock garden and pool. The bar begins dishing out free pupus from 11am.

There's another K.K. restaurant that you should know about. At 413 Kilauea Ave. (tel. 935-5216), is **K.K.'s Place,** a Japanese-American fast-food operation, sparklingly clean, and offering tasty plate lunches—with two entree choices like fried fish, chicken hekka, pork cutlet, and meat cutlet—from $3.50 to $4.50. Meals are served day or night at the same price. A good place to remember whenever you feel hungry and in a hurry.

What brings the Mercedeses and other fancy cars to the modest Puainako Town Center? Although not many tourists know of it, the Chinese population has discovered the **Ting-Hao Mandarin Restaurant** (tel. 959-6288), and they come to enjoy the wizardry of Ting Cheng, the master chef recently of Taiwan, whose repertoire includes some 200 banquet dishes. He cooks Peking, Mandarin, Szechuan, and Cantonese style so there is quite a variety on the menu. Everything we've tried—and we've dined here many times—has been special. And they never use MSG! Corn egg-drop soup is unusual and subtly flavored; pot stickers, those tasty dumplngs that are both steamed and fried (on one side), are a great beginning to your meal. Outstanding main courses in the Mandarin style include shredded pork with fungus and golden egg, shredded pork with garlic sauce (watch out, it's hot!), and the eggplant with garlic sauce, each $5. Unusual and delicious, too, are the Kung Pao ika (that's cuttlefish) with spicy paprikas, $7; and the Kung Pao shrimp with spicy paprikas, $8; the minced chicken with lettuce, $9; and the chicken with cashew nuts, $6. Most of the entrees are inexpensive and hearty enough to fill you up for many hours. In fact, we usually find the portions here so generous that we wind up taking containers back to our kitchenette apartment for the next day's lunch. At lunch, between 10:30am to 2:30pm Monday to Saturday, there are four daily specials, served with spareribs or an egg roll, for $4. Vegetarians can enjoy a number of good dishes. Ting-Hao is a large, very clean restaurant, simply decorated, with fans and prints on the wall. Service is helpful and friendly; there's a warm, family feeling here. Dinner is served from 4 to 9pm daily, from 4:30pm on Sunday. Puainako Town Center is past the airport, and not far from Prince Kuhio Plaza; the restaurant is near the big Sack 'n' Save store.

Although it's one of the city's newer dining establishments, **Restaurant Osaka,** 762 Kanoelehua St. (tel. 961-6699), is fast becoming a Hilo tradition, and it's easy to understand why. From the clean, modern decor and cozy family atmosphere to the varied menu, very tasty food, and generous island portions, Restaurant Osaka is simply a very good place to eat. At lunch, you have your choice of sandwiches, American dishes, noodle dishes, and a full Japanese menu of tempuras, teriyakis, ginger pork, chicken or beef tofu, and fried fish, priced from $4.50 to $5.65, all served with soup, rice, tsukemono, and tea. Prices for sushi are the same at lunch and dinner (from $5.25 to $8.25); the nigiri we tried was delicious. Dinner offers similar bargains. Complete meals start at $4.65 on the American menu, at $5.25 on the Japanese menu. Children's combination dinners are $4.75. Be sure to try the exotic desserts: pumpkin mousse, peanut-butter fudge pie and frozen New York cheesecake with blueberry topping are a treat at $2. If you're in a hurry, the take-out sushi is reasonably priced: $14.50 buys you 34 pieces of a varied selection, great for a picnic or a meal at home.

Restaurant Osaka is open for breakfast, lunch, and dinner, from 7am to 9pm Sunday through Wednesday, to 11pm Thursday, Friday, and Saturday; the bar, which serves free pupus with drinks, stays open every day until 11pm.

Want to eat the freshest fish in Hilo? Then head for **The Seaside** at 1790 Kalanianaole Ave. (tel. 935-8825), a few miles out of Hilo town in the Kaukaha area, where the mullet or aholehole or rainbow trout on your plate will be taken out of the pond when you call to make your reservation! The Seaside, highly respected by Hilo people for years and virtually unknown to tourists, is actually a fish farm, and the Japanese family in charge have been cultivating fish here for over 50 years, in the same way that mullet was historically fattened in special fish ponds for the alii of old

Hawaii. They catch fingerlings from the Wailoa River, keep them in pens for six months, then release them into the pond for almost five years. Rainbow trout thrive in Hawaii's warm waters and take less time to mature—just a year. The 30-acre pond, leased from the state, is set amidst 50 acres of land in a rural area. Susuma Nakagowa, a former research entomologist with the U.S. Department of Agriculture, took over the fish farm from his parents; now, he and his wife and son Colin, the restaurant manager, are in charge. If you come before dinnertime, while it is still light, somebody will be able to show you around and explain the operation to you. (The place is a favorite stop for school groups and those interested in aquaculture.) Then on to the simple dining room where you can have your fish prepared in the traditional way, steamed in ti leaves, with onion slices and lemon juice, or fried. The menu is quite simple: for dinner, there's mullet or trout at $11.50; a combination of any fish with chicken, $12.50; chicken only, $9.50; a combination of one steamed fish and one fried fish (perhaps the best choice for first-timers), $12.50. At lunchtime, the fish is $8.50, chicken $5.95, and combination plates, $10.50 and $12.50. Lunch includes rice, vegetable salad, and beverage. Bottled wine is available. And for dessert—homemade apple pie. This place is not fancy, but the fish is the freshest, and coming here is a real experience in nontourist, old-time Hawaii. Be sure to call first, as they serve only when they have fish available. A nice adventure for the kids, too.

Lunch is served from 11am to 1pm, dinner from 5 to 8pm.

Overlooking the Ice Pond at Reed's Bay is one of Hilo's most upbeat restaurants. It's **Harrington's,** 135 Kalanianaole St., near Banyan Drive (tel. 961-4966). There's an atmosphere of casual elegance here in the open-air dining room and lounge, a lively mood, and delicious food. Plan on this one for a splurge meal, since most entrees—like mahimahi forestière, New York steak, chicken marsala, sautéed scallops, and the like—are in the $12 to $18 range (they are accompanied by rolls, soup, choice of salads and starch). However, there is a way to eat here inexpensively, albeit lightly. Ask to be seated in the lounge rather than the main dining room, and along with your beer or drink you can order from the appetizer and side-dish menu, which means that items like deep-fried calamari strips, mushrooms tempura, etc., ranging from $2.75 to $6.95, will be served cut up, pupu style. You could even have a stuffed potato for $1.75 and a house salad (Caesar or pasta or tossed greens) for $2.75. Be sure to make reservations if you do sit in the dining room, since this is a very, very popular scene. Open nightly from 5:30pm.

Note: Harrington's also has a restaurant on the west side of the island. Harrington's at Kawaihae Center in Kawaihae overlooks the harbor, offers the same menu, open-air dining, and a great sunset view. It's open nightly from 5:30 (tel. 882-7997).

Don's Grill, at 485 Hinano St. (tel. 935-9099), near the Waiakea Villas Hotel, has everything a good family restaurant should have: It's large, comfortable, inexpensive, and the food is fresh and good. Owner Don Hoota has won a large local following for this place. Tuck into one of the booths, and treat yourself to a complete dinner—honest!—from just $4.50 to $6.95 (only the seafood platter and New York steak at $7.95, are higher); along with your main course of rotisseried chicken, (the house specialty), or barbecue ribs, or filet of fish, you get a choice of soup or salad, a starch, hot vegetables, rolls, and a beverage. They also have good sandwiches, burgers, plus local favorites like loco moco, saimin, and homemade chili; it's hard to go wrong. Don serves his good food from 10:30am to 9pm daily except Sunday.

Reuben's Mexican Food, 336 Kamehameha Ave., across from the waterfront (tel. 961-2552) is a real local hangout. Aside from its shocking-pink color scheme and Mexican murals on the wall, it has little in the way of decor, but it's large (there's plenty of breathing room between the tables), has a big bar, and the food is good. Reuben's is run by Chef Reuben and Sue Villanova (he's from Mexico, she's from Hilo). Our appetizer of nachos ($2.75) was hot and tasty; so was our chicken flautas (a flour tortilla with chicken, shredded lettuce, guacamole, and sour cream) combination plate for $7.50. Some 34 combination plates, which include beans and rice, run from $6 to $8. There are a few interesting house specialties, like gallina adovada (baked chicken), filete al mojo de ajo (grilled fish with garlic butter), and a crab salad, from $5 to $8. You'll find lots of local families here enjoying the food, the low prices, and the memorable margaritas. Open daily except Sunday from 11am to 9pm; same menu all day.

Downtown at 168 Keawe St. is another place the locals like very much: **Restaurant Satsuki** (tel. 935-7880). It's small, very clean, plain, and neat, with partitions and a screen dividing the room. Formica and vinyl chairs and tables. Might as well go with Satsuki's Special Teishoku; $5.75 at lunch, $6 at dinner, it includes any two choices of either fried shrimp, shrimp tempura, yakitori, pork teriyaki, beef teriyaki, or butterfish, served up with various side vegetables, plus soup, rice, and tea. Donburi dishes with soup, tsukemono, and tea, are $4.65 to $7.15. Open for lunch and dinner.

Another local place where you can't go wrong is the 10-table **Tomi Zushi,** 68 Mamo St., where $5 to $6 buys you a good Japanese dinner, in the company of lots of island people who are heartily lapping up the food. There is no attempt at decor here: walls are institutional green, and tables are just tables. You come for the food. Here's what the average $5 to $6 buys: a choice of any two main courses like fried shrimp Tokyo style, or shrimp or vegetable or fish tempura, accompanied by soup, pickled vegetables, rice, and tea. Plate lunches are under $4. Plan on this when you want to eat quickly, as it's no place to relax and visit. Tomi Zushi closes at 8:30pm and is open every day but Wednesday. Only dinner is served Sunday.

Hilo has a new Chinese restaurant that locals like a lot, and it's called, appropriately enough, **New China Restaurant,** 510 Kilauea Ave. (tel. 961-5677). It's large, pretty, traditionally decorated, with wood veneer tables; the food is fresh and tasty, and prices are appealingly low. Start with one of their soups, like shrimp with eggflower soup or scallop soup, $4 and $5. Sizzling platters are the specialty of the house, and servings are really generous: A delicious seafood sizzling platter is $5.50, chicken or duck sizzlers, $4 and $5. Seafood is well done, in dishes like the steamed butterfish with black-bean sauce at $6. You can't go wrong here. Open daily from 10am to 10pm.

Jimmy's Drive Inn, at 362 Kinoole St. (tel. 935-5571), is a popular place offering some of the best prices in town. The "drive inn" is misleading; you don't eat in your car but at clean chrome tables or at the counter. Japanese meals go from $4.95 to $7.25, and there are daily dinner specials like chicken-katsu, beef stew, fish tempura, breaded scallops, and captain's platter, which go from $5.45 to $7.25, quite a bargain considering that they are accompanied by rice, vegetables, and coffee or iced tea. On the regular menu, there are about half a dozen complete dinners and complete seafood dinners, most priced between $5 and $5.95; and these include such entrees as barbecued steak, liver and bacon, ahi, butterfish, and shrimp tempura, all accompanied by soup or salad, fries or rice, vegetable, bread, dessert, and beverage. Open from 8am to 9:30pm daily except Sunday.

At Prince Kuhio Shopping Plaza

You'll want to spend some time seeing Hilo's big, new multimillion-dollar Prince Kuhio Shopping Plaza out on Hwy. 11, and while you're at it, you can have some pretty good meals, too. Best bet is **Kow's Deli & Chinese Restaurant,** which looks like a cute coffee shop dressed up with large fans and Chinese prints on the wall. The food is excellent and inexpensive—most dishes are between $4 and $6— and all the favorites are here, like chicken with oyster sauce, shrimp Canton, beef broccoli, and a variety of noodle dishes (soup style), which are big local favorites. Chinese cookies and dem-sem are sometimes sold out front. *Note:* There are two more branches of the popular Kow's: one at Kaiko'o Hilo Mall, and another at 87 Kawailani St., corner of Kinoole. Local people love this one.

Also at Prince Kuhio is a pleasant **Woolworth's Restaurant,** which offers inexpensive meals on the order of roast turkey, crispy fried chicken, tempura shrimp platter, and beef stew island style, plus sandwiches, burgers, and breakfast and fountain specials. **Arby's,** a member of the popular chain, offers its roast beef sandwiches, plus good breakfast specials. There's a **Mrs. Field's Cookies** and an **Orange Julius.**

And the sparkling **Boomer's Fountain** is fun, decked out like a 1950s diner, with "I Like Ike" slogans and other memorabilia on the walls. It offers daily hot lunch specials, complete with rice and vegetables. Service is quick and efficient and prices go from $2.50 (for a fish burger) to $3.50. Ice-cream cones, milk shakes, and other fountain treats are popular here.

Eating at the Hotels

The popular **Hukilau Restaurant** in the Hilo Hukilau Hotel, Banyan Drive, is managing to hold the price line on three good meals a day. They have a lunch special every day at $3.45, which includes entree, salad bar, rice or potato; and at least a dozen à la carte entrees (filet of mahimahi steak, calf's liver, Reuben sandwich) are just $2.85 to $3.95. Dinner features two menus, seafood and regular. Most seafood dinners are priced $8.95 to $13.95 for the likes of salmon steak, fresh fried oysters, fresh abalone steak, rainbow trout, soft-shell crab, and fresh fish of the day, all served with soup of the day and salad bar. On the regular dinner menu, entrees go from $7.95 to $14.95 for the likes of pork chop, prime rib roast, teriyaki steak, and steak and lobster, again accompanied by soup-and-salad bar. Breakfast here is fun, too, especially when you have the pineapple hotcakes or french toast with macadamia nuts. The dining room is pleasant, and the staff has plenty of aloha.

For a traditional Japanese meal—and for an excellent bargain as well—count on **Restaurant Fuji**, in the Hilo Hotel, 142 Kinoole St. (tel. 961-3733). This is one of those gracious, relaxed places where you can really get comfortable; you can sit either at the tempura bar (where you watch your dishes simmer and sizzle), at the comfortably spaced tables in the dining room, or at tables with hibachi grills overlooking the pool. The hotel is owned by Japanese interests and caters to a Japanese clientele, so you can be sure the food is authentic. At lunchtime recently, we sampled the very good butterfish ($9.60), and the barbecued chicken and egg ($5.90) with green salad, soup, vegetables, rice, and tea. Dinner features a number of dishes for under $10, like the tasty yosenabe teishoku at $9.50, a mélange of seafood, chicken, and vegetable tempura at $9.70. Restaurant Fuji serves lunch from 11am to 2pm, dinner from 5 to 9pm, every day except Monday.

Meals on the Run

One of the most popular coffee shops in town is **Dick's** in the Hilo Shopping Center, a lively local place with sporting pennants on the walls. On the à la carte dinner menu, you could choose entrees like chicken cutlet, grilled fish filet, teriyaki steak Oriental, grilled pork chops, most in the $3.95 to $4.90 range, with New York –cut steak under $7. And along with your main course comes soup or salad, starch, rolls and butter. Lunch features burgers from $2.85, gourmet sandwiches like pastrami on French bread or steak sandwich for under $3.50—and homemade pies and cream pies for dessert for around $1! And there are daily lunch specials for $2.45 to $2.60. In addition, there are five weekday lunch and dinner specials under $3.50. Breakfast is inexpensive, too: You could have a complete breakfast of grilled mahimahi, with toast, and hash browns or rice, for $2.25. A local friend raves about the fried chicken and the rhubarb pie, but advises that you come early, as only one rhubarb pie is baked each day. Dick's serves all three meals, Monday through Saturday; on Sunday it's breakfast only, 7 to 10am.

If you're shopping at Kaiko'o Hilo Mall, behind the government buildings, you might want to stop in at the original **Kow's Deli** (see above, under Prince Kuhio Shopping Plaza). Hearty plate lunches and dinners feature entrees like roast duck, chicken broccoli, char siu, and sweet-and-sour spareribs, and run $3.35 to $4.95. Special breakfasts are $2.50; house specialties include homemade pork hash, crisp wonton, and hot steamed manapua. This place caters mostly to local people and is usually thronged with busy shoppers, so you know the values have to be good. Even if you're not eating here, you might want to stop by for some of those luscious Chinese pastries—wedding cake and black-bean cake—in the window. Kow's is open every day except Sunday, from 7:30am to 6:30pm.

Whenever we'd drive by **Cafe 100,** 969 Kilauea Ave., we'd notice huge lines of island people at the windows of this popular drive-in. We joined them one day and found out why: it's hard to spend more than $4.50 for a full hot lunch. Fried chicken, beef stew, breaded mahimahi, and teriyaki steak are all served with rice and potato-macaroni salad. Hiloans swear by the local favorite, which is reputed to have been invented here: loco moco, a hearty meal of a hamburger patty and fried egg on rice, topped with brown gravy; it's $1.25. They even have loco moco T-shirts! Chili and sandwiches of all kinds start at 85¢. Try their specialties: yummy mahi sandwiches and goody-goody sherbet. Good to remember when you're in a hurry and the traveler's checks are running low.

Ken's House of Pancakes, at the intersection of Hwy. 19 and Hwy. 11 (tel. 935-8711), serves breakfast 24 hours a day. That means that whatever time of day you're hungry for, say, macadamia-nut pancakes or fresh banana pancakes, or eggs Benedict or eggs with Scottish bangers or Portuguese sausage, Ken's will dish them up, and at very reasonable prices—from about $3 to $5. The restaurant, a Hilo tradition for many years, had just changed hands at the time of this writing, but word has it that the all-day breakfast menu will remain intact, and that many local dishes will be added for lunch and dinner. Prices will stay low. Pop by Ken's from midnight until 6am, and you'll be treated to an early brunch—all the pancakes, plus imaginative omelets with an international flair in the $3.95 to $5.95 range.

McDonald's of Hilo, at the corner of Haili and Ululani streets, is an enclosed, air-conditioned restaurant, with Hawaiian-designed stained-glass murals, and tile floors. . . . You'll find a familiar **Dairy Queen** at 317 Waia Nuenue Ave., just up from Kinoole Street. There's another Dairy Queen on Banyan Drive at the Kamehameha intersection. . . . You can get salads, spaghettis, sandwiches, and, of course, those thick and crusty pizzas at **Pizza Hut,** 233 Kilauea. . . . **Kentucky Fried Chicken** is just one block from Kaiko's Hilo Mall, at 348 Kinoole St. . . . There's a **Burger King** at 510 Kilauea Ave. . . . **Subway,** the attractive sandwich shop chain that bakes its own bread and serves up super subs, hot and cold, for low prices, has a sparkling new outlet at Puainako Town Center at 2100 Kanoelehua Ave.

Best bet at the Waiakea Kai Shopping Plaza, 88 Kanoelehua, is **T's Saimin Shop:** bright, sparkly clean, with nice booths and tables, and Japanese fans on the wall. In addition to saimin (fried saimin is $2.95), they also have a mahimahi plate at $4.75, teriyaki-beef sandwiches at $2.75, a variety of noodle dishes from $2.75 to $4.50, and regular meat sandwiches, from $3.75.

The most interesting restaurant in this Waiakea Square area is **Fiascos,** at 200 Kanoelehua Ave. (tel. 935-7666). It's done up attractively, with lots of plants and wood, and a lively, upbeat atmosphere. And the food (notwithstanding the rather precious menu descriptions depicting the journeys of one mythical Hans Fiasco), has been consistently good, and there are enough possibilities to appeal to a variety of tastes and budgets. Examples: appetizers ($2.25 to $6.95) include potato skins, nachos, "yummy drummies" (batter-fried chicken drumettes with hot BBQ sauce), and a fantastic baked brie, topped with macadamia nuts and served with fresh fruit and hot sourdough bread. Many Hilo folks swear by their salad bar entree; it's a bountiful table of fruits and vegetables, served with homemade dressings, $5.95 alone, $6.95 with soup, $2.95 with any meal. If you come here on a weekday between 11:30am and 2pm, you can have a choice of four soups and salad bar for $5.95. There are also lots of imaginative sandwiches, like the one they call Mary's Melt; it consists of snow crab liberally drenched in garlic butter, piled atop a toasted bun, and served with sharp melted cheddar. There's also a fresh fish sandwich every day. Hot entrees, served at both lunch and dinner, include many items from $5.25 to $8.25, like stir-fry chicken, herb chicken, country-fried steak, and kalbi ribs. And there are good pastas, too, including pasta Alfredo at $6.95. Desserts? Their strawberry crêpe filled with ice cream or their chocolate macadamia-nut mousse could be a meal in itself. Upstairs at **Fiascos,** a 1950s and 1960s dance club swings into action on Thursday, Friday, and Saturday nights, from 8:30pm to 2am. Fiascos is good fun and good food for the price. It's open daily from 11am to 11pm.

Bears' Coffee, that stylish little place (marble-topped tables indoors and out, hand-stenciled walls) that adjoins The Most Irresistible Shop in Hilo at 110 Keawe St. (tel. 935-0708) is also proving to be irresistible—so much so that its original menu of a variety of coffees and pastries keeps expanding: now they start the day (at 7am weekdays, 8am Saturdays) with breakfast items like "souffled eggs" (steamed light and fluffy on the espresso machine) and "egg busters" (eggs, cheese, and ham on English muffin), and offer deli and vegetarian sandwiches ($3.25 to $3.60), salads, designer bagels (create your own toppings), hot and cold soups, in addition to the original coffee and pastry menu, until closing at 5pm, weekdays, 4pm. What fun to indulge in coffee and espresso drinks like caffè latte or Mexican chocolate, not to mention the likes of carrot cake, lemon–poppy-seed coffee cake or raspberry cheesecake, plus their luscious chocolate brownies. You can also buy fresh-roasted coffee beans by the pound to take home. House coffee is 75¢ per cup, and pastries run $2.50 to $3. Bearvo! Closed Sunday.

THE NIGHT SCENE IN HILO

Nightlife is quieter than it used to be in Hilo, with the closing or conversion into condominium apartments of several major hotels. However, there's still enough to keep you busy making the rounds of some of the favorite places.

For an inexpensive, family-style evening in Hilo, try **Uncle Billy's Restaurant** at the Hilo Bay Hotel. The hotel and restaurant are owned and operated by Uncle Billy and his Hawaiian family, and each night at 6 there's a free hula show, a totally nonslick warm-hearted revue. After that, it's Hawaiian dinner music, from 7:30 to 9pm nightly. Dinners feature fish just caught in Hilo waters, from $14.95. Sandwiches are available for light eaters. . . . Watch the local papers for news of entertainment at the posh Hawaii Naniloa Hotel; name performers from Honolulu sometimes play the Crown Room. At their Karaoke Bar, which stays open from 11am until late at night, music to sing along to starts about 7pm.

If it's just drinks, music, and maybe dancing you're after, there are several good spots around Hilo. **Harrington's,** 135 Kalanianaole St., has a scenic location overlooking the Ice Pond at Reed's Bay. You can enjoy live entertainment in the lounge Tuesday through Saturday nights, and have reasonably priced appetizers and drinks in a wonderfully romantic setting. . . . Dance the Hilo night away at posh **Reflections Restaurant,** 101 Aupuni St., in the Hilo Lagoon Centre. They have a large dancing area, with live musical entertainment Tuesday to Saturday from 8pm on. Or watch sporting events on a 10-foot satellite TV screen. During their "Attitude Adjustment Hour"—now there's an interesting name for it—between 4 and 8pm weekdays, there are free pupus along with the drinks. . . . The upstairs area of **Hans Fiascos,** 200 Kanoelehua Ave., becomes a dance club on Thursday, Friday, and Saturday, from 8:30pm to 2am. Music of the 1950s and 1960s is featured.

KK Tei's Restaurant and Lounge, 1550 Kamehameha Ave., turns into a karaoke spot Wednesday through Saturday nights; you can sing along in English or Japanese, take your choice. . . . The plush **Hilo Hawaiian Hotel** has a **Menehuneland Lounge** with the little people scrambling all over the walls. It's Hawaiian music beginning every night at 5, then contemporary music from 8:30pm to closing. Local friends rave about the authentic Hawaiian show presented on Wednesday nights by Alberta and Alvin Kalina, who have their own hula halau. No cover, no minimum, and some of the best prices for beer and house wine in town. From 4 to 6pm, happy hour prices on domestic beer and house wine, plus free pupus. . . . In historic downtown Hilo, on 60 Keawe St., there's elegant **Roussells,** a French-Créole restaurant in a converted old bank. You can have cocktails there or after-dinner drinks nightly, perhaps treat yourself to some dark French-roast coffee, brewed right at your table, along with a traditional dessert like New Orleans bread pudding with a sweet whisky sauce; on weekends, there's usually jazz music and dancing, no cover or minimum, in the lounge. . . . There's no entertainment and scarcely any atmosphere at the **Hukilau Hotel** bar, but always a local crowd full of fun, a big TV screen, and drinks at some of the lowest prices in town. . . . When the bars close down, you can get some nourishment over at **Ken's House of Pancakes**

(see above), where they serve pancakes and omelets through the wee hours of the morning.

2. Between Hilo and Kona

In our next chapter we'll describe the drive from Hilo to the resort center of Kona, a trip you should take. Right now we'll tell you about some hotels and restaurants at which you might stop en route.

HOTELS, GUESTHOUSES, AND RESTAURANTS ON THE NORTHERN ROUTE

Forty-four miles north of Hilo on the northern, or Hamakua Coast, route, and not far from the cattle country of the Parker Ranch, is the venerable **Hotel Honokaa Club,** Honokaa, HI 96727 (tel. 775-0533), which has been serving local business people and hunters for over 50 years now. Undemanding types will find the $32 singles, $35 doubles with private bath and TVs possible. The hotel's inexpensive restaurant and bar are very popular with the local people. If you're driving through on a weekday, between 11am and 2pm you can get sandwich specials with salad bar for $4.35, or daily lunch specials from $4.75 to $6.50.

Two miles from the center of Honokaa, on the ocean side, is **Waipio Wayside,** one of the most charming new B&Bs to open in this area. Jacqueline Horne, a recent escapee from California's Silicon Valley, settled in these peaceful parts, found a 1938 sugar plantation home, and renovated and decorated it to express the charms of old Hawaii. Bordered by a white picket fence and set amidst 4½ acres of tropical fruit and vegetable gardens, the house overlooks sugarcane fields and the ocean far below. The outside deck with its Japanese furo surrounded by hammocks and the gazebo for sunset watching are popular spots; so, too, are the kitchen, where Jackie, a gourmet cook, often whips up special treats (she serves a full breakfast) and the living room with its 31-inch TV/VCR, where she might schedule a "Japanese film festival" complete with popcorn. There are five rooms, each beautifully decorated with antique furniture, Chinese rugs, and silk drapes hand-painted by a local artist. Two rooms at the front of the house, the Moon Room with a full-size bed and the Plantation Room with twin beds, share a bath and rent for $45 a night. The Garden Room, detached from the main house, has its own entrance and overlooks the anthurium and vegetable garden, banana trees, and the ocean; it has a full-size bed and shares a bathroom, also $45. At the back of the house is the Chinese Room, with its antique Chinese reclining barber's chairs; it overlooks the deck and gazebo, has a half-bath, and rents for $55. Our favorite is the Bird's-Eye Room at the back of the house, a spacious private bedroom suite with its own bath, blond wood paneling and a patchwork quilt on the bed. Double doors open onto the deck and a view of gardens, sugarcane fields, and ocean beyond; it rents for $65. A great spot for a peaceful retreat. Write Waipio Wayside, P.O. Box 840, Honokaa, HI 96727, or call toll free 800/833-8849. The local phone is 775-0275.

Searching for the perfect romantic hideaway? Search no more. We've found it 7 miles north of Honokaa, at **Hamakua Hideaway,** a charming home perched high on a cliff and affording magnificent views of breathtaking Waipio Valley and the dazzling ocean below. Kristan and Jim Hunt, a friendly couple who have built the home themselves, have also created two quite separate guest accommodations, one connecting to the main house, the other down the way a bit, out on the cliff. The Tree House Suite, which connects to the main house, is nestled into a mango tree, has sunshine and windows on all sides, a private bath, and a kitchen, and is beautifully furnished. It comes complete with its own TV and cassette recorder. Rates are $50 a night. The Cliff House, nestled beside a 50-foot waterfall, is more like a little house, with its own wood stove, a loft with a futon above, TV, complete kitchen, and a private bath with sunken tub. It rents for $60 a night. Weekly and monthly rates are available. Guests will have use of a swimming pool, which was under construction at the time of our visit. Both units have glorious views and as much privacy as one would wish. The Hunts' three tow-headed little boys, aged 3, 7, and 10, add to the overall charm. Write Hamakua Hideaway, P.O. Box 5104, Kukuihaele, HI 96727.

Remote and hardly populated Waipio Valley, which can only be reached by a four-wheel drive vehicle or by hiking down the steep cliffs, actually has two places where you might spend a night or two. It's like living in the jungle, with all its lush beauty—but also with the possibility of jungle rains. Tom Araki's **Waipio Hotel** has all of five rooms and one bath, and has absolutely no truck with such modern amenities as hot water, telephones, restaurants, or even electricity. A friend of ours, a very successful businesswoman in Honolulu, swears she'd rather spend her vacations here, at Tom Araki's $15-a-night hotel, than anywhere else. For reservations, write to Tom Araki or Waipio Hotel, 25 Malama Pl., Hilo, HI 96720, or phone 935-7466 in Hilo or 775-0368 in Waipio. You no longer have to bring your own sleeping bag: Linens and blankets are furnished.

Waipio Valley also offers a possible haven for incurable romantics who won't mind spending $125 a night for a home in the trees. **The Treehouse,** 30 feet up in a 60-foot monkeypod tree, faces a 1,000-foot waterfall, sleeps three, and even has a kitchen. A skylight offers moonlit views through the leaves. You can swim under the waterfall or in the ocean, about a 1½ mile walk from here. Hot furo baths are available in an adjoining building. Fresh fruits can be picked on nearby paths. If you have your own four-wheel drive vehicle, the rate goes down considerably. For details, write Linda Beech, Box 5086, Kukuihaele, HI 96727, or phone 775-7160.

From Honokaa, it's 15 miles on Hwy. 19 to Kamuela (or Waimea), heart of the Parker Ranch cattle kingdom. A good place to stay in this deliciously cool mountain town is the **Kamuela Inn** (tel. 885-4243), an old standby in this area that has been recently taken over by a new management and attractively renovated. All of the 21 rooms have color cable TV and private baths. Single or double rooms range from $44 to $55 without kitchen (the Chinese Room at $55 is quite handsome), from $66 to $72 for rooms with kitchens, which are well equipped with all utensils, even including rice cookers. Two penthouse suites are $72 each, or can be rented together for $118.80, which would give, say, a large family or two couples traveling together a nice arrangement; the front suite, which sleeps two on a queen-size bed, has an expansive mountain view, a full bath and a private lanai with wet bar; the rear suite has a full kitchen and bath and generous-size bedroom, which sleeps three with a king-size and a single bed. At the time of this writing, 10 more units were under construction. Eight will rent for approximately $55, double. There will also be two luxury suites, each with a king-size bed, two singles, a full kitchen, a full bath, and a lanai with hot tub. The price should be around $100 a night. Continental breakfast is free, served in a cheery coffee lounge with broad windows admitting the morning sun. Scenic grounds (there's a "bottlebrush" tree with red flowers that really look like bottle brushes) just outside the hotel and a friendly management are pluses here. Write to Kamuela Inn (attn: Earnest Russell, Manager), P.O. Box 1994, Kamuela, HI 96743. There are restaurants nearby and good swimming 12 miles away at Hapuna Beach Park.

Also very pleasant in this area is **The Parker Ranch Lodge,** a modern 20-unit motor hotel within walking distance of the Parker Ranch Center and all its sightseeing, shopping, and eating facilities. Horseback riding and golf are nearby, some excellent beaches a reasonable drive away. Each room boasts quality furnishings, attractive decor, color TV, and beamed ceiling. From this cool, 2,500-foot elevation you have a view of rolling green meadowlands and mountains. Prices, which include tax, are as follows: singles, with one king-size bed, are $62.36; doubles, with two queen-size beds, are $76.59; a single with kitchen, with one king-size bed, is $70.02; and a double with kitchen, with two queen-size beds, is $78.78. An additional person in the room is charged $8. For reservations, write The Lodge, P.O. Box 458, Kamuela, HI 96743 (tel. 885-4100).

Waimea Garden Cottages in Waimea has to be one of our very favorite places on the Big Island. This is the perfect rustic retreat, two elegant country cottages where you can live in graceful surroundings, do your own cooking if you wish, spend your time riding or hiking in the mountains, or swimming at Hapuna Beach or the Mauna Kea Beach Hotel, just eight miles down the road. (The hosts provide beach towels, back rests, and coolers for the beach.) Barbara and Charlie Campbell, a charming local couple, have created the cottages near their own home, incorporating some of the materials found on the site of an old Hawaiian homestead into a striking new architectural design. In the first cottage, a small foyer leads down a step or two to the main room, furnished in eucalyptus and other natural woods, with antique furniture, two single beds that can be made into a king, plus a futon, beautiful rugs, and wall hangings, and color TV, of course. Japanese robes hang in the bathroom. The second cottage has a living/sleeping area with a queen-size bed, wooden floors, country touches, a fireplace, TV, and radio. Not only are the kitchens in both cottages complete, but the refrigerators are filled with freshly picked local fruits and eggs taken from the chickens a few hours before. In fact, you are invited to pick your own limes, bananas, lemons, and oranges and gather your own eggs from the chickens right on the grounds! The Waiaka Stream meanders right behind the property. If you are lucky enough to get into this place, you're in for a treat: rates are $85 nightly, $550 a week, $15 a night for an additional person. There is a three-night minimum stay. Write to Barbara and Charlie Campbell, P.O. Box 563, Kamuela, HI 96743, or phone them at 885-4550.

Ask local people about the best restaurants in Waimea and the first name you're likely to hear is **Merriman's**. In fact, ask anybody on the Big Island the same question and you'll get the same answer. **Merriman's,** Opelo Plaza, Route 19 (tel. 885-6822), is rated four stars by just about everybody, and Peter Merriman, the young 35-year-old owner, is rapidly gaining as a reputation as one of the most innovative young chefs in the country. Stop by for a meal and see why. Merriman uses only the freshest and finest local products—like 10 different kinds of mangoes, each with a subtly different flavor, or white pineapples, or shellfish he may have gone diving for himself—to produce an imaginative, contemporary, and highly sophisticated cuisine. And the setting is lovely: a Hawaiian Art Deco room done in soft peach/green colors, with comfortable upholstered chairs, and many plants and flowers that create a light, airy feeling in the daytime. In the evening, the atmosphere is more intimate, with flickering candles on the tables highlighting the original paintings on the walls and the island memorabilia of the 1920s, '30s, and '40s.

At dinner, many of the dishes, especially the fresh fish, approach the $20-and-up mark, but you can still eat well on the low side of the menu, with such choices as the wonderful seafood cioppino at $17, the wok-charred marlin (blackened on the outside, sashimi inside) at $15, the Thai-style shrimp curry for $18.50, or the delicious herb-grilled chicken with peanut dipping sauce and star fruit for $14.50. A salad of fresh Waimea greens, a vegetable, and starch accompany all dishes. Among the appetizers and salads, roasted peppers with goat cheese is special, and so is the Caesar salad, done a little differently, with sashimi, at $5.50. Lunch is very reasonable and still of the same high-gourmet quality. We could happily make an entire meal of the bouillabaisse, its fresh fish, and shellfish piping hot in a saffron broth, $7.75. Or, try the salad niçoise, again with the distinctive Merriman difference—it is made with artichokes, potatoes, and grilled fish on a bed of tossed greens, $6.75. Smoked salmon and pasta salad, $8.50, is another treat. Desserts are great at both meals, like the fabulous chocolate mousse. With such a creative chef as Merriman, the menu changes frequently—but you can be sure it will be outstanding.

Merriman's serves dinner nightly from 5:30 to 9pm, lunch weekdays only, 11:30am to 1pm. Dinner reservations advised.

Another famous gourmet restaurant in Waimea is **Edelweiss** on Kawaihae Road (tel. 885-6800), a homey place with a European country feeling, seating only about 50 guests. So renowned has master chef-owner Hans Peter Hager's reputation become that there's usually a wait of an hour or so at dinnertime, and reservations are not taken. But it's usually not too crowded at lunchtime; just be sure you get there before 1:30pm or you will not be seated. Hans Peter's cuisine does not disappoint. The luncheon specialty of bratwurst and sauerkraut is $4.95; also popular is the Puu Haloa ranch burger at $5.75, or in a more continental mood, the sautéed chicken breast with champignons and Monterey Jack cheese, $6.50. Several light dinners are offered at $8.50; regular dinners go from $12.50 to $20 and more for the likes of chicken-liver omelet, roast duck bigarade, and calves' liver with onions, including soup of the day, salad, vegetable, and beverage. The house specialty of sautéed veal, lamb, beef, and bacon with pfefferlinge (European wild mushrooms) is very tasty. Since Hans Peter is also a master pastry chef, you'd be well advised to save room for dessert, especially if the incredible Grand Marnier parfait is available that day. Black Forest cake, chocolate mousse, fresh peach pie, or Edelweiss tart with raspberry sauce are also heavenly. Edelweiss serves lunch daily from 11:30am to 1:30pm, and dinner from 5pm to closing. Closed Monday.

There's something about eating in a bakery that's, well, warm and homey and smells delicious. Maybe that's why **The Bread Depot** at Opelo Plaza is such a big hit with everybody in Waimea. Chef Georges Amtablian is both baker and cook, and his cinnamon buns and sourdough French bread, which he sells to local restaurants, are famous in these parts. Doors open at 6am, and soon folks are lining up for those giant cinnamon buns ($1.49) or a variety of healthful muffins, apple turnovers, and delicious ham-and-cheese brioches ($1.49). At lunchtime, 11:30am to 3pm, you can choose a sandwich on a fresh-baked roll for $3.95; or have a soup-and-sandwich lunch at $5.75. Georges, a stickler for fresh and natural ingredients, prepares a special soup every day: Boston clam chowder, cream of potato with leek, and old-fashioned chicken-noodle soup are among the possibilities. Or, try one of his daily specials: It could be boneless chicken leg with stuffed rice, with soup and salad; or chicken enchiladas; or tuna casserole; or quiche, around $5. This French chef knows his stuff! If you're en route to one of the nearby beaches, you can pick up a nice picnic lunch here, too. The Bread Depot is open every day until 5:30pm.

When a noted chef leaves a place like the Mauna Kea Beach Hotel after 23 years and opens his own restaurant, that's big news on the Big Island. Which is why all the local food buffs are eagerly acclaiming **Bree Garden Restaurant** on Kinohou Street in Waimea (tel. 885-5888), the creation of Chef Bernd Bree and his wife, Diana. The exquisite two-level restaurant does look like a garden, indoors and out, as it is built around a gigantic East Indian banyan tree whose root system is above ground. One wall of the restaurant is a tropical greenhouse, with an abundant collection of cacti and succulents grown by the chef. The menu reflects creativity, too, and everything is done to perfection. Dinner, the only meal served, is not inexpensive, but good value considering that the price of the entree includes soup or salad of the day, a choice of rice or potatoes, rolls, and fresh garden vegetables. Stick to the low side of the menu with a $16 pasta dish (one of Chef Bernd's specialties), a seafood creation like the Pacific Northwest salmon sausages on a bed of linguine, at $17, or with one of his German specialties like wienerschnitzel with crispy spinach leaves or smoked pork chops with juniper-apple sauerkraut, $15 each. Fresh fish of the day is $19. For a vegetarian creation, notify the chef in advance, and he'll prepare something wonderful for you. As for desserts, try the deep-fried ice cream, the strawberry shortcake or an old-fashioned hot chocolate sundae.

Bree Garden Restaurant serves from 4:30 to 9pm every night. The cocktail lounge opens at 4:30pm, and it's fast becoming known for its tropical drinks and great pupus—Korean mun-doo, and a pasta special of the evening, to name just two.

Note that if you're planning to drive from Waimea to Waikoloa to visit the Hyatt Regency Waikoloa (about half an hour's drive), you can have a perfectly lovely lunch for about $10 to $12 at the **Orchid Café,** where you can feast on *cuisine naturelle;* see Chapter XIV, "Seeing Hawaii," for specifics.

For a meal on the run in this area, you can join the local families at the **Kamuela Drive-in Deli,** next to the Parker Ranch Center. It's a plain, unpretentious spot where you can eat either in your car or at the indoor tables. The prices are low and the portions big. They open at 5am for breakfast, when they cook up a storm of hotcakes, and bacon and eggs. But have the Portuguese sausages instead; they're the real thing. The rest of the day they serve sandwiches like roast beef, $1.75 to $1.95

(no doubt from the Parker Ranch); and hot platters like curry or beef stew or teriyaki steak for around $4. The only thing high here is the elevation—almost 3,000 feet.

You can get other quick meals in Waimea at **Masayo's,** across from Edelweiss, a luncheonette with hearty local specialties like curry stew, loco moco, and pigs'-feet soup, from $3 to $4. In the Parker Ranch Visitors Center, **Auntie Alice's Restaurant and Bakery** is cozy for a quick bite. Lunch, offers salads, sandwiches, burgers, fried fish baskets ($3.95 to $6.25); and breakfast is fun with eggs Benedict, Belgian waffles, and french toast made from Portuguese sweet bread. Open from 6am to 4pm.

If you're driving on Hwy. 19 to Kona, it's no trouble at all to stop off first at the harbor town of Kawaihae, where, at **Kawaihae Center,** you'll find the highly praised **Café Pesto.** So popular has this gourmet pizza-pasta restaurant become that it's regularly patronized by folks staying at the plush resorts of the Kohala coast, as well as by food fans from all over the island. We have to agree with all the Big Island friends who told us that this pizza was worth going out of your way for. It is. Café Pesto is the brainchild of two noted Big Island chefs, Jim Williams, former owner-chef of Redwater Café in Waimea, and David Palmer, a former chef at the Mauna Lani Bay Hotel. They've put their not inconsiderable talents into creating a "pizza-pasta–provocative menu"—which translates into exotic pizzas and pastas, gourmet hot sandwiches, and some satisfyingly rich desserts. It's all served in a sophisticated café atmosphere with black-and-white tile floor, black tables, white chairs, and a single rose on every table. Fine Italian wines and cold beers are available, and paintings by local artists change every month. Have someone in your party order one of the pastas, someone else one of the pizzas; that way, you get a chance to sample. As for the pastas, $4.95 to $7.95, the ceviche pasta salad with cilantro pesto is delicious, with its Tahitian lime-marinated scallops and shrimps; the Thai-curry pasta salad, with shrimp, sundried tomatoes, red onions, and spinach, is another taste treat. As for those pizza pies, they begin with a base of handmade and baked-to-order crust (a blend of white, rye, and wheat flours, plus olive oil and honey); they are topped with gourmet cheeses, fresh herbs, sundried tomatoes, and the like. The house special, and our favorite, is the pizza al pesto—fresh basil pesto, roasted garlic, sundried tomatoes, Japanese eggplant, $9.95 small. Seafood pesto with bay shrimp, steamer clams, tarragon pesto, and roasted garlic is also quite special, $10.95 small. Or, you can create your own pies with such toppings as Maui onions, feta cheese, prosciutto ham, Gorgonzola cheese, and the like. Soup of the day is always homemade: It might be a Hawaiian version of a bouillabaisse, or an Italian saffron, garlic, and potato soup, or a smooth and creamy shrimp bisque. For dessert, we like the giant chocolate macadamia-nut cookies at $1.50, and the chocolate truffles, $1.95.

Café Pesto is open every day, from 11am to 9pm Sunday through Thursday, from 11am to 10pm Friday and Saturday. Phone ahead (tel. 882-1070) and they'll have your orders ready for take-out if you wish.

It's possible that there will be branches of Café Pesto in Kona and possibly in Hilo, too, by the time you read this.

HOTELS, GUESTHOUSES, AND RESTAURANTS ON THE SOUTHERN ROUTE

Driving the southern route (Hwy. 11) from Hilo to Kona, and vice versa, you have several delightful possibilities if you want to spend a night or two. Remember, though, that the weather is highly changeable here, and the rains come and go. First, there's the famed and venerable **Volcano House,** right on the brink of Kilauea Crater, where the ancient kahunas (priests) once gathered to make sacrifices to Pele. This hotel has changed hands several times in recent years, and, alas, rates have gone up quite a bit. It's now $75, double or single, for rooms in the Ohia wing (a separate building, away from the main building), which are the least desirable. Better rooms, in the main building, are $100 for a noncrater view, $125 for crater view; an extra person is charged $10. If this puts Volcano House out of your budget range, do at least come by to soak up the atmosphere or have a meal. Enjoying a breakfast here in the early-morning mountain air, seated at a table near the window where you can gaze right into the volcano as you savor your ono french toast and ohelo-berry preserves, is one of the special treats of Hawaii. Reservations: Volcano House, P.O. Box 53, Hawaii Volcanoes National Park, HI 96718; or phone 967-7321.

The most beautiful rooms in this area are undoubtedly the ones to be found at the new **Kilauea Lodge,** one mile Hilo-side of Volcanoes National Park, in Volcano Village. There are only five of them at present, but six more are in the offing. When you see the Lodge—set amid 10 acres of greenery, bordered by magnificent ferns and towering pine trees—you'll know why everybody on the Big Island is excited about it. This former YMCA mountain retreat has now become a restaurant offering excellent meals (sorely needed in this area) and an inn offering exquisite rooms at B&B prices. Lorna and Albert Heyte (she comes from Honolulu, he hails from Germany) are in charge here; he performs the magic in the kitchen, she's created the magic in the guest rooms. You'd never believe this used to be a YMCA dorm! Architects have opened up the top of the building to create a skylight, flooding the rooms with natural light. Hawaiian quilt patterns (some of the quilts are antiques) set the mostly soft pastel color schemes for the woodwork. Furniture is made of light oak, even down to the oak tissue box. Each room is decorated differently—most are in the country style, one is strikingly Japanese—but all have private baths, toasty electric blankets, and working fireplaces. Full breakfasts at the Lodge—papayas, pancakes with fruit, eggs any style, Portuguese sausages and more—are included in the price of $75 single or double; an extra person on a futon is $15. There is also a one-bedroom cottage with a queen-size bed in the bedroom and a queen-size sofa in the living room; it can sleep two at $90, up to four at $15 for each extra person. More units should be ready by the time you read this.

For reservations write: Kilauea Lodge, P.O. Box 116, Volcano Village, HI 96785 (tel. 967-7366).

The Volcano area is perfect for the guesthouse life style. We found several local residents who have charming cottages to rent. Remember, these aren't hotels; they're country cottages or houses where you can bring the kids, relax, drive off to the volcano or to the black-sand beaches further south, or just savor the simple charms of country life. Bonnie Goodell is in charge at **The Guesthouse at Volcano,** P.O. Box 6, Volcano, HI 96785 (tel. 967-7775), which consists of a living room downstairs with a double hideaway bed, a complete kitchen, and a nice bedroom upstairs with two twins and a queen-size fold-out bed. The apartment is fully furnished, including phone, black-and-white TV, books, magazines, games, electric heater, and even wool socks! The big outside porch has a hibachi, kids' toys, and a big sink area for "cookouts, muddy boots, berries, etc." Price is $50 a day for two people ($40 a day off-season), $5 for each extra person more than 2 years old. There's a two-day minimum; the seventh day is free. If Bonnie is booked, she will probably be able to help you find another similar place. (See Readers' Selections for a personal comment on The Guesthouse at Volcano.)

Dallas and Beverly Jackson are the proprietors of **Hale Ohia Cottage,** P.O. Box 599, Volcano, HI 96785 (tel. 967-7986). The comfortable cottage, on the grounds of a beautiful kamaaina home, has an attractive large living room and a full-size, well-equipped kitchen with dining facilities both inside and on the large covered lanai. Three bedrooms offer sleeping accommodations for up to five people. Rates are $50 for two, $5 for each additional person. Weekly rates are available.

Volcano Vacation is quite grand, a luxury two-bedroom, one-bath cottage not far from the Volcano Golf Course. It has its own sauna, fireplace, a fully equipped kitchen with washer/dryer, and a half-acre yard. Four people can stay here for $70 daily, $430 weekly. Write Volcano Vacations, P.O. Box 608, Kailua-Kona, HI 96745, or phone 325-7708.

Jim and Sandy Pedersen have a cozy little country house set in a pretty landscaped area, which they call **Volcano Bed & Breakfast.** The entire house is turned over to the pleasure of their guests, who are free to enjoy the downstairs area, with its sunroom, reading room, fireplace, piano, cable TV—and they even make bicycles available! It would make an ideal spot for a small family reunion. There are two nicely decorated sleeping rooms with double beds upstairs, and one room done in bright yellow downstairs; baths are semiprivate. Rates of $45 to $55 double, include a full breakfast, which features Sandy's french toast and homemade jams and jellies. The Pedersens describe themselves as "friendly, gracious Christian hosts with inside information about where to go and what to see." They can be reached at P.O. Box 22, Volcano, HI 96785 (tel. 967-7779).

Although they reside in Maui most of the time, JoLoyce and John Kaia make their Volcano area home available to guests. **Volcano Heart Chalet** is a two-story cedar house surrounded by trees and consists of three bedrooms (all with private locks), containing either queen or twin beds, warm comforters for cool nights, and either private or shared baths. All guests can use the glass-enclosed porch for cooking and eating and the carpeted lounging and exercise room. Guests are provided with coffee, tea, and cocoa to make their down drinks, and a hostess leaves fresh pastry. Adults only; no smoking. Rates are $50 single or double, with a weekly rate of $300; two-night minimum. Write to JoLoyce Kaia, P.O. Box 404, Hana, Maui, HI 96713 (tel. 248-7725).

Hosts Tom and Brenda Carson, who run **Carson's Volcano Cottages,** love meeting new people and try to provide them with a welcome and peaceful environment. They have a private, cozy cottage that can sleep five, and a three-unit cottage; all rooms have private baths and private entrances, and two have kitchenettes. Rooms are furnished in Victorian Polynesian, Asian, country, or southwestern style, with many unique pieces, homey touches, and fresh flowers indoors and out. The Carsons leave a basket of island fruit, muffins, Kona coffee, tea, and cocoa for the guests to prepare at their leisure; there's a hot tub on the deck of the main house. Rates begin at $50 for two and go up; family rates are available. Write to P.O. Box 503, Volcano, HI 96785 (tel. 967-7683).

Any former Boy Scouts or Girl Scouts in the crowd? You might try one of the 10 cabins at **Namakani Paio Campground,** in Volcanoes National Park, three miles beyond Volcano House, at approximately 4,000 feet elevation. Designed for those "who desire true outdoor living," they are of Polynesian design, frame construction, and they're furnished with a double bed and two single bunk beds. You have your own lanai, but you share a common bathhouse with your neighbors. Cost is $24 single or double, including a linen bag (sheets, pillows, towel, soap, one blanket) for the double bed. It's $5 more for a third or fourth person, including single linen bags. Extra blankets or sleeping bags are recommended; it gets cold at this elevation. Write to Volcano House (the concessionaires) at Hawaii Volcanoes National Park, HI 96718, or call them at 967-7321.

Drs. Keith and Norma Godfrey, retired chiropractors from Alaska, have settled in Hilo and built a guesthouse on a lava bed where the ocean meets the volcanic flows at Kapoho Beach in the Puna area, about half an hour's drive from Hilo. It's a stark setting, but the house is warm and cozy, beautifully decorated and with every comfort. Each of the two stories is a complete apartment with a superb kitchen and all modern appliances, a living room and three attractive bedrooms. Considering that you can rent an entire apartment for $60 for one or two guests, $80 for three or four, $90 for five or six, this is an extraordinary bargain. What a place for a family reunion! Weekly and monthly rates are also available; three-day minimum. You can swim in a warm pool right in front of the house, or walk a short distance to tidal pools and a black-sand beach that provide your view. The Godfreys call their place **Champagne Cove,** the name of their Alaska residence. Write them at RR2, Box 3943, Pahoa, HI 96778.

Although most of its guests come to **Kalani Honua** for intercultural conferences and retreats (see Chapter XVIII), there's no reason why just plain travelers cannot enjoy its lovely facilities. Kalani Honua means "harmony of heaven and earth," and it is situated in a harmonious location, near the black-sand beach at Kalapana, with dramatic views and vistas in this area where ancient lava flows have reached the sea. Spacious grounds house conference facilities, a dining hall and café that turn out gourmet natural-food meals, a rainwater-fed pool and Jacuzzi, and a sauna with a window from which you can watch the stars of the night sky. Nearby is

Hawaii's only natural warm springs and steam bathing, and a secluded beach where swimmers play with friendly dolphins. Massage is available. There are bicycles for touring. You might even want to join a study retreat: on music, the arts, holistic health, shamanic training, the inner dance of yoga—or whatever. Rooms are attractively decorated and quite comfortable, located in four cedar lodges and private cottages. Regular rooms with private bath are $50 single or double. Rooms with shared bath are cheaper: $40 single, $24 per person double, $18 per person multiple. Tent space (you bring the tent and linens) is $13 per person. Now, if you'd prefer a private cottage, each containing two separate units, that's $72 or double, single, $70 double, for a living room with bedroom and bath.

For information, write Kalani Honua, Box 4500, Pahoa-Kalapana, HI 96778, or phone 965-1828. For reservations only, call toll free, 800/367-8047, ext. 669.

Kalani Honua has an attractive gift shop (see Chapter XIV, "Seeing Hawaii") and a mostly vegetarian restaurant, **Café Cashew,** which offers breakfast at $6, lunch at $7, dinner at $11, or $13 with a fish or fowl option. Call in advance, however, as it is not always open (tel. 965-7827).

You have several interesting choices of atmosphere for lunch on this trip. The traditional lunch stop here has long been **Volcano House** (tel. 967-7321), noted for its lovely buffet—a tempting array of salads, fruits, and main dishes, served with beverage and dessert, in a spectacular setting overlooking Halemaumau Crater. The cost is $11 for adults, $6.75 for children. The dining room at Volcano House, named Ka Ohelo, in honor of the sister of Madame Pele, the fire goddess, has been attractively enlarged, so that seating on two levels can provide views for up to 260 people However, since lunch is a very busy time, what with all the tour buses disgorging hungry passengers, we prefer to come here for a superb and quiet breakfast, served up to 10:30am. Just remember to offer some of the ohelo-berry preserves to Madame Pele first, as a sign of respect. (Ohelo is sacred to Pele; you can also sample it in ohelo-berry pie, served at Volcano House's snackshop.) The dinner menu includes teriyaki chicken ($10.95), hamburger steak ($9.50), and sautéed mahimahi ($12.50); entrees are served with rice pilaf or white rice, plus homemade sweet breads and rolls. (Prices subject to change.)

Two miles south of Volcanoes National Park entrance, watch for the sign that reads "Golf Course," directly across from the Kilauea Military Camp. It will lead you to the **Volcano Golf and Country Club** (tel. 967-7721). Here's where many local people take visitors to avoid the Volcano House crowds. The clubhouse, open to the public, has a rustic modern dining room with glass windows, huge ceiling, and wood-burning fireplace. From the windows, you can gaze at Mauna Loa and often sight the rare Hawaiian Nene goose. Complete lunches, including soup or salad, vegetable, rice or fries, offer such dishes as mahimahi, honey-stung chicken, chili, and pastas, and run from $3.75 to $7. Excellent burgers cost $4.75. Lunch is served daily, from 11am to 3pm, late lunch to 5pm.

Kilauea Lodge, one mile Hilo-side of Volcanoes National Park (tel. 967-7366) is the new "hot" place for dining in this area. The huge room is dominated by the "Fireplace of Friendship," its rocks donated by civic and youth organizations from 32 countries around the Pacific during the years when this was a mountain retreat of the YMCA. The place is still warm and friendly, the dining room is spacious and attractive, and Chef Albert Jeyte is known for excellent continental dinners. Entrees come with tiny loaves of freshly baked bread and homemade soups. There are at least five specials every day—perhaps ahi, roast duck, lamb provençale, or hassenpfeffer (that's rabbit in wine sauce); there is often venison and game on the menu. Regular entrees, which run from $8.50 to $18.50, include seafood, beef, chicken, fresh fish of the day, plus a few vegetarian dishes, like eggplant supreme and fettuccine primavera. Pies are the thing for dessert: lime, macadamia nut, lilikoi chiffon, and ohelo berry are all quite special.

Kilauea Lodge no longer serves lunch, but it does present dinner, Tuesday through Sunday from 5:30 to 9pm. Closed Monday. Reservations advised.

If you can hold out for another hour or so before lunch, continue your drive on the southern route until you come to Punalu'u, home of the famous Black Sands

Beach—and of the **Punalu'u Black Sands Restaurant** (tel. 928-8528). In a dramatic indoor-outdoor setting, in full view of the ocean, is a delightful restaurant under the direction of a creative chef. It's great fun to stop here for their buffet lunch, since the spread is truly lavish, including fresh tropical fruits on ice, island greens, fresh and pickled vegetables, a tropical Waldorf salad, Oriental pasta dishes, fruit and vegetable molds, as well as a choice of three hot entrees (meat, fish, poultry), plus steamed rice and butter rolls. Delicious Punalu'u sweet bread comes from their own country bakery, as do a variety of desserts. Coffee, tea—hot, minted, or fruit ice tea—round out the meal, all for $9.50 for adults, $6.95 for children. Salads and sandwiches are available on the à la carte menu. If you're in the area at night, come by for another delicious meal: fresh fish of the day runs from $13.95 to $15.95, broiler specialties like teriyaki chicken and Korean kal-bi ribs are $11.95 to $16.95; a sautéed-vegetable plate is $8.95. The buffet lunch is served from 10:30am to 2pm Monday through Saturday and a Sunday brunch is served from 10am to 2pm. The à la carte luncheon menu is served daily. Dinner is available from 5:30 to 8:30pm daily.

On your way to the Puna area of the Big Island (see "Seeing Hawaii," Chapter XIV), you'll pass through the little town of Keeau. An enjoyable restaurant here is **Mama Lani's,** in the shopping center (tel. 966-7525). Mama Lani (and Papa Budd) have created a charming Mexican restaurant with a warm feeling and a clean, crisp look: darkwood tables, white-stucco walls, tile floors. Everything is made on the premises, utilizing the finest of ingredients. Dinner entrees, served with homemade refried beans or Spanish rice, run from about $7 to $9 for the likes of tacos, enchiladas, burritos, and chimichangas. Or create your own combination plate for $9. Fresh fish and hamburgers are also available, served with a green salad, or Mexican style, with rice and beans. Lower-priced lunch specials are also served from 11am to 9pm. Desserts like apple empanada and Mexican flan are homemade, and they boast the "best margaritas" around. Mama Lani's is open every day from 8am to 9pm, Saturday and Sunday from noon to 9pm.

Natural-food types should look in on **Tonya's Café,** (tel. 966-8091), just across from the shopping center and next door to Keeau Natural Foods. Tonya Miller spent 15 years cooking vegetarian foods "all over California," and now she's on the Big Island, offering international vegetarian cuisine, with many dishes of Thai, Italian, Mexican, and especially Jamaican inspiration (she learned many of her recipes in Jamaica). For about $5.75, you can get a complete meal with a hot entree, salad, and bread. There are also vegetable drinks, fruit smoothies, homemade corn muffins, and some wonderful peanut-butter macadamia cookies. This is a tidy little place, very small, with just a few tables inside and out: eat here, or take food out. Tonya's Café is open weekdays only, from 11am to 7pm.

Just about halfway between Hilo and Kona you come upon an oasis in the lava flows. This is the beautiful town of Naalehu, the southernmost community in the United States. As you drive through town, keep your eyes peeled for the **Naalehu Fruit Stand,** next door to the library. Locals swear by this one! You get your food at the counter, then take it to eat at tables outside. Try one of their unique pizza sandwiches on homemade Italian bread, $4 to $5 for a whole sandwich. They also have the more usual kinds of pizzas, homemade pies, health foods, and deli sandwiches.

Also in town is the venerable **Naalehu Coffeeshop,** where lunch and dinner entrees, served with salad, vegetable, bread, and rice or potatoes, run from $7.95 to $11.95. There are also good sandwiches: the Hawaiian fishburger, the Farmer John baked ham, oven-baked turkey sandwich, and others are all served with relishes and salad, $3.95 to $5.95. After your meal, check out the art gallery and Menehune Treasure Chest, and browse among the local handcrafts. It it's anytime between September and March, be sure to see the flaming sphere poinsettias blooming out back. If you approach from Naalehu, make your third left when you pass the school; from Kona, turn right when you pass the theater. The coffee shop is just 100 feet on the left-hand side, across from the shopping center—where, incidentally, owner Roy Toguchi's brother runs the **Green Sands Snack Bar,** a little take-out place for plates like chicken hekka, pork tofu, chopped steak, and chili, from about $2.50 to $4.95.

---

3. Kailua-Kona

The Kona Coast is to the Big Island what Waikiki is to Oahu: the resort area. Unlike Waikiki, though, it still has a small-town charm. Once the playground of the Hawaiian alii, Kona lures deep-sea fishermen (its marlin grounds are the best in the Pacific), families, anyone looking for relaxed, tropical beauty. A handful of hotels offer pretty decent rates.

HOTELS

Kona Bay Hotel, right in the center of town on Alii Drive, is a sister establishment to Uncle Billy's Hilo Bay Hotel, and run by the same family management. They have landscaped their newer hotel with bridges and ponds and a Polynesian longhouse restaurant surrounding a large circular swimming pool. The thatched roof over the registration desk and the koa-wood tables in the lobby create a warm Hawaiian feeling. All rooms are of comfortable size, smartly done up in gray, blue, and mauve color schemes, with air conditioning, TV, bathrooms with full tubs and showers, and good-size lanais. Every room has a refrigerator, and many have two double beds. During summer, April 1 to December 15, standard rooms are $64, single or double; superiors are $69; deluxe are $74; and ocean view are $79. Children under 12 are free; extra adults are $10. Rates go up $10 in high season. Room, car, and breakfast packages for two are available at $74, $84, and $89 in summer, $10 more in winter. Rates are subject to change. For reservations, phone directly to Hawaii toll free, 800/387-5102, or write Kona Bay Hotel, 87 Banyan Dr., Hilo, HI 96720.

If you want more luxury and still a good price, try, also on Alii Drive, the **Kona Islander Inn,** a rambling, plantation-style complex that boasts some of the nicest hotel rooms in the area, plus a pool set in a glorious garden and a barbecue pit out by the pool. All rooms here are identical, but the price is $65 for garden or poolside rooms, $85 for ocean-view rooms. From December 23 to April 15, rates go way up, $80 and $99. Third and fourth persons in the room are not charged extra. Rooms are beautifully decorated in earth tones, with rich-orange carpets; all have two twin beds, plus a queen-size sofa bed, shower (no tub), and a private lanai furnished with a table and two director's chairs. An extra person is charged $10. There's a refrigerator in every unit, and the kitchenette package of hot plate and utensils is available for $6 more. For reservations at Islander Inn, call toll free 800/922-7866, or write to Aston Hotels & Resorts, 2255 Kuhio Ave., Honolulu, HI 96815. The local phone is 329-3181.

A good choice smack in the center of town is the **Kona Seaside Hotel** (tel. 329-2455) and Kona Seaside Pool Wing, both of which have been newly renovated. Kona Seaside is at the intersection of Kuakini Hwy. (Hwy. 11) and Palani Road (Hwy. 19), and just a parking lot away from the shopping and restaurant excitement of Alii Drive. Size is the byword—large rooms, spacious lanais, and an extra-large pool. Blue is the theme of the well-appointed rooms, all of which are equipped with color TV, air conditioning, and a direct-dial telephone.

Some of you will remember the Kona Seaside Pool Wing as the former Hukilau Hotel, whose sister hotel we've told you about in Hilo. This is a very similar place, with most of the rooms overlooking the large lovely pool. The rooms are smartly furnished, have twin- or king-size beds, air conditioning, and TV, and from many you can see the harbor across the road. Or you may just want to laze on the sun deck, which looks out on Alii Drive and the harbor, and watch the world go by below you. The pool wing leads directly into **Stan's Restaurant,** which serves three reasonably priced meals every day. Prices are not bad: standard rooms are $55 to $65, single or double; deluxe, $72 to $82; and deluxe with kitchenette, $76 to $86. A third person in the room is charged $12. Add $14 per unit for a room-and-car package. For reservations, write to Sand & Seaside Hotels, 2222 Kalakaua Ave., Suite 714, Honolulu, HI 96815, or phone toll free 800/367-7000.

In a garden setting overlooking the ocean, a bit away from the bustle of Alii Drive and very close to the Kona Hilton, is the petite **Kona Tiki Hotel** (tel. 329-1425), a longtime budget stop in Kona. All the rooms have private oceanfront lanais looking out on the blue-green pounding surf (and it really does pound—noisily—against the sea wall). The ocean is great for fishing and snorkeling; there's a freshwater pool for gentler swimming. Rooms include queen-size beds, ceiling fans, and a small refrigerator in every room, even those without kitchenettes. So popular has this small, unpretentious place been over the years, that its rooms have seen a great deal of use, however, management has advised us that they intend to spiff the place up. Regular rooms go for $40, kitchenettes for $45, single or double; extra persons are $5 each; maximum of three to a room. Friendliness abounds at the Kona Tiki; it's the kind of small, family-owned hotel where guests usually get to know one another. You can help yourself to Kona coffee and doughnuts in the morning. You can drive from here to the center of town in 3 minutes, or walk it in 15 minutes. For reservations, a month in advance usually, two months in advance in busy seasons, write: Manager, Kona Tiki Hotel, P.O. Box 1567, Kailua-Kona, HI 96740. Specify first and second choices on rooms with or without kitchenette; very few kitchenettes are available. Minimum stay is three days.

Condominiums are very big in Kona these days, and surely one of the nicest is the **Sea Village,** an idyllic spot overlooking the ocean just outside of town at 75-6002 Alii Dr. This is a large resort complex, with a tennis court, a swimming pool, and Jacuzzi whirlpool bath on the premises, snorkeling off the rocks in front of the hotel for strong swimmers. Living quarters are outstanding: The apartments are beautifully furnished, ultra-spacious and luxurious, with huge living rooms, one or two bedrooms, shiny modern kitchens fitted with every appliance including dishwashers, washer-dryers, and refrigerators with automatic ice makers. Bathrooms are lovely, and there is ample closet and storage space, weekly maid service, private lanais. Although rates here are higher than our usual budget ones, if you come during off-season (May 1 through December 15), you can get a one-bedroom garden-view apartment for two persons for $70; it's big enough to sleep four, at $10 per extra person. A two-bedroom garden-view apartment for up to four persons is $94; it can sleep six. Ocean-view apartments go up to $82 and $106; oceanfront apartments run even higher, to $86 and $112; high-season rates add $16 more per unit. There is a discount of 10% on monthly stays in summer. A minimum stay of three nights is required. For reservations, write to the Sea Village Condominium Resort, c/o Paradise Management Corp., Kukui Plaza C-207, 50 S. Beretania St., Honolulu, HI 96813 (tel. 538-7145); or call toll free 800/367-5205.

Aston Royal Sea Cliff must certainly be considered one of the top condominium resorts on the Kona coast. This all-suite resort enjoys a superb oceanfront location at 75-6040 Alii Drive (tel. 329-8021), an architecturally stunning building, a variety of splendidly decorated and furnished apartments, plus something no other resort we know offers: a *free* Budget car rental for every day of one's stay, included in every price category. Luxury, comfort, convenience—this place has it all. Guests are offered a number of activities, including free tennis, the use of two swimming pools—salt water or fresh water—plus a sauna and jet spa. Pools are located at the ocean, which is a bit rocky for swimming, but good swimming beaches are nearby. Rooms are among the nicest we've seen, very large, handsomely furnished with wicker, light woods and Polynesian fabrics, air conditioning, cable TV, direct-dial phones, washer/dryers. The large and fully equipped kitchens have both microwave and conventional ovens. Lanais are large enough for dining, soaking up the sun by day, watching the stars by night. Yes, there is daily maid service. Studio suites with garden view are $115 to $135; one-bedroom suites for four guests with garden view are $130 to $150; with ocean view, $140 to $170; and superb two-bedroom, two-bath apartments, which can easily sleep up to six people, at $150 to $170 garden view, $160 to $190 ocean view. For reservations, phone toll free 800/922-7866, or write Aston Hotels & Resorts, 2255 Kuhio Ave., 18th floor, Honolulu, HI 96815-2658.

Kona Riviera Villa, oceanfront at 75-6124 Alii Drive (tel. 329-1996), is the kind of place we like best: charming, intimate, low-key, and affordable. It's an older condominium complex, set just far enough back from the water to bring in the cooling breezes—and not too much ocean noise. A freshwater swimming pool and patio with barbecue grill overlooks the ocean, too rough here for swimming, but fine for snorkelers and surfers. Each apartment is comfortably furnished and nicely decorated: All units have one bedroom, and some of the living rooms have sofa beds, so that up to four people could be accommodated. Kitchens are electric, equipped with dishwashers and garbage disposals. Rates are very modest for this luxury area: From April 1 to December 1, a one-bedroom garden apartment for one or two persons is $50 per day; a one-bedroom oceanview apartment is $60; and a one-bedroom oceanfront is $70. Add $10 for each extra person. The rest of the year, all rates go up $10. This is a congenial place, so much so that many of the same guests come back year after year. Make reservations well in advance by writing to Kona Riviera Villa, 75-6124 Alii Dr., Kailua-Kona, HI 96740, or phone 329-1996. A minimum stay of three nights is required.

A few miles further along Alii Drive is another lovely condominium resort, the 155-room **Kona Bali Kai,** fronting the ocean at 76-6246 Alii Dr. (tel. 329-9381). Rooms are exquisitely and individually furnished, with every convenience—full kitchens, washer-dryers in oceanside units, color TVs, direct-dial phones, daily maid service (unusual in most condominiums), and lanais from which those in the main building can watch the spectacular surf and tireless surfers (other buildings afford partial views of mighty Mt. Hualalai or lush gardens). Although the surf is too strong here for casual swimmers, a good swimming beach is a mile away, and right at home is a sunning beach amid the coral-reef tidal pools, a swimming pool, Jacuzzi, and sauna. There are barbecue grills on the beach, and a Pupu Pantry in the lobby area for essentials, groceries, and sandwiches. Arrangements can be made at the activities desk in the lobby for golf (three miles south), tennis (two miles north), or for a variety of adventures nearby. Studio rooms for one or two persons are $75 mountainside of road, during the summer season. One-bedroom apartments for one to four persons are $100 mountainside, $125 oceanside; and spectacular two-bedroom, two-bath apartments, which can comfortably sleep up to six people, are $145. Add $15 to $25 per unit from December 20 through March 31. For reservations, phone toll free 800/367-6040, or write Kona Bali Kai, 76-6246 Alii Dr., Kailua-Kona, HI 96740. FAX: 326-6056.

Each and every apartment at **Kona Magic Sands Condominium,** 77-6452 Alii Drive (tel. 329-9177), overlooks the pounding ocean and the glorious sunsets of Kona. This is one of the older condos in the area, not as luxurious as some, but it's very beachy and cozy—the kind of place where it feels good to kick off your sandals and take life easy. These are studio apartments, of good size, with full kitchens and TV; instead of a separate bedroom, they have a sleeping alcove off the living room, with either a double, queen, or sofa bed. There are palm trees outside your window, a freshwater pool for swimming, and the convenience of having **Jameson's by the Sea,** a top restaurant, right downstairs. A minimum stay of three nights is required. Apartments come in two categories: standard, which rent for $65 a night, and large, which go for $70. A few extra-large apartments at $75 have lanais overlooking the beach. Apartments are furnished to accommodate two guests; extra persons pay $10 more. Write to Kona Vacation Resort, P.O. Box 1071, Kailua-Kona, HI 96745, or phone toll free 800/367-5168 from the mainland, or 800/423-8733, ext. 329 from Canada.

Thirteen miles south of Kailua, on Hwy. 11—and 1,400 feet high in the coffee country—is the place where you'll find some of the most reasonable accommodations in the Kona area, the **H. Manago Hotel** in the village of Captain Cook (tel. 323-2642). But staying here means more than getting a clean, comfortable room for rock-bottom prices; it's a way to get to know the nontourist Hawaii. For the Manago Hotel is part of the history of the Kona coast, a favorite with island people since 1917, when two young Japanese immigrants, Kinzo and Osame Manago, started serving meals in their own house and gave the salesmen and truck drivers who wanted to stay overnight a futon to sleep on. The dining room and hotel grew over the years, and now a third generation of family management has taken over. The older rooms, with community bath, are strictly for nonfussy types: They rent for $18 single, $21 double, $23 triple. Rooms in the newer wing, with private baths and lanais, are modern and comfortable. These rooms are $29, $30, and $32 single, $32, $33, and $35, double. An extra bed is $3. The gardens that they overlook, incidentally, are tended by 92-year-old Osame Manago, who grows rare orchids and anthuriums in one garden, and fresh vegetables, which are served in the restaurant, in the other. She also creates the hand-knotted patchwork quilts found in some of the rooms. A Japanese-style room, with futons and its own furo (deep hot tub), is dedicated to Kinzo and Osame, and rents for $46 single, $49 double. It's delightfully quiet and cool here throughout the year. The hotel restaurant is a favorite with local people for its home-style Japanese and American cooking; breakfast starts at $3.75, lunch and dinner about $5.50 to $10 (a typical meal is beef or fish with three kinds of vegetables, and beverage). They're known for their pork chops. And incidentally, the three-story frame building looks down the foot of the mountain to Kealakekua Bay, where Captain Cook met his end. Owner Dwight Manago advises reserving about three weeks ahead in season, two weeks other times. Address: P.O. Box 145, Captain Cook, Kona, HI 96704.

There's only one youth hostel on the Big Island, and it's right in this area, up mauka in the country town of Honalo; it's 1,400 feet above and 7 miles south of the tourist world at Kailua-Kona. **Kona Lodge & Hostel** is simple, rustic, and very friendly, popular with older adventurous types as well as with bikers, athletes, school groups, and others accustomed to the hostel life-style. Nicest of all, it's set on an acre of land that grows organic papayas, mangoes, avocados, pineapples, bananas, and even macadamia nuts—offering the possibility, in season, of pick-your-own fruit salads! Other pluses are hot showers outdoors and a volleyball area. Everybody shares the communal kitchen. A large coed dorm sleeps 25; beds cost $14 a night, $12 if you're an AYH member (minimal chores are expected). There are also six rooms with a double bed, which go for $24 for one, $29 for two; and two rooms with two double beds, $35 for one, $40 for two, bath down the hall. Tenting is $7. Don't expect TV as the folks here don't believe in it, but there's enough going on so that nobody seems to miss it. Reservations in advance are advisable, especially if you'll be here during the annual "Ironman Triathlon" in the fall, when the place is positively jumping. Write to the managers, Dave and MaryJo McJunkin, P.O. Box 645, Kealakekua, HI 96750 (tel. 322-9056 or 322-8136).

BED & BREAKFAST UP MAUKA

Grander than most B&B's, smaller than most hotels, **Holualoa Inn** is in a class by itself: an exquisite small inn set high up in the mountains in the farming community/art colony of Holualoa, about a 15-minute drive from the ocean at Kailua-Kona, which provides its magnificent views. The three-level mansion set in a 40-acre estate was originally built as a mountain hideaway for *Honolulu Advertiser* president Thurston Twigg-Smith. Now his nephew Desmond Twigg-Smith and his wife, Karen, have taken it over and superbly decorated its four guest bedrooms, which they rent out on a B&B basis to those lucky enough to find this serenely beautiful spot. The house is built of cedar wood, its floors of eucalyptus, its windows of spun glass. The handsome living room has a fireplace, reading areas, even a billiard table. The formal dining room is the scene of morning breakfasts of fresh fruits, juices, pastries, and muffins from The French Bakery in Kailua town. And the rooms are enchanting, each one done differently: one with an Asian theme, another in Balinese style, a third in Polynesian decor, the fourth with a Hawaiian hibiscus motif. In addition to the use of the living and dining rooms upstairs, guests also have a common room on the lower level, where they can store food in the refrigerator. There's a large swimming pool outside, a tower from which to watch the sunset, and everywhere, the song of birds. The Twigg-Smiths hope to add a new wing with 10 more units, maybe even a restaurant, in the near future. Rates are $60 single, $75 to $125 double, $15 for an extra person. No children under 12, no smoking except outdoors; minimum stay of two days, maximum stay of two weeks. There's a 15%

discount for stays of one week or longer. For information, write Holualoa Inn, P.O. Box 222, Holualoa, HI 96725 or phone 324-1121.

There's another unique hideaway in this same up-country area overlooking Kailua town. **The Mango Cottage,** as charming as its name suggests, is the creation of Barbara and Kevin O'Brien, who have traveled the world over and brought back splendid antiques with which to furnish their Hawaiian plantation-style home. The spacious veranda with its wicker chairs is where guests gather to watch the ocean below and the sunsets; it overlooks a koi pond, a swimming pool, and a superb garden full of fruit trees from which guests may pluck tangerines or lemons, limes, or bananas or passion fruit. Indoors are several rooms with private baths, all furnished with antiques and graceful touches; one even has an old-fashioned wicker sleigh bed under the mosquito netting. A room facing the garden boasts office equipment; several cottages with kitchenettes are available, as are more accommodations at the Kona Cabanas, the nearby home of Kevin's sister, Diane O'Brien. A full breakfast is served. Rates are $75 to $100 a night, $300 to $500 per week. Mango Cottage is also available for small parties and weddings—which, in such a setting, should be pure enchantment. Write or phone: The Mango Cottage, P.O. Box 5095, Kailua-Kona, HI 96745 (tel. 326-7220).

In the hills overlooking the Keeahou area is **Kona Walua Lodge,** one of the more reasonably priced B&Bs in this area, and good value for the money. The spacious home, set in a lovely tropical area approached by winding country roads, has five rooms; two have double beds, two have a king-size bed, and one has twin beds. Each room has a private bath, and there's a large common area with fireplace, TV, and many comforts. Rooms are not fancy, but they are of good size, clean, and comfortable. Guests have use of a swimming pool, pretty with its wall of bougainvillea and banana trees. There's a barbecue grill and burner out here. Healthy breakfasts are served. Jennifer Babiak, a capable young woman, is in charge part of the year; her parents are on hand the rest of the time. During the winter season, rates begin at $40 single; $60 double; $10 per extra person; $5 per child (children under 2 and over 14 preferred). In summer, May 1 to December 1, rates are even cheaper: $30 and $40. Room-and-car packages with Tropical Rent-A-Car average another $20 a day. Write or phone Kona Walua Lodge, P.O. Box 2302, Kailua-Kona, HI 96745-2302 (tel. 324-0627).

Barbara Moore and David Link, the lovely couple who run **The Dragonfly Ranch** (a flower farm) in Honaunau, offer their place for families and small groups for reunions, workshops, and private retreats. They also have extraordinary accommodations for travelers, and you'll be happy if you luck into one of these unusual spaces. Our favorite is the Outdoor Water-Bed Suite, in a jungle setting with private bathroom, outdoor shower with an old-fashioned sitz bath, and a kitchenette. The king-size bed has a marvelous view of Honaunau Bay, while the adjoining redwood room (viewing the "pink garden") has a queen-size sofa bed. This suite accommodates four people, but is ideally suited for two as a romantic getaway. Depending on the season, it's $75 to $100 for up to four people. The self-contained Redwood Cottage in the meadow is super cozy, with a hammock out on the deck, a double bed, kitchenette, toilet and outdoor shower; it's $60 a night, $360 a week for two (extra guests can squeeze in on the futons). For the same price, a spacious 20-feet-by-22-feet studio apartment with a cheery bright yellow accent has its own kitchen, private bathroom, outdoor shower, king-size bed, and additional futons. Discounted longer stays can be arranged. For music lovers, David has a vast selection of music, a piano, a professional recording studio—and he also gives music lessons. All units have stereo cassette players and, upon request, guests are provided with cable TV, VCR, and video tapes. For breakfast, there are baked goods (such as whole-wheat croissants) and fresh home-grown fruits. Guests are welcome to harvest their own bananas and papayas, as well as the more exotic star fruit, soursop, or chocolate zapote in season. And Barbara offers the use of a massage chair, dream pillows, aroma therapy, and flower essences. For plant lovers, there are beautiful flower arrangements, a Fragrance Walk, and the Rainbow Vision Garden—as well as fresh herbs and vegetables when the organic garden is happening.

The Dragonfly Ranch, in itself a refuge, is just a two-minute drive from the ancient Place of Sanctuary (Pu'uhonua o Honaunau National Park), with some of the world's finest diving and snorkeling. An assortment of snorkeling gear is available for guests' use. If you're lucky, you might even get to swim with the dolphins. It's 19 miles south of Kailua-Kona, and great for total escape. As one guest put it: "Peacefulness personified." Write: The Dragonfly Ranch, Box 675, Honaunau, HI 96726, or call 328-2159 or 328-9570.

Adrienne and Reginald Ritz-Batty are a hospitable couple who really like people, so if you book a room at **Adrienne's Bed & Breakfast,** in Honaunau, (about half an hour's drive from Kailua town) you'll be treated like a personal friend. Not only will they share their knowledge of the Big Island with you, but they'll invite you to join them in the living room in the evenings to choose a film from the more than 1,000 movies in their collection to watch on their VCR—or the one in your room. Of course, Adrienne will have blueberry–macadamia-nut muffins, homemade Hawaiian coconut bread, cheese, cinnamon raisin breads, made daily, to enjoy along with Kona coffee, fresh fruits (papayas, white pineapples, tangerines, avocados), from their gardens, and she'll serve them to you out on the lanai, with its unobstructed view of the ocean. You're also invited to soak in the hot tub out on the lanai or just laze in the hammock. As for the rooms, there are three with private baths, all nicely decorated; one room has a king-size bed plus a queen-size sofa bed, which makes it a good bet for a family. All rooms have private baths, color cable TVs with VCRs, and small refrigerators. Prices are modest: $40 to $60 for up to two, $10 for children; for two couples traveling together, it's $15 per adult in the same room. Write to Adrienne's Bed and Breakfast, R.R. 1 BE, Captain Cook, HI 96704, or phone toll free 800/242-0039. The local phone is 328-9726.

RESTAURANTS

Every time we dine at the **Ocean View Inn,** smack in the middle of Alii Drive (tel. 329-9988), we realize why it has survived and thrived for so many years while other newer, flashier establishments come and go. This business has been owned by the same family for over half a century. It's a big, comfy place, nothing fancy; the view across the road is ocean all the way, the tables are filled with local residents, and the waitresses are old-timers who know their trade. American and Chinese meals are inexpensive and generous. And it has a wide variety of Chinese vegetarian dishes that are surprisingly delicious. Vegetarians bored with yet another salad bar had best make tracks for this place. Dishes based on vegetarian beef (textured vegetable protein) and tofu run from $2.75 to $4.75; the sweet-and-sour crisp vegetarian wontons rank with the tastiest Chinese food anywhere. Dinners offer good value: they include soup or fruit cup, rice or mashed potato or fries, green salad (with a choice of dressings, including bleu cheese), tea, and coffee. At a recent meal we dined on broiled ahi (the fish of the day), and for the same $7.50 could have had broiled ono, breaded mahimahi, or butterfish. There are at least 24 other choices between $5.50 and $8.95, including corned beef and cabbage, fried chicken, and roast pork with apple sauce. And there are over 80 Chinese dishes beginning at $2.75; a Chinese plate dinner is $4.50; roast duck and roast chicken are $4.75 each. Lunch is also a good buy, with many hot plates to choose from, like shoyu chicken or teriyaki steak, from $4.95 to $6.50. These are served with rice or potato, salad, and beverage. Breakfast too, with everything from ham and eggs and french toast to beef stew, saimin, and poi. Open daily except Monday, serving breakfast from 6:30 to 10am, lunch from 11am to 2:45pm, dinner from 5:15 to 9pm. The bar is open 6:30am to 9pm.

The **Rusty Harpoon** has long been one of our favorite restaurants in Maui, so we were delighted to find another Rusty's here on the Big Island, in the Kona Market Place (tel. 329-8881). The lovely second-floor lanai dining room, done all in tones of peach, is right on Alii Drive, and looks out across the road to the ocean. The paintings by local artists that grace the walls are for sale. Like its Maui counterpart, this Rusty's draws the crowds with its fresh, imaginative cuisine, excellent service, and lively atmosphere. Rusty's prices are medium-range, but if you come for their Sunset

Dinners, from 5:30 to 7pm, they're even lower than that: for $8.95, you receive a choice of chicken marsala, seven ounces of top sirloin, and fresh fish of the day, along with pasta or rice, vegetables and delicious French bread. On the regular dinner menu, as you sip your daiquiris (for which the restaurant is famous), you can begin with onion rings, kal-bi, short ribs, deep-fried calamari or prawn cocktail, among other pupu possibilities, $2.95 to $5.95. Among the chicken, seafood, and beef entrees, you can't go wrong with deep-fried chicken macadamia in a sweet-and-sour sauce ($10.95); shrimp scampi ($12.95); or their outstanding boneless prime ribs, wrapped and cooked in rock salt (which seals in the juices and is removed before serving) in the ancient Hawaiian way ($13.95 and $15.95). There's always fresh fish of the day, market priced. Now, if you'd like a dinner salad, have the freshly broiled ahi salad or the shrimp Louis ($8.95 and $8.50); and if a burger is all you want, Rusty's has the best, half-pound burgers with fries at $6.95. Lunch offers similar entrees ($6.95 to $7.95), more salads, and sandwiches. At either meal, you should not miss dessert, especially the island macadamia-nut pie, lined with chocolate inside the crust! Then there's breakfast, and fabulous Belgian waffles with your choice of toppings ($5.50)—enough to make waking up positively pleasurable. There are also good three-egg omelets, and for those who want to go local, "da kine rice and eggs" with really good fried rice and two eggs any style ($3.95).

Rusty's is open daily, serving breakfast from 8 to 11:30am, lunch from 11:30am to 2pm, dinner from 5:30 to 9:30pm. Dinner reservations are a good idea.

So you want to live the good life dining at the **King Kamehameha Hotel** restaurants? There are several not-expensive possibilities. The pretty **Kona Veranda Coffee Shop** has luncheon entrees like Polynesian chicken, mushroom burger, sandwiches, and a salad of fresh Hawaiian fruit, from $6 to $8. Or have dinner in the atmospheric **Moby Dick's**, selecting one of the lower-priced dishes, like the pesto vegetable mélange at $12.95, the baked fresh fish with taro, $13.95, the spicy Malaysian sauté of shrimp and chicken at $13.95, or the Thai or Hawaiian chicken at $14.95. Come between 5:30 and 6:30pm for a Sunset Dinner and you have a choice of four entrees—among them seafood pasta, Kahlua pig and cabbage, or saké chicken—served with steamed rice, sautéed fresh vegetables, and a house salad, for $9.95. You can get subs, salads, hot dogs, and Hawaiian favorites at **King Kam's Beach Walk** at small prices in the afternoons. Or go all out and treat yourself to a big-splurge champagne brunch at Moby Dick's on Sunday, from 9am to 1pm at a cost of $18.95 for adults, $9.95 for those 12 and under. The enormous buffet table is laden with a dozen hot entrees, bountiful salad, and fresh-fruit selections, an omelet station, as well as a fabulous fresh pastry buffet. And there's live entertainment throughout the brunch.

There's an outpost of Middle Earth right on Alii Drive, across from the Kona Hilton Hotel, known as **Tom Bombadil's Food and Drink.** And while murals and decor and names on the menu are mythic (Aragorn Pizza, Misty Mountain sandwiches, Smeagols' Fine Fishes), the food is downright substantial and filling. Tom Bombadil's is known for its broasted chicken (the unique taste is a result of its being deep-fried under pressure), about $6.55 for a two-piece dinner; for pizzas (from $3.30 for a small); and for hot or cold sandwiches (roast beef dip, turkey, bacon, and avocado, and such), direct from Goldberry's Pantry. Sandwiches range from $5.75 up to $9.85 for the huge submarine. There are also tasty appetizers such as batter-fried zucchini and an appetizer platter that two or three hungry hobbits could share, plus salads, pastas, and flame-broiled specialties, which include fresh fish of the day, chicken teriyaki, hamburgers, and New York steak. You can enjoy ocean-view dining from the covered lanai, maybe relax in the cozy pub area with a drink, or view live satellite coverage of sporting events on their cocktail patio. Tom Bombadil's is open daily, serving continuously from 11am to 10pm. All food is available for take-out by phoning 329-1292 or 329-2173.

If you like homemade Italian food served in a friendly, unpretentious atmosphere, you're going to love **Poki's Pasta,** in the Kailua Bay Shopping Mall (tel. 329-7888). Poki Goold, who has been a chef at much fancier restaurants, shines in her own place, which is just two small rooms including the counter. The emphasis is on terrific fresh pasta, wonderful homemade sauces, and an imaginative treatment of everything—all at modest prices. Poki's appetizers, $4.25 to $6.75, are special: We like deep-fried mozzarella and the jumbo elephant garlic with French bread (an experience!). The spinach salad Mediterranean ($6.25) and the Cobb salad ($7.75) are practically meals in themselves. But do save room for the hearty homemade minestrone soup and one of the pasta or spaghetti dishes ($6.75 to $9.25), like the tasty frizzled spinach (sautéed with Italian ham) or the fettuccine al pesto, with macadamia nuts. There's usually a daily special at $7.95 and $8.95; the day we were there, it was beef-and-cheese lasagne and chicken-and-broccoli lasagne, served with a tossed green salad. Popular entrees include calamari sautée, chicken alla parmigiana, and seafood marinara, from $11.75 to $13.75. Desserts are the standard Italian gelato and sorbets, and there's no liquor license, so BYOB.

Poki's Pasta serves one menu all day, from 11:30am to 9pm. Everything on the menu is available for take-out.

Poo Ping, on the top floor of the Kona Inn Shopping Village on Alii Drive (tel. 329-2677), was one of Kona's first Thai restaurants. It's been so successful that it's opened a second restaurant, **Poo Ping 2 Thai Cuisine** in Kamehameha Square (tel. 329-0010). Both restaurants are attractive and offer basically the same menu, but the new location is much larger, with a courtyard, many plants, whirling fans—plus the advantage of an all-you-can-eat luncheon buffet offering Thai, Chinese, and Indonesian dishes for around $6. If you have a car, buzz out to that one; if you're on foot, the original Poo Ping is for you. It's a large and pretty room, modestly decorated, with blue oilcloth tablecloths. All the traditional Thai dishes are here—spring rolls, vegetable satés, hot and sour soup, noodle dishes like pad thai (fried-rice noodles with shrimp, chicken, eggs, bean sprouts, and peanuts—a classic), curries such as red curry with chicken and bamboo shoots, main dishes on the order of broccoli chicken, boiled squid with mint leaves and chili, or charcoal shrimp with lemon grass and onions (the dinner menu has a greater variety of seafood dishes than lunch, and some of these are quite unusual). Everything can be ordered mild, spicy, or very spicy. Vegetarians will be happy here, since they can choose to have any item without meat. Prices are reasonable: most main dishes at lunch are $5.75 to $6.50; at dinner, $5.75 to $8.50. Wine and beer are available: imported Singha or Singha Gold are favorites. And do try the Thai Tea, a spicy iced tea with cream and sugar that tastes like flowers! Poo Ping is open for lunch Tuesday to Saturday from 11am to 3pm; for dinner Tuesday to Sunday, from 5 to 10pm. Poo Ping 2 is open for lunch from 11am to 3pm; for dinner from 5 to 9:30pm, Monday to Saturday. Closed Sunday. Takeout orders are available at both places.

Once you develop a taste for Thai food, you want more and more. So another good possibility is to drive over to the industrial area, close to town, and treat yourself to a meal at **Lanai's Siamese Kitchen,** 74-5588A Pawai Place (tel. 326-1222). This is a lovely indoor-outdoor spot (ask to be seated on the lanai), where you can sample authentic Thai cuisine, cooked with fresh and natural ingredients and Asian spices, at very modest prices. An especially good deal is the $4.95 to $6.95 luncheon when, in addition to a complimentary pupu (have it with your wine or beer), you choose from such main dishes as Lanai Thai Noodle (rice noodles sautéed with a nuts and plum sauce), chicken curry with cucumber sauce, spicy garlic and pepper sautéed with cabbage. At dinner (when you might want to be seated in the dining area in the garden), you might start with one of the flavorful soups (co co soup is chicken or fish in spiced coconut milk; thom yum is a hot and sour concoction with lemon grass and chicken or seafood), proceed to similar entrees as at lunch ($5.25 to $8.95), or have noodles and fried rice, "adventure dishes" like squid with chile and mint, or crab claw in a pot, all priced from about $6.95 to $8.95. Your dishes can be ordered mild, spicy, or very spicy; we chose the mild and were perfectly content. No MSG is used. Along with your meal, have some sun tea or homemade lemonade, $1.25.

Lanai's Siamese Kitchen serves lunch from 11am to 3pm, dinner from 5 to 9pm, Monday through Saturday. Closed Sunday.

While you're here in the industrial area, it might be fun to drive over to 74-

5467 Kaiwi St. and check out **The French Bakery** (tel. 326-2688), which supplies many top restaurants in the area and also sells directly to the public. Although the name is French and the pastry chef is German, it's actually an international bakery, with quite an array of interesting goodies, including French bread, whole-wheat croissants, blueberry brioches, rum balls, German three-seed muffins, and a selection of sandwiches, too. For something different, try the Tongan bread (some of the employees come from Tonga), and fill it with either chicken or spinach or a sausage/bacon combo, $2.25 and quite good. There's a table for coffee and your selection. The French Bakery is open daily except Sunday from 6am to 5pm.

Honolulu has its Restaurant Row, and Kailua-Kona now has its Waterfront Row, a handsome on-the-ocean, multiple-level dining-shopping complex, with a boardwalk and plenty of space from which to watch the pounding surf. It's fun to come here just to catch the scene—you can climb a 45-foot observation tower (the Crow's Nest) and look for whales or stars through the telescopes; see the historical wall with its collection of fishing artifacts; survey the shops, the model ships, and other nautical memorabilia. And it's also fun to eat here: You can do so very inexpensively by visiting the Food Arcade, a little more expensively by patronizing the restaurants. Among the latter, you'll always do well at the architecturally striking **Chart House** (tel. 329-2451) with huge sails hanging from the tall ceilings, an upstairs open-air lounge, a waterfall, koa-wood booths, beautiful fabrics and decor within. Note the photographs of legendary Hawaiian athletes on the walls. If you've ever dined at a Chart House restaurant (there are very popular ones in Maui and Honolulu), you know you can expect nothing but the best from these establishments in the way of food, service, and ambience. The Chart House is a bit above our usual price range, but stick to their fabulous salad bar and you have a meal for $10.45. Or, stay on the low side of the menu with items like teriyaki steak kebab at $13.95, teriyaki chicken at $14.65, broiled smoked chicken at $14.95, or scallops at $15.75. All of these come with unlimited salad bar, fresh vegetable, and freshly baked squaw or sourdough breads. Daily seafood and fresh-fish selections run about $22. As for desserts, we wouldn't dream of passing up their mud pie, even at $4.25. An alternative is to come here simply for pupus and a drink in the outdoor cocktail lounge, and watch the sunset as you munch on the likes of garlic jalapeño cheese bread, New England clam chowder, or baked brie with roasted almonds ($2.95 to $8.25). The Chart House serves dinner only, from 4:30 to 10:30pm; pupus until midnight daily. Reservations suggested.

Phillip Paolo's Italian Restaurant at Waterfront Row is liable to make you think you're dining somewhere on the Mediterranean—it's open to the sea with sweeping views, colorful murals of Venice grace one wall, there are wicker chairs, pink tablecloths with green napkins, and a sparkling, blue-sky ambience. Come here at lunch for best buys, because at dinnertime most entrees, except for four pasta dishes at $12.95, go from about $16.95 way up to $24.95. At lunch, however, you can enjoy traditional pastas like cannelloni, manicotti florentine, shrimp scampi, or crab fettuccine from $7.95 to $10.95. There are many hero sandwiches, including a broiled chicken breast with sautéed onions, from $7.95 to $9.95; and a full complement of tropical salads (the papaya stuffed with chicken salad, $8.95, is a favorite), antipasti, and hearty Italian soups. Lunch is served from 11:30am to 2:30pm, dinner from 4:30 to 11pm daily. Reservations are a must at dinner: 329-4436.

Having a meal at the fast-food restaurants at **Waterfront Row** is no hardship at all; there's a nice variety of places and numerous oceanfront tables to which you can take your food. Our favorite here is **Spinnaker's Sailboat Salad Bar:** It is actually a sailboat, complete with mast, upon which is set a very attractive buffet that includes not only plenty of fresh, green vegetables, but also dishes like tabbouleh, brown rice with steamed veggies, unusual pasta salads, pesto, homemade breads (herb cheese, garlic parmesan, sourdough, squaw bread), plus soup of the day. The nice thing about this place is that you pay for your salad by the pound ($3.99), so you alone determine how much you wish to eat and spend. They also have fabulous Häagen-Dazs ice-cream concoctions, like a volcano sundae and a mocha double-nut-fudge mud pie.

Next door to Spinnaker's is **Crazy Ed's Little Chicken Shack,** where Ed, who is far from crazy, deep-fries skinless chicken breasts or fish filets in canola oil (97% saturated-fat free and 100% cholesterol free). Plates, which are served with french fries, rice and macaroni or potato salad, go from $3.55 to $4.95 to $5.95. Our suggestion: Have a big salad at Spinnaker's, combine it with one or two pieces of chicken or fish ($1.85 each) from Ed's, for a healthful and delicious meal. Then you can feel justified in treating yourself to a dessert and an espresso at **The Coffee Pub of Kona,** right across the way; or perhaps a nifty fresh-fruit shake (piña colada is $4.25) or a chocolate-covered strawberry or two from **Flying Fruit Fantasy.** Hot-dog lovers can pig out at **Hot Diggety Dog,** which bakes its own buns and tops them with gourmet hot dogs and sausages, including turkey franks.

A bit north, but still on Waterfront Row, you'll find the **Jolly Roger** (tel. 329-1344), which old-timers will recognize from the days when it was the Spindrifter Restaurant. The on-the-water location is superb, and the food is the kind you remember from the popular Jolly Rogers in Waikiki: good American fare with full-course meals from about $10 to $12, including entrees of teriyaki steak, barbecued beef ribs, fish-fry platter and chicken Polynesian. (Watch the local papers for two-for-one dinner offers for about $17.) Jolly Rogers also has lots of sandwiches and salads at lunch, plus hearty breakfasts, which many people consider their best meal. Eggs Benedict, delicious Mac-Waples (waffles with cinnamon apples and macadamia nuts), and steak and eggs go from about $3.45 to $5.95. Jolly Roger serves food continuously every day from 6:30am to 10pm, with contemporary music groups playing from 9pm to 1:30am. Nice for a drink at sunset, too.

There's not much Chinese food available in the Kona area, so **King Yee Lau,** situated atop the Kona Inn Shopping Village on Alii Drive (tel. 329-7100), is very welcome. It's a large and attractive room, open on one side to the ocean breezes; "Lazy Susan" tables make it easy to sample the goodies. Both Cantonese and Mandarin cuisines are served here, but the house special is called the "Sizzling Plate"; this means that such dishes as pepper steak, fresh-seafood platter, and boneless sautéed chicken are served on hot platters (hear them sizzle and see them smoke), with gravy on the side. They are priced from $8.95 to $12.95. Mongolian beef, lemon chicken, and Kona fresh fish with vegetables of the season are other popular choices. Most dishes are in the $6 to $9 range. Lunch is served from 11am to 4pm, and dinner from 4 to 9:30pm (to 9pm on Sunday), every day. **Sam's Kamaiina Lounge** offers cocktails and pupus from 10am to 11:30pm. Parking is free.

There are lots of places for quick meals in town. **McGurk's Seafood & Sandwiches** (tel. 329-8956), for one, is a good choice for a quick lunch or dinner. Located on Alii Drive, near Hulihee Palace, and decorated in white and blue with nautical accents, McGurk's has both indoor and outdoor tables. You might take out fish and chips, shrimp and chips (three pieces at $6.95), or sandwiches ($2.95 to $3.95); or stay and have a fresh mahimahi sandwich ($4.95), dinner, and chef salads ($2.25 to $3.85), or a scallop and chips plate with macadamia-nut coleslaw ($5.65), while enjoying a splendid ocean view. Wednesday night, from 4:30 to 8:30, it's all the fish you can eat for $5.95.

Bagels go Hawaiian at **Da'Kine Fresh Juices and Bagelry,** (tel. 329-5552), a neat little spot on the upper level of Kamehameha Square. Where else but in the islands could you get the Tropical Breeze Bagel, topped with cream cheese, fresh pineapple, and coconut? Believe it or not, this unlikely combination is actually delicious. So too, are the Pink Flamingo (cream cheese blended with lox and green onions) and the Bagel Italiano (a ricotta and pesto spread topped with pine nuts). These house specialties cost $2.75 to $3.95; if you're hungry, you may want two. Or, choose a basic bagel—anything from plain to cinnamon raisin, from poppyseed to blueberry—and build your own toppings. Freshly squeezed tropical-fruit juices and Kona coffee are available to accompany your little feast, which you can eat on their lanai if you wish. Owner Greg Haggenson and Ann Schwarzmann take justifiable pride in this attractive little family operation. Open Monday to Friday, 7am to 4pm, Saturday 8am to 4pm. Closed Sunday.

Exotic **Sibu Café,** in Baynan Court on Alii Drive (tel. 329-1112), is a semi-open place where you can sample the mood and food of Indonesia. Balinese decorations, tables topped with sarongs covered with glass, and revolving fans overhead set the scene. House specialty is saté: skewers of marinated meats or vegetables broiled over an open flame, from $6.50 to $6.75. Far Eastern dishes like Balinese chicken, spicy pork, ginger beef, Indian curries, and vegetarian stir-fries are also reasonable ($6.25 to $7.50); and everything is accompanied by either brown or fried rice plus a marinated cucumber-and-onion salad. Combination plates are excellent, and so is their special peanut sauce. Prices go up a few dollars at dinnertime. Daily Indonesian and international specials are also available, spiced to taste, and there are always several vegetarian entrees. Sibu Café is open every day from 11:30am to 9pm.

It's not really a restaurant, but **Suzanne's Bake Shop** on Alii Drive, a few doors from Mokuaikaua Church, serves as a breakfast place and snack shop for many people. The doors are open at 4:45 every morning, and that's when fragrant and flavorful muffins, doughnuts, danish, breads, croissants, and other goodies start coming out of the ovens. Danish are 85¢ to $1.30 each, and the caramel/macadamia-nut danish is a special treat. Sandwiches, Kona coffee, cold sodas, and ice cream are also available. A few chairs and tables outside afford a view of the passing parade and the ocean across the street. Open daily til 9:30pm.

For those who like hearty buffet meals, the **Kona Chuckwagon Buffet,** 74-5565 Luhia St. at Kaiwi Square (tel. 329-2818), is a good bet. The breakfast buffet is $4.25, the lunch one is $5.50, dinner, $8.25. Dinner and lunch see at least three meats on the table (perhaps ham, prime rib, barbecued beef ribs, fried chicken), plus chili, potatoes, vegetables, rices, and a soup and salad bar with a selection of 20 items. (Kaiwi Street is the first street as you enter Kailua from the airport.)

The lovely **Kona Inn Restaurant** (tel. 329-4425) in the Kona Inn Shopping Village is a splurge for us at dinner, but it's such a special spot, with a spectacular view of the bay and some tables perched right at water's edge, that it's worth your while to have lunch here. You can have chowder and salad for $4.95, Hawaiian chicken for $6.95, calamari for $5.95, pasta and chicken salad, $6.95, and a host of good sandwiches on a croissant roll, for $4.95. Having cocktails out on the oceanfront lanai is lovely, too.

Fisherman's Landing Waterfront Restaurant, on the oceanfront of the Kona Shopping Village on Alii Drive (tel. 326-2555) is a seafood restaurant in a spectacular setting. Splashing fountains and pools and nautical decorations all set the stage for the grand show put on by the pounding surf smashing up on the beach. It's most reasonable to come here at lunchtime, when broiler items like teriyaki beef, chicken Hawaiian, a variety of salads, go from about $6 to $9. They often have a $6.95 lunch buffet, consisting of salads, cold meats, and the catch of the day; you can create your own sandwiches. If you're willing to splurge, then enjoy superb fresh fish (about $18 to $20), Far Eastern and wok specialties ($13.75 to $17.95), and meat entrees like veal Oscar and New Orleans blackened steak ($17.95 to $18.95) at dinner. All entrees are accompanied by soup or salad (their Oriental salad is superb) and freshly baked bread from the restaurant's own ovens. Save room for dessert, too, like the lava macadamia-nut ice-cream pie.

Fisherman's Landing is open daily, from 11:30am to 2:30pm for lunch, from 5 to 10pm for dinner. There's music every night, Hawaiian and contemporary. Reservations are essential, especially at night. The cocktail lounge is open from 11am to closing.

Keauhou

Keauhou is one of the loveliest areas of the Kona coast, with its historic sites, glorious views of the bays and mountains, and grand resort hotels. It's well worth a short drive out here to enjoy the fabulous buffets for which the **Kuakini Terrace of the Keauhou Beach Hotel** has become known. Set in an open-air atmosphere, the Kuakini Terrace affords views of the hotel's lush and beautifully landscaped grounds, and provides an enticing view of Kahaluu Bay. The buffet table is also enticing: Monday through Thursday evening, it's a super Chinese feast, the tables laden with many unusual Far Eastern salads, greens, hot dishes like Chinese roast duck, steamed clams with black beans, sweet-and-sour shrimp, Chinese barbecued spareribs; there's a complete dim-sum table, and a table of luscious desserts, as well. And the cost for all you can eat is a mere $10.95 for adults, $5.95 for children. Considering the setting, the charm, and the quality of the food, this is definitely one of the best buys in town. Also very popular is their Seafood Buffet, served Friday through Sunday; it's all you can eat at $17.95 for adults, $8.95 for children. Sunday champagne brunch is another winner, with a wide selection of local favorites; it's $16.95 adults, $8.95 children. Kuakini Terrace is open daily from 6:30am to 9pm, serving all three meals (tel. 322-3441). Buffets begin at 5pm. Reservations are recommended.

Drysdale's Two (tel. 322-0070), in the graceful Keauhou Shopping Village, is a popular gathering spot, especially with sports fans who will be sitting in the huge, pennant-bedecked bar area, watching their favorite teams on the TV. There are several attractive dining areas here, too, as well as very good food on a popular-priced menu that is served all day, from 11am to midnight. Possibilities include such specialties as barbecued pork back ribs, breast of chicken teriyaki, and a vegetable stir fry, from $6.95 to $12.95; excellent hamburgers, including low-fat buffalo burgers (honest!), from $4.50 to $5.95; hearty meat sandwiches, croissant sandwiches, homemade chili, and a good variety of salads including a fresh Hawaiian fruit salad with sherbet at $6.50. Just about any taste can be accommodated here. Fabulous tropical drinks and ice-cream/liquor drinks are great for sipping out on the lanai; Peggy's peanut-butter ice-cream pie is a must for dessert, $2.95. Drysdale's Two is open daily from 10am to 1am, serving continuously from 11am to midnight.

For a change of ambience from the tourist world of Kailua, drive out on Hwy. H-11 (one block mauka from the main street of Kailua), a few miles south to **Teshima's,** at Honalo in coffee-growing country, a very popular place for about 45 years with the local Japanese, Hawaiians, Filipinos, and haoles. You might spot Senator Dan Inouye there—he always comes in for a meal when he's in Kona. Say hello to Mrs. Teshima—she's a great lady. On one visit she proudly showed us the report that Teshimas's had won first prize—the Gold Plate Award—for the best Japanese cuisine on the Big Island, from the *Gourmet Guide of Hawaii.* You can have a complete teishoku lunch of miso soup, sashimi, sukiyaki, plus various side dishes, served on an attractive black-lacquered tray, from $6 to $7.25. At dinner, vegetable tempura and shrimp tempura run $6.75 and $6.25, and there are plenty of dishes like sashimi, beef, pork, or chicken tofu, from $6.50 to $8.25, all served with miso soup, tsukemono, rice, and tea. Sashimi is market-priced. Teshima's is open from 6:30am to 2pm and from 5 to 10pm daily.

Take your choice of food and mood at the **Kona Ranch House** (tel. 329-7061), on Hwy. 11, on the corner of Palani and Kuakini. For a splurge, choose the lovely Plantation Lanai, so pretty in wicker and green: dinner features steaks and seafood ranging from $10.95 to $19.95. For a meal that's right within our budget, choose the adjoining Paniolo Room or "family-style" room, open for dinner from 5 to 9pm. There are several light dinners at just $6.95—thinly sliced roast pork, broiled or sautéed fish filets, broiled teriyaki, chicken breast, and thinly sliced roast beef—which are served with a choice of soup or salad or starch. Heartier appetites can enjoy dishes like grilled liver and onions, paniolo stew, ratatouille, lemon chicken with capers, vegetarian spaghetti with garlic bread, served with soup or salad *and* a choice of starch, from $6.95 to $9.25. Feeling really famished? Indulge in the Ranch House barbecue platter—entrees might be broiled half-chicken, barbecue beef ribs, pork spareribs, pork chops, combo chicken and ribs, or barbecue sliced beef. With them comes soup or salad, corn on the cob, a choice of rice, fries, onion rings, baked beans, or mashed potatoes, all for $12.95. Children's menus, burgers, tasty tropical drinks, luscious homemade desserts—Kona Ranch House has all of this, and reasonably priced lunches and breakfasts, too. The Kona Ranch House is open every day from 6:30am to 9pm.

The lively **Kona Coast Shopping Center,** near the intersection of hwys. 11 and 19, offers you a chance to mingle with the local folk at some inexpensive restaurants.

The branch of the **Sizzler** national chain is always busy, for they offer consistently good value in steaks, seafood, and huge salad bars. There's always a special on fresh fish of the day and a variety of all-you-can-eat specials, like all the steak and ribs you want for $13.99. Prices are low: fish platter, $9.89; teriyaki steak platter, $8.49; quarter-pound hamburgers, $4.99, served with toast and baked potato, french fries, or rice. The salad bar alone is enough for a meal, $6.99; with a regular platter, it's $3.99. Open 6am to 10pm Sunday to Thursday, till midnight on Friday and Saturday. The answer to a hungry family's prayer . . . **Bianelli's,** a new gourmet pizza shop, has been drawing kudos from the local crowd. You can have traditional hand-tossed New York–style pizza, or deep dish Chicago-style, with the usual toppings, most pies about $8.95 small, as well as some gourmet specialties like Greek, Mexican, Gourmet Vegetarian, or Gourmet Garlic (if you dare) pies, from $11.95. There are also pasta dinners, sandwiches, calzones, salads, and good desserts; not a bad choice at all. **Kim's Place** is a small Korean take-out shop, where traditional dishes like kalbi, bulgogi, Korean chicken, and the like, are all around $4—and all very good . . . **Betty's Chinese Kitchen,** small but sparkling, offers Chinese food in serve-yourself cafeteria style; most dishes are $3.35 for two portions, $4.05 for three, $4.65 for four. . . . Betty also has an interesting selection of dim sum—pork manapua, brown sugar manapua, egg rolls, and Chinese doughnuts, from 25¢ to 80¢ each. . . . **Monster Burger** is true to its name: it offers a half-pound Monster Burger at $3.25, a quarter-pound Mama Monster at $1.99, and a Baby Monster at 75¢. They also have lunch and dinner plates of items like roast beef, boneless chicken fry, mahimahi, from $3.75 to $5.99, including salad and rice or french fries. Breakfast special at $2.25, too. They also have excellent ice creams and sherbets, two scoops for $1. . . . You can't go wrong with the big avocado, cheese, and tomato sandwich on cracked wheat bread sold at the health-food store, **Kona Healthways.** It's $2.95, hearty and delicious.

Across the road is a newer shopping plaza, **Lanihau Center,** and it, too, has several restaurants and fast-food places. **Royal Jade Garden** is a cheerful, attractive Chinese restaurant, with large round tables, fans, and paintings on the walls, and a good menu with many reasonably priced entrees. Pork and beef dishes run $4.95 to $5.95 and there are almost two dozen seafood dishes—spicy shrimp, deep-fried oysters, abalone with black mushrooms—that go from $5.95 to $10.95. . . . We've already told you about McGurk's at Alii Drive. Now there's a **McGurk's at Lanihau,** and all the good things—fish and chips, shrimp and chips, fish and shrimp dinners, sandwiches—are here, too, at reasonable prices. There are daily specials, like Cajun BBQ, teriyaki breast of chicken sandwich, for $3.99. On Wednesday and Sunday, it's all the ono you can eat for $4.95. Homemade soups like cream of broccoli and New England clam chowder hit the spot. . . . **Buns in the Sun** is a cute little bakery/café with pretty glass-topped tables, with everything from cinnamon rolls to sourdough breads and challah twists. Breakfast sandwiches are served on butter croissants, and a variety of luncheon sandwiches, $3.75 to $4.50, on freshly baked breads. They always have a daily special, like their striped marlin fish sandwich, on a French roll, with salad and pickle, $4.50. . . . You could pick up some **Kentucky Fried Chicken** here, or snack on natural, fat-free (and quite delicious!) frozen yogurt at **Penguin's Place,** the first local branch of the popular West Coast chain.

On your way to City of Refuge at Honaunau (see Chapter XIV), there are some good places to stop. The **Aloha Café** (tel. 322-3383), in the lobby of the Aloha theater in Kainaliu, has wonderful, healthful food and an unusual atmosphere. The artistically decorated counter-service café is in the lobby of the theater, but it's even more fun to sit out on the terraced lanai that borders the building, especially all the way down near the meadow. The menu features homemade vegetarian soups, veggie salads, eggplant sesame cheeseburgers, vegetarian burritos, tostadas, nachos, and quesadillas, lots of sandwiches, and even a non-health-food item or two like great charbroiled burgers. These items run about $4.95 to $5.95. Dinner, served from 4pm to closing, adds filet mignon at $14.95, fresh fish (market-priced), and several vegetarian specials like lasagne or phyllo pie, $8.25 to $8.95. Wines and beers are available. If you get there in time for breakfast, you'll be treated to three-egg omelets, pancakes, and whole-wheat french toast, $4.25 to $5.95. Even if you don't have a meal here, stop in for some of the homemade fresh baked goods. The day we were there it was raspberry linzer tortes. Ono! Their baked goods, sandwiches, and burritos are also served at the World Square Theater in Kailua, and you don't have to pay admission to the theater to get the food. Aloha Café, by the way, seems to be local headquarters for transplanted mainlanders to hang out, so it's always a fun stop. Open every day except Sunday from 8am to 8pm only. Their adjoining health-food and gift store can provide picnic ingredients—cheeses, organic fruits (we recently tried organic lichees!), and vegetables. They also offer a large selection of gifts and cards, specializing in children's gifts and books. The store is open daily Sunday 9am to 5pm; other days, 8am to 8pm.

Down the street from the Aloha is the quaint **Kona Coffee Roasters,** with its old-world charm. Coffees, espresso, cappuccino, pastries, and bagels and cream cheese, are served in this café from 7am to 5pm. Tuesday through Friday. Coffee is roasted right on the premises. You can also buy fresh coffee beans here, and they ship.

The dining room of the **H. Manago Hotel** in Captain Cook (tel. 323-2642) is the place to catch a slice of local life. This big, family-style restaurant has enjoyed a good reputation for years among the local people, although very few tourists make their way here. Everything is served family style: big plates of rice, salad (macaroni salad is especially good), vegetables, and whatever the cook has made that night are brought out and served to everyone at the table, along with such entrees as pork chops, liver, ahi, opelo, ono, mahimahi, or steak; the prices go from about $5.50 to $10. The menu is limited and the food is not fancy, but this is a good chance to experience the nontourist life of the Kona coast. Very pleasant. They serve all three meals, dinner from 5 to 7:30pm weekdays; to 7pm Friday, Saturday, and Sunday.

Everybody likes the **Canaan Deli** in Kealakekua, across the street from the Bank of Hawaii. It's a New York–type deli started in 1972 by several young Christians with a mission: high-quality food served with aloha. The deli features New York-style sandwiches using fresh island beef and locally baked breads (hot pastrami and rare roast beef run around $4.95), homemade salads, and Italian specialties. All sandwiches come with a choice of salad and kosher pickle. They even have lox and bagels! Scrambled eggs and omelets are breakfast favorites, with a $2.25 breakfast special from 7 to 9am. And the homemade Italian dinners are fun: accompanied by a minestrone soup or salad, and garlic bread, entrees like fettuccine Alfredo, eggplant parmigiana, spaghetti, and meatballs run from $5 to $8. There's New York–style pizza, too.

THE NIGHT SCENE IN KAILUA-KONA

There's plenty of nighttime entertainment in these parts, even if you don't make it to one of the big hotel luaus (they cost around $40 at the **Kona Hilton** and the **King Kamehameha Hotels,** around $50 at the exotic **Kona Village Resort** at Kaupulehu). If you don't mind skipping the pig and poi, you can see an exciting Polynesian show every Tuesday and Friday night from 5:30 to 6:30pm at the Kona Surf Resort & Country Club, for the cost of a few drinks at its Nalu Terrace. It's worth the drive just to see the Kona Surf anyway, one of the most beautiful resorts in the area. Other nights, it's happy hour at the Nalu Terrace from 4 to 6pm, and there is always a group playing soft music as the sun sinks into the sea.

You will, of course, want to see a torchlighting ceremony. Happily, there's no charge at all for that. Just take yourself to the beach in front of the **King Kamahameha Hotel** at luau time on a Sunday, Tuesday, or Thursday evening just before sunset and watch the beautiful ceremony, as torches are lit on land and sea, in the shadow of an ancient heiau. Then you might proceed to the **Billfish Bar,** situated around the lovely pool, where there is a variety of musical entertainment every night from 5 to 10pm. Happy hour prices prevail from 5 to 7pm.

The Keauhou Beach Hotel is the place for fans of Hawaiian music. Much beloved here is Uncle George, who sings and plays on Monday, Tuesday, Thursday, Friday, and Saturday at the Makai Bar. Hawaiian Heart, another popular group, plays at the Makai Bar earlier in the evening. Kapio and Kalehua entertain at the

Kuakini Terrace on Friday, Saturday, and Sunday, while the seafood buffet (see above) is being served.

One of the most popular lounges in town is **Don Drysdale's Club 53,** where the exotic drinks—like Frozen Babbon, Fuzzy Willie, and Hawaiian Sunset—are unique, and where the pupus-shrimp scampi and deep-fried, spicy buffalo wings and potato skins are really special. There are burgers and sandwiches, too, to go along with the drinks.

Have you heard about Karaoke? It's been the rage in Japan for years, and now it's here, Tuesday, Wednesday and Friday from 7 to 9:30pm, at the **Windjammer Lounge** of the Kona Hilton. Karaoke means "empty orchestra," the orchestra minus the singer. Here, a laser-disc video machine provides the words, and guests—that could be you—take turns at providing the singing. Lots of fun, inexpensive drinks, and a $2 beer special.

The terrace overlooking the ocean at **Fisherman's Landing** is a wonderfully romantic spot, great for sunset watching or star gazing. Hawaiian and contemporary music every evening, from 6:30pm on. . . . The cocktail lounges at **Spindrifter, Kona Inn, The Chart House,** and **Phillip Paolo's** are all seaside, offering super scenery along with the libations.

If you're in a disco mood, go to romantic **Eclipse**—candles, wooden beams, mirrors, and the disco sound. Sunday nights it's Big Band music. Eclipse is on Kuakini Hwy., across from Foodland. Dinner from 5pm, dancing begins at 10pm every night but Monday. **The Poo Ping 2 Thai Cuisine Restaurant** at Kamehameha Square turns into the Poo Ping Discotech every night from 10pm until 2am. It's rock and roll of the '50s and '60s, plus Top 40s music. . . . **The Windjammer Lounge of the Kona Hilton** has become another rock music venue: Silk & Steel, Kona's "top rock ensemble," give out with oldies, contemporary, Hawaiian, and country-western music, Saturday, Sunday, and Monday.

The Windjammer Lounge, by the way, is one of the most scenic spots around, where you can listen to the sound of the surf smashing up against the rocks as you sit out on the patio and watch the Pacific perform. Walking around the big hotels like the Hilton, examining the gardens and lagoons by moonlight and floodlight, is like a show in itself.

READERS' SELECTIONS ON HAWAII: "The **Keauhou Beach Hotel** at Keauhou-Kona was exceptional! It was lovely in every way. It had such a Hawaiian atmosphere, with its oceanside bar, torchlit gardens, pool with waterfall, and restaurant over the lagoon. Their weekend seafood buffet was exceptional at $16.95. They even upgraded our partial oceanview rooms to full oceanview at no extra charge ($80 for partial oceanview). I highly recommend this place" (Martha Farwell, Illinois City, Ill.). . . . "The **Manago Hotel and Restaurant** at Captain Cook on the Big Island was GREAT!!!! Nice room, excellent food, fast service, and the people were friendly and helpful" (Louise Walter, Iuka, Ill.). . . . "We found **The Dragonfly Ranch** a place to exceed the expectations of even the wildest, most demanding imagination. Gifts from the heart abound there. It is a beautiful feeling to have lived, even for a bit, in such a romantic, fertile, nurturing, and beautiful environment" (Dori Dorkin, Haiku, Maui).

"There was one restaurant in particular that we returned to several times. It is the **Golden Chopstix Restaurant** in Kailua-Kona, located in Kaahumanu Plaza on Kaiwi Street, in the industrial area. They serve huge portions, are reasonably priced, and the biggest bonus of all is that they don't saturate their food with MSG, so we didn't experience any of the usual after-effects. Superb food with an out-of-this-world special sauce. Aloha! . . . Secondly, a word of advice—don't mess with Madame Pele!!! Even with forewarning, my skeptical husband took a piece of lava rock from the recent lava flows and was in a minor fender-bender with a local Kona lawyer the very next day! Needless to say, he gave the rock back to Pele! We made the mistake of not purchasing any rental-car insurance (because my husband had an excellent driving record and insurance coverage back home). Damage had to be paid on the spot, putting a real dent in our vacation money. Worst of all, we forgot about our $300 insurance deductible, so we *won't* be getting it all back eventually. Expensive lesson learned!" (Sandy and Dave Heinrich, Forks, Wash.)

"Our visit to the **Hilo Hotel** on Kinoole Street in Hilo found newly redecorated rooms. The carpeting and upholstered furnishings were brand new, everything was spotless, service was pleasant, free coffee and sweet breads are served by the pool in the morning. Our spacious and quiet two-bedroom, two-bath apartment was a bargain at $68 a night" (Joanne G. Schmidt, Newark, Del.).

"I have a lovely bedroom and sitting room in my home in Volcano, 12″×24″, with its own private entrance and private bath. It has a king-size bed and double futon on a frame, TV, and VCR. I can accommodate up to four people at $50 for two, $5 for each additional person. I also rent out my new two-bedroom, two-bathroom cedar home at $75 a day for two, $15 for each additional person. The seventh night is free on weekly stays. I love to bake and cook—I do a full breakfast with things like buttermilk pancakes, quiches, Hawaiian french toast made from Portuguese sweet bread, and my guests really enjoy it. They can write me at The Country Goose, P.O. Box 597, Volcano, HI 96785, or call 808/967-7759" (Joan Earley, Volcano, HI).

"**The Hotel King Kamehameha Luau** in Kona was the best we have seen. The food was terrific and plentiful. The show was very authentic and the right length of time. The hosts were very gracious and attentive. High recommendations" (Jim and Deb Phillips, Hastings, Neb.). . . . "The food and dancers at the **King Kamehameha Hotel Luau** were better than at the luau we saw in Kauai. Dancers in Kauai were mostly kids: seeing kid dancers is like paying to see a Broadway musical and watching a chorus line made up of grammar school and junior high school girls. . . . The **Ocean View Inn** on the waterfront is an inexpensive, joyful place to eat" (Naomi Kashiwabara, San Diego, Calif.).

"Our two-bedroom, one-and-a-half bath condo at **Sea Village** was terrific. We can't speak highly enough of this place. The kitchen was equipped with every utensil you'd ever need, right down to dishwasher detergent, the furnishings were lovely and rooms spacious, the gas BBQs on the lawn made it a cinch to grill steak or hamburgers, and the pool and Jacuzzi were beautiful. I was even able to stand next to the stone wall surrounding the pool and watch the whales in the ocean [*Authors' Note:* See text for details on Sea Village]. . . . The Jamboree breakfasts at the **Sizzler** in Kona were terrific *and* a bargain at $2.99. Also, **Ken's House of Pancakes** in Hilo had incredibly good macadamia-nut pancakes, banana pancakes, you name it—and again, *very* reasonably priced" (Cheryl Reese, New Richmond, Wisc., and Becky Gardner, Hammond, Wisc.).

"I'd like to add my raves to those that everybody else seems to give the **Dolphin Bay Hotel.** The room was quite adequate and even included a kitchenette for its amazing $31 a day, but the real plus here was the people. I never met the fabled John Alexander, but the motherly lady named Donna who took me in hand was no less wonderful" (Lisa Yount, Richmond Annex, Calif.). . . . "We stayed at the **H. Manago Hotel** in Captain Cook. At your suggestion, we asked for the Japanese room. What a treat! Only $49 per night. It was furnished in the Japanese fashion, including a futon, a deep tub, and a Go game board" (G. Vaughan Parker, Santa Barbara, Calif.). . . . "I spent a week-long retreat at **Kalani Honua,** which also rents rooms to individuals or couples. We found the accommodations comfortable, but on the rustic side (no hot water during nighttime hours and limited bathrooms). Prices were reasonable and the food was the best I've had anywhere at any time—mainly vegetarian with a few fish/chicken meals—very gourmet! Nearby is a "clothes optional" black-sand beach, lava tubes, and the volcano" (Dorene Carrel, Clearwater, Fla.) [*Authors' Note:* See text for details on Kalani Honua.]. . . . "We found the Thai restaurant in Kona, **Poo Ping,** delicious and inexpensive. They will pack some of their family's special recipe peanut sauce (used in satays) in $2-, $3-, and $5-size containers. It should last about three weeks—if you don't eat it all up first" (Lois-Ellin Datta, Bethesda, Md.).

"The **Dolphin Bay Hotel** made our stay in Hilo very special. As you and your readers rightfully point out, John Alexander is most helpful on what to see and do in the Hilo area. His suggestions on which trails to take at Volcanoes National Park were especially instructive. The maps and signs provided by the park are somewhat misleading (I'm not sure why), so do ask John specifically which trails to take when visiting the Volcano. . . . In the Kona area, the **Keauhou Beach Hotel** is beautifully run. The service is impeccable and the grounds are lovely. Every person we had the pleasure of dealing with at the hotel was friendly and eager to assist in any way. They had an arrangement with Tropical Rent-a-Car which provided us with an economy room *and* a car. I can't recommend this splendid hotel highly enough. . . . For a superb, inexpensive dinner, **Drysdale's Two** in the Keauhou shopping mall is one of the finest choices in town. The restaurant and bar is adorned with numerous sports trophies, and four color TVs —each one tuned to a different sports broadcast. Tables are available inside and on the terrace. We found fresh fish to be surprisingly expensive at most of the restaurants in Kailua, but at Drysdale's, you could get a delicious ahi sandwich, complete with fries or a green salad, for only $6.50. And for those who relish tropical drinks, Drysdale's has the best mai tais in town!" (John F. Stark, Santa Monica, Calif.).

"The **King Kamehameha Hotel,** in Kona has so much to offer visitors. The **Kona Veranda Coffeeshop** had the best hamburger of any—the Mauna Loa Burger with a fine garnish of onion curls and the best steak fries, adorned with a Vanda orchid. Across the street, **Quinn's**—plain out front but with a pleasant dining area out back—had an outstanding vegetable omelet with mushrooms and a mouth-watering sandwich of fresh avocado, beansprouts, and delicious cheese. In fact, Kona restaurants served the most reasonable and delicious food we had on our trip" (Beth and Bake Baker, Englewood, Fla.).

"Above all else, **Volcano House** must not be missed. Sitting on the rim of Kilauea Crater, it invokes the feeling of a mountain lodge. Volcano House is small and intimate with a friendly staff. It has a wood fireplace in the lobby, but no TVs (who needs them here in this setting!). We live in the mountains of New Mexico, but I have never seen stars like those at Volcano House. Where else but in Hawaii can you stand on a tropical island shivering in the chill below a 10,000-foot-plus mountain with snow in early October" (Nancy Goertz, Sandia Park, N.M.).

"We have just returned from Hawaii and want you to know that the **Dolphin Bay Hotel** in Hilo is the best, cleanest, and most friendly hotel we have stayed at in 12 trips to the islands. Fresh bananas, papayas, and mangoes each day free, and beautiful grounds to surround you, and very reasonable cost, $42 a day with kitchen. We have found that we can see Hawaii without paying a fortune. Thanks for telling us about the little hotels, especially the Dolphin Bay in Hilo and Kona Tiki in Kona. They are like old Hawaii" (Tom and Marg Keall, Surrey, B.C., Canada).

SEEING HAWAII

Count on a minimum of four days on the Big Island for relaxed sightseeing: the first day for touring in and around **Hilo;** the second for visiting the **Puna area** and **Hawaii Volcanoes National Park;** the third for driving across the island from Hilo to **Kailua-Kona** on the western coast; and the fourth for exploring the **Kona coast.** This gives you two nights at a hotel in Hilo and one or more in Kona. You can, of course, add a few more days at either end. It's also possible to arrive at Hilo, drive immediately to the volcano area for a few hours, and then continue right across the island to Kona, where you can then relax in the sun for as long as you want. Or fly into Kona and reverse the trip, from west to east. The following itinerary will give you the basic information, around which you can do your own improvising.

1. Around Hilo

Most of the residents of Hilo are convinced that this is the world's greatest little city, and they wouldn't consider living anywhere else. The fact that they live between the devil and the deep-blue sea bothers them not a bit. See those huge mountains that dominate the skyline? The bigger one, Mauna Kea, is an extinct volcano, but her smaller sister, Mauna Loa, is still very much alive.

If you've read Michener's *Hawaii,* you'll remember how the Alii Nui Noelani went to Hilo in 1832 to confront Pele and implore her to halt the fiery lava that came close to destroying the town. Pele has toyed with the idea more than a few times since, as recently as 1935, 1942, and 1984, but she has always spared the city—even without the intervention of priestesses. The citizens are convinced she always will. They feel just as nonchalant about tidal waves—at least they did until 1960. On the May morning when seismic waves hurtled across the Pacific headed for Hawaii, the citizens of Hilo had hours to evacuate; instead, some of them actually went down to the bridge to watch the show. This time the gods were not so kind. Sixty-one people were swept into the waves, and a big chunk of waterfront area was wiped out. For several years after, one could see the devastation along the ocean side of Kamehameha Avenue; now there is grass and palm trees. Past Pauahi Street, however, look to your right and see the surprisingly modern architecture of the county and state office buildings. The construction of these buildings caused one of the liveliest controversies in the history of the city; the reasoning was to inspire confidence in the devastated bayside area. The optimists won the day, and Hilo continues to defy further tsunami activity.

This knowledge impresses itself strongly on the mind of the visitor, making Hilo far more than a make-believe world for tourists. It forms a curious backdrop to the beauty and gentleness of this city arching around a crescent bay (Hilo's name means new moon). Once a whaling port of the Pacific, Hilo is still a seaport, from which raw sugar (note the bulk-sugar plant on the waterfront) and cattle are shipped to the other islands and the mainland. Flowers are big business, too; 132 inches of rainfall a year (most of it at night—but there are plenty of misty mornings, too) make the orchids and anthuriums grow as crabgrass does on suburban lawns elsewhere. Nearly a quarter of a million tropical blossoms are sent from Hilo via airplane all over the world.

GARDENS, GARDENS, GARDENS

And here's where our sightseeing tour of Hilo begins, with a visit to **Hilo Tropical Gardens.** Follow Hwy. 12 to the eastern strip of town where you'll find the gardens at 1477 Kalanianaole Ave., about two miles from the airport. Paved walkways (accessible to the disabled) lead you through a tiny jungle of tropical flowers, shrubs and trees, splendid orchids, native Hawaiian plants and herbs, past water-lily pools, waterfalls, even a Japanese pond with a footbridge and statuary. After you've seen the gardens and used up a little bit of film, stop in at their gift shop for Hawaiian handcrafts, wood products, photographs, notecards, food items, and, of course, flowers. Anything can be shipped home. Free admission. There's even a free hula show Saturday at 10am. Open daily from 8:30am to 5:30pm. Phone 935-4957 for driving directions.

If you haven't been surfeited by all this, you might also try **Orchids of Hawaii,** 2801 Kilauea Ave., which allows you to view its nursery and packing operations. Tropical cut flowers, orchid sprays, and leis are available to take back with you or ship home without any restrictions. To get there, drive southward on Hwy. 11 and turn right at Palai Street and left onto Kilauea Avenue. You'll see Orchids of Hawaii just after you cross the one-lane bridge on the left. Open weekdays from 8am to 4pm, closed on major holidays. Free admission.

Another very pleasant place to visit is **Hirose Nurseries,** 2212 Kanoelehua Ave. They give you free flowers, and you explore the beautiful hothouse and gardens on your own. Hirose Nurseries is about three miles out of town on Hwy. 11, on the left-hand side of the road, near Kahaopea Street.

On the way back toward town, stay on Manono Street as it crosses Kamehameha Avenue and continue on the drive along Hilo Bay. Soon you'll spot the **Nihon Japanese Culture Center** which, in addition to serving authentic and excellent Japanese cuisine (see Chapter XIII), has an art gallery, a tea room, and spaces for music, dancing, films, and other entertainment. Check to see if anything special is going on. Now there's **Liliuokalani Gardens** coming up on your right, lovely with its Japanese bridges, ponds, plants, and stone lanterns; you can picnic here. It's believed to be the largest such formal Japanese garden and park outside Japan. Look for the authentic Japanese tea ceremony house. Now on your left is **Coconut Island,** a favorite picnic spot for the local people. If you continue around the park, you'll find yourself on Banyan Drive, which takes you past many of the resort hotels in the city. The magnificent trees are labeled in honor of the celebrities who planted them: James A. Farley was one, Amelia Earhart another; Cecil B. De Mille has a tree, and so does Mrs. De Mille. At the end of the drive is **Reed's Bay Park,** a cool picnic spot on the bay.

To see one of our favorite gardens, however, you'll have to drive in another direction, about three miles south on Hwy. 11 (the road to the volcano) from Hilo Airport, then turn left onto Makalika Street just after Hwy. 11 divides. Drive 7/10 of a mile (look for the familiar Hawaiian warrior sign for the turn-off), and you'll

HAWAII — THE BIG ISLAND

N

Upolu Point   Kapaau
Hawi   NORTH KOHALA
                Kohala   Coast
         270   Waipio
              250   Waipio   240   Honokaa
                     Valley   Hamakua
Kawaihae   19   Waimea   19   Laupahoehoe
                     Waimea-Kohala   Coast
                     Airport
QUEEN KAAHUMANU HWY.   190   Mauna Kea   Akaka Falls
                                               Honomu
         19   IMAMALAHOA   Boiling Pots   Hilo Bay
              HWY.   Mt.   Hilo
Keahole Airport   Hualalai   SADDLE RD.   Rainbow   Hilo Airport
                                                     Falls
Kailua-Kona   200   Kee'au
         180
              Kealakekua   130   Kapoho
Napoopoo   Captain Cook   Mauna Loa   11   Pahoa   132
Kealakekua   137
Bay   Pu'uhonua o Honaunau   Kilauea Crater   Black Sand   Kaimu
              Nat'l Hist. Park   Beach
                                                     Road closed by
         Kealia   K   CHAIN   recent lava   Kalapana
                                         A   OF   activity
              Manuka State Park   Pahala   U   CRATERS
                                                  RD.   Hawaii Volcanoes
         11   Punaluu   Nat'l Park

                   Naalehu

              Kelae
              (South Point)

soon find **Nani Maui Gardens,** a wonderland of 20 acres full of the fruits and flowers of many lands; their orchid garden alone, with thousands of varieties, is the largest in Hawaii. A ginger/heliconia garden, an anthurium garden, a tropical water-lily and carp pond, an enclosed nursery and an artificial waterfall and stream are also featured. Nani Mau has been taken over by new management, which is planning many new developments to turn it into a world-class attraction: a restaurant is set to open shortly and, in the future, they'll have a native Hawaiian herb garden, a rose garden, a wedding chapel, a palm garden, and much more. You can tour the gardens by foot, on a tram ($2 per person), or by renting a golf cart, which seats four people, at $6. You can sit in the gardens as long as you like, to picnic or just relax. Open daily, from 8am to 5pm, with an admission charge of $5. Phone 959-3541 for information.

Most of Hilo's gardens are lovely, but manicured: **Hawaii Tropical Botanical Garden** is something altogether different. Located seven miles north of Hilo on the four-mile scenic route at Onomea Bay, it's a one-of-a-kind combination of tropical rain forest and wild jungle. Its 17 acres are dotted with myriad waterfalls, meandering streams, and more than 1,600 species of tropical plant life (many of them rare and endangered); there's a lake with tropical water lilies and a stretch of rugged ocean coastline. Many have called it "the most beautiful valley in Hawaii." The garden is the altogether remarkable creation of one man, Daniel Lutkenhouse, a San Francisco businessman who visited Onomea Valley in 1977, fell in love with its rugged beauty, and then spent 10 years of hard work and over $1 million of his own money in transforming the neglected rain forest into a botanical showcase that has received world wide acclaim. Working seven days a week for eight years, Lutkenhouse and three helpers did all the physical work themselves, clearing the jungle paths, equipped only with cane knives, sickles, picks, and shovels. Lutkenhouse is still working hard; he's recently bought 40 new acres, and he and his wife, Pauline, travel every year to new tropical destinations to gather exotic seeds and plants and bring them back to Hawaii.

For serious students of nature and lovers of natural beauty—not to mention photographers—it's a paradise. Admission is $10 (children under 16 free), which is tax deductible, because the garden is a nonprofit foundation. It's open every day, rain or shine (they furnish umbrellas), from 8:30am to 4:30pm. Phone 946-5233 for driving directions. You park at the Visitors Center (a historic, restored church), and then are taken down into the valley for a self-guided tour; most people spend at least an hour or two here. No food is sold and there are no picnicking facilities.

A HAWAIIAN ZOO AND AN ENVIRONMENTAL CENTER

While you're visiting the gardens in this area, you might also want to take in a charming Hilo attraction: the **Panaewa Rain Forest Zoo.** It's just outside the city as you drive on Rte. 11; turn right on the Stainback Hwy. and watch for signs on the right to the zoo. This is by no means the big time, as zoos go; it's a small place but with its own special Hawaiian charm. You'll see denizens of the South American rain forest, the rare Hawaiian "nene" (goose), the Hawaiian "pueo" (owl), many brightly plumaged birds, and peacocks roaming the grounds; cutest of all are the monkeys, especially the capuchins, who seem to enjoy the funny humans walking about. Free admission. Open every day from 9am to 4pm.

THE TRAIL OF KAMEHAMEHA

Now it's time for some Kamehameha lore, since the Big Island is where that doughty old warrior was born and where he first started dreaming his dreams of glory and conquest. Continue your journey on Kamehameha Avenue, turn left at Waianuenue Street, and drive three blocks to the modern county library on the right side. See the two stones out in front? The bigger one, the **Naha Stone,** was Kamehameha's Excalibur. According to Naha legend, only a chief of the royal blood could even budge the gigantic boulder; any warrior strong enough to turn it over would have the strength to conquer and unify all the islands of Hawaii. Kamehameha did the deed, but since the stone weighs at least a ton, no one has bothered, as yet, to repeat it.

HILO'S NATURAL SIGHTS

Best time to see the next sight, **Rainbow Falls,** is early in the morning. Come between 9:15 and 10am, when the sun gets up high enough over the mango trees so that you're apt to see rainbows forming in the mist. But it's pretty at any time, and so are the beautiful yellow flowers growing near the parking lot. You reach the falls by taking Rainbow Drive off Waianuenue Avenue. If you'd also like to see the **Boiling Pots,** deep pools that appear to be boiling as turbulent water flows over the lava bed of the river, continue along Waianuenue about two miles, past some of the nicest homes in Hilo and a huge monkeypod tree, to Peepee Street. From the parking lot you can walk over to the edge and observe the show below. Both Rainbow Falls and the Boiling Pots are part of the **Wailuku River State Park.**

Now we head for the **Kaumana Cave** and a chance to see some of the work of Pele at close range. The cave is a lava tube, created in 1881, when Pele came closer to wiping out Hilo than at any other time. Lava tubes are sometimes formed when lava flows down a ravine or gully; the top and sides cool while the center keeps racing along. Millions of years of volcanic eruptions have left hollow tubes like this all over the islands; in many of them are hidden the bones of the alii, which were always buried in remote, secret places. Of the two tubes here, only the one on the right— whose entrance is an exquisite fern grotto—is safe for exploration. The one on the left is treacherous, and who knows—perhaps the bones of Kamehameha, never discovered, are buried here? To get to the caves, return to the fork at Hwy. 20 and turn right to the other branch of the fork, Kaumana Drive. The cave is about three miles out; an HVB marker indicates the spot.

A CHURCH AND A MUSEUM

On we go, from paganism to Christianity. When you get back to Kamenameha Avenue, watch for Haili Street; turn onto it in a mauka direction (away from the bay and uphill); cross Keawe, Kinoole, and Ululani streets, and on the left-hand side you'll see **Haili Church.** Its architecture is pure New England, but its fame stems from its great Hawaiian choir. Continuing up Haili Street, you next cross Kapiolani Street, and on the right-hand side you'll find the **Lyman House Memorial Museum Complex** at 276 Haili St. You can visit either the old missionary house and the newer $1-million museum addition, or both. The original Lyman House is another of those old mission homes that the grandchildren and great-grandchildren turned into a museum, and this one, originally built in 1839, has been fully restored and furnished as a home of the late 19th century. Hilo's oldest structure, the white-frame building contains hand-molded New England glass windows, doors made of native koa wood, and the original wide koa floorboards. As you tour the rooms, you'll see how the missionary family lived: the clothes, old four-poster beds, white marble-topped table stands and dressers. The fascinating Hawaiian artifacts and worldwide curios that used to be displayed here have now been transferred to the recently built Lyman Museum building. In this very modern museum, you begin at the Island Heritage Gallery on the first floor where a raised relief map shows routes taken by all the groups that came to Hawaii. Then you can see the artifacts of each group and study their cultures; the Hawaiian exhibit includes a full-size grass house, Stone Age implements, feather leis, etc. Other ethnic exhibits include an intricately hand-carved Taoist shrine brought to Hilo piece by piece in their luggage by early Chinese sugar-plantation workers. There are also Japanese, Portuguese, Korean, and Filipino displays.

The second floor also has fascinating exhibits, among them the Earth Heritage Gallery with its display of volcanic eruptions and worldwide gem mineral collections, one of the finest and most extensive such collections in the country; a worldwide shell collection, covering many examples of beautiful and rare shells. The Chinese Art Gallery has pieces dating back as far as the Shang Dynasty, 13th century B.C.; and the Artists of Hawaii Gallery features works by early Hawaiian artists as well as contemporary art of Hawaii.

Lyman House is open from 9am to 5pm Monday to Saturday; closed Sunday and major holidays. Admission is $3.50 for adults, $2.50 for children 12 to 18, $1.50 for ages 6 to 12.

SHOPPING IN HILO

Shopping is concentrated in three areas here: downtown, where stores and boutiques are housed in quaint wooden buildings; at the Kaiko'o Hilo Mall; just behind the county and state buildings; and out on Highway 11, at the newer mega-bucks Prince Kuhio Plaza Shopping Center. Let's start out **Kaiko'o Hilo Mall;** with a big supermarket and stationery and drug stores, it's mostly of interest to local people, but we always do very well at the **J.C. Penney's** here, where values and selections are excellent in every department. It's a good place to shop for muumuus, and luggage, too. And we always like to have a look at **Book Gallery 2,** especially to browse through their wide selection of island cookbooks: They carry all the local cookbooks of church groups, women's groups, and the like. They have a good selection of Hawaiiana, books for the keikis back home, and some unique Petroglyph Press paperbacks, printed right here in Hilo.

If you're in Hilo on a Sunday morning, and you don't mind getting up early, take yourself to the bus terminal at the corner of Mamo Street and Kamehameha Hwy., downtown, at about 6am in the morning. This is the scene for Hilo's biggest Farmer's Market, and people come from all over to pick up produce, lots of flowers, some fish, and some arts and crafts, too, at low, low prices. They sell out quickly, so it's best to be there early. A Farmer's Market is also held on Wednesday morning, but Sunday is the big event.

Just down the street from the mall, crafts-minded people should stop in at **Hawaii Modelcraft,** located at the Hilo Shopping Center, 1221 Kilauea Ave. This is a great hobby store for kids of all ages. The people here freely dispense hospitality and travel tips to visitors along with know-how on local crafts.

The only natural food store in Hilo is **Abundant Life Natural Foods Store,** now settled into its new location on the bayfront at 292 Kamehameha Ave., in downtown Hilo. Almost 15 years old, it is the Big Island's most complete natural grocery store. Along with the top major brands of supplements, quality skin-care products, groceries, and the like, Abundant Life carries a unique selection of local and imported items. Their deli section is great for a healthy and hearty meal on the run, and their produce section features locally grown fruits and vegetables—strawberry-papayas, apple-bananas, mangoes, local watermelons, tangerines, avocados, and more. Organic, raw, unsalted macadamia nuts and honey from the Big Island are also treats. Lots of gift items to take home for friends—or yourself.

You can't miss seeing those ads for Hilo Hattie wherever you go in the islands, so you might as well visit one of the **Hilo Hattie Fashion Centers** right here in Hilo. The company is the largest manufacturer of aloha wear in the state. The facility in Hilo houses a production line, so you can see garments being made, as well as explore the large retail area, which carries gifts, candy, and jewelry in addition to clothing, all at less-than-usual prices. Everybody gets a complimentary shell lei and refreshments, too. Hilo Hattie's is on the main highway, just a few blocks past the airport at 933 Kanoelehua. Call 961-3077 for free transportation. Open every day.

If you'd like to take some anthuriums home with you, be sure to stop at **Anthuriums of Hawaii,** 530 Ainaola Dr., where you can see anthuriums of every color and description (green and red "hula dancer" or "lipstick" anthuriums, for example), and enjoy the friendly hospitality of the owners. They're the kind of people who, simply because we inquired about different varieties of ginger, rushed to our car as we pulled out with a big stalk of fresh ginger to take with us—compliments of the house. They'll pack and ship anthuriums anywhere, and prices are reasonable. Everyone gets two anthuriums and whatever fresh fruit is in season free—just for visiting. The owners ask that you call 959-8717 for directions before you come.

Across the street from the Hawaii Visitors Bureau, at 195 Kinoole St., is **Hale Manu Craft,** which has hats, baskets, place mats, and other lauhala weavings made by local craftspeople. . . . **Grassroots,** 197 Kinoole St., is a women's shop with an ethnic flavor—some items from Bali and other parts of Indonesia, some locally made—all at moderate prices. . . . A few doors along, at 201 Kinoole St., is **Old Town Printers & Stationers,** the retail store of the Petroglyph Press, which has been publishing books on Hawaiiana since 1962. Drop in to browse through their publications, notes, and postcards, including many Hawaiian designs. Better yet, walk around the corner to their other store, at 169 Keawe St., called **Basically Books,** which specializes in Hawaii and the Pacific, with videotapes and a complete selection of maps of Hawaii including USGS topographic maps, NOAA nautical charts, road and street maps. They also carry travel books and maps for destinations worldwide.

There's an artistic touch to a handful of downtown shops, all of them on or close to Keawe Street. The **Potter's Gallery,** located on the corner of Waianuenue Avenue and Keawe Street, features contemporary works by Big Island artists and craftspeople. There is a wide selection of quality work including functional pottery raku, koa furniture, etched glass, paintings, jewelry, textiles, and sculpture. They also have a full calendar of shows spotlighting Big Island artists. . . . **Sig Zane Designs,** 140 Kilauea Ave., is known for its distinctive designs in Hawaiian sportswear. You'll see them elsewhere in the island, but this is the source: muumuus, T-shirts, aloha shirts, pareaus, handsome quilted designer jackets, jewelry, accessories, all bearing Sig's signature touch. Everything is 100% cotton. Prices are not inexpensive, but this is top of the line.

The **Most Irresistible Shop in Hilo,** at 110 Keawe St., is always worth a look-see, since owner Sally Mermel is always coming up with something new and exciting for her flocks of loyal customers. On a recent visit we spotted lots of one-of-a-kind jewelry by local artisans (earrings made of Hawaiian woods, dolphin rings); Hawaiian quilt-design mugs in a variety of pastel colors; lovely pareaus from Tahiti, Hawaii, Indonesia, and Italy, some of them exclusive here; a variety of perfume essences made on the Big Island, with wonderful names and fragrances—tuberose, pikake, plumeria, gardenia, orange blossom, at $5.25; koa cutting boards and rice paddles. There are some exclusive "Hilo, Hawaii" T-shirts, and also some T-shirts with all-around designs: These come in whale, shark, volcano, and turtle motifs—and are hot! Hawaiian jams and jellies make great small take-home presents: Take home some poha berries mixed with strawberries, made in Waimea—delicious. Speaking of which, adjoining the shop is **Bears' Coffee** (see Chapter XIII), with wonderful coffees, light foods, and desserts, all with a bear theme—Bear Claws, Teddy Bear Pie—and more.

The renovated and quite attractive 1922 Pacific Building, which houses The Most Irresistible Shop in Hilo, is also home to several other tasteful boutiques. The **Cunningham Gallery** features prints and paintings by local artists like Pegge Hopper, John Thomas, Robert Nelson, Tom Rossacher, and Kim Taylor Reese. Attractive koa-framed mirrors start at around $50. Cards by Guy Buffet, Herb Kane, Jane Chao, and others begin at just $1. . . . A lot of the items at **The Futon Connection** are too big for you to carry home, but do have a look at their crystals and jewelry, their lovely Japanese rice-paper shades ($25, and they can be mailed), cotton kimonos, colorful wall fans, and lots more.

Prince Kuhio Shopping Plaza will remind you of Kaahumanu Center on Maui or Kukui Grove on Kauai; it's vast, it cost millions to build (in this case 47.5), it boasts the traditional big department stores like **Liberty House, Sears** and **Woolworth's,** plus a handful or more of charming little boutiques. **The Most Irresistible Shop in Hilo,** which we mentioned above, has cloned its downtown location (except for Bears' Coffee) and is now here as well, with the same kind of tasteful merchandise. . . . **Imagination Loves Toys** is an educational toy center, with all kinds of creative playthings. . . . Across from it is **Kay-Bee Toys and Hobby,** fun for kids and hobby fanatics. . . . And **Once Upon a Time** is a charmer, full of stuffed animals, whimsical teddy bears, Victorian dolls, funny slippers, and more. You could buy a Star Wand or a Bubble Wand for $5.95. . . . **Contempo Casuals** is known for trendy sportswear, beach clothing, disco wear, and creative costume jewelry at reasonable prices. . . . **Tee's 'n' Togs** has lots of cute tops that can be imprinted with your choice of design, or personalized . . . and **Casual Corner** has nice contemporary women's fashions. . . . **The Candy Store** is great fun, full of hard-to-find local delicacies like dried abalone and a large variety of preserved seeds, sweet-and-sour apricots, shredded mango seeds, and such. Lots of imported and local cookies, like macadamia-nut snowball cookies, too. . . . Speaking of cookies, **Mrs. Field's Cookies** is here, with no fewer than four kinds of chocolate brownies and divine peanut-butter dream bars. There are some pleasant places to eat here, like **Kow's Chinese Deli** and **Boomer's,** with the mood of a 1950s diner, but keep in mind that you're about a two-minute drive from the Puainako Town Center, home to **Ting-Hao Mandarin Restaurant,** one of the best in town (see Chapter XIII).

MUUMUU MADNESS

We found a great source for reasonable muumuus and aloha shirts right on Kamehameha Avenue, at no. 210: it's called **Island Fashions.** Island Fashions has sister shops on the other islands and one in Kona (at 75-56630 Pulani Rd.); at all of them you'll find very reasonable prices, at least 20 to 30% off what comparable clothes would cost elsewhere. Always worth a look to see if they have something for you.

WAILOA CENTER

The building that looks like a volcano, just behind the state office building, is actually the **Wailoa Center,** a continuing free exhibit that accents the natural history and culture of the Big Island. Wall niches and free-standing displays are changed every month or two, so you might get to see an exhibit of Hawaiian-born artists, a display of the history and culture of the island, or one on ancient Hawaiian antiques. There's a permanent exhibit on tsunamis (tidal waves); a tsunami monument stands next to the building. Check out the Mini Fountain Gallery with changing art displays each month. The people here are happy to provide information and suggestions for visitors. Services and admission are free. The entrance is on Piopio Street, between the state office building and Kamehameha Avenue. It's open weekdays 8am to 4:30pm, noon to 8:30pm Wednesday, Saturday from 9am to 3pm.

TIME FOR A SWIM

Your ramblings have worn you out, your budget hotel doesn't have a pool, and you want a swim. Where do you go? We'd head out on Kalanianaole Avenue, drive three miles to **Onekahakaha Beach Park** or a mile further to **James Kealoha Park,** where the swimming in the rocky bay is okay if not memorable. But it's pleasant to drive through this Keaukaha area, the most beautiful part of Hilo, to see the exquisite private homes, some with their own tranquil Oriental fish ponds. Picnic and swimming spots continue until the end of the paved road. Watch for the signs pointing to **Richardson's Ocean Park,** the home of an outdoor marine recreation and interpretive center. You can swim, snorkel, fish, and surf in waters that front the center; tour a coastal trail which features coastal plants and brackish water ponds, and picnic on the lawn areas. The center contains marine life displays that interpret nearby ocean and coastal environments. Open Monday through Saturday, 8:30am to 4:30pm. Free admission. Phone 935-3830 for details.

If you favor pool swimming, join the local people at the Olympic-size **Sparky Kawamoto Swim Stadium** (tel. 935-8907) at Kuawa and Kalanikoa streets, near the civic auditorium. Admission is free. Open weekdays from 11am to 1pm for adults, from 1 to 4pm for everybody; on weekends 10am to noon for adults and 1 to 4pm for everybody.

---

2. Puna and Volcanoes National Park

You must not leave the Big Island without paying homage to the goddess Pele. Not to visit her residence at Halemaumau, the firepit crater of Kilauea (this is the smaller volcano nestled along the southeastern slope of Mauna Loa), would be unthinkable. If Pele is entertaining, you're in for one of the world's great natural spectacles; if not, just a look at a volcano and what it can do will be a big experience.

Although everybody goes to the volcano, a lot of tourists miss one of the most fascinating places of all: the Puna region east of the volcano, where you get a feeling of what a volcanic eruption means, not as a geologic curiosity, but in terms of the farms and stores and orchards and graveyards and cucumber patches that got in its way. Make the volcano trip your first priority; if you have a little extra time, this one is fascinating, too

THE DRIVE TO PUNA

This outing begins on Volcano Hwy. (Hwy. 11), which branches off from Kamehameha Avenue southward past the airport. About six miles out of town, you'll come to a possible stop, the **Mauna Loa Macadamia Nut Mill and Orchard,** the world's leading grower, processor, and marketer of macadamia nuts. Macadamias— Luther Burbank called them "the perfect nut," and they taste better than peanuts— are a big crop of the islands. On the drive from the highway to the Visitor Center (past roads with names like Butter Candy Trail or Macadamia Road), you'll see hundreds of thousands of macadamia trees planted in this area. From an observation gallery you can see the processing and packing operation, and observe colorful displays on history and horticulture. You can also take a mini Nature Walk through a macadamia-nut grove with papaya, monkeypod, and banana trees. Open daily from 9am to 5pm.

At **Keaau,** you may want to turn left off Volcano Hwy. and drive through town until you find Rt. 130 and Keeau, an old, rather rundown plantation town that is now home to many artists and craftspeople. Just mauka of the Keeau Police Station is **Puna Tropical Buds** (in the historic Plantation Store), a good stop if you're planning to send flowers to anybody back home. You can buy a dozen anthuriums here and, with packaging and mailing, the cost is a mere $15, which is at least $5 less than what you'd pay at shops in Kona. They also sell inter-island airline tickets at substantial discounts. And once you're back home, send the nice people here $29, and they'll ship you, pronto, a gorgeous tropical bouquet. (Write to Jonna & Scotty, P.O. Box 1593, Keeau, HI 96749, tel. 966-8116). On the same street, across from the shopping center, is **Keeau Natural Foods,** one of the best-stocked health-food stores on the Big Island, with lots of organic produce, a nice selection of items (dips, tabbouleh, vegetarian sandwiches, carrot juice, etc.), and homemade goodies to munch on. You can also stock up on guilt-free temptations like Russian tea cake and date bars, made only with unbleached flour and little or no sugar. Also in stock: incense, candles, hammocks, sandals, T-shirts, and the like.

Back on Rte. 130 now, **Pahoa** is about 10 miles further along; here you'll enter the area that received the brunt of the 1955 eruption of Kilauea. This had been peaceful farm country for a hundred years, dotted with papaya orchards, sugarcane fields, coffee farms, pasture lands. Then a rift in the mountain opened, and the lava fountains began to spout erratic cauldrons that turned a farm into ashes, but left a gravestone or an old building untouched. You'll see cinder cones along the road and tiny craters still steaming. The most spectacular—and chilling—scenery comes later.

Downtown Pahoa is a funky little town you may want to explore a bit, especially if you're interested in art. Stop in at the **Pahoa Arts and Crafts Guild** on the boardwalk, a co-op gallery/shop run by local artists. Oils, watercolors, prints, metals, baskets, jewelry are all represented, and prices are fair. You can get natural deli foods at **Pahoa Natural Groceries.** And keep your eyes open for the local vendors who can sometimes be found downtown, selling anthuriums, puka products, papayas, and the like—all at very reasonable prices. Look for the one selling six papayas for $1. Don't be lazy: Get out of your car and stock up! Nowhere else can you beat these prices.

Hungry? **The Pahoa Coffee Shop** is a favorite, open from 7am to 2pm only, but that should give you enough time to sample some three-egg omelets, Belgian waffles, or a hearty T-bone steak with eggs, hash brown potatoes, rice, and toast—all very reasonably priced. **Paradise West** stays open until 9pm daily, whips up a neat eggs Benedict and a fresh catch Benedict, does homemade soups, salads, vegetarian dishes, steaks, and lots more.

Continue along Rte. 130 now, and prepare yourself for a chilling sight: a look at the lava flow that destroyed the idyllic garden community of Kalapana in May of 1990. Flows from the Pu'u o'o vent of Kilauea, which began erupting in 1983, finally reached the sea seven years later, but not before destroying in its terrible path at least 123 houses, a church, local stores, and the idyllic Harry K. Brown Park. Also in its path was the Star of the Sea Painted Church, one of the two "painted churches" on the island, known for its colorful, indoor murals painted there in 1931. The church was removed before the lava flow could consume it, and was to be relocated somewhere in this area (check local sources for its exact whereabouts).

First, following the signs to Kalapana, you will come to one of the most incredible beaches in the world: the black-sand beach at Kaimu. The unexpected color effects are the results of explosion of black lava from a much older flow hitting the sea. Graceful palm trees make the picture idyllic, but don't try swimming here, for the currents are treacherous. Continue on Rte. 130, bypassing the turnoff to Kaimu, to see the lava flows. Then, backtrack two miles to the junction of Kaimu and Rte. 130, and turn left, turn around and retrace your path to Hwy. 137, toward Kapoho and a fantastic 15-mile trip across one of the most exciting coastlines in Hawaii. From the red rollercoaster of a road, you'll see where the tropical jungle alternates with black rivers of lava that laid waste miles of earth before they reached their violent end in the steaming Pacific. The sea pounds relentlessly on the black lava rocks, eventually to grind them into more black sand; on the land the jungle creeps back slowly, reclaiming the land for itself and breaking it down into what will one day again be red earth. This is how the islands of Hawaii—and many of the earth's surfaces—were formed, and no textbook description will ever leave such a vivid picture in your mind.

En route to Kapoho on Hwy. 137, between the 17- and 18-mile marker, you'll see a sign on the left that reads, "Kalani Honua." **Kalani Honua** is a cultural and arts conference center and retreat, offering classes, workshops, dance performances, and special events, as well as lodgings (see Chapter XIII). You may want to stop in at this point to have a look at their lovely gift shop, which shows, among other artistic offerings, silk-screened pareaus made by Richard Koob and other craftspeople. On a recent visit, we noted that these pareaus had been turned into bedspreads for the guest rooms by the center's talented seamstress, Sylvie. We liked the bedspreads so much that we persuaded Sylvie to make them up for sale. She borders the vividly colored pareaus with white cotton; the results would look wonderful in a summer home or beach cottage. A single bedspread is $58, a double $68, and a pillowcase is $10, all including the cost of the fabric. Sylvie will make these to order and mail them home to you. If she's not at the gift shop, she asks that you leave her a message. Call 965-7828. While you're here, have a peek to see if **Café Cashew,** right next door to the gift shop, is open. If so, you can have a pleasant, mostly vegetarian meal there at $6 for breakfast, $7 for lunch, $11 for dinner, or $13 with a fish or fowl option.

Continuing toward Kapoho on Hwy. 137, you'll find two good spots for picnicking, fishing, or hiking (no swimming: **MacKenzie State Park** near Opihikao and **Isaac Hale Park** at Pohoiko. Continue on Hwy. 137 until you reach Kapoho, a Hawaiian Pompeii that was buried under spectacular lava flows in 1960. The day-by-day fight to keep the village from being overwhelmed by the lava flow and pumice cinders from the new cinder cone (which now overlooks the sad remains of Kapoho) was one of the most dramatic episodes in recent Hawaiian history. A cinder cone on the concrete floor is all that remains of Nakamura's Store, and nearby, a desolate lighthouse stands inland from the new coastline created by the lava flow. Come back from Kapoho on Hwy. 132 and stop, perhaps at the **Geothermal Visitors Center** in Pohoiki. Free tours are held from 7am to 5:30pm every day. Nearby is **Lava Tree State Park.** An old lava flow encircled the trees here, and they were eventually burned out, but the lava trunk molds remain, surrealistic witness to the whims of Pele

You'll note that we've now described a triangle almost back to Pahoa; from here it's Rte. 130 back to Keaau, and then home to Hilo.

THE VOLCANO

It's more exciting than ever to visit the volcano, because for several years there has been a great deal of activity in Mauna Ulu, Pauahi Crater, and others. These new eruptions on the flanks of Kilauea have been big enough to spurt enormous fountains of fire 1,800 feet up above the crater's rim. In 1984 both Kilauea and Mauna Loa were active at the same time, the first time this has happened since 1868. Lava flows came dangerously close to the city of Hilo. As of this writing six years later, Pele is still acting up. You can call the park rangers at 967-7311 before you start for news of the latest eruptions and viewing conditions. Call 967-7977 anytime for recorded information on eruptions. But whether or not anything is happening, the volcano trip is a must.

Your excursion to the volcano will start on Hwy. 11 out of Hilo, just as the Puna trip did, but this time you stay on that road all the way to **Hawaii Volcanoes National Park.** It's a drive of about 30 miles. Be sure to take a warm sweater and a raincoat; the air gets refreshingly cool 4,000 feet up at Kilauea Crater. The weather can change quickly and dramatically, as sunshine gives way to mist and fog.

There are several possible stops en route for flower fanciers. The first, at the 14-mile marker in the tiny town of Mountain View, is the **Hawaiian Flower Garden Nursery,** which specializes in anthuriums—and sells tham at very low prices. (While you're on the main street of Mountain View, look for the Mountain View Bakery and see if they have some of their "stone cookies.") The next stop—at the 20-mile marker—could be at Hirano Store, which, at the time of our last visit, had an excellent view of the ongoing eruption of the volcano at ground level. At the 22-mile marker is **Akatsuku Orchid Gardens,** a lovely botanical-type garden, where you can view many varieties of orchids and receive one free as a gift. Just before you get to the park, it's fun to stop in at tiny **Volcano Village and Volcano Store** (on Hwy. 11, make a right at Haunani Road directly to the store). Half of the porch is the home of a snack bar and small restaurant called Volcano Diner; the other half is the place where local people go to scoop up reasonably priced flowers: just to give you an example, we saw Birds of Paradise for 50¢ a blossom, a dozen calla lilies for $2.25, king protea for $4 and less. The store will pack and ship, anywhere in the United States, at very reasonable prices: a dozen anthuriums and a sprig of orchids, $20; or two dozen large anthuriums, $18. Poke around inside a bit—it's great for local color. On our last trip, we discovered Lilikoi Butter (7 ozs. for $2.50), a preserve made from passion fruit: fabulous! The bulletin board out front often has leads on cottages to rent and news of local events.

Once you reach the park (entrance $2 per person, free for those over 62), signs will direct you to the **Kilauea Visitor Center,** which should be your first stop. Check with the very helpful park rangers here for directions on the current eruption—if any. Be advised that if an eruption is going on, extreme caution must be exercised on the hiking trails, as there may be earth cracks, hundreds of feet deep, anywhere, and a fall could be deadly. Those with heart and respiratory problems should beware of noxious fumes, children must be kept under control, and everyone should protect himself from the intense rays of the sun. Most visitors, however, simply drive to the important points on Crater Rim Drive (more about that ahead), which is much safer. If you can afford it, there is, of course, nothing to compare to the spectacular helicopter flights directly over the lava flows.

First, though, explore the Visitor Center a bit. You can get information here on self-guided walks, the Kipuka Puaulu Walk, which is a one-mile loop, and the Halemaumau Trail, a 6½ mile round-trip hike. Trail guides for both are available at the Visitor Center. And try not to miss the terrific color films of the latest eruptions, shown every hour on the hour from 9am until 4pm. Until recently, there was a display case here consisting of letters from people who had taken rocks from the volcano—despite being warned never to do so—and had spells of bad luck, and sent the rocks back. Many of the letters ask forgiveness of Madame Pele. For example: "My friends are no longer in my life, I am divorced, I've lost my business, my property is being foreclosed. Pele is angry about something . . . I took the rock . . . Pele is a very busy woman and surely she would not miss a handful of stones from the firepit. Right? Wrong!" More letters and more rocks continue to make their way back to Hawaii.

Now that you know not to break any Hawaiian kapus by taking lava rocks back home, walk a few doors from park headquarters to the **Volcano Art Center.** Here, in the 1877 original Volcano House Hotel, a nonprofit group shows the work of some 200 artists and craftspeople, most of them from the Big Island. Fine arts reflective of Hawaii, bowls and sculptures of native Hawaiian woods, and posters (many by the Art Center's founding director, Boone Morrison) are for sale, as well as small items that would make distinctive gifts. Note the Jack Straka native wood bowls, the Chin Leong raku pottery, the Dietrich Varez block prints, the "trashface jewelry" by Ira Ono, considered collector's items. There are excellent fine and performing arts programs for long-term visitors, as well as concerts and special events. During the month of December, Christmas is celebrated with a blazing fire, hot apple cider, holiday music, and Santa Claus, too. Write P.O. Box 104, Hawaii Volcanoes National Park, HI 96718, or call 967-7511 for more information. Always a worthwhile stop.

The Volcano Art Center is also the place to pick up a "Tales of Old Hawaii" self-guiding tour tape to accompany you on your explorations of the volcano. Created and narrated by Dr. Russ Apple, a noted authority on Hawaiian history, it affords an insight into the natural history, legends, and lore of the area. Rental of the tape and a tape deck is $10. Tapes can also be picked up and/or returned at the Lyman House Museum, the Hawaii Naniloa Hotel, and the Hilo Hawaiian Hotel back in Hilo.

Just across the road is **Volcano House,** which we've described in Chapter XIII. Situated as it is on the rim of the crater, it's also a great spot for sunset watching—best done from the cocktail lounge where the bartenders, volcanologists all, have whipped up something called "Pele's Delight," a combination of rum and lilikoi that manages to be pink at the bottom, fiery orange at the top. Eruption movies are shown in the lobby every night at 8:30 and 9pm. And it's so cozy just to sit here for a few minutes in front of the fireplace, where the fire, so it is said, has been burning continuously for over 100 years. Burning ohia logs fill the air with a wonderful aroma.

But enough of these handmade frills. It's nature you came here to see. There are some simple nature trails that begin right in back of Volcano House, and we urge you to take at least one. The upland air is fragrant, the vegetation glorious, the views spectacular. The silvery trees that look something like gnarled birches are ohia, and their red-pompom blossoms are lehua, the flower of the Big Island, sacred to Pele. (It's rumored that if you pick one, it will rain before you arrive home.) That's the big bald dome of **Mauna Loa** towering 10,000 feet above you into the heavens; you're on **Kilauea,** which rises on its southeastern slopes. Pele hangs out in Halemaumau, the firepit of this enormous, 2½-mile-long crater.

To see the important views, you merely take Crater Rim Drive, the 11-mile circle road in either direction around the rim of Kilauea Crater. The rangers' map is easy to follow. We'll begin our trip around this wonderland of rain forests and volcanic desert at the **Sulfur Banks,** just west of park headquarters. The banks have that familiar rotten-egg odor. Further along the road you'll see eerie wisps of steam coming out of some fissures, but don't be alarmed—they've been puffing along for centuries. You can stop to enjoy a hot blast from the steam jets, a natural underground "sauna."

Just beyond the Kilauea Military Rest Camp, there's a road that swings off to the right and across the highway that brought you here; if you follow this side path, you'll come upon an interesting clump of tree molds, formed in the same freakish way as the ones at Puna. The 100-acre **bird park** (Kipuka Pualu) is here, too, a sweet spot for a picnic or a nature ramble through many rare trees; but you'll have to be sharp to spot the birds chirping away above your head

Driving back to the rim of the crater road, turn right and continue the journey into the weird world ahead. You'll get your first view of Halemaumau, that awesome firepit 3,000 feet wide and 300 to 400 feet deep, from the lookout at the **Thomas A. Jaggar Museum**. Stop inside, too, to learn something about the history and development of volcanoes, and to see the murals by artist Herb Kane on the legends of Pele. The museum is named in honor of Thomas A. Jaggar, the first person to understand the necessity of having trained observers on site before and after volcanic eruptions.

Continue along the well-marked Crater Rim Road now to **Halemaumau Overlook** itself, the home of Pele. When Pele decides to act up, everyone from here to the Philippines seems to descend on the area; whole families sit bundled in their cars all night long watching the awesome fireworks. Nobody can say when Pele will blow her top again. It is still local custom to appease her, but now that human sacrifice is out of fashion, she is reputed to accept bottles of gin! For a more intimate glimpse of Halemaumau, the three-mile (one-way) hike through a hushed forest to the eerie heart of the volcano is recommended. The walk, a tough one, starts at Volcano House; be sure to get the descriptive pamphlet at park headquarters to guide you.

The drive now takes you to the area hit by the 1959 eruption of Kilauea Iki (Little Kilauea; all the volcanoes have little sisters here). A boardwalk has been set up over the cinder ash here; and a walk along this **Devastation Trail** will take you past the twisted ghosts of white trees felled by the lava. At the end of the trail you can look down into the **Kilauea Iki Crater.** (This walk takes about 15 minutes, so to conserve energy you might send one member of your party back to the parking lot to bring the car around to the lookout area at the end of the walk.) A favorite four-mile hike around the crater's edge begins here.

The forest takes over at **Thurston Lava Tube** a few miles further on, and a magnificent prehistoric fern forest it is. The lava tube shaded by this little grotto is another of those volcanic curiosities, even more spectacular than the one you saw in Hilo.

Now, if you have some more time to spend—at least two to three hours—and are feeling adventurous, continue around Crater Rim Drive until you come to the **Chain of Craters Road.** It's a dramatic drive, the road descending 2,700 feet in 24 miles, all the way to the point where, if the current eruption is still going on, the lava flows enter the sea. They create steam clouds that are visibly white during the day and glow orange to red at night. You'll pass a jungle of ferns, an ohia forest, historic lava flows, and sea arches, as you go all the way down to the sea. Somewhere near the **Kamoamoa Campgrounds,** you'll find the mobile visitors center, built after the Wahaulua Visitors Center burned last year, destroyed by fire sparked by a lava flow from Kilauea. This area may still be active by the time you read this, so there is no telling exactly where the visitors center will be. *Note:* Since a lava flow has covered part of Chain of Craters Road, blocking the park's eastern boundary, there is no longer any way to continue on Rte. 130, which leads to Kalapana and the black-sand beach at Kaimu, so you will have to return to park headquarters the same way you came, via the Chain of Craters Road. Note also that there is no food or gasoline available along this route, but both are available in Volcano Village, one mile Hilo side of Volcanoes National Park.

BIKING DOWN VOLCANOES

There's another way to experience the grandeur of the volcano—and that's on a mountain bike, descending downhill 4,000 feet along the Chain of Craters Road. **Hawaiian Eyes—Big Island Bicycle Tours** is a new outfit that takes riders on a variety of downhill tours—not only at Hawaii Volcanoes National Park ($99), but also at Mauna Kea Iki ($48), Kohala Mountain ($60), and the Saddle Road ($90). Trips last from one to four hours on the bike, and include round-trip transportation from pickup points in Hilo or Waimea, a mini-mountain bike lesson, a mountain bike and helmet, and all necessary equipment, a support van, even snacks on fresh local foods. Riders have ranged in age from 10 to 65, and initial reports have been enthusiastic. For information, phone 885-8806.

DANGER AHEAD

There may be trouble in paradise, according to conservationists and local people who are launching a mighty protest to stop the industrialization of the Big Island. Already, geothermal drilling is getting under way on the slopes of Kilauea Volcano, in the midst of a Hawaiian rain forest. Planned for the near future are geothermal wells, power lines crisscrossing the southern part of the island, a metals smelting plant, and an underseas cable, all of which could produce huge quantities of toxic waste and severely harm the environment. Native Hawaiians also consider the drilling a desecration of their religion and their respect for the goddess Pele and her sacred places. If you'd like to get more information, perhaps help them in their cause, write to Pele Defense Fund, P.O. Box 404, Volcano, HI 96785.

HUNTING AND CAMPING IN THE VOLCANO AREA

If you're brave enough to tackle Mauna Loa (the largest mountain in the world, more than 32,000 feet from sea floor to summit—18,000 of them below sea level), make your requests for information and permits for overnight trips to the superintendent, Hawaii Volcanoes National Park, Hawaii. The area is under the jurisdiction of the federal government and is administered by the National Park Service, U.S. Department of the Interior. There is an overnight camping area at the **Namakani Paio Campground,** two miles from Volcano House. Ten cabins, nicely furnished, with beds and cooking utensils, each sleep four people, at about $24 per night (more details in Chapter XIII).

In addition, Hawaii Volcanoes National Park manages three drive-in campgrounds on a first-come, first-served basis at no charge: these are the above-mentioned Namakani Paio on Hwy. 11, 2½ miles west of park headquarters, with eating shelters, fireplaces, water, and rest rooms; Kipuka Nene, on Hilina Pali Road, 11½ miles south of park headquarters, with eating shelters, fireplaces, water, and pit toilets; and Kamoamoa in the coastal area, with eating shelters, fireplaces, pit toilets, and water at a nearby area. Wood is not provided at any site. You cannot reserve sites in these campgrounds in advance. There is no camping fee, and no permits are required. However, your stay is limited to no more than seven days in any one campground.

Backpackers who wish to camp in the volcano area must register at the Kilauea Visitor Center before beginning their trip (shelters and cabins are managed on a first-come, first-served basis at no charge). They may use the two Mauna Loa Trail Cabins (one at Red Hill at an elevation of 10,000 feet, 10 miles from the end of the Mauna Loa Strip Road, and another on the southwest side of Mokuaweoweo, the summit caldera, at an elevation of 13,250 feet, each with bunks but no mattresses), or the Pepeiao Cabin, another patrol cabin on the Ka'u Desert Trail at Kipuka Pepeiao.

Oddly enough, Mauna Loa's sister, **Mauna Kea,** belongs to the state, and is administered by the State Department of Land and Natural Resources, which is responsible for the maintenance of the camping facilities on the mountain. This is great hunting country, and not a few of the sportsmen use bow and arrow. Mammal game consists of wild pigs and sheep; the birds are pheasant, chukar partridge, and quail. For all the details on seasons and licenses, write to Division of Forestry and Wildlife, P.O. Box 4849, Hilo, HI 96720.

Slightly higher up the mountain, in the saddle at 6,500 feet, **Pohakuloa** is the base camp for recreational activities in the Mauna Kea area. It has seven housekeeping cabins that sleep up to six each, rates from $10 for one person to $30 for six people. Again, these are completely furnished and equipped, from bedding and dishes to an electric range and refrigerator. Also available are two immense barracks, each containing four units, each with eight beds—just great for a huge family or a U.N. convention. Prices range from $8 for one to $2 per person for 64 persons. One huge mess hall with a restaurant-size kitchen is shared by both buildings. You can write to the Department of Land and Natural Resources, Division of State Parks, P.O. Box 936 (75 Aupuni St.), Hilo, HI 96721 (tel. 961-7200).

For additional information on camping around the Big Island, details on current conditions of parks, fees, etc., contact the County Department of Parks and Recreation, 25 Aupuni St., Hilo, HI 96720. Remember that summers and holidays get booked far in advance.

---

3. Across Hawaii

There are three possible routes across the Big Island from Hilo to the Kona coast.

THE CHOICES

(1) If you're continuing on from the volcano, simply follow the excellent Hwy. 11 another 90 miles. You pass through the Ka'u Lava Desert (where an explosion of Kilauea in 1790 routed an army of Kamehameha's chief enemy, Keoua) and can stop off at Punalu'u to see the black-sand beach. You hit the pretty little village of Naalehu before encountering mile on mile of lava flows, until you get to the other side of Mauna Loa and the welcoming Kona coast.

(2) If you're starting from Hilo, however, and have already been to the volcano, it's impractical to take this 126-mile route, when you can reach Kona directly in 96 miles, and sample in-between terrain so varied that Hawaii seems more like a small continent than a large island. We're referring to the drive along the majestic Hamakua coast, through the rolling pasture lands of the Parker Ranch, and then around Mauna Kea and Hualalai Volcano to Kona.

(3) An alternative route for the first 50 miles of this trip crosses over the saddle between Mauna Loa and Mauna Kea, giving you wild, unforgettable views of both—but also a not-so-comfortable ride. Car-rental companies prohibit driving on this Saddle Road—Hwy. 20 out of Hilo—mostly because help is so far away. If your car breaks down, the tow charge is enormous, not to mention your being stranded in the wilderness! The presence of a military camp in this area is another negative factor. Definitely not recommended.

(The drive in the opposite direction, from Kona to Hilo, is described briefly at the end of this section.)

THE HAMAKUA COAST DRIVE

The drive we prefer—and the one that we'll explore in depth—starts from Hilo on Hwy. 19, paralleling Kamehameha Avenue along the waterfront and heading for the northern shore of the island and the Hamakua coast. This is sugar-plantation country, miles of cane stretching inland to the valleys (the produce eventually goes to the bulk-sugar plant in Hilo and then to the mainland), the coastline a jagged edge curving around the sea, broken up by gorges and streams tumbling down from the snow-capped heights of Mauna Kea. The views from the modern and speedy Hwy. 19 are good, but if you really want to soak up the scenery, get off now and then on the old road that winds through the gullies and goes to the sea.

Ten miles out of Hilo, at Honomu, the HVB marker indicates the way to **Akaka Falls.** Four miles inland on a country road, you'll find not only the falls—perhaps the most beautiful in the islands, plunging dizzily 420 feet into a mountain pool—but also a breathtakingly beautiful bit of tropical forest turned into a park, lush and fragrant with wild ginger, ancient ferns, glorious tropical trees and flowers. It's a rhapsodic spot, very difficult to leave. Console yourself, then, with a bit of snacking and shopping in Honomu. At **Ishigo's General Store** you can pick up a hot cup of Kona coffee, as well as some scrumptious pastries at the bakery adjoining it. A few steps down the road is the **Akaka Falls Flea Market** (fun and inexpensive) and the **Crystal Grotto,** a new age headquarters of sorts for this part of the island, with a good collection of crystals, jewelry, books, tapes, and Hawaiiana. We love the bumper stickers that read: "May the quartz be with you."

The little town of **Laupahoehoe**—you can drive down to it from the highway

—is a "leaf of lava" jutting into the Pacific, its local park another idyllic spot for a picnic. But it's also a grim reminder of the savagery of nature that is always possible in Hawaii; it was in a school building here that 20 children and their teachers were swept away into the sea by the 1946 tidal wave.

If you have time for a little hiking and nature study now, watch for the signs leading to **Kalopa:** this is the 100-acre Native Forest State Park containing trees, shrubs, and ferns indigenous to pre-Polynesian Hawaii, with trails through the ohia rain forest and many spectacular views—a nice spot for a picnic. Cabins are available for rental here, through the County Department of Parks and Recreation.

Thirty miles past Akaka Falls you reach **Honokaa,** second-largest city of the Big Island, the site of the **Hawaiian Holiday Macadamia Nut Plant,** where you can view the plant and visit the retail store, which features a mind-boggling array of 200 macadamia-nut products. A macadamia-nut festival is held here in late August. Follow the warrior signs to the "Macadamia Nut Capital of the World," open daily 9am to 6pm. On your way down the hill to the factory, you might want to stop in at **Kamaiina Woods** on Lehua Street, a factory and gift shop that turns out distinctive carvings in koa, milo, and other local woods. A glass panel separates the visitors from the artisans who are busy transforming raw koa logs into finished products. Handcrafted items begin under $5. (There is another Kamaiina Woods in Waimea, in Opelo Plaza.) Open Monday to Saturday, 10am to 5pm.

Honokaa is best known as the takeoff point to pastoral **Waipio Valley.** This side trip from your cross-island route takes you eight miles from Honokaa, branching off to the right on Rte. H-240. The best way to explore this spectacular valley (where 7,000 full-blooded Hawaiians lived less than 100 years ago; today there are fewer than 10, plus a few hippie families) is by the **Waipio Valley Shuttle,** a 1½-hour four-wheel vehicle tour starting and ending at the Waipio Valley Lookout. The tour takes you down into the valley, through taro fields, a $200,000 Ti House, the Lalakea fish pond, a black-sand beach, and the dramatic Hiilawe Falls (the water drops 1,200 feet here when it's running. Cost of the shuttle trip is $20 for adults, $10 for children under 12. Trips leave daily on the hour from 8am to 4pm. Make reservations by calling 775-7121 in Kukuihaele.

It costs more—$45—than the four-wheel drive trip, but an excursion into Waipio Valley on a mule-driven wagon would surely be memorable. **Waipio Valley Wagon Tours** runs a three-hour tour each morning at 9:30 and again at 12:30pm to explore the sights of the valley, as mule power takes you across Waipio's streams and rivers. The tour includes a stop at a swimming hole in the river and at the largest black-sand beach in Hawaii. Reserve at least 24 hours in advance by phoning 775-9518.

Whether or not you go down into Waipio Valley, you should make a stop at **Waipio Valley Lookout,** for one of the most spectacular views in the islands. From the steep pali, the waves below are bits of foamy lace. In winter, you can often see whales frolicking offshore. There are picnic tables and rest rooms; it could be an ideal spot to break your trip. And by all means, pay a visit to **Waipio Woodworks,** snuggled in the sleepy town of Kukuihaele, which overlooks the valley (turn at the sign that reads "Kukuihaele 1 mile"). Here at Waipio Woodworks, local craftspeople and artisans display some incredible island wood products. Although prices can go way up, there are a number of modestly priced items: wooden earrings at $5.50, switchplate covers airbrushed with Hawaiian designs at $7, hand-painted T-shirts from $24 to $34. Open every day, 9am to 5pm.

The Parker Ranch

On the next leg of your trip you'll begin to see why Hawaii is so often called a continent in miniature. West of Honokaa, winding inland on Hwy. 19, the sugar plantations of the tropics give way to mountain forests of cedar and eucalyptus as you climb up the slopes of Mauna Kea toward a vast prairie of rangelands and the plateau of Kamuela (also known as Waimea) and the 225,000-acre **Parker Ranch,** one of the largest cattle ranches in the United States under single ownership.

King Kamehameha started the whole thing, quite inadvertently, when he accepted a few longhorn cattle as a gift from the English explorer Capt. George Vancouver. The cattle multiplied and ran wild until a young seaman from Newton, Massachusetts, John Parker, tamed them and started his ranch. The Parker family still owns it today, and many of the current generation of paniolos are descendants of the original Hawaiian cowboys. Parker Ranch is the biggest, but certainly not the only one; ranching is a way of life on the Big Island.

For years, visitors have wanted to tour the Parker Ranch, but only recently has that become possible. If you can spare about two hours, you'll find the **Paniolo Shuttle Tour** very worthwhile. It begins at the visitor center with a video presentation, then proceeds via mini-bus to Pukalani Stables, to see artifacts from the ranch and observe the orphaned-calf program. Then it's on to Puhihale, a working area in the pastures. Final stop is at the historic homes at Puuopelu and their beautiful gardens. Mana, the 1847 home of the ranch founder, is built entirely of koa wood and is open for touring; and you may view the splendid art collection, with the works of many Impressionist masters, at Puuopelu, home of current ranch owner Richard Smart. The tour operates daily from 9am to 3:30pm, with shuttles leaving every 10 to 15 minutes: cost is $15 for adults, $7.50 for children under 12. Visitors with more time (and money) can take the four-hour **Paniolo Country Tour,** which includes all of the above sites plus a drive deep into the pastures to the original homestead site of Mana and the Parker family cemetery. Lunch is included. Tours cost $38 for adults, $19 for children, and leave at 9am and at noon. If time is very limited, at least try to visit the **Historic Homes at Puuopelu** ($5 adults, $2.50 children) or the **Parker Ranch Visitor Center** (video plus historic exhibits ($4.50 adults, $2.25 children). For information and reservations, phone 885-7655.

Shopping and Sightseeing in Waimea

The bright little mountain town of Waimea is one of the fastest-growing shopping areas on the Big Island, with delightful boutiques and galleries opening all the time. A good place to start your wanderings is at the **Parker Ranch Shopping Center.** At the Parker Ranch Store, adjacent to the Visitor Center, you can buy many Parker Ranch logo items, including sweatshirts and jogging outfits. . . . Of all the many treasures at **Setay,** a jewelry shop a few doors away, the ones we covet most are the "Swinger Rings," which revolve continuously on tiny roller bearings. Not inexpensive (they start at $450 and go up into the thousands), but foolproof conversation-starters. . . . **Hilo Hattie's** and **Reyn's,** well-known island shops, have outposts, here, too. . . . You'll find quality women's fashions (dresses, tops, bags, accessories) at **Lady L. . . . At Fiber Arts,** everything—quilts, clothing, pillows— is handcrafted, usually by an island artisan. They also serve one of the best cups of espresso in town. . . . And at its sister store, **Fiberarts,** we bought a darling patchwork quilt for a baby's crib with whale motif, for just $25. . . . **Big Island Natural Foods** may be just the ticket if you're in need of chakra T-shirts or organic chickens. . . . **Kamuela Delights** serves colossal ice-cream cones in a variety of flavors and toppings.

Parker Square is one of our favorite shopping complexes in town, with a group of tasteful boutiques. The most exciting is **Gallery of Great Things,** which shows an extraordinary collection of works by local and Pacific island artists; we coveted the stunning appliquéd quilts from Tahiti and the handcrafted silver jewelry from Bali. Prices can go way up, but many things are surprisingly affordable: We saw koa-wood rice paddles at $5, koa hair sticks at $4, Tutu Nene potholders at $8, feather necklaces at $38. . . . **Waimea General Store** is a tasteful bazaar with a highly sophisticated potpourri of merchandise: distinctive handcrafts, kitchen gadgets, toys and games, handmade baby quilts, men's clothing, ceramics (note their "Morris Platters"). There's an excellent collection of Hawaiian books. Fans of the artist Guy Buffet, who does wonderful, whimsical paintings of Old Hawaii, can find the Guy Buffet Calendar and cards here. . . . **Mango Ranch** has the feeling of the Southwest: Pendelton Indian blankets, belt buckles, kachina dolls, cowboy hats, silver and turquoise jewelry. Many well-priced items. . . . **Bentley's** is an exquisite store, like a French country home, with furniture, hand-painted wicker baskets, dried flower wreaths, and much more. . . . Lovely, lacy lingerie can be found at **Christel's Collectibles . . . Gifts in Mind** has a fine array of clothing plus.

A visit to **Hale Kea** gives you a chance to step back a bit into Hawaii's past, as well as to browse, shop, enjoy the views, and maybe have a meal as well. Originally built in 1897, the splendid estate house is set on 11 acres of rolling hills and gardens; it was once the home of Parker Ranch managers, and later became a country place for Laurance Rockefeller (developer of the Mauna Kea Beach Hotel). Its indoor rooms, completely restored with antiques and period pieces, is the scene of **Hartwell's at Hale Kea,** where you could have a pleasant lunch for under $10 (poached fish salad, croissant clubhouse, papaya salad, etc.) Dinner and Sunday brunch are also served. The cottages and guest quarters of the estate now house a number of upscale shops. Of these, we especially like **Maya Gallery,** which shows a combination of Japanese folk art and fine art, as well as some works by local artists. Admire the paintings and prints, maybe come home with a trinket like a notepad made of rice paper, $10.50. . . . Tutu Nene is the original source of those stuffed nene birds that one sees around the island. Some of the proceeds go to help the nene, the rare Hawaiian goose, make a comeback. Prices begin at $10. . . . The new **Vintage Country Shoppe** features charming old-fashioned clothing for women and children. . . . And you can find beautiful carved ivory scrimshaw at **Golden Nugget. . . . Noa Noa** has a new store here, with wild tropical prints on its hand-painted clothing. . . . **China Clipper** is a wonderful shop, full of 1930s memorabilia, gifts with art deco themes, like the old Pan American posters from the '30s, plus Hawaiian perfumes, Balinese wooden flowers, unusual jewelry, and much, much more. When you've done shopping, stroll up to the gazebo to savor the view—you might find a wedding party here, as it's a popular spot for festive occasions.

The newest shopping mall in town, **Waimea Center,** seems to be of interest mostly to local folks, but a visit to **Ackerman Gallery** is well worthwhile. **Capricorn** is an excellent bookstore, and Princess Kaiulani Fashions has some great muumuus. For meals on the run, there's **Subway** for hero sandwiches, and **TCBY**—The Country's Best Yogurt—for low-cal shakes, parfaits, fruit sundaes, crêpes, and Belgian waffles.

Yugen is a delightful shop on Hwy. 19, and, for women who love distinctive clothing, a must. Designer Carolyn Ainsworth fashions silks and cottons into beautifully simple, elegant clothing. Most of it is expensive, but have a look, anyway: stunning tops begin at just $30. Adjoining Yugen is **Nikko Gallery,** which houses fine arts and crafts by island artists, as well as a collection of Japanese antiques and folk art.

C&C Cycle and Surf is a madly popular store with the local people. It has just about everything needed for the active life, including skateboards, boogie boards, and skate, surf, and bike clothing and accessories. There are often free giveaways: Who knows, you could win a boogie board or a water-balloon slingshot or even a mountain bike! Look for owner D'Armand Cook's shop behind the Dairy Queen, near the blinking traffic light.

Your last stop in this area could well be the **Kamuela Museum** (tel. 885-4724), the largest private museum in Hawaii, founded and owned by Albert K. Solomon, Sr., and Harriet M. Solomon, great-great-granddaughter of John Palmer Parker, the founder of Parker Ranch. You'll see ancient and royal Hawaiian artifacts (many of which were formerly in Iolani Palace in Honolulu) alongside European and Asian objets d'art, plus cultural objects brought to the islands by various ethnic groups in the 19th century. A charmer. The museum is at the junction of Rtes. 19 and 250; open daily, including holidays, from 8am to 4pm; $2.50 admission for adults, $1 for children under 12.

Painting Hawaii

Robert Althouse, an artist who makes his home in Waimea, believes that just about anybody can paint—and what could be better to paint than the fabulous landscapes of the Big Island! He takes small groups of people out on one-day trips to some of the island's most magnificent spots—Waipio Valley, the Kona coast, tropical rain forests, ancient Hawaiian villages, and the like—and provides instruction, inspiration, and all materials: canvas, paints, brushes, smocks, French easels. At the end of the day, your painting is yours to take home as a very personal memento. Upon request, his wife June, a naturalist, accompanies the group, providing a fount of information on plants, wildlife, ecology, and native Hawaiian legends and myths. The tariff of $125 per person includes transportation to and from your hotel and a picnic lunch. Not inexpensive, but what you take home will be an original! Phone 885-6109 for information.

The Lively Arts

Waimea, by the way, is something of a cultural center for the Big Island. While you're here, you may be lucky enough to catch performances by such groups as the Peking Acrobats, the Honolulu Symphony, or the Morca Dance Theatre at the 500-seat **Kahilu Theatre and Town Hall,** just across from the Parker Ranch Visitor Center. It's a handsome facility (a gift by Parker Ranch to the community) for professional touring productions and contemporary films. For ticket information, phone 885-6017.

A SIDE TRIP FROM WAIMEA

From the cool green oasis of Waimea you can make another side excursion, 22 miles to the little town of **Hawi,** on the northernmost tip of the Big Island. The drive is along Rte. 250, winding uphill through the slopes of the Kohala Mountains, and the sights are unforgettable—the Pacific on your left, looking like a blue-velvet lake lost in misty horizons; the shimmering, unearthly peaks of Mauna Kea, Mauna Loa, and Hualalei, their slopes a jumble of wildflowers, twisted fences of tree branches, and giant cactus. Your destination, Hawi, is an end-of-the-world spot, recommended for those who like to be far away from the nagging complexities of civilization. There's Kohala Lodge, an inexpensive hotel, a more expensive inn called the Hawaiian Plantation House, and a visitor center, but that's about as much truck as they'll have with any newfangled amenities.

Hawi's riches—and those of its neighboring **Kohala district**—are in its memories. The great Kamehameha was born in this area, and if you travel east a few miles to **Kapaau,** you'll see a statue of the local hero that looks amazingly like the one you saw in Honolulu. Actually, this one is the original; it was made in Florence, lost at sea, and then found after another just like it had been fashioned for the capital. The trip to this North Kohala area is thrilling, but remember that you've got to come down the road again (Hwy. 270), which links up to Hwy. 19 and the Kona coast, adding a total of 44 miles to your cross-island trip.

TO KONA VIA THE KOHALA COAST RESORTS

From Waimea, you could zip right along the coastal road, Hwy. 19, and be in Kailua-Kona within an hour. However, it's fun to stop off along the way to have a look at some of the fabled Kohala coast resorts that dot these shores, and maybe have a meal or a swim. **Anae'hoomalu Bay,** a splendid crescent-shaped white-sand beach with public facilities and picnic tables, is actually the beach fronting the glorious Royal Waikoloan Hotel. And very close to that is the megaresort that everyone in Hawaii seems to be talking about and wants to see: the **Hyatt Regency Waikoloa.** Yes, you should see it and plan an hour or two to enjoy it: If you can't squeeze the time in on your cross-island trip, then come back once you've settled in Kona.

Although guests of the $360-million fantasy resort, which opened in the fall of 1988, pay anywhere from $200 to $2,700 a day for their accommodations, you can enjoy many of the resort's facilities as a visitor. For something organized, phone the Hyatt at 885-1234, ext. 2715, and reserve a space on one of their guided tours: an art tour, a garden and wildlife tour, a petroglyph tour, a facilities tour, and a back-of-the-house tour. What we like to do is simply to hop one of the canal boats or space-age tubular trams that continually circle the property, and stop where fancy leads us. There are lush tropical gardens and a wildlife collection; a mile-long museum walkway filled with superb examples of Pacific and Asian art; a shopping arcade with upscale boutiques; enormous swimming pools with slides, waterfalls, grottoes (one even has a "riverpool," and its currents float guests from level to level); and a million-gallon saltwater lagoon, teeming with tropical fish, which is the home of six tame bottle-nose dolphins. Definitely get off the boat here, for here's your chance to play—or watch other folks play—with these highly intelligent and loving mammals. By winning a daily lottery, guests and visitors alike can get to swim with the dolphins. Conservation issues are emphasized in this 30-minute learning session. And up to 20 children a day can join a "Dolphin Discovery" program to meet the friendly mammals. A portion of the encounter fees goes to the Waikoloa Marine Life Fund. Even if you don't get to take part in a session, it's fun to have a drink or a bite at **Hang Ten**, the snack bar overlooking Dolphin Pond, and watch. You're also welcome to watch the daily training sessions at 12:30pm. Kids will adore this one.

Feeling hungry? Nothing could be better than lunch (11am to 5pm) at the outdoor-indoor **Orchid Café,** near the main swimming pool, which features *cuisine naturelle.* Lunch need not cost you more than $10 to $12, and the food is remarkable—among the best of its kind we've had anywhere. Just to give you an idea, at a recent meal we started with a spicy tortilla soup and an exquisitely delicate, chilled guava-papaya soup topped with macadamia-nut cream; went on to main courses of a grilled tuna-steak sandwich with mustard mayonnaise and a tomato-avocado salad with roasted scallops, artichokes, and mozzarella; then topped off our meal with a fabulous Mandarin lime pie with papaya sauce—and each dish was better than the last. We can hardly wait to eat there again. When you're feeling flush come back and have a fabulous dinner at **Donatoni's,** a formal dining room decorated with masterpiece paintings, which serves perhaps the best northern Italian cuisine on the Big Island. A number of other restaurants, lounges, and entertainments are available here, including a traditional luau called **Legends of Polynesia;** it's held every Monday, Wednesday, and Friday at 6pm; you can see the show and have a cocktail for $22.

If you can tear yourself away from the Hyatt now, and still feel like seeing more playgrounds of the rich and famous, look for the entrance to the **Mauna Lani Bay Hotel,** five miles north on Rte. 19; to our way of thinking, it is one of the most purely beautiful resorts anywhere, especially in its landscaping and gardens and the massive indoor waterfall in the Grand Atrium. Golfers rave about the Francis Ii Brown golf course here, an 18-hole championship course carved out of barren lava. The hotel has won numerous awards for excellence, including the coveted Five-Diamond Award from AAA. If time permits (or if not, come back later once you're snugly ensconced in Kona and) have a splurge meal at one of the most enchanting of its seven restaurants, the newly opened **Canoe House,** which features Pacific Rim cuisine by a master chef in an al fresco oceanfront setting—incomparable! (Phone 885-6622 for reservations.) You can then continue along the coastal road, Queen Kaahumanu Hwy. (Rte. 19), until you reach Kailua-Kona. Or, alternatively, you can leave Waimea on Rte. 19 and drive about 12 miles to the deep-water port of **Kawaihae,** where you descend through prairie land, grazing cows, and ocean vistas all about you, until you're suddenly in sultry tropics. On the road above the harbor is **Puukohola Heiau National Historic Site,** a well-preserved heiau and historical park that figures importantly in the history of the islands. It was here that Kaahumanu, the sweetheart-queen of the great Kamehameha, after his death began the breakdown of the dread kapu (taboo) system by the startling act of eating in public with men (previously, such an act would have been punished by death). But the place is better remembered for a bloody deed that should forever disencumber you of notions that Stone Age warfare was all good clean fighting. Remember Keoua, Kamehameha's biggest rival, the one who lost an army at K'au? Kamehameha had decided to dedicate this heiau to the war god Kukailimoku, and invited Keoua to a supposed peace parley in the new temple. Instead, he had him speared as he approached the land and sacrificed him to the god. Then he was free to unify Hawaii and the other islands.

After digesting this gory bit of history, you deserve a change of pace. A mile and a half back, on a right fork just past Samuel Spencer Park, is the landmark **Mauna**

Kea Beach Hotel, the original world-class resort on the Kohala Coast. The architecture and landscaping are elegantly imaginative, the rooms nestling along the brow of a hill overlooking the crystal waters of Mauna Kea Beach below. You can wander a little about the public areas of this seaside caravanserai, perhaps bumping into a celebrity or two en route to the golf course. Note the magnificent plantings, the authentic Hawaiian quilts, and the splendid art collection, which ranges from Asian bronzes and a gigantic 7th-century Indian buddha to primitive masks and wood carvings from New Guinea. After many years the beach was opened to the public (but only 10 parking spaces provided!), and you can also join the leisure class at lunch: a lovely, splurge buffet runs around $22. (Considering that there are hot dishes like stuffed Cornish hen and beef Wellington among the dazzling array of fresh fruits, salads, cheeses, hors d'oeuvres, home-baked breads, and scrumptious desserts, it's worth the money.) The Sunday buffet brunch is reported to be even more spectacular! Not far away are two public beaches where you might want to stop for a picnic: **Samuel Spencer Park** (popular with campers and sometimes a bit unkempt) and, about three miles further south, the more spacious **Hapuna Beach** (watch, however, for signs indicating possible dangerous tides and rip currents). Continue on Rte. 19 through the lava desert, with the possibility, on clear days, of glorious views of all the volcanoes of Hawaii and perhaps of Haleakala on Maui, too. Lava flows from Mauna Loa and Hualalai mark the eerie landscape, punctuating the miles until you emerge at last into the verdant world of the Kona coast.

(*Note:* We're sorry to have to issue this caveat, but we've been told that rowdies sometimes hide in the bushes near these beaches, wait for tourists to dutifully put their valuables in the trunks of their cars, and then proceed to pick the locks while the tourists are out on the beach. If you're going to put anything in your trunk, do so a few miles before you reach your destination.)

FROM KONA TO HILO

If you've arrived at Kona first, you could drive across the island to Hilo on Hwy. 11, through the K'au Desert and miles and miles of lava flows, desolate enough to be reminiscent of Doré's engravings. But before the landscape turns bleak, there's plenty of magnificent scenery. Should you make the drive in November or December, you'll see unbelievably beautiful poinsettias, riot upon riot of red color. For a swim, you might try **Hookena Beach Park,** 22 miles from Kailua. It's a long drive down the road to an almost-deserted, lovely sandy beach. **Manuka State Park,** further on, with its arboretum of extraordinary plants and trees, is a good spot to stretch your legs and perhaps have a picnic lunch. The approach to the little village of **Waiohinu** is marvelously scenic, and the village itself, once a small farming center, is one of the quaintest on the Big Island. Have a look at the monkeypod tree planted by Mark Twain, and a few miles further on you can make a side trip (about a mile and a half off the highway) to the black-sand beach at **Punaluu.** Another favorite jaunt is the 12-mile drive off the highway outside Naalehu down to **Ka Lae** (South Point). Local people fish here on this wild shore of cliffs and surf, the southernmost point in the United States. Now you approach the desolate K'au region where Pele obligingly destroyed an army of Keoua, Kamehameha's archenemy, in 1790; the footprints of the victims can be seen under glass. The landscape is moonlike, and we don't mean that only poetically; space scientists are studying the lava fields of the Big Island in the belief that actual conditions on the moon may be similar. The lava flows lead you to Kilauea, Hawaii Volcanoes National Park, and on to Hilo.

4. The Kona Coast

A man we know in Kona, a refugee from the Bronx, swears he will never go back home. "I've found my bit of paradise right here, and I'm staying!" A lot of other people have waxed ecstatic about Kona, the vacation resort of Hawaiian royalty ever since the word got out that the sun shines here about 344 days a year. (Kona winds, that nasty stuff they get in Honolulu, should be properly called southerly winds, say the Konaites.) It's such a deliciously lazy spot that you may be very contented doing nothing at all in Kona. Of course, looking at the surf as it smashes along the black-lava coast, noting the brilliant varieties of bougainvillea, the plumeria, the jasmine tumbling about everywhere, and lazing on the beach can keep you pretty busy. But we suggest that you take a day off from these labors and have a look at the sights. Kona is an important historic center; within the space of a few miles, Captain Cook met his end, the New England missionaries got their start, and Kamehameha enjoyed his golden age.

The tiny village of **Kailua-Kona** is the resort center, modern enough to be comfortable, but still unspoiled. Ami Gay, the very helpful lady at the Hawaii Visitors Bureau office, in the Kona Plaza Shopping Arcade, can help you with all sorts of practical information. There's a U.S. Post Office in the General Store at the Kona Shopping Village, across the street.

TOURING THE TOWN

There's only one street, Alii Drive, running down the length of Kailua, so you won't get lost. Start up at the King Kamehameha Hotel, in the northern end of town, at the site of the monarch's heiau, which has been restored. There are tasteful museum-caliber displays highlighting Hawaiian history throughout the lobby and various free activities: ethnobotanical, historical, and "hula experience" tours are held several times a week. Inquire at the hotel for a schedule. Just about 150 years ago, Kamehameha ruled the Hawaiian Islands from a grass-roofed palace on this very site (Lahaina became the next capital; Honolulu did not become the capital until 1820). The old king died here in 1819, only a year before the first missionaries arrived from Boston, bringing with them the purposeful Protestant ethic that would effectively end the Polynesian era in Hawaii.

They were responsible for the **Mokuaikaua Church,** standing on the mauka side of Alii Drive, a handsome coral-and-stone structure that is the oldest Christian church in Hawaii, built in 1838. Note the sanctuary inside; its architecture is New England, but it is made of two Hawaiian woods, koa and ohia. Across from it, on the ocean side of the street, is **Hulihee Palace,** until 1916 a vacation home for Hawaiian royalty. Now it's a museum, full of Hawaiian furniture and effects, as well as more primitive curiosities like Kamehameha's exercise stone (it weighs about 180 pounds, so maybe that story about the Naha Stone isn't so crazy after all). Check out the charming little gift shop; it has an especially nice selection of native woods (handsome koa-wood dinner plates are $35), plus books and jewelry. Profits go to the Daughters of Hawaii. The museum is open from 9am to 4pm daily; closed federal holidays. Admission is $4 for adults, $1 for students 12 to 18, 50¢ for children under 12.

KONA "UP MAUKA"

The shore road extends for about six more miles, but we're going to leave it temporarily, taking a left at Hualalai Street and heading out of town on Hwy. 11 (the mauka road). Kona "up mauka" is far removed from the tourist scene at Kailua. It is, for one thing, the place where Kona coffee, that dark, rich brew you've seen all over the islands, is grown. Hawaii is the only state in the union that has a commercial coffee crop. There are no big plantations, only small farms where everybody in the family pitches in to bring in the crop. Watch the road for the shiny green leaves of the coffee bushes with little clusters of red berries at harvest time. There are small cattle ranches here, too, although they're not visible from the road. You'll see the local folk at places like the H. Manago Hotel in Captain Cook.

The drive is a beautiful one, winding through the cool mountain slopes, with fruit trees and showers of blossoms all around. If you're in the mood for a little off-beat shopping here, there are several possibilities. A number of interesting stores are clustered in tiny Kainaliu Village. **Kimura's Fabrics** is a favorite old-timer: Some say Mrs. Kimura has the best collection of fabrics in the islands. Hawaiian and Japanese prints are specialties, and prices are reasonable. . . . A favorite newcomer here is

Crystal Star Gallery, local "new age" headquarters. Quartz crystals, jewelry, pendants, paintings, carvings, books, all at good prices and nicely presented. . . . Look for the **Aloha Theater and Café** in Kainaliu now, and perhaps stop in for a tempting pastry or snack (see the preceding chapter). . . . Next door is the **Aloha Village Store,** where you'll find cards, baskets, toys, gourmet items, plus healthy snacks and vitamins. Across from it is **Blue Ginger Gallery,** a showcase for about 50 local artists. You'll find stained glass, ceramics, jewelry, hand-painted silks, and more, plus many crafts from Bali. An enticing collection. . . . **Paradise Found Boutique** is the place for unique clothing, like raw silk outfits designed here and made in China, a line of batik designer clothes, beautifully cut lacework garments from Indonesia, as well as sought-after antique aloha shirts. Gift items by local artisans as well as Asian ports, too. They have another shop down in Kailua town.

A popular shop in Kealakekua is the **Grass Shack,** a real grass shack with bananas growing out front—it's been here almost forever. The inside is laden with tasteful and authentic Hawaiian and South Pacific handcrafts, including one of the largest collections in the islands of locally made wood items. Burmese jade is sold at the most competitive prices around. The nice people here will give you a native flower and some coffee beans for planting as you leave; within three to four weeks (the time it takes for the seed to germinate) you'll be on your way to having your own potted coffee plant.

If it happens to be a Thursday or Saturday and it's between 8am and 3pm, stop in at the **Kona Scenic Flea Market** in Kealakekua, just off Hwy. 11 on Haleki Street. Vendors from the now-defunct Kona Garden Flea Market have reconvened here to sell everything from apples to antiques, from crafts to clothing, and a great time is had by all.

After about 12 miles from the beginning, the road winds gently down the slopes of the mountain (watch for the HVB marker), past the **Royal Kona Coffee Mill** and Museum, the only remaining mill still in operation, through the lush tropical village of Napoopoo on to **Kealakekua Bay.** Visitors are welcome at the mill.

A monument to Captain Cook is visible across the bay, erected at a spot near where he was killed in 1779. It was here that Cook and his men pulled into the Kona coast a year after their first landing on Kauai, were again treated as gods—and wore out their welcome. When their ship was damaged in a storm and they returned to Kealakekua a second time, the men got into a fight with the natives, and Cook was killed trying to break it up. You can't see the monument up close unless you approach it from the water. There's a **"Captain Cook Cruise"** that leaves Kailua wharf daily; it gives you a good look at the monument and lets you swim and snorkel in the bay. It's a good way to combine a suntan and a history lesson for $36.40 for adults, $18.20 for children 2 to 12 (tel. 329-6400). The cost includes a continental breakfast and a barbecue lunch.

There are two plaques you can see on the Napoopoo shore: one commemorates the first Christian funeral in the islands; the other is in honor of the remarkable Opukahaia, a young Hawaiian boy who swam out to a ship in 1808, got himself a job as a cabin boy, converted to Christianity, and convinced the missionaries that they were needed here in the pagan, ignorant Sandwich Islands. Right near the shrines are a very few jewelry stands that offer good buys in clothing and necklaces of local seeds and kukui-nut leis.

THE KONA SHORE

Continuing along the shore road now to Honaunau, you'll pass **Keei Battlefield,** a lava-scarred stretch where Kamehameha started winning wars. In the tiny fishing village of **Keei,** there's a beach with good swimming.

But the best is yet to come: Honaunau and **Pu'uhonua o Honaunau National Historical Park.** This ancient, partially restored Pu'uhonua still has about it the air of sanctuary for which it was built over 400 years ago. In the days when many chieftains ruled in the islands, each territory had a spot designated as a place of refuge to which kapu breakers, war refugees, and defeated warriors could escape; here they could be cleansed of their offenses and return, purified, to their tribes. (There is another such place on the island of Kauai, near Lydgate Park, but this one is far better preserved.) The heiau, Hale-o-Keawe, the temple of the purifying priests, has been reconstructed (it was in such temples that the bones of the high chiefs of Kona—which had mana, or spiritual power—were kept), and so have the tall ki'i built for the god Lono. After you've driven into the park and left your car in the parking lot (an improvement over the old days when the only way to get here was to run, or, if one came from the north, to swim, since the feet of commoners were not fit to tread on the Royal Grounds on the north side of the place of refuge), we suggest you take in one of the orientation talks given daily at 10, 10:30, and 11am, and at 2:30, 3, and 3:30pm, in the spacious amphitheater staffed by the National Park Service, which administers this facility. Besides explaining the concept of refuge, the park ranger also talks about the plants and trees of the area. Then you're free to have a swim (but sunbathing is not allowed), a picnic, go snorkeling or fishing—or just absorb the peace on your own. Or you can tour the area by yourself with a self-guiding leaflet. "Cultural demonstrators" are usually on hand, carving woods, weaving, and performing other such ancient Hawaiian tasks. Canoes, fishnets, and traps are on display, and often are being used outside the huts. Entrance fee is $1.

There's one more curious sight in Honaunau, which you reach by turning north on a side road as you go back up the highway. This is **St. Benedict's Church,** which everybody calls the "Painted Church." The Catholic missionaries, more adaptable than their Protestant predecessors, created biblical murals that gave a feeling of spaciousness to the tiny church, presumably so that the congregation would have more of a feeling of the outdoors—to which pagan nature worship had accustomed them.

Between Pu'uhonua o Honaunau and the Painted Church, you might want to stop in at **Wakefield Gardens and Restaurant,** which offers free, self-guided tours through its five-acre botanical garden and macadamia-nut orchard, with some 1,000 varieties of plants and flowers. The gift shop sells those little macs very reasonably ($5 buys 2½ pounds in the shell), and also features items made by local artisans (note the koa-wood cribbage boards at $24.95). They also have a very pleasant restaurant offering daily specials at $5.95, moderately priced soups, salads, sandwiches —plus delicious, prize-winning homemade desserts on the order of freshly baked macadamia-nut cheesecake. And they have the best macadamia-nut brittle anywhere! They're on Hwy. 160, open daily from 11am to 3pm (tel. 328-9930).

Back on Hwy. 11 and headed toward Kailua now, you continue for about 11 miles until you come to a turnoff to the left that brings you back to the shore at Keauhou Bay. Before you descend, though, you might want to stop off to have a look at the handsome **Keauhou Shopping Village,** where you could have a drink or a meal with the local sports fans gathered around the large-screen TVs at Drysdale's Two (see Chapter XIII), or an espresso or cappuccino at Henri's Fine Candies and Coffee. There are some attractive small shops here, like Alapaki, with top-quality gifts made in Hawaii—handcrafted native woods, hand-carved coral sculptures, feather hatbands and leis, and much more; the **Keauhou Village Book Shop,** where, in addition to a vast array of books, we found wonderful old postcards reading, "Aloha from Waikiki, 1935"; **Possible Dreams,** with prints, gift items, silk flowers, kaleidoscopes, and an enchanting collection of circus animals, starting at $15.95, from Carousel Memories; **Small World,** with a large selection of both clothing and toys for children. At **The Showcase Gallery** you're likely to see an exhibit by such leading island painters and craftspeople as Herb Kane, Jane Chow, John Thomas, among others. Among the small treasures here, we found feather pendants beginning at $15, prints and serigraphs from $15 to $450.

Drive down to the shore now to explore the grounds and public areas of the fabulous **Kona Surf Resort.** The Asian and Polynesian art objects scattered about, the glorious use of natural materials, the 14½ acres and 30,000 plants on the property make it a sightseeing stop in its own right. Complimentary garden tours are given Monday, Wednesday, and Friday at 9am, but you're welcome to come on your own and have a look.

A possible shopping stop in this area might be the **Liberty House Clearance**

Center at the Keauhou Bay Hotel. No telling what you'll find at a place like this on any particular day, but we've seen $40 jeans for $10, $50 bathing suits for as low as $7, $50 leather bags for $25. Items are from various Liberty House shops on the island; worth a look.

Continuing back to Kailua now, the old vies with the new for attention everywhere. To your left is a modern small-boat harbor; to your right, faintly visible on the mountain slopes are the remains of a rocky royal slide, down which the alii of Hawaii once scooted into the water. Coming into sight soon is Kahaluu Beach Park, and your sightseeing labors are over.

THE LAZY LIFE

Now you can concentrate on the important business of Kona, sun-worshiping. **Kahaluu Beach Park** is a fine place for swimming, snorkeling, and picnicking. Snorkelers claim it's the best place on the Big Island. There's a pretty lagoon, the swimming is safe, and the sand, once a fine white, is now salt-and-pepper, thanks to an ancient lava flow that came pounding across it. Even prettier is **White Sands Beach** (sometimes called "Disappearing Beach," since the high surf occasionally removes and then returns the sand), a gorgeous, if tiny, spot. Palm trees arch across the sand, the surf is a Mediterranean blue, and the brilliant reds, yellows, and purples of tropical blossoms are everywhere. It can be dangerous, though, when the surf is rough. Back in Kailua, you can swim in front of the luxurious King Kamehameha Hotel; the beach here is a public one, something that old King Kam would probably have approved of. The water is very gentle, safe for kids.

UNDERWATER ADVENTURE

Definitely "thrill-of-a-lifetime" experience is a dive aboard the submarine *Atlantis,* which takes passengers 80 to 100 feet below the clear waters of Kona Bay to explore an exotic world usually seen only by scuba divers or research scientists. You'll feel as if you're in a Jacques Cousteau documentary, gazing out of the portholes as schools of brightly colored tropical fish—butterfly fish and saddle wrasses, moray eels and often a barracuda or two, all denizens of the coral reefs—surround the sub: It's something like an aquarium in reverse, with you inside the glass. Divers are sent down to feed the fish, so there's always something to see. (Bring cameras with high-speed film, 400 ASA, as flashbulbs will not work through the portholes.)

The 65-foot submarine, one of a growing fleet of such high-tech recreational subs (others have been operating in Barbados, St. Thomas, the Cayman Islands, and Guam for several years), is superbly equipped for safety and comfort; it is air-conditioned and maintains normal atmospheric pressure. Everyone from youngsters (over 4) to septuagenarians enjoy it. Although the cost of the dive, $67 for adults, $33 for children, is high, this is a unique adventure, well worth a splurge. On Wednesday nights, spectacular night dives take place: These cost $87, or you may purchase two dives, one day and one night, for $99. There are six dives daily, departing from the office of Atlantis Submarines in the Hotel King Kamehameha: A launch takes you out to the boarding site in the bay. For reservations, phone 329-6626. Another Atlantic sub is now operating in Waikiki, from the Hilton Hawaiian Village (tel. 522-1710).

THE SPORTING SCENE

There is, of course, no dearth of sporting activities in Kona. Deep-sea fishermen consider Kona their favorite place in the world. Most fishing charters are beyond our budget, but whether you go out fishing or not, you can view the catch of Kona's fishermen. The morning weigh-in of the giants is from noon to 1pm, the afternoon one from 4 to 5pm, at the pier in front of the King Kamehameha Hotel.

A number of our readers have written over the years to recommend an idyllic snorkeling adventure aboard the *Kamanu,* a 36-foot catamaran run by **Kamanu**

Charters (tel. 329-2021 for reservations, or write to P.O. Box 2021, Kailua-Kona, HI 96745). The great thing about this trip is that it's just as simple for nonswimmers as it is for Red Cross lifeguards, since those who wish to may enter the water in an inner tube. Jay Lambert, who runs the tours, claims that snorkeling is even easier than swimming, requiring little exertion or water knowledge. And everybody likes to hand-feed the many varieties of small tropical-reef fish abounding in the crystalline waters where the boat drops anchor. Those who only want to sail without getting wet are welcome, too. One of our readers, Marty Iabis of Prospect, Illinois, wrote us: "The cruise was organized by two very congenial fellows who make each trip cozy and informal, unlike the mass atmosphere most tourists have to put up with—this was on a first-name basis and only 10 to 15 persons aboard. My husband and I found it to be one of our most memorable experiences on the island!" You receive free transportation by van to the boat, then sail to an isolated reef; equipment, professional instruction, and even a glass of guava juice or beer and wine and fresh local fruit are provided, all at $35 for adults, $20 for children 12 and under (free for toddlers under 2). Prescription masks are free; and underwater cameras are available. Jay also runs exclusive sunset/cocktail sails.

Golf? That's easy too. The place to play is at the beautiful **Keauhou Kona Course,** six miles south of Kona; make arrangements at your hotel. If it's tennis you're after, try the free public court at the **Kailua Playground** near the Kona Sunset Hotel, or the four courts at the Old Airport Tennis Court. Courts are also available at nominal cost at the Hotel King Kamehameha, the Keauhou Beach Hotel, the Kona Hilton Beach and Tennis Resort, and the Kona Surf Hotel.

Those who would like to hike through the Big Island's beautiful trails are advised not to hike on their own outside of the national parks, but to consult local hiking clubs and try to join one of their excursions. If no group hikes are scheduled, they can advise you on where you can hike safely. The offices of the **Hawaii Visitors Bureau** can give you information on local clubs, or, write to the local office of the **Sierra Club,** P.O. Box 1137, Hilo, HI 96721.

If you can afford a fee of about $80 for a roughly nine-hour trip, you can have a great adventure with **Paradise Safaris,** an outfit that takes small groups almost 14,000 feet up to the top of Mauna Kea to experience extraordinary sunsets (visibility is 100 miles) and have a look at the night sky at a world-class telescope facility. They pick up at West Hawaii hotels and, thankfully, even provide warm parkas and hot drinks against the chilly mountain air. Be sure you're capable of handling high altitudes for this one. Phone 322-2366, or write in advance to Paradise Safaris, P.O. Box A-D, Kailua-Kona, HI 96745.

This is great country for those who like to ride. Ten minutes away from Kailua-Kona are the slopes of Hualalai, where you can ride at elevations of from 1,500 to 3,000 feet, through beautiful pasturelands, courtesy of **Waiono Meadows.** Rates are $20 per person per hour, $34 per person for a two-hour ride. Call them at 324-1544 for information and to inquire about some of their more ambitious rides, like a barbecue ride, the four-hour Mountain, Fishing, Riding Adventure, which includes fishing for largemouth bass and a lakeside lunch. A large selection of horses is available to meet various levels of riding ability.

Note: For complete listings of Big Island sports facilities, stop in at the office of the Hawaii Visitors Bureau. For information on adventure and wilderness excursions, see Chapter XVIII.

CRUISES—DAY AND NIGHT

A variety of cruises run by **Capt. Bean** are a venerable institution on the Kona coast. They offer that something for everyone, and prices are reasonable. For reservations, tel. 329-2955.

The one-hour glass-bottom boat ride is a bargain at $10 for adults, $5 for children under 12. Enjoy the underwater marine life and hula dancing as well. Boats depart at 1:30pm.

Want to go native? Well, the captain has a half-day Kealakekua Bay cruise in an authentic Polynesian war canoe, and it's the largest glass-bottom boat in Hawaii.

Learn the history of the Kona coast, swim or snorkel in the clear blue waters, enjoy a light lunch with the crew (purchased separately), and sing along to the old songs and dances of Hawaii, all for $25 for adults, $12.50 for those under 12. The boat departs at 8:30am.

Let's not forget romance. Capt. Bean's two-hour dinner sail cruise is a truly fun-tastic experience with an open bar, all you can eat, and a troupe of authentic Polynesian dancers. For two hours, these 25 young people will regale you with an unparalleled display of energy and enthusiasm as they perform the dances of the Pacific islands. Before you know it, you're dancing, too! Adults only, $42. Departure time at 5:15pm.

All boats depart from the Kailua Pier near the King Kamehameha Hotel.

SHOPPING IN KONA

The Kona shopping scene has blossomed like everything else in this bubbling resort town. At last count, there must have been something like 100 stores and shops, some in quaint arcades, some in small centers and hotels, others just there, all on or just off Alii Drive.

A good place to begin might be the shopping arcade in the **Hotel King Kamehameha. Island Togs** has some attractive women's clothes, and prices are quite reasonable. We've always had good luck here. . . . There's no longer a real live mynah bird at the **Mynah Bird,** but everything else is in good order. There's a collection of lovely fabrics, from $6 a yard, all cotton; clothes can be custom-made from these fabrics and mailed to you at home. Attractive handmade and imported women's clothing, starts at about $24, for dresses.

In the Kona Square Mall is a longtime favorite, **Island Silversmiths.** A sign on the door reads, "We only look expensive," and they're right. We saw coral rings here for $6 that were $15 in hotel gift shops nearby. They're known for their sterling silver charms: The most popular is the Humuhumunukunukuapua's (oh well, just ask for Hawaii's state fish), $34. Also nice is their Cleopatra silver perfume ring at $25. . . . Right across the road is another neat jewelry store called **Goldfish Jewelry.** "We catch your eye" is their motto. Their specialty is 14-karat-gold charms—pineapple, marlin, reef fish, whale's tails, and the like: prices start at $10, average $40 to $50.

Whatever else you do, don't miss the **Kona Arts & Crafts Gallery,** across from the sea wall in this area of Alii Drive. It's one of the few places that deal solely in *genuine* Hawaiian crafts: their wood carvings, for example, are made only of native woods such as milo, ohia, or koa; monkeypod is not used, because it is not indigenous to Hawaii. Prices can go way up for the works of fine art here, but there are many small treasures, too: Hawaiian sand-art petroglyphs from $6.95, banana-bark paintings, notecards by local artists, bookmarks made from the flowers of Hawaii, limu art (limu is an edible seaweed). Do note their chime collection: They bear the imprints of native ferns grown on volcanic soil, pressed into the lava, and then fired, and have a worldwide reputation; from $12.95. The shop also carries genuine hula instruments (made of gourds with seeds), and much more. Owners Fred and Sally Nannestad are knowledgeable about their collection and take time to explain the intricacies of these native arts. Very worthwhile.

If you haven't brought the right walking shoes with you (doesn't it always happen?), pay a visit to **Sandal Stop** in Seaside Mall. They have a great selection, helpful service, and plenty of shoes to wear in the water, like "Aquasox." **Sandal Basket** on Alii Drive also has an excellent collection of shoes; it's been in business for over 29 years.

Cross the street now to the ocean side where you'll find the biggest cluster of shops in town at the rambling **Kona Inn Shopping Village.** With more than 40 shops and restaurants and a waterfront location, it's always pleasant for browsing about. Shops come and go here, but you'll certainly find much to attract you. The **Original Maui Divers,** an island tradition, is a top place for black, pink, or gold coral jewelry. . . . Women will come away with a different look from **Noa Noa.** Joan Simon's wild tropical designs on natural fabrics are stunning, and prices are not unreasonable. They also carry a selection of Balinese artifacts, which range from duffel bags at $36 and scarves at $45, up to collector's items like Indonesian IKAT textiles, which would make splendid wall hangings, starting around $240. . . . Imagination runs wild at **Alleygecko's,** which boasts "colorful gifts from all over the world." Hundreds of Balinese wooden "guardian" figures hang from the ceiling; there is all manner of stuffed geckos, an enormous collection of brightly colored magnets, Japanese prints, Indonesian shirts, and lots more. Don't miss. . . . Boys and girls Hawaiian clothing is well priced at **Kona Children's Wear,** whose selections go from infants through young teens. . . . Light cottons for women and darling dresses for little girls, too, are featured at **Dragonfly Hawaii.** . . . Like to sew? Check out **Fare Tahiti,** a fabric shop with Hawaiian and Tahitian prints, mostly cottons, from $7.50 per yard. Note, too, their hand-decorated pareaus, made on Maui, airbrushed in rainbow colors, at $26.50. They also sell men's tapa shirts, women's short and long dresses, and needlepoint and cross-stitch charts and kits.

Still at Kona Inn Shopping Village, **Crystal Visions of Hawaii** is charming, with crystals, jewelry, mystical gifts and cards, and even a "Visionary Art Gallery" . . . . We found stylish modern and vintage fashions for women, and vintage jewelry at **Flamingo's.** . . . The hand-painted and hand-silk-screened cotton women's fashions at **Elizabeth Harrison** are very tasteful. Some 16 local artists contribute their designs. Popular "cropped tops" start about $22. . . . Need a hat to keep the sun off your head? **Big Island Hat Company** has plenty to choose from, including custom-blocked Panamas. They also have handcrafted Hawaiian feather-lei hatbands. . . . Prices are not cheap at the **Kona Inn Flower, Gift and Lei Shop,** but we did find a couple of fantastic bargains: dried-bougainvillea leis, beautiful and just $4! (Fresh bougainvillea leis are $10.) Purple-flowered bozo leis will also last for a long time, $6. . . . **Island Life Tee Shirt Company** sports some exclusive Kona designs on their T-shirts, which are silk-screened by owner Roberta Fair. The same shirts are also available at **Island Salsa,** in the Kona Marketplace, about $16. . . . Lovely handmade items, including handmade pareaus and many tie-dyes (around $32) can be found at **Ta-Yu Silks.**

Hawaiiana at the Kona Shopping Village is one of those places collectors of vintage aloha shirts seek out, and it's one of the best in the islands. Do people actually wear these shirts? We know that celebrities love them, but with prices going from $100 to $1,000 for silk and rayon shirts of the 1940s and 1950s, our guess is that most of them wind up framed, on somebody's walls. Also fun: the vintage aloha items that collectors snap up, like "nodders" (hula dolls with nodding heads) from $45 to $75, and menu covers from the Royal Hawaiian Hotel and cruise ships of the Matson Line of the 1930s and 1940s, from about $25 to $125.

If calories are irrelevant, pick up some coconut shortbread or macadamia-nut cookies at **Mrs. Barry's Kona Cookies.** One of our readers, Charles Rabin of New York, writes that "these cookies were one of the many reasons I regretted departing Kona!"

Have an ice cream or snack on a breezy lanai overlooking the ocean at the **Be Happy Cafe;** or soups or salads, drinks, and pupus, at the popular big lanai at **Don Drysdale's Club 53. Kona Inn,** and **Fishermen's Landing** are both top-notch restaurants here, and both are right out on the waterfront.

Running out of things to read? Help is at hand in the **Middle Earth Book Shoppe,** across Alii Drive and one flight up in the **Kona Plaza Shopping Arcade,** stocked with a good selection of maps and charts as well as books. . . . Downstairs in this same arcade is **Coral Factory,** a huge place with every kind of coral imaginable, and many good gift items at reasonable prices. We also like **Marlin Casuals** in this same arcade; it always offers very tasteful resort wear at competitive prices. . . . **Paradise Found,** next to Suzanne's Bakery, specializes in resort wear that is elegant and casual at the same time; prices are good. Note their hand-painted items on raw silk.

There aren't many shops at Waterfront Row, but for those who love fine Hawaiian crafts, a visit to **Alapaki** is in order. Everything here is made in Hawaii, from traditional music instruments, calabashes, and poi bowls, up to modern interpretations of traditional handcrafts; we were impressed with the koa-wood necklaces by Curtis Wilmington of Honolulu (around $200) and the koa carvings by Bob Holder. A good place for special, one-of-a-kind gifts.

Near the intersection of hwys. 11 and 190 is the **Kona Coast Shopping Center.** Here, the old Taniguchi's, razed when the King Kamehameha Hotel was rebuilt, has been relocated in a modern supermarket setting and renamed **KTA.** The store is slick and modern now, with none of its pretourist local character, but it's still a good place to stock up on food for your kitchenette apartment. It also might pay to join the local folks at places like **Pay'n'Save,** a huge drugstore with very low prices for film and other items, and **Kona Health Ways,** with a large selection of herbs, roots, teas, spices, and some fresh produce.

On the other side of the highway at 75-5595 Palani Rd. is the newer **Lanihau Center.** It's mostly of interest to local people, but you can shop for produce, baked goods, national brands, beers, and wines at low prices at the cavernous **Food4Less** supermarket, which is open 24 hours a day, seven days a week; browse through the fashion racks and get a free shell lei and cup of Kona coffee at the **Hilo Hattie Fashion Center;** explore **Long's Drugs** and **Waldenbooks.**

If candy is your passion, be sure to visit the **Kailua Candy Company** at 74-552C Kaiwi St., in the industrial area, a few blocks from Alii Drive (take your first right after the intersection of hwys. 11 and 190, look for the "Hawaiian Warrior" marker). You'll be taken on a tour of the kitchen and given lots of free samples of chocolates and dry-roasted macadamia nuts. It will be hard to resist buying some to take home with you, even though the average price is $15 a pound, for these are handmade and hand-packed candies, made with real butter, no preservatives, and a great deal of pride by the family that operates the business. They call them the best-tasting candies in Hawaii, and you might just agree. They have received national recognition from *Chocolatier* magazine and *Bon Appetit.* Their newest treats: Kona Café Olé and Tropical Truffle.

As long as you're in the industrial area, you might as well stop in at a local favorite, **Pot Belli Delli,** to pick up some of their New York–style deli sandwiches (about $2.45 to $4) and you'll be all set for a picnic down the road at the old airport beach. Call in for special or large orders by 10am for a noontime pickup (tel. 329-9454).

A BIG ISLAND CALENDAR

Can't decide when to come to the Big Island? Here's a list of some events that may help you make your plans. April is the time for the **Merrie Monarch Festival,** including competitions, workshops, and miniperformances at Wailoa Center, lots of free shows at the tennis stadium, and more hula than you can shake a hip at. Tickets must be reserved many months in advance. . . . May Day is **Lei Day:** there's usually lei-making in the hotel lobbies. . . . A major event for local artists is the **Big Island Spring Arts Festival,** held in May or June. A wonderful chance to see the best of island arts. . . . **July 4** is a big time for community gatherings: rodeos in Waimea and Naalehu, rough-water swims in Hapuna, and an anniversary celebration for Pu'uhonua o Honaunau in Kona, showing off old Hawaiian crafts in a cultural festival. . . . Also in July is the **International Festival of the Pacific** in Hilo, including free Shakespeare in the park performances, parades, dances, and displays of the multi-ethnic peoples of Hawaii. . . . **Bon Dances** are big events in both July and August. . . . In late July or August, sportsmen from all over gather for the **Billfish Tournament** in Kona. . . . August brings a cast of thousands for the **Strongman Triathlon World Championship.** The **Honokaa MacNut Festival,** featuring unusual races with macadamia-nut bags, nut balls for a golf tournament, and more, is held in late August. . . . **Aloha Week** festivities in October are special on the Big Island: the opening ceremony is at Halemaumau with dance performances and offerings to Pele. . . . The **Kona Coffee Festival** is held in mid-October.

READERS' SIGHTSEEING AND SHOPPING SUGGESTIONS ON THE BIG ISLAND:

"I love Hawaii and have just completed my fourth trip to the islands in five years. I have learned to travel on moderate funds and have seen more of the islands and met many locals and learned much about the real Hawaii by doing so. I no longer feel like a tourist when I go, but rather like a friend returning to a familiar, heart-warming home away from home. On my last trip, I spent five days on a 54-foot sailboat, *Christina,* with the **Oceanic Society,** whale watching and snorkeling—what a wonderful trip! The leaders were Mark and Beth Goodoni, who also run the **Eye of the Whale Expeditions.** I cannot speak highly enough about these people and this trip: Oceanic Society Expeditions, Fort Mason Center, Building E., San Francisco, CA 94123; Eye of the Whale, P.O. Box 1269, Kapaau, HI 96755. The *Christina* also goes out on private trips run by a delightful Hawaiian-born and raised skipper named Kaua. This is a great snorkel cruise, with lunch or dinner and all equipment and trolling lines for fishermen provided. There are no crowds; six people maximum. Price is $65. **Aloha Kona Cruises,** P.O. Box 5320, Kailua-Kona, HI 96745. . . . The senior citizens put on a wonderful show free of charge at the lobby of the King Kamehameha Hotel on Fridays; I spent a whole afternoon there enjoying them. They also make beautiful crafts which are on sale there. . . . Snorkeling at Kahaluu Bay with the locals was great and so was the family-run sandwich stand, with very reasonable prices, like $1.25 hamburgers" (Marilyn Kintz, Mohena, Ill.). [*Authors' Note:* See Chapter XVIII, "Alternative and Special-Interest Travel," for details on Eye of the Whale and Oceanic Society Expeditions.]

"We highly recommend combining deep-sea fishing and snorkeling on the **Party Boat out of Kona.** For $30, we cruised the coast on this catamaran for 4½ hours. We snorkeled for over an hour, all gear provided, and were served breakfast and lunch. The boat had bathrooms and a bar. The crew even grilled the barracuda we caught for lunch. We girls had a much better deal than our fellows, who sat on a fishing boat 4½ hours for $75 and never caught a thing! They even had to bring their own food. Check this out" (Martha Farwell, Illinois City, Ill.).

"**Kamanu Charters** in Kailua-Kona was everything your book claims. Jay runs his snorkel-sails very professionally. Spinner dolphins swam along with the bow of the boat as we sailed along, so close you could almost touch them. Highly recommended" (Joanne G. Schmidt, Newar, Del.). . . . "The visit to **Waipio Valley,** via Waipio Valley Shuttle, was one of the high points of our visit. Scenically it is overwhelming in its beauty, and the historical insights provided by our driver, who was raised there, enhanced our enjoyment. There is another spot that, in a way, complements Waipio Valley. It is the **Pololu Overlook** at the end of the road going east from Hawi, on the north Kohala coast of the island. Not as grand as Waipio, but still very scenic; it is the western boundary of these Hawaii sea cliffs, while Waipio is pretty much the eastern one" (William S. Connell, Durham, N.H.).

"We took a one-day **Scenic Tours fly-bus tour** of the Big Island to see the volcano, and it was the highlight of our trip. The pilot of our eight-seater flew close to the volcano, then doubled back several times so that passengers on both sides could get good pictures. (Take a seasick pill before you take this trip.) The bus took us to a place where lava had recently flowed over a road; we could see it bubbling up and felt the heat. Awesome!" (Dorothy Nichols, Arcola, Mo.).

"Please tell your readers that for anyone traveling alone, Hawaii is perfect. Many places and people, I feel, gave me preferential treatment *because* I was alone. They seemed to go out of their way to see that I had a good time. Two places that are an example are **Orchids of Hawaii** and **Hale Manu Lauhal Weaving.** I spent a long time in both places just enjoying the good conversation" (Patricia Kelly, Pascagola, Mo.). . . . "We highly recommend **Kamanu Catamaran Cruises** (formerly Pacific Sail and Snorkel). Jay Lambert is a great catamaran captain. The snorkeling was super, and fruit and juices awaited us on the boat afterwards. Jay will even pick you up at your hotel. A highlight of our trip! . . . We hopped aboard **Captain Bean's glass-bottom boat** and had a great morning watching colorful fish along the coastline. While on board we were treated to a hula show, free juices, Hawaiian music, and a 'general hula class.' They will even dress you up in native costume for pictures. I advise those prone to motion sickness to take Dramamine beforehand. I'm usually not prone, but they stop the boat to watch the fish and the waves take over" (Patti Connor, Arlington, Mass.). [*Authors' Note:* Ginger pills, sold in local health-food stores, also work well in preventing motion sickness.]

"The highlight of our trip had to be the black-sand beaches. Not the ones 'everybody' goes to, such as the one at Kalapana, but ones we found with the help of locals. As we were studying our maps at a small drive-in restaurant/general store, a young local woman asked what we were looking for. We told her, 'the black-sand beaches.' As she was heading there herself, she gave us directions: we were to drive until we saw the 'Road Closed' signs, drive *around* the signs and keep going until the lava flows blocked the road and park the car there. We followed these directions as we hiked over the fairly recent flows toward a small column of steam; farther to the right was a *big* column of steam; we hiked toward the smaller one. During the hike, we were much more emotionally impressed than we were when we later visited Volcanoes National Park. At the park, most of what we could see seemed far away and old. On our hike we saw, up close, remains of cars, homes and furnishings that had been in use only months before. Then, at the end of the hike, about 15 minutes, we were treated to a black-sand beach only months old. It was majestic! The 'sand' looked like millions of pieces of tiny black onyx—so very black and sparkling. We could have stayed all day! The water was *so* blue and the sand *so* black and we had it all to ourselves. We couldn't help but say, "Now *this* is Hawaii! We'll be back!!!" (Cheryl Reese and Becky Gardner). [*Authors' Note:* Despite the beauty of such a trip, local authorities definitely warn against straying off beaten paths and ignoring 'Road Closed' signs. New lava often looks safe but may actually be very thin, and one wrong step could be disastrous. It's always best to stay on safe paths.]

"Allow yourself enough time when planning your vacation to be able to see and do everything you want, and some extra time for just relaxing and enjoying the Hawaiian way of life. We did the Big Island in five days and moved on to Kauai for four more days. It just wasn't enough time! We managed to see everything, but didn't have the time to stop and really enjoy the beauty of the areas. . . . The highlight of our trip was the snorkeling cruise on the *Fairwinds* in Kona. The crew was great and took us to Kealakekua Bay. I'm ready to go back just to snorkel and relax on the beaches; which I got to do only once!" (Sandy and Dave Heinrich, Forks, Wash.).

"In my opinion, the best shop in all of the Hawaiian Islands is the **Volcano Art Center** on the Big Island, which sits next door to Volcanoes National Park headquarters and across the road from the current Volcano House. This art center, housed in the original Volcano House built in 1877, contains handcrafted items of the finest quality from island artisans. Beautiful koa, mango, milo, and other native-wood bowls, boxes, and cutting boards, may be purchased, as well as feather leis, ivory jewelry, petroglyph notecards and postcards, among others. They will package and mail any item purchased there" (Teresa M. Zent, Taneytown, Md.). . . . "A United Airlines employee at Kahului gave me this helpful tip. If your plane stops in Hilo en route home, buy flowers at the airport—fresher and cheaper. I bought a beautiful orchid, carnation, and plumeria lei, and orchid plants were $1 to $2 less than at other flower stands elsewhere. The saleswomen were extremely helpful and cordial" (Elizabeth C. Greer, El Cerrito, Calif.).

"**Parasailing** is available at the Kona wharf area. The day my daughter 'flew,' participants included both sexes, aged 21 to 75—that's right, 75, a woman—who enjoyed the flight at the end of a 300-foot tow rope. Usually the driver of the towboat can start you off and land you dry on their launching raft anchored out from shore—but wear a bathing suit just in case you get dunked. Parasailing is also available at Lahaina, Maui, but is more expensive" (Janet Bryan, Stockbridge, Ga.).

"We snorkeled at Hanauma Bay in Oahu, and Poipu Beach and K'ee Beach in Kauai, but we found the best snorkeling by far to be at **Kahaluu Beach Park** in Hawaii, about five miles south of Kona. One day I took out some bread and when I let some pieces go, we had hundreds of fish within reaching distance of us. This definitely was a highlight of our entire trip" (Richard Marks, Lodi, Calif.).

"One of the big athletic events in the islands is the **Triathlon**. It's said to be the single most grueling athletic contest in the world; it's much harder to be a participant in this than in the Olympics. Over 600 brave souls entered the contest twice last year. Briefly, it is a 2½-mile swim, then a 117-mile bike race, then about a 50-mile run with no resting in between. It starts about 8am, and many do not finish until the wee hours. . . . There's an interesting **Fourth of July Rodeo** in Waimea. Instead of the typical bucking broncos you would expect from a mainland rodeo, they have hilarious 'wild cow milking,' and also relay races on horseback. . . . Kailua-Kona's annual **Billfish Tournament** in July features a parade bearing floats and entries from countries like Samoa, Fiji, and New Zealand" (Barbara King, Kailua-Kona, HI.).

"John Alexander, the delightful host at the **Dolphin Bay** in Hilo, gave us a helpful hint that we want to pass on. He told us to buy our flowers at an inexpensive place, such as a grocery store or small florist, obtain a carton, and pack them carefully with shredded, wet newspapers, covered with plastic, to keep them moist. We did this, and carried them on the plane with us. I am writing this over a week later and they are still in good shape. I have four dozen anthuriums and six birds of paradise to give to my friends, and all for just a little over $15" (Mrs. Dean James, Celina, Ohio).

"For those who enjoy snorkeling, we would like to recommend a lagoon only five miles south of Kailua-Kona at milepost 5. **Kahaluu Beach Park** has picnic tables, showers, rest rooms, and a beautiful large lagoon from one to three feet deep. Part of the lagoon is closed from the sea by a row of rocks. According to the local groundskeeper, the Menehunes were to create a fish pond in trade for some land. Since the Hawaiian who bargained with the Menehunes had second thoughts about the deal, he would crow like a rooster from a coconut tree every morning at 3am. The Menehunes, who worked by night, thought morning was approaching, so they stopped work, never completing the fish pond. All types of fish are present in this lagoon, including a few Crown of Thorns" (Charles Kinney, Hayward, Calif.). . . . "When visiting the **petroglyphs at Puako,** be sure to take along some material suitable for making rubbings. Burlap and wax crayon (seen in the Lyman Museum) were very effective. There are two sites; the second one, about a quarter mile past the first, has a much wider variety of carvings" (Patricia Scruggs, Chino, Calif.).

"We took a nice side trip to Pololu Valley Lookout on the northern tip in the **Kohala** district. After viewing the beautiful valley we stopped about three miles back down the road from the lookout on Hwy. 27 at **Keokea Park,** which had a lovely view, picnic tables, outdoor showers, and a little sea pool. There is a sign off Hwy. 27; you can drive in from the road about one mile" (Mr. and Mrs. Donald Plumlee, Santa Clara, Calif.). . . . "We found canvas shoes much more desirable than sandals when we visited **Volcanoes National Park** and the Pu'uhonua o Honaunau at Kona; the volcanic pebbles are difficult to walk on and get between your toes, and the canvas shoes give you a firm footing. Since we were in Hawaii in November and December we did have rain, and my washable canvas shoes were not ruined by the red mud I encountered several times or the deluge of rain we had to paddle through in Hilo" (Mrs. Jack Morgan, Vacaville, Calif.).

"The **fishing pier** across from Liliuokalani Gardens Park has a very interesting fish auction at 7:30am weekday mornings, when the boat operators sell to licensed fish markets. The auction takes only a few minutes, and visitors may ask questions. In Kona, the weighing in of marlins and tuna is very interesting and starts at about 4pm" (Mrs. Charles H. Gould, Seattle, Wash.). . . . "It is interesting to drive up the 13-mile road on the slope of **Mauna Loa** for the view. From there the trail leads to the summit. On this ride in the morning at 7am, I saw plenty of wild pigs and wild goats. Before Waiohini, it is worthwhile to drive nine miles down to the left to the **South Point** (Ka Lae), the southernmost point of the U.S. There is a lighthouse and steep cliffs. The fishermen have to tow the fish over the cliffs from their boats" (Prof. Dr. W. K. Brauers, Berchem-Antwerp, Belgium).

THE ISLAND OF MAUI

Even though she lives two blocks away from highly celebrated Waikiki Beach, a woman we know in Honolulu regularly spends her vacations in Maui. The reason? To go to the beach! In addition, however, to possessing some of the world's most marvelous beaches, this second-largest island in the Hawaiian archipelago boasts one of the great natural wonders of the planet: Haleakala, the world's largest dormant volcano. Add to all this a string of gorgeous little jungle valleys where the modern world seems incredibly remote, a picturesque whaling town kicking its heels after a long sleep in the South Seas sun, and a wonderfully hospitable local citizenry intent on convincing you that Maui *no ka oi*—Maui is the greatest. You just might end up agreeing.

Maui has been going through the throes of enormous expansion. But while new hotels and condominium apartments have been and are being built at a formidable rate, the island still manages to retain a graceful, unhurried feeling. The laws here are stricter, and nowhere on Maui has there been such wanton destruction of natural beauty as there has been in Waikiki.

Although most of the new condominium apartments are in the luxury category, some are fine for us. But even with these additions to the hotel scene, a room in Maui is probably going to be more expensive than one in Waikiki. Meals go from budget to luxury, but there are plenty of opportunities to do your own cooking. Again, your biggest expense will be car rentals or guided tours, your only alternative on an island with very limited public transportation.

CHOOSING A BASE

Maui is small enough so that you can logically make your headquarters at one hotel and take off each day for various sightseeing and beach excursions: to **Haleakala,** to the historic old whaling town of **Lahaina,** and to remote, romantic **Hana.**

The **Wailuku-Kahului** are, closest to the airport, is centrally located for sightseeing excursions but lacks a really good beach. The best beach area close to Kahului is **Kihei** (about a 15-minute drive) and this also enjoys a central location. The liveliest and most beautiful area, to our taste, is the **Lahaina-Kaanapali-Napili** region, about 40 miles from Kahului, generally more expensive than the Kihei area, which has a far greater number of condo accommodations. All of these places work as a base; the only place on the island that is inconvenient as a base if you want to move around is **Hana;** you might want to plan an overnight stay there as the drive each way is a long one, although most people do it on a one-day trip.

ARRIVAL IN KAHULUI

Your plane will land at the very modern and airy Kahului Airport. The terminal is located in the seven-mile-wide valley that binds together the two great volcanic masses of Maui—the West Maui Mountains and Haleakala on the east—and accounts for the name Valley Isle. You're just a few miles here from modern Kahului and graceful old Wailuku, neighbor towns competing peacefully for the title of largest city. There is shuttle service from the airport to Kihei and Kaanapali. If you need assistance, stop by the state information kiosk at the airport. The **Maui Visitors Bureau** is a short drive from the airport, at 380 Dairy Rd., directly en route to Lahaina or Kihei. They have an extensive supply of visitor information (tel. 871-8691).

If you're going to be staying in West Maui, you can save some driving time by flying directly to the new Kapalua-West Maui Airport via either Hawaiian or Princeville Airlines.

U-DRIVES

As in all the neighbor islands, the major low-cost, all-island car-rental companies, like Dollar, Alamo, National, Budget, Tropical, etc., are all represented in Maui. The best place to make your reservations with these companies is in Honolulu (see Chapter V, "Transportation Within Honolulu," for details). Some of the local agencies can also offer you good deals, at either flat rates or time plus mileage. **Sunshine of Hawaii** (tel. 871-6222 in Kahului, 661-5646 in Lahaina, toll free 800/367-2977) is an excellent company. Rates begin at $19.95 daily, $99 weekly for a compact standard; a compact automatic with air conditioning is $23.95 daily, $119 per week. (Rates are subject to change.) They're right at the airport. At **Trans Maui**

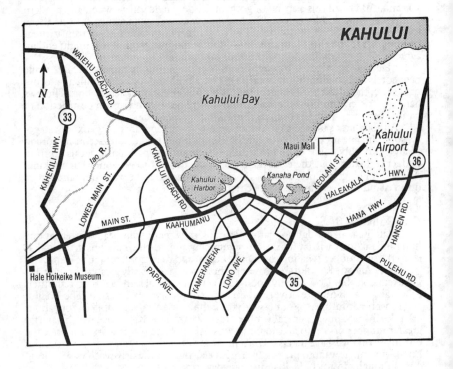

Rent A Car (tel. 877-5222, or toll free 800/367-5228), charges can sometimes be as low as $17.95 flat rate for either a stick-shift or automatic compact.

Atlas Rent A Car (tel. 871-2860, or toll free 800/367-5238 U.S.A., 800/433-5906 Canada) offers a late-model compact from $12.64 per day with "absolutely no hidden charges." All sizes of cars are available. They rent the Suzuki Samurai four-wheel drives, for as low as $29.95 per day. They will provide prompt and courteous airport service. Write them at P.O. Box 126, Puunene, Maui, HI 96784.

In the Lahaina-Kaanapali area, you can get a good deal on flat rates from **Rainbow,** 741 Wainee St., Lahaina (tel. 661-8734), which charges $21.50 per day for Toyota Tercel compacts.

---

1. Hotels

IN KAHULUI

Kahului has a string of four hotels within minutes of the airport and across the road from three very attractive shopping centers dotted with inexpensive restaurants. The ocean, here, however, is rocky and can be fairly rough. With the development of a very good beach area in Kihei, just 15 minutes away, these hotels have become largely the place for local business travelers and for very large tour groups, since Kahului does offer a central location for touring all of Maui. If you choose to stay here, your best bet is the **Maui Seaside,** which now encompasses the old Maui Hukilau Hotel, which is known as its pool wing. And there is a new sand beach. The entire complex has recently been renovated and is very attractive: Rooms are large, light, and tastefully furnished, all boasting air conditioning, color TV, and two double beds. Refrigerators are available on request, in deluxe tower rooms. From April 1 to December 14, standard garden rooms are $55, single or double; deluxe poolside rooms are $59; superior tower rooms are $68; kitchenette rooms are $79. The rest of the year, add $10 per room per night. You can realize savings by renting a car for another $16 per night in each category. You can save even more by dining at Vi's, which offers a long menu of dishes—seafood, American, Mexican, Italian, and Oriental—most from $6.50 to $10.50. For reservations, write to Sands and Seaside Resorts, 2222 Kalakaua Ave., Suite 714, Honolulu, HI 96815, or phone toll free 800/367-7000.

IN WAILUKU

Here's good news for the active budget crowd—travelers, hikers, scuba divers, windsurfers, bikers, etc. **Northshore Inn,** 2080 Vineyard St. (tel. 242-8999), is a new hotel right in the heart of historic Wailuku town that's offering just about the most reasonable rates in Maui. Chris Dunkel, who hails from Germany, and his wife, Katie, from Kent, Washington, decided to settle in Maui after traveling around the world, and looked for a way to create an inexpensive, comfortable, friendly lodging. They discovered the old Wailuku Grand Hotel and have completely renovated and remodeled the old building, so that it's now quite pleasant. A path leads from the busy street back to a tropical garden that has sitting areas and a barbecue, and one flight up is the hotel, with 24 sleeping rooms, a common room with TV, VCR, games, and a shiatsu massage table. There's a place to store bicycles, surfboards, and the like. Rooms are small but cozy, with white stucco walls, roll-up blinds, color TV, a small refrigerator, and either double or twin beds; these rent for $29 single, $39 double. There are two community rooms, with three double-decker beds each, that rent for $15 per night per person. There are no private bathrooms, but there are five shared bathrooms, all with showers. The Dunkels had not yet completed the place at the time of our visit, and it was already full—it attracts a lively international crowd—so our guess is that this is going to be hugely successful. Hopefully, the Dunkels will be able to expand soon and create more rooms. Northshore Inn is located right above Hazel's Café, a popular local eatery; other inexpensive restaurants abound. Good beaches are about a 15-minute drive away.

IN KIHEI-WAILEA

The closest beach area to Kahului (about 15 minutes away) is the Kihei-Wailea section of Maui—a windswept stretch of sea and sand, with miles and miles of unspoiled ocean beach, the waves lapping at your feet, air warm and dry, and the mighty volcano of Haleakala and its changing cloud colors to gaze at from the shore. It's blessed with the least rain and best weather in all of Maui. Full-scale tourist development began here not so long ago, and the area has blossomed mightily since then, with scores of condominiums, plus new restaurants and small shopping centers opening to keep pace. There are four luxury-class hotels in Wailea and Makena: the Hotel Inter-Continental, the Stouffer Wailea Beach Hotel, the Maui Prince, and the Makena Surf. Beaches here can be rather windy in the afternoon (get your swims in the morning and save sightseeing for later). Despite its beauty, the Kihei-Wailea region remains less glamorous and exciting, at least for us, than the Lahaina-Kaanapali region (see ahead), but if you like a quiet vacation, you'll do well at any of the places described below.

When a hotel has a very large return clientele—as much as 75% year after year —you know it's doing something right. Such is the case with **Nani Kai Hale,** at the very entrance to the Kihei area, blessed with a location on an excellent swimming beach, nice accommodations, and the ministrations of managers Jeanne and Larry Forseth, who do a lot to create that old-time aloha spirit. Guests receive a pineapple in their room on arrival, are invited to a coffee-and-doughnuts party at the beach on Saturday morning, and sometimes to a hukilau run by the native Filipino family that lives next door (a hukilau, once common but now quite rare on the islands, is a 700-foot fishing net pulled in by hand). There's always a congenial group around the pool or out on the sandy beach; swimming is excellent, but snorkeling is limited. The apartments are condominiums, and decor varies with the individual owners, but all are attractively furnished, have either queen or twin beds, good sofa beds in the living rooms, well-equipped kitchens, private lanais; most do not have telephones. In summer, a three-day minimum is required. Rates begin at $32.50 for a room and bath only (no kitchen or lanai); a studio with kitchen and lanai is $47.50; a one-bedroom, two-bath apartment with kitchen and ocean view is $65; a one-bedroom, two-bath apartment with kitchen and beachfront is $75. All these rates are for one or two people. For four people, a two-bedroom, two-bath apartment with kitchen is $95. During the winter, December 16 to April 15, rates are $42.50, $73.50, $90, $105, and $125, and a seven-day minimum stay is required. An extra person is charged $8 in summer, $10 in winter; children under 5 stay free. For reservations, write Nani Kai Hale, 73 N. Kihei Rd., Kihei, Maui, HI 96753, or call toll free 800/367-6032 U.S.A., 800/367-3705, B.C. and Alberta only. The local number is 879-9120.

Koa Resort is one of those places you could easily spend a long time living in—and many people do—it's so cozy and comfortable. It's an inviting setup, across the road from the ocean, but with many charms of its own. Five two-story wooden buildings stand amidst over 5½ acres of green gardens and lawns and house 54 units. On the property are two tennis courts, an 18-hole putting green, an oversize pool spanned by a bridge, a Jacuzzi, barbecues, and shuffleboard courts. Apartments are spacious and comfortable, with nice furnishings, cable TV, fully equipped kitchens, and large lanais. Rates are decent for Maui. Best buys are the one-bedroom, one-bath unit for four people: $80 from April 1 to November 30, $100 for the rest of the year. Two-bedroom units with one bath are $95 and $115 for four; and two-bedroom units that can sleep six are $105 and $125. Should there be eight of you, you can spread out in three-bedroom, two-bath units for $130 and $150, three-bedroom, three-bath units for $155 and $175. An extra person is $10 per night. Minimum stay is five nights; a 10% discount is given for monthly stays. For reservations, write Koa Resort, 811 S. Kihei Rd., Kihei, Maui, HI 96753 or phone toll free 800/367-8047, ext. 407, from U.S.A., 800/423-8733, ext. 407, from Canada.

Two former readers of this book, Milt and Eileen Preston, started traveling to the islands some years back and then decided to settle there. They've had their own place in Kihei for quite a while now, and will give you a warm welcome at the **Sunseeker Resort,** across the road from Kihei Beach. They've recently done another major remodeling, so that their half-dozen studios, plus the one- and two-bedroom units, all have king-size beds; color schemes are cheerful, there's original artwork, color TV, upholstered furniture on the lanais, cross-ventilation, and either a kitchenette or a full kitchen. Picture windows face the ocean. Hawaiian pitched roofs add a Polynesian touch. The studio apartments with kitchenette are $50 per day; one-bedroom apartments with full kitchen are $60 per day, and two-bedroom, two-bath apartments, with full kitchen and a huge fenced, private Polynesian garden behind, are $80 per day. An extra person is charged $6; minimum stay is three days. These rates apply from May 1 to October 31; add $5 the rest of the year. The Prestons will provide you with free barbecue equipment. For reservations, write them at P.O. Box 276, Kihei, Maui, HI 96753 (tel. 879-1261).

Close by, the **Nona Lani** consists of eight individual cottages, each standing alone in a grassy tree-filled area. The cottages afford an ocean view, and there is a beach for swimming and walking 20 yards away. Delightfully furnished and decorated, with rich wood panels and thick carpets, they feature a living room, full bedroom (with a queen-size bed), kitchen, bath, color TV, and an open lanai with dining table. Since there are two beds in the living room, a family of four could be comfortable here. From April 16 to December (when there is a four-night minimum), rates are $60 for two, and weekly and monthly rates are available; from December to April 16 (when there is a seven-night minimum), prices are $79 for two. For reservations, write to Dave and Nona Kong, 455 S. Kihei Rd., Kihei, Maui, HI 96753 (tel. 879-2497).

Both these places are near the beach at the stop where the 1792 arrival of Capt. George Vancouver is commemorated by an HVB marker and a Thunderbird totem carved by the Nootka Indians on Vancouver Island.

The **Lihi Kai Cottages** have been a staple in the Kihei area for many years. The complex of nine one-bedroom cottages is set in a garden and looks out over a protected bay and small-boat landing. Although the furnishings here are showing their age and may seem a bit spartan compared to the newer, more lush condominiums elsewhere, the rooms are acceptable, each with wall-to-wall carpeting, kitchen, color TV, and a private lanai with floral landscaping. Kalama Park, a lovely, uncrowded swimming beach, is right at hand. Managers Tad and Kimberly Fuller, truly go out of their way to help their guests. They ask that you book reservations as far in advance as possible, especially during the high season, December 1 to April 30, because so many guests keep coming back year after year. During that period, daily rates are $59 a couple, for a minimum of three days, $10 for an extra person. The rest of the year, the rate drops to $54, and weekly rates are available. Write to Lihi Kai Cottages, 2121 Iliili Rd., Kihei, Maui, HI 96753 (tel. 879-2335) or call toll free 800/LIHIKAI. (See the Readers' Selections, ahead, for comments on Lihi Kai.)

Condominium Rentals Hawaii is a large real estate agency with a number of vacation properties. Two of these could fit into our budget category, especially during the summer season. Kihei Akahi, 2531 St. Kihei Rd., has the lowest rentals; during the summer (April 16 to December 14), you can rent an attractive studio for $60; a one-bedroom for $70; and a two-bedroom, two-bath apartment for $95. In winter, expect to pay rates of $80, $95, and $125. The property is located across the road from a beautiful swimming beach, and right at home are two swimming pools, barbecue grills, and a tennis court. Units have full kitchens, washer-dryers, telephones, color TVs, private lanais. These rates apply to stays of four to six nights.

The second possibility here is Hale Kamole, 2737 S. Kihei Rd., a low-rise apartment complex also right across the street from a fine swimming beach. No studios, only lovely one-bedroom units and split-level two-bedroom, two-bath apartments. In summer, the one-bedrooms rent for $70; the two-bedrooms for $95; in winter, the rates are $100 and $125. All units are nicely furnished, have telephone, color TV, complete kitchens. A tennis court, two pools, and barbecue grills are right on the grounds. Again, these rates are for stays of four to six nights.

For information on the above two resorts, write to Condominium Rentals Hawaii, 2439 S. Kihei Rd., #205-A, Kihei, Maui, HI 96753, or call toll free 800/367-5242 (from B.C. and Alberta, 800/663-2101; from other Canadian provinces, collect 808/879-2778). FAX: 879-7825.

We've always shied away from high-rise condominiums, but after we visited **Kahale Makai Resort (Village by the Sea)**, we were convinced that, in this case at least, bigger also means better. The two five-story buildings house some 168 units, and some have been superbly decorated by their owners. All have full kitchen, laundry, central air conditioning, and color TV. The two buildings, right on the ocean, are separated by a well-tended lawn on which there is a pool and putting green, Jacuzzi, barbecues. Also available are saunas and shuffleboard; tennis courts and golf are nearby. An in-house convenience shop makes housekeeping easy in case you've forgotten something at the supermarket in Kihei, or in Kahului, 15 minutes away. As with most condominiums, several rental agents handle units here, but the one offering the most reasonably priced units is Village Rentals, Azeka's Place, P.O. Box 1471, Kihei, Maui, HI 96753, which can also be reached toll free at 800/367-5634. Studios for one or two persons go from $40 to $45 a night during the off-season (April 15 to December 15), and from $55 the rest of the year. One-bedroom units begin at $60 off-season, $80 in; two-bedroom units at $80 a night off-season, $100 in.

Kahale Makai Resort is right on the ocean, but you may want to walk a bit to a good swimming beach, as this one tends to be a bit rocky.

Tennis buffs will be in heaven at the **Leinaala Oceanfront Condominiums** because this cozy little complex of 24 apartments is sandwiched on both sides by public courts. After your game, you can cool off in the freshwater swimming pool, or snorkel or windsurf in the ocean right out front. The best swimming beaches in Kihei are about a mile away. All of these one- and two-bedroom apartments are nicely and individually furnished, with air conditioning, color TV, and fully equipped kitchens. Every one of them is oceanfront, with glorious ocean and sunset views, and the place is very quiet. Off-season (May 1 through December 1) rates are $75 for the one-bedroom unit for two, $100 for the two-bedroom unit for four. In winter the one-bedrooms are $85, and the two-bedrooms are $110. An extra person is charged $10. There's a five-night minimum stay. Monthly rates are available. For reservations, phone toll free 800/334-3305, or write Leinaala Oceanfront Condominiums, 998 S. Kihei Rd., Kihei, Maui, HI 96753 (tel. 879-2235).

The traditional big hotel in this area is the casually relaxed **Aston Maui Lu**, a collection of low-rise, Polynesian-style buildings on 30 acres of tropical grounds, complete with a large Maui-shaped swimming pool, sandy beach, tennis courts, and a spirit of "ohana" or "family" reminiscent of an older, more gracious Hawaii. The rooms are modestly priced, especially when one considers that they all have those handy conveniences—refrigerator and coffee maker, as well as phone, color TV, and air conditioning. Furnishings are attractive. Many units offer kitchenettes and some even have full kitchens. For those not cooking in, the Long House serves excellent dinners. From December 23 through April 15, standard rooms, single or double, run $83; superior, $93; deluxe, $98. From April 15 to December 21, prices go down considerably, to $73, $83, and $93. An extra person is $10; no charge for children under 18 sharing a room with their parents and using existing bedding. Inquire about hotel-and-car packages. For reservations, write Aston Hotels and Resorts, 2255 Kuhio Ave., Honolulu, HI 96815, or phone toll free 800/922-7866 from the mainland, 800/922-3368 from Oahu, 800/342-1551 from the neighbor islands. Maui Lu is at 575 S. Kihei Rd., Kihei, Maui, HI 96753, and the local number is 879-5881.

On the beach at Kihei, the **Menehune Shores** offers family accommodations in a big, beautiful condominium complex. You could almost stay here and not want to leave the grounds—there's the ocean, a conventional swimming pool (heated), and the "Royal Fishpond," a protected stone and reef formation built by the ancient Hawaiians, right on the premises, as well as a restaurant. There's a whale-watching platform on the roof garden. All apartments face the ocean, are individually decorated, and have a full electric kitchen, with refrigerator-freezer and washer-dryer. From April 16 to December 14, the one-bedroom, one-bath units for two people go for $70; the one-bedroom, two-bath units for two people, for $82; the two-bedroom, two-bath units for four people, $92; the three-bedroom, two-bath apartment for four people, $112; and the three-bedroom, two-bath apartment for six people, $115. The rest of the year, the rentals are $85, $102, $112, $122, and $140. An additional person is $7.50 per day; there's a five-day minimum stay. For reservations, write Kihei-Kona Rentals, P.O. Box 556, Kihei, Maui, HI 96753 (tel. 879-5828, toll free 800/558-9117; or Menehune Reservations, P.O. Box 1327, Kihei, Maui, HI 96753 (tel. 879-3428).

We'd have to call **Luana Kai,** 940 S. Kihei Rd., one of the nicest condos in the Kihei area. This low-rise complex is gracefully situated on eight acres of beautifully landscaped grounds, and wherever you look from its 113 rooms, you'll see garden or ocean views. Step from your room—well, almost—to the ocean or swimming pool, heated whirlpool, saunas, tennis courts, putting green, barbecue area; everything is close at hand. Best of all, there's a peaceful feeling here. Inside, carved wooden doors lead to one-, two-, and three-bedroom luxuriously furnished apartments in light woods, all with full electric kitchens, telephones, TVs, lanais, and every comfort for vacation living. During the long off-season, from April 1 to December 19, one-bedroom garden apartments for up to two persons are $85; two-bedroom garden apartments for up to four, $100; three-bedroom garden apartments for up to six, $145. During high season, the rates are $115, $130, and $185. One-bedroom ocean apartments are $95, two-bedroom ocean apartments are $115 during off-season; in high season, rates go up to $125 and $145. Weekly rates are also available. An extra person is charged $10; children under 6 stay free; minimum stay during high season is two nights. For reservations, call toll free 800/367-7042. The local phone is 531-7595. You may also write to Hawaiian Islands Resorts, P.O. Box 212, Honolulu, HI 96810.

A unique hotel in this area—or in any area, for that matter—is the **Mana Kai Maui Condominium Hotel,** 98 rooms big, and offering a combination of condominium apartments and regular hotel rooms in a lively, upbeat setting. Situated on a beautiful crescent of beach (it's known as one of the best snorkeling beaches around), with a pool, an open-air restaurant, and all sorts of activities going on, it offers a lot under one roof. The hotel rooms have the lowest rates; these are small bedrooms with either a king-size bed or twins, telephone, color TV, and an attractive bathroom with a large vanity sink. The daily rate is $85 to $90, including a car with unlimited mileage and daily breakfast for two. If you want to splurge, take one of their one-bedroom apartments at $136 to $152, or a two-bedroom apartment for four people at $162 to $180, including car. Both units include full kitchen with refrigerator, range, dishwasher, dishes, etc. (All rates are subject to change without notice.) For reservations call toll free from the mainland and Canada, 800/525-2025. Or write: Mana Kai Maui Condominium Hotel, 2960 S. Kihei Rd., Kihei, Maui, HI 96753 (tel. 879-1561). FAX: 874-5042.

Although it's across the street from the ocean, all units are oceanfront at **Shores of Maui,** an attractive, two-level condo complex of one- and two-bedroom apartments. Snorkeling is good right across the street, and there's a sandy swimming beach just a block away. You can relax in the good-size swimming pool, soak in the spa, play a little tennis, enjoy a barbecue here. Apartments are nicely and individually decorated, all with dishwasher, washer-dryer, TV; and summer rates, May 1 to December 19, are quite modest: $55 per day for a one-bedroom/one-bath unit; $80 per day for a two-bedroom/two-bath unit. The one-bedroom units can sleep up to four; the two-bedroom unit, up to six. It's $5 per night for each extra guest. In winter, the one-bedrooms are $75 daily, and the two-bedrooms are $100. For reservations, write to Shores of Maui, 2075 S. Kihei Rd., Kihei, Maui, HI 96753, or phone toll free 800/367-8002. The local phone is 879-9140. FAX: 879-6221.

An on-the-beach location and some of the more moderate prices in the area are big pluses for the **Surf & Sand Hotel** at the entrance to the Wailea Beach Resort. Two championship golf courses and 14 tennis courts are within walking distance of the hotel; and right out front is a beautiful crescent of sandy beach, perfect for swimming and snorkeling. No need for a pool here, but there is an oceanfront Jacuzzi. The Maui Outrigger Restaurant, so pretty with its oceanfront views, is right on the premises. Rooms are comfortable, nicely furnished, with air conditioning, TV, direct-dial telephone, private bath with shower, and daily maid service. Most of the 88 rooms are in the standard category, which means they have either double or twin beds and a garden view. During the off-season, April 1 to December 20, they are $57 single, $60 double; in season, December 21 to March 31, they are $67 and $70. Superior rooms which have a double bed and an ocean view are $65 and $68 off-season, $75 and $78 in season. Deluxe rooms, which have either a double or queen-size bed and are oceanfront, are $75 and $78 off-season, $85 and $88 in season. What makes these rates even better is that they include the use of a Budget Rent-A-Car subcompact, with air conditioning and unlimited mileage, free. For reservations, contact Hawaiian Pacific Resorts, toll free 800/367-5004 from the U.S. mainland, 800/367-5004 from Canada, or write them at 1150 S. King St., Honolulu, HI 96814. Surf & Sand is at 2980 S. Kihei Beach Rd., Kihei/Wailea, Maui, HI 96753 (tel. 879-7744).

B&B Maui Style is headquartered in the Kihei area, and many of its accommodations are right here. But they also have discoveries all over the island, in Lahaina, Iao Valley, and upcountry in Kula, Haiku, and Olinda. They delight in being "matchmakers," finding just the right accommodation, the right host, and the right price for their clients. On their roster are rooms in private houses, which run mostly from $45 to $60 single or double, and vacation rentals in condos, cottages, studios, and homes, which go from $65 to $100. A very popular car-and-condo package starts at $84. And they also have some secluded, romantic hideaways at higher prices, and even magnificent properties suitable for retreats or executive conferences. The staff is available for advice and assistance once you're in Maui. Phone toll free 800/848-5567 or locally, 879-7865, or write to B&B Maui Style, P.O. Box 98, Puunene, HI 96784.

AT MAALAEA BAY

Down by the small boat harbor at Maalaea Bay, a few miles from Kihei, is a wonderful beach area, and perched here, at Maalaea Village, is a small group of condominiums. **Hono Kai Resort**, one of the most reasonably priced of the lot, would make an ideal place for a family vacation (minimum stay is five days). You can swim in front of your door or at the public beach 50 yards away—or try your luck with surf at the harbor, which, according to some of the locals, is "the fastest surf in the world." All units are on the ocean side of the street and have at least one or two bedrooms, and all are pleasantly furnished. Shoji doors separate the living room and bedroom; the two-bedroom units all have lofts. There are full kitchens, including dishwashers, cable TV with HBO on request, even use of boogie boards and surfboards free. There's a swimming pool, washers and dryers on every floor, and two good restaurants—Buzz's Steak House and The Waterfront—nearby. We've had several good reports from our readers about this place and about manager Jeanne McJannet, who also manages two adjoining properties: **Makani A Kai** and **Kanai A Nalu**. Rates at Hono Kai, slightly lower than at the others, average around $60 for the one-bedroom garden view, $75 for the one-bedroom oceanfront during the summer; during the winter the rates go up about $10. Ask if they still have summer specials. For reservations, write Hono Kai Resort, RR 1, Box 389, Maalaea Village, Maui, HI 96793, or phone toll free 800/367-6084. The local phone is 244-7012.

A beachfront location and sensible prices are pluses for the **Kealia Condominium Resort**, a high-rise building with nicely furnished studios and apartments, all of which have air conditioning, color TV with cable, full kitchens, washer-dryers, and lanais with ocean views. There's an attractive swimming pool and sunning area on the grounds, as well as that glorious beach. From May 1 to December 1, studios are

$65, one-bedroom units are $75. The rest of the year, the rates are $80 and $90 (rates are subject to change). An extra person is charged $10; there is a minimum stay of four nights in summer, seven nights in winter. Write to Kealia Condominium Resort, 191 No. Kihei Rd., Kihei, Maui, HI 96753, or phone toll free 800/367-5222. The local phone is 879-0952.

A GUESTHOUSE IN PAIA

With a name like **Salty Towers,** you just know this place has to be interesting. Proprietor Claire Christen, like us, is a fan of the zany British comedy series about that improbable hotel called "Fawlty Towers." She long dreamed of owning a house on Maui that she could call Salty Towers; now she has it, and she is graciously sharing it with folks lucky enough to commandeer one of its three rooms. Not only are they beautiful, but their price is ridiculously low. This is an old plantation house built in the 1920s and completely restored; it is beautifully decorated, filled with works of art, antiques, Hawaiiana, and memorabilia collected from Ms. Christen's worldwide travels. The second floor has two large rooms, each with a queen-size bed (one room also has a twin bed), private bath, small refrigerator, and cable TV. These rent for $50. On the main floor is a smaller room with queen-size bed, TV, and shared bath; the price is $40. Minimum stay is two nights. Coffee and tea are provided in the rooms; guests staying for a while can use the light cooking facilities in the kitchen. The downstairs living room is lovely, and there's a sun-filled porch where guests can gather. And the garage is big enough for storing windsurfing equipment—a help if you're planning to join the throngs at Ho'okipa Beach, which many consider the windsurfing capital of the world (it's a 5-minute drive away). Paia itself is one of our favorite places, for its small-town charm, intriguing shops and restaurants, and great beaches. It's a 10-minute drive from Kahului Airport on Maui's north shore, the last town on the road to Hana.

Write Claire Christen, Salty Towers, Drawer E, Old Paia Town, Maui, HI 96779 (tel. 579-9669).

IN LAHAINA, KAANAPALI, AND ON NAPILI BAY

The area surrounding the historic old whaling town of Lahaina, about 30 miles from Kahului, might be a good place to move on to after a day or two in the Kahului or Kihei areas; or it could serve as a base of operations for your entire stay in Maui. In the heart of it all, out on the wharf overlooking the harbor, is the **Pioneer Inn,** an island landmark and a historic sight in its own right. For years, kamaiinas, tourists, movie stars, sailors, and beachcombers sat out on the big lanai in front, wondering what was happening back in civilization. Well, Lahaina is very civilized now, but the old hotel is still there, quaint and colorful, and the old rooms, clean but not at all fancy, have the lowest prices in Lahaina: $25 without a bath, $30 with, single or double. Much nicer rooms in the mauka building are air-conditioned, have private bath and lanai, and go for $60 single or double for a superior room; $70 for a deluxe room; an extra person is $10, a child under five is $5. Most rooms have a queen-size bed plus a twin. Fun for adventurous types. And the food is still good. The Harpooner's Lanai serves breakfast and lunch (and more potent stuff all day), and at night it's broil-your-own steak around the patio. The Pioneer Inn is at 658 Wharf St., Lahaina, Maui, HA 96761 (tel. 661-3636). Honolulu phone: 836-1411, weekdays.

Without a car, almost any vacation on Maui is difficult. But lack of wheels will not be a hindrance to anyone who chooses to stay at the **Maui Islander,** a hotel that affords peace and privacy (its units are spread out over nine acres of tropical grounds) while providing proximity to everything you could want in the area: it's a three-block walk to a sandy beach, a two-block stroll to the activities of Lahaina Harbor, a block away from the shops and restaurants of Front Street, two blocks to the supermarket, and a short bus ride to the resort life at Kaanapali Beach. You can be picked up at the airport and taken to the Maui Islander at a nominal cost. And the hotel-condo itself is lovely: the 372 units are simply but very nicely decorated in island style with light woods, tile bathroom, color TV, telephone, tidy kitchen (hotel rooms have refrigerators only). Right at home is a swimming pool, a barbecue and picnic area, and a tennis court that is lit at night. Rates have gone up here recently (and are subject to change), but still offer good value in this pricey area, especially considering that you won't need a car. In summer, it's $81 for two people in a hotel room, $93 for up to three people in a studio, $105 for up to four people in a one-bedroom suite. In the winter, all rates go up another $12. For reservations, phone toll free 800/367-5226, or write to Maui Islander, 660 Wainee St., Lahaina, Maui, HI 96761. The local phone is 667-9766. FAX: 661-3733.

Considering that you can swim right in front of the hotel, beachfront **Lahaina Shores Hotel,** might be worth stretching your budget for a bit. It's composed of 200 units, all with complete electric kitchens, wall-to-wall carpeting, air condition-ing, and lanais offering ocean or mountain views. The seven-story building, a charming example of Victorian architecture, is very much in keeping with the rest of old Lahaina—a welcome contrast to the burgeoning concrete high-rises flourishing all over the rest of the island. A swimming pool with adjacent heated therapeutic Jacuzzi sits ocean side, just off the huge, airy lobby. During the summer season, April 1 to December 1, a mountain-view studio is priced at $98, an oceanfront studio is $110, single or double. In the luxury category are the one-bedroom units at $121 ocean view, $140 oceanfront, single or double. Penthouses go up to $145 for a mountain view, and $165 for oceanfront rooms. During the winter, these prices climb to $105, $117, $136, $146, $166, and $195. (Prices subject to change.) No charge for children under five (cribs available); additional persons $10. You can swim in Lahaina Harbor, right in front of the hotel, play tennis across the street. For reservations, phone toll free 800/628-6699, or write to Lahaina Shores, 475 Front St., Lahaina, HI 96761. The local phone is 661-4835. FAX: 661-0147.

Anyone who remembers the shabby old Lahainaluna Hotel will be stunned to see the magical transformation it has undergone, emerging as the Lahaina Hotel, 127 Lahainaluna Rd. (tel. 661-0577 or, for toll-free reservations, 800/669-3444; FAX 677-9480)—an intimate, 13-room inn with all the grace and charm of turn-of-the-century Lahaina. The hotel was re-created from the ground up (the electrical wiring and plumbing were completely replaced), at a cost of $3 million, by Rick Ralston, of Crazy Shirts fame, and Alan Beall, developer of Restaurant Row in Hon-olulu. Ralston, one of Hawaii's most avid preservationists, saw to it that every detail of the period restoration was complete, from the turn-of-the-century wood, brass, and iron full-size beds, Oriental rugs, and wood wardrobe closets to the marble mantle clocks, leaded glass lampshades, and even the lace runners on the dressers. All the antiques are from his personal collection. Modern conveniences include new private baths, air conditioning, telephones, ceiling "fly fans," and incredibly luxuri-ous decorator fabrics and wall coverings. Guests are served a continental breakfast that they may enjoy either in bed or in the wicker rocking chairs on their balconies, which overlook busy Lahainaluna Street in the midst of Lahaina town. All rooms are one flight up, on the second floor; downstairs, there's a small graceful lobby and, adjoining it, David Paul's Lahaina Grill, an upscale restaurant serving New Ameri-can Cuisine. If you can afford the tab—doubles from $110 to $120, parlor suites at $175—a stay here is clearly a special experience.

A few miles outside of Lahaina, on Maui's exquisite west coast, you approach the Kaanapali-Napili region, one of Hawaii's most desirable vacation areas, blessed with miles of gorgeous beach and stunningly blue skies, with the famed Royal Kaanapali Golf Courses thrown in for good measure. The luxury hotels here are way beyond our budget, but just in case you're wondering which of the hotels has the lowest prices, it's the **Kaanapali Beach Hotel.** There are a number of standard rooms that go from around $135, single or double, $20 for each extra person. (Rates are subject to change.) The rooms are large and well decorated, and have TVs, refrig-erators, and private lanais facing into a garden. The Kaanapali Beach has a spacious open feeling, with its huge garden, a whale of a swimming pool (yes, it's in the shape of a whale), a beautiful ocean beach right next to the rock formation (which makes it good for snorkeling) on which the neighboring Sheraton Maui sits, and all the com-forts of the luxury life. Certainly worth a splurge—if your pocketbook is up to it.

The Kaanapali Beach aims to be "the most Hawaiian of the hotels," and its gracious staff and unusually sensitive management live up to that ideal. Reservations: Kaanapali Beach Hotel, 2525 Kaanapali Hwy., Lahaina, Maui, HI 96761-1987; the toll-free phone is 800/367-5170, local phone, 661-0011. FAX: 667-5616.

For families with lots of kids, or for two couples traveling together, an apartment at the **Maui Sands** is ideal. Imagine an enormous living room (about the size of two average hotel rooms put together), beautifully decorated, with two small but comfortable bedrooms, twin beds in one, a double in the other; a full electric kitchen; tropical ceiling fans; air conditioning; color TV; a view of gardens or ocean from your private lanai, and enough space for six people to stretch out in—for a cost of $125 (garden view) to $145 (oceanfront) per day for four and $9 for each additional body. You'd expect to pay twice as much for anything comparable at the luxury resorts. This attractive hotel, just past the Kaanapali gold coast area, also has one-bedroom apartments at $85 or $130 double; and apartments close to the road (for heavy sleepers) at $65 for the one-bedroom, $80 for the two-bedroom. (Rates are subject to a slight increase.) There is a four-day minimum most of the year, longer at the peak of the winter season. Since the Maui Sands was built when it was feasible to buy large lots of land, there is plenty of it to spare; the grounds are abloom with lovely trees and plantings, there's a big laundry, a comfortable swimming pool and sunning area (free coffee is served there in the morning), and a narrow sliver of beach (it's been washed away by storms but, hopefully, will return). At sunset, it's pure enchantment as you watch the sun seeming to sink right between the islands of Molokai and Lanai off in the distance. The hotel is completely refurbished, including new furniture. Managers Kay and Adel Kunisawa are cordial hosts, and some weekends they provide Hawaiian entertainment and free mixers for a cocktail party. Off-season, April 15 to June 15 and September 1 to December 15 (with the exception of the 14-day holiday period surrounding Thanksgiving and Easter), there's a 10% discount for a stay of seven days or more, a 20% discount for 30 days. Readers continue to praise this one. Write to Maui Sands, 3559 Honoapiilani Rd., Lahaina, Maui, HI 96761. The toll-free reservation number is 800/367-5037, and the local number is 669-4811.

The same Maui Sands management is in charge at some of the select units at **Papakea,** right next door, and these little homes are even more luxurious. Creature comforts include two pools, two Swedish saunas, two tennis courts, shuffleboard, barbecues, putting green, and picnic areas. Of course it's all on the beach. During the off-season (see above) two can stay in a garden studio for $94, a group of four in a one-bedroom for $122. Phone the same toll-free number—800/367-5037—any time between 8am and 5pm Hawaii time to make reservations. FAX: 669-8790.

Honokawai Palms is one of the older apartment complexes in this area, not as luxuriously furnished as some of the newer condos, but good value for the money. There's a beach across the street, but at this writing it was in bad shape, and not particularly desirable at night. So, drive elsewhere for the beach, and enjoy the prices here. Apartments are spacious and comfortably furnished. One-bedroom apartments for two people, with ocean view and lanai, are $65; with neither view nor lanai, $60. Two-bedroom apartments for two people, without ocean view or lanai, are $65. On stays of 7 nights or more, there is a 10% discount. The one-bedroom apartments can accommodate four, the two-bedroom apartments can hold six; each additional person is charged $6 daily. There's a large pool to dunk in, barbecue area, and ample all-electric kitchens to make cooking easy. The management is friendly and helpful; there's a warm, cozy feeling here. Minimum stay is four days. For advance reservations, phone toll free 800/843-1633 or write to Honokawai Palms, 3666 Lower Honoapiilani Hwy., Lahaina, Maui, HI 96761 (tel. 669-6130 in Maui).

There's a new economy hotel in this same area, just across the road from Honokawai Beach Park, and it's proving very, very popular. **Maui Park,** under the aegis of Aston Hotels & Resorts, offers 228 units in six separate buildings surrounding a nearly Olympic-size swimming pool and sunning area. It features apartment-size studios and one-bedroom suites, attractively furnished, with full kitchens, direct-dial phones, cable TVs, clock radios, large closets, daily maid service. The three-story buildings do not have elevators and there is no air conditioning. Five rooms are handicapped-accessible. There's 24-hour service at the desk, and a grocery and sundry store right at hand makes cooking at home very easy. Rates include the use of a Budget Rent-A-Car for every day of your stay. From April 16 to December 21, the studios rent for $79, with a maximum of two people; the rest of the year, $89. The one-bedroom apartments, with a maximum of four people, go for $99 in summer, $109 in winter. Maui Park is at 3626 Honoapiilani Hwy. (tel. 669-6622). For reservations, phone toll free 800/922-7866, or write Aston Hotels & Resorts, 2255 Kuhio Ave., Honolulu, HI 96815-2658.

Just across the street from Maui Park, the Aston people are also in charge at **Paki Maui**, a lovely condominium suite resort right on the oceanfront. The grounds are lush, with a waterfall, a swimming pool, and a pond with koi fish in the center of the property. Rooms are individually furnished with a great deal of charm, and all boast fully equipped kitchens, TVs, direct-dial phones, and private lanais for splendid views of Molokai and Lanai out there across the waters. Guests have the use of a Budget Rent-A-Car for every day of their stay. Considering all this, rates are not bad: From April 16 to 21, oceanfront studio suites are $109 for one or two people; the rest of the year, $129. One-bedroom suites with kitchen are $109 and $129 for up to four people garden view, $129 and $149 oceanfront. And two-bedroom, two-bath suites for up to six people are $150 and $170 superior oceanfront, and $160 and $180 deluxe oceanfront. Paki Maui is at 3615 Lower Honoapiilani Hwy. (tel. 669-8325). For reservations, phone toll free 800/922-7866, or write Aston Hotels & Resorts, 2255 Kuhio Ave., Honolulu, HI 96815-2658.

Continuing oceanside along this same stretch of Lower Honoapiilani Road in this beautiful West Maui area, you'll find the graceful **Hale Kai**, whose 40 condominium apartments look out on flowering gardens, a park, and a good-size pool that fronts on the ocean beach. Each is decorated differently and each has a different view: some guests come back year after year for the ocean view, others for the quiet parkside units. Rooms on the upper levels have handsome cathedral ceilings. All are furnished nicely with electric kitchens, TV, private lanais. One-bedroom apartments for two persons go for a daily rate of $80. Two-bedroom apartments for four persons average $115 daily, $770 to $805 weekly. An additional person is charged $8 a day. Minimum stay is three nights, except for Christmas, when it is two weeks. No credit cards are accepted. For reservations, write to Hale Kai, 3691 Lower Honoapiilani Rd., Lahaina, Maui, HI 96761 or call toll free 800/446-7307. The local number is 669-6333.

Hans and Eva Zimmerman have been in charge at the **Hale Maui Apartment Hotel** for almost 22 years now. It's a small hotel, right on the ocean, with just a dozen one-bedroom suites, newly refurbished, that can sleep up to five people. All of them have private lanais, radios, TVs, and good kitchens. There's a nice barbecue area out back. There's no pool, but steps from the lawn lead right into the water. Values are best here in the off-season, April 1 to December 15, when the apartments go for $60 to $70; in winter they go up to $80. For more than two people in a unit, the charge is $8 per person. Minimum stay is three nights, one week at Christmas. Weekly rates are available. Write Hale Maui, P.O. Box 516, Lahaina, Maui, HI 96767 or phone 669-6312.

Further north in this lush, oceanfront area, you'll find **Kaleialoha,** a lovely condo resort with 67 studio and one-bedroom units. The units are all of good size and pleasantly furnished; studios have two punees (couches), one-bedrooms have a queen-size bed and a sofa in the living room that opens up to sleep two. The well-equipped kitchens boast dishwashers and washer-dryers; phones are available at $1 a day, and there's color TV. As for swimming, you can relax around a pool sheltered from the parking area out front by an interior courtyard, or try the ocean out back; swimming is not bad within the protective outer reef. Studio rooms with mountain view are $65 for up to four people; one-bedroom studios with ocean view are $75 for up to four; and one-bedroom deluxe studios with ocean view are $85; $7.50 for an extra person over two. Write to Rental Agent, Kaleialoha No. 17, 3785 Lower

Honoapiilani Hwy., Lahaina, Maui, HI 96761, or phone toll free 800/222-8688. The local phone is 669-8197.

It's ocean all the way at **Polynesian Shores,** the kind of small, relaxed place where everybody feels right at home—so much so, reports General Manager Diane Elwood, that many of the same people keep coming back year after year. Every one of the 52 vacation apartments here has an ocean view from its own private lanai, there's a deck on the oceanfront with barbecue facilities, and it's a great place to watch for whales. Snorkeling is good right out front, swimming is better at nearby sandy beaches. The grounds are so lush that guests can pick bananas right off the trees. On Thursdays, there's a pupu party right out on the Tiki Deck. Apartments are nicely furnished, with separate living rooms, color TVs, telephones, private baths with tub and shower. During the summer season, from April 15 to December 15, one-bedroom units go for $95; the rest of the year, they're $105. Two-bedroom, two-bath loft units for two people are $115 and $125; two-bedroom, two-bath units for four are $135 and $145; and three-bedroom, two- or three-bath units for four are $145 and $155. A stay of three nights minimum is required. For reservations, phone 800/433-MAUI from the U.S. mainland, or 800/423-8733, ext. 503, from Canada; or write to Polynesian Shores, 3975 Lower Honoapiilani Rd., Lahaina, Maui, HI 96761.

You get the feeling of gracious retreat at **Hoyochi Nikko** (Resort of the Sunbeam), from the Asian architecture of the two-story, 18-room condominium to the spacious oceanfront lawn and garden where you could easily laze away peaceful days. You can walk down the lawn stairs to the ocean and swim and snorkel inside the reef, swim in a freshwater pool in the garden, relax in the units, which range in size from standard to large to "special." All have private lanais with full ocean views, "long boy" twin beds (a few queens), color cable TV, fully equipped kitchens with washer-dryers. Standard rooms are $80 a day; larger rooms are $90. Minimum stay is usually seven days; discounts in summer. There's a grill for barbecues, and sometimes mai-tai parties are held out in the garden. Despite the Japanese name, most of the guests here—many of them repeats from year to year—are North American. Write to Hoyochi Nikko, 3901 Lower Honoapiilani Rd., Lahaina, Maui, HI 96761, or phone 669-8343.

The condominium units, all oceanfront, at **Noelani,** in the Kahana area, are beautifully furnished, and the view from your oceanfront lanai—of Molokai and Lanai, blue seas, and tropical gardens—is even more beautiful. There are two freshwater swimming pools at seaside (heated for evening swimming), good snorkeling right in front, and a wide sandy beach adjacent to the property. Managers John and Donna Lorenz host mai-tai parties at poolside several times a month so that guests can get to know one another. Readers have praised the warm, homey atmosphere here. All rooms now have microwave ovens and in-room videos. The studios, which rent for $77, are furnished in Pacific decor, with dressing room, bath, and kitchen. The one-bedroom, two-bedroom, and three-bedroom units have their own washer-dryer and dishwasher and are $97, $120, and $145. Those in the studios have the use of a launderette. Weekly and monthly rates are available, as well as car-condo packages: three-day minimum stay. Write Noelani, 4095 Honoapiilani Rd., Lahaina, Maui, HI 96761 (tel. 669-8374). The toll-free number from the mainland and Alaska is 800/367-6030. From Canada, call collect.

Everytime we have a look at the **Pohailani Maui,** it grows a little bit more. The original 8-unit complex now has 29 units at the water's edge, plus another 85 two-bedroom duplex apartments on the mountainside. Two tennis courts, two pools, and other facilities are spread out over eight acres—not to mention a stretch of sandy beach, perfect for gentle ocean swimming. Each of the seaside units is spacious, attractively furnished in studio style (with such touches as big, old-fashioned ceiling fans), and boasts large kitchenette, color TV, private phone, plus a lanai that is perfectly enormous. Low-season rates, April 16 to December 16, are $65 for two in a studio, $75 for a deluxe studio, $80 for the two-bedroom town houses. High-season rates, December 16 to April 16, are $80 and $90. There is a 5-night minimum stay (14 nights from December 20 to January 5) and a 5-night deposit necessary to confirm reservations. For reservations, contact Rainbow Reservations, P.O. Box 11453, Lahaina, Maui, HI 96761, or phone toll free 800/367-6092 (tel. 667-7858 locally). The hotel's phone is 669-5464. FAX: 661-8691.

The **Mahina Surf** is a fine place to settle in for real at-home living. The units are not only charming and attractively furnished, but well priced for the area: from April 15 to December 15, it's $80 per night (minimum stay of three nights), $532 a week; during the high season, December 15 to April 14, it's $90 per night, $598.50 per week. These rates are for two people in a one-bedroom unit with complete kitchen and accessories, color TV, telephone, and an ocean view. These units can actually sleep four: each extra person is charged $8 per night. Two-bedroom units are available for an extra $15 per day, and two-bedroom/two-bath units for an additional $20. Sizes of the apartments vary, but all are little "homes"; the cutest are those with a loft area upstairs that serves as a second bedroom, and these are big enough to sleep six. The 56-unit complex is situated on a rocky strip of ocean, and snorkeling is fine, but there is no sandy beach; there is, however, a big pool as compensation. Write to Mahina Surf, 4057 Lower Honoapiilani Rd., Lahaina, Maui, HI 96761 (tel. 669-6068 or toll free 800/367-6086). Inquire about their excellent deals on car rentals. FAX: 669-4534.

Now you're approaching Napili Bay, a gorgeous little stretch of sea and sand where not very long ago the breadfruit, papaya, and lichee trees ran helter-skelter to the sea. For us, this area is the end of the rainbow, and we don't mean the one likely to be arching across the sugarcane fields, as you approach: The setting is perfect, and the swimming, from a gentle reef-protected beach, among the best in the islands. Here you'll find the **Mauian Hotel,** with 44 attractive studio apartments big enough for four, each with private lanai, all-electric kitchen, including microwave oven, one queen and one trundle bed (that opens into two), and all the conveniences of home. From April 15 to December 14, doubles are $75 garden view, $80 ocean view, and $100 oceanfront; in high season, it's $90, $95, and $115. For those capable of tearing themselves away from the idyllic beach, there's shuffleboard and a freshwater swimming pool (a big laundry and ironing area, too). Write to Mauian Hotel, 5441 Honoapiilani Rd., Lahaina, Maui, HI 96761 (tel. 669-6205). Toll-free reservations: 800/367-5034. FAX: 669-0109.

One of the very nicest places in this area is the **Napili Surf Beach Resort,** which has 54 soundproof luxury units perched on the tip of Napili Bay, on a particularly lovely curve of beach. Each of these units is completely equipped for easy housekeeping, and has color TV and handsome furniture; the private lanais overlook the pool, garden, or ocean. It's $98 double for the studios, $134 for the huge one-bedroom units. But wait—managers Bob and Marge Putt also have garden units, at $88 double. These 18 off-beach studios, called Napili Puamala (garden of flowers), are small but super-neat and functionally designed; they come with color TV, radio with digital clocks (something rather rare in hotels), full kitchens, dishwashers, the works. There may be a special summer rate for these units. All these units overlook the pool. No matter where you stay, though, it's fun to get together with the other guests out on the lawn in the evenings when Bob and Marge often bring in entertainment. It may be a well-known island group like the No Ka Oi Four, or just some friends or guests who like to sit around with a guitar and sing the old songs. In such a gracious setting, with such warmly hospitable people in charge, the coconut palms swaying in the evening wind and the sea lapping gently at your feet, it's hard to remember what you were planning to worry about. Write to Napili Surf, Napili Bay, Maui, HI 96761 (tel. 669-8002). An advance deposit is required.

If snorkeling is your passion, you're going to be very happy at **Honokeana Cove,** a lovely resort condominium located directly on a private, rocky cove where the snorkeling is tops. Swimmers need walk only about five minutes to a gentle sandy beach. Each of the condo's 38 units is close to the water and the pool oceanside; the grounds are also ideal for whale-spotting. We were told that a whale once gave birth at the entrance to the cove! When you're not busy watching whales, snorkeling, or admiring the grounds with its beautiful trees—we spotted a 160-year-old Kamani nut (or false almond) tree—you can be enjoying the view from your lanai and the comforts of your apartment, each individually owned and decorated. Rates can go up quite a bit here for the larger apartments and town houses; your best bets are the one-bedroom apartment for two people at $95 to $115 and the two-bedroom, two-bath unit for four people at $135. An extra person is charged $10, regardless of age; minimum stay is five nights. Discounts on stays of a week or more. No credit cards are accepted. The management is cordial, arranging a pupu party every Friday to bring the guests together. For reservations, write Honokeana Cove Resort Condominiums, 5255 Lower Honoapiilani Rd., Lahaina, Maui, HI 96761, or phone toll free 800/237-4948. From Canada, call collect: 669-6441.

Not a hotel, not a condo, but a country inn in the European manner is what the **Coconut Inn** calls itself. Just five minutes away from Kapalua, and sharing the glorious views and scenery of that lush resort, Coconut Inn is a two-story, 40-unit retreat on a hill overlooking Napili Bay. The inn is situated mauka—several blocks up the hill on the mountain side of the road and a 10-minute walk or five-minute drive to the ocean—which gives it more of a country than a beachy feeling. Prices are reasonable for this area: rates from $79 for a studio, $89 for a one-bedroom unit, and $99 for a loft unit. (Rates are subject to change.) Maximum occupancy for the studio is two, for the one-bedroom and loft it's four; each additional person is charged $10. Units are nicely decorated in the island style, not large, but comfortable enough, and with fully equipped kitchen and bath with both tub and shower. All have color TV, phone, and twin or king-size beds. The two buildings are set in a small garden that shelters a pool, a hot tub, and a special "quiet area" surrounding a small pond and brook. You're welcome to cut flowers from the garden to brighten your room, or herbs from the garden to brighten your cooking. And as if all this weren't enough, a continental breakfast of freshly baked banana bread, island fruit, and brewed Kona coffee (there's a choice of coconut, chocolate, or regular), is included in the price of your room. For reservations, write to Coconut Inn, 181 Hui Rd. F, Napili, Maui, HI 96761, or phone toll free 800/367-8006. In Hawaii, call 669-5712. FAX: 669-4485.

MOUNTAINSIDE BED AND BREAKFASTS

If you like mountains better than beach, charming private homes better than impersonal hotels or condos, and refreshingly old-fashioned prices best of all, we've got some good news for you. We've discovered nine delightful "up-country" guest-houses and vacation rentals—four in Kula, three in Makawao on the slopes of Haleakala volcano (ideal locations if you want to drive to the summit to catch the sunrise), and two on the Hana road, in Paia and Haiku. You can't go wrong at any of these, although each has a slightly different style and personality.

IN KULA: We'd call **Elaine and Murray Gildersleeve's** splendid home in Kula probably the best value for the money. The Gildersleeves are a retired couple from Alaska: Murray devotes a lot of attention to his pineapple farm right on the premises; and Elaine looks after the guests. Their Hawaiian pole house is designer-elegant, with three guest bedrooms on the ground floor sharing their own kitchen and living room. Guests are welcome to use the refrigerator and to cook breakfast or whatever meals they like: a rare privilege in a guesthouse. The three bedrooms are beautifully furnished, have private baths, either twins or a king-size or queen-size bed, and splendid views of the West Maui mountains and Haleakala. The charge is only $45 a night for two, $7.50 for a third person using a futon. Next to the main house is a delightful cottage made to order for a family: With a queen-size bed in the bedroom, twin beds in the loft, and two window seats in the living room that can also be used as extra beds, six people can sleep comfortably. There's a complete kitchen, windows on three sides, bougainvillea growing outside, a charming decor within. Cost is $75 a day for a party of four; an extra adult is $10, an extra child, $7.

The Gildersleeves ask that guests do not smoke or drink. Write to Elaine and Murray Gildersleeve, 2112 Naalae Rd., Kula, Maui, HI 96790 or phone 878-6623).

Jody Baldwin calls her cozy English country-style home in Kula "Kilohana"; it's an old plantation house (various parts were built from 55 to 85 years ago), and its mood is one of country charm, with antiques, collectibles, cozy nooks, old quilts, and queen-size beds. Rooms would work better for singles or couples than for families. Jody is a cordial hostess who makes everybody feel right at home. She delights in whipping up "light and healthy" breakfasts: she bakes her own breads and muffins, serves tropical fruit juices, fresh fruit and yogurt, hot and cold cereals, and "the best coffee" (chocolate raspberry and vanilla macadamia nut are among the possibilities), as well as herb teas. In the evening she offers wines and after-dinner liqueurs. Rates are $55 single, $65 double for the two rooms with shared bath; a third room, separate from the house, with a private bath and garden, is $70 to $75. There is a two-night minimum. No smoking is allowed indoors.

Write to Jody Baldwin, Kilohana, 378 Kamehameiki Rd., Kula, Maui, HI 96790, or phone 878-6086.

Bloom Cottage stands by itself, behind a pretty house in Kula owned by Lynne and Herb Horner, a busy young couple who work for the *Maui News* and the Maui Oil Company, respectively. Their kids are fans of the cartoon "Bloom County," and "things bloom here," says Lynne Horner, so that's how this charming little cottage got its name. It's tastefully decorated, has a four-poster bed in the sleeping area plus a single bed in the second bedroom, in the living room, plus a double fold-out futon, which would be so nice by the fireplace (yes, they have them up here in the mountains). There's color TV, as well as a microwave oven in the fully equipped kitchen. Lynne and Herb stock the refrigerator with Maui eggs, coffee, fruit juices and muffins, put out fresh bouquets of flowers for their guests, and invite them to pick a wide variety of culinary herbs that grow in the garden. Rental for the cottage is $75 for two people on stays of two to seven nights ($85 if you stay only one night); $10 for each extra person. No smoking in the cottage; no pets.

Write Lynne and Herb Horner, Bloom Cottage, Box 229, Kula, Maui, HI 96790.

Rusty and Frank Kunz own a lovely modern home on Lower Kimo Drive in Kula, set on eight acres of lawns and pastures at the 3,000-foot level, 20 miles from the summit of Haleakala Crater. The views are of the West Maui mountains, a carnation farm, and Kihei beach way below in the distance. The Kunzes divide their time between this home and one on Oahu. On Maui, they always have a vacation apartment available for rental: It's an excellent bargain at just $65, for a two-bedroom apartment with its own private entrance, a deck (perfect for sunset watching), a carpeted metal fireplace, a kitchenette (refrigerator, toaster-oven, two-burner hot plate, sink), and a private bath. Children can be accommodated. It's $10 for an extra person. When they're not in Maui, the Kunzes will, on occasion, rent their own quarters, a handsome home with a large fireplace that goes through from the living room to the master bedroom, full kitchen, private bath, etc.; it rents for $100 a night, for either one or two couples. Inquire also about their reasonable vacation rentals in Lanikai on the island of Oahu, a block from the beach.

Write to Rusty and Frank Kunz, R.R. 1, Box 513, Lower Kimo Drive, Kula, Maui, HI 96790, or phone 878-2137 in Maui, 263-4546 in Oahu.

OFF THE HANA ROAD: You park your car and follow a tree-lined path to the front door. The cottage sits in the midst of a tropical jungle filled with flowering plants, bananas, and palm trees. The picturesque screened lanai leads to a charming living room and bedroom filled with antiques and Oriental rugs. No electrical poles mar the landscape; an alternative energy system provides utilities and phone. You swim in natural pools half a mile away, stroll along moonlit paths, listen to the sound of the surf pounding the cliffs. Does this sound like the ultimate retreat from civilization? It is, and it's located in Haiku, a mile off the Hana Hwy. (18 miles east of Kahului), going toward the ocean. Ann DeWeese, an artist whose studio is on the premises, is the proprietress of **Hamakualoa,** which she calls a Bed & Breakfast Tea House Cottage, and she makes it available to guests who can appreciate the simple life. She provides fresh fruits, home-baked breads, and very good coffee and teas for breakfast. She charges $50 single, $55 double: Sorry, there's no indoor bath; it's outside and requires a flashlight to get to at night. Other than that, this could be heaven. Smoking is permitted outdoors only.

Write to Ann DeWeese, P.O. Box 335, Haiku, Maui, HI 96708, or phone 572-5610.

Clark and Denise Champion were the pioneer B&B hosts upcountry, and their home in Haiku, set amid an acre of garden with fruit and flower farms all around, is delightful. **Haikuleana** is an old plantation house built around 1850 for a doctor from Scotland, decorated in country style with old quilts on the walls, comforters on the beds. Two guests rooms (one with twin beds, the other with a queen-size bed) share a common bath. Guests also have their own living and dining room and may keep wine and other perishables in coolers out on the porch. Denise grows her own flowers and decorates with them, so bedrooms and common areas bloom with proteas and orchids and mountain flowers. She usually bakes muffins, and serves four or five seasonal Hawaiian fruits, Hawaiian teas and coffees for breakfast. Tea is always available. "We try to be supportive and helpful—for example, we give people down jackets when they go up to Haleakala for the sunrise—but we don't interfere with their privacy," says Denise. Smoking is allowed, but not in the bedrooms. Rooms go for $65 a night. Since they are small, Denise advises that families with children over the age of 2 take both rooms.

Write Denise and Clark Champion, Haikuleana, 69 Haiku Rd., Haiku, Maui, HI 96708, or phone 575-2890.

IN MAKAWAO AND OLINDA: Makawao is Maui's own little cowboy town, fast turning into a mecca for people who love the rural life. Among these are Pam and Lee Muller, whose vacation cottage, **Pua Kaha Farm,** is right in front of their own home, overlooking broad lawns with a view of pasture lands, Kahului Harbor far below, and the summit of Haleakala. Pam, an artist and professional jeweler (you can see her porcelain jewelry in island gift stores under the name "Kaha"), has furnished the spacious cottage with many artistic touches, including Hawaiian paintings on the walls. There's a queen-size bed in the living room and another one in the bedroom, a refrigerator, a microwave oven, and a TV. Best of all is the wall of windows; you can usually see peacocks and pheasants strutting on the grounds. The rate is $55 for two people, $10 more for each extra person. Smoking is not allowed indoors. Pam starts her guests out with banana bread, and leaves necessary supplies for breakfast. For reservations and information, write Pam & Lee Muller, Pua Kaha Farm, 511-A Olinda Rd., Makawao, Maui, HI 96768, or phone 572-7994.

Haleakala Bed & Breakfast is a huge, beautiful home on two acres on the slopes of Haleakala in this same Makawao area. Owner Mara Marin, a local environmental activist, makes three rooms available for guests, and her rates are very reasonable: $45 for the two rooms that share a bathroom, and $55 for a master bedroom suite, complete with king-size bed, vanity area, bathroom, huge walk-in closet, and lovely views of the mountains. Guests have their own living room with a TV set and a deck from which to watch the magnificent Maui sunsets or sip wine under the stars. The front door looks out directly on the 10,000-foot summit of Haleakala. Rates include a continental breakfast of juice, coffee, and danish, rolls, or muffins, or sometimes a treat, like Mara's homemade bread pudding with raspberry jam and orange-passion-fruit juice. Write Mara Marin, 4 Manienie Rd., Makawao, Maui, HI 96758, or phone 572-7988.

Five miles up the hill from Makawao, on a country road that winds through a forest of 150-foot-tall blue gum eucalyptus trees, lies the village of Olinda; and it's here, at the top of Olinda Road, at the 4,000-foot elevation, that lucky travelers will find one of the nicest cottages and B&Bs in Maui. **McKay Country Cottage** sits amidst a 12-acre protea farm with its own driveway, a short distance from the home of Shaun and Stewart McKay. Shaun, a member of the noted Baldwin family, among Maui's missionary founders, and Stewart, a painter and decorator from Scotland, are very special hosts, indeed; their warmth and graciousness are evident everywhere on the property. They've furnished the cottage handsomely with original art by Maui artists, protea from their own garden, lace curtains, a king-size bed in the bedroom, a queen-size pullout sofa in the living room (futons are available for the kids), a full kitchen, and a working fireplace with enough wood for cool mountain nights. What fun to sit on the cushioned window seats, or out on the deck, and gaze at central Maui and famed Hookipa windsurfing beach far below! First-day breakfast supplies are left in the refrigerator for you. There's such a feeling of peace and relaxation here that it could be hard to leave. Rates are $85 for two, including children under 16; $10 per night for an extra adult.

Inside the McKays' own home, which has an almost baronial splendor with its cathedral-ceiling living room and huge wood-burning fireplace, is a charming bedroom that they rent as a B&B accommodation. It is furnished with century-old Italian antiques (the twin beds belonged to Shaun's grandmother), lace curtains, brass rubbings from England, an original sculpture by Stewart. There's a dressing room and private bathroom with bidet. And, of course, always fresh flowers in the room. As for breakfast, be prepared for surprises, as Stewart loves to cook, and you never know when he might whip up Scottish bangers, or serve smoked salmon or, more simply, a papaya filled with fresh fruit and sprinkled with coconut. The rate is $65 a night for two. Minimum stays of two days are requested at both the cottage and the B&B room. Write to McKay Cottage, 536 Olinda Rd., Makawao, Maui, HI 96768, or phone 572-1453.

IN HANA

Since Hana is one of the more remote, untouched areas in Maui (in all Hawaii, in fact), you might well want to spend a few days here just relaxing and being utterly away from civilization. Happily, the number of reasonably priced accommodations is growing.

The most inexpensive accommodations in Hana are available courtesy of the Division of State Parks. These are the housekeeping cabins in **Waianapanapa State Park,** a few trails away from a black-sand beach. Local families like to come here to escape from civilization. The attractive bungalows are snuggled among the pandanus trees, some overlooking the ocean, and are supplied with bedding, towels, cooking utensils, dishes, electricity, and plenty of hot water. The only fly in the ointment may be mosquitoes: A reader who spent a hot August week here advised taking insect spray and repellent. Each two-room cabin has its own lanai, can sleep six persons, and rents for $10 per person a night. The maximum stay is five nights. For reservations, write to Department of Land and Natural Resources, Division of State Parks, P.O. Box 1049, Wailuku, Maui, HI 96793 (tel. 244-4354). Reservations should be made six months to a year in advance as this idyllic spot continues to grow in popularity. A campground for tent camping is also available, and it is free of charge; reservations are required.

For deluxe studio and one-bedroom apartments where you can prepare your own meals (almost a necessity in Hana, where there are very few eating places), the **Hana Kai–Maui Resort Condominiums** are a fine choice. They are located oceanfront on lush, tropical grounds. The rates for the studios are $80 double, $6 for each additional person (no charge for children under 2). These studios, maximum of three persons, include a bath with tub-shower combination, dressing vanity, well-equipped kitchen, and private lanai—a spacious open room where you can enjoy the ocean just a few feet away. One-bedroom apartments are $95 double and can sleep up to five. (Rates are subject to change.) There is a $10 additional charge for more than two persons; children under 11, free. Pluses include a large patio area a few steps away from the ocean, with gas barbecues, Ping-Pong, shuffleboard, horseshoes, and snorkeling equipment. The beach is better for surfers than swimmers, but good swimming beaches are within an easy drive. For reservations, write Hana Kai–Maui Resort, P.O. Box 38, Hana, Maui, HI 96713, or phone toll free 800/346-2772 (the local number is 248-8426). FAX: 248-7482.

Sina Fournier is the rental agent for **Hana Kai Holidays,** and she has a number of options for Hana vacationers, starting at just $35 a night. For this price, one gets a comfortable twin-bedded room with a shared bath; for $45, a room with a private bath is available. Then there are studio cabins at $65 a night, some oceanfront, one-bedroom cottages at $80 a night, all the way up to condominium apartments at Hana Kai–Maui Resort (see above), and private houses, which begin at $125 a night and ascend to $225, for a large house with swimming pool and spa. You can write to Sina Fournier, Hana Kai Holidays, P.O. Box 536, Hana, Maui, HI 96713; or phone her or her son, Duke Walls, toll free at 800/548-0478 or locally, at 248-7742, and they will try to find the right setup for you. Many accommodations are within walking distance of the beach; some of the houses are directly on Hana Bay.

Mrs. Alfreda Worst, the owner of **Heavenly Hana Inn,** has created a miniature Eastern garden—like atmosphere in her four units, each of which has two bedrooms, a light-cooking facility, TV, a dining area, bath, screened lanai, and its own private entrance. The inn is small but charming, and the inside door of each unit leads to the lobby and lounge. Outside, leading to the street, is a winding walkway through a screened Japanese gateway guarded by stone lions, symbols of good fortune. Rates are $70 single, $80 double, $90 triple, $100 quad. An additional person is charged $10. Mrs. Worst also has two separate rental units away from the Inn: a small beach cottage on Hana Bay for one to four adults, at $70 to $100 per night,and a two-bedroom family cottage in town overlooking the ocean and Kauiki Hill, for families of up to six. The latter, called Li'l Barn-by-Sea, rents for $65 to $100. Write to Mrs. Worst at P.O. Box 146, Hana, Maui, HI 96713 (tel. 248-8442).

Blair Shurtleff and Tom Nunn, the people who run **Hana Plantation Houses,** aim to provide their guests with "a vacation that will leave you feeling rejuvenated and thoroughly relaxed." We're sure they succeed, for just contemplating the lovely custom homes they've created for visitors is relaxing in itself. The main compound, on five superbly landscaped acres abloom with ginger, heliconia, banana, and papaya (which guests are welcome to pick), includes a plantation-style home that accommodates up to four guests at $130, a Japanese-style studio for two at $75, a Japanese-Balinese–style two-bedroom cottage for four at $95, and even a tiny studio inside a banyan tree, very rustic, with an outside bath, for one (or two very close friends), for $45. A few miles away, near Hana Bay and picturesque beaches, is a two-story plantation house with two accommodations (upstairs, for four people, $130; downstairs, for two people, $85), and a superb solar-powered beach house for four, for $150 (with annex for two, $185). Amenities are plentiful. There are Jacuzzis indoors and out. Each house has its own kitchen and even its own coffee grinder, with Hana Plantation House's own labeled coffee beans. Hosts Blair and Tom are always on hand to advise guests on activities and to help them meet the people of Hana. A three-minute walk from the main compound is a secluded, natural spring and ocean-fed pool, surrounded by lush, tropical plants and a few steps from the ocean. Beautiful Hamoa Beach is less than a mile away. Waterfalls and jungle trails abound. Write Hana Plantation Houses, P.O. Box 489, Hana, Maui, HI 96713 (tel. 248-7248). For reservations only, phone toll free 800/657-7723. FAX: 248-8240.

Manager Stan Collins of **Hana Bay Vacation Rentals** rent a dozen properties scattered throughout the Hana area, with a wide variety of locations, including on the beach, in and out of town, plus some in very secluded and private places. They offer apartments, cabins, and homes, with either one, two, or three bedrooms, with ocean and mountain views. All are fully equipped with the essentials for comfortable vacation living. They can accommodate as few as 1, as many as 15 in a group, at prices ranging from $65 to $200 per night for two people, plus $10 to $25 for each additional person. Each cabin and home is private, and all have full kitchens, telephones, and cable TV. A half-million-dollar home sleeps six, at rates of $200 per night, three-day minimum. Stan can also arrange car rentals in Hana if you decide to fly direct; he will have you picked up at the airport. For reservations or more information, write or phone Hana Bay Vacation Rentals, P.O. Box 318, Hana, Maui, HI 96713 or phone toll free 800/657-7970. The local number is 248-7727.

Located conveniently close to Hana Bay and the stores are the **Aloha Cottages.** Each redwood cottage has two bedrooms (queen-size bed in one and twin beds in the other), a living room, complete kitchen, and bathroom. Each has a view of Hana Bay or Kauiki Head. The cottages are well ventilated, comfortably furnished, and clean. All necessities are provided, including daily maid service. Rates range from $50 to $80 for two and $10 each additional person. Write to Mrs. F. Nakamura, P.O. Box 205, Hana, Maui, HI 96713 (tel. 248-8420). *Note:* See the Readers' Selections at the end of this chapter for several rave reviews for the Aloha Cottages.

---

2. Restaurants

IN KAHULUI

If you like buffet meals as much as we do, then you should know about the Rainbow buffet lunch served in the pretty main dining room and pool terrace of the **Maui Beach Hotel.** It's on daily from 11am to 2pm, and it's $8.50 for all you can eat, $6.50 for kids 10 and under. Local people like it because it includes many Asian dishes not usually seen on buffet meals: We ourselves are partial to the tsukemono (pickled-vegetable salad) and kamaboku (fish cakes). Also there for the taking—and still more taking—are those delicious Kula onions, Maui potato chips, lots of greens, rice, hot breads, three hot entrees daily (fish, chicken, and a beef item, plus a noodle dish), soup and cakes baked daily by the hotel's own bakery shop. *Note:* Prices are subject to change.

In and around the big shopping centers across the way from the hotels—the Kahului Shopping Center, the Maui Mall, and the Kaahumanu Shopping Center—are several places that are fine for a modest meal. The **Maui Mall** is fairly bursting with inexpensive places to eat. Sir Wilfred's Coffee, Tea, Tobacco, known for the best selection of pipes and cigars in Hawaii, has enlarged its popular espresso bar; now it's **Sir Wilfred's Espresso Caffè,** which also serves breakfasts and light lunches, soups, home-baked croissants, and fine wines by the glass at good prices. Decorated with island woods and featuring paintings by local artists, it's a very attractive and inviting spot: prices are low, and the quality of the food, atmosphere, and service is high. You can try their breakfast special of "fluffy eggs" (which manage to be just that with no fats or oils being used), served on a whole-wheat croissant at $2.80 any time of the day. The chef's talents are shown to good advantage in his flavorful tarragon chicken salad, the Wailea pea salad (peas, celery, nuts, bacon, and sour cream) and in the unusual Boboli pizza. Also good are the lox and bagels and brie or other cheeses with French bread—all from $1.75 to $5.25. And the cappuccino comes in flavors —chocolate, coconut, almond, mint, or orange—take your choice. Look for their other place at The Cannery in Lahaina.

When you've seen one Sizzler, you've seen them all. And, as far as we're concerned, the more there are in the islands, the better. The **Sizzler** at Maui Mall (at 355 Kamehameha Ave., just outside the main shopping area) is a beauty, with handsome decor and a large area for lanai dining. Sizzlers are as much into seafood and salad as they are into steak these days, so take your choice. On Maui, seafood is an especially good choice: where else can one get the fresh catch of the day—mahi, ahi, swordfish, ulua—for $5.59 to $6.59? Add salad and soup bar for $3.50 more and you've got quite a meal. There's an all-you-can-eat rib special for under $13. Complete luncheon specials, which include soup bar and salad bar, plus beverage, run from $6.99 to $9.69. Sizzler's has also added a hot pasta and tostada bar. There are special menus for senior citizens and children, and great steaks from $6.79 to $8.69 for sirloin. Cocktails are available. Always a good bet. Open from 6am to 10pm, until midnight Friday and Saturday (tel. 871-1120).

Luigi's Pasta & Pizzeria is one of the liveliest spots, not only in the Maui Mall, but in Kihei and Kaanapali as well. The atmosphere is upbeat, the food is good and reasonably priced, and at night things really get rolling with dancing, disco, Karaoke, and live music. Pizzas run from $7.99 to $27.99, burgers and sandwiches from $5.99 to $7.99. Make a meal with a pasta dish as a main course (lasagne with meat, fettuccine Alfredo, pasta primavera, among a variety of choices); the price will range from $3.99 to $9.99 at lunch, from $8.99 to $14.99 at dinner. Or dine on such house specials as chicken parmesan, veal with marsala and cream, or calamari sauté; entrees go from $13.99 to $19.99 and are served with soup or salad, toasted garlic bread, and breadsticks. Open for lunch and dinner from 11:30am to midnight, daily.

Still hungry? **Restaurant Matsu** at Maui Mall is a sparkling clean little Japanese place for tasty sushi, noodles, fish, and luncheon or dinner plates ($4.20 to $4.60), with good Bento (take-out) specialties as well. Next door to it is **Siu's Chinese Kitchen,** with American-Chinese breakfasts, family-style Chinese dinners, and fast-food Chinese lunches, from 11am to 5pm. A lunch plate with three choices is $4.35, a tasty house noodles special, $4.95.

The homemade, super-rich ice creams at **Dave's Ice Cream** in Maui Mall are really good: so good, in fact, that *People* magazine recently voted Dave's coconut-and-macadamia-nut flavor as one of the top five exotic ice creams in the United States. Try it, or cast your vote for green tea, lichee, mango, or other far-out flavors. They're also at the Wharf in Lahaina.

Before you leave Maui Mall, you owe it to yourself (if not to your diet) to try a Guri Guri. You get one at a stand called **Tasaka's Guri Guri,** and if you're not sure what it is, just ask anybody who lives on Maui; it's been an island favorite for more than half a century. We'd call it a cross between ice cream and sherbet; it's served in a scoop, comes in only two flavors—pineapple and strawberry—and tastes divine. Better than ice cream.

At Kaahumanu Center, our favorite café, C.D. Rush's, was changing hands and menus at the time of our last visit, so we'll report on the new place in our next edition. Meanwhile, a local Japanese friend put us on to a special find for all of you sushi lovers out there. He suggested you go to the bento (take-out) section at **Shirokiya's,** the Japanese department store in Kaahumanu Center, order an assortment of sushi for about $4.50 to $6.75, and have yourself a picnic. The food—including futomakki, California roll, and cone sushi—is scrumptious (other Japanese dishes are also available), and the price is about half of what it would cost to have sushi in a restaurant. Their barbecue chicken, $3.50, is excellent.

The benefits of higher education can definitely be enjoyed by those who find their way to **Class Act** at Maui Community College, 310 Kaahumanu Ave. Students in the college's food service program get a chance to try their skills; you get a chance to have a five-course gourmet meal for a flat $6. What a deal! The decor is pleasant enough with all new furniture and drapes, and the food can be excellent. For appetizers, you might be served fried scallops with spicy tartar sauce, or calamari sauté; then there's soup or salad and a choice of two entrees, one of which is termed "traditional" and the other "nutritious"—i.e., low-fat, low-cholesterol, and all of those good things. Sample dishes would include broiled butterfly lamb, Cajun Cornish game hen, mahimahi with shoyu sesame butter. Then comes dessert and beverage. Yes, there's a catch. Students serve lunch only, on Wednesday and Friday between 11am and 12:30pm, and only when school is in session: from August up until mid-May. On Wednesday, half of the students cook, and the other half serve; on Friday, they switch. Reservations are a definite requirement: phone 242-1210. High marks for this one!

Maui Bagel, 201 Dairy Rd., is an idea whose time has come. It is the only bagel bakery on Maui (there aren't so many bagel bakeries elsewhere in the islands, come to think of it), and it's been doing a thriving business ever since its owners opened two years ago. A recent remodeling has added plenty of seating and a full deli. Since Maui Bagel is near the airport and on your route to Hana or Haleakala, it's a good first—or last—stop on the island, as well as a good spot to get a picnic lunch for your sightseeing trips. It's a cute little place, with blue-and-white café curtains and a warm, friendly atmosphere. You'll find not only bagels, seven varieties, coming warm from the oven, but also delicious French bread as well as rye and wheat breads baked daily and challah on Fridays. They carry seven flavors of cream cheese, Maui onion being a favorite ($1.25) to put on your bagel or take out. Lunch possibilities include meat sandwiches like kosher corned beef and pastrami, tuna fish, veggie bagels, pizza bagels, lox and cream cheese. There's an excellent selection of salads, meats, and cheese by the pound. Prices range from $2.50 to $5. The store is open from 6:30am to 6pm Monday to Saturday, until 2pm Sunday. For take-out, phone 871-4825.

Attractive, moderately priced Chinese restaurants are hard to find on Maui, so praise be for **Ming Yuen** at 162 Alamaha St., in the Kahului Light Industrial Park, off Hwy. 380. The food here just gets better all the time, and the service, by many long-time employees, provides a "family feeling." The specials here are authentic Cantonese and the spicier Szechuan cuisine. We always like to start off with crispy wonton and Chinese spring rolls, $3.75 and $3.95. The menu offers a very wide choice of entrees, like Mongolian beef, lemon chicken, mushui pork (a personal favorite), and scallops with black-bean sauce, all about $5.95 to $8.50. If you prefer something spicier, choose the hot Szechuan eggplant, $5.50, one of their excellent vegetarian dishes. The desserts here are a little different: We like the Mandarin or chocolate mousse. Should you happen to be on Maui during Chinese New Year's in February, don't miss their 10-course banquet, complete with firecrackers. Fabulous! Even if it's not New Years, all you need is a party of eight people and you can enjoy a splendid banquet anytime, starting at about $13 a person. Ming Yuen serves lunch all day, beginning at 11:30am; dinner is on from 5 to 9pm seven days a week. Reservations requested (tel. 871-7787).

IN WAILUKU

Local-style food served in hearty portions, at old-fashioned prices, and in gracious surroundings: that's the combination that made **Chums**, 1900 Main St. (tel. 244-1000), a favorite right from the start. It's so pretty with koa-wood booths, many plants, and old, classic posters on the walls, a great place for "chums" to hang out. And the food is delicious, from the homemade oxtail soup with grated ginger, two scoops of rice and Chinese parsley, practically a meal in itself ($4.75); to the burgers and sandwiches ($3.75 to $4.95); the Hawaiian-special plate meals (around $5.25); and the broiler specialties ($5.95 to $7.25). Every day the chef comes up with a few delicious specialties: perhaps poached mahimahi with white wine and mushroom sauce, plus rice or macaroni salad, and veggies at $5.75; broiled ono with garden vegetables, and lemon herb butter, plus accompaniments, for $6.75. As you can see, prices like this went out of style years ago! Chums opens at 6:30am for hearty breakfasts served until 11am, (french toast made of Portuguese sweet bread stuffed with fruit jam, fried rice and egg, Hawaiian chop steak are favorites), and then serves the regular menu all day long to 11pm, to 10:30pm weekends.

Lunch at **Naokee's Restaurant,** at 1792 Main St. (tel. 244-9444), is a long-time budget tradition in Wailuku. Naokee's is a modern, attractive three-level restaurant, with steakhouse decor, a bar, table service, and a very cozy feeling about it. At night, most steak and fish dinners begin at around $9, but lunch is another story, and that's where we come in. That's when just about everything on the menu goes for $6 and under—and that includes broiled filet of fish, sirloin butt, Korean barbecue, and chopped steak, all served with rice, vegetables, and a little kim chee on the side. The dinner prices are not bad, considering that everything is served with rice, soup, salad, and a basket of delicious garlic bread, and that there are a few entrees in the lower price categories—but you can't beat lunch. There's also a special New York–cut steak served lunch or dinnertime for around $8.95. Naokee's is just past the bridge on the right, as you head for Wailuku from Kahului. Lunch is from 11am to 2pm, dinner from 5:30 to 9 or 9:30pm every day.

Canto's, 2092 Vineyard St., at the corner of Church St. (tel. 242-9758), is an unusual place. If you like gourmet food and low prices, you should know about it. Primarily, it's the catering business run by Anne and Paul Canto, Jr., but they'll also do a bit of "catering" right in their restaurant, a tidy little place with just about six tables and booths, curtains hiding the tables from outside view. If you call them in advance—at least 24 hours in advance—and tell them what you would like to have for dinner, they will create a meal that meets your needs perfectly. What a boon for those on special diets and health programs! They are expert at doing anything from spa cuisine to the most lavish gourmet meals; they often use recipes from

The Silver Palate Cookbook. Dinner is thus by reservation only, but at lunchtime just walk in. You can order off the regular menu, or go for one of their daily specials. It might be creole baked opakapaka with wild rice and fresh vegetables, salad, and freshly baked French bread, all for $8.95; or perhaps it will be the mochi chicken salad with fresh snow peas, sprouts, and a tangy sweet-and-sour sesame dressing, for $5.25. On the regular menu, there is always a homemade soup at $3, a ham-and-Cheddar-and-Swiss omelet, French dip, and a parmesan chicken salad or sandwich, enlived with a Caesar dressing. Prices range from $4.50 to $6.75. The Cantos' aim to keep prices low, so they save you money by serving on paper plates and using plastic utensils; you serve yourself water and beverage. Hopefully, they will have freshly ground chocolate-raspberry-truffle coffee that day; they always serve a flavored coffee. You probably won't even need a dessert with that, but go ahead, indulge yourself with a home-baked chocolate peanut-butter or oatmeal-date cookie, or some such.

Canto's is open weekdays only for lunch, officially from 11am to 2pm, but you can usually get something good to eat until 5pm.

Tokyo Tel, at 1063 E. Lower Main St. (tel. 242-9630), is a favorite Japanese restaurant with the local people. The atmosphere is simple and pleasant, the quality of the food high, and the prices easy to take. Lunch and dinner meals include rice, miso soup, and pickled vegetables along with such entrees as teriyaki pork, beef sukiyaki, and sashimi, all priced between $4.50 and $7.50. You'll know why the restaurant is famous for its tempura dishes once you bite into the shrimp tempura—four large, flavorful shrimp, served with rice and soup, along with the traditional Japanese accompaniments. And their teishoko combination plates, $7.25 to $8.75, are very popular. This is a nice place for families, as children are treated graciously here. Lunch is served from 11am to 1:30pm, when there are a number of specials from $2.75 to $5.25; dinner is from 5 to 8:30pm, Sunday to 8pm.

A big favorite with local people who live in East Maui is **Siam Thai** at 123 N. Market St. (tel. 244-3817). It's inexpensive, the food is delicious, and authentically Thai. It's a pretty place, too, typically Asian in decor, with travel posters, plants, a reclining Buddha near a small aquarium. Most dishes are $5.95 to $7.25. You won't go wrong with the Evil Prince dishes (take your choice of beef, chicken, pork, or vegetables); the meat is sautéed in hot spices with fresh sweet basil and served on a bed of chopped cabbage. Even those who hate eggplant are converted by the Eggplant Tofu dish; it's sautéed with fresh basil and hot sauce, and available either hot, medium, or mild. Then there's Tofu Delight, tofu and other vegetables sautéed in a special sauce and served over steamed bean sprouts. Thai ginger shrimp sautéed with string beans and ginger, served on cabbage, is another winner. No way you can go wrong here! Siam Thai serves lunch Monday through Friday from 11am to 2:30pm, dinner nightly from 5 to 9:30pm.

Sam Sato's, 318 N. Market St. (tel. 244-7124), is your totally local, totally down-home Wailuku restaurant. It has a big lunchroom, no decor to speak of, but it's always filled with local families and office workers happily gobbling up the likes of chow fun or wonton soup or plate lunches and sandwiches. Try their wonton special: It's hearty, it's satisfying, it's delicious, and it's a meal at $3.55. This is the place where you should sample those local-filled pastries called manju, as Sam Sato's is reputed to have the best in Maui. Open only from 8am to 2pm, closed Thursday and Sunday.

If you're still in the mood for local color—and flavor—cross N. Market Street diagonally, and you'll find **Takamiya Market,** an old-time grocery store that has a huge selection of prepared foods to go, like sushi or smoked salmon belly or mahi tempura or whatever, all at small prices. Our local spies tell us they are "outrageous." While you're there, throw in a piece or two of their equally outrageous "lemon booze cake" or "pistachio booze cake" for very good measure.

PAIA AND ENVIRONS

Paia is one of our favorite little towns—full of seekers from everywhere who've found the natural life-style they were looking for in these Hawaiian uplands. Since the area is only a 15-minute drive from Kahului, at the beginning of the road to Hana and just past the cutoff to Hwy. 37 (the Haleakala Hwy.), a visit to the restaurants here can be worked into almost any itinerary.

Our favorite place in Paia—at 89 Hana Hwy.—is **Dillon's Restaurant** (tel. 579-9113), which calls itself "a tropical hideaway," and that's just what it is. The bamboo walls, tropical decor, outdoor garden, and orchid paintings on the wall are all the art and craft of Casimir (Charles Powell), an island painter; the inspired menu is the work of his wife, Nancy Powell. The Powells are transplanted New Yorkers who have brought a touch of both sophistication and homeyness to their restaurant, and the local people and visitors have responded enthusiastically. Travelers on their way to Hana often stop by between 7 and 8am for the eggs Benedict special at $5.95, french toast with Kahlua, or those great fresh raspberry pancakes with compote syrup. The kitchen and bar are open every day for breakfast, lunch, and dinner, with a continuous pupu menu available until closing. There is always a wonderful quiche with salad, a superb frittata (an open-faced vegetable omelet topped with hollandaise), the "best hamburgers you ever ate" (could well be, with fresh Maui onion, crispy french fries, kosher dill pickle), and the Coral and Jade sandwich (veggies, onion, avocado, and cheese on whole-wheat bread), which comes with french fries and a slice of orange; all are reasonably priced, and portions are large. New England –style clam chowder, made from scratch, is a welcome treat out here in mid-Pacific. For a more extensive meal, you might have a mahimahi lunch at $8.95 or a complete fresh fish dinner at $15.95; dinners include a choice of soup or salad, fresh garden vegetables, rice or fries, and hot French bread. Dillon's house pasta is a caloric wonder: artichoke, spinach, and semolina homemade pasta generously sautéed in butter, mushrooms, fresh cream, garlic, basil, and parmesan cheese, $12.95 for the complete dinner. There's New York steak, too, and steak and pasta combinations. Also very popular is the "Lite Dining" meal, which includes meat or vegetarian lasagne, and "really Italian" spaghetti with meatballs, $8.95. Desserts are a must: Nancy brought her recipe for New York–style cheesecake and offers a blue-ribbon chocolate layer cake, too. Dillon's is a homey place, homey enough, Nancy advises, to make whatever you want. Everything is cooked to order here, so sit back and sip one of the fresh tropical fruit drinks of the day, while your meal is being prepared; the last time we were there it was passion-fruit daiquiri! This food is worth waiting for.

If you need a picnic lunch for your trip to Haleakala or Hana, the place to stock up is **Pic-nics,** on Baldwin Avenue right in Paia (you'll recognize it by a bright orange-and-yellow awning), a cheerful, clean, Formica-table-and-benches place, which is known all over the area for its sandwiches: especially the spinach-nut burgers, served on whole-wheat sesame buns, and piled high with lettuce, tomato, sprouts, and dressing; they are $4.25 and terrific. They also serve a filet of mahimahi for just $5.25. Everything is delicious, since they use, as much as possible, only freshly grown local produce and organically raised island beef. The very popular excursion lunches include sandwiches, Maui potato chips, salads, seasonal fruits, beverages, homemade cookies and desserts, plus many other basket stuffers, and begin at $8.50. No need to call ahead: your order will be prepared quickly. Picnics also features cappuccino, freshly baked breakfast pastries, and muffins for breakfast while you're waiting for your order. Great. Open daily from 7:30am to 3:30pm.

Folks who live in East Maui and are accustomed to driving long distances for a gourmet meal can't believe their luck, now that **Haliimaile General Store** has opened right in their area, in the midst of farm lands, at 901 Haliimaile Rd., in the town of Haliimaile (tel. 572-2666). Owners Beverly and Joe Gannon (Bev is also known as the operator of a highly successful catering business called Fresh Approach) have created a charming place with super-high ceilings, walls covered with shelves of lovely pottery and china, chairs painted a sparkly blue green; it's bright and busy, with the feeling of a sophisticated San Francisco dining spot. Best time to check out the gourmet touch is at lunch (it's not far from the roads to either Haleakala or Hana so it can fit into one of our excursions), when you can get imaginative sandwiches like fresh grilled ahi on an onion roll with homemade tartar sauce for $7.95; or "upcountry turkey"—that's tarragon turkey salad on whole-grain bread

—for $6.75; or chicken club—grilled chicken breast with bacon and provolone on an onion bun—for $6.25. There are daily pasta, quiche, sautéed fish of the day, and boboli (pizza) specials. Dinner is a more pricey affair—appetizers like salmon tamales with cilantro cream and duck-liver mousse run about $5.25 to $10.95, and entrees go from $12.95 to $24.95. If you choose carefully, however, you can stay on the low side of the menu with a vegetarian lasagne for $12.95, or half of a smoked chicken served with homemade pineapple chutney for $15.95. A wonderful mandarin orange and Maui onion salad, with sourdough bread, accompanies all dinners. Menus change every two weeks.

Haliimaile General Store is open from 11am to 3pm and 6 to 9:30pm Tuesday to Sunday. Closed Monday. Dinner reservations are recommended.

EN ROUTE TO HALEAKALA

Since there is no food to be had in Haleakala National Park, you might want to eat on your way to—or from—the crater. In Pukalani, about halfway between Kahului and the park entrance, you can get an inexpensive snack at **Bullock's of Hawaii:** delicious hamburgers, cheeseburgers, "moonburgers" (a meal in themselves), from $2 to $3.25. Try the shakes, a combination of nectars, juices, and ice cream; we loved the guava, but they also have pineapple, mocha, and coffee, each $2.75. Breakfasts, complete with hash browns, toast, rice, and upcountry jumbo eggs delivered fresh daily, range from $2.75 to $6.25, for steak and eggs. Open daily from 7:30am to 3pm.

The most scenic spot for a meal in this area is venerable **Kula Lodge** (tel. 878-2517), on the slopes of Haleakala in the delightful mountain town of Kula. This is a charming country inn, with a real fireplace and a nonpareil view. Go ahead, feast at breakfast time on their eggs Benedict, served with cottage fries and a rich hollandaise; it's $7.25 and delicious. Lunch offers sandwiches and burgers, soups, salads, and such entrees as teriyaki chicken, sautéed mahimahi and shrimp curry, reasonably priced from $5.25 to $6.95. Prices escalate for gourmet dinners, which feature Caesar salad, escargots, and entrees like pepper steak Madagascar, fresh fish of the day, sesame chicken, and shrimp scampi, from $10.95 to $18.95. Breakfast is served from 6:30 to 11:30am, lunch until 5pm, dinner 5:30 to 9:30pm daily.

Another enjoyable place to eat is in nearby Makawao, a few miles off your route to Haleakala, but worth making a little detour for; turn right at Pukalani. Here, at 1188 Makawao Ave., you'll find **Casanova Italian Restaurant and Deli** (tel. 572-0220), which looks as if it belongs more in Rome or Milan, Bologna or Naples, than it does in cowboy town Makawao. These cities are, in fact, the homes of the four young partners, all professionals, who came to Maui after working in New York restaurants and deciding they wanted their own place. In four short years, they've created a stir: people come from all over Maui for their fresh pastas and divine pastries; Casanova supplies them to some of the best hotels and restaurants on the island. There are two parts to the operation. One is the original deli, which opens at 8:30am and serves breakfast, lunch, snacks, and dinner-to-go entrees until 7:30pm; that's probably the part you'll visit if you're enroute to the crater. However, at 5pm, the restaurant section opens, and that's when visitors and up-country folk gather for some fabulous Italian country fare. The front part of the restaurant, done in Hawaiian woods and with works by local artists on the walls, is divided into a café and bar on one side and a huge dance floor and stage area on the other; the fine dining area is in back. Our personal favorite is the café area, dominated by a huge, wood-fired pizza oven from Italy, from which emerge delicious crispy-crusted pizzas with a decidedly imaginative flair, like the Genova (pesto sauce, prawns, and fresh tomato) or the Romana (goat cheese, roasted peppers, thyme, and garlic). They're all under $10, and they're all delicious. So are the antipasti, and an incredible salad of chicory with Gorgonzola cheese, walnuts, and fresh pears, $5.50. The wine list is moderately priced. On Wednesday and Thursday nights there's disco and dancing, and live entertainment on weekends, featuring some of Hawaii's major performers, and an occasional jazz great from the mainland, too.

During the daytime, however, the restaurant is closed, so join the happy folks in the deli. There's not much in the way of eating space here—just a few tables in back and a few seats up front; it's mostly take-out. Everything is made fresh every day, including their own croissants and Italian bread. It's hard to choose from the array of pastas, salads, lasagnes, and vegetable rolls, and the imaginative sandwiches ($4.50 to $5.50), with an international flair, such as: Paris (brie with artichoke hearts); Parma (prosciutto and tomatoes); Brooklyn (hot pastrami and Swiss). Whatever you choose, though, be sure to end your meal with one of their pastries ($2 to $3); lemon-brandy cheesecake and chocolate cheesecake are worthy of bravos, and the tiramisu—a traditional Italian cake made with Amaretto and cognac—is the one people drive miles for. If you stop here in the morning, you can have omelets and fresh croissants up until 11am. Lots of Italian provisions, too—cheese, garlic bread, pesto sauce, espresso by the pound. Nifty.

An old standby in this quaint little cowboy town is **Polli's Cantina,** a cute little place at 1202 Makawao Ave. (tel. 572-7808), at the corner of Olinda Road, which specializes in "cold beer and hot food." The decor is Mexican, the clientele is local, the music is lively, and the food is very tasty. Taco salad is $6; cheese enchiladas, $7.50 for two; a bowl of chili, $4.50. Fresh fish, steak, and lobster, and many vegetarian dishes are available, too. We love their desserts, especially the buñuelos: Mexican pastries topped with vanilla ice cream, drizzled hot pure maple syrup, and cinnamon, $3.50. *Muy bueno!* Polli's is open daily from 11:30am to midnight, with live entertainment Wednesday through Saturday evenings. Happy hour is from 2:30 to 5pm; and Sunday brunch is on from 10:30am to 2pm. There's another great Polli's—Polli's on the Beach—in the Kihei area (see below).

To pick up some sandwiches or snacks, check out the attractive deli section of the **Rodeo General Store,** at 3661 Baldwin Ave., which receives early-morning bakery deliveries of plain and stuffed fresh croissants. Sandwiches start around $3.50; there is also teri chicken. The store is known for a great selection of wine at very reasonable prices.

If you're driving to Tedeschi Vineyards after you come down from the volcano (see next chapter), **Grandma's Coffee House** on Hwy. 31 (tel. 878-2140) in the tiny town of Keokea, makes a nice stop. It's a green building right next to the gas station. Alfred Franco, a young man whose family has been growing and roasting coffee in Maui since 1918 (you can buy a pound to take home), opened this little mom-and-pop café about two years ago. It's always busy, filled with neighborhood people who come for his wife's freshly baked breads, coffee cakes, cinnamon rolls, and such. Sit down, have a sandwich or a bread pudding (75¢) or a pineapple coconut square (80¢), and some fragrant coffee—perhaps cappuccino or café au lait. Photos on the wall, café curtains, and antique bottles make for a cozy scene. Grandma's Coffee House is open daily, from 7am to 5pm.

IN KIHEI AND WAILEA

Remember the name **Azeka's Place:** this lively shopping center is a good spot for budget watchers to get a good meal in Kihei. In addition to pancakes, omelets, waffles, burgers, and such, the **International House of Pancakes** offers some 20 dinner specialties from $5.95 to $10.95—and these include breast of chicken parmigiana, steak and shrimp, London broil, and delicious spit-roasted chicken. The price of the entree includes green salad or soup of the day, natural-cut fried or other potatoes, steamed vegetables, and dinner rolls with whipped butter. And dinner, lunch, or breakfast is available any time this place is open, which means from Sunday through Thursday, 6am to midnight, Friday and Saturday 6am to 2am. The high-ceilinged dining room has comfortable booths and a pleasant atmosphere. There's another IHP at Maui Mall, in Kahului.

Luigi's, which we've told you about in Kahului (above), has another popular restaurant in the same Azeka Place (tel. 879-4446). Pasta, pizza, and low-priced Italian specialties are featured. The cocktail lounge stays open all day and until late at night. A lively crowd gathers after dark for dancing, disco, karaoke (singing to video accompaniment), and live music. Open from 11:30am to 2am daily.

Tucked away in a corner of Azeka's Place is **Island Thai** (tel. 874-0813), a pleasant little Thai restaurant that the local people recommend. It's neat and pretty with wooden tables, pink napkins, a few wall decorations. Lunch is a good deal, because all the favorites—spring rolls, curries, noodle dishes, etc.—are modestly priced; à la carte entrees are $5.95 to $6.95. At dinner, the special is the Thai spicy steak, $10.95. Lunch is served weekdays only, 11am to 3pm; dinner, every day from 5 to 9:30pm.

La Familia, in Kai Nani Village at 2511 S. Kihei Rd. (tel. 879-8824), is one of the happiest spots in Kihei. Happy hour lasts almost all day (from 10:30am to 6pm and then again from 10pm to midnight), so once they start pouring those cool margaritas for $2.50, the large, circular tiled bar and its lanai become the "in" place in town for a smart singles set. Food service starts at 11:30am and continues to 10pm. Come around sunset time and you're in for a special treat: The dining room is open-air on three sides, affording a splendid view of the ocean. You might even catch a view of humpback whales. Mexican specialties are reasonably priced, from $6.99 to $9.95 for such dishes as steak ranchero, Judy's sour-cream enchiladas, crab tostada, and chimichangas. Combination plates are $9.95. Steak and seafood entrees go from $9.95 to $15.95. Desserts include a delectable mud pie (cookie crust topped with ice cream, fudge sauce, and whipped cream). La Familia is open every day and serves cocktails until midnight.

There's a new **La Familia** in Wailuku now, in a Hawaiian garden setting at 2119 Vineyard St., serving Monday to Friday from 11:30am to 10pm, with a daily happy hour 3 to 6:30pm. There's live music Thursday and Friday from 7 to 11pm.

In the same Kai Nani Village, **Kihei Prime Rib House** (tel. 879-1954) has long been an island favorite. It's a bit high for our budget, but arrive early—between 5 and 6pm—and enjoy their Early Bird specials; prime rib dinner, Polynesian chicken, or fresh island fish, starting at $9.95. Their salad bar, included with all dinners, uses only locally grown fruits and vegetables, and can be enjoyed alone at $8.95. Regular entrees, including salad bar, run from $16 to $22. Ocean-view dining and the work of internationally known artists on the walls add to the warmth and charm.

In the rear courtyard of Kai Nani Village is a new little place called **The Greek Bistro,** 2511 S. Kihei Rd (tel. 879-9330). It has just about 10 tables, some of them outside (the bar is inside), so it's fun to sit under the blue-and-white striped umbrellas, listen to the Greek music, sip some wine, and pretend you're sitting by the Mediterranean. Breakfast, served from 7:30am to 9:30pm, is largely American-style, with the exception of the Greek omelet (Greek cheese, olives, herbs and spices), at $6.25. But the lunch and dinner menu, served from 11am to 9:30pm, has all the classic Greek specialties, and very nicely prepared: moussaka, lamb kebab, spanakopita, as well as fresh fish Greek-island style. Most entrees are priced from $7.95 to $12.95. A lamb gyro sandwich (spiced roast of lamb) served in pita bread makes a tasty lunch for $5.95. For dessert, go with the homemade baklava, $2.95. Open daily.

You may remember Polli's Mexican Restaurant from up-country Makawao; you'll be even happier to find the same good food and good drinks here in a perfectly wonderful location at Kihei, at the Kealia Beach Plaza, 101 N. Kihei Rd., at the entrance to Kihei (tel. 879-5275). **Polli's on the Beach** has tall, beamed ceilings, wooden tables, straw chairs, tile floor, plants, and piñatas; best of all is its huge dining lanai with umbrellaed tables that juts right out over the beach, so that you feel *that* close to the water. What a spot for sunset watching, whale watching, people watching, or just sitting in perfect contentment as you sip your margaritas and munch on delicious Mexican food with an island flair! Everything is made from scratch each day by Polli, who combines fresh Maui ingredients with spices and chiles sent by her family in Arizona. Polli's Munchies (appetizers) are great, including buffalo wings, fajitas, and chili queso ($4 to $8.95), and some of them are filling enough to make a meal on. Also quite filling are the baked bajas on the à la carte menu—that's a large potato stuffed with either beans, chicken, beef, or taco mix (a vegetarian soy substitute that can be used to fill anything), and topped with sour cream, olives, and tomatoes ($5 to $6). Most à la carte entrees average $3 to $6. Combination plates run $8.50 to $13.95, the latter for a neat chicken-and-crab combo topped with melted jack cheese, tomato and avocado. Try the house dressing with your salad; it's an unusual blend of cashews and garlic. Steak, lobster, and fresh fish are also featured, at higher prices. Los niños can have their own plates at $5.50. Good desserts include buñuelos and mud pie. Polli's is open every day, serving lunch between 11:30am and 2:30pm, dinner from 5 to 10pm, drinks throughout the day. Happy hour is on from 2:30 to 5pm, and there's Sunday brunch, from 10:30am to 2:30pm. Live entertainment and dancing, Friday and Saturday night, 9pm to midnight, and Sunday 5 to 7:30pm.

We'd have to agree that the new **Bonanza Restaurant** at Kukui Mall, 1819 S. Kihei Rd. (tel. 879-2525) is aptly named. It's a large, handsome room with windows on two sides, pleasant seating areas, and as far as the food goes—it's a bonanza! For $5.99 at lunch, $6.99 at dinner, you can help yourself to all you want of their "Freshtastiks" Food Bar, a giant buffet laden with vegetables, salads, cheeses, hot dishes (pastas, rice dishes, chile and fixings), soups, hot breads, and desserts; there's a lighter fare section with low-sodium soups. And this bountiful buffet comes free with all the other dishes—a variety of steaks, chicken, fish, and seafood entrees, all reasonably priced, from about $7.99 to $13.79. Beer and wine are at hand. Sandwiches are available at both lunch and dinner, there are special meals for children, and free refills on coffee, tea, and soda. Breakfast offers good value, too, with three-egg omelets at $4.99 to $6.29. Definitely a place where the whole family can eat cheaply and well. Open daily, serving breakfast from 7 to 11am, lunch from 11am to 4pm, dinner from 4 to 9pm.

If you like to eat sandwiches at any and all hours of the day, you should also know about the branch of the popular **Subway** chain in Kukui Mall (tel. 879-9955). At a Subway, you can get hot and cold subs—seafood and crab, roast beef, vegetarian, meatball, steak and sirloin, to name a few—served on super-fresh breads and rolls; you know they're fresh because you can watch them being baked right up front. Fresh, fast, and inexpensive: Most six-inch subs are under $4. There are just five or six stools at the window, no tables; take your subs out to the beach. (There are three other Subways on Maui; in Kahului at 340 Hana Hwy.; in Lahaina at The Wharf Cinema Center on Front Street; in Pukalani at Pukalani Terrace Shopping Center. All are open daily from 9am until midnight.)

The **Sand Witch** is a cozy bar at Sugar Beach, 145 N. Kihei Rd. (tel. 879-3262), which, in addition to turning out great tropical drinks, cooks up a variety of hot dogs, pupus, burritos, burgers, and "Sheer Witchery" sandwiches to go with them. Piled high with meats, cheeses, onions, tomatoes grown on Maui, sprouts, and romaine lettuce, they are a meal in themselves, from $3.95 to $6.95. Eat indoors or proceed directly to the beach. Open daily from 11am to 11pm.

People appreciate good value when they see it, and that's why **Rainbow Lagoon,** upstairs at Rainbow Mall, 2439 S. Kihei Rd. (tel. 879-5600), is kept busy every night. The food is top quality, the atmosphere is pleasant and cozy (wood paneling, many windows, blue captain's chairs, lots of plants), and value for the dollar is very good. It's especially good if you come for one of the Early Bird specials served from 5 to 7pm; along with either soup and a turn or two at the fabulous 44-item salad bar, you get a choice of white rice, rice pilaf, or baked potato, to go along with such entrees as fish and chips, mahimahi almondine, broiled chicken breast, New York steak, or prime rib au jus with creamy horseradish, from $9.95 to $12.95. During the rest of the evening, the Café Menu offers inexpensive burgers, fish and chips, spaghetti, French dip and pizza for one; most regular entrees of seafood, meats, and poultry go from $14.50 to $18.50. Dinner is served every night from 5 to 10pm and there's entertainment from 7pm. Reservations advised.

Dolphin Plaza, 2395 S. Kihei Rd., has two establishments we like a lot: **Pizza Fresh** and **The New York Deli.** Doug and Georgann Malone, the couple who run Pizza Fresh, came to Maui with a reputation to live up to; their pies had been voted "Best Pizza in Dallas." They may also be the best pizza in Maui. Their motto, "We make it, you bake it," means this is something to take back to your condo rather than eat there. We sampled their Garden Lite pizza—a whole-wheat vegetarian special with a variety of veggies, light on the cheeses, and with a thin crust—$10.45 small,

$15.75 medium, and quite delicious. Other possibilities include Hawaiian-style (Canadian bacon, pineapple, mushrooms, etc.) and the traditional pies. Open daily from 3 to 9pm. For free delivery in the Kihei, Wailea, and Makena areas, call them at 879-1525.

Just across the courtyard from Pizza Fresh is The New York Deli (tel. 879-1115), which should be a must for any homesick New Yorkers—they even have a picture of ex-mayor Ed Koch on the wall. The wonderful bagels air-expressed from the homeland daily, the hot pastrami and corned-beef-on-rye sandwiches ($4.95), the hot and cold heroes, and the pasta and potato salads, sold by the pound, will all soothe the pangs of Manhattan separation anxiety. This is a tiny but sparky place, with brick floors, red-checkered cloths on all of three tables. Have an espresso or cappuccino and a slice of their New York cheesecake, or pick up your lunch and take off for the beach (you won't miss New York a bit). Open from 9am to 8pm daily.

Wailea and Makena, just beyond the Kihei area, is wealthy condo country, and the home of four stunning hotels: the Maui Inter-Continental Wailea, the Stouffer Wailea Beach Resort, the Maui Prince, and the Makena Surf. When we get rich, we're going to have all our meals at Raffles' at the Stouffer Wailea Beach Resort. Definitely. Until that happy day, however, it's fun to play rich by having a "Big Splurge" Sunday champagne brunch in this lovely dining room, 10-time winner of the coveted *Travel Holiday* Award. Brunch is priced at $23.50 for adults, $10.50 for children under 12, and is considered to be the most elaborate Sunday champagne brunch on Maui, which is perhaps a bit of an understatement. Consider just a few of the delights on the table: omelets made to order, gravlox marinated in dill sauce, lox and bagels, sushi, rack of lamb, prime roast beef, homemade breads and rolls, crab salad in avocado, several pastas, green salads of arugula, radicchio, and spinach, and the world's most incredible pancake dish: Pancakes Romanoff—thin pancakes layered with fresh raspberry purée, topped with meringue, with strawberry sauce for ladling! And a staggering dessert table as well. You can come for this feast as early as 9am and stay until 2pm, if you like, or any portion in between. Of course, the glasses of champagne and the cups of steaming coffee are bottomless. Reservations are a must: 879-4900.

Remember **Ed and Don's** at the Wailea Shopping Center for a pleasant snack or lunch in this area: They have gourmet sandwiches of pastrami, turkey, Reubens, curried chicken, and French dips, etc., from $2.95 to $4.95, and lots of good ice creams and sundaes.

IN LAHAINA

Lahaina's restaurants reflect its easy, relaxed approach to living. A good place to relax and soak up some sea breezes while you dine is the new **Lahaina Broiler,** 889 Front St. (tel. 661-3111), a complete makeover for the venerable Lahaina eating place. The building is open to the waterfront—try to get a table right on the sea wall—and the decor is a study in pinks and whites, from the pink awnings over the water to the pink-cushioned white chairs and tables shaded by pink umbrellas. The building is large, but rooms are partitioned to create a more intimate feeling. The price range is middle-of-the-road; breakfast pancakes and french toast under $5, omelets $5.50 to $6.50, lunch sandwiches and burgers from about $4.25 to $7.95. Although the Broiler's dinner specialties like the roast prime rib of beef, the seafood fettuccine and the cioppino (a simmering stew of seafood and fresh fish, the restaurant's most popular dish) go from $16.95 to $22.50, there are at least half a dozen dishes on the low side of the menu, like baked chicken or mahimahi, teriyaki steak or Cajun shrimp, which afford a complete meal for $9.95 to $5.95; they are accompanied by either seafood chowder, Portuguese bean soup or tossed greens, plus a starch, hot vegetables, and bread. Desserts are the usual: cheesecakes, pies and cakes, and ice cream.

The Lahaina Broiler is open every day, from 7am to midnight.

In Arthurian legend, Avalon was another name for Paradise, the place where heroes went to reap their eternal reward. You can reap some culinary rewards right here and now by going to **Avalon,** in the courtyard of Mariners Alley, 844 Front St.

(tel. 667-5559), which is, quite simply, the best new restaurant to open in Lahaina in many a year. The creation of a transplanted southern Californian, chef Mark Ellman, Avalon provides an exuberant and imaginative dining experience without a drop of pretension. It sits modestly in the courtyard of a shopping mall, prettily decorated with old posters and antique Hawaiian shirts on the wall, oversized Fiestaware and flowered cloths on the tables. If you're watching the budget, come just for lunch (under $12), or order one of the exotic vegetarian dishes on the dinner menu ($8.95 to $12.95). Better still, throw caution to the wind and indulge yourself this once. This is the kind of restaurant people write home about.

Avalon presents contemporary Asian cuisine—original recipes influenced by all the cultures of Asia, using many fresh, local ingredients. Many ingredients are grown a farmyard away. The chef will not use MSG, not even salt, and does all his seasoning with herbs. All sauces are made to order, and all dishes may be ordered mild, medium, or spicy. If you're on a special diet, they will do their best. Now then, what to order? While you're sipping something pleasant to start, perhaps the KGB Cooler (Absolut Citron with freshly squeezed lemonade over ice) or a glass of champagne with crushed fresh raspberries, discuss the daily specials with the waiter. Chef Mark is always trying something new, so you can never tell what heavenly treats may be in store (at a recent meal, for example, we started with homemade shrimp ravioli with shiitake mushrooms and sun-dried tomatoes in a Szechuan cream sauce). Always on the menu are such treats, among the appetizers ($4.50 to $7.50), as Vietnamese summer rolls, Maui onion rings with a homemade tamarind-chipotle catsup, and guacamole made tableside. Salads? There's hearts of romaine with a spicy anchovy dressing, an incredible salad of scallops lightly sautéed with shiitake mushrooms and served over mixed greens, accompanied by a ginger-sesame dressing, to name just two. Among the entrees, fresh fish of the day, fresh sea scallops and large Asian prawns can be ordered with a choice of sauces that include garlic black bean and sun-dried tomato, basil, and cream. Vegetarians will love the Gado Gado salad, a classic Balinesian dish of steamed vegetables on brown rice, with peanut sauce and condiments. Entrees run from $8.95 (for Chinese tofu salad) to $26.95 (for mixed seafood grill), with most in the $18 to $23 range.

Still with us? How can we describe the Caramel Miranda, the only dessert offered? Imagine a plate of fresh raspberries and strawberries, framed on one side by an incredibly delicious, thick, warm caramel sauce, on the other side by a giant scoop of Häagen-Dazs macadamia-nut brittle ice cream. Unforgettable! Depending on the season and the availability of exotic fruits, it might include, instead, coquitos (full grown mini-coconuts from Chile), or Kula blackberries and huckleberries. If you don't get to have dinner here, at least come by afterwards for coffee and dessert (about $5).

Avalon is open every day, from noon to midnight. Reservations are advised, especially at night, when people clamor for tables.

Lahaina Coolers Restaurant & Bar, 180 Dickenson St., just two blocks from busy Front Street (tel. 661-7082) is exactly the kind of place Lahaina needed: a place where you can get creative, upbeat food at almost any time of the day, in a relaxing setting and at a reasonable price. No wonder it's become so popular so quickly! The restaurant looks like somebody's summer porch, with open windows on three sides (windsurfing sails provide shade), blue-and-white tiled floor, white chairs, whirling fans overhead, lots of potted plants—a very summery ambience. You can order anything on the lunch and dinner menus from noon to midnight—and there's a wealth of choices. For a snack or a starter ($3.50 to $4.90), the spinach and feta cheese quesadillas and the green apple and brie quesadilla with walnuts are both great. Among the salads, you can't go wrong with the sesame chicken with water chestnuts and papaya, the Greek salad, or the mandarin chicken ($5.75 to $6.50). Or maybe you'll want to try a tropic-pizza: Evil Jungle pizza, Thai-style chicken in a spicy peanut sauce, is a whimsical takeoff on the popular Thai dish ($8.75). There are burgers from the grill, as well as sautéed chicken breast, Moroccan chicken spinach enchilada, and New York steak ($6.75 to $12.50). Perhaps you better come here with a little group so you can sample a lot. But don't miss dessert: crème brûlée, cheesecake, and chocolate mousse pie ($3.50 each) are all special. And breakfast, served from 7am to noon, is fun, too, with a variety of omelets and egg specialty dishes. The lively bar is popular, especially during the 4-to-6pm and 10pm-to-closing happy hour, when drinks and pupus are less. Lahaina Coolers is open every day, from 7am to midnight.

You'll think you've stepped back to the '50s, or even the '40s, when you eat at **Happy Days, Café of Yesterday,** in the Lahaina Marketplace (tel. 661-3235). And well you might have. The place looks like an old-fashioned malt shop, complete with a soda fountain behind the counter, seven seats at the counter itself, where you could order a malted or a cherry Coke or a hot-fudge sundae, and a large dining room open to the air on both sides. Old movie posters, antique sheet music, advertising slogans, record albums of Elvis, and such memorabilia provide the decor. And the food is the same as they used to serve at the corner malt shop way back when; they specialize in burgers, hash browns, hot dogs, homemade chili and beans, hearty soups. Breakfast, served from 7 to 11am, features three-egg ranch omelets (most at $5.50), made the way the Toddle House Coffee Shops used to make those "Humpty Dumpty" omelets back in the '30s, old-fashioned buttermilk hotcakes, and strawberry french toast. Then there's lunch and dinner, served continuously from 11am to 9pm, when you can have burgers from $3.95, hot dogs from $2.50, hearty sandwiches, good salads, and yummy hash brown potatoes. Open daily from 7am to 9pm.

Everybody seems to like **Longhi's,** 888 Front St. (tel. 667-2288), an on-the-sidewalk, across-from-the-ocean café where the Italian-accented specialties are fresh and luscious, the mood convivial (lots of plants, koa tables, backgammon tables, a lively bar, and friendly service), and the desserts—and sunsets—super-special. Sit upstairs or downstairs—the rooms are similar, but there's an even better ocean view upstairs. Owner Bob Longhi goes to great lengths (like to New York and Italy) to bring in the finest and freshest cheeses, produce, and Italian cold cuts, makes his own pastas, bakes his own breads and pastries, and maintains a gourmet standard throughout. Because everything depends on freshness, the menu is always verbal: the night we were there, linguine with a delicious pesto sauce was $15, eggplant parmigiana was $11. It was $20 for shrimps, scallops, and pasta scampi, and $21 for fresh Maui fish. It's easy for the bill to climb here since the entrees are served alone, and side dishes can add up (salad at $5, vegetables, etc.), so our recommendation is either go all out and consider this a big splurge, or tell the waiter how much money you want to spend, and let him plan the menu for you. (You can also ask for a menu with prices before being seated.) It's wise to eat lightly and save your strength, in fact, for Longhi's otherworldly desserts; they've become something of a legend around town, since there have been 1,000 different ones in the restaurant's 13-year history. You never know what they'll come up with, but you might sample, as five of us once did, an incredible strawberry shortcake, a superb macadamia-nut pie (better than any pecan pie we had ever tasted), an unusual chocolate-cake pie (chocolate cake between pie crusts with custard between the layers), a mouthwatering mango-topped cheesecake, and a cooling strawberry mousse. All desserts are priced at $5, and they are huge, so be sure to bring a friend to help you. There's an extensive wine list, including selections that you can order by the glass. Longhi's opens at 7:30am for breakfast (frittatas, omelets, homemade coffee cake, and strudel), and serves continuously until about 10pm or later. On Friday and Saturday nights there's live music and dancing until 1am. Complimentary valet parking from 5pm.

Mr. Sub, long one of Honolulu's most popular submarine shops, is repeating its quality act in Lahaina. It's at 129 Lahainaluna Rd. (near Front Street, next to Nagamine Camera), with wonderfully fresh ingredients, 7 varieties of breads and rolls, great salads, quick service, and low prices. You can eat right in their air-conditioned shop, but the best bet is to choose from the 31 combination sandwiches (or create your own combination) at about $3.50 to $4, and head for your picnic. Special picnic packages, with coolers for the beach, include a sandwich, chips, fruit, and a drink, and run $5 to $7. Phone them the day before at 667-5683, and everything will be ready for pick-up by 8am. Open weekdays from 7am to 5pm, Saturday to 4pm, closed Sunday.

Moose McGillycuddy's Pub & Café, 844 Front St. (tel. 667-7758), which you may remember from Waikiki, offers the same brand of good food, good booze, and good fun here in Lahaina. It's one flight up, with a big bar, a lively atmosphere, and some tables set out on the lanai overlooking busy Front Street. The Moose is known as a "bargain" in pricey Lahaina, and its dinners, served from 5pm, offer good value: entrees like teriyaki chicken, stuffed mahimahi, prime rib, range in price from $7.50 to $12.95, and come with soup or salad, baked potato or rice or fries, and hot garlic bread. Early Bird dinners, served from 5 to 7:30pm, feature prime rib, mahimahi almondine, and half a charbroiled chicken for only $7.95, plus steak and lobster at $14.95. Then there are other favorites like the giant taco salad at $6.95, Mexican specialties like sizzling beef or chicken fajitas at $8.95, a variety of burgers like the University Burger ("highly ranked bacon and intelligent cheddar") from $4.25 to $7.50. Three-egg omelets are served with fresh fruit and Texas toast, up until 4pm. Margaritas and daiquiris are the big booze selections here, along with coffee drinks, Hawaiian exotics, and way-out house specialties. The Moose's breakfast specials are considered the best deals in Lahaina: the Early Bird, served from 7:30 to 9am, $2.69 for two eggs, bacon, toast, and orange juice; and the Beggar's Banquet, $3.29 for three eggs any style, with potatoes or rice, Texas toast, and fresh-fruit garnish. Open from 7am until late, late.

What a surprise the **Kobe Japanese Steak House** is! Just one block behind traditional Baldwin House at 136 Dickenson St. (tel. 667-5555) is what could pass for an authentic Japanese country inn, magnificently decorated with traditional Japanese arts and artifacts, and serving delicious food in a most entertaining setting. You could eat at the enormous sushi bar (sushi assortments run from $8.50 to $15.90), but we prefer to take our seats at one of the communal tables, and, along with other diners, spur the master chef on as he whips up our meal at the center grill, teppanyaki-hibachi style. In such a setting, people dining alone, friends dining together, even families with children can all feel comfortable. Every meal begins with grilled teppan shrimp pupus, followed by shabu-shabu soup. Then the chef takes whatever you've chosen—steak, chicken, shrimps—and sautés it with fresh vegetables and flavorful sauces. For dessert, wonderful green-tea ice cream and green tea itself, hearty because it is roasted with rice. Teriyaki chicken is $11.50, hibachi steak $17.90, teppan shrimps $17.90, and a steak and chicken teriyaki combo is $16.90. Other steak, fish, and lobster choices go higher. We like to start the meal with warm saké; Japanese beer goes well with this food, and regular drinks and cocktails are also available. Special children's menus are available.

Kobe serves dinner only, every night from 5:30pm. Cocktail service begins at 5pm, and there's a late-night happy hour, from 10pm to 1:30am, when draught beer and wine are $1.50, standards $3. Plenty of free parking.

Call **Kimo's,** 845 Front St. (tel. 661-4811), your quintessential Lahaina-style restaurant. It's been there forever, right out on the waterfront, serves good fresh fish and steaks, is a perfect place to nurse a drink, discuss the meaning of life and/or watch a sunset. The oceanfront dining room is open only for dinner, from 5 to 10:30pm; that's when, by sticking carefully to the low side of the menu, you can dine quite reasonably: a cheeseburger is $6.95, New York–steak sandwich, Polynesian chicken, and kushiyaki (marinated chicken breast and sirloin brochette) are all $9.95. Health nuts are kept well in mind with the "spa-cuisine style" marinated chicken breast, low in calories, salt, and cholesterol; it's called ginger chicken and is $9.95. And everything you order comes with tossed green salad with house dressing, a basket of freshly baked carrot muffins and French rolls, and steamed herb rice. There's limited service downstairs during the day: the bar menu features lunch from 11:30am to 2:30pm with fish, meat, and veggie sandwiches as well as a large fruit salad, from $5.95 to $9.95; pupus are served at the bar between 3 and 5pm.

Not only does **The Wharf Cinema Center,** a nifty shopping complex at 658 Front St., have some of the most tasteful boutiques in the area, it also has a good supply of quick-service restaurants. For breakfast or lunch al fresco, **Lani's Pancake Cottage** (tel. 661-0955) is the place to go. The indoor area with its counters and

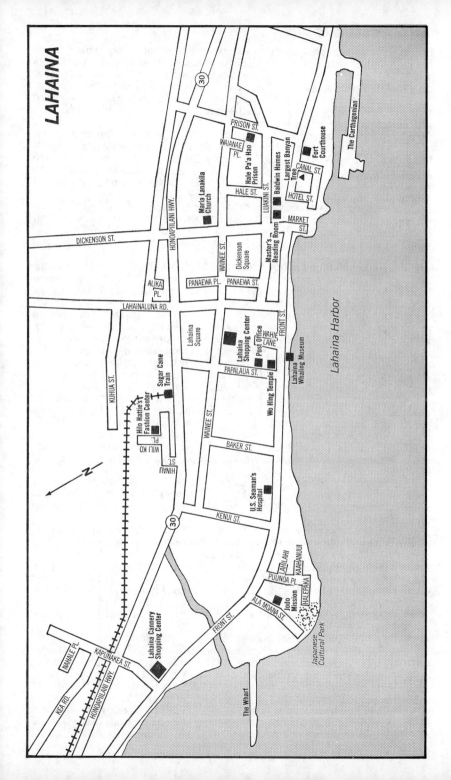

booths is pleasant enough, but they also serve on a large umbrellaed terrace. Breakfast is on until closing, so any time is fine for banana or strawberry pancakes ($3.95 and $4.50) or the omelet to end all omelets: the Chef's Mess Omelet, made of five eggs and filled with the likes of Ortega chili and cheese, bell peppers, Swiss cheese, etc.—$12.50 for two of you, $15 for three. Their tuna melt sandwich—grilled tuna and cheese with a small green salad—makes a good lunch at $4.50, and so do such entrees as a chile relleno burger, a bowl of chili, or honey-dipped fried chicken, from $5 to $6.50. Beer and wine are available. Open 6:30am to 3:30pm only.

Next door to Lani's, sharing the same outdoor terrace area, is **Mama's Original Maui Pizza** (tel. 667-2531), where you can get thin-crust pies (from $7.80 and $8.30, small) as well as individual slices ($1.35); spaghetti entrees with salad bar and garlic bread ($3.75 to $5.30 at lunch, $4.59 to $5.50 at dinner), and Italian hot and cold sandwiches. Free delivery from Lahaina to Kapalua.

Tucked away in a cozy corner on the first floor of The Wharf is a Mexican restaurant the local people like a lot: **Pancho and Lefty's,** with a bar up front, booths and tables in back. Nachos are $6.95, taco salad $6.95, Mexican plates $8.95. On our last visit, they were also serving a definitely nonspa-cuisine special: pizza with rice and beans, $5.95.

You might call **Blue Lagoon Steak and Seafood** (tel. 661-8141), up in the front area of The Wharf, a medium–fast-food operation: you place and pay for your order at the cashier's, then proceed to sit either indoors at booths or outdoors under umbrellaed tables in the very pretty patio bar (tropical mixed drinks are excellent here). The same menu is served throughout the day, from 11am to 9:30pm, which means that you can get good values on good food, like a 6-oz. serving of sirloin for $8.95, a pound of teriyaki ribs for $8.95, or platters of shrimp, clams or fish and chips for just $6.95 and $7.95. Good burgers and meat sandwiches begin at $5.95. At 5pm, the specials of the day go into effect, and they really can be special: imagine 10 ounces of prime ribs for $9.95 (Friday and Saturday), or two fried chicken dinners for $7.95, including potato or rice or snappy Texas toast (Friday).

Chicago-style pizzas and pastas are the specialties at **Pizza Patio,** an attractive new addition to The Wharf. We like their designer pies, like the Pestey Tomato (pesto sauce, fresh tomatoes, mushrooms, mozzarella), $9.50 small, $14.50 medium, and the Spicy Polynesian (peanut sauce, shredded chicken breast, onions, pineapple, macadamia nuts, and mozzarella), $9.95 small, $14.95 medium. Their special house calzones, with similar varieties of toppings, are also fun. Cold beer and wine are available.

Subways, one of our favorite sandwich shops, has a new branch here (see above, under Kihei Restaurants). And for an Asian plate lunch, you'll do well at **Song's Kitchen** at the rear of The Wharf. All is tidy and clean, and lunches run $3.85 to $4.95.

For those who savor the bookish life, the most charming place at The Wharf will have to be **The Whalers Book Shoppe and Coffee House.** Here, in a shady corner at the top of The Wharf, people are sitting quietly on the patio engaged in such un-Lahaina-like pursuits as reading or writing letters—all the while munching on light snacks like quiches and sipping some wonderful coffees, English teas, hot Ghirardelli chocolate, and the like. There are also good homemade cookies, cakes, and pastries. (Don't miss the fresh coconut macaroons—divine!) You can also buy Kona coffee by the pound—and books, of course, to give you something to do out on the patio.

Stick to the pasta and chicken dishes on the low side of the menu, and you can have a very reasonable and atmospheric meal at **Bettino's,** at 505 Front St. (tel. 661-8810). Bettino's is tucked away in the rear of this little shopping complex, affording oceanfront views from every table. The menu is mostly Italian, and the food is good. Along with your orders of, say, fettuccine Alfredo or marinara, chicken breast parmesan, or broiled breast of chicken, all from $9.50 to $13.95, you'll get soup or salad, fresh vegetables, rice or pasta or fries, and freshly baked breads. Fish and steak dishes are higher. Lunch is moderately priced, and specials include mahimahi, fish and chips, and Maui-style ribs, from $6.90 to $7.95, plus a goodly array of burgers and hot sandwiches. It's a nice place, too, for breakfast: omelets and pancakes. Bettino's serves breakfast from 7am to 2pm (full bar service starts at 8am), lunch from 11am to 2pm, and dinner from 5pm to closing. Open every day. *Note:* It's easy to park here in the underground garage.

A tapas bar in Lahaina? No need to go to Spain for tapas now—a Mediterranean restaurant on the order of a Spanish tapas bar has opened in Lahaina. **Tasca,** 608 Front St. (tel. 661-8001), is the first of its kind in Hawaii, and it's a charmer. Spanish, French, and Greek music plays in the background, there are good paintings on the walls, a fountain in the back, cute little white-tile tables, fans, plants all about. In case nobody told you, tapas—hot and cold—are small portions of a variety of foods, perfect for grazing. At Tasca, the dishes come in three sizes (small, medium, and large). Best to come here with a few people and share. If you're watching the budget, we suggest you come when you're not *too* hungry, as small portions are just that; if you're really hungry, you won't be satisfied except with the large portions, and then the bill will add up. At a recent meal, four of us started with the satisfying Mediterranean soup ($2.75), and went on to a delicious green salad with shrimps and olives in a raspberry vinaigrette ($3.95 small, $7.25 medium, $11.25 large). Then came a respectable fettuccine Alfredo ($4.95, $7.25, and $12.95); a flavorful dish of prawns Mediterranean, sautéed in a brandy sauce with garlic, tomatoes, mushrooms, and dill ($4.95, $9.25, $15.95); followed by a very good saffron chicken ($8.95, $14.95). We all agreed that the sautéed opakapaka Grenobloise was the best ($9.95, $15.95). Desserts like baked brie cheese with strawberries and nuts and "chocolate decadence" were a bit on the overkill side; fresh Kula raspberries with crème anglaise were just fine.

Tasca is open Monday to Saturday from 11:30am to midnight, Sunday from 5:30pm; the bar stays open until 1:30am.

Lahaina Square (just behind Lahaina Shopping Center) is a good place for hungry budgeteers to note. Here you'll find **Amilio's Delicatessen,** which has good sandwiches, some with an Italian flair, to take out or eat here; the price range goes from $3.35 for tuna or cheese, to $4.50 for Amilio's special of many meats and cheeses. There's apt to be a special offer, like one sandwich at 99¢ when you buy another deli sandwich at full price. There's a choice of good breads, deli meats, and cheese if you wish to make your own sandwiches. Local-style plate lunches are good buys at $2.95. Open most days from 9am to 1pm, until 9pm on Friday, on Sunday from 10am to 4pm.

Christine's Family Restaurant at Lahaina Square (tel. 661-4156) is just the place to bring a hungry family; they'll eat heartily and well, and there won't be a big dent in the budget. It's very popular with the local people for its home-style cooking. The neat thing about Christine's is that breakfast, lunch, and dinner are served any time of the day; so if you get an urge for, say, a pancake sandwich stuffed with meat ($4.50), or another local favorite, the loco moco (rice, hamburger steak and an egg, topped with gravy, $5.15), it's yours whenever. Lunch and dinner are abundant meals, with something like 20 entrees under $7.85, including the likes of teriyaki pork, ham steak, grilled tuna patties, roast beef, and grilled lemon chicken, all served with two scoops of rice or french fries, a choice of salad or soup, plus vegetables. There are burgers, sandwiches, chili dishes; beer and wine, too. Nothing fancy about Christine's, but it is large and comfortable, with a smaller counter up front, and booths and tables in the back, a large sunset painting on the wall. It's open Tuesday to Saturday from 6am to 9:30pm, on Sunday and Monday to 2pm.

More family choices in the same Lahaina Square include a familiar **Jack in the Box,** as well as a **Baskin-Robbins,** and a large **Denny's.**

The local people have given a warm reception to **Thai Chef,** a cute little restaurant in the Lahaina Shopping Center (tel. 667-2814), offering Thai specialties in a pleasant setting: Thai decorations on the walls, lacy curtains, white tablecloths under glass. Tell the waiter if you want your food mild, medium, or hot, so he can help you choose from among salads, soups (we like the chicken soup simmered in coconut milk with giner at $7.25), a variety of curries, noodles, and such specialty dishes as stuffed chicken wings or fried crab legs with bean sauce. Vegetarians have a complete menu of their own: appetizers, soups, noodles, and main dishes. It's all reasonable; most dishes are priced from $6.95 to $9.95. Thai Chef serves lunch Monday to Friday from 11am to 2:30pm, dinner nightly from 5 to 10pm.

Marie Callender's in the Lahaina Cannery (tel. 667-7437) is a restaurant as American as apple—or chicken pot pie. Both are served with gusto at this charming place, which has just about everything the cost-conscious diner could desire: a gracious, pink-and-pretty setting, comfortable seating that invites relaxing with friends, a wide variety of dishes, and wholesome American cooking—all at very realistic prices. As for that chicken pot pie, it's as good as we've tasted, with a flaky, all-vegetable crust, lots of chicken chunks and vegetables, and makes a satisfying meal, with soup or salad, at $8.25. Salads are also a specialty: spinach, chicken curry, tostada, and cobb are all delicious, as are the fresh pasta dishes, the quiches, omelets, and a variety of burgers and sandwiches. Most items run $8 to $10. After 4pm, dinner entrees like chicken teriyaki, fajitas, and meat loaf are added to the menu, and are served with salad or soup, pasta or rice or fries, plus cornbread with honey butter, $10.75 to $16.85. Now for dessert: Marie Callender's is known for its home-baked pies, so have a slice here—of fresh peach or sour-cream blueberry, rhubarb or butterscotch or macadamia-nut cream ($2.50 or $3.25), and see if you can resist taking a whole pie back to your hotel with you.

Marie Callender's opens at 7am for breakfast (try the banana macadamia-nut waffles) and stays open to 10pm daily. The Lahaina Cannery is at 1221 Honoapiilani Hwy., on the Kaanapali side of town.

We've already told you about **Sir Wilfred's Espresso Caffè** at the Maui Mall in Kahului: there's a newer Sir Wilfred's here at the Lahaina Cannery, serving the same delicious light foods and that wonderful array of flavored coffees, cappuccinos, and espressos. Rest your feet, and try something delicious. Pastries are delivered every day from The Bakery in Lahaina, bagels from Maui Bagel in Kahului. Open daily, from 9:30am until closing.

A variety of fast-food outlets and a big central courtyard for seating makes it possible to have an inexpensive meal on the run at the Lahaina Cannery. Our favorite: **Pappoule's II** for gyros, shish kebab, chicken-a-bab, all $3.95, $1.85 spinach pies, and other Greek tasties. Also on hand for those in a hurry are **Yami Yogurt, Burger King, McConnel's Ice Cream,** and **Orange Julius.**

There's no natural-foods restaurant in Lahaina at the moment, but the local health-food store, **Westside Natural Foods** at 136 Dickenson St. (tel. 667-2855), does have salads, sandwiches, soup of the day, smoothies, and hot food to eat informally at outdoor tables or to go. Entrees like lasagne, chili, and enchiladas run from $3.10 to $5.50. You can get unsprayed pineapples here, and star fruits grown in Lahaina. Open daily from 10am to 9pm, until 7pm Sunday.

Just past the railroad depot on Honoapiilani Hwy. you'll spot a familiar building: it's a **Pizza Hut,** the home of those thick, crusty pizzas with the chewy, cheesy taste. This attractive spot, with its red curtains at the window, cozy booths and tables, attracts a large family crowd, since both pizza and pasta are filling, tasty, and inexpensive. If you come between 11am and 2pm Monday through Friday, they'll guarantee that your personal pan pizza ($2.69 for the supreme, $2.99 for the pepperoni) will be ready in five minutes, or the next one's on them. As for the regular pies, create your own with any two ingredients chosen from the scores available at $6.50 small, $9.99 medium, $12.99 large. Beer and wine by the glass and the pitcher. Open from 11am to 11pm Sunday to Thursday; to midnight Friday and Saturday.

Stacks of kiawe wood and Hawaiian ranch decor set an up-country mood, but here we are in tropical Lahaina, at **Chris's Smokehouse BBQ** at the corner of Honoapiilani Hwy. and Hinau Street, just opposite Pizza Hut. The baby back pork ribs and kiawe chicken are good and tasty—they're smoked over kiawe wood and broiled over kiawe charcoal to give them a very special flavor. There are five complete dinners on the menu under $10—and that means that along with your rack of baby back pork ribs, hot links, half a smoked kiawe chicken, charbroiled boneless breast of chicken, or beef ribs, you also get freshly baked cornbread with honey-macadamia-nut butter, coleslaw, and a choice of ranch-style baked beans, homemade steak fries, or steamed rice. Higher-priced dinner entrees include various combination plates, New York–strip steak, and charcoal-broiled fresh fish, about $11 to $14. A la carte dishes run from about $6.95 to $10. Come at lunchtime and you can sample Chris's tasty smoked meats in open-face sandwiches with barbecue sauce at $4.50 to $5.50, served with coleslaw, cottage cheese, or steak fries. For the last three years, their $4.95 burger has been chosen "Best Hamburger for Lunch" by the *Maui News*. You're given a plain, white paper place mat and crayons for doodling while you're having a drink and waiting for your meal. Chris's serves dinner every night from 5 to 10pm, lunch Monday to Saturday from 11:30am to 4pm; happy hour is 2:30 to 5pm.

Next to the train depot (the Lahaina-Kaanapali Railroad) at 991 Limahina Pl. is a "Maui secret." Many of the fine restaurants in town get their bread and pastries from **The Bakery**. It's a popular spot, crowded with locals who come early in the morning for the best croissants around: brioches, pain au lait, hot from the oven. Chocolate cream cheese croissants and coconut macaroons are memorable. Herb bread, $1.25, is their specialty. They also offer gourmet-quality deli items and sandwiches to go (on the order of cheese broccoli or smoked pork loin and cheese). Worth stopping by just to inhale the aromas! *Note:* Local friends advise that their prices on California wines, Maui champagne, and imported champagne, too, are so good that they should be kept a secret!

BARGAINS AT KAANAPALI BEACH

The strip of luxury hotels along Kaanapali Beach boasts a goodly share of luxury restaurants, but very few where the budget diner can relax. So it's good news that the beautiful **Maui Marriott Resort** (tel. 667-1200) offers reasonably priced Sunset Special meals in three of its dining rooms. At the Moana Terrace, you can get Sundowner Specials between 5 and 6pm; complete dinners, with entrees of pasta marinara, catch of the day, chicken breast macadamian, teriyaki beef, and prime ribs of beef run from $8.95 to $12.50. These include visits to the extensive soup-and-salad bar, plus beverage: a complete Sundowner Buffet is $13.50. **Lokelani,** an island fish house, offers Sunset Specials between 6 and 7pm, and they include prime rib and the fresh catch of the day, at $14.95. Homemade crusty bread, dessert, and beverage are also included. You can get a complete Japanese meal between 6 and 6:30pm at Nikko: soup, rice, teppanyaki vegetables, green-tea ice cream, and tea accompany such dishes as sukiyaki steak, scallops, shrimp, and breast of chicken, from $12.95 to $16.95. All three restaurants offer inexpensive children's menus, too.

There's another popularly priced eating spot at the hotels: the **Kaanapali Beach Hotel Koffee Shop.** Breakfast begins at 6am, lunch at 11am, and dinner at 5pm. Be sure to check the luncheon specials, perhaps pot roast, an island dish, beef stew, or roast chicken, plus hot and cold sandwiches, $5.95 to $8.95. At dinner you can have hot platters such as roast turkey, fried shrimp, breaded veal cutlet or New York–cut steak, in the same $5.95 to $8.95 price range, plus a nightly dinner special which includes entree, vegetable, potatoes or rice, rolls and butter. Service is cafeteria-style, and since the coffee shop is at the entrance side of the hotel, you can walk right in after parking your car, without having to go through the hotel lobby.

Luigi's at Kaanapali Beach is still another branch of this popular Italian eatery. You'll find it just off Kaanapali Hwy., as you head down toward the Westin Maui Hotel and Whaler's Village. Like its sister restaurants in Kahului and Kihei, this Luigi's (tel. 661-8934) serves pizza, pastas, and Italian specialties, and also has a game room and billiard center. Open daily from noon to midnight.

For a lovely treat in the Kaanapali area, and at prices that are not too hard to take, take yourself to dinner at **Mango Jones**. The restaurant is at the top of the hill in Kaanapali (adjacent to the Kaanapali Royal), and the dining room, open on three sides and decorated in a tropical mood, overlooks the Kaanapali resort and ocean down below. Yes, there are mangoes here—in the chutney that's served with the chicken and shrimp curries, in the mango-pineapple-banana bread that accompanies all meals and, if you're lucky and mangoes are in season, in a spectacular flambéed dessert called Torch Mango. The pupus are imaginative: We especially like the lomi-lomi salmon mousse served on Hilo soda crackers (a local favorite), and the light and crispy seafood lumpia; pupus run from $5.99 to $7.99. Most entrees run from about $15 to $20, but stick to the low side of the menu and enjoy the delicious curried chicken or stir-fried chicken at $14.99; the BBQ chicken, teriyaki steak kebab, or machimahi macadamia at $15.99. No matter what you order, you get that delicious fruit bread, and a choice of fruit-filled papaya, Molokai fish soup, or a green salad with delicious dressings (try the papaya seed). Cooked banana comes along with your entree. Dessert features (wouldn't you know it—mango ice cream, mango cheesecake, and a mango trifle) that's banana cake layered with mango ice cream and strawberries. There's a special menu for children; this is one of those places where the whole family is welcome and will have a good time.

If you don't mind having dinner early, take advantage of the Sundowner Special offered between 4:30 and 6pm: Dishes like beef kebab, stir-fried chicken, and mahimahi Polynesian are available for $9.95. Free pupus are offered during the happy hour in the Long House Bar, also from 4:30 to 6pm.

Mango Jones is open daily, from 4:30pm until closing, with entertainment from 6pm. Light lunches were being contemplated at the time of this writing. Reservations advised: phone 667-6847.

AT WHALER'S VILLAGE

There's a salty but slick flavor to the handsome complex of shops and museum attractions at Maui's Whaler's Village, and you can be sure that old-time seamen never had food as good as you'll find in the village's restaurants. From the red and green umbrellas over the outdoor tables to the fully stocked deli case and banners inside, the flavor of **Ricco's Old World Delicatessen,** on the lower level of Whaler's Village, is definitely Italiano. Their sandwiches, generous and tasty, are served on French roll, deli rye, or whole wheat, with lettuce, tomato, Maui onion, Italian dressing, and pickle: You might have lean corned beef, picnic ham, rare roast beef, turkey breast, or veggie, at $4.75 Mama size, $5.25 Papa size. Oven-toasted specialties, like Ricco's Italian combo, deli club, and the "Kula Kraut" Reuben, are all one size, $5.75. Ricco's pizzas are fun, too (try the Aegean with feta cheese and Italian sausage, or the Hawaiian with pineapple and ham) for something different. Pasta dishes, $6.95 to $8.25, include an excellent veggie lasagne, and a regular one, too. Salads, homemade cannolis, cheesecake, and carrot cake for dessert, and a big selection of ice-cold beers, wines by the glass, carafe or bottle, plus espresso and cappuccino, add to the enjoyment. A fun place, good for a quick and tasty meal. Open daily from 11am to 10pm.

The **Rusty Harpoon** (tel. 661-3123) has been a Whaler's Village standby for many years: It's been totally renovated, with a handsome interior (green colors, beautiful woods, a view of the ocean as well as the kitchen from every table), and a new menu concept: "nouvelle California–Maui cuisine." And it's still known for excellent value for the dollar. Come for the Early Bird specials, nightly between 5 and 6pm, and for $10, you can have dishes like linguine with clam sauce, salsa chicken, prime ribs, or fresh fish of the day, including fresh vegetables and rice pilaf or pasta. Most regular dinner entrees range from $10.95 to $14.50, and that includes chicken piccata, stir-fried beef, shrimp scampi, chicken, fettuccine primavera, or four-cheese lasagne. Five fresh-fish dishes are offered every night. Rusty's still has its famous half-pound burgers at $7.50 and $7.95, and there are some super salads—shrimp Louie, chicken walnut, fresh fruit, three-salad taster—from $7.95 to $8.95. Appetizers have an international flavor, from fried mozzarella to kalbi to pizzas to nachos and sashimi and sushi. Rusty's uses only fresh local produce, rolls its own sushi, and makes its own pastas and wonderful fresh island desserts. Of course those famous fresh-fruit daiquiris (how about banana or pineapple?) are still there and still called the "finest in the Western world." There's a full bar, a lively crowd, lots of fun.

Rusty's serves breakfast from 8 to 10:45am, lunch from 11:30am to 3pm, dinner from 5 to 10pm. And, oh yes, that sunset over the ocean is terrific! You'll find another Rusty Harpoon in Kona, on the Big Island.

Is **Chico's Cantina** (tel. 667-2777) the best Mexican restaurant in Maui? Our local friends rave about this place, and we can see why. It's got a great tropical atmosphere, open-air yet protected from the elements, with white adobe walls, colorful Mexican hangings, heavy wooden furniture; the service is friendly; the food is both imaginative and delicious, and served in generous portions; and the price is right. Combination plates, for example, which include rice and beans, are $9.50 to $9.95. House specials, accompanied by soup or salad, run from $11.95 to $16.95. Some of the specials include fresh fish in an imaginative presentation, with chile orange butter and a blue corn seafood enchilada; lobster enchiladas; and a unique southwestern sampler, which includes shrimp guayamas, blue corn duck taco, and stuffed California chile served with sweet peppers. Start your meal with some nifty nachos, end with flan or "el hula pie." Carmelita's Taco Bar is fun; it has its own tortilla machine and lots of specials. Chico's Cantina has a large seating capacity, so even waiting is comfortable. A *simpático* choice. Lunch is on from 11:30am to 2:30pm, dinner from 5 to 10:30pm, cocktails from 11:30am, and the Taco Bar is open from 11:30am to midnight.

Yami's Soft Frozen Yogurt, with a few outside tables to sit at on the lower level of Whaler's Village, is fine for a quick bite. Relax with one of their yogurt shakes like the Queen's Quencher, yogurt plus lemon and coconut, $2.45; or snack on a papaya stuffed with yogurt and topped with fruit, $2.99; or try one of their good sandwiches—tuna, avocado, raw milk cheese, and egg salad—served on cracked-wheat bread with tomato and alfalfa sprouts, for $2.95 to $3.25. Their cheesecake frozen yogurt is a winner.

The only restaurant we know of with its own pool, right on a glorious beach, is **El Crabcatcher** at Whaler's Village. This is a glamorous place, with dinner too pricey for us, but you can make do at lunch with sandwiches starting at $5.95. Sit at an outside table, relax, have a drink and pupus, and enjoy a swim in the pool or ocean.

AT KAHANA

The **Longshot Bar & Broiler,** formerly the Kahana Keyes Restaurant, is still a big favorite in the Kahana area. It's located in the Valley Isle Condominium, three miles north of the Kaanapali area (tel. 669-8071). People like it because it has one of the best salad bars in the area (reputed to be Maui's largest), as well as Early Bird dinners (from 5 to 7pm) at $8.95; entrees change nightly. The regular menu features seafood (including lobster) and steaks, with prices from about $12 to $20. The Longshot Challenge, a 64-oz. New York steak, is free, provided you can eat it all! The restaurant is open for breakfast and lunch from 8am to 3pm, dinner from 5 to 10pm every night. There's usually live entertainment and dancing.

IN HANA

Outside of the famed—and very expensive—Hotel Hana-Maui, there are very few public restaurants in Hana. The best place for a reasonable lunch (or breakfast) is **Tutu's,** which has been holding forth at Hana Bay for many years. Tutu's specializes in local-style plate lunches for around $5, plus very good fresh-fruit salads, green salads, sandwiches, ice cream, and such. You can call them at 248-8224 to order a picnic lunch.

The Hana Ranch Restaurant (tel. 248-8255), a bit away from the Hotel Hana-Maui, but still in the same Hana Ranch complex, is a medium-priced choice, with an indoor dining room that features a nice buffet lunch at $8.95; it's served from 11:30am to 3pm. A takeout counter serves up burgers, sandwiches, hot dogs, and the like, from 6:30am to 4pm.

The Hotel Hana-Maui is wonderful, but forget about dinner here until you strike it rich—it's prix fixe at $55.

3. The Night Scene

IN KAHULUI

Nightlife is relatively limited in this area. Your best bet, as usual, is in the big hotels. On Friday and Saturday, from 8pm to midnight, you can dance to Top 40s rock and contemporary music at the East West Dining Room of the **Maui Palms Hotel**. . . . At the Red Dragon Room of the **Maui Beach Hotel**, the mood is more mod than Hawaiian: a DJ keeps the crowd happy Friday and Saturday from 10pm to 2am. . . . **Luigi's Pasta and Pizzeria** at the Maui Mall is always a popular place at night. There's ladies' disco dancing on Wednesday from 10pm to 1am, Thursday night disco dancing from 10pm to 1am and Karaoke singing Sunday and Monday nights from 9 to 11:30pm and Friday and Saturday nights from 9pm to midnight. (In case you hadn't heard, Karaoke is a Japanese craze of singing along live to a video background that's becoming big in Hawaii.) Luigi's also has an Aloha Friday lunch every week, from 11:30am. . . . Check the shopping centers for free Polynesian shows, presented several times a week. Maui Mall, for one, sometimes presents top revues from Honolulu clubs—free.

IN LAHAINA

Lahaina at night is the place for the drinking set, with no shortage of swinging bars. The **Pioneer Inn**, a must for sunset watching and "characters," is the center of much activity; there's a big drinking scene at its Old Whaler's Grog Shop and Harpooner's Lanai, and on Friday and Saturday nights there is entertainment and dancing at its South Seas Patio. . . . The **Whale's Tale Restaurant** on Front Street always attracts a lively crowd. Beer from $2.75, plus good burgers and sandwiches around $9.95. **Moose McGillicuddy's Pub & Café** is the place for a young crowd who love their rock 'n' roll. There's a 4 to 8pm happy hour every day, special prices on Tijuana Tuesdays, Ladies' Night on Thursdays, videos every night, and on Friday and Saturday, live bands from 9:30pm until closing. . . . Count on good jazz at **Blackie's Bar**, Monday, Wednesday, Friday, and Sunday from 5 to 8pm. . . . Prices are low at the late-night happy hour at **Kobe Japanese Steak House**, from 10pm to 2am.

Should you be in the mood for a luau, we can't think of a nicer one than the **Old Lahaina Luau**, right out on beach behind Whaler's Marketplace at 505 Front St. (tel. 667-1998). This is a smaller and more personal, old-time luau than many of the slick hotel presentations: *Maui Magazine* called it "the best on the island." And the setting, on the grounds of Kamehameha's royal compound, is picture perfect: you dine as the sun sets over the water, watch the traditional hulas of Hawaii by starlight. There is an open bar. After—or before—the luau, check out the native crafts at the **Old Lahaina Luau Gallery;** guests receive 20% discounts. The luau is held Tuesday through Saturday evenings at 5:30pm at a cost of $42 for adults, $21 for those 12 and under. Phone for reservations.

Even if you don't get to the luau, you should stop in at the **Old Lahaina Café**, which overlooks the ocean and the luau grounds. Run by the same management, it's Maui's only full-time Hawaiian-music nightclub, and features local musicians as well as recording artists like Teresa Bright, Kekua Fernandez, Kawaii Cockett, and Hawaiian Heart. They have great tropical drinks for $4, a variety of pupus and authentic Hawaiian food—luau plate, teriyaki beef plate, mahimahi plate, even fruit in a pineapple boat, and a chicken macadamia-nut-salad sandwich—reasonably priced from $5.50 to $6.25. No cover, no minimum, and open until 2am.

IN KIHEI AND WAILEA

The place to dance in the Kihei area is at the **Rainbow Lagoon Restaurant** at the top of the Rainbow Mall, where pianist Dennis Manawaiti and guitarist Miles Yoshida keep the crowds happy at the piano and organ bar, from 6:30pm on. Then, from 11pm on to the wee hours, it's video disco. **Luigi's Pizzeria and Pasta** at Azeka Place is a popular place to dance to live music and disco on Friday and Saturday; other nights, it's Karaoke.

You can take your choice of luaus in this area: famed island entertainer Jesse Nakaoka presents **Luau Polynesia,** one of the best shows in the islands, at 145 S. Kihei Rd. (tel. 879-7227 for reservations) on Sunday, Wednesday, and Friday at 5:30pm. The price is $39 for adults, $20 for children under 12 (free under 3). . . . There's another super luau at the **Maui Lu Resort** on Saturday at $32 for adults, $19 for children (reservations: 879-5881). . . . If it's Monday or Thursday, it must be the luau at **Stouffer Wailea Beach Resort,** a traditional Hawaiian luau held in a beachfront garden setting and featuring "Memories of the Pacific." Luau time is 6pm; adults pay $38, children under 12, $21 (for reservations, phone 879-4900).

At the same time Stouffer Wailea Beach Resort, the Lost Horizon nightclub offers disco entertainment Thursday through Saturday. There is a $3 cover charge Friday and Saturday for nonhotel guests. Live Hawaiian entertainment at the Sunset Terrace very night: Sunday and Monday, 5:30 to 10pm; Tuesday through Saturday, 5:30 to 8pm.

Note: Check local listings when you arrive: prices, days, and entertainers change frequently.

AT KAANAPALI BEACH

More fun and games await you at the big beach hotels at Kaanapali. One of the greatest shows in town takes place every night at the **Sheraton Maui,** and it costs absolutely nothing to be in the audience. As the sun begins to set over the water, torches are lit all the way to the point. A native Hawaiian boy stands atop Black Rock (that eerie perch from which the souls of the dead were supposed to depart to the other world), throws his leis into the water, and then looks down some 20 feet or so to the waiting ocean below. The crowd—on the beach, lining the lobby floors—holds its breath. He plunges in, surfaces, and the evening festivities are underway.

If you need something to steady your nerves after that spectacle, make your way to the nautically decorated **"On the Rocks" Bar.** The ship models, volcanic rock floor-to-ceiling columns, and the tables with compass designs are all unusual and handsome, but somehow we never notice anything except the view; from the crest of this black-lava cliff overlooking the sea it's a spectacular one, a must for us collectors of Hawaiian sunsets.

Choosing among all the luau and dinner shows in the Kaanapali area can be difficult: all of them are good, none is inexpensive (most run about $40).

The Royal Lahaina Luau at the **Royal Lahaina Resort** is considered one of the best; it's presented nightly, September through May, at 5:30pm, June through August at 6pm, costs $38 for adults, $18 for children 12 and under (tel. 661-3611 for reservations). . . . *Drums of the Pacific* at the **Hyatt Regency Maui** is one of the few to offer a cocktail show: the $24 tab includes a mai tai and a souvenir lei, tax, tip, and a chance to see a spectacular production of Pacific dancing (Samoan slap dances, Tahitian drum dances and shimmies, spear and knife dances, fire dances, etc.). The dinner show is $42 for adults, $34 for children 6 to 12, free under 5. Call Hyatt at 667-4420 for reservations.

For us, just walking around the Hyatt is another kind of show: Its displays of Asian art, gracefully situated throughout the public areas, are worthy of any fine museum. Be sure to stroll the grounds, too, of its exquisite next-door neighbor, the **Marriott Resort.** Friday night is a good time to come by: A Hawaiian buffet is held from 5 to 9pm, with an Imu Ceremony at 4pm, $17.50 for adults, $7.50 for those under 12. Stop to sit in the Marriott lobby and you can enjoy the sounds of music coming from the lobby bar, where Lauren Nakano and her Karaoke machine are featured Tuesday to Saturday nights, 7 to 11 or 11:30pm. For something a bit more organized, try the Banana Moon nightclub here; it's Maui's only video disco and one of the hottest nightspots for dancing and mingling. The two-level club with in-house DJ, a state-of-the-art video system, and backgammon tables allows you to enjoy the music on the dance floors and conversation in the surrounding cocktail areas. Disco is on from 9pm to 2am. An attractive crowd enjoys the good pupus, good conversation, live music (and comfortable seating, as well) at the over-the-water, open-air Makai Bar.

Need a laugh? Then try the Lobby Bar of the **Maui Marriott,** which presents stand-up comics, imported from Honolulu's popular Comedy Club, on Fridays at 8pm. Tickets are $10.

The Kaanapali Beach Hotel's Tiki Terrace, located oceanfront on Kaanapali Beach, hosts a hula show nightly from 6:30 to 7:30pm, and it is 100% free: no cover, no minimum, no anything. Hooray! Preceding the hula show is a torchlighting cere-mony in the courtyard area. On Friday nights, Kaanapali Beach Hotel hosts a luau with a price of $37.50 adult, $18.75 children 5 to 12; children under 5, free.

There's always music at the Colonnade Lounge of the **Westin Maui;** guitarists Sam and Conrad Ahia play Tuesday through Saturday from 9 to 11pm, Felipe and Keoki are heard on Sunday and Monday. . . . At the same Westin Maui, fans of Ha-waiian music gather from 2 to 5pm every day at the Beach Bar, a cocktail lounge perched atop the central island of the hotel pool. Pohaku is the featured performer, Monday through Friday, other performers on Saturday and Sunday. . . . Another popular Hawaiian artist is Hapa, who performs both traditional Hawaiian and con-temporary music poolside at El Crab Catcher at **Whaler's Village,** Sunday, Monday, and Thursday, 5 to 7pm.

Another of Maui's best entertainment happens to be free. It's the presentation of **Hula Kahiko O Hawaii** at The Shops at Kapalua, every Thursday morning at 10. Unlike most hulas done in commercial shows, these are the authentic ancient dances of Hawaii, presented by a local hula halau (school), with Kumu Hula Cliff Ahue re-lating enchanting stories of Hawaii's history and ancient religion. It's all done in the spirit of Tutu Inez Ashdown, a great lady who originated these programs and is Maui County's historian emeritus. Local friends call this one of the best-kept secrets on the island!

IN MAKAWAO

Maui's cowboy town, Makawao, has suddenly become an entertainment ven-ue, with the opening of **Casanova Restaurant.** Weekends one might see jazz greats like Mose Allison and other mainland entertainers ($4 cover); on Wednesday and Thursday, it's disco dancing with a live DJ from 10pm to 1am. And there's music to dine by from 7 to 9pm most nights (for information, phone 572-4978). **Polli's Can-tina** in Makawao (tel. 572-7808) often has entertainment, as well.

READERS' HOTEL AND RESTAURANT SELECTIONS ON MAUI: "Thank you for your recommendation of the **Noelani Condominiums.** This place is real heaven for a family looking to relax on the beach. We rented a three-bedroom and two-and-a-half-bath duplex overlooking Molokai and Lanai for only $145 a day. The rooms are beautifully decorated and have fully equipped kitchens. Adjacency to the two pools, swimming beach, and the use of three barbe-cues helped make our stay all the more enjoyable. The managers, Donna and John Lorenz, keep everything immaculate and are very friendly (yes, they did have a mai-tai party poolside for guests). There is a homey, family atmosphere here. The place is terrific!" (Michael P. Gaertner, Huntington, N.Y.).. . . "I booked six days at the **Lihi Kai Cottages** based on the information I received in your book. Maui itself was exquisite, but the accommodations at the Lihi Kai were fantastic. The cottage was clean, well kept, within half a block of the beach, conveniently lo-cated and, most importantly, the owners (the Fullers) were friendly, helpful, and contributed to making my stay most memorable. There is no doubt in my mind that when I return to Maui (and I will), I will stay at the Lihi Kai. Thank you for recommending such a fantastic accommo-dation" (Rita K. Borzillo, Esq., West Chester, Pa.).

"We stayed in Kihei at a cottage near the road and found the noise from constant traffic overwhelming. With the massive construction going on in Wailea, in a few years it will take 15 or 20 minutes to cross S. Kihei to get to the beach! However, the first part of our trip spent at the cottages at Waianapanapa State Park were incredible! I hesitate to mention this as I want to keep them the way they are—private and incredibly wonderful" (Bette and Tom DuBay, Santa Rosa, Calif.).

"We stayed at the **Lahaina Shores,** in our opinion a perfect spot because you can walk to town if you wish, but have peace and quiet, a fantastic view, beautiful gardens, kitchen facilities, and a friendly staff. We got an unexpected weekly rate which made our stay (a repeat visit) even more enjoyable. Staying here, we were able to watch the Old Lahaina Luau almost every night and we agree, it is the best. Not the usual commercial offering, but varied, and exciting to watch. Best of all, if you don't have the $40 you can stand on the beach and watch. The dancers come right on to the beach as they go to the platform, and with the torches lighting up the beach, it is quite something to see. We have been to luaus throughout the islands and thought this one the best so far" (Elizabeth Lundh, North Vancouver, B.C., Canada). [*Authors' Note:* See text for details on Lahaina Shores and Old Lahaina Luau.]

"**The Chart House** in Lahaina, is not to be missed! It was simply wonderful—service excellent, food delicious, atmosphere tops!" (Sue Tamny, Hersham, Pa.). [*Authors' Note:* We agree. It's a great place. The Chart House is at 1450 Front St., specializes in steak and seafood, and serves dinner daily from 5pm, tel. 661-0937. Dinner should run about $20 or more. There's another Chart House in Kahului, tel. 877-2476.]

"As a 14-year resident of Lahaina, I hope you'll find these comments useful. The (French) **Country Kitchen** in Lahaina Square has complete dinners at $13.95, and an excellent à la carte menu, from $5.95 to $7.95. Both lunch and dinner are offered. . . . **Take Home Maui** handles shipping fruit, but has a great sandwich deli with exotic fruits. Very inexpensive and only four outdoor tables. It's on Dickenson Street, near Front Street. . . . The Haliimaile General Store in Haliimaile has upbeat food and is considered a top restaurant by Maui restaurant owners. Open for lunch and dinner" (Robin Ritchee, Lahaina, HI).

"I made reservations at the **Luana Kai,** and my husband originally had some doubts, but after we checked in, all his misgivings disappeared. Our oceanfront condo had lovely decor, a full kitchen and two full bedrooms and baths. One night with the trade winds coming in the open windows and the ceiling fans on convinced us we wouldn't miss the air conditioning. The Luana Kai has everything a vacationer could want. We were able to truly relax and enjoy our stay. Staying in a condo is the only way to go—we ate dinner out only once (which was disappointing), preferring to cook out on the barbecue grills provided. A real money saver, and you're guaranteed to enjoy your dinner" (Carol and John Slupski, Lincoln Park, Mich.).

"I have to recommend the **Kaanapali Beach Hotel** to anyone who can afford it. They had some vacancies when we checked in and gave us a deluxe room even though a less expensive room had been reserved and paid for. The view was absolutely gorgeous—just what you dream about. The courtyard is pretty just to wander through, and the snorkeling was also pretty good, considering there were no rocks where fish are usually found" (Carol Robinson, Lubbock, Tex.).. . . "**Mana Kai Maui** at Kihei is one of the best places we have ever visited. It has a terrific location and is kept up in great condition" (Jim and Deb Phillips, Hastings, Neb.).. . . "We spent a week at **Noelani** in the Kahana area, mentioned in your book. All units are oceanfront. Our two-bedroom, two-bath apartment was beautifully furnished and the view was breathtaking. There is nothing more peaceful than falling asleep listening to the sound of the surf. We highly recommend Noelani; it is quiet and so relaxing" (Rebecca Areford, San Diego, Calif.).

"Our big find was **Hana Kai Holidays,** Box 536, Hana (toll free 800/548-0478 or locally, 248-7742), which has several small guesthouses. On a two-day notice in February, we got a very clean, comfortable and basic twin-bedded room with a spotless bath shared by two other rooms for $35 a night. The guesthouses are within easy walking distance of the beach and the Hana Maui big splurge inn. . . . Makawao has our all-time-great cheap eats. At **Kitada's,** a place where the locals eat, you can get a clean, simple booth, a friendly proprietor and really good Japanese-style food such as a $3 steak teriyaki lunch plate, including rice and a cucumber-like salad. Sandwiches are around $2. Two of us ate well one lunchtime for a total of $6" (Lois-ellin Datta, Bethesda, Md.). [*Authors' Note:* See text for details on Hana Kai Holidays.]

"**Kaia Ranch** was a delightful 'real old Hana' experience—very clean and well kept" (Mark Bendich, Washington, D.C.). [*Authors' Note:* Kaia Ranch is a 27-acre flower and fruit farm that welcomes guests to share its ranch house; guests have the use of a large, enclosed patio, furnished with a queen-size bed and two twins, and share the bath with the hosts, John and JoLoyce Kaia, a friendly and generous couple. Johnny is active in the local rodeo: JoLoyce loves to share local tips. No electricity, just old-fashioned kerosene lamps, plenty of dogs, cats, and horses on the property. Smoking permitted only on the outside lanai. Adults only, two-night minimum. Included in the fee of $50 single or double, $90 for two couples, is a big breakfast. Write to Kaia Ranch & Co., P.O. Box 404, Hana, Maui, HI 96713, or phone 248-7725.]

"**Hong Kong Restaurant** in Kihei is cheery and reasonable. They will cook to order, and

I had my shrimp and broccoli prepared with garlic hot sauce ($7.65), while my partner enjoyed beef with snowpeas ($6.25). Both were delicious. With tastes developed in New York's China-town, we will always remember the Hong Kong when we're up for tasty Chinese fare in Maui" (Ronald P. Marsh, Newport, R.I.).

"Our best bet for food in Maui was the **Safeway Supermarket** at The Cannery Shop-ping Center, combined with an efficiency lodging, with refrigerator and cooking facilities. On the way back from Hana, Paia is worth a stop. **Mama's Fish House** at top dollar is Beverly Hills atmospheric. You can get a quiet table in the corner and still see the windsurfers at an early dinner. In Makawao, **Polli's** Mexican food was outstanding and provided generous, inexpen-sive servings. Polli's is where all the locals go" (Michael and Arlene Goldstone, Merrick, N.Y.). . . . "**Swan Court** in the Hyatt Regency at Kaanapali is by far the most delightful place for 'the big splurge.' The restaurant is open to a pond/garden setting with black and white swans glidding by, service is very attentive, and food is excellent. Most entrees are in the $20 to $35 range, and there is a huge dessert buffet at dinner. Breakfast is also served here, buffet style, as well as from menu selections. Swan Court accepts reservations until 5pm at 661-1234, ext. 420, and after 5pm at ext. 4455. However, hotel guests have first priority on reservations be-tween 7 and 9, so it's easier for 'outsiders' to get reservations between 6 and 7 or after 9pm. . . . **La Bretagne** off Front Street serves very good French food in a charming garden atmosphere and takes reservations at 661-8966. . . . In Lahaina, our favorite was the **Oceanhouse**, right on the harbor at 831 Front St. (661-3359), which serves breakfast, lunch, and dinner. We espe-cially enjoyed dinners with fresh seafood. The catch of the day prepared Créole style was excellent, as were both the blackened fish and steak. No reservations accepted. . . . We figured out how to beat the system at the **Chart House,** which serves a terrific dinner, but never takes reservations. Put your name down on their list and then go shopping in Lahaina; they'll let you know when to be back. . . . We have stayed at **Kahana Village** five times. The units are very spacious and well appointed. When two couples share a two-bedroom unit, the rate is quite reasonable in today's world, or if three couples share a three-bedroom unit. Kahana Village also attracts families and, unless you are terribly fond of children, should be avoided during school holiday periods" (Bob Harrison and Hal Goodstein, Provincetown, Mass.). [*Authors' Note:* Kahana Village is a beautiful oceanfront resort located on a sandy beach. Off-season rates for two-bedroom apartments are $140 ocean view, $170 oceanfront; three-bedroom apartments are $185 ocean view, $250 oceanfront. Address: 4531 Honoapiilani Rd., Lahaina, Maui, HI 96761. Call toll free 800/824-3065.]

"We went to Maui in November. We stayed at the **Maui Sands,** and it is everything you said it was and more. Our favorite restaurant in Lahaina was **Kimo's**—a splurge, but the food, service, and view were fantastic. We tried the Rainbow Buffet at the **Maui Beach Hotel** on our last day. It was all there for the taking, and did we ever take! Among the four of us, I think we managed to try everything. This is the best place to sample Asian dishes" (Don and Donna Hammons, Mesquite, Tex.). . . . "After some very windy days in Kihei (not typical, we were told), we moved on to the **Papakea Beach Resort** in Kaanapali for the remainder of our stay. It was everything we dreamed a vacation would be! We had a one-bedroom unit with a huge sleeping loft (really a two bedroom). Papakea is a vision of loveliness everywhere you look. The grounds are meticulously tended and filled with beautiful plantings. Other bonuses were two putting greens, two pools, two Jacuzzis, 'swimmercize' classes each morning, tennis clinics, and a rum-punch party by the pool with entertainment on Friday. This is a quiet, family-oriented resort, yet very close to the abundant restaurants, supermarkets, and shops of Kaanapali" (Frances S. Kielt, West Hartford, Conn.). [*Authors' Note:* Current rates would be about $122 in season, $110 in summer. Call toll free 800/367-5037 for information.]

"The overall price increase was more obvious on Maui than elsewhere, but we found the **Denny's** in Lahaina Square to be a treat. The decor is like no other Denny's seen by us across the country: lovely fans in motion, live plants on each table and in the rest room, along with attractive, framed prints and a decorated, vaulted ceiling. And I found a delicious pine-apple boat served with a choice of bread or crackers for $6.49. What an unexpected treat" (Elizabeth Greer, El Cerrito, Calif.). [*Authors' Note:* There's another excellent Denny's in Kihei, at Kamaole Shopping Center.]

. . . . "**The Bakery** in Lahaina, on the same street as the Lahaina-Kaanapali Railroad depot, has delicious blueberry or cinnamon-apple muffins. They are so huge you could make a meal of one of them. Their sticky buns, encrusted with pecans, go perfectly with a cup of fresh Kona coffee" (Deanne M. Miltoma, Sacramento, Calif.). [*Authors' Note:* Agreed. See text for details.] . . . . **Safeway,** behind Maui Mall in Kahului, had the best food prices on the entire island. Very clean, lots of fresh produce, a bakery, a deli. . . . We highly recommend **Napili Point**

Condos. Clean, spacious, well equipped, lovely grounds—and what an incredible view" (Ted and April Ziegenbusch, La Palma, Calif.).

"We loved the **Nona Lani Cottages.** When my wife mentioned to Mr. Kong that Oahu had been rather disappointing in regard to fruit—especially since in New York we can buy any type 24 hours a day—he immediately gave us a tour of the luscious garden and picked tamborines (a cross between an orange and a tangerine), cherry guavas (another fruit we didn't know of before), as well as regular guavas and lemons, which he allowed us to pick any time we felt like eating some. It was great. The atmosphere of the cottage was also just right and the location perfect—although the sound of the highway was a little bit disturbing at first, but soon absorbed by the sound of the breaking waves" (Isabel and Horst Cerni, New York, N.Y.).

"We were totally delighted with **Shores of Maui** in the Kihei area. We were greeted by a very pleasant resident manager who led us to our beautiful apartment. It was not only beautifully decorated, but equipped beyond what we expected. Microwave oven, even a cooler for picnic lunches. A lovely lanai for breakfast and dinner overlooking the pool area. Everyone was in agreement that Shores of Maui had everything, including a central location for sightseeing. At $55 per night—unbelievable!" (Mrs. Donald Phillips, Drexel Hill, Pa.). [*Authors' Note:* See text for details on Shores of Maui.]

"We highly recommend the **Napili Bay,** close to Kaanapali Beach and Lahaina. These are studio apartments with one queen-size bed and two singles and kitchen; they are reasonably priced. We had clean, fresh linens each day, including beach towels; the rooms are not air-conditioned, but have adjustable shutters so you can feel the incredibly refreshing trade winds and hear the ocean at night. It cost us $50 for groceries for two people for a week and we ate well. Efficiencies are great! The owners were like grandparents to us, extremely friendly and accommodating" (Francine Schept, White Plains, N.Y.). [*Authors' Note:* Napili Bay's address is 33 Hui Dr., Lahaina, Maui, HI 96761 (tel. 669-6044).]

"The **Aloha Cottages** that you mention in Hana are wonderful. When we arrived, Mr. Nakamura gave us a basket of local fruits. He immediately suggested some good places to see in the area. He is also the barber in Hana, and I got a good haircut for $3.50 and learned all about Hana from him: He has lived here 30 years. We highly recommend it. Be sure to ask Mr. Nakamura how to get to the secluded *red sand* beach in Hana" (Peter Sinclaire, New Britain, Conn.).. . . "I want to thank you for listing Mr. Nakamura's Aloha Cottages at Hana. We had not even unpacked before he shinned up a papaya tree and plucked the ripe fruit for our pleasure. We stayed in his larger cottage and can hardly express the feeling. It is large, and as the old saying goes, 'you could eat off the floors'—and I really mean it. The furnishings are spare, but it is one of the most peaceful places we have ever stayed. One could easily stay a week instead of just overnight" (Bart and Lynda Esterly, Capistrano Beach, Calif.).

"I called **Maui Sands** on their toll-free number (tel. 800/367-5037) because their rates were among the best in the Kaanapali area. And I thought I'd ask them if they had a discount rate for clergy. As it turned out, they gave me a 20% discount. Other clergy would, I'm sure, be glad to know this" (Rev. Bob Waliszewski, no address given).. . . "We discovered why **condos** are so much cheaper than hotels; their services are meager. Maid service is usually every other day. It is harder to obtain touring advice and assistance than in a full-service hotel. We recommend that first-timers stick to hotels, unless they have their trip very well planned" (Jeff and Chris Jacobsen, Rinton, Wash.).. . . "Your readers may be interested in hearing about the cabin at **Poli Poli Springs State Park,** on the slopes of Haleakala at 6,472 feet. The cabin is in a heavily wooded camping area—there are even redwoods—and the view, of central and western Maui, as well as Molokai and Lanai, is outstanding. The park is crisscrossed with miles of hiking trails, some of which lead to Haleakala Crater. The cabin has three bedrooms and will sleep up to ten. There is some furniture, a wood heating stove, a gas cooking range, complete cooking utensils, and bedding. There is no electricity. For information and reservations, write or call the State Department of Land and Natural Resources, Division of State Parks, P.O. Box 1049, Wailuku, Maui, HI 96793 (tel. 244-4354)" (Roberta Rosen, Long Beach, Calif.). [*Authors' Note:* A campground for tent camping is also available, free of charge; reservations are required.]

SEEING MAUI

Three or four days are the absolute minimum for savoring the varied charms of Maui, figuring one day in the **Kahului-Wailuku** and **Kihei-Wailea** areas, and **Haleakala,** another at **Lahaina** and **Kaanapali** in western Maui, and a third day for the trip to and from **Hana.** And this is going at a pretty rugged pace. If you can manage a few more days, we strongly urge you to do so. It's so pleasant to relax here after you've seen the sights. *Note:* Excellent maps are available in the *Maui Drive Guide,* which your car-rental company will give you free.

1. Kahului-Wailuku and Kihei-Wailea

THE KAHULUI AREA
Kahului is too new to have any historic sights, but it's considered a good example by city planners of what a model city should be. You can spend a pleasant hour or so browsing through its shopping centers. Maui's biggest shopping complex, **Kaahumanu Shopping Center,** was opened a few years back, and a better name for it might be Ala Moana No. 2. Like its Honolulu counterpart, it has **Sears** at one end, **Liberty House** at the other, and that fascinating Japanese department store, **Shirokiya,** in between. Most of the 50-odd stores here are geared to local residents, but there are a few places catering to gift buyers. Our favorite of these is **Maui's Best,** a store which features crafts and candy made on Maui. Lovely craft items include handmade jewelry, potpourri oils and creams, koa-wood carvings, Christmas tree ornaments, children's clothing, great hand-painted T-shirts, sweatshirts silk-screened with Japanese prints, all reasonably priced. They also have coffees, teas, and delicious Island Princess candies; be sure to sample the chocolate-covered Kona coffee beans, and the cooling sherbet drops. Texas customers swear the macadamia-nut popcorn and macadamia-nut brittle is even better than the kind at Neiman-Marcus! . . . **The Coffee Store** is always fun, with a large roaster and sacks of coffee up front, every kind of coffee and coffee accessories to buy, and a neat little coffee bar and café area, with tables and bakery selections in back: café mocha, cappuccino, filled croissants, bagels, quiches, and lasagne, from $1.75 to $4. Among the attractive gift

items here, huge Hawaiian quilted potholders at $13. . . . You can get island Asian prints by the yard, well priced, at **Sew Special,** which also has some wall hangings that would make neat gifts. . . . Kids and hobbyists will enjoy **Kay-Bee Toys,** a very large shop with good values. . . . **Hopaco,** a well-known stationery shop, is the place to pick up the "Mauiopolo" game. . . . You might find some saké cups to take home with you, or charming Hakata dolls, at **Shirokiya,** which also has those wonderful sushi take-out lunches we've told you about in the preceding chapter. . . . In case you haven't sampled crackseeds yet, **Camellia Seeds** is the place.

It's also fun to visit the **Maui Mall,** a busy scene with its frequent sidewalk sales and entertainment. . . . You can get some good buys in muumuus and aloha shirts too, at **Island Muumuu Works.** This is a wholesale outlet for Hilda of Hawaii (there are several stores in Honolulu), and most of the beautiful, first-quality muumuus are just $43. Lace muumuus are $55 to $65, aloha shirts are $20.50. Alterations can be done for a very nominal fee. What a treat! They also carry handsome tote bags, with patterns on both sides, by Mauheali'i of Honolulu; the one with a breadfruit quilting pattern, red on white, is particularly striking, $20. Although this company has another store in Lahaina (at 180 Dickenson Square), you'd be wise to make purchases here instead, as they will do alterations at a nominal charge. . . . Children's clothing is very special at **Baby's Choice,** which also carries bedding, cribs, and furniture, in addition to darling items like tiny happi coats for little girls. . . . **Allison's Place** and **WOW! Swimwear** feature youngish sportswear. . . . **JR's Music Shop** has some very good selections. . . . **Long's Drugs** offers some of the best values for souvenirs and sundry items. . . . And you can stock up on groceries at **Star Super Market,** where the locals shop; if you're going to be cooking in your kitchenette apartment, it pays to stop here after getting off the plane before driving on to the more expensive resort areas. . . . You can pick up a T-shirt that reads "Just Mauied" at the **T-Shirt Factory.** . . . **Roy's Photo Center** probably has the most complete supply of camera accessories and films on Maui. . . . **Sir Wilfred's Coffee, Tea, Tobacco Shop** has more than its name implies; in addition to a great selection of pipes, cigars, tobacco, and coffee beans, it also has gourmet gifts and gadgets, plus an espresso bar, a full bar, and a delightful menu of light foods at **Sir Wilfred's Espresso Caffè.** They always have tasteful handmade ceramic mugs, from about $7. . . . Stop in at **Waldenbooks** if you've run out of reading material, and at **Maui Natural Foods** for anything and everything in the health-food line; it is the most complete store of its kind in the area.

Woolworth's has an inexpensive coffee shop here, **Dave's** is great for exotic ice-cream flavors, and **Luigi's** has pizza and pizzazz. Free entertainment is held here often; check the local papers for announcements.

Another good stop on anybody's itinerary is at **Airport Flower & Fruit,** 460 Dairy Rd. (first stop sign from the airport on Hwy. 38). Visit this one just before you get on the plane to leave Maui, or better still, phone the owner, a delightful lady named Mrs. Sally Anne Goodness (honest!), at 871-7056, tell her what flowers and fruits and other goodies you want to take home with you, and she will have everything ready, efficiently boxed and certified for export. All you do is carry it on the plane. Her prices are surprisingly low, her range of products wide—anything from sweet Maui onions to pineapples to candies to mustards to cut flowers and orchid plants—and her service most helpful. We also spotted small gift items here at prices lower than elsewhere, as well as beautiful leis at $5.95 (at the airport, similar ones were going for $9.95). When you're thinking about Christmas presents, remember that Sally Anne welcomes mail orders, too: Airport Flower & Fruit, 460 Dairy Rd., Kahului, Maui, HI 96732 or phone toll free, 800/922-9352. Sally Anne now has a second location, at 640 Front St. in Lahaina (tel. 667-7463), where you can make your selections and arrange to have everything packed and delivered to the airport on the day of your departure.

Kahului also boasts the only deep-water harbor in Maui, a bulk-sugar loading plant, the cannery of the Maui Pineapple Company, and the Hawaiian Commercial and Sugar Company, the driving force behind the town's development (most of the homes belong to plantation workers). Out near the airport, at the **Kanaha Pond**

Waterfowl Sanctuary, you can see where migratory birds from our northwest mainland take their winter vacations.

THE WAILUKU AREA

Historic old Wailuku, the commercial and professional center and the seat of Maui County (which also includes Molokai and Lanai), is quite different from Kahului—even though it's right next door. It's a bit ramshackle, strictly local. Drive westward along Kaahumanu Avenue out of Kahului about three miles; you'll pass the Maui Professional Building at High Street on the right, and then, about one block further, to the left on Iao Road, you'll reach the **Bailey House Museum.** These buildings, on beautiful shaded grounds, once housed in the Wailuku Female Seminary (where young females could be kept safely "away from the contaminating influences of heathen society") and the home of Mr. Edward Bailey, the seminary instructor. Today they are full of fascinating bits of Hawaiiana, from ancient petroglyphs and necklaces of human hair worn by the alii of Maui to missionary patchwork quilts and furnishings. Dating back to 1833–1850, the building itself was completely restored in 1974–1975, and is an excellent example of Hawaiian quality work and Yankee ingenuity. This smaller building, once the dining room of the school and later Mr. Bailey's studio, has been restored as a gallery with rotating exhibits. The museum is open daily from 10am to 4:30pm. A donation of $2 for adults is appreciated.

Just off Kaahumanu Avenue, across from the Wailuku War Memorial on Kanaloa Street, you may want to make a stop at the **Maui Zoological and Botanical Garden.** Beautifully and lovingly maintained, the botanical garden contains an abundance of native Hawaiian plants, many of which can no longer be seen anywhere else. At the very front of the garden is the Maui Zoo, a new little zoo that has been stocked largely by its big sister, Honolulu Zoo. The majority of the collection consists of lovable farm animals—we like the noisy feral sheep or "hipa," as they're called here; there are also some very happy monkeys and a few tropical birds, notably peafowl and parrots. Admission is free.

Shopping in Wailuku is offbeat. Shops are unpretentious, not a bit touristy. Antique lovers will be in heaven at **Antique Row,** a cluster of shops and galleries on N. Market Street offering one-of-a-kind items from around the globe as well as from times gone by. Start at **Traders of the Lost Art** where, hopefully, you will find owner Tye Hartall, unless he happens to be on one of his yearly journeys to New Guinea to collect ancestral carvings and primitive ritual art. His shop is reminiscent of a New Guinea spirit house, complete with split drums, crocodile tables, and a host of spirit masks and figures. An appointment may be necessary: phone 242-7753.

Next door to Traders of the Lost Art, at 158 N. Market St., is **Memory Lane,** where Joe Ransberger shows the unusual and one-of-a-kind items he's collected from all over the world. We've seen rare Japanese netsukes, vintage aloha shirts, and lots more. At the far end of Antique Row, where Market Street dips toward Happy Valley, is **Able Antiques,** where proprietor Kyle Kinter shows period furniture, exotic jewelry, ethnic collectibles, fine porcelain and glass, signed prints and paintings. Adjacent to Able Antiques is Eddie Kirsch's **Wailuku Gallery,** which features original art by Maui artists. Noted artist Don Jusko is shown here exclusively. Across the street is **Alii Antiques,** 1608 N. Market St., known for its fine collection of Asian art from the Ming and Ch'ing dynasties, as well as items from Europe and the mainland. A recent browse turned up antique guns from the Civil War, Persian rugs, paintings by local artists. More antique and offbeat emporiums are in store for this neighborhood, so if antiques are your thing, be sure to save some time for exploring this area.

Miracles Unlimited, 81 Central Ave., is where you go if you're into matters spiritual and esoteric. The quaint little blue shop houses a nice collection of metaphysical books, tapes, crystals, cards, and such, and some very beautiful crystal jewelry creations. They also show art-to-wear clothing by local craftspeople (from

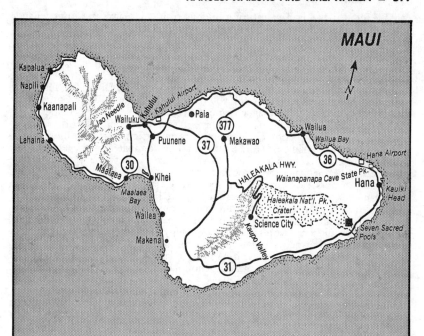

$30), and fine arts by such visionary artists as the Japanese painter Ki. Check the bulletin board and the free "Island Calendar of Events," published nearby by Alaya, to find out who's lecturing or giving a meditation workshop.

Now, if you need to stock up on local produce, natural foods, vitamins, and the like, you can do so at bargain prices at **Down to Earth Natural Foods** at 910 Vineyard St. Local folks praise their lunch special, which is served weekdays only, from 10am to 3pm. (The store is open daily.)

Did you know they brewed beer on Maui? If you'd like to try a free sample of Maui Lager, you may be able to stop in at the tasting room of the Pacific Brewing Company, located at the Millyard on Ima Kala St., in an industrial park in Wailuku. There are frequent tours, except on bottling days, so call first, 244-0396, for information and driving directions.

Not far from Wailuku, in the sugar-plantation village of Waikapu, you can sightsee, shop, eat, and have an educational experience—all under one roof (or better yet, one sky)—at **Maui Tropical Plantation.** Designed as a showplace and marketplace for the tropical agriculture of the islands, Maui Tropical Plantation does offer free admission to its official agricultural pavilions and exhibits. But you may want to hop aboard the Tropical Express ($8 for adults, $3 for kids) for a 45-minute tour that traverses some 50 acres planted in bananas, papayas, coffee, pineapple, macadamia nuts, sugarcane, and other crops. The tour leaves every 45 minutes starting at 9:15am until 4pm, daily. Then you'll want to visit the **Tropical Market,** where a huge variety of made-on-Maui products, plantation-grown fresh fruit, and gift items are available. (A mailing service makes this a convenient place for sending gifts back home.) Mailing service is also available at their Tropical Nursery, where you can get orchids, hibiscus, or anthuriums. And you may end up at the **Tropical Restaurant** for a buffet luncheon or à la carte service featuring sandwiches, fresh-fruit ice-cream sundaes, and banana cream pies. There's a Hawaiian Country Barbecue every Monday, Wednesday, and Friday, featuring Buddy Fo and his Hawaiian Country Band. The fun starts at 5:30pm, with beverages, square dancing, and a quick tram ride through the fields. Dinner is an all-you-can-eat Hawaiian country feast. Cost is $42 for adults, $21 for children. **Maui Tropical Plantation** is on Honoapiilani Hwy. at Waikapu, open daily from 9am to 5pm. Inquire about transportation available from Lahaina, Kaanapali, Kihei, and Kahului for the Hawaiian Country Barbecue.

Back to sightseeing: Continue on now in the direction of Iao Valley, and about two miles from Wailuku, on the right, you'll note a sign reading **"Black Gorge President Kennedy Profile."** The jagged mountain cliff ahead of you, which does bear a resemblance to JFK's profile, has been there for centuries, but not until relatively recently, of course, did people begin to notice its timely significance. In another mile you'll come to **Iao Valley,** a wildly beautiful gorge dominated by the **Iao Needle,** 2,250 feet of green-covered lava rock reaching straight up into the sky. In this dramatic setting, Kamehameha won the battle that was to give him the island of Maui; the local warriors, accustomed to spears and javelins, were no match for Kamehameha's forces supplied with cannon by two English sailors. The carnage was so intense that the waters of Iao Stream were dammed up by the bodies of the conquered, giving the stream its present name: Kepaniwai, damming of the waters. Now all is tranquil here, save for the shouts of happy keikis wading through the pools at **Kepaniwai Park,** where present-day Mauians love to go for a picnic or a swim. Beautifully landscaped gardens with Asian pagodas, swimming, and wading pools provide a palatial playground in this crisp mountain valley.

A SUGAR MILL MUSEUM, AND ON TO KIHEI AND WAILEA

If you're staying in Kahului, Kihei is your nearest beach, about a 20-minute drive, via Hwy. 350, and then Hwy. 311 right to Kihei. This is a good time to make a stop at the Alexander & Baldwin Sugar Museum, which is at 3957 Hansen Rd. in Puunene (Puunene is on Hwy. 311; look for the tall stacks of the sugar mill). This former residence of superintendents of the mill (still in operation next door) has been transformed into a tasteful museum with artifacts dating back to 1878, absorbing photo murals, and authentic scale models, which include a working model of sugar-factory machinery. Educational for the kids, entertaining for grown-ups, too. Be sure to visit the museum shop, with unique items relating to the sugar industry and plantation life, including contributions of the various ethnic groups who came to the islands to work the plantations. Open Monday through Friday from 9:30am to 4:30pm. Admission is $2 for adults, $1 for students 6 to 17, free for children under 6 (tel. 871-8058).

Back in the car, continue on Hwy. 311 until you see the signs for Kihei. Kamaole Beaches I, II, and III are fine, but the beach is public everywhere, and you can swim where you like. Look for **Azeka's Place,** a lively shopping center on the side of the road, and browse a bit. **Rainbow Connection,** is a tasteful boutique which, in addition to its many condo decorative items, has a unique jewelry collection: We admired the handmade, hand-painted porcelain jewelry (from $25 to $90), the earrings and necklaces made of Hawaiian volcanic glass (from $12 to $45), the brass shell items, and jewelry and hand-carved wooden mirrors from Bali. . . . Browse through a good selection of books at **Silversword Bookstore,** pick up some beachwear at **Leilani** or **Tropical Traders.**

You may want to stop in at **Vagabond,** where you cannot only rent a surfboard, but also stock up on bags, tank shirts, and all kinds of necessities for the beachcomber's life-style. . . . **Wow Swimwear** has something for "everybody." . . . **Maui Dive Shop** can outfit you for scuba or snorkeling and take you on a tour. . . . **O'Rourke's Tourist Trap** is a good place to get any necessities you forgot to pack, as well as postcards, monkeypod souvenirs, and the like. . . . Look to **Liberty House** for its usual excellent selections. . . . There are plenty of bathing suits and beach fashions at **Maui Clothing Company.** . . . And **Little Polynesians** is great for kid's stuff.

If you're really in a shopping mood, Kihei is the place. Shopping malls are going up here at a great rate; you'll see them as you drive along. Kukui Mall, one of the newest ones, is well worth a stop. Specialty boutiques include **The Cactus Tree** for sophisticated women's clothing, **Brass Gecko** for tasteful gift items and jewelry, and **Whale of a Shirt,** where they silk-screen T-shirts while you wait. **Breezy Bay** has fashionable women's sportswear, and **Ashante** has smart clothing for larger women. There's a large natural foods store here (not too easy to find in Maui) called **The Health Spot,** a branch of **Waldenbooks,** and a **Local Motion,** the surfing store. Lunch and snack possibilities include **Bonanza** for steak, salad, seafood, and such, and the popular **Subway** for sandwiches on bread and rolls baked right before your eyes.   *Note:* Check the local papers for news of the swap meet and flea market usually held on Saturday in the courtyard of St. Theresa's Church, near Azeka's Place on Kihei Road. Many local artisans take part. We saw some beautiful hand-painted blouses here for $17; the next day, we spotted them in a gift shop for $35! Hours are 7am to 3pm. . . . Pick up some Molokai watermelon, Hana sweet corn, or other locally grown produce at the **Maui Farmer's Market,** Tuesday and Friday from 2 to 5:30pm on the grounds of the Suda store. Cheeses, juices, and freshly baked breads are also available. (The farmer's market moves to Kahana, in West Maui, Monday and Thursday from 8am to 1:30pm).

Practically a farmer's market under one roof, the **Paradise Fruit Stand,** 1913 S. Kihei Rd., is a Maui tradition. Fresh produce is featured, plus good sandwiches and salads, smoothies, cakes, and cookies for your picnic lunch. They're open almost around the clock. A good place to buy local fruit for shipping back home. Check their bulletin board for news of local happenings.

The Wailea Shopping Village in this area is always worth a stop. Many artistic and cultural events are held here, free, and the shops are of high quality. Yes, there sometimes is a herd of elephants at **Elephant Walk.** Last time we were there, the cute creatures were made of clay and priced from about $35 up. **Lahaina Printsellers** shows their excellent collection of maps and prints here. **Maui's Best,** which we've told you about (above) at Kaahumanu Center in Kahului, has a location here, with a more extensive clothing collection (beautiful, but expensive). Other tasteful shops here include **Alexia Natural Fashions** (natural-fabric clothing from Greece, for women), and **Sea and Shell,** which has nicer-than-usual island gifts, with a good selection of wind chimes.

Drive a little further and you can explore the **Makena Resort Maui Prince Hotel,** very modern and elegantly understated. Two waterfalls run down into the central courtyard and lead to the Japanese rock garden. You may want to stop in at the Café Kiowai on the garden level for an exotic dessert (like macadamia-nut brittle flan) and a cup of coffee.

Ready to call it a day and relax on the beach? This area has some of Maui's best swimming spots. Look for the public-access sign that reads "Ulua/Mokapu Beaches" near the Stouffer Wailea Beach Resort, park your car (there's a small paved area), and head for a lovely stretch of sand and ocean, with public rest rooms and showers.

---

2. Haleakala, the House of the Sun

Any schoolchild on Maui can tell you the story of the demi-god Maui, the good-natured Polynesian Prometheus who gave man fire, lifted the Hawaiian Islands out of the sea on his fishhook, and trapped the sun in its lair until it agreed to move more slowly around the earth—so that his mother could have more time to dry her tapa before night came! And where did this last, most splendid achievement take place? Why, right at **Haleakala,** 10,023 feet up in the sky, just about the closest any Stone Age person—or god—ever got to the sun.

With or without benefit of legends, Haleakala is an awesome place. The world's largest dormant volcano (its last eruption occurred two centuries ago), its 33-mile-long, 24-mile-wide, 10,000-foot-high dimensions make Vesuvius seem like a mud puddle. Even more spectacular is the size of the volcano's crater: 7½ miles long, 2½ miles wide, big enough to swallow a modern metropolis or two within its moonlike desert. Haleakala is one of the great scenic wonders of Hawaii.

TO THE SUMMIT

Plan on at least three hours for the Haleakala excursion (37 miles from the airport each way) and bring a warm sweater or jacket with you (it gets surprisingly cold and windy two miles up). Note that anyone with a cardiac condition is advised not to make this trip because of the stress of the high altitude. We feel it's best to get an early start on this trip, since there's less likelihood of clouds early in the day. You might call the park headquarters (tel. 572-7749) to check on cloud, road, and weather conditions before you start out. There's no place to eat once you enter **Haleakala National Park,** but you might pack a picnic lunch and stop at Hosmer's Grove on the lower slopes. You can get sandwiches at **Subway,** in the **Pukalani Terrace Shopping Center,** in Pukalani, about halfway between Kahului and the park. You might also stop off at the **Pukalani Superette,** a real upcountry store, where you can get mangoes for about half of what they cost in town, plus delicious homemade sushi and lumpia, and local Japanese and Filipino delicacies. The drive starts in Kahului on Hwy. 32; head eastward to Haleakala Hwy. (Hwy. 36), on which you turn right. Shortly after Hwy. 36 swings left, it's intersected on the right by Hwy. 37, which takes you to Hwy. 377, the Upper Kula Road, where you head up into a cool forest of flowers, cactus, and eucalyptus.

Now watch for the turnoff to Hwy. 378 to the left, Haleakala Crater Road, a snaky two-lane highway curving through the clouds. You'll see cattle and horses on the pasture lands of Haleakala Ranch as you climb the slopes of the volcano. At 6,700 feet, you reach the entrance to Haleakala National Park. You'll then see **Hosmer's Grove** on the left, a scenic place to picnic (or camp) among rare trees and plants. Temperate tree seedlings from around the world have been planted here, along a half-mile trail of native shrubs and trees that are home for a variety of birds; you may see a pueo (short-eared owl) or a ring-necked pheasant. Stop at park headquarters a mile ahead at 7,030 feet, where the friendly and knowledgeable rangers will give you maps, instructions, directions for hiking the trails, and camping permits. Admission to the park is $3 per car and $1 for bicycles. Senior citizens admitted free. The choicest way to see Haleakala is to go into the crater on foot or horseback, but you must check with the rangers before you do.

Now you're ready for the ascent on this South Seas Everest, to the **Haleakala Observatory Visitors Center,** two miles up on the edge of the crater. Inside the octagonal observatory, you learn that the early Hawaiians used the crater as a highway across eastern Maui, camping in its caves and building rock shelters. The last eruption from the crater was prehistoric, although there was an eruption from the flanks of Haleakala just 200 years ago, and very likely the volcano will erupt again; it is dormant, not extinct. But the most thrilling show is what lies beyond the glass: a dark kaleidoscope of clouds and colors and light played against what might well be the deserts of the moon. On a clear day you can see over a hundred miles to the horizon, your field of vision encompassing 30,000 square miles of the Pacific; from this altitude, the volcano's vast cones look like so many sand dunes. Their rustlike colors change as the day grows old. At sunrise the crater is in shadow; it seems to give birth to the sun. From midday to sunset the play of sun and shadow is more subtle, and sunset, according to some, is the most muted and lovely of all. One of the easiest ways to get a spirited debate going among Mauians is to ask whether sunset or sunrise is more superlative at Haleakala; suffice it to say that both are considered among the great natural sights of the world.

The summit of Haleakala is a half-mile beyond, at **Red Hill,** atop a cinder cone 10,023 feet high. Nearby, there's a satellite-tracking station and a **Science City** complex (the clear air here in mid-Pacific permits research that could be done nowhere else), which you reach via the Skyline Drive.

On the way down from Haleakala, you should stop for some different—and spectacular—views of the crater at **Kalahaku** and **Leleiwi** lookouts. (Because of safety hazards, you cannot stop at these places on the drive uphill.) At Kalahaku, you view the vast crater on one side; on the other you'll spot western Maui and your first silverswords (unless you've seen some on the Big Island). The silversword is a botanical rarity, a plant that will grow only on lava rock, at the highest altitudes. These curious, oversize cousins of the sunflower have swordlike leaves, and when they're ready to blossom (between June and October) they shoot up a stalk the size of a man. The whole thing turns into a tower of pink and lavender flowers, blooms once, and dies, scattering its seeds into the cinders to begin the phenomenon all over again. At the next lookout, Leleiwi, you may, with great luck, get to see the rather spooky specter of the Brocken; the sun must be strong at your back with misty clouds overhead in order for you to see your own shadow in the rainbow-mist of the crater. It doesn't happen often, but when it does, it is unforgettable; a ranger told us that he has seen it many times, and with as many as seven rainbows!

Coming down from the heights of Haleakala, it's pleasant to stop on the lower slopes at **Sunrise Market,** and **Protea Farm,** near the beginning of Crater Road. You can have a free sample of Maui pineapple, buy some sandwiches, homemade fudge, or local fruits, get a cup of coffee and a muffin (maybe mango or banana or walnut) to go with it. If you like, take your picnic lunch out to the tables surrounding the protea fields outside. Sunrise Market has just about the best prices around on pineapples to carry home, plus a variety of gift items. As for the protea farm part of the operation, this is a good chance to walk around and see protea growing in their natural habitat (several protea farms dot these Maui uplands; protea are becoming a big commercial crop). Their protea gift shop displays fresh protea bouquets, as well as dried arrangements, and crafts, which can be shipped home.

CAMPING AND RIDING IN HALEAKALA

Strong hikers, take note: You can spend a magnificent two or three days in Haleakala for spectacularly low prices. At Haleakala National Park there are three primitive cabins, each sleeping 12, for overnight lodging. The cabins have woodburning stoves and cooking and eating utensils. All you need bring is food, water, a sleeping bag, and matches! The three form a sort of triangle in the crater, and you can go from one to the other on your exploration. **Kapalaoa Cabin** is at the middle of the southern end of the crater, **Paliku Cabin** is northeast of Kapalaoa at the eastern tip, and **Holua Cabin** is northwest of Paliku across at the western tip of the crater. Write to the Superintendent, Haleakala National Park, P.O. Box 369, Makawao, Maui, HI 96768, to make reservations for use of the cabins. Give the details of your proposed trip, the number in your party, dates of the stay, and names of the specific cabins you wish to use each night. The price is minimal: $5 per person per night, $2.50 for children 12 and under, with a minimum of $15 per night, plus a $15 key deposit, plus the $3 entrance fee to the national park. There is an additional charge of $2.50 per person per night for firewood. Cabins may be occupied for no more than three consecutive nights, with a maximum of two nights' stay in any one cabin. So popular are these cabins that assignments for each month are chosen by lottery 60 days prior to the beginning of the month. In other words, if you want a reservation sometime in the month of July, be sure your request is received before May 1.

We should note that these cabins—and these trails—are for experienced hikers in good physical condition: The Park Service warns that "wilderness travel is arduous; the elevation and exertion required to return from the crater floor place excessive physical demands upon the body. Pits, cliffs, caves, and associated sharp rocks are dangerous."

If you'd like to ride down into the crater, get in touch with the people at **Pony Express Tours,** who offer half-day rides, down to the crater floor and back up, lunch included, at $90 per person. No experience is needed. A full-day ride, nicknamed "heavy duty," is for rugged types only, explores the crater floor extensively, and costs $120 per person. Gentler one- and two-hour rides are also offered at Haleakala Ranch, on the beautiful lower slopes of the mountain, for $25 and $45. For all trips, you must wear long pants and closed-toe shoes. You must be at least 10 years of age and weigh no more than 230 lbs. Contact Pony Express Tours, P.O. Box 11746, Lahaina, Maui, HI 96791, or phone 667-2200. You can also reach them through any of the Activity Desks in Lahaina and Kaanapali.

Did you know that you can coast downhill on a bicycle, all the way from the 10,000-foot summit of Haleakala to sea level below? You must be a skilled rider and in good physical condition, and it helps if your nerves are in good shape. Several outfits offer these tours: our local correspondent, who lived to tell the tale, claims that **Cruiser Bob's Haleakala Downhill** offers the best experience. They have both a sunrise trip (departure at 3am), which includes a continental breakfast, and a day trip, which departs at a more civilized 7am and includes continental breakfast and a sit-down picnic lunch halfway down the slopes. Riders of all ages are welcomed, but there is a five-foot-minimum height requirement. The price is approximately $90 and may vary slightly from season to season. For reservations, phone 667-7717. A neat family adventure.

MAKAWAO

On your way back down from Haleakala, it's easy to make a visit to Makawao, Maui's very own cowboy town, the scene every Fourth of July of the famed Makawao Rodeo. Turn right at Pukalani for just a few miles and you'll find yourself on the main street, whose clapboard storefronts make it look like something out of the Old West. This is a good place to stop off for a snack: Local people swear by the fried doughnuts on a stick at **Komoda's General Store**—as well as by their great macadamia-nut cookies and cream puffs. **Kitada's Kau Kau Korner** is known for the best saimin up-country; many of the local people come here for home-cooked meals. **Casanova Italian Restaurant & Deli** (see preceding chapter) is right here on Makawao Avenue. You could have a light lunch (Monday to Saturday) at **Your Just Desserts** (quiches, French onion soup, baked potatoes, soups, salads, frozen yogurt, pastries) in the handsome restored building at the corner of Makawao and Baldwin avenues, or perhaps pick up some sandwiches at the **Rodeo General Store** (see preceding chapter), or splurge on dinner at the **Makawao Steak and Fish House** at 3612 Baldwin Ave., which has long been popular in these parts. As a sophisticated, upscale group moves into Makawao and other up-country towns, the local shops are changing, too, with blacksmith shops and barber shops and pool halls giving way to trendy boutiques and art galleries. Examine the fashionable women's clothing, leather goods, and jewelry collection at **Maui Moorea and Legends;** check out the hand-painted handbags, hats, and silk-screened T-shirts by noted island artists at **Gecko Trading Company;** browse through Hawaiian crafts, vintage aloha shirts, plus more antiques and collectibles at **Coconut Classics.** Check **Glassman Galleries** for wildly experimental art; **Klein, Fein and Nikki** for work by local artists; **Crater Gallery & Design** for a tasteful, eclectic collection. Stop in to see the handsome clothing, gift items, and jewelry at **Collections.** If you've got the kids with you, they can sit and read while you shop at **Maui Child. Mountain Fresh Market** is the place to stock up on health-food items. The gift section of Your Just Desserts (see above) is called Heartsong, and it's enchanting, with nostalgic items including Hawaiian-style quilt patterns, afghans, hand-stitched patchwork quilts; you may want to take home some Maui Pohi Jam or Maui Banana Butter. New shops and galleries are opening here steadily, so shopping and browsing is enjoyable. (*Note:* Most of the shops are closed on Sunday.)

There's another attractive gift shop at the **Hui Noeau Visual Arts Center,** at 2841 Baldwin Ave. You may be lucky enough to sit in on a class or workshop if you're staying in the area: phone 572-6560 for a schedule. Open every day from 9am to 4pm.

Unless you're planning to stop at **Paia** on the way to Hana (see below), we recommend that you do so now. Instead of taking the road back to Pukalani, just take Baldwin Avenue a few miles into Paia, where you can shop for gifts and antiques and hobnob with the local people before heading back home.

HAWAIIAN VINEYARDS

An unusual side trip you might want to take on your way back from Haleakala is to the **Tedeschi Vineyards,** on Hwy. 37 in the beautiful Maui up-country at the Ulupalakua Ranch. It's about 10 miles—via winding mountain roads—from the town of Kula. Hawaii's only winery, Tedeschi cultivates 22 acres of grapes on the slopes of Haleakala to produce a champagne, a blush, and a red table wine in the Beaujolais Nouveau tradition. It also produces a pleasant light, dry pineapple wine. You're welcome to take a free guided tour daily, from 10am to 5pm, to observe various phases of the bottling operation. After the tour, stop in at the tasting room in one of the early 18th-century buildings, sample the wines, perhaps purchase some. If you've brought your picnic lunch, there are tables outside the tasting room, amid beautiful scenery and spectacular views.

---

3. The Road to Hana

Ten thousand feet down from the moon canyons of Haleakala, curving around the base of the old volcano, is a world light years away, a place of such tropical lushness and splendor that it conjures up the word "primeval." This is remote Hana and the curving road leading to it—a road carved under the fringe of the lava cliffs, plunging down on one side to the sea, emerging on the other from overhanging jungle watered by the thousand streams of Haleakala.

In all of Hana, there are just a few dozen modestly priced hotel rooms. (The town's chief industry is the exquisite Hana-Maui Hotel, which caters to wealthy travelers only.) If you can reserve one of these (see the preceding chapter), it would be worth your while to stay overnight; otherwise, you'll have to do Hana in a one-day trip. Count on two to three hours each way, more if you want to savor the magnificent scenery. And be sure to check with the Highway Department about road conditions before you take off. If the weather has been wet, you could get stuck in landslides or mud. If it's raining heavily, forget the Hana trip altogether. Parts of the road are easily washed away, and it may take hours for you to be rescued (which happened one year to friends of ours). There's always tomorrow, or the next visit to Maui.

Even though extensive highway repaving has made it much easier to drive the Hana road, it is still rugged and winding. There are plenty who love it as well as some who think that, despite the glory of the scenery, it's just not worth the effort. A picnic lunch is essential, unless you want to eat at the expensive Hana-Maui or one of the little snack shops on the road or in Hana. Besides, you'll be traveling through the kind of country for which picnics surely were originally invented.

Hana glories in its remoteness. Rumor has it that a road is not being built because the local people like to keep Hana the way it is—difficult to get to. The current road was not completed until 1927, and by that time, the Hasegawa General Store had already been in business 15 years and a hotel was already operating there. Hana's lush isolation attracted the late aviator and environmentalist Charles Lindbergh, who spent his vacations in Hana and is now buried there (the Lindbergh family has requested that his gravesite be kept private).

Because of its remoteness, Hana has been slow in accepting change. Throughout its history it has assimilated new cultures, new religions, and new institutions, but Hana has not become part of them; rather, they have become a part of Hana.

STARTING IN PAIA

Start eastward on Hwy. 32 in Kahului or Wailuku and switch (right) to H-36. You may want to stop at **Dillon's Restaurant** on the Hana Hwy., or **Pic-nics** on Baldwin Avenue in Paia, to pick up a picnic lunch (see Chapter XV), or take some time now, or on the return trip, to browse in some of the antique, decorator, and gift shops that have sprung up in this unspoiled, upcountry community. Be sure to visit the **Maui Crafts Guild** at 43 Hana Hwy., a cooperative gallery showing outstanding work by local craftspeople. The two-story gallery carries a variety of crafts, ranging from bamboo (directly from the bamboo groves of Maui) to wooden bowls and boxes, jewelry, quilting designs, ceramics, woodblock, and lithographic prints to hand-painted clothing designs on silk and cotton. Prices are practically wholesale: artist/members, who run the business themselves and wait on visitors, take only a 10% markup. Prices can go way up for some of the furniture, wall sculptures, and stained glass, but there are many items at small prices, too: We recently spotted printed tablecloths at $22, Raku pottery at $22, and lauhala ornaments at $9.

The nice thing about shopping in Paia is that it is a local, not a tourist, area. Rents are not as high as in Lahaina or Kihei, so shopkeepers can afford to give you lovely things at good prices. One of the nicest of the local shops is **Tropical Emporium** at 104 Hana Hwy., where Veronica Popejoy specializes in natural fabrics (cottons, silks, rayons), and will coordinate a "look" for you that will work back home, too. . . . Another popular shop in this little cluster (they're all on either side of, or across the road from, Dillon's Restaurant on Hana Hwy.) is **Jaggers**, 100 Hana Hwy., where you'll find hand-painted, mostly made on Maui clothing. They also have men's trunks, T-shirts, and aloha shirts with a windsurfing theme. . . . **Nuage Bleu** has high-style women's wear and accessories . . . We like the adorable kiddy clothes—especially the slippers with animal faces for $10—at **Just You and Me, Kid**. . . . Posters, pottery, and locally woven baskets of natural fibers are among the varied wares at **Paia Gallery and Gifts** . . . A small sawmill in nearby Haiku supplies the beautiful woodcrafts that you can see at **Exotic Maui Woods**, 85 Hana Hwy. We've seen a mango-wood nene goose at $30, dolphins and whales of koa wood at $110. Baskets begin at $10. . . . **Summerhouse**, 124 Hana Hwy., is an old favorite here. Their specialties are casual Island wear in natural fibers, Asian imports, and a swimsuit collection extraordinaire. . . . **Trade Winds Natural Foods** has whole-wheat croissants, bagels, muffins, and other munchies, in addition to the usual health-food line . . . And the **Paia General Store** has everything a general store should have—including, because this is Maui, those wonderful macadamia-nut brownies and chocolate-chip macadamia nuts.

Around the corner from these shops, at 12 Baldwin Ave., is **The Clothes Addict**, a spot that has been sought out by customers like Billy Joel, Cindy Lauper, and Ringo Starr for its collection of vintage rayon and silk aloha shirts. This is one of the major sources for these shirts in Hawaii: The collection, from the '30s, '40s, and '50s, comes from Canada, the mainland, and Japan. If you can't afford the prices ($50 to $500), just browse and have a look at some of their other fashionable sportswear. Back in the car, now, continue on your trip.

Before you get back on the road to Hana, however, you might want to make a short detour in Paia to **Hookipa County Beach Park**, otherwise known as "windsurfing capital of the world." Windsurfing, or sailboarding, as it is also known, is an enormously popular new sport (it was introduced as an exhibition sport at the Los Angeles Summer Olympics in 1984), and nowhere are conditions better for it than right here on the northern shore of Maui. It's fun to watch the windsurfers anytime, and if there happens to be a competition going on (make local inquiries), you're in for a special treat. The park is right on the road. Get out your cameras; the views are incredible.

Now it's back on the road to Hana. The highway runs straight and easy, through cane fields, until you get to Pauwela. Here's where the road becomes an Amalfi Drive of the Pacific; the view is spectacular, but keep your eye on the curves. The variety of vegetation is enough to drive a botanist—or photographer—wild. Waterfalls, pools, green gulches beckon at every turn. You'll be tempted to stop and explore a hundred times, but keep going, at least until you get to **Kaumahina Park**, where you might consider picnicking high on the cliff, looking down at the black-sand beach of Honomanu Bay below, watching the local folk fish and swim.

Believe it or not, from here on the scenery gets even better. From the road, you can look down on the wet taro patches and the peaceful villages of **Keanae** and **Wailua,** to which a short side trip, to see the old Catholic church built of lava rock and cemented with coral, is eminently worthwhile. It seems that this coral was strewn ashore after an unusual storm in the 1860s, providing the villagers with the necessary material to construct their church. To commemorate this miracle, they constructed the **Miracle of Fatima Shrine,** which you will see on the Wailua Bay Road, at the 18-mile marker (turn left at the road sign).

Not far from the shrine is **Uncle Harry's Fruit Stand and Living Museum,** which, in the few years that it's been open, has become one of the most popular spots on the Hana Road. And with good reason: not only can you pick up locally grown fruit, get a sandwich, and buy a souvenir, but you can also get to know the native Hawaiian family who runs the place, and who makes all of the crafts—rare-wood tiki carvings, hand-carved wooden bowls of native woods, delightful Hawaiian Christmas ornaments, Hawaiian shell jewelry, and more. "Uncle Harry" Mitchell, his son, Harry Jr., and his daughter-in-law, Joanne, abound with aloha. Their little stand is on their home property; you're welcome to take pictures of the fruit trees, flowers, and lush greenery and visit an authentic grass shack filled with Hawaiian artifacts. They often give free samples of fruits, breads, coconut huskings; maps and visitor information—as well as rest rooms—are available. Refreshing.

In a little while, you get another vista of Keanae from Koolau Lookout. In the other direction you look through a gap in the cliff over into Haleakala. A little further on is **Puaa Kaa Park,** another made-in-heaven picnic spot. The flowers are gorgeous here, and so are the two natural pools, each with its own waterfall. You might have a swim here before you continue. On you go, past grazing lands and tiny villages, to **Waianapanapa Cave,** another possible side excursion. This lava tube filled with water is the place where a jealous Stone Age Othello was said to have slain his Desdemona. Every April, the water is supposed to turn blood-red in remembrance. Near the cave is a black-sand beach (not always safe for swimming), another great place for a picnic. Just before reaching Hana, you arrive at **Helani Gardens,** a five-acre tropical botanical garden, through which you may take a self-guided tour. They also have rest rooms and a picnic area. Admission is $2 for adults, $1 for children 6 to 16.

HANA

Not a little history was made at Hana. The Big Three—Captain Cook, the Protestant missionaries, and the vacationing Hawaiian royalty—were all here. You can even follow the road to a historic Stone Age delivery room near the cinder cone of **Kauiki Head,** where Kamehameha's favorite wife, Kaahumana, was born (there's a plaque near the lighthouse). Or you can just walk around the town for a while and soak up the atmosphere. A must on your list of sights should be the **Hasagawa General Store** where, it is reported, you can get anything and everything your heart desires (just like at Alice's Restaurant) in one tiny shack. A song was written about the place some years ago, and it has not changed in spite of all the hullabaloo. As for practical matters, the store has everything from soup to nuts and bolts to gasoline and muumuus, but because of the scarcity of restaurants in Hana, the food department—plenty of local fruit, some vegetables, mostly sausage meats, and some staples—will be of most interest to you. And you may not be able to resist—as we couldn't—the bumper stickers that read: "Fight Smog—Buy Horses, Hasagawa General Store" or "We visited Hasagawa General Store—far from Waikiki."

A visit to the **Hana Cultural Center** in the middle of town will fill you in on a bit of the history and background of this quaint town. Opened in 1983, the cultural center got most of its collection from local residents, and it's full of wonderful old photographs, Hawaiian quilts (note the unusual Hawaiian-flag quilt dating from the 1920s), plenty of memorabilia from the '30s and '40s, as well as artifacts and tools, and rare shells. Admission is free; the center is open daily, 10am to 4pm (tel. 248-8622).

Hana's best beach, **Hamoa,** is at the Hotel Hana-Maui, but you can also swim at the public beach on Hana Bay, at the black-sand beach at Waianapanapa State Park, and at the "red-sand" beach (ask locals how to get there). Most visitors drive about 10 miles past Hana on to Kipahulu, an unspoiled extension of Haleakala National Park and **Ohe'o Gulch** (formerly, but incorrectly, known as the Seven Sacred Pools), a gorgeous little spot for a swim. Here the pools drop into one another and then into the sea. But it's a roller-coaster ride on a rough, narrow road filled with potholes, and again, unless you dote on this kind of driving, it may not be worth your nerves.

En route to Ohe'o Gulch, you'll pass **Wailua Gulch** and a splendid double fall cascading down the slopes of Haleakala. Nearby is a memorial to Helio, one of the island's first Catholics, a formidable proselytizer and converter. A tribute to his work stands nearby—the *Virgin of the Roadside,* a marble statue made in Italy and draped every day with the fragrant flower leis of the Hawaiians. The good road runs out a little farther on at Kipahulu, so it's back along the northern route, retracing your way past jungle and sea to home base.

Now for the fourth of your day-long trips.

---

4. Lahaina

If Haleakala and Hana are nature's showplaces on Maui, Lahaina is humanity's. It was there that some of the most dramatic and colorful history of Hawaii was made: a hundred years ago Lahaina was the whaling capital of the Pacific, the cultural center of the Hawaiian Islands (and for a time its capital), and the scene of an often-violent power struggle between missionaries and sailors for—quite literally—the bodies and souls of the Hawaiians.

Your trip to Lahaina and the western Maui coast happily combines history with some of the most beautiful scenery in the islands. Take your bathing suit and skip the picnic lunch, since there are plenty of places en route where you can eat. Since there's no paved road completely circling the western tip of Maui, we'll take the road as far as Honokahua, and return by driving back along the same road to Kahului—a route that is more interesting and comfortable than the drive on the unpaved portion between Honokahua and Waihee on the northern shore. The trip begins on Hwy. 32, which you follow through Wailuku to Hwy. 30 (High Street), where you turn left. At Maalaea the road swings right at the sea and continues along the base of the West Maui Mountains, along a wild stretch of cliffs pounded by strong seas, until it reaches Lahaina, 22 miles from Kahului. During the winter months, whale sightings are frequent along this stretch of ocean.

THE SIGHTS OF LAHAINA

Lahaina today is a comfortable plantation town, with pretty little cottages, a cannery, sugar mill, and acres of cane and pineapple stretching to the base of the misty western Maui hills. Thanks to its having been declared a National Historic Landmark property, it still retains its late 19th- early 20th-century architectural charm. New buildings must fit in with this architectural scheme, so there is no danger that it will ever look like Waikiki. For some years, Lahaina has been in the process of a restoration that will cover the 150 or so years during which Lahaina rose from the Stone Age to statehood—from the reign of King Kamehameha I to the annexation of Hawaii by the United States. Re-created will be the days when Lahaina was the capital of the Hawaiian monarchy (before the king, in 1843, moved the palace to Honolulu, where there was a better harbor); the coming of the missionaries; the whaling period; and the beginning of the sugar industry. The restoration is being lovingly and authentically carried out by the Lahaina Restoration Foundation, a devoted group of local citizens and county and state interests. You may visit their office in the **Master's Reading Room** at the corner of Front and Dickenson streets, open weekdays 9am to 4pm, or phone them at 877-3224, then 0001 for further information.

As you tour Lahaina, you'll notice various signs reading "Lahaina Historic Site"; those with a square at the bottom indicate buildings that are either original or restored; those with a circle indicate structures that no longer exist. A booklet called "Lahaina Historical Guide," free at many Lahaina locations, provides useful maps and descriptions.

Begin your exploration out on the old pier in the center of town, where you can gaze at the famed **Lahaina Roads;** from the 1820s to the 1860s this was the favorite Pacific anchorage of the American whaling fleet. Over on your left are the soft greens of Lanai, to the north the peaks of Molokai, on the south the gentle slopes of Kahoolawe. During the winter and early spring, you may get to see some nonpaying tourists sporting about in the water; there are the sperm whales that migrate from their Aleutian homes to spawn in the warmer waters off Lahaina.

For the whalers, this place was practical as well as beautiful; they were safe here in a protected harbor, they could come or go on any wind, there was plenty of fresh water at the local spring, plenty of island fruits, fowl, and potatoes. And there were also Hawaiian women, who, in the old hospitable way of the South Seas, made the sailors feel welcome by swimming out to the ships, and staying a while. To the missionaries, this was the abomination of abominations, and it was on this score that violent battles were fought. More than once, sailors ran through the streets setting houses on fire, rioting, beating up anyone who got in their way, even cannonading the mission house. You can see the evidence of those days at **Hale Paaho,** the old stone prison (on Prison Street, off Main), where sailors were frequent guests while the forays lasted.

Across the street from the waterfront, you'll see the **Pioneer Inn,** which may look oddly familiar—it's been the set for many a South Seas movie saga. Back in 1901 (it has since been tastefully renovated and enlarged) it was quite the place, the scene of arrival and departure parties for the elegant passengers of the Inter-Island Steamship Company, whose vessels sailed out of Lahaina. And since it was too difficult to make the hot trek to central Maui immediately, arriving passengers usually spent the night here. Walk in and have a look around: note the lovely stained-glass window one flight up from the entrance to the **Harpooner's Lanai** and the grandfather's clock at the foot. The lanai itself is a wonderful place to waste a few years of your life while soaking up the atmosphere.

Across Wharf Street from the hotel, a little to the north of the lighthouse, is the site of a palace used by Kamehameha in 1801, when he was busy collecting taxes on Maui and the adjoining islands. And across from that, where the Lahaina Branch Library now stands, is another spot dear to the lovers of the Hawaiian monarchy, the royal taro patch where Kamehameha III betook his sacred person to demonstrate the dignity of labor.

The huge banyan tree just south of the Pioneer Inn covers two-thirds of an acre; it's the favorite hotel for the town's noisy mynah-bird population. In the front of the tree is the **Court House,** a post office, and police station, the post office part of which has been functioning since 1859. Between the Court House and the Pioneer Inn, you'll see the first completed project of the Lahaina Restoration, the **Fort Wall.** It's built on the site of the original fort, but since rebuilding the whole fort would have destroyed the famed banyan tree, the authorities decided to reconstruct the wall instead, as a ruin—a ruin that never existed.

Now that you've seen how the whalers lived, let's see how their arch opponents, the missionaries, fared. Walk one block mauka of the waterfront to Front Street and the **Baldwin Home**—so typical, with its upstairs and downstairs verandas, of New England in Polynesia. The old house, built in the late 1830s with walls of coral and stone, served as a home for the Rev. Dwight Baldwin, a physician and community leader as well as a missionary (and incidentally, the founder of a dynasty; the Baldwins are still an important family in Maui). Thanks to the Lahaina Restoration Foundation, the house has been faithfully restored; you can examine Dr. Baldwin's medical kit (the instruments look like something out of a Frankenstein film), kitchen utensils, and china closets, old photographs and books, the family's furniture and mementos, all the little touches of missionary life 100 and more years ago. Open daily. Admission is $2 for adults and free for children accompanied by their parents for a personally guided tour.

After you've seen Baldwin House, stop next door to visit the **Master's Reading Room,** a former seamen's library and chapel that now houses the office of the Lahaina Restoration Foundation. Then on to the **Spring House** in the same compound, which houses a special exhibit: the Molokai lens. The 5,000-lb. lens, formerly installed in a lighthouse on Kalaupapa in Maui, was once the brightest light in the Pacific; it was dismantled and replaced by a modern electric beacon in 1986. Eventually, it will be returned to Molokai; right now, it's here, in a free exhibit, open daily from 10am to 6pm.

Next stop might be the **Wo Hing Temple,** on Front Street, near Mariner's Alley. The restored 1912 fraternal hall is now a museum, with a display on the history of the Chinese in Lahaina. Stop in at the Cook House Theater adjacent, which shows movies of Hawaii taken by Thomas Edison in 1898 and 1903. Open daily, 9am to 9pm, admission donation requested.

The Restoration Foundation also operates the floating museum ship *Carthaginian,* moored opposite the Pioneer Inn. Its "World of the Whale" exhibit features a series of colorful multimedia displays on whaling, whales, and the sea life of Hawaii. Maui's own humpback whale, which comes to these waters each winter to mate and calve, gets special treatment through videotape presentations made on the spot by the National Geographic Society, the New York Zoological Society, and others. The ship is a replica of a 19th-century brig and is open daily from 9am to 4:30pm. Admission is $2 for adults, free for children with their parents. (If you visit between January and May, when the whales are "in town," be sure to drop by the Whale Report Center at the *Carthaginian* berth where sightings pour in by phone and radio, and you can add your personal observations to the scientific data being compiled.)

Head now for Wainee Street (to the right of Lahainaluna Road); here, where the recently built **Waiola Church** now stands, is the site of Wainee, the first mission church in Lahaina, to which the Reverend Baldwin came as pastor in 1835. The old cemetery is fascinating. Buried among the graves of the missionary families are some of the most important members of the Kamehameha dynasty, including no fewer than two wives of Old King Kam: Queen Keoupuolani, his highest-born wife, and Queen Kalakaua.

On the grounds of Lahainaluna High School stands **Hale Pai,** the original printing house of Lahainaluna Seminary, which the missionaries built in 1813. From the hand press here came the school books and religious texts that spread the Word. The coral and lava structure has been turned into a charming museum by the Restoration Foundation. Open Monday to Saturday, 10am to 4pm.

Outside of Lahaina proper, opposite Wahikuli State Park, is the **Lahaina Civic Center,** an auditorium and gym, with a dramatic mosaic by one of Maui's most famous artists, Tadashi Sato.

Five miles east of Lahaina, on the highway headed toward Kahului, are the well-preserved **Olowalu Petroglyphs.** Two to three hundred years old, these rock carvings depicted the occupations—fishing, canoe-paddling, weaving, etc.—of the early Hawaiians. Unfortunately, they are rather difficult to get to.

On the other side of Lahaina, on the road leading toward Kaanapali, is another historical spot, the **Royal Coconut Grove of Mala.** Mala, one of the wives of Kamehameha, brought the trees from Oahu over a century ago. They are now being replaced by local citizens as part of the restoration.

For those interested in Asian culture, it would be unthinkable to leave Lahaina without a visit to the **Lahaina Jodo Mission Cultural Park.** In a beautiful spot perched above the water is a 3½-ton statue of Amitabha Buddha, erected to commemorate the centennial anniversary of Japanese immigration in Hawaii. It is the largest Buddha outside of Japan. You can meditate here as long as you wish, strike the huge temple bell, and perhaps leave a small donation in the offertory (there is no admission charge).

Note: It's easy to miss this place. As you drive along Front Street, look for the big sign that reads "Jesus Coming Soon." Then turn makai on Ala Moana Street and you'll find the Buddha.

If you want to continue your sightseeing out in the Kaanapali resort area now, there are two ways to go, in addition to driving your own car. The first is free; it's the **Lahaina Express,** a quaint green trolley that provides shuttle service between Banyan Tree Square and the hotels in the Kaanapali Resort every 35 minutes from 9am on. The last trolley leaves The Wharf Cinema Center in Lahaina at 10pm. For information, phone The Wharf Shops at 661-8748. It's more fun, however (and also more expensive: $9 round trip, $6 one way, half fare for children), to hop the old-timey **Lahaina-Kaanapali & Pacific Railroad,** a reconstructed, turn-of-the-century sugarcane train, for the 12-mile round trip between Lahaina and Kaanapali. You'll be entertained with songs and stories en route by a singing conductor, and kids will get a kick out of the hoot of the locomotive's whistle. The railroad terminal is on Honoapiilani Hwy., one block north of Papalaua Street; the bus service from the Pioneer Inn, Boat Harbor, Shopping Center, etc., to the terminal is free. Before or after the trip, you might want to check out the stand at the station that sells fresh coconuts, chilled for eating and drinking, plus fresh-trimmed sugarcane.

A FILM TO REMEMBER

If there's one sightseeing/entertainment experience in Lahaina not to be missed, it has to be the movie *Hawaii: Islands of the Gods,* at the new **Hawaii Experience Dome Theater** at 824 Front St. (tel. 661-8314). To call it a movie is really an injustice, for the traditional boundaries between viewer and film are broken down here as the floor of the planetariumlike theater seems to give way under you, and off you go, soaring into space. Soon you're flying over a burning volcano on the Big Island or swooping down into Kauai's Waimea Canyon, bicycling at breakneck speed down the slopes of mighty Haleakala, or scuba diving far below the surface of the ocean to the breeding grounds of the humpback whale off the coast of Maui. It's all courtesy of state-of-the-art technology. The screen is 60 feet around and more than 25 feet from the center, and your vision is a full 180°, which makes you feel you are part of the picture. The Dome Theater was created here by Jim and Liz Dankworth, who originated the concept in Alaska. "Hawaii is like Alaska," says Jim, "in that it has so many extraordinary areas that are largely inaccessible to the average visitor. We wanted to capture that—to show the natural beauty, the history, the culture of the islands in a way that has never been done before." They have succeeded to an astonishing degree. The 45-minute film is shown daily, every hour on the hour, between 10am and 10pm; at $5.95, this has to be the best bargain on Maui. We can hardly wait to see it again.

SHOPPING IN LAHAINA

We must confess: the thing we love to do most in Lahaina is shop. While the reconstruction of the historical sights is proceeding slowly, Lahaina (and Whaler's Village at Kaanapali Beach, see below) is fast emerging as one of the best shopping areas in the islands, second only to Honolulu. On each one of our visits there are new and exciting shops, boutiques, galleries to visit. Perhaps it's the influence of the young people and other newcomers moving into the area; they keep everything constantly stimulating and alive.

First, let's get your car parked. Finding a spot on the street is not easy, although it's often possible on Front Street, on the ocean side. Also try the Lahaina Shopping Center, the area behind the Wharf Shopping Center, at the corner of Front and Prisons streets and at the corner of Front and Shaw streets. If that doesn't work, however, drive in to one of the commercial parking lots like the one behind Baldwin House, at the corner of Luakini and Dickenson streets: charges are reasonable. Across from the parking lot is a place where you can get fresh island produce to take home, and in front of that is a stand selling ice-cold coconut juice.

Cool and refreshed now, let's start our wanderings, perhaps at the **Lahaina Marketplace** (on Front Street, just south of Lahainaluna Road). Walk all the way to the back and you'll find **Donna's Designs,** three little booths where Donna Sorenson does some fanciful hand-painted T-shirts and coverups (100% cotton, machine washable), and sells them for the lowest prices around: $10 to $26. Bags are $38. Donna points out—and we agree—that since shops directly on Front Street come and go at a rapid rate because of the high rentals, you're apt to get better bargains if you go slightly "off Front Street."

Also at Lahaina Marketplace is an old favorite of ours, **Apparels of Pauline,** the place where the hand-painted craze in the islands started many years ago. Most of the artwork for their unique hand-painted pieces—blouses, T-shirts, dresses, hats, handbags, and so on—is done in Maui. The emphasis here is on silks and cottons, natural fabrics, and fair prices. Hand-painted T-shirts start at $20, sundresses begin at $50, and silk pareaus (gorgeous!) are about $48 to $65. A shop a bit different from most others in Hawaii.

Our favorite men's shop in Lahaina Marketplace is one that caters to men: It's called **Kula Bay Tropical Clothing,** and it's come up with a novel idea. Realizing that most men don't want to spend several hundred dollars on an antique aloha shirt, they've taken the prints from vintage shirts of the '30s, '40s, and early '50s, had them printed in more muted colors, put them on long-staple cotton (instead of rayon or silk), accessorized them with coconut or mother-of-pearl buttons, and come up with a winning collection. Shirts are $45. There's also a good array of classic design clothing in this "gentlemen's shop." Also in Honolulu and Kauai.

Not too many places like the **South Seas Trading Post** at 851 Front St. are left in Lahaina, places where the owners still search out and find authentic South Seas and Asian treasures. Although there are many collector's items here—primitive art from New Guinea, bronzes and buddhas from Thailand, precious jades from China—most of the items are surprisingly affordable: consider, for example, one-of-a-kind jewelry designs using antique pieces, $25 to $75; freshwater pearl necklaces with precious gemstones, from $18; hundred-year-old porcelain spoons from China, at $10; Christmas ornaments in the shape of Hawaiian tutus, $3.50—and much more. . . . **The Whaler, Ltd.,** at 866 Front St., is just about the only honest-and-true nautical shop in the old whaling port of Lahaina. They have lanterns that run on oil, brass lamps and hooks in various shapes, scrimshaw and ivory carvings, whaling prints and boxes, carvings of whales and whalers, and more unusual items and collectibles.

Central to the Lahaina shopping scene is **The Wharf Cinema Center,** 658 Front St., a stunning three-story arcade built around a giant tree, with a fountain and a stage on the lower level, a glass elevator, a triplex theater complex, a number of attractive eating places, and dozens of shops reflecting quality and taste, some more so than others. Here you'll find places like **Seegerpeople,** which offers three-dimensional photo sculptures—of you, your family, your kids, your group. Photo sessions last an hour, it takes another hour for proofs, and then (in about four weeks) you have a sculptural collage unlike any other. Prices begin at $35 for one person, one pose; each additional pose is $20. Have a look around and admire. . . . We've always liked the fashions—in good taste and well priced—at **Luana's Originals.** Much of the clothing—for both men and women—is made on Maui. Luana shows distinctive prints by Island Silks, and has a good selection of totes and beach bags (there's another Luana's at 869 Front St.). . . . The people at **Earth & Co.** are doing such good work that you really ought to buy something here. They carry a large selection of Greenpeace and Earthtrust products—artwork, posters, jewelry, T-shirts, and many gift items—at moderate prices.

Steve Mitchell, the owner of **Coat of Arms International,** comes from a family involved in heraldic research for four generations. Now Mitchell is in Maui, researching and reproducing family coats of arms from all over the world. He has 375 family pedigrees here: 800,000 more can be researched. Should your name be one of the 375, right on the spot you can pick up tiles, bells, coffee mugs, beer steins, tumblers and the like, all with your coat of arms emblazoned on them. Most items are under $20, which makes them great possibilities for amusing gifts.

Have you always wanted a genuine Panama Hat? The **Maui Mad Hatter** has them, plus scads of other chapeaux—every known type of hat weave, including Maui lauhala, for men, women, and children. Proprietor Shell Hansen, who invites visitors to his factory in Paia, claims, "If you've got the head, I've got the hat!" Most hats run from $10 to $30. . . . Children can be nicely outfitted with island clothes at **Little Polynesians.**

We've already told you about the restaurants at The Wharf, but if all you want is a brownie or a muffin to nibble on, or perhaps a cup of coffee to go with it, try the delicious homemade goodies (courtesy of The Bakery) at **Whaler's Book Store,** a combination bookstore and European café, where you can sip and sit in un-Lahaina-like peace. We often find stunning local books of art and photography and Hawaiiana here that are not readily available elsewhere: especially lovely is a book called *The Hula,* by Jerry Hopkins.

Check the local papers for news of frequent entertainment at The Wharf **Cinema Center;** on one visit, for example, Kamalu Kekahuna's Mau Kaukau Hula Halau was presenting (for free) a full Polynesian revue, including Samoan knife dances done by women on the center state. Shops stay open late, so a visit here can be a good evening's activity. The free Lahaina Express trolley makes its last run to Kaanapali at 10pm.

Our favorite shop at the 505 Front Street arcade is **The Old Lahaina Luau Gallery** (it's also the ticket office for the Old Lahaina Luau: see preceding chapter). Everything here is authentic and in good taste, the work of island craftspeople; you'll find traditional woven baskets, hand-carved wooden items, Niihau shell necklaces, jewelry, posters, even authentic Hawaiian hula instruments like *uli ulis,* and the seed-filled gourds called *ipus.* Lovely pareaus by Sig Zane are $28. Luau guests are given a 20% discount on these items. . . . **Lee Sands,** the eelskin wholesaler with many shops in the islands, had a branch here, showing a wide selection at very good prices. . . . and **Lace Secrets** is full of pretties for women.

If you happened to miss **Island Muumuu Works** in the Maui Mall, make up for that now by going to their new branch in Lahaina, 180 Dickenson St., in Dickenson Square. Almost all the muumuus at this outlet store for the famous Hilda of Hawaii manufacturer are just $43, and their styles are truly flattering (we always note how many Maui women are wearing them each year). Men's aloha shirts, too, plus tote bags and some attractive haku leis, all at low prices.

Cover-Pix, at 819A Front St., has come up with a novel idea: They take your photo, then turn it into a full-size magazine cover for just $15. What a neat idea! If you want postcards, they are three for $5.

Once it was a pineapple cannery. Now the heavy equipment and the factory workers are gone, and in their place are a supermarket, a drugstore, scads of boutiques and restaurants, and plenty of tourists. Lahaina's newest shopping center, and its first enclosed, air-conditioned one, **The Cannery,** at 1221 Honoapiilani Hwy., is a very pleasant place to shop: It's sunny but cool, with lots of light and space. It's a boon to people staying out this way, since the Safeway Supermarket stays open 'round the clock, and Long's Drugs fills a variety of needs. There is ample parking. As for the smaller shops, there are branches of popular island stores, like **Sir Wilfred's Coffee, Tea & Tobacco,** one of our favorites from the Maui Mall; **Reyn's** for tasteful men's casual wear (they now have some of their classic prints in T-shirts, for $16); **Alexia Natural Fashion** for stylish women's clothing in raw silk, linen, and cotton; and **Blue Ginger Designs,** where everything is made of hand-blocked batik fabrics; and **Super Whale,** which always has wonderful children's clothing. **Plantation Clothiers** is also a winner for children's clothing, mostly of the handmade and hand-painted variety, and there are equally lovely (and pricey) items for mom, too. We like the fanciful women's clothing at **Arabesque,** and the array of high-flyers at **Kite Factory. Lahaina Scrimshaw** (see description ahead, under "Whaler's Village") has an impressive collection here, too.

Maui on My Mind is one of the more tasteful shops around, with a variety of wearable crafts and handmade jewelry. They even have T-shirts with prints by some of Maui's favorite artists: We like the animal scene by Guy Buffet proclaiming, "It's a jungle out there." It's $22. Floral wind chimes are $21.

Rocky Mountain Chocolate Factory will dip frozen bananas in chocolate for you, and will mail their famous fudge, chocolate-covered macadamias, and what-not anywhere. While you're thinking of food, you can check out the variety of fast-food outlets here, sit down and have a bite at one of the tables in the big central courtyard. For a more serious meal, try **Marie Callender's,** an outpost of the Oahu favorite known for its wonderful pot pies.

The Cannery presents a vast number of free entertainment, so be sure to see if anything is going on while you're there. You may be lucky enough to catch someone of the caliber of noted island funny man Frank De Lima, as we did on a recent visit. Fabulous!

Attention chocoholics and or potato-chip junkies, or any combination of the above: before you leave The Cannery, stop in at **Long's Drugs** and treat yourself to Maui's latest gourmet munchie craze: **Chocolate Chips of Maui.** Believe it or not, these are original Maui potato chips, dipped by hand in either rich dark chocolate or milk chocolate, packed in an elegant box, and signed by the dipper. They can be gobbled as is or, if you can wait, frozen and served with ice cream or sherbet or brandied whipped cream! A four-ounce box is $3.99.

You can hardly miss the ads for **Hilo Hattie's Fashion Center** at 1000 Limahana Pl., in the industrial area, near the sugarcane train. Hilo Hattie's provides free van service from the courthouse at Lahaina Harbor seven times daily, and once you're there, they'll give you free seed leis and refreshments. You can choose from some 10,000 garments at good prices. Phone 661-8457 for information. While you're in the industrial area, have a look around, too, at some of the outlet stores. These include **Coral and Gifts, Posters Maui, Lahaina Printsellers, J.R.'s Music Shop,** and the **Lobster and Roses** sportswear outlet. Merchandise varies from day to day, but value can be excellent.

ART NIGHT

Lahaina boasts numerous galleries, and the best time to visit them is on Friday night. Friday evening, from 7 to 9pm, is "Art Night" in Lahaina; galleries present special appearances by artists and offer free entertainment and refreshments. Great fun! Check the local papers for what's happening where. Among the numerous galleries involved are **South Seas Trading Post, Dolphin Galleries, Wyland Gallery, Center Art Galleries-Hawaii,** and the **Lahaina Arts Society.**

---

5. Kaanapali and Kapalua

Head out of Lahaina now for a bit of sightseeing at some glamorous hotels, shopping, and swimming. Your first stop should be at the splendid **Hyatt Regency Maui,** where you can have a look at the $80-million, 20-acre complex, lush with waterfalls, gardens, tropical birds, an acre-long swimming pool with its own bar in a lava cavern, an atrium lobby surrounding a 70-foot-tall banyan tree, and an elegant shopping arcade that rivals Rodeo Drive. A walk here is like touring a park-botanical garden and an indoor-outdoor museum of priceless Asian art. This aesthetic and architectural tour de force offers gorgeous vistas wherever you look. You might want to pause and have a drink at the Weeping Banyan Bar beside a lagoon—and please don't throw crumbs at the penguins! Note, too, the unusual ceilings in the shops—there is one in stained glass—and perhaps pick up a trinket at a place like **Elephant Walk,** where prices go way up for safari exotica, but are relatively down-to-earth for elephant-hair jewelry.

By all means, pay a visit to the **Maui Marriott Resort** on Kaanapali Drive, next to the Hyatt Regency. This is an example of modern hotel architecture and landscaping at its best, especially beautiful at night, when lights, flowers, and tropic moon over the ocean create dazzling effects.

Your next stop should definitely be the new **Westin Maui Resort,** a sensational $165-million remake of the old Maui Surf Hotel. It's a toss-up as to whether this or the Hyatt Regency Maui (both Christopher Hemmeter creations) is the more sumptuous; you decide. This gorgeous pleasure palace by the sea has $2½-million worth of artwork gracing the public areas and gardens, a spectacular, multilevel swimming pool complex fed by waterfalls and bridges (twice as big as the giant pool at the Hyatt Regency), and swans gliding just a few feet from the registration desk. Art tours are held Tuesday and Thursday at 9am and last an hour; wildlife tours are held Sunday, Monday, Wednesday, and Friday at 10am; a great chance to photograph the flamingos, swans, and macaws. You'll need reservations: phone 667-2525.

As you continue driving, you may want to stop at the **Sheraton Maui Hotel,** which sits atop **Black Rock,** the perch from which the souls of the dead Hawaiians were said to leap into the spirit world beyond. The majestic hotel, not in the least bit haunted, is worth having a look at, especially for the 360° view from the top, a sweeping panorama of ocean, islands, and mountains. The tasteful Polynesian formal lobby is on the top floor; you've got to take the elevators down to everything else, including Kaanapali Beach.

WHALER'S VILLAGE

The main shopping attraction out here is Whaler's Village, recently done over and now bigger and better than ever. The one- and two-story buildings are of uniform design and materials, authentic reproductions of the type of buildings that the New England missionaries constructed in Lahaina between 1830 and 1890. First, pay a visit to the **Whaler's Village Museum** (on the third floor of Building G), study its absorbing collection of whaling memorabilia, and perhaps see the whaling film shown every half hour in the museum's theater. After you've boned up on history and soaked in some gorgeous views, you can concentrate on the serious business of shopping, and there's plenty to concentrate on.

One-of-a-kind, rare, unusual—these are words to describe the very special offerings at **Sea & Shell,** one of our favorites here. Everyone connected with this place seems to be talented; many of the employees do watercolors, create belts and hair jewelry; owners Michael and Madaline Abrams do all the beautiful mountings and mirrors and offer unique jewelry by island artisans. Take a look at the earrings and pins made of multicolored "Kroma Glass" (a new technology called "Thin Line Physics" produces stunning effects), from $35. Hand-carved napkin rings from Bali begin as low as $4.50; wonderful "bird bags" in the shapes of swans, flamingos, and toucans are $32, and a conversation piece anywhere. The same people also run the **Madaline and Michael Gallery,** which features the work of Mexican artist Sergio Bustamente and a lot of other amusing, whimsical art. And in Lahaina, at 713 Front St., they are responsible for Madaline and Michael's Collectibles. . . . **Ka Honu Gift Gallery** is a delight, with lots of Hawaiian handmade works: dolls, ceramics, bowls of milo and koa wood, and Christmas ornaments like Santa on a surfboard, $12.95. They have a large collection of Niihau shell necklaces. . . . **Maui on My Mind** has the best that Maui has to offer in the way of handcrafted baskets, pottery, and jewelry. They carry Guy Buffet T-shirts, Robert Lyn Nelson posters, beautiful koa-wood jewelry boxes. Kathleen Barker's eyeglass cases, with leaf prints on raw silk, are delightful at $13. . . . If money were no object, we'd simply buy out all the fabulous designs by local Hawaiian designers at **Silk Kaanapali, Ltd.** In addition to hand-painted and unusually tailored clothing, the shop carries striking bags and other accessories, starting at about $30. . . . **The Painted Lady** is another mecca for beautiful women's clothing, much of it hand painted—great splashes of color and designs in gauze and cottons. . . . If you've forgotten your sunglasses, pick up a pair at **Eyecatcher Sunglasses.** The selection is huge and distinctive, albeit pricey.

The Sharper Image is now in Maui, and you can have a great time here—free! Work out on the exercise bikes, then massage your back as you experience a Japanese shiatsu massage table or a luxury recliner. Great fun! Oh yes, you could buy something here, too—they have the "perfect travel alarm clock" for $35. . . . Scrimshaw collectors should head straight for **Lahaina Scrimshaw,** where there's an impressive selection of quality art executed by over 45 different scrimshaw artists, most of them residents of Maui. There's a prize antique collection as well, with prices going up into the thousands. Do-it-yourself scrimshaw kits are available, too, from $7.95 to $17.95. Since the people here are fervent "Save the Whale" supporters, they will continue to create fine-quality scrimshaw on nonendangered fossil walrus ivory. They've become so popular that they now have six shops in the area. . . . **Lahaina Printsellers** has some fascinating antique maps and prints that would look great on those walls back home. **Esprit, Aca Joe, Cotton Cargo,** and **Waldenbooks,** island regulars, are all represented here. And there's a cute kiosk on the bottom level called **Maui Fishmarket,** which features bold fish prints—in bags, T-shirts, and the like.

We've already told you about some of the nifty restaurants at Whaler's Village —**Rusty Harpoon, Chico's Cantina,** and **Ricco's Old World Delicatessen** (see the preceding chapter).

THAR SHE BLOWS!

From mid-December until the end of April, some 400 celebrities arrive in Maui, and everybody wants to see them. It's estimated that approximately 400 North Pacific humpback whales migrate 3,000 miles from their home in Alaska to mate and bear their young in the warm waters off Hawaii. You can probably spot a few whales from the beach or your lanai, but it's also fun to take one of the whale-watching excursion boats that leave daily from Maui harbors. All of the cruises are good, but we like to support the ones run by the **Pacific Whale Foundation;** when you travel with them, you're in the company of expert research scientists, and proceeds benefit the foundation's research and conservation efforts to save the endangered humpback whale. Cruises depart daily from Maalaea Harbor, last 2½ hours, and cost $25 for adults, $12.50 for children 3 to 12. Be sure to bring your cameras for some spectacular shots. Call the Whale Hotline at 879-8811 or Maui Discoveries at 667-5358 for more information.

TO KAPALUA AND THE NEARBY BEACHES

One of the nicest things about the Hawaiian Islands is that all beaches—even those at the fanciest hotels—are open to the public. As you stroll by the beachfront hotels (the Sheraton Maui, the Royal Lahaina, the Kaanapali Beach, the Marriott, the Westin Maui, the Hyatt Regency), you can stop by for a snack or a drink and treat yourself to a swim. Kaanapali Beach is wider in some places than others (storms occasionally carry away some of the sand), and we personally prefer the areas in front of the Westin Maui, the Royal Lahaina, and Sheraton Maui; the latter is known for fabulous snorkeling at Black Rock, right in front of the hotel. Unfortunately, there is very little public parking in this area, and hotel parking lots may be crowded. You may want to swim behind Whaler's Village, which has a good beach, but you will have to pay for parking in their indoor lot.

As you drive north along the coast, **Honokawai Beach Park** is another possibility for a picnic or a swim. However, it is not always as good as it should be (and in the evening, a hangout for an undesirable crowd), so best to drive further along until you come to some better beaches. One is **Napili Bay,** which has a small sign showing the public right of way; look for it—and park—when you see the sign for the Napili Surf Beach Resort. Our favorite, still further north on this road is **Fleming Beach** (also known as Kapalua Beach), a perfect crescent of white sand, gentle surf, the ideal spot for the whole family to swim, play, and snorkel. There's a public right-of-way sign past the Napili Kai Beach Club, which leads to a small parking lot for this very popular beach. If it's full, we'll let you in on a secret: the parking lot at The Shops at Kapalaua, adjacent to the plush Kapalua Bay Hotel, usually has plenty of space and you can walk from it, through the hotel, and down through the lovely grounds to the ocean.

The Kapalua Bay Hotel itself is exquisite, and well worth a look. And we always stop to visit **The Shops at Kapalua,** one of the most serenely tasteful of island marketplaces. Most of the shops here are way beyond our budget, but there are many affordable items at places like **Kapalua Kids,** which can outfit teens as well as children, and at **The Kapalua Shop,** where you can pick up T-shirts, bags, and many accessories with the distinctive trademark logo: the Kapalua butterfly. **By the Bay** is a gift gallery with many delightful items from around the world. **Distant Drums,** "a cultural art gallery," showcases art, handcrafts, and jewelry from Bali, New Guinea,

Asian and South Pacific shores, much of it museum quality. But there are some charming low-priced items, too, like bracelets handmade in Hawaii from woods indigenous to the islands, laminated and lacquered so you can wear them in the water, from $15 to $30; straw baskets from Sri Lanka at $15; handmade earrings from Bali, starting at $18. Enormously popular are their hand-carved, hand-painted tropical fish, the kind you see when you're out snorkeling in Maui waters: They go from $5.50 to $29, small to large, and are made in Sri Lanka.

If you can, try to time your visit to The Shops at Kapalua for a Thursday morning at 10 o'clock; that's when you can watch "Hula Kahiko O Hawaii," a local hula halau, present the ancient dances of Hawaii. The performance is free, and it's a delight.

Have a sandwich and an espresso, now, at the European-style Market Café, which also purveys cookbooks, cheeses, wines, and deli items. Or, walk through the lobby of the hotel itself and wander out to the Bay Club. Here you can have a fancier lunch, a drink, or simply a walk outside to see the breathtaking views, with blue sea at every vista. Beautiful Fleming Beach is right below you. Let the peace and beauty stay in your memory as you turn around and go back the way you came—the road continuing around the island is a poor one, and usually off limits to drivers of rented cars.

Note: Despite any information you may receive locally, nude sunbathing is definitely against the law in the state of Hawaii.

SAILING TO LANAI

If sailing, snorkeling, swimming, whale watching, and rustic sightseeing—or any combination of the above—appeal to you, splurge this once and spend a perfect day sailing to the island of Lanai aboard one of the sleek, multihulled yachts of **Trilogy Excursions.** Jim and Randy of "The Sailing Coon Family" pioneered these trips back in 1973, and they are recognized today as the best on the Maui docks; these people know how to do everything right. And now that Lanai is beginning to undergo full-scale resort development (two Rockresorts, the upcountry Lodge at Koele and the beachfront Manele Bay Hotel, have just opened) after many years as a sleepy pineapple plantation, this is a great time to see Lanai while it is still unspoiled. The all-day excursion begins at 6:45am; watching the morning light brighten as you sail out of Lahaina Harbor is magical. Hot coffee and Mom Coon's home-baked cinnamon buns are served on board, and within about an hour-and-a-half you're at Lanai. Then it's superb snorkeling (lessons for beginners) at the **Hulupo'e Bay Marine Preserve,** swimming on a crystal beach, an excellent lunch of barbecued chicken prepared over kiawe wood by the captain and served in a comfortable dining lanai overlooking the water. Another highlight of the trip is the tour around Lanai in an air-conditioned van; the native guides are delightful and will fill you in on island lore. (Should you want to stop off here at the venerable Hotel Lanai for the night, you can arrange to do so in advance and pick up another Trilogy boat the next day.) Then it's back to Lahaina, and, with luck, a sighting of whales in season. On a recent voyage, not only did whales come close to our boat, they turned over to show us their bellies! A fellow passenger reported dolphins dancing around the boat on another trip she had made (many passengers are repeats). Whales and dolphins cannot be guaranteed, but a thoroughly enjoyable day—and a return to Lahaina around 4:30pm—certainly can be. Bring the kids and the cameras.

The Trilogy Excursion costs $125 for adults, $62.50 for children 3 to 12; reservations are essential, as space is limited. Call 800/874-2666 from the mainland; the local phone is 661-4743.

HIKE MAUI

So you want to get off the beaten path, away from the tourist routine, and explore the backcountry, the mountains, the jungles, and waterfalls and rain forests, perhaps even trek into the crater of mighty Haleakala, on foot? The best way we know to do all this is to team up with an amazing gentleman named Ken Schmitt, a professional nature guide and much more. Schmitt has lived in Maui for 11 years, most of the time in the open, sleeping under the stars, living on wild fruits and vegetables on the jungle paths. He is a scholar, an explorer, an expert in the natural history and geology of Maui, and in the ancient legends and wisdom of Hawaii. He leads very small groups, or individuals, on a variety of 50 different hikes, which range from easy walks to arduous treks, and cost anywhere from $60 per person for a half-day tropical-valley hike to $100 for an excursion into Haleakala (children under 16 are charged $40 to $65). Personalized trips concentrating on special interests can be arranged. We've had ecstatic reports on these hikes.

We asked Ken what he might suggest for our budget-conscious readers: "Take one or two of my day hikes to find out everything necessary to enjoy camping or backpacking on Maui. Then you can live for free, fishing and eating wild fruit, taro, and sweet potatoes. Of course, not everyone wants to live this way, but it can be done, and I will show you how. Each of my excursions is a workshop in natural history and environmental knowledge. In one day I can teach people as much as they could learn in weeks of research, including the following: locating safe and beautiful places to camp; selecting an itinerary appropriate to current weather conditions and personal interests and abilities; finding trailheads and following the trails; what fruit is in season and where to find it in the wilderness; where to rent equipment and what is needed; possible hazards in the environment and how to cope with them; how to get around without a car; where to buy inexpensive groceries, including farms that sell their own fresh fruit and vegetables. The emphasis of my programs is enhancing our connection with our natural environment and teaching the skills that we need to feel comfortable in Hawaii."

Sounds great to us. You can write in advance to Ken Schmitt at Hike Maui, P.O. Box 330969, Kahului, HI 96733, or phone him when you arrive, at 879-5270.

READERS' SIGHTSEEING AND SHOPPING SUGGESTIONS ON MAUI: "On Maui we found a service that I would recommend highly to anybody planning to take the road to Hana. 'Hana Cassette Guide' is available for $20 from Craig at the Shell Service Station on Hwy. 380, before Hwy. 36. Craig is a local photographer who narrates the tape himself, and he is a joy to listen to. He is well versed in local lore, legends, and facts about the 54 bridges, the uncountable waterfalls, and scenic views. We took the tape player out of the car whenever we stopped and the people around were interested in hearing the comments. Also included is a picture book of the wildflowers and a souvenir map. We consider this our 'Best Buy' on our trip to Maui" (Dennis N. Benson, Uniontown, Ohio). [*Authors' Note:* Craig also has an excellent cassette tour of Haleakala. He can be reached by phoning 572-0550.]

"We found we saved $5 each by dealing direct with **Akamai Tours** in Kahului for our trip to Hana. We saved $15 by driving to their office, then another $5 for arranging our trip direct with them rather than through an agent. We agree that it was much better to take this tour than to drive ourselves, and all the passengers felt the same way. Also, our driver, Frank Bernard, took us all the way through to Hana and back to Kahului without turning back, while our rental car would have had to return the same way. We started out in sunny weather but ended up in a real downpour, but the trip was kept exciting and interesting by Frank. He got us to pick guava from the trees at the side of the road as we toured along, and his botanic knowledge was informative and interesting. He pointed out the home of the famous people, too, but it was his interesting facts about the flora and fauna that made the trip really worthwhile. We saw peacocks, bird's nests, etc., some of which we would have missed had it not been for Frank. . . . **O'Rourke's Tourist Trap** in Kihei had by far the cheapest postcards—good ones" (Elizabeth Lundh, North Vancouver, B.C., Canada).

"One of the prettiest beaches on Maui was just down the road from Kihei, in Makena. It's called **Big Beach** and it is lovely, with no hotels in sight. We spent some time playing in the waves, which can get rough in midafternoon, but went back again and found the water to be much calmer" (Carol and John Slupski, Lincoln Park, Mich.). . . . "We took the **Ocean Activities Center Molokini Snorkel Trip**. Great crew and fun trip. The crew was very helpful in helping my nonswimmer wife get in some snorkeling adventure, and the boat was in excellent shape. We had a great time. . . . I went biking down Haleakala in late November, the rainy season, and felt it was more a survival trip than a fun thing to do. Check on the weather first before booking. It rained the whole way down and the leader tried to make it fun, even though everyone was very cold and soaked to the bone" (Jim and Deb Phillips, Hastings, Neb.).

"One of our most pleasant experiences was taking a private charter boat to Molokini for snorkeling. The cost was the same as for the large boats, and the individualized attention from the owners was terrific. We heartily recommend the **Aquatic Charters of Maui** (tel. 808/879-0976), with Jim and Robyn Friend" (Lindsay and Jay Johnson, Columbus, Ohio). . . . "Your readers may want to know about **Tom Barefoot's Cashback Tours** (tel. 661-8889). You can book any and all of your activities through them and get an immediate 10% cash back at time of purchase" (Pat McCallum, Bethesda, Md.). . . . "On Baldwin Avenue in Makawao is **Gecko,** a store specializing in wearable art from local artists. We got two unique, beautifully colored T-shirts using leaf and flower prints of local flowers by an artist called Glory—and only wished we had gotten more" (Lois-ellin Datta, Bethesda, Md.).

"Best bet for shopping in Lahaina: **The Salvation Army Thrift Shop** off Front Street, near the Lahaina Shores Hotel, had very reasonable used and *new* clothing selling a few blocks away for five times the amount. The best sales appear to be on Saturdays. . . . The road to Hana is more bark than bite. It rained despite a good weather forecast that morning and although it was gloomy, the scenery was worth stopping for. In fact, there were many tourist vehicles clogging up the road during the long trip. Expect a tropical rainforest ambience and you'll probably be satisfied. The **Seven Sacred Pools** is also worthwhile, weather permitting. The 10 miles from Hana to the pools is strictly pothole-city. For us, Maui sums up the Hawaii experience: scenery, solitude, and plenty of options to pursue your own interests" (Michael and Arlene Gladstone, Merrick, N.Y.).

"We certainly endorse your recommendation to visit **O'Rourke's Tourist Trap;** the shops do have outstanding bargains in all kinds of souvenirs, including T-shirts and Polynesian instruments. They also are very willing to handle special orders. . . . The Lindbergh family has requested that local tourist information services not reveal the location of Charles Lindbergh's grave; it seems that some tourists have taken to removing portions of the grave stones as souvenirs! . . . While Maui has many scenic beaches, there aren't many easily accessible from hardtop roads that are consistently suitable for novice snorkelers. In calm conditions, several of the west side beaches are acceptable. But when swells or windy conditions exist, your choices rapidly dwindle. One very notable exception is **Black Rock Cove** at Kaanapali. This sheltered cove has clear water and scores of colorful, small fish. If you are staying outside of this immediate area, just park in the Whaler's Village lot, walk to the beach, and head north about a quarter-mile; the cove is just below the Sheraton Maui Hotel. Tourists should also be advised that the many boat services that offer snorkeling excursions to Molokini Island are subject to weather effects; if conditions at Molokini are choppy, they will go instead to some alternate site (but this generally won't be announced until you're well under way)" (Dale Knutsen, Ridgecrest, Calif.).

"Ask anyone at the **Information Tourist Booth** in front of The Wharf in Lahaina for specialized personal tourist trips. They are always coming up with new things to show tourists. One day they took us to a windsurfing competition at Hookipa Beach; another time they arranged for three of us to hike into the interior with a native Hawaiian guide" (Rue Drew, New York, N.Y.). . . . "We took advantage of riding at the **Rainbow Ranch,** near Kaanapali Beach. A variety of riding tours is available at all levels of experience for reasonable prices. Good quality horses and great guides" (Patti Connor, Arlington, Mass.).

"For those who enjoy island artists, but don't have the hundreds of dollars needed to purchase an original David Lee or Robert Lyn Nelson painting, I suggest a stop at the **Village Gallery,** at their main location just mauka of Baldwin House in downtown Lahaina and the **Village Gallery at the Cannery,** also on Front Street. The Gallery carries works by many excellent local artists not found in the more commercial galleries: this is a good place to see the great variety of ways in which island artists interpret their surroundings. There is a wide range of sizes, styles, media (including wood), and prices. I noticed prints by Dietrich Varez (whose work adorns the lobby of Volcano House, on the Big Island) for only $15. (There is, however, a better selection of Varez's works at the Volcano Art Center.) In short, the Village Gallery is a good place to sample the local art scene."

"Our most enjoyable **snorkeling** spot was near the rocks below the Maui Sheraton. The area is so beautiful, and public walkways lead right to the beach. Our daughter loved it here because she didn't have to go out too far to snorkel, and the water was calm, so we could lay across an air mattress to see the fish. This is a perfect way for youngsters or beginning swimmers to view the underwater world. It was also fun watching the windsurfers and natives diving off the cliffs." (Julie Martin, Huntington Beach, Calif.).

"Maui has some 150-odd miles of coastline with some superb beaches. But if you're bored with sun and sand, try something different—say, a **hike into Maui's backcountry,** and enjoy some of the pristine beauty seldom seen by the average tourist. Pick up the book *Hiking Maui*, by Robert Smith (Wilderness Press); it's splendid reading. It also covers a large variety of hikes, complete with maps, difficulty ratings, where to obtain permission if needed, with a sensitive, no-nonsense approach to hiking. Our favorites: the Iao Stream (no. 16) or, for the more history minded, the King's Highway (no. 15) in La Perouse Bay" (J.A. Drouin, Edmonton, Alberta, Canada).

"We have our own snorkeling equipment and enjoy seeking the less-crowded spots. If you drive on the road that goes past Kihei and Wailea, south of Wailea the road continues to Makena. At the end of the road is a massive lava flow that forms **La Perouse Bay,** which is now an official sanctuary for over 90 species of exotic reef fish. We were the only ones snorkeling there. A word of caution: It is quite rocky, so be sure to wear something on your feet" (Mr. and Mrs. Dennis W. Randall, Seattle, Wash.). . . . "The whale-watching cruises are expensive (around $30) for what you see. By law, they can only go within 300 yards of a whale. You can see the **whales** romping just as well from La Familia lanai on Kamoole Beach II, and drink $2.50 margaritas as well. The whales are most active when the wind blows in the late afternoon" (Mary Popovitch, Calgary, Alberta, Canada).

"You should warn people about the highway to Lahaina and Kaanapali. **Highway 30** is two-lane and very heavily traveled. There are lots of slow-moving trucks and it is almost impossible to pass. If you aren't staying at one of the hotels in that area and plan to drive there for dinner from Central Maui or Kihei, allow plenty of time. At night, watch out for the drunks. Driving that road at night is not a fun experience. . . . We thoroughly enjoyed **Haleakala.** It is fantastic. However, for those who want to stop at the various look-outs, particularly the area near the silversword plants, be sure and have some insect repellent. We were pestered by some of the meanest flies we have ever seen. They love faces and bare legs. You mention insect repellent, but it was for Hana. We saw only one mosquito on our trip to Hana" (Don and Nancy Gossard, Bellevue, Wash.). [*Authors' Note:* In the tropics, mosquitoes come (and thankfully, go), depending on seasons and changing climatic conditions. Our advice: Always have your insect repellent handy in country areas.]

"It's becoming very popular to get up early to catch **sunrise on Haleakala.** The total experience of leaving the hotel at about 3am, driving up the mountain in pitch blackness, meeting other people with the same crazy idea, then slowly waiting for the sun to rise over the crater is absolutely breathtaking. At that hour, however, a sweater, jacket, and blanket *may* suffice for only some. It was cold! Bring breakfast/lunch and enjoy amid other sun/nature worshipers or on your own" (Francine Schept, White Plains, N.Y.). . . . "On the early-morning drive to **Haleakala Crater** for sunrise it took me an hour and ten minutes from Kahului, and I am a cautious driver. It was freezing at the visitors center—about 45 degrees in late August—so I would suggest gloves, especially for photographers; my 'shutter finger' was stiff from the cold! First light—30 to 40 minutes before sunrise—is as lovely as the sunrise and should not be missed. On the way down, I was the only person to stop at Leleiwi Lookout, sharing it with a park ranger for two hours; I think the view from the lookout is superior to the one at the visitors center" (Martha F. Battenfeld, Brighton, Mass.). . . . "For calm and shallow **snorkeling,** pull off Hwy. 30, south of Olowalu General Store. This is not a park, just a shallow beach. So good, they give beginner scuba lessons here" (Vic and Bev Suzuki, Thornhill, Ontario, Canada).

"Our four nights at **Waianapanapana Park** were at our No. 1 idyllic spot. Hana was having a week-long Aloha Week festival. We went to a real Hawaiian luau with great performers for $6; the previous night the ladies of the village gave a real hula show at the village soccer field—free. October is a great time to go to Hana, as there are very few guests. Try the red-sand beach for snorkeling at **Hana Park,** near the old frame schoolhouse, now a library, and follow the trail down a meadow, around a cliff, to a secluded beach behind a natural lava breakwall. Caution: Young couples still swim in the buff here! For golf in Maui, got to **Wailuku Golf Course:** 18 holes, most overlooking the ocean. A real fun place!" (Richard Welse, Westfield Center, Ohio).

"The book *Hiking Hawaii* by Robert Smith (Wilderness Press: Berkeley, 1977) is excellent. It has lots of hikes from family outings to those that are very tough going. . . . One of the nicest waterfalls and swimming holes is located exactly 2.8 miles toward Hana from the Seven Sacred Pools at a bridge. It was still going even when lots of others were dry" (Dr. Michael Baron, San Francisco, Calif.). . . . "We found the prettiest part of Maui to be that short section of Hwy. 30 that goes past the **Napili Bay** area: towering cliffs, crashing waves, lush valleys. Few tourists seem to drive up here because they know the road ends. We packed a picnic dinner and ate it in total isolation on a cliff overlooking the water. It was one of the best moments of our honeymoon" (Sue and Terry Young, Crystal Lake, Ill.). . . . "The road past **Nakalele Point to**

Kahakuloa marked 'impassable' on most tourist maps is definitely just that! The trip is 14 miles, not 5 as stated in most brochures, and a total disaster. We ventured a couple of miles on the road ourselves and had to turn around when the road became too narrow for our car. However, a couple we were traveling with covered the entire 14 miles, and it took them several hours, which they say were harrowing at best. The scenery is not any more spectacular than you can find on other island roads and the driving is so nerve-wracking it is unlikely you will be able to spare any time to view the scenery anyway. The road to Hana is described as treacherous in some brochures, but it is no comparison to this road—save yourself some time and nerves and just don't bother with this route" (Mr. and Mrs. Wes Alton, Edmonton, Alberta, Canada).

"We found the **municipal beach** between Lahaina and the hotel beach complex great! Protected and much less surfy than in front of our hotel" (Mrs. Morris Finck, Shaker Heights, Ohio). . . . "The best snorkeling beach on Maui (we discovered it ourselves and it was later pointed out to us by islanders) is **Honolua Bay** on the north end of the island near the end of Hwy. 30. Overnight camping permits should be obtained from the Maui Pineapple Company in Lahaina, but we did not have one and had no problems" (Sandra Johnson, Santa Paula, Calif.). . . . "South of Kihei is **Kamaole Park,** which is actually three beaches. Each is calm, sandy-bottomed, and almost deserted on weekdays. On this and a previous visit we saw a whale frolicking just offshore" (Bob and Doris Ryan, Grand Island, N.Y.).

"**Camping** is still inexpensive. On Maui, you pay for County Park Baldwin Park, $3 per adult and 50¢ per child. State parks are free. For County Park permits: War Memorial Gym (next to Baldwin High School), Kaahumanu Avenue, Wailuku, Maui, HI 96793. Office hours are 8am to 4pm Monday to Friday. For State Park permits: State Office Building, 54 High St., Wailuku" (Frank Bogard, Pasadena, Calif.). . . . "Taking the road to Hana, we stopped at the **arboretum,** which is on the main road just before the turnoff to the rock and coral church mentioned in the book. This was the highlight of our Hana trip, as the gardens were beautiful with the exotic trees and plants clearly labeled for the haoles. There are about two miles of path to hike (all level), it's free, and would make a lovely place for a picnic—there are some picnic tables available" (Barbara L. Mueller, Tucson, Ariz.). . . . "The best snorkeling we found was at the southern edge of the **Kaanapali Airport.** The water was clear and safe for children, the coral plentiful and well below the surface, and the variety of fish amazing. Even beginning snorkelers will enjoy this beach, which is reached by turning in at the last Kaanapali sign going north, then walking about 50 yards down to the beach" (Nick Howell, Camp Springs, Md.).

"I'd like to pass on some information I learned the hard way. I mentioned to a clerk in a market that I was planning to drive to Hana the next day. He said, 'If it's raining when you get halfway, turn back, or you can get stuck out there.' I assumed he was being overly cautious. It sprinkled off and on as we drove to Hana, but it's a long trip and we didn't want to waste our day. The sun was shining as we visited the Seven Sacred Pools, and water rushed from the very top pool to the ocean. On our way back, cloudy but no rain, we were stopped in a line of about 30 cars, trapped by a landslide on a narrow, cliff-hugging road. Rescue crews had been called, but it took two hours with men, shovels, and a bulldozer to clear the road so we could get by. It could have been a tragedy, and we learned to take seriously what the Hawaiians say. They know best!" (Mrs. Donald B. Newton, Saratoga, Calif.).

XVII

THE ISLAND OF MOLOKAI

1. **ISLAND HOTELS**
2. **ISLAND RESTAURANTS**
3. **THE NIGHT SCENE**
4. **SHOPPING**
5. **SEEING THE SIGHTS**

What's the most Hawaiian of the Hawaiian islands? If you're thinking in terms of the Hawaii of 50 years ago—the Hawaii before high-rises and shopping centers, before billboards and commercialism, then it might well be the little island of Molokai. The closest of the Neighbor Islands to Oahu, 261-square-mile Molokai remains the least developed and most sparsely populated of the major Hawaiian Islands. Its resident population (only about 6,000) has the highest percentage of people with native Hawaiian ancestry anywhere in the islands (with the exception, of course, of privately owned Niihau). The environment is rural and the life-style traditional. Imagine a place with no buildings over three stories high, no elevators, no traffic lights (let alone freeways!), no movie theaters, no fast-food or supermarket chains. Instead, think of great natural beauty, vast uncrowded spaces, and ideal conditions for golfing, hunting, riding, windsurfing, big-game fishing, boating (swimming is not ideal here, since the beaches can be beautiful but the water rough), and leading the lazy life in an unspoiled setting. If that's the kind of relaxed Hawaii you're thinking about, then you should definitely visit Molokai.

Molokai sometimes gets overflow visitors from better-known tourist destinations, people who didn't even know what or where Molokai was. Yet once they start to unwind here, they find they like it, and come back again. Kamaainas have been in the know about Molokai for a long time: It's a favorite weekend spot for family holidays.

In the past, Molokai was known mostly for its treatment center for Hansen's disease—leprosy—at Kalaupapa, and as a pineapple plantation island. And somehow, the tidal wave of progress that has swept the islands since statehood has left Molokai behind; it appears, at first glance, like a midwestern town in the Depression '30s. Yet there's a down-homeness and a realness here that most people find appealing, and a genuine friendliness among the locals. Artists and craftspeople, seeking a last refuge from overpriced civilization, are beginning to settle here. In some parts of the island there is a sense of tranquility that is almost palpable. And Molokai is changing. Although the pineapple industry has been phased out, and many of the local people are experiencing hard economic times, luxury facilities for visitors are on the rise. Before Molokai changes too much, come see what rural Hawaii is still like. A visit to Molokai can be a rewarding experience, especially since you won't have to break the bank to do it: prices here are still somewhat lower than elsewhere in the state.

GETTING THERE

Molokai is 20 air minutes from Honolulu, 15 minutes from Maui. It is easily reached via **Hawaiian Airlines,** which runs 50-seat DH-7 aircraft into Hoolehua Airport on a frequent schedule. Two commuter airlines, which run small planes (anywhere from 9- to 18-seaters), also call at Molokai: These are **Aloha Island Air** (which recently took over from Air Molokai) and **Panorama Air,** a company also well known for its all-island sightseeing flights. Flying low on these small planes can be quite thrilling, as we discovered on a recent Panorama flight. Molokai lies between the islands of Oahu and Maui (it can easily be seen from western Maui) and is, in fact, part of Maui County. Route it on your way to or from either Maui or Honolulu. A one-day trip is quite feasible.

A more leisurely—and scenic—way to get to Molokai is to take the inter-island ferry, *The Maui Princess,* a 118-foot luxury vessel that plies the routes between Maui and Molokai every day. It's about an hour-and-a-quarter trip. One-way fare is $21 for adults, $10.50 for children. The tour is narrated, there are plentiful opportunities for taking pictures, and if it's between December and May, you may spot a few humpback whales taking the same trip you are. For reservations, phone 533-6899 from Oahu; 661-8397 on Maui; 553-5736 on Molokai. From the mainland phone toll free 800/833-5800.

DESTINATION MOLOKAI

Molokai is serious about putting out the welcome mat for visitors and, to that end, has set up the Destination Molokai Association to promote tourism. If you phone their toll-free number, they'll send you a comprehensive brochure listing hotels, resort condominiums, tour companies, auto-rental companies, restaurants, visitor activities, and airlines serving the island, as well as individual brochures put out by these firms. From continental U.S., as well as Alaska, Puerto Rico, and the Virgin Islands, phone toll free 800/367-ISLE. If you're already in the islands, phone 567-6255.

MOLOKAI, PAST AND PRESENT

Although Molokai is known as "The Friendly Isle," that friendliness has really not been tested yet, as far as mass tourism goes. You might easily be the only mainland visitor on the few minutes' flight from Oahu or Maui, and your fellow passengers will more than likely be island people visiting relatives, or plantation people arriving on business.

The Friendly Isle was once known as the Lonely Isle. The power of Molokai's kahuna priests was feared throughout the other islands. Warring island kings kept a respectable distance from Molokai until, in 1790, Kamehameha the Great came to negotiate for the hand of the queen, Molokai's high chieftess, Keoupuolani. Five years later he returned with an army to conquer Molokai on his drive for Oahu and dominion over all of Hawaii.

Today Molokai presents a tranquil scene, a Polynesian island untouched and unspoiled. A thickly forested backcountry populated with axis deer, pheasant, turkey, and other wild game makes life exciting for the hunter. For those of you who just like to look and sightsee, there is magnificent Halawa Valley with its healing pool at the foot of Moaula Falls; the less-rugged Palaau Park with its Phalic Rock; Kalaupapa Lookout and Kalaupapa itself, an isolated peninsula (refuge for the victims of the once-dreaded leprosy), which today you can visit on a guided tour. But more about that later.

You won't have to rough it on Molokai. The few hotel facilities are excellent, the roads are for the most part quite good, and you'll be able to get whatever comforts and supplies you need—from rental cars to color movie film. The drinking water is as pure as you'll find anywhere in the world, and the restaurants, most located in the three major hotels on the island, serve very good meals.

One word of advice: Go directly to your hotel from the airport and get comfortable and adjusted to Molokai before visiting its nearby principal town, Kaunakakai. This sleepy village, made famous by the song "Cock-eyed Major," is best appreciated once you're in the Molokai mood. Especially after Waikiki.

To get a little head start on your sightseeing, you might note that, between the airport and town, on the ocean side of the road is Kapuaiwa, one of the last surviving royal coconut groves in the Hawaiian Islands, planted in the latter part of the 19th century. It was planted in honor of Kamehameha V and given his pet name. Opposite the grove is Church Row, a lineup of tiny rustic churches.

CAR RENTALS AND TAXIS

You're going to need a car if you want to explore Molokai on your own, and it won't be difficult to get one, since Molokai now has local outlets of four major all-island rental companies: **Budget Rent-A-Car, Dollar Rent-A-Car, Tropical Rent-A-Car,** and **Avis.** (See Chapter V for details on all-island rentals.) And they're all right at the airport. Rates vary according to the season and business, but on a typical day on our last visit, here was where the rates stood. **Budget Rent-A-Car** had the lowest rates: $21.99 for stick-shift economy cars, $22.99 for economy automatics with air conditioning. For toll-free reservations, phone 800/527-0700. . . . **Dollar Rent-A-Car** offers two-door, standard compacts for $23.99, and compact automatics for the same price. They also rent Jeeps. Phone toll free 800/367-7006. . . . At **Avis,** rates are about $30 a day for a four-door compact with air conditioning. Call toll free 800/367-5140. . . . **Tropical Rent-A-Car** charges $27.95 for an economy car (without air conditioning), $29.95 for a subcompact automatic with air conditioning, $32 for a four-door compact automatic with air conditioning. Call toll free 800/367-5140. All rates quoted include unlimited mileage. Again, remember, these rates are always subject to fluctuation, so it's wise to shop around.

Need a taxi? Up until a year ago, there was no such animal on Molokai but now the island has a fleet—well, four, at least—of cabs, courtesy of **Molokai Taxi,** which has drivers at the ready 24 hours a day: to pick you up at the airport and take you to your hotel or to take you on personalized tours. And since they have a four-wheel drive AMC Cherokee, they can also provide service to remote and scenic sites accessible only by dirt road, such as Waikolo Lookout, the Sandalwood Pit, and Moomomi Beach. (If you rent a car, you must stick to paved roads.) A phone call to the Molokai Taxi Desk at the Kaluakoi Hotel and Golf Club, 552-2555, ext. 510, brings them to you, *wiki-wiki.*

---

1. Island Hotels

Molokai at this moment has a grand total of eight hotels and condos plus a few bed-and-breakfasts—and that's more than twice what they had a few years ago! Since there are so few, we'll give you the details on all of them; they're not all budget, but they all offer good quality for the money.

The drive from Hoolehua Airport to the town of Kaunakakai takes about 10 minutes, across what seems to be typical western grazing land. About a quarter mile from the town, following Hwy. 45 along the beach, you'll see the **Pau Hana Inn,** the best choice in town for us budgeteers, the most local and the most laidback. Pau Hana is a relaxed, cottage-type hotel with about 40 units, some in the garden, others facing the ocean or pool. All rooms and public areas have been newly refurbished. Rates start at $45 single or double for small, plain but clean budget rooms, with two twin beds and shower, in the longhouse. Superior units, which have two double or queen-size beds, are $69 for up to four persons poolside, $85 for up to four oceanside. Superior studios with kitchenettes are $85 for up to four; deluxe oceanfront suites are $125 for up to four. An extra person is charged $10; a crib is $5. A swimming pool compensates for the rather poor ocean beach. The oceanfront dining room is open for three reasonably priced meals a day. On weekends, it's the local hot spot for dancing. Write to Pau Hana Inn, P.O. Box 546, Kaunakakai, Molokai, HI 96748, or call toll free 800/423-MOLO, from the USA, or 800/423-8733, ext. 250, from Canada. Pau Hana is now affiliated with Aston Hotels and Resorts in Honolulu, which also operates Hotel Molokai (below).

The prices are just a bit higher at **Hotel Molokai,** a modern Polynesian village that maintains the aura of the gracious past. In separate three-unit cottages are lovely rustic bedrooms with baths and all the modern-day comforts, including wall-to-wall carpeting and deliciously comfortable basket swings out on the furnished lanais. There's a swimming pool (the waterfront here is a shallow lagoon behind the reef, popular for snorkeling but not good for swimming), a comfortable open lobby, and an excellent dining room where the "family" (staff) entertains their guests at dinner nightly. Although this is an oceanfront hotel, the waves break a quarter mile out, leaving the lagoon tranquil and still, with only a lapping sound to lull you to sleep. (*Note:* light sleepers may want to ask for a room away from the restaurant area.) Now for the rates: standard rooms, single or double, are $55, superior (garden floor) rooms are $69; deluxe accommodations on the upper floor, with lanai, go for $85; oceanfront deluxe rooms are $99, and family units, for up to six, are $115. Only deluxe rooms can accommodate one or two extra persons, $10 per person. Crib charge is $5. In conjunction with Tropical Rent-A-Car and Panorama Air, the hotel often runs a "2-nighter for 2" special deal, which includes round-trip air fare from Honolulu or Maui, two days at the hotel, and the use of a rented car for two days, at prices beginning at $112.50 weekdays, $125 weekends, per person, based on double occupancy. The nice thing about this is that the return portion of the trip can be used to continue in the direction you're going—that is, from Honolulu to Molokai to Maui, or vice versa. Let's hope this package is available when you're there. Prices are subject to a slight increase. For toll-free reservations, call 800/423-MOLO from the USA, or 800/423-8733, ext. 250, from Canada. From Oahu, 922-7866. The local address is P.O. Box 546, Kaunakakai, Molokai, HI 96748. The local phone is 553-5347.

The grandest of Molokai hotels is the sparkling **Kaluakoi Hotel and Golf Club** (which started life as the Sheraton-Molokai), a luxury resort situated about 15 miles from the airport next to the glorious, 3-mile stretch of almost-deserted Kepuhi Beach. The 117 rooms in two-story buildings (overlooking ocean or golf course) all are beautifully appointed (some have high-beamed ceilings) with wood, rattan furnishings, and vibrant Polynesian colors. All rooms have a refrigerator. Besides the beautiful ocean (often not safe for swimming), there's a handsome free-form swimming pool, bar service at poolside, the championship 18-hole Kaluakoi Golf Course (a golfing friend tells us that at night deer come out to drink at the water hazards!), four lighted tennis courts and a tennis pro, all sorts of shops and services, and the Ohia Lodge for excellent meals. As we sipped a cool drink by the pool recently, one of the guests smiled at us and said: "I think I'll never leave." We could understand that feeling; it's like being at one of the beach hotels at Kaanapali in Maui, but with nothing else around.

Kaluakoi is not inexpensive, but their Colony Club program is definitely the way to go. One inclusive price (and it really is inclusive) covers your room, transfers to and from the airport, all meals (run of the menu, no limitations, unlimited tennis, bicycles, snorkeling, nightly movies, and one round of golf per person, based upon double occupancy per room night. For a stay of four days/three nights, a room with a garden view is $440; with an ocean view, $470; a garden-view villa is $495; an ocean-view villa $540; and on up for suites and cottages. Stays of five days/four nights begin at $570; eight days/seven nights, $935. For reservations, phone Colony Hotels and Resorts toll free at 800/367-6046. The local phone is 552-2555.

If you want to settle into your own apartment in this area, there are three excellent condo choices: Paniolo Hale, Kaluakoi Villas, and Ke Nani Kai, all of which are part of the larger Kaluakoi Resort, a 6,700-acre development, which also includes the Kaluakoi Hotel and Golf Club and the beautiful, three-mile long, Papohauu Beach. Next door to the Kaluakoi Hotel, on Kepuhi Beach, **Paniolo Hale** is adjacent to the golf course (in fact, one must cross the fairway to get to the beach). Wild deer and turkeys are frequently seen on the grounds. There is a swimming pool and a paddle-tennis court, and guests receive a reduced rate when golfing at Kaluakoi. The Kaluakoi Hotel also offers its four lighted tennis courts to Paniolo Hale guests for a nominal fee. This is a luxury condominium complex. Best buys here are the one-bedroom/two-bath units, at $95 for up to four persons. Studios rent for $75 for two, and two-bedroom, two-bath units go for $115 for up to four persons, with a maximum of six; extra persons over four in a unit are charged $8. Car-and-condo packages are also available: $93 for the studio for one to two persons, $113 for the one-bedroom for one to four persons, and $133 for the two-bedroom for one to six persons. There are also ocean-view units. Hot tubs are available on the lanais of all two-bedroom units for an additional charge. All the apartments have full kitchen, TV, telephone, and attractive Island furnishings. Each unit has its own screened lanai (a touch of old Hawaii), which you walk right onto from your room, without going through a door. Minimum stay is three nights. The nearest restaurant is at the Kaluakoi Hotel, about one block away along the sea wall, and the nearest grocery store seven miles away. We continue to receive good reports on this one. For reservations, phone toll free 800/367-2984. From Canada and Hawaii call collect 808/552-2731 for reservations, or write to Paniolo Hale, P.O. Box 146, Maunaloa, Molokai, HI 96770.

Kaluakoi Villas is new, very luxurious, and very lovely. It consists of some 100 condominium units, studios, and one-bedroom suites. All have private lanais affording ocean views, and are richly decorated in the island mood with rattan furnishings. They boast color TV, refrigerator, a counter-top range, cooking utensils, china and glassware: The Golf and Ocean villas have a full range and a dishwasher. All of the amenities of the resort—the restaurants, day-and-night tennis courts, and 18-hole championship golf course—are available to guests. On the property are a free-form swimming pool and Jacuzzi. During the winter, rates begin at $105 for partial ocean-view studios, $125 for ocean-view studios, $185 for golf and ocean villas. During the summer months, the rates are $85, $110, $120, and $165. Golf and tennis packages are available. Reservations: toll free 800/525-1470, or write to Kaluakoi Villas at Kaluakoi Resort, P.O. Box 200, Maunaloa, Molokai, HI 96770. FAX: 552-2201.

There's an air of tranquility about **Ke Nani Kai** that makes you feel this is the kind of place where you could stay for weeks and simply unwind, never missing civilization a bit. Located at the entrance to the Kaluakoi Hotel (actually between the 8th and 17th fairways of the golf course), this is a superb condominium resort, with some 55 units available to the general public. One- and two-bedroom apartments are handsomely and individually furnished, with very large living rooms, cable color TVs, bedrooms with sliding doors, lanais affording splendid views, superbly equipped kitchens, washer and dryer in every unit. On the grounds are an enormous swimming pool (with a shower in the shape of a tiki god), two tennis courts, a whirlpool spa; the beach is just a short walk away. Hanging flowers cover the trellises of the units. A one-bedroom apartment with garden view is $105 for up to four guests; with ocean view, $115. A two-bedroom garden-view unit is $125 for one to six people; with ocean view, $135. Cribs are available for $8 per night. Minimum stay is two nights. All rates are subject to change. For reservations write to Pacific Basin Management Corporation, P.O. Box 126, Maunaloa, Molokai, HI 96770 (tel. 552-2761). For toll-free reservations, phone 800/888-2791. FAX: 552-0045.

Molokai Shores is located just a mile from Kaunakakai, between the Pau Hana Inn and the Hotel Molokai. The three-story, 102-unit oceanfront apartment building has very pleasant one-bedroom/one-bath and two-bedroom/two-bath units, all with ocean views, color TVs, well-equipped kitchens, and private lanais overlooking tropical lawns. Picnic tables, barbecue units, and a putting green make outdoor life pleasant, and there's a pool for swimming (the beach is not particularly good here). The one-bedroom units begin at $70 daily during low season for two people, and most can accommodate four ($10 for each additional person per night); and the two-bedroom/two-bath units are $100 for four, and can accommodate six. Weekly rates available. For reservations, phone 800/367-7042, or write to The Hawaiian Islands Resorts, P.O. Box 212, Honolulu, HI 96810.

The east shore of Molokai is a newer area for tourist development, and it's quite lovely, a good base of operations for some nice swimming beaches and excursions to Halawa Valley. Nestled against the East Molokai mountains is **Wavecrest Resort,** with tennis courts, a swimming pool, and all the amenities necessary for at-home resort living. There's not much of a beach, but it's okay for fishing. The 126 one- and two-bedroom condominium apartments are all smartly furnished with fully equipped electric kitchen and color TV. From your private lanai you can see Maui, right across the water. One-bedroom apartments run $56 ocean view, $66 ocean-front for two people; for $77 and $87, you can also have the use of a car. Two-bedroom units for up to four people are $76 ocean view, $86 oceanfront; with a car, they are $97 and $107. From December 20 to April 20, add $5 per night; additional persons are $5 a night. For reservations, call toll free 800/367-2980. The local phone is 558-8101.

In this same area, just past the 16-mile marker at Pukoo, is **Swenson's Vacation Cottage.** Here's a perfect retreat for those who really want to get away from it all. Diane and Larry Swenson, whose house fronts on a sandy swimming beach, are renting a fully equipped beachfront cottage with living room, kitchen, bedroom and bath, which can sleep four people. The rate is $50 per night for two, $66 per night for four; there is a two-night minimum stay. You're welcome to pick bananas, papayas, and mangoes in season from the trees, and since the house sits in a coconut grove, the ground is usually covered with coconuts, which the owners will husk for you. Within walking distance is Pukoo Lagoon, and from your window, views of Maui, Lanai, and the ocean. Write to Diane and Larry Swenson, P.O. Box 1979, Kaunakakai, Molokai, HI 96748, or phone 567-6822. FAX: 567-6155.

It's an easy walk to the beach from **Honomuni House,** a country cottage that can accommodate up to four adults. There's a private enclosed sleeping area; a large living/dining area with color TV and a sofa bed; a nicely equipped kitchen, a full bath plus a Hawaiian shower outdoors, and a covered lanai. Rates are $65 per day for two, $10 for each additional adult, $5 for a child. The weekly rate is $375. Hosts Jan and Keaho, who are educators in marine biology and Pacific studies, are available to answer questions and they invite guests to enjoy the papayas and other tropical fruits fresh from their garden. Phone them at 558-8383 or write: Honomuni House, Star Route 306, Kaunakakai, HI 96748.

Also on the eastern end of Molokai, in the town of Kamalo, Herb and Marina Mueh, longtime Hawaii residents, have a private B&B country cottage on their grounds; it faces a large lawn surrounded by five acres of flowers and trees. The cottage is fully equipped with cooking and dining facilities, has two couches that convert to twin beds at night, a stall shower, and a pleasant deck for lounging and watching the birds. Breakfast items are provided. Maximum occupancy is two adults (no children); minimum stay is three days. Snorkeling/swimming beaches are about an 8-to-10-mile drive. Rates are $50 a day. Write or call Herb and Marian Mueh, Star Rt., Box 128, Kaunakakai, HI 96748, tel. 558-8236.

---

2. Island Restaurants

There aren't many restaurants to choose from in the only business district on Molokai, on Ala Malama in Kaunakakai. Local friends advise that you keep your eyes peeled (especially on Tuesday and Friday) for Christita Reyes, a Filipino lady who parks her bright-blue station wagon in town around lunchtime and sells local delicacies from the back of the wagon. All dishes are cooked in a certified kitchen, and you can usually get shoyu or teriyaki chicken, vegetable tempura, coconut candy on a

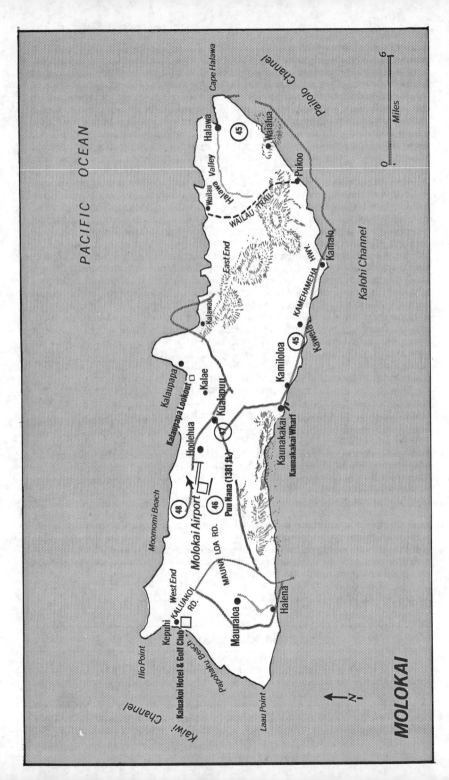

stick, and other goodies, at very reasonable prices. Another local lady also sells food from her station wagon, this one an older model but also painted a shiny blue. Her lunches, too, are both affordable and delicious. **Outpost Natural Foods,** at the west end of town (behind Kalama's Service Station) is a natural-foods store and juice bar/restaurant with picnic tables outside that's quite pleasant for a light and health- ful meal. In addition to freshly squeezed Molokai orange juice, carrot juice, and the like, they offer vegetarian sandwiches for under $3 (the wholegrain bread is baked fresh in Hawaii, the organic lettuce and greens are grown on Molokai), salads, burritos, and a special hot lunch every day. The hot lunch has to be one of the best buys in town, since it always includes an entree such as a pasta or tofu dish or stir-fry veggies, plus salad, for $3.50. Everything is available for take-out. Very popular here is the self-service Vitari machine, which dispenses a luscious all-fruit ice cream. Open every day except Saturday from 9am to 6pm.

Kanemitsu Bakery and Coffee Shop on Ala Malama is primarily a bakery, but it does serve great inexpensive breakfasts (two eggs with meat, hash browns, and coffee for $2.75), and offers sandwiches, plate lunches, and daily specials for lunch and dinner until 9pm. Kanemitsu is famous for its flavorful Molokai French bread (a great gift item, by the way, for friends in Honolulu). They also bake excellent cheese and onion breads and even sell fresh fish—if the fishermen bring them in that day. This humble bakery actually turns out up to 1,500 loaves a day, and will deliver bread to the airport in cartons. It opens at 5:30am, and is closed on Tuesdays.

There are three other pretty good possibilities: a Chinese restaurant quaintly called Hop Inn, Mid-Nite Inn, and a local Filipino place, Oviedo's. Don't let the dreary outside appearance of **Hop Inn** put you off; just about every building in town shows its age, and inside you'll find a clean place and good Chinese cooking. The à la carte dishes are reasonable: We spent $5.15 for almond duck, $4.75 for lemon chicken. A Mongolian beef sizzling plate is very good at $6.95. Open daily from 11am to 9pm. Watch for Hop Inn on the left as you drive up Ala Malama Street from Kam Hwy.

We don't know why they call it **Mid-Nite Inn,** since it's never open at midnight: 5:30am (they get up early on Molokai) to 1:30pm and 5:30 to 9pm are more like it at this venerable local establishment, with tables, booths, and tasty, inexpensive food. Owner John Arthur Kikukawa and his staff are super-friendly, and you know they've got to be nice people if they're offering delicious fresh fish dinners, fried and served with rice and kim chee, for less than $7! Fresh grilled akule, one of their spe- cialties, is almost always available. Most non-seafood entrees, like breaded veal cutlet, fried chicken thighs, teriyaki steak with fried onions, go for $4 to $5.50. Piz- za is served at lunch and dinner on Thursday, Friday, and Saturday. You're welcome to bring your own bottle of wine; they'll gladly uncork it and provide glasses at no charge. Breakfast is also available at good old-fashioned prices like $1.50 for hotcakes and coffee. (For a solution to the name mystery, see the Readers' Selections, at the end of this chapter.) Open daily, except for Sunday dinner.

To sample Filipino food, sit down for lunch or get a take-out plate at **Oviedo's,** a simple, home-style restaurant on the main street in Kaunakakai. Oviedo's is open from 10am to 7pm every day, and features such Filipino specialties as pork adobo (adobo is a kind of stew), tripe stew, and roast pork, $6 for a lunch or dinner plate.

Take-out Filipino food is also available at **Kaunakakai Market** on Ala Malama, next door to Molokai Fish and Dive. Here, in addition to groceries, meat, vegeta- bles, liquor, and such, one can get a good rice and adobo dish, a different one every weekday, for about $6, served "from 11am until food pau," according to the owner, Mrs. Rabang. She also suggests you try the Filipino dessert called *halohalo*—ask her to explain what it is. (If you've been to Molokai before, you might remember the Rabangs' former little restaurant up in Kualapuu.) Open 9am to 9pm daily.

If you're driving the long 25 miles out to Halawa Valley, you'll want to know about the **Neighborhood Store 'n Counter** at the 16-mile marker going east. New owners have recently expanded the food menu, with the largest selection of local- style plate lunches on the island. They also have fresh fish (in burgers, tacos, and by the pound), regular burgers, traditional Hawaiian food, fresh baked pies, bento and sushi plates, chicken buckets, plus ice cream and sodas. You can take your food and eat outside under the trees. The new owners, incidentally, are local native Hawaiian activists who share a closeness to the land and the environment. It is a "pro-Molokai" establishment, where a large selection of reading materials and T-shirts are available for socially conscious folks.

Hotel Molokai has long boasted an excellent restaurant, **Holo Holo Kai** (tel. 553-5347), right on the edge of the ocean and open to its charms. Lunch is very pleasant here, since $6.50 gets you a bountiful salad (the fruits and vegetables are fresh from the garden), plus a soup and a hot entree. At dinner, fresh catch of the day, $16.95, with soup and salad bar, is very popular. Honey-dipped chicken with rice and vegetables is $10 without the salad bar. Beef stew, a local favorite, is served with rice or poi, and elicited from one of our readers, Jack Lindberg of San Jose, California, the comment that "it is a bottomless bowl of hearty munching: It approaches my Irish mother's blend—ummm!" Entertainment by singer-guitarist Kimo Paleka accompanies dinner, served daily from 6 to 9pm, on Thursday, Friday, and Saturday night. Lunch is served from 11:30am to 2pm. Box lunches, around $6, are, to our appetite, big enough for two.

Now here's a special tip for those of you who are going to be in Molokai only for one day. Take an early-morning flight out from Honolulu or Maui, and go directly from the airport to the Hotel Molokai, where breakfast is served up until 10:30am. Treat yourself to either of their famous breakfast specialties—Holo Holo Kai french toast (which is Molokai bread in a banana-egg batter, with a choice of meats) or our personal favorite, papaya pancakes (these are hot cakes dipped in a special papaya batter, topped with crushed macadamia nuts, plus a choice of breakfast meats). Both of these treats are under $5. Now, after your coffee, you're set for a day of exploring Molokai.

Dining at the **Banyan Terrace** of the Pau Hana Inn (tel. 553-5342) is also extremely pleasant. Both indoor and outdoor seating is available: indoors in a big rustic dining room with a tremendous fireplace, outdoors under the enormous, spreading Bengalese banyan tree out on the beach, which is also the scene of night-time entertainment. The banyan, also known as an East Indian fig tree, has been standing sentinel over the ocean here for almost a hundred years. Dinner is well priced, with most entrees—like catch of the day, honey-dipped chicken, barbecued beef short ribs, top sirloin—in the $7.95 to $16.95 range. Specialty of the house is prime ribs, a 10 oz.-cut for $13.95. The price of the entree includes a salad bar, a hot vegetable, fries or rice or mashed potatoes, Molokai bread and butter. At lunch their daily specials are around $5, like spaghetti with garlic bread and salad, fried chicken, plus sandwiches, from about $3.50 to $6.85.

Banyan Terrace is generally open from 6:30 to 10:30am, 11:30am to 2pm, and again from 6 to 9pm, but it's all "Hawaiian time."

Many of the local people feel the glamorous **Ohia Lodge** of the Kaluakoi Hotel (tel. 552-2555), a South Seas spot overlooking the water, is the best dining room on Molokai. There's music for dancing here every night. Most reasonable items on the menu are the pasta choices, from $12.95 for pasta Alfredo to $16.75 for a seafood jamboree of shrimp, scallops, and island fish. Steak, rib, and lamb dishes are $17.50 to $21, and fish freshly caught from Pacific waters is market priced. We like their Oriental specialties: the Indonesian chicken at $15.75, and the Hunan duck with plum sauce at $18.75. Entrees come with rice pilaf and fresh sautéed vegetables. Appetizers have an Oriental flavor, too—spring rolls, teriyaki sticks, and chicken sate, $2.95 to $3.50. You could have a salad buffet of tropical fruits, garden vegetables, and cheeses for $8.75, and a bowl of Portuguese bean soup for $2.75. Lunch is fun, too, with a variety of light meals, good salads (chicken salad in papaya boat, sesame chicken, tropical fruit salad, etc.) from $6.95 to $7.25, sandwiches (vegetarian to flame-broiled steak), and lovely desserts: We like the cappuccino crunch pie at $3.75. Molokai Country Breakfasts are hearty ways to start the morning. Breakfast is served from 6:30 to 10:30am, lunch from noon to 2pm, dinner from 6 to 9pm.

For a real budget meal in this area, dine with the islanders at **Jo Jo's Café** (tel.

552-2803), not far from the Kaluakoi Resort; it's in Maunaloa, in the tavern section of the old Pooh's Restaurant. Jo Jo Espaniola is no longer there, but new owners have maintained the down-home atmosphere. The old antique bar is still here. The menu is the same all day, and prices are low for the likes of chopped steak, Korean ribs, teriyaki plates and such, from about $4.50 to $7. All entrees are served with vegetables and a scoop of rice. Jo Jo's specialty is fish; they serve several different fish dishes every day, either frozen or fresh, whenever it's available, so you may be lucky enough to get ahi, mahimahi, ono, aku, or opakapaka, very reasonably priced from $4.75 to $6.95. Hamburgers, surfburgers, hot dogs, saimin, and salad, too. For dessert, try one of their fresh island homemade toppings on an ice-cream sundae, or have a piece of pie—all from $1.50 to $1.99. Funky and fun. Open daily from 11:30am to 7:30pm.

You'll probably be driving through the little town of Kualapuu at some point in your stay on Molokai, perhaps to visit the Kalaupapa Lookout, the Mule Barn, or the Meyer Sugar Mill (see below), so it's good to know that there's now a charming little café in this old plantation town. Look for **Kualapuu Cook House** (tel. 567-6185) as you head up Kalae Road and then take a left turn onto Farrington Road. It actually was a cook house, back in the days of the Del Monte Plantation. Now owner Nanette Yamashita has turned it into a quality eating place, with seating either indoors or on an outdoor patio. Fresh foods are featured at very reasonable prices, like $3.79 for a complete breakfast—eggs, meat, rice, and pancakes or french toast. At lunch and dinner, nothing on the regular à la carte menu is over $8; local favorites are served, as well as gourmet burgers, made from hamburger ground fresh every day. A daily plate special gives you a full meal for $5 to $7, including entree, salad, rice, and beverage. And for dessert, you must have one of Nanette's homemade pies and cakes. She bakes daily and always makes pumpkin, custard, and apple pies. Cream or chiffon pies are made from fresh local fruits in season. Honey-butter cake is another popular specialty.

Kualapuu Cook House is open from 7am to 8pm weekdays, to 3pm Saturdays, closed Sundays. A welcome addition to restaurant-poor Molokai.

---

3. The Night Scene

Nightlife on Molokai, as we travelers know it, is almost all in the major hotels. A dance band plays every night at the **Ohia Lodge** of the Kaluakoi Hotel. You might want to try a Molokai Mule (it has a kick!) in the cocktail lounge; you get to take home the mug. . . . The bar at the **Hotel Molokai** is a pleasant place to be, since it's in between the pool area and the open-at-the-sides dining room; so you can have a drink and watch the entertainment by Kimo Paleka on Thursday, Friday, and Saturday night. During the 11am to 6pm happy hour, beer is $2 to $2.75, drinks run $1.50 to $3.50. At the **Banyan Terrace** of the Pau Hana Inn, a local group called the Ebb Tides, takes to the stage under the banyan tree and gives out with its special brand of Hawaiian, country and western, rock music and what-have-you, Friday and Saturday evenings until about 1am. A very popular local scene. Happy hour is on from 2 to 6pm.

In general, one might say that nightlife on Molokai is impromptu. It all depends on when local people feel like doing things (people here are not apt to let work interfere with their lives!). But check the local papers; there may be a hula show or even a luau at the Pau Hana Inn when you're in town.

---

4. Shopping

Molokai is perhaps the only place in the islands that is *not* heaven for shopping buffs—so much so, that many locals go off-island (they'll fly to Honolulu on one of the little commuter planes) to do their shopping—and that even includes grocery shopping.

The local supermarkets, grocery shops, and liquor stores on Ala Malama, the main street of Kaunakakai, a general store here and there in the country, and a handful of craft shops just about do it.

To stock up on organic local produce—papayas, bananas, avocados, sprouts, etc.—try **Outpost Natural Foods** (next door to the laundry), which sells the usual natural-food-store fare plus other items at the lowest possible prices. They also have an excellent juice bar/restaurant (see above). Pick up a sandwich or get some Cosmic Cabbage or Maui Onion Salsa, a local delicacy. . . . For the best selection of books on the island, try **Molokai Drugs,** also on Ala Malama. They have a particularly good selection of Hawaiiana, and also sell local crafts and gift items in addition to the usual drugs and sundries. . . . **Port of Call** on Ala Malama (on the second floor over the bank) has the only hairstyling salon in town, unisex. . . . To learn where the fish are biting, and to get fishing, diving, snorkeling, and camping gear, plus boogie boards and golf balls, the place to go is **Molokai Fish and Dive,** also on Ala Malama. But they're more than just a sporting goods store; they have the largest collection of Molokai souvenirs on the island, including a huge selection of T-shirts, designed and printed for them and sold exclusively here. And next door is their boutique for island fashions, called **Molokai Island Creations.** Here you'll find muumuus, swimwear, clothes for kids, ivory and coral jewelry, books, cards, and more. There's plenty to catch your eye here. . . . You can shop late, until 10:30pm every day, at **Molokai Wines 'n' Spirits Unlimited,** for groceries, meats, even T-shirts. (On holidays they close at 6pm.) **Imamura's** on Ala Malama has a little bit of everything, and is lots of fun to poke around in.

Our favorite Molokai shopping is out in **Maunaloa** (not far from the Kaluakoi Resort). Once a thriving plantation town, Maunaloa has been declining since Dole closed shop in 1975; however, young artisans are seeking it out and showing their wares here. We should tell you at the start that this is the most laidback "shopping area" we've ever come across, with shops staying open more or less as inspiration moves the owners, who often seem to be out fishing or surfing or visiting Honolulu. However, one owner who's always on hand and happy to greet visitors, is Jonathan Socher of the **Big Wind Kite Factory.** Jonathan and his wife Daphne not only create some beautiful, high-flying kites (which are sold in many neighbor island shops, as well as in Fiji), but they even offer free flying lessons with modern 100-mph "aerobatic kites." It's also fun to take a mini-tour of their mini-factory, where they demonstrate the techniques of kite making. Their most popular items are pineapple windsox and mini-kites at $14.95, and rainbow-spinning windsox at $15 to $35. Note Daphne's award-winning "cheetah kite" with a 20-foot tail. Also popular are their kite kits for kids to color, cut out, and fly, at $2.95. A great browsing spot, open Monday to Saturday from 8:30am to 5pm, and Sunday from 10am to 2pm.

Adjacent to the kite factory, Jonathan has created **Plantation Gallery,** which shows the work of several island artisans. One is the **Tao Woodcarver** (Bill Decker) who creates beautiful hand-carved bowls and boxes of rare Hawaiian woods; large items, like desks and sculpture, are available on commission. You'll probably find Butch Tabanao and his deerhorn jewelry, hair combs (from $12), and cribbage boards (around $40) made from the axis deer of Molokai—unless the surf is up. There's raku pottery sculpture by Katie Leong from $20, and Hawaiian pillowcase quilts by Ginger La Voie at $25. Several local artists do hand-painted shirts at $25, long-sleeved tops at $42. On our last visit, Jonathan proudly showed us his new collection of personally chosen imports from Bali and Southeast Asia: He calls this the "Bali Hale Gift Shop." It's full of delightful surprises, such as colorful wooden bird mobiles and birds of paradise stalks, $25 and $35; batik pillow covers; pareaus; wonderful Balinese masks called "guardians" or "crib angels"; magnificent batik quilts for $400; and colorful wooden bird and fish earrings at $7.50, and you get another pair free. Note, too, the collection of books, cards, and prints by leading island artists. The gallery/shop is decorated with orchid plants and an aquarium, and there's a garden outside. For lovers of the unusual, a must stop.

Across the road from the Plantation Gallery are several small cottages. In one of them, Lori Cavanaugh, the owner of **Dolly Hale** (that's pronounced "holly" and means house) creates charming handcrafted dolls, priced from around $7.50 to $20. Angel dolls are made of coconut fiber with macadamia-nut heads, then decorated with shells, dried flowers, seeds, and ti leaves that have been collected locally. One-of-a-kind, these are a must for the doll or Christmas-tree-ornament collector. Molokai Tita Dolls are rag dolls with hand-painted faces and hand silk-screened dresses of Hawaiian flowers. No regular hours here; let's hope she'll be open when you're there.

Hotel shopping is limited in Molokai, but do stop in at **The Molokai Gift Shop** at the Hotel Molokai, where proprietor Maria Watanabe offers clothing, T-shirts, books, sundries, and crafts by Molokai artists. We've found some nice things here, and prices are usually lower than on the other islands.

5. Seeing the Sights

Sightseeing on Molokai requires a bit more determination on the part of the visitor than it does on the other islands. A visit to the island's most spectacular scenic spot, Halawa Valley, involves some rugged driving and an hour's hike. To reach Kalaupapa, the major point of interest on the island, you have to either fly, hike, or ride a mule down a steep pali. But if you're willing to put up with a few obstacles, you might find sightseeing on Molokai among the most rewarding adventures of your trip to Hawaii. Sightseeing tours and local guides are especially helpful on this island.

PURDY'S NUT FARM

We don't know of any other macadamia farm in Hawaii where either the owner or his mother will greet you personally and take you on a tour of his orchards. But a visit to Purdy's All Natural Macadamia Nut Farm, the only working macadamia-nut grove on the island, is different. Owner Tuddie Purdy and his mother conduct a very good tour, and not only do they tell you all you ever wanted to know about macadamia nuts, but they also show you a variety of Hawaiian fruits and flowers. Most fun of all, you get to crack some macadamia nuts and try them raw. Then you'll be given some fruit and macadamia-blossom honey to taste, plus samples of their toasted macadamia nuts, which are remarkably light, surprisingly non-oily—and absolutely delicious. They'll give you the recipe for their Ono Toasted Macadamia Nuts, and you can also buy them right on the spot. They also sell raw macadamia nuts out of the shell, as well as the honey. The farm is located on 1½ acres in Hoolehua Hawaiian Homesteads, and open every day from 9am to 1pm, or by appointment: phone 567-6601 daytime, 567-6495 in the evening. It's not far from the airport, but it's best to ask for driving directions there. If you're in Molokai for a one-day trip, this could be a fun way to start the day.

THE TRIP TO HALAWA VALLEY

For a beautiful day on Molokai, get up early, have your hotel pack you a picnic box lunch (or put one together from the supermarkets in town), hop into your car, and head for Halawa Valley. The trip is just about 25 miles from Kaunakakai along Kamehameha IV Hwy., but it will probably take you two hours to get there, since the last part of the driving is rough going. This is Molokai's southeastern coast, dotted with ancient heiaus, old fish ponds (some of which are used for scientific studies), and many coastal churches built by Father Damien and others. You won't be able to see the heiaus unless you get permission to go on private property, but you can stop in at **St. Joseph's Catholic Church** in Kamalo. The church, and the lovely statue of Father Damien beside it, were designed and built by Father Damien, who was a skilled carpenter. A little further on is Father Damien's **Our Lady of Sorrows Church,** where you'll see a statue of Damien in a pavilion near the church. As you drive by the Kamalo mountains, watch for rainbows and double rainbows—they're not uncommon here. When you get to Mapulehu, at mile 15½, look on the right for a sign to the **Mapulehu Mango Grove,** the largest mango patch in Hawaii, with over 2,000 mango trees of many varieties, plus a coconut grove. You can stop to pick up some tropical fruits here, as well as mango and other fruit juices at a little stand fronting the ocean. (Snorkeling tours and equipment are also available.) You'll begin seeing sandy beach again in the Pukoo area. There are many secluded little beach coves along this coast, but they are unmarked and difficult to find, so best to ask local people for directions. From the beach here, you can see Maui, only nine miles across the water.

About 20 miles out, past Pauwalu, the broad country road begins to narrow, and soon you're on a one-lane road where the sharp turns force the car to practically creep along while the scenery becomes more beautiful every minute. Then you begin to climb up, up, through the ranchlands of **Puu O Hoku Ranch,** from which a narrow road takes you into the Halawa Valley. We hope you do make it into the valley, because this is veritably a tropical paradise, a remote Shangri-La that one may find difficult to believe still exists. Once a populous area, it was swept by a tidal wave in 1946 and largely deserted. You can explore the valley (a few people still live here), have a swim in the bay, or make a roughly two-hour hike to the valley's most spectacular point, **Moaula Falls.** (You'll probably need mosquito repellent.) The rewards are a picnic or a swim at the base of a waterfall that plunges relentlessly down from dizzying heights. The water is cold and delicious, but according to Molokai legend, it is only safe to swim here if the ti leaf that you throw in floats. If it should sink, you'll have to make your own decision. Remember to make this trip in the morning, since, after a hike back to your car, you'll have to drive another two hours or so back to your hotel.

Note: Since so many people have difficulty finding the falls, we refer you to Mr. and Mrs. Wayne Ditmer's letter in the Readers' Selections, ahead.

KALAUPAPA OVERLOOK

Even if you don't get to Kalaupapa itself, you should pay a visit to the Kalaupapa Overlook in Palaau Park. It's an easy trip on very good roads, about 10 miles from Kaunakakai on Hwy. 460. After you make your right on 470 and begin to climb to Upper Molokai, the air becomes fragrant with eucalyptus and pine. Park your car at **Palaau State Park,** a well maintained and popular camping and picnicking spot for the local people. A short walk through towering cypress and pine and suddenly you're high, high up, looking down immense cliffs to the Kalaupapa peninsula below. From the overlook, you can see the world's tallest sea cliffs, 3,300 ft. high at Umilehi Point. A series of six informative plaques tell the Kalaupapa story, but official descriptions seem superfluous. Just standing here, gazing down at the peninsula below, you are caught up in some of the tremendous sorrow of those who lived their lives of exile at Kalaupapa.

There is another trail, this one a bit longer (and steeply uphill some of the way) that leads to the **Phallic Rock.** According to legend, barren women who made offerings to the rock and spent the night here would then become capable of bearing children. Supposedly, an unfaithful husband of one of the minor goddesses was transformed into this rock and his mana still remains there.

While you're pondering this story (wrongdoers were often turned into stone in Hawaiian mythology), get back into your car and drive down the hill. Two miles below the overlook, on Hwy. 470, you may want to pay a visit to the **Meyer Sugar Mill,** an authentic restoration of an 1878 sugar mill that has been restored to operating condition after almost a century of neglect. The only surviving 19th-century sugar mill in Hawaii, it is listed on the National Register of Historic Places. Local volunteer labor spent several years on its restoration. The original machinery, including the mule-drive cane crusher, is still in operating condition. Photos and memorabilia of the mill's original owner, and of his Hawaiian-born wife, Kalama Waha, provide a glimpse into early Molokai history. The mill is open from 10am to noon Monday to Saturday and on Sunday from 1 to 5pm, for guided and self-guided tours. Admission is $2.50 for adults, $1 for students (tel. 567-6436). Continue down the road now to the little town of Kualapuu, where, now that the Del Monte pineapple plantation has been phased out, diversified agriculture is a growing industry (Molokai is now the state's leading producer of watermelon). Here's where you'll also find the pleasant little **Kualapuu Cook House Restaurant** that we've told you about (above). Turn left on Puupeelua Avenue, and you arrive back at the airport road.

If you're in the mood for traveling, continue west on Hwy. 460 past the airport, and you're on Maunaloa Road, which goes 10 miles to the old Dole pineapple village to Maunaloa, about 1,300 feet high with its unusual little crafts shops (see above).

MOLOKAI RANCH WILDLIFE PARK

Yes, you can go on a safari of sorts in Molokai, a camera safari to see over 1,000 African and Asian animals that live on the grounds of the 1,000-acre natural wildlife preserve known as Molokai Ranch Wildlife Park. The dry terrain of western Molokai happens to be quite similar to that of the Kalahari Desert of Botswana, in Africa. The animals, which include giraffe, zebra, Barbary sheep, Indian black buck, eland, oryx, greater kudu, sika and axis deer, East African crowned crane, rhea, and wild turkey, thrive here. Safari Chief Pilipo Solitario, known as "the man who talks to animals," leads visitors on an hour-and-a-half tour in an air-conditioned van, stopping often for photos and allowing the animals, who appear out of the thickets and ravines when they hear his horn, to feed out of his hand. After the tour of the park, visitors adjourn to the picnic and petting area, where they are given free snacks and soft drinks, and where they can feed the curious and friendly giraffes who gather around to see the funny people. Cost of the tour is $25 for adults, $10 for children 12 and under, and arrangements can be made at the Kaluakoi Hotel Travel Desk, or by phoning 552-2555. We get good readers' comments on this one.

MOLOKAI WAGON RIDE

This new Molokai adventure is a delight. Your horse-drawn wagon stops first at the Ili Ili O Pae Heiau, one of Hawaii's largest and best preserved temples, built in the 13th century, where a guide explains the historical background; then it's back down the trail to the Mapulehu Mango Grove, the largest mango grove in the world. Then it's on to the beach for a Molokai-style barbecue and a fabulous party, complete with Hawaiian music, traditional Hawaiian net throwing, fishing, coconut husking, and many surprises. Guests are invited to try their hand at all the activities. Cost is $33 for adults, $16.50 for ages 5 through 12 (free for those under 5). Guided horseback rides are also available. For reservations, phone Larry Helm at 567-6773 from 6 to 8am and after 6pm, or at 558-8380 (the wagon-ride site) from 10am to 3pm daily, or write Molokai Wagon Ride, P.O. Box 56, Hoolehua, Molokai, HI 96729.

SAILING AND BOATING

If you love to sail, consider the 42-foot sloop *Satan's Doll*, docked at Kaunakakai Wharf (tel. 553-5852), which takes a minimum of four people for its sailing adventures.

The boat cruises run by **Hokupaa Ocean Adventures** (tel. 558-8195) are a bit different, since they depart from Halawa Valley and tour Molokai's north coast, cruising beneath the world's highest sea cliff. The four-hour cruise aboard their 25-foot twin diesel-engine cabin cruiser, *Mahealani*, costs $50 per person. At scenic spots along the way they stop for bottom fishing and snorkeling. Summer only.

BEACHCOMBING

Papohaku Beach, on Molokai's western shore, part of Kaluakoi Resort, is the largest white-sand beach in the Hawaiian Islands, almost three miles long. It's the ideal spot for a beach picnic, but not—alas—for ocean swimming, since the water here is usually quite rough in winter. During summer, waters are generally calm.

There's access at Papohaku Beach Park, which has picnic grounds, barbecues, showers, a pavilion with rest rooms and changing area, plus parking. Camping is also available.

THE TRIP TO KALAUPAPA SETTLEMENT

Even some of those who have never been to Hawaii have heard about Father Damien and what he did for the destitute lepers on Molokai about a century ago. In 1989, on the 100th anniversary of the death of Father Damien, a Damien Centennial Year was declared by both the state of Hawaii and the government of Belgium. Representatives of the Roman Catholic Church (Father Damien is a candidate for canonization), government officials, and the faithful from throughout the world gathered in Molokai to honor him. Kalaupapa is where he performed his labors, and it is still in operation as a center for the treatment of leprosy—which is now politely called "Hansen's disease." Less than 100 patients and former patients are still on Kalaupapa, and to visit their island home is a moving experience. It is not, however, a trip we advise everyone to make. It is not for those who get nervous just thinking about diseases (although leprosy has been arrested by modern drugs and is presumably not contagious), and it is definitely not for those with idle curiosity. The people of Kalaupapa do not wish to be patronized. Getting to their beautifully but tragically isolated home takes a bit of doing, and the emotions the trip can raise have been overwhelming to more than one visitor. We can promise only one thing: It is a special kind of experience, and one not easily forgotten.

There are a couple of ways to get to Kalaupapa. The one that's the most exciting is the famous mule trip run by **Rare Adventures/Molokai Mule Ride.** Mule riders should be between 16 and 70 years of age and weigh no more than 225 pounds. We might add that only those who are accustomed to riding should attempt this one, although many nonriders do take the trip. It's an unforgettable experience as the mule descends a spectacular, steep switchback trail 1,600 feet below the towering cliffs at Kalae into Kalaupapa. You are met at the peninsula, given a tour and a picnic lunch, and then returned to the trail for the ride to the top at 2pm. Cost is around $85, plus tax. Call the stables at 567-6088. You can make reservations in advance by writing to Rare Adventures, Ltd., P.O. Box 200, Kualapuu, HI 96757 or phoning toll free from the U.S. mainland, 800/843-5978.

It's more economical, of course, to hike down the trail; it's a scenic 3⅛-mile cliff walk that should take about an hour and a half. It's safe for most hikers; the hike *up* the pali, however, is arduous, and if you hike down, you must also hike up. You must be at Kalae Stables by 8:30am, since all hikers must go down before the mules do. **Rare Adventures "Molokai Hike-In"** costs $30 and includes a pass to enter Kalaupapa Peninsula, a picnic lunch, and the ground tour of the settlement. Call the above numbers in advance.

There is, of course, an easier way to get to Kalaupapa, the one we personally favor, and that's by air. Call Richard Marks' **Damien Molokai Tours** at 567-6171 (the only tour service operated by former patients who know Kalaupapa from the inside out), and they will arrange for you to fly in from upper Molokai via an 18-passenger shuttle flight for $30 (best time to call is between 7 and 9am and 5 and 8pm) round trip. Keep in mind that you cannot walk past the gate at the top of the cliff trail or around the peninsula without a permit, according to Health Department rules (Damien Molokai Tours will handle all permits). Minors under 16 are not allowed at Kalaupapa. Bring some lunch, as there are no stores or restaurants open to visitors at Kalaupapa. Yes, you may bring your camera and binoculars. Advance reservations for the tour are a must: phone 567-6171, or write Damien Molokai Tours, Box 1, Kalaupapa, Molokai, HI 96742. The full, four-hour grand tour costs $19 per person.

What you'll see on the tour—the early settlement of Kalawo where St. Philomena Church, built by Father Damien and now lovingly restored, still stands; the cemetery where he was buried before his remains were returned to Belgium; the grave of Mother Marianne; Siloama Church; and a glorious view of Molokai's towering mountains—is just the beginning. (Mother Marianne, by the way, is also a candidate for canonization by the Roman Catholic Church.) All the tour guides are expatients, people who can give you a look at Kalaupapa off the record. It is a magnificent sight—a testimony to the patients who took barren lands and turned them into Eden, a testimony to the medical pioneers and missionaries who preserved so many lives; and yet it is a strangely paradoxical place. Despite the fact that many of the inhabitants live in cozy little houses and spend much of their time gardening and watching TV, Kalaupapa is one of the most silent places on earth. There are no children on Kalaupapa. Only a small minority of the residents have their spouses living with them; when pregnancy occurs, the expectant mother is usually flown from the island for the delivery, where she either remains to raise her child without its father or chooses to return to Kalaupapa alone. And this is the deepest of sorrow of all the sorrows of Kalaupapa.

There is another sorrow of Kalaupapa—the fear that, since there are so few patients left and since all of them have been cured or at least "arrested"—that Kalaupapa will one day soon give way to the gods of progress. The state government once talked about phasing out the patients at Kalaupapa and eventually turning the area into another giant tourist facility. Although the former patients may be physically able to return to society, it is hard for them to imagine a society in which their disfigurement—many are fingerless, toeless, scarred—would not, indeed, turn them into the social lepers of biblical days. Most are silent about this, a few are vocal and protesting. As wards of the state, they have little voice in determining their own future. Happily, their dream has come true: Under legislation passed by Congress, Kalaupapa will be left as it is until the last of the residents has died. It is now known as Kalaupapa National Historic Park. The remaining residents, most in their 50s and 60s, like to joke about themselves as an "endangered species." But all of them now live here by choice. What was once a veritable prison has now become a sanctuary.

Like so many visitors who come to Kalaupapa, you may want to stay here a few days to really get to know the people. But it is almost impossible; except for family members and "officials having business in the settlement," overnight stays have not been permitted. However, we have been informed that Damien Tours may have overnight accommodations available for selected groups or couples—not for mule-train passengers. Inquire to see if these are available.

The newest addition to the tour is a visit to the Kalaupapa Visitors Center, which has an excellent bookshop dealing with the history of Kalaupapa and Molokai. If you're lucky, your tour might include Richard Marks's own collection of Kalaupapa memorabilia, including antique bottles and clocks.

Note: On a recent visit to Kalaupapa, flying direct from Honolulu, we met two women who were making the exact same trip that we were; however, because they had booked the entire trip as a "tour" via a well-known tour operator, their cost was almost double ours. All you need do is make your own air arrangements and contact Damien Tours as we suggested: No need to waste your money.

READERS' SELECTIONS ON MOLOKAI: "The drive out to Halawa Valley is very scenic. When parking in the Moaula Falls parking lot (the yard of a resident), make sure any food is secured. A cat jumped in through our open car window and devoured my tuna sandwich. So much for the Friendly Isle! The parking attendant sells snacks, soda, and local fruit. This might be a nice time to try Granny Goose Taro Chips, since taro grows here in the valley, identifiable by its large heart-shaped leaf. . . . For things to do, consult the *Molokai News* or the *Molokai Dispatch,* free at the local stores. That's how we learned of Lei Day festivities on April 29 at several local schools. A very nice way to get to know the natives. . . . At **Purdy's Macadamia Nut Farm** I bought about three pounds of nuts in the shells for $7. They also sell local honey, and Mrs. Purdy makes and sells leis. They do have a mail order service. Write Purdy's Macadamia Nut Farm, P.O. Box 84, Hoolehua, Molokai, Hawaii 96729. Local phone is 567-6601.

"**Hotel Molokai** was lovely, and it did help to have a room away from the lobby/bar/restaurant area. One day was more than enough to drive around the island. The best part of Molokai was the **Mid-Nite Inn.** We had five meals on the island, and all five were at Mid-Nite. The prices were low to moderate, the service was quick and friendly, and the fish was marvelous. Mid-Nite fries fish with a pinch of light oil and soy sauce, not a greasy batter. The side dish with the fish is not the hot and garlic Korean kim chee, but a crunchy cucumber and daikon tsukemono" (Fred Shima, Los Angeles, Calif.).

"Our favorite gift item was the raw keawe honey produced by the **Molokai Honey Company** and available at most of the grocery stores in Kaunakakai. It, and Molokai bread from **Kanemitsu Bakery,** are also available at **Kepuhi Sundries** in the Kaluakoi Hotel, but at higher prices. . . . Be sure to try the fresh fish at Mid-Nite Inn. As a resident of Hawaii (Honolulu), I assure you that the akule and mullet (fish) served there is authentically 'island style' and very delicious" (June Honda, Honolulu, HI). . . . "The **Mid-Nite Inn** is as good as you said. We had a steak dinner, an ahu dinner, a side order of kim chee, Coke, coffee, and one dessert—*all* delicious—for under $16. We're going back tonight" (Pam Corwin, Olympia, Wash.).

"You can get to **Kalaupapa** by foot, on a mule, or by air. We chose air and were glad we did. We had four fascinating hours with **Richard Marks,** a fine guide. By mule the stay is only one-and-a-half hours, not nearly enough. We understand the mule trip is not all that easy, especially for us seniors. We saw some mule riders as they returned, and they looked pooped" (William S. Connell, Durham, N.H.). . . . "Our tour with Richard Marks was one of the most informative, inspiring tours we've ever taken. I would go again in a minute, only this time I would take a battery-operated tape recorder and tape what Marks had to say. What a remarkable man he is!" (Marymae H. Seaman, Lakewood, Colo.). . . . "We stayed at the **Molokai Shores Condos.** Of all the places we had stayed in the islands, this was the most pleasant. Every room has a view of the ocean. The rooms are very homey and comfortable. We found a great secluded beach with excellent snorkeling at a public beach park on the southeast end of the island. It also had barbecue grills and picnic tables. Above all, the residents really are friendly" (M.H.C., Lawai, HI).

"Readers should be warned that on the road going two miles northwest of Hoolehua, the two-lane paved road gets to the top of a hill and ends with an eight-inch drop and goes right into a one-lane dirt road. There is no warning as to the dead end, and there is even a painted strip in the middle of the road about 20 feet from the end. We were going about 50 mph in the rain and went off the end right into a huge, deep puddle of water and were fortunate to get out without being stuck" (Kenneth Kendall, Omaha, Nebr.)

"The **Molokai Ranch Wildlife Safari** is a great tour. The animals come right up to your van—fantastic. You can sign up for horseback riding at the Kaluakoi Hotel, even if you are not staying there. We were picked up for our ride by H. 'Nobu' Shimizu, who took us on a personal tour of the island after our horseback ride. He showed us the true aloha spirit" (Nancy Grant, South Easton, Mass.).

"Molokai is no place for swimming. Heavy surf along the north and western shores during winter months makes the beaches unswimmable except for experienced surfers. Residents claim that swimming is unsafe even in summer because of undertow and riptides. The local swim team has to practice off the wharf in Kaunakakai, as there is no other real swimming area. Snorkeling enthusiasts coming to Molokai should also be prepared for the fact that there really isn't any of note. You can get out to the reef from the Jay Cee beach on the south shore at about mile 20 if the tide is not too low. There is also a good spot at a tiny piece of beach just over the rocks to the east of Jay Cee, where a channel through the rocks takes you to deeper water and some nice coral heads. The current there, however, is very strong" (Judy Rosen, Alexandria, Va.).

"Visit the **Big Wind Kite Factory** in Maunaloa. The charming, hospitable owners are also technical giants when it comes to explaining the aerodynamics of various styles of kites. These are not the remembered paper-and-stick creations of long ago, but modern, jet-age wonders. With kites imported from all over the world, the shop is a delight, even if just to browse. If you are fortunate, the owner may take out his 'triple-decker' stunt kites and bedazzle you with dives and twists as the kites rattle crisply in the breeze. Beware, though—it is tough not to buy at least two! . . . It is still possible to be the 'only one' on a beach in Hawaii. Take a stroll along three-mile **Popohaku Beach,** just south of the Kaluakoi Hotel. Most of the water farther along is free of coral and slopes gently to wave level—good for body surfing, but the undertow may be dangerous, so 'know your water.' Snorkel toward the east end, past the 19-mile marker at a pretty little park. Lots of coral. Very shallow, lots of interesting fish. Great for poor swimmers since it is only waist deep way out" (Jack Lindberg, San José, Calif.).

"Molokai was the highlight of our 10-day trip to Hawaii. We enjoyed the **Hotel Molokai.** . . . We enjoyed shopping at **Takes,** a variety store on the main street in Kaunakakai. After returning our Datsun station wagon to **Avis,** their employee drove several miles out of her way to show us some sights we had missed. Molokai is indeed 'the friendly isle'" (Marion Montgomery, St. Paul, Minn.).

"I advise your readers to forget their budget when visiting Molokai, for if bound to the budget they would not have the experience of visiting **Kalaupapa**. I flew to the settlement on Polynesian Airways for $30. The Damien Tour costs $19. The returns from the investment will continue, for the experience was filled with love, sensitivity, and affection for a special group of proud people who ask for nothing but their dignity. I suggest that your readers read *Holy Man* by Gavin Daws, published by Harper & Row, prior to their trip. It will give them a broader insight and background" (A. Willet, Jr., Redwood City, Calif.). . . . "We found out why they call it **Mid-Nite Inn** the August 1981 issue (vol. 160, no. 2) of *National Geographic* in an excellent article, 'Molokai.' I quote: 'Art Kikukawa's restaurant, the Mid-Nite Inn, began as modestly as the bakery—with a saimin stand his mother opened. Four nights a week, departing travelers would eat the zesty noodle dish while waiting until midnight to board the interisland steamer. Hence the name'" (Marceile Gresch, Waukesha, Wis.).

"I went **snorkeling** just south of the Kaluakoi Hotel by the golf course after 5pm. The water was not clear enough to see the vivid colors of the fish (which I had remembered from prior snorkeling at Hanauma Bay on Oahu), but I wanted to give it a try anyhow. What I had not counted on, however, was the unpredictable currents near the large rocks. I barely avoided being swept into them, and/or out to sea. In discussion with the locals later, I learned that such experiences are not uncommon there. A safer area would be about 20 to 22 miles east of town on the route to Halawa Valley. I rented full snorkel gear at **Molokai Fish and Dive** (tel. 553-5926) in downtown Kaunakakai" (Mr. and Mrs. Ronald Sandberg, Pleasanton, Calif.).

"If you are leaving Molokai to go back to the mainland, there is no agriculture inspector there. Consequently, you must check all your luggage to Honolulu, pick it up there and take it to the agriculture inspectors, then to your airline back to the mainland. This is a real chore as both Aloha and Hawaiian Air are miles from the main terminal and a porter costs $4 and a taxi about the same, to say nothing of the walk you have to put in! In other words, if you're doing Molokai, don't do it last before you return" (Howard S. Walker, Sequim, Wash.). . . . "We found it very difficult to locate the trail to **Moaula Falls,** and could never have done it without the help of some of the local people. The hike was definitely worthwhile, however. I made the walk down into the **Kalaupapa Settlement.** The trail is a little over three miles long, and descends about 1,600 feet over 26 switchbacks. It is a difficult, rocky trail, but if you are in good hiking condition, you will find it well worthwhile. Coming up took a little longer, but wasn't as difficult as I had imagined, when going down. The tour through the area was a fascinating experience" (Rev. H.W. Schneider, Church of St. John the Apostle, Minot, N. Dak.).

"To get to **Moaula Falls** you must go up the dirt road in front of the small green church on the left side of the river as you face the falls. The small parking lot across from the church is the best place to leave your car. As you go up the road, stay on the main road until it ends; you go by several houses on the way. A trail takes over where the road ends. Go up this trail *only* about 100 yards and you will come to a row of rocks across the trail. Turn to the right here and follow the trail down to the stream. You have to cross *both* forks of the stream here. When you get to the other side, find a trail that goes up the hill perpendicular to the stream. (When you cross a mud flat, you will see an orange mark on a tree. Here, go right through some heavy grass. When you leave the grass, look behind you as you go up the trail. If you see some more orange marks, you know you are on the trail.) Shortly you come upon a major trail that has been blocked off to the right. Turn left and now follow the white plastic pipe and white arrows marking the trail to the falls for a spectacular hike and view of the falls and the pool below. The trail by the houses and through their fields on the right side has been closed off" (Mr. and Mrs. Wayne Ditmer, Mott, N. Dak.). . . . The trail of **Moaula Falls** is not well marked and is difficult to find. My suggestion is this: the walker's trail and the horse's trail are one and the same for most of the way. When starting out, cross both forks of the stream and keep a sharp watch for hoof prints. When you find the hoof prints, you will know you are going the right way. In **Halawa Valley,** a local resident has set up a parking lot on his property. He will watch your car for a small fee" (Thomas M. Nickel, San Diego, Calif.).

XVIII

ALTERNATIVE AND SPECIAL-INTEREST TRAVEL

1. ADVENTURE, WILDERNESS, AND ACTIVE TRAVEL
2. EDUCATIONAL TRAVEL
3. HOLISTIC HOLIDAYS: NURTURING BODY, MIND, AND SPIRIT

Everybody has a different idea of what travel should be like. If your ideas include some hands-on participation tours as opposed to the "just looking" variety; or if you wish to learn something new while you're on vacation; or if you're interested in going to a spa or to a New Age center where you can cultivate body, mind, and spirit—all against a background of the natural beauty of the Hawaiian Islands—read on.

You'll see that for these tours and trips, you'll need to break our usual $60-a-day budget. But while these may be considered "Big Splurges," all of them represent excellent value.

Note: Other active adventures—snorkeling, horseback riding, helicopter trips, and the like—are listed in their appropriate chapters.

1. Adventure, Wilderness, and Active Travel

The spectacular beauty of the Hawaiian Islands means that there's plenty of exciting adventure travel opportunities. Here are just a few ideas and resources to guide you.

BICYCLING TOURS
Backroads Bicycle Touring, 1516 5th St., Suite 422, Berkeley, CA 94710 (tel. 415/527-1555 or toll free 800/533-2573 outside California, FAX 415/527-1444). This well-known outfit runs bicycling tours in Europe, China, the U.S., and the Pacific. From November through April, they take a number of tours to Hawaii. Couples, singles, and families of all levels of ability are welcome, including seniors. Tours, which average $140 a day, include all meals and accommodations at attractive inns. Write for their free 64-page color catalog.

Island Bicycle Adventures, 569A Kapahulu Ave., Honolulu, HI 96815 (tel.

808/955-6789 or toll free 800/233-2226). Ron Reilly and a dedicated staff lead small groups (maximum 14) on six-day, five-night cycling tours through the mountains and valleys, shorelines and valleys and jungles of Maui, Kauai, or the Big Island. The only cycling tour group based in Hawaii, they can share local expertise. All-inclusive cost of approximately $785 excludes air fare, includes accommodations, meals, maps, support van, and services of two experienced leaders. Bicycle rental extra.

On The Loose Bicycle Vacations, 1030 Merced St., Berkeley, CA 94707 (tel. 415/527-4005 or, outside of California, toll free 800/346-6712). Choose a ten-day circle tour of the Big Island or a 10-day tour combining the Big Island with Maui, where the highlight is a bicycle trip 10,000 feet down to sea level from the summit of Mount Haleakala. Tours run from November through March, host a maximum of 16 guests, and are van-supported. People of all levels of cycling ability are welcome; they clock 30 to 60 miles per day. Cost is $1,295 for the Big Island alone, $1,495 for the two-island trip, both plus bicycle rentals. Rebecca and Edward Tilley are the people in charge.

ADVENTURE, WILDERNESS, AND HIKING/CAMPING TOURS

Crane Tours, c/o Bill Crane, 15101 Magnolia Blvd., H10, Sherman Oaks, CA 91403 (tel. 818/784-2213, or Ron Jones 714/773-5570), offers moderate to moderately strenuous trips for experienced backpackers. Seven-day excursions explore the Kona coast on the Big Island; and Waimea Canyon, the Alakai Swamp, and the Na Pali coast on Kauai; a Na Pali coast kayaking trip is also offered. Bring your own tents and backpacks. One or two nights are spent in mountain cabins, the last night of the seven-day trip in a hotel. The price, from $450 to $700, includes ground transportation, breakfast and dinner; participants make their own lunches. Groups are usually 10 to 15 people. Day hikes are also offered. Summer only.

Note: Those intent on seeing the July 11, 1991, total solar eclipse take note. Crane Tours is offering a special Solar Eclipse Tour. Several four-wheel-drive vehicles will take participants high on either Mauna Loa or Mauna Kea to the center of the four-minute totality zone for the highest probability of clear weather conditions. This trip will cost about $700; there will be day hiking and camping during the week, but no backpacking. As we go to press, practically every accommodation on the Big Island is sold out for that day, so if this is important to you *act immediately.*

Action Hawaii Adventures, P.O. Box 75548, Honolulu, HI 96815 (tel. 808/732-4453). Unique island tours with Action Hawaii Adventures include snorkeling, underwater photography, wave riding/boogie boarding, and a mountain walk to the summit of Diamond Head. Expert guides and certified lifeguards accompany small groups of no more than 14 persons, and make learning safe, fun, and easy for everyone. The cost of this eight-hour daily tour is $79 for adults, $69 for students, and includes narration on Hawaii's land, water, legends, and people; use of all gear; underwater camera; with transportation from Waikiki hotels.

Pacific Quest, P.O. Box 205, Haleiwa, HI 96712 (tel. 808/638-8338). Neophyte adventures and experienced outdoorspeople alike can enjoy the 14-day, four-island adventure trips planned by the islands' leading adventure travel company. Zane Bilgrav, the young owner, tries to avoid "just looking" types of activities, and instead, leads small groups in sailing, snorkeling, scuba diving, hiking, camping, and more on the islands of Kauai, Maui, the Big Island, and Molokai. Two nights of camping at the beach alternate with two nights of lodging in rustic cabins in mountainous volcano areas. Most participants are in the 25-to-40 age group, but there are many older couples and young family groups as well. The cost, around $1,550, includes all expenses—meals (except for one dinner), group camping equipment, the services of two guides, ground and air transportation, and boat charters within the islands (the trip starts in Kauai and ends in Honolulu).

Sierra Club, 730 Polk St., San Francisco, CA 94109. Trips of from seven to ten days' duration are run by the Sierra Club from spring through Christmas; most are on the Big Island; several are on Maui, Kauai, and sometimes on Molokai. These are considered leisurely trips, with some backpacking portions; bicycle tours are also available. There's often a choice of activities: hiking a trail or lazing on a beach. Price range is from $700 to $1,200 per week, including all ground costs. For the current catalog, write to the above address, enclosing a $2 check made out to the Sierra Club. Profits from these trips help support the conservation efforts of the Sierra Club.

Wilderness Hawaii, P.O. Box 61692, Honolulu, HI 96839 (tel. 808/737-4697). Shena W. Sandler leads a unique wilderness experience designed to promote personal empowerment and enhance self-esteem. An accomplished outdoors-woman and former instructor for the Hawaii Bound School, Sandler leads backpacking trips in Hawaii Volcanoes National Park that are designed to be adventurous and challenging, to take people beyond their set limitations. Although most of her work is with Hawaii's teenagers, she will put together 4- to 15-day trips for groups of at least six people, of any age. Cost of the 4-day trip is $275, the 15-day trip, $900; the 21-day teenage trip is about $1,200.

Hiking and Camping on Oahu

Hawaiian Trail and Mountain Club, P.O. Box 2238, Honolulu, HI 96804. Visitors are welcome to join weekend and holiday hikes with an avid group of outdoor enthusiasts. Check the schedule printed in Thursday's "Today" section, Bulletin Board column of the *Honolulu Star-Bulletin,* or, several weeks before your visit, send a stamped, self-addressed long envelope for their current schedule. Add $1 and you will receive a packet of valuable information about hiking and camping in Hawaii.

Sierra Club, Hawaii Chapter, P.O. Box 2577, Honolulu, HI 96803 (tel. 808/538-6616). Write or call the office for hiking information. They also have groups on Maui, Kauai, and the Big Island.

Hiking and Camping on the Big Island

Hawaiian Walkways, P.O. Box 1264, Kailua-Kona, HI 96745 (tel. 808/325-6677. Psychologist Dr. Ken Sanborn and his wife, Esther, longtime Hawaii residents, lead groups of 12 people in three exciting, day-long or half-day hikes. One walk is along the Ala Kahaki Trail, an ancient Hawaiian shoreline trail on a terrain marked by black lava flows, white-sand beaches, freshwater ponds, palm trees, and turquoise ocean waters. Another is a valley walk in the Kohala Mountains, following jungle streams, visiting a rain forest and seeing ancient petroglyphs. A third is a hike down Mauna Kea, beginning at 13,000 feet and descending about 2,000 feet to the ancient Hawaiian caves and to visit Lake Waiau, one of the highest lakes in the world. All day hikes, which include lunch, cost $80; half-day hikes cost $45. For minimum groups of six, the Sanborns will also lead three-day/two-night camping trips along the Ala Kahaki Trail, stopping to swim and take the sun, explore historical artifacts, visit petroglyph fields. At night, around the campfire, the groups learn the history, legends, chants, and hulas of old Hawaii. All camping equipment is provided; no backpacking is necessary. The trip is for those who are "reasonably fit" and can handle about six hours a day of hiking under a hot sun. No children under 12. Cost is $395 for the Thursday-to-Saturday trips.

Wilderness Day Trips on the Big Island

Waipio Valley Shuttle, Kukuihaele (tel. 808/775-7121). This four-wheel-drive tour into remote Waipio Valley, through taro fields, fish ponds, a black-sand beach, and a waterfall is a perennial favorite. Cost is $20 for adults, $10 for children under 12.

Waipio Valley Wagon Tours, P.O. Box 1340, Honokaa, HI 96727 (tel. 808/775-9518). Here's a way to explore Waipio Valley by mule-powered wagon transport. Three-hour tours depart from Kukuihaele at 9:30am and 12:30pm weekdays only, at a cost of $45 per person, half-price for children. The trip includes time at a hideaway swimming hole in the river and on the magnificent black-sand beach for fun in the surf.

For the most rugged way to explore Waipio Valley, consider the **Waipio Valley Naalapa Trail Ride.** No more than six riders at a time are guided along the lesser used trails of the spectacular valley. A four-wheel drive takes you down into the valley, and then it's a four-hour ride to all the major sights. Riders must be at least eight years old. Cost is $60.32 per rider. Write Waipio Naalapa Trail Rides, Box 992, Honokaa, HI 96727, tel. 808/775-0419.

Paradise Safaris, P.O. Box A-D, Kailua-Kona, HI 96745 (tel. 808/329-3600.) Sunset-watching, star-gazing expeditions to the top of Mauna Kea, almost 14,000 feet up. A visit to a world-class telescope facility is included. Price is $80 per person and includes pickup at West Hawaii hotels, warm parkas and hot beverages. Be sure you're in good physical condition and can handle high altitudes for this one.

Wilderness Adventures on Maui

Hike Maui, P.O. Box 330969, Kahului, HI 96733 (tel. 808/879-5270). Ken Schmitt is everybody's favorite naturalist and tour leader (see "Seeing Maui"). In addition to his regular day hikes, he offers special programs of backpacking as well as trekking programs with lodgings in country inns. Prices vary with accommodations and other services desired, such as sailing, bicycling, yoga, massage, etc., and typically start at $1,000 per week. All of these are offered by request, and dates are flexible.

Kauai Day Trips

Kauai Mountain Tours, P.O. Box 3069, Lihue, Kauai HI 96766 (tel. 808/245-7224). No need to hike the Na Pali coast now—this knowledgeable guide will take you on a one-of-a-kind trip into the Na Pali Kona Forest Reserve in an air-conditioned four-wheel vehicle that traverses the winding mountain roads around the back of Waimea Canyon. It's $75 for a seven-hour tour, lunch and light continental breakfast included.

Outfitters Kauai, P.O. Box 1149, Koloa, Kauai, HI 96756 (tel. 808/742-9667). Bicycling through Kauai's backcountry can be an exciting experience. This company rents mountain bikes of high quality, which are well maintained and suited for off-road riding. They provide helmets, water bottles, spare tubes with pumps, and extensive trail information based on years of riding and exploring on Kauai. Car racks are available to carry bikes to other locations. Bikes rent for $25 a day, $75 for four days, and $125 a week.

WATER SPORTS

Hawaii holds out myriad opportunities to experience snorkeling, scuba diving, underwater photography, windsurfing, and more.

Kayaking Trips

Pacific Outdoor Adventures, P.O. Box 61609, Honolulu, HI 96839 (tel. toll free 800/52-KAYAK). Whether you're a beginner, intermediate, or advanced paddler, you'll find a trip to suit you here. This company designs and builds its own boats and designs day, overnight, and up-to-five-day tours and clinics on all of the Hawaiian Islands. You can choose from 19 different itineraries on five islands, or have one custom-made for your own group of 4 to 12 people. Rates, averaging $150 per day, include paddling, snorkeling, hiking, camping, all equipment, meals, local and inter-island transportation. Nonswimmers, beginners, and disabled are welcome and can enjoy adventures like the popular 1½-hour Waikiki Sunset Paddle ($32); they are teamed with more experienced paddlers in two-person inflatable boats. All trips are designed to go downwind and to avoid any areas where there might be high surf or storms. All-inclusive airline and hotel packages can also be arranged. Write for a free brochure or visit the Windward Nature Center at 559-A Kapahulu Ave. for classes, day and overnight trips.

Outfitters Kauai, P.O. Box 1149, Koloa, HI 96756 (tel. 808/742-9667). In addition to simple half-day kayaking trips for beginners ($44) and one-day sea-kayaking adventures along Kauai's southeast coast in the shadow of 2,000-foot cliffs ($95 for a full-day excursion), this outfit also offers an escorted Kayak Experience along the Na Pali cliffs, either as a one-day trip from Haena to Polihale with following trade winds and currents, or as a two-or-more-day expedition featuring camping at Kalalau and Miloli'i, some of the most breathtakingly beautiful spots in the islands. Two-person inflatable kayaks may also be rented for self-guided tours to jungle rivers. Each boat comes with racks/straps to secure it to your car, maps, and personal information to help you select the ideal river. Cost is $45 per day.

Kayak Kauai Jungle Outfitters, 41-1340 Kuhio Hwy., Kapaa (tel. 808/822-9179), or on the Main Street in Hanalei, P.O. Box 508, Hanalei, HI 96714 (tel. 808/926-9844). Summer (May to September) journeys along 14 miles of Kauai's dramatic north shore coastline attract thrill seekers for some of the most challenging wilderness paddling to be found in Hawaii. Five-day packages cost $650 per person. The same company offers guided one-day canoe/kayak trips around the Na Pali cliffs, including lunch on an isolated beach ($95), and a three-hour Hanalei Wildlife Refuge Tour ($45). Their private canoe/kayak rentals at $42 for two persons, are very popular; they'll tell you how to get to barrier reefs, wildlife refuges, the Fern Grotto and waterfalls. You are the captain, crew, and navigator!

Sailing Cruises

Honolulu Sailing Company, Box 1500, Honolulu, HI 96744 (tel. 808/235-8264, toll free 800/367-8047, ext. 264). Sail away aboard a sleek, modern yacht to the islands of Oahu, Maui, Lanai, and Molokai. This company runs day, overnight, and one-week cruises out of Honolulu Harbor, combining sailing and snorkeling, at rates of about $60 for a half-day, $130 overnight. Boats sleep from four to ten passengers. Captain, crew, and cruise comforts: hot and cold running water, private state rooms for couples. One-day sailing, snorkeling and Zodiac trips on Oahu are also available for about $95 per person.

On Hawaii

Eye of the Whale, Marine/Wilderness Adventures, P.O. Box 1269, Kapaau, HI 96755 (tel. 808/889-0227 or toll free 800/657-7730). With a goal of promoting understanding of Hawaii's delicate ecosystem through first-hand experience. Beth and Mark Goodoni lead 7- to 10-day hiking/sailing adventures for groups of no more than 6 to 10 people. Days are spent outdoors, hiking through mountain valleys and jungles or sailing the Big Island's Kona coast, but nights are spent either on boats (for sailing trips) or in scenic inns and B&Bs. There is no backpacking or camping. Beth, a marine biologist and seasoned naturalist, introduces participants to the natural history of Hawaii, emphasizing the origin and identification of tropical flora, the development and exploration of coral-reef ecosystems, and the biology and observation of marine mammals. On the boat, she's the crew; husband Mark is the licensed U.S.C.G. captain. Costs are about $125 to $140 per day, including meals, accommodations, transportation, and inter-island fares. A highlight of the trip is a private luau, where guests learn to dig the imu, string their own leis, and dance the old-time hulas.

Snorkeling

Windward Expeditions, 789 Kailua Rd., Kailua, HI 96734 (tel. 808/263-3899). This company runs hour-and-a-half tours on the southeastern coastline of Oahu. You can see Turtle Canyon and various coastal sea caves, among other sights. Snorkeling equipment and instruction is included. Cost is $35. The first tour begins at 9am, Monday through Saturday.

Scuba Diving Package Tours on Oahu

Aaron's Dive Shop (tel. 808/262-2333). Custom-designed package tours to suit a variety of needs. Four-day certification courses offered. Phone for details.

Scuba Diving Package Tours on Kauai

Aquatics Kauai (tel. 808/822-9213, toll free 800/822-9422). Beachfront condos. Tropical Rent-A-Car. Seven nights, three dives, from $599.

Sea Sage Diving Center (tel. 808/822-3841, toll free 800/821-6670). Individual dives from $37.50 to $90, depending on equipment. Multipackage deals available.

Scuba Diving Tours on the Big Island

Gold Coast Divers (tel. 808/329-1328 or 329-4025). Lodging at Keahou Resort Condos, National Car Rental of Hawaii. Seven nights, three dives, from $499 and up.

Jack's Diving Locker (tel. 808/329-7585, toll free 800/345-4807). Lodging at Kona Makai Condos. Dive packages available.

Kohala Divers (tel. 808/882-7774). Lodging at Shores at Waikoloa, Budget Rent-A-Car. Continental airfare from the West Coast, plus inter-island flights. Seven nights, three dives, $1,000.

Kona Coast Divers (tel. 808/329-8802, toll free 800/KOA-DIVE). Lodging at Kona Billfish Condos. Transportation provided to dive sites. Three nights, two days, four dives—single $318, double $228 per person. Five nights, six dives—single $507, double $357 per person.

Sea Paradise Scuba (tel. 808/329-2500, toll free 800/322-KONA). Lodgings at Kona Surf Resort, Keahou Beach Hotel, and Kanaloa at Keahou. Dollar Rent-A-Car. Packages available.

Scuba Diving Packages on Maui

Central Pacific Divers (tel. 808/661-8718, toll free 800/433-6815). Lodging at Plantation Inn, Sunshine Rent-A-Car. Seven nights, seven dives, $595.

Dive Maui (tel. 808/661-4363 or 667-2080). Lodgings at Kuleana Condos. Customized packages.

Lahaina Divers (tel. 808/667-7496, toll free 800/657-7885). Lodgings at Maui Islander Inn, Dollar Rent-A-Car. Six nights, three dives, $499 per person, based on double occupancy.

Windsurfing Packages on Maui

Maui Windsurfari, P.O. Box 330254, Kahului, Maui, HI 96733 (tel. 808/871-7766, toll free 800/367-8047). Here's the ticket for an ideal windsurfing vacation, especially designed for the windsurfing enthusiast who can stay in Maui for a week or longer. Customized packages include choice of accommodations (ranging from quiet North Shore studios to deluxe oceanfront condos near prime sailing spots), rental cars with unlimited mileage, and hi-tech sailboard equipment. Also available are windsurfing lessons using Hawaiian Sailboard Techniques (HST) by world-famous sailor Alan Cadiz. Complete seven-day land packages start at $425 per person (double occupancy), or $390 per person (quad occupancy). Low airfares are also available.

Tradewinds Glider Flights, P.O. Box 2099, Lihue, Kauai, HI 96766 (tel. 800/2-GLIDER). If you've ever wanted to ride in a glider, here's your chance. Tradewinds has several flights, which glide out of Port Allen Airport and sail over Salt Pond Beach Park and Hanapepe Valley. The cost is anywhere between $45 and $125 per person, depending on the length of the trip and the altitude.

---

2. Educational Travel

You've had enough of sightseeing, swimming, shopping, and the usual tourist pleasures. Want to learn something new, stimulate your imagination and curiosity? The following will provide some suggestions.

FOR SENIORS ONLY

Elderhostel, 80 Boylston St., Suite 400, Boston, MA 02116 (tel. 617/426-7788). If you're 60 or older, or the spouse or companion of someone of that age, you are eligible to participate in one of the splendid Elderhostel educational programs, held all over the world, and sometimes in Hawaii. Write or phone for their latest catalog. Rates are reasonable.

FOR ALL AGES

The Nature Conservancy of Hawaii, 1116 Smith St., Honolulu, HI 96817 (tel. 808/537-4508). This local affiliate of The Nature Conservancy, a national, nonprofit conservation organization, runs week-long natural history tours of Maui and Molokai, which include in-depth tours of nature preserves and accommodations at luxury hotels. Fees are on the high side. Weekend tours and day trips may also be offered. Write or phone the Field Trip Coordinator at the above address for information or reservations.

Oceanic Society Expeditions, Fort Mason Center, Building E, San Francisco, CA 94123 (tel. toll free 800/326-7491). This national nonprofit organization, dedicated to preserving and protecting the ocean and coastal environments, has been leading outstanding journeys of discovery to the natural world since 1972. Among a wide variety of trips scheduled for 1991—which include expeditions to Africa, Antartica, the Amazon, and Indonesia—are two educational excursions to Hawaii. From January 27 to April 4, 1991, there are six different departure days for the five-day Hawaii Whale Watching, Sailing, and Snorkeling trip on the Kona coast of the Big Island. The group spends three full days sailing aboard a 41-foot ketch, the *Pacific Pearl*, to observe the courting, mating, and breeding activities of the endangered humpback whales. They will also look for bottlenose, spinner, and spotted dolphins, as well as pilot and false killer whales. Participants will collect baseline data on humpbacks, photo-identify individual whales, and perhaps record their mating songs, as part of ongoing research for the North Gulf Oceanic Society. Mark and Beth Gooden (who are also in charge at Eye of the Whale) are the naturalists who lead the group. Cost, not including airfare, is $925.

Five trips between December 1990 and December 1991, are scheduled for Hawaii Earth, Fire, Air, and Sea, a six-day land-based and sailing trip focusing on the different ecosystems of the Big Island. Participants visit Waipio Valley and its rain forest, investigate the world's most active volcano at Kilauea, sail the Kona coast searching for whales and acrobatic dolphins, and snorkel amidst the coral reefs. Cost, not including airfare, is $895.

Detailed itineraries, the Society's catalog, and reservations are available at the address above.

University Research Expeditions Program, Desk M05, University of California, Berkeley, CA 94720 (tel. 415/642-6586). A number of research programs are held in the United States and abroad; the cost of the programs is tax-deductible. Write for information about current offerings: previous trips included a three-week expedition to the island of Lanai to study the social patterns and behavioral interactions of spinner dolphins, and a two-week $1,395 expedition to Hawaiian petroglyph fields on the Kona coast of the Big Island to compare the ancient rock art of Hawaii with that of other Polynesian sites. The rock-art project will continue this year.

---

3. Holistic Holidays: Nurturing Body, Mind, and Spirit

SPA AND FITNESS CENTERS

At **The Plantation Spa,** 51-550 Kamehameha Hwy., Kaawa, HI 96730 (tel. 808/237-8685 or 808/237-8442), 14 lucky guests at one time can be pampered in the first health spa in Oahu, housed in one of the last true Hawaiian retreats, snuggled between the ocean and mountains in Kaawa. The seven-acre estate stretches all the way to the mountains, has its own waterfall, a nearby river, a pool on the grounds, and the ocean just across the street. Director Bodil Anderson, who hails from Sweden, runs her retreat more like a European health spa than a fitness center, and combines exercise classes, beach walks, mountain hikes, canoeing, massages, herbal wraps, and the like with mind exercises, iridology, and classes in cooking, food combining, and how to maintain the proper alkaline/acid balance in the body

European juice fasting is available, and very popular. Don't be surprised if you see familiar television and movie faces here, as it's a popular place for celebrities to come and unwind and shed a few pounds (Richard Chamberlain and Margaux Hemingway have been guests). The six-night program costs $1,450 per person, double occupancy, $1,750 single occupancy. Shorter stays of three nights are sometimes possible, and can be booked, upon availability, with short notice. Write or call for a brochure.

Kauai Lagoons Spa, at the Westin Kauai Resort, Kalapaki Beach, Lihue, Kauai, HI 96766 (tel. 808/246-5062). You needn't be a guest at the fabulous Westin Kauai Resort to enjoy the facilities and services of its plush European health spa. Visitors can sign up for a massage, facial, full-body skin treatment, or wellness screening, all of which include unlimited use of the spa facilities and exercise classes for the day. If you're feeling especially indulgent, treat yourself to one of their comprehensive day packages, like the Spa Experience, which includes a massage, in-depth facial, and full-body skin treatment of your choice for $160. Or experience the Total Wellness Package, which includes a range of wellness screenings by a qualified health professional, consultations, and a take-home fitness program for $175. Separate facilities are available for both men and women, each with a Turkish steam room, inhalant Finnish sauna, whirlpool, and exercise equipment. A variety of pampering services are offered, including facials, four types of massage, and three types of full-body skin treatments: herbal wrap and body buff, Hawaiian salt-glow rub, and Pacific full-body masque.

After your visit to the spa and/or the Wellness Center, have a lovely light lunch at The Terrace, an indoor/outdoor restaurant featuring spa cuisine and overlooking the swimming pool and the mountains beyond. Then wander and explore the other features of this fabulous seaside playground (see "Seeing Kauai," Chapter XII).

NEW AGE CENTERS AND ACTIVITIES

The New Age has spawned several programs and retreats in the serene Hawaiian environment.

On Oahu

Foundation of I, Inc. (Freedom of the Cosmos), 2143 N. King St., Honolulu, HI 96819 (tel. 808/842-3750). The Foundation of I presents evening lectures and classes on Ho'oponopono, an ancient Hawaiian process of problem solving that has been updated for today's world by native Hawaiian Morrnah Simeona. Classes are presented in Honolulu, throughout the islands, and in many other parts of the world. For information, contact the Foundation of I at the above address.

Maitreya Institute, 2327 Liloa Rise, Honolulu, HI 96822 (tel. 808/942-9051). Founded by His Eminence Tai Situ Rinpoche, Maitreya Institute is a nonprofit corporation dedicated to promoting "peace, harmony, and loving kindness among people of all races and religions." To that end, it sponsors three annual sessions of courses in spirituality, art, and healing from various traditions. The sessions cover the months of February-March, June-July, and October-November. Outstanding speakers are presented. Offerings range from free evening lectures to moderately priced weekend events and evening classes. Recent subjects have included: Process-Oriented Psychology; Taking the Path of Zen; Hawaiian Spirituality; Culture and the Arts; the Yoga of Healing; and Perspectives on Peace. Write for a brochure, available two weeks before the start of each session.

Science of Mind Center of Hawaii, 2909 Waialae Ave., Honolulu, HI (tel. 808/735-6832). Classes, workshops, seminars presented by a nondenominational metaphysical organization. Sunday services at 11am.

Silva Mind Control Training, P.O. Box 4466, Kaneohe, HI 96744 (tel. 808/247-5458), offers occasional free introductory lectures, graduate reinforcement meetings, and three-to-four-day training sessions to activate creativity, intuition, and problem-solving ability.

Unity School of Hawaii, 3608 Diamond Head Circle, Honolulu, HI 96815 (tel. 808/735-7666). Visitors are welcome to attend classes and workshops on a variety of spiritual and educational topics, including "A Course in Miracles," Yoga, Tai Chi Chuan, Relationships, Assertiveness Training, and Holistic Healing. **Common Ground,** 47-155 Okana Rd., Kaneohe, HI 96744 (tel. 808/239-7190). Alternative newspaper reporting on nonsectarian spiritual events in the islands. Pick up a copy for news of latest workshops, lectures, and classes in a wide variety of New Age subjects.

Big Island

The Dragonfly Ranch, Honaunau, HI 96726 (tel. 808/328-2159 or 328-9570). The Dragonfly Ranch is a private retreat on the Kona coast, within walking distance of Honaunau Bay, an ancient "Place of Sanctuary," with beaches and snorkeling. Hosts Barbara Moore and David Link will work out arrangements to provide guests either with total privacy or total attention: The Royal Treatment can include lomilomi (Hawaiian massage), health-oriented meals, fasting, flower essences, dance therapy, and references to many healers. Amenities of this two-bedroom country home include private sun decks, an outdoor canopied waterbed, cable TV, fireplace, badminton court, organic garden, and beautiful landscaping. Also available for B&B rentals. The donation is comparable to what one would spend at a quality hotel. For information, contact Barbara Moore and David Link at the address above.

Kalani Honua, Box 4500, Kalapana, HI 96778 (tel. 808/965-7828). Kalani Honua is Hawaii's prime intercultural retreat and conference center, offering a varied program of workshops and seminars in everything from dance and the arts to sports, health, and personal growth. Kalani Honua itself sponsors a limited number of programs, including an African/Hawaiian Dance Festival in June, and a Merrie Monarch Festival Cultural Celebration, which coincides with the annual hula competition held on the Big Island every spring. The cost of programs varies with each group. Kalani Honua is located in a spectacularly beautiful spot on the Kalapana coast, near black-sand beaches, and consists of four two-story wood lodges, each with an ocean-view meeting room/studio space on the upper level and a common kitchen on the ground floor. There are accommodations for individuals, couples, families, and groups (see Chapter XIV, "Seeing Hawaii," for specifics). Meals are largely vegetarian, with fish or fowl option. There's a pool and a Japanese-style spa with sauna and a hot tub. Guests are welcome to attend conferences, schedule their own, or use the facilities for their own personal vacations or retreats.

Maui

Alan Cohen, 170 Kawelo Rd., Haiku, HI 96708. Alan Cohen is a well-known workshop leader who holds a number of events in Maui, often with associates Michael and Maloah Stillwater. Write the above address for a schedule of his programs.

Miracles Unlimited, 81 Central Ave., Wailuku, Maui HI 96793 (tel. 808/242-7799). This charming store selling jewelry, crystals, fine art, art-to-wear, books, cards, gifts, and more, should be a first stop for anyone interested in where the classes, workshops, lectures, and other New Age happenings are taking place. On the first Wednesday of each month they have an Ohana Luncheon at which they present speakers; cost is $13, and much networking takes place. Once a month, they publish a complete calendar of events through their Alaya Unlimited office; it's yours free at the bookstore, or write them before your visit to get a copy. The shop is open every day except Sunday from 10am to 5:30pm.

Romi Lea, the founder and director of Miracles Unlimited, is also in charge at **Island Adventures,** a new service that offers "magical journeys in nature." Romi custom-tailors programs for small groups or individuals and encourages them to feel a new communion with Mother Earth. Programs include hiking in Hana and in Haleakala Crater, a hike to birthing pools used by ancient Hawaiian women, a trip to bamboo forests and waterfalls, canyons, and ocean-fed pools, and more. Off-island trips to Lanai and Kauai are also available. Romi provides a safe, easy, and loving environment for people of all ages. Hikes are provided on a donation basis, of which 10% will be sent to a nonprofit environmental organization. Out-of-pocket expenses (plane, boat, meals, lodging, etc.) will be charged accordingly. Write to Island Adventures, 760 S. Kihei Rd., #608, Kihei, Maui, HI 96753, or phone 808/879-0108.

Natalie and John Tyler, who describe themselves as "Fun-loving and spiritual psychotherapists who specialize in PAIRS" (practical application of intimate relationship skills), have opened their lovely home in the Kihei area as a B&B accommodation for "nonsmoking, conscious people." Their house is a mile from the beach and is filled with books, fine arts, and classical music. Guests can watch the sunset over the ocean with cool drinks and pupus on the deck and enjoy morning breakfast on the screened porch to the sound of birds. They offer an ocean-view room for $80 a night ($75 per night for three days or more, $60 a night for a week), a mountainside room for $75 ($70 per night for a three-day stay, $55 a night for a week's stay), an office for $50 per day, and a library for $25. Optional extras include a daily "Course in Miracles" meditation; gourmet dinners with wine on the screened porch; and individual, couple, and family therapy. Snorkeling, scuba lessons, and special trips are also available. For reservations, write to John and Natalie Tyler, 3270 Kehala Dr., Kihei, HI 96753, or phone 808/879-0097.

Kauai

Hawaiian Shaman Training, c/o Aloha International, P.O. Box 665, Kilauea, HI 96754, tel. 800/367-8047, ext. 888, from the U.S. mainland and 808/826-9097 from Hawaii and Canada. Dr. Serge Kahili King, who was adopted and trained by a Hawaiian family in the ancient traditions of Polynesian Huna, presents frequent workshops in the islands. For information on his classes in Kauai, contact the above numbers. His organization also operates the Hawaiian Art Museum & Bookstore in Kilauea (tel. 828-1309) and the Kauai Village Museum & Gift Shop in Kapaa (tel. 822-9272).

The Source, P.O. Box 1259, Koloa, HI 96756 (tel. 808/246-9535). Pick up a copy of *The Source,* a free bimonthly newspaper, for listings and notices of New Age activities on Kauai, and on the Big Island and Maui as well: retreats, workshops, classes—everything from crystals and channeling to rebirthing, self-transformation, and yoga.

A HAWAIIAN VOCABULARY

FROM AA TO WIKIWIKI

As we pointed out in the introduction, there are just 12 letters in the Hawaiian alphabet: the five vowels—*a, e, i, o, u*—and the seven consonants—*h, k, l, m, n, p, w.* Every syllable ends in a vowel, every vowel is pronounced, and the accent is almost always on the next-to-the-last syllable, as it is in Spanish. Consonants receive their English sounds, but vowels get the Latin pronunciation: *a* as in farm, *e* as in they, *i* as in machine, *o* as in cold, and *u* as in tutor. Note also that when a *w* comes before the final vowel in a word, it is given the "v" sound, as in Hawaii. Purists say Ha-vye-ee for Hawaii, but most people call it Ha-wye-ee.

The following glossary will give you a pretty good idea of what the Hawaiian language sounds like. No one, of course, expects you to go around spouting phrases like "Holo ehia keia?" to ask what time it is, but a familiarity with the most important words is what distinguishes the kamaainas from the malihinis.

rough lava	**aa**	
eat	**ai**	(eye)
friend, as in "Aloha, aikane"	**aikane**	(eye-kah-nay)
smart	**akamai**	(ah-kah-my)
road, as in Ala Moana (ocean Road)	**ala**	(al-lah)
noblemen, the old royalty of Hawaii	**alii**	(ah-lee-ee)
welcome, farewell, love	**aloha**	(ah-low-hah)
no	**aole**	(ah-oh-lay)
alas! woe!	**auwe**	(ow-way)
in the direction of Ewa, a town on Oahu "Drive Ewa five blocks."	**Ewa**	(ehvah)
the pandanus tree, the leaves of which are used for weaving	**hala**	(hah-lah)
pineapple	**halakahiki**	(hah-lah-kah-hee-kee)
school (as in hula halau)	**halau**	(hah-lau)
house	**hale**	(hah-lay)
to work	**hana**	(hah-nah)
Caucasian, white	**haole**	(how-lay)
white man	**haolekane**	(how-lay-kay-nay)
white woman	**haolewahine**	(how-lay-wah-hee-nay)
a small part, a half	**hapa**	(hah-pah)

pregnant, originally "to carry"	**hapai**	(hah-pie)
happiness	**hauoli**	(how-oh-lee)
ancient temple	**heiau**	(hey-ee-au)
to go, to walk	**hele**	(hey-lay)
to sleep	**haimoe**	(hee-ah-mow-ay)
ashamed	**hilahila**	(hee-lah-hee-lah)
to run	**holo**	(ho-low)
to have fun, to relax	**holoholo**	(ho-low-ho-low)
formal dress with train	**holoku**	(ho-low-koo)
a cross between a holoku and a muumuu, long and without a train	**holomuu**	(ho-low-moo)
to kiss, as in "Honikaua wikiwiki!" (Kiss me quick!)	**honi**	(ho-nee)
to flatter	**hoomalimali**	(ho-oh-mah-lee-mah-lee)
angry	**huhu**	(hoo-hoo)
a club, an assembly	**hui**	(hoo-ee)
a fishing festival	**hukilau**	(hoo-kee-lau)
a dance, to dance	**hula**	(hoo-lah)
underground oven lined with hot rocks, used for cooking the luau pig	**imu**	(ee-moo)
sweetheart	**ipo**	(ee-po)
the	**ka**	(kah)
ancient (as in hula kahiko)	**kahiko**	(kah-hee-ko)
sea	**kai**	(kye)
money	**kala**	(kah-lah)
to bake underground	**kalua**	(kah-loo-ah)
old-timer	**kamaaina**	(kah-mah-eye-nah)
man	**kane**	(kah-nay)
tapa, a bark cloth	**kapa**	(kah-pah)
crooked	**kapakahi**	(kah-pah-kah-hee)
forbidden, keep out	**kapu**	(kah-poo)
food	**kaukau**	(kow-kow)
child	**keiki**	(kay-kee)
help, cooperation	**kokua**	(ko-koo-ah)
south	**kona**	(ko-nah)
sun, light, day	**la**	(lah)
porch	**lanai**	(lah-nye)
heaven, sky	**lani**	(lah-nee)
leaf of the hala or pandanus tree	**lauhala**	(lau-hah-lah)
garland	**lei**	(lay)
stupid	**lolo**	(low-low)
massage	**lomilomi**	(low-mee-low-mee)
feast	**luau**	(loo-au)
thank you	**mahalo**	(mah-hah-low)
good, fine	**ma'i ka'i**	(mah-ee kah-ee)
toward the sea	**makai**	(mah-key)
stranger, newcomer	**malihini**	(mah-lee-hee-nee)
free	**manawahi**	(mah-nah-wah-hee)
toward the mountains	**mauka**	(mau-kah)
song, chant	**mele**	(may-lay)

a mysterious race who inhabited the island before the Polynesians. Mythology claims they were pygmies	**menehune**	(may-nay-hoo-nay)
loose dress, Hawaiian version of missionaries' "Mother Hubbards"	**muumuu**	(moo-oo-moo-oo)
lovely	**nani**	(nan-nee)
coconut	**niu**	(nee-oo)
big, as in "mahalo nui" ("big thanks")	**nui**	(noo-ee)
sweet taste, delicious	**ono**	(oh-no)
belly	**opu**	(oh-poo)
stubborn	**paakiki**	(pah-ah-kee-kee)
precipice	**pali**	(pah-lee)
Hawaiian cowboy	**paniolo**	(pah-nee-oh-low)
finished	**pau**	(pow)
trouble	**pilikia**	(pee-lee-kee-ah)
crushed taro root	**poi**	(poy)
hole	**puka**	(poo-kah)
couch	**punee**	(poo-nay-ay)
hors d'oeuvre	**pupu**	(poo-poo)
crazy	**pupule**	(poo-poo-lay)
rain	**ua**	(oo-ah)
speech, mouth	**waha**	(wah-hah)
female, woman, girl	**wahine**	(wah-hee-nay)
fresh water	**wai**	(why)
to hurry	**wikiwiki**	(wee-kee-wee-kee)

PHRASES

Be careful	**Malama pono** (mah-lah-mah po-no)
Bottoms up	**Okole maluna** (oh-ko-lay mah-loo-nah)
Come and eat	**Hele mai ai** (hey-lay-my-eye)
Come here	**Hele mai** (hey-lay my)
Come in and sit down	**Komo mai e noho iho** (ko-mo my ay no-ho ee-ho)
For love	**No ke aloha** (no kay ah-low-hah)
Go away	**Hele aku oe** (hey-lay ah-koo oh-ay)
Good evening	**Aloha ahiahi** (ah-low-hah ah-hee-ah-hee)
Good morning	**Aloha kakahiaka** (ah-low-hah kah-kah-hee-ah-kah)
Greatest love to you	**Aloha nui oe** (ah-low-hah noo-ee oh-ay)
Happy Birthday	**Hauloi la hanau** (hah-oo-oh-lee lah hah-nah-oo)
Happy New Year	**Hauoli Makahiki Hou** (hah-oo-oh-lee man-kah-hee-kee ho-oo)
Here's to your happiness	**Hauoli maoli oe** (hah-oo-oh-lee mah-oh-lee oh-ay)
How are you?	**Pehea oe?** (pay-hay-ah oh-ay)
I am fine	**Ma'i ka'i** (mah-ee kah-ee)
I am sorry	**Ua kaumaha au** (oo-ah cow-mah-hah ow)
I have enough	**Ua lawa au** (oo-ah lah-wah ow)

I love you	**Aloha wauia oe** (ah-low-hah vow ee-ah oh-ay)
It isn't so	**Aole pela** (ah-oh-lay pay-lah)
Let's go	**E hele kaua** (au-hey-lay cow-ah)
Many thanks	**mahalo nui loa** (mah-hah-low noo-ee low-ah)
Merry Christmas	**Mele Kalikimaka** (may-lay-kah-lee-kee-mah-kah)
Much love	**Aloha nui loa** (ah-low-hah noo-ee low-ah)
No trouble	**Aole pilikia** (ah-oh-lay pee-lee-kee-ah)
What is your name?	**Owai kau inoa?** (oh-why kah-oo ee-no-ah)

AND THEN THERE'S PIDGIN

Despite the earnest efforts of educators to stamp it out, pidgin, that code language of the islands, continues its not-so-underground existence. The Chinese developed it in their first contacts with English-speaking people, but you'll hear it spoken today by all the racial groups, from haoles to Hawaiians. Beachboys, cab drivers, university students, a few who don't know better and a lot who do, all occasionally descend into pidgin. Although its subtleties are unintelligible to the newcomer (that's part of the idea), you'll be able to pick up a few words: *wasamala, wasetime, lesgo, da kine.*

You'll hear all kinds of theories about the indestructibility of pidgin. Some sociological types feel it's a subtle form of rebellion by the dispossessed Hawaiian, not unlike the jargon of mainland blacks. The psychological types call it more of an adolescent code, a desire for teenagers to have their own language. Others say it's just plain bad English. Take your choice, whatever *da kine* reason, pidgin is "in" in Hawaii.

Note: After you've been in the islands a bit, get yourself a copy of Peppo's *Pidgin to Da Max*. It's one of Hawaii's most popular humor-cartoon books (over 130,000 copies in print), available in any bookstore, and an absolute hoot! We reprint the "Word of Caution to the Non-local: If you don't already speak pidgin, you might need some help from local friends to understand this book. Remember: *Pidgin to Da Max* is not a tourist guide to pidgin. So don't try to speak after reading this book. You'll just get into trouble." We agree. Don't try to speak pidgin. Just read the book —maybe on the plane trip back home—and try to keep yourself from rolling in the aisles. It's $4.95, published by Bess Press, Honolulu. There is, in fact, a whole series of Peppo's Pidgin books now, another one of which is *Fax to Da Max*, which lists "Everything You Never Knew You Wanted to Know About Hawaii," plus lots of "useless fax," too. Another howler.

And so this 26th edition of *Hawaii on $60 a Day* is *pau*. As every writer knows, no travel book is holy writ; establishments go out of business, owners change, prices go up, quality improves or falls off. Don't become angry with establishments if their prices are higher than those quoted as we went to press; inflation is a fact of life. The book is brought up to date every year; be sure you are reading the latest edition available. And we will be grateful to all readers who give us their up-to-the-minute reports on the places mentioned in the book. If you've discovered something new—a hotel, a restaurant, a shop, a beach—we hope you'll share it with us and with readers of future editions of this book. Send your suggestions, comments, criticisms to us, Faye Hammel and Sylvan Levey, c/o Frommer Books, 15 Columbus Circle, 15th floor, New York, NY 10023. We regreat that we cannot personally answer the many hundreds of letters we receive each year. You can be certain, however, that your letter is carefully noted and appreciated, and that your input is very important to us. Please note that we reserve the right to make minor editorial changes for the sake of clarity and brevity.

And now you're ready to strike out on your own, to sample for yourself the charms of what Mark Twain called "the loveliest fleet of islands anchored in any ocean." Ahead of you lies the newest, and most unique, of the United States.

Aloha!

INDEX

GENERAL INFORMATION

SIGHTS AND ATTRACTIONS

Hawaii — The Big Island

Honolulu & Environs

Kauai

Maui

Molokai

Oahu

ACCOMMODATIONS

Hawaii—The Big Island

Honolulu & Environs

KEY TO ABBREVIATIONS: All accommodations fall into the $60-A-Day price range; the only other categories for you to consider are: B&B = Bed-and-Breakfast; S = Splurge

Kauai

Maui

Molokai

RESTAURANTS

Hawaii—The Big Island

NOTE: S stands for Splurge

Honolulu & Environs

Kauai

Maui

Molokai

NOW, SAVE MONEY ON ALL YOUR TRAVELS!
Join Frommer's™ Dollarwise® Travel Club

Saving money while traveling is never a simple matter, which is why the **Dollarwise Travel Club** was formed 31 years ago. Developed in response to requests from Frommer's Travel Guide readers, the Club provides cost-cutting travel strategies, up-to-date travel information, and a sense of community for value-conscious travelers from all over the world.

In keeping with the money-saving concept, the annual membership fee is low —$18 for U.S. residents or $20 for residents of Canada, Mexico, and other countries—and is immediately exceeded by the value of your benefits, which include:

1. Any TWO books listed on the following pages.
2. Plus any ONE Frommer's City Guide.
3. A subscription to our quarterly newspaper, *The Dollarwise Traveler.*
4. A membership card that entitles you to purchase through the Club all Frommer's publications for 33% to 50% off their retail price.

The eight-page **Dollarwise Traveler** tells you about the latest developments in good-value travel worldwide and includes the following columns: **Hospitality Exchange** (for those offering and seeking hospitality in cities all over the world); **Share-a-Trip** (for those looking for travel companions to share costs); and **Readers Ask . . . Readers Reply** (for those with travel questions that other members can answer).

Aside from the Frommer's Guides and the Gault Millau Guides, you can also choose from our Special Editions. These include such titles as **California with Kids** (a compendium of the best of California's accommodations, restaurants, and sightseeing attractions appropriate for those traveling with toddlers through teens); **Candy Apple: New York with Kids** (a spirited guide to the Big Apple by a savvy New York grandmother that's perfect for both visitors and residents); **Caribbean Hideaways** (the 100 most romantic places to stay in the Islands, all rated on ambience, food, sports opportunities, and price); **Honeymoon Destinations** (a guide to planning and choosing just the right destination from hundreds of possibilities in the U.S., Mexico, and the Caribbean); **Marilyn Wood's Wonderful Weekends** (a selection of the best mini-vacations within a 200-mile radius of New York City, including descriptions of country inns and other accommodations, restaurants, picnic spots, sights, and activities); and **Paris Rendez-Vous** (a delightful guide to the best places to meet in Paris whether for power breakfasts or dancing till dawn).

To join this Club, simply send the appropriate membership fee with your name and address to: Frommer's Dollarwise Travel Club, 15 Columbus Circle, New York, NY 10023. Remember to specify which single city guide and which two other guides you wish to receive in your initial package of member's benefits. Or tear out the next page, check off your choices, and send the page to us with your membership fee.

FROMMER BOOKS
PRENTICE HALL PRESS
15 COLUMBUS CIRCLE
NEW YORK, NY 10023
212/373-8125

Date_____

Friends:
Please send me the books checked below.

FROMMER'S™ GUIDES

(Guides to sightseeing and tourist accommodations and facilities from budget to deluxe, with emphasis on the medium-priced.)

☐ Alaska	$14.95	☐ Germany	$14.95
☐ Australia	$14.95	☐ Italy	$14.95
☐ Austria & Hungary	$14.95	☐ Japan & Hong Kong	$14.95
☐ Belgium, Holland & Luxembourg	$14.95	☐ Mid-Atlantic States	$14.95
☐ Bermuda & The Bahamas	$14.95	☐ New England	$14.95
☐ Brazil	$14.95	☐ New York State	$14.95
☐ Canada	$14.95	☐ Northwest	$14.95
☐ Caribbean	$14.95	☐ Portugal, Madeira & the Azores	$14.95
☐ Cruises (incl. Alaska, Carib, Mex, Hawaii, Panama, Canada & US)	$14.95	☐ Skiing Europe	$14.95
☐ California & Las Vegas	$14.95	☐ South Pacific	$14.95
☐ Egypt	$14.95	☐ Southeast Asia	$14.95
☐ England & Scotland	$14.95	☐ Southern Atlantic States	$14.95
☐ Florida	$14.95	☐ Southwest	$14.95
☐ France	$14.95	☐ Switzerland & Liechtenstein	$14.95
		☐ USA	$15.95

FROMMER'S $-A-DAY® GUIDES

(In-depth guides to sightseeing and low-cost tourist accommodations and facilities.)

☐ Europe on $40 a Day	$15.95	☐ New York on $60 a Day	$13.95
☐ Australia on $40 a Day	$13.95	☐ New Zealand on $45 a Day	$13.95
☐ Eastern Europe on $25 a Day	$13.95	☐ Scandinavia on $60 a Day	$13.95
☐ England on $50 a Day	$13.95	☐ Scotland & Wales on $40 a Day	$13.95
☐ Greece on $35 a Day	$13.95	☐ South America on $35 a Day	$13.95
☐ Hawaii on $60 a Day	$13.95	☐ Spain & Morocco on $40 a Day	$13.95
☐ India on $25 a Day	$12.95	☐ Turkey on $30 a Day	$13.95
☐ Ireland on $35 a Day	$13.95	☐ Washington, D.C. & Historic Va. on	
☐ Israel on $40 a Day	$13.95	$40 a Day	$13.95
☐ Mexico on $35 a Day	$13.95		

FROMMER'S TOURING GUIDES

(Color illustrated guides that include walking tours, cultural and historic sites, and other vital travel information.)

☐ Amsterdam	$10.95	☐ New York	$10.95
☐ Australia	$9.95	☐ Paris	$8.95
☐ Brazil	$10.95	☐ Rome	$10.95
☐ Egypt	$8.95	☐ Scotland	$9.95
☐ Florence	$8.95	☐ Thailand	$9.95
☐ Hong Kong	$10.95	☐ Turkey	$10.95
☐ London	$8.95	☐ Venice	$8.95

TURN PAGE FOR ADDITONAL BOOKS AND ORDER FORM

FROMMER'S CITY GUIDES·

(Pocket-size guides to sightseeing and tourist accommodations and facilities in all price ranges.)

☐ Amsterdam/Holland	$8.95	☐ Montréal/Québec City	$8.95
☐ Athens	$8.95	☐ New Orleans	$8.95
☐ Atlanta	$8.95	☐ New York	$8.95
☐ Atlantic City/Cape May	$8.95	☐ Orlando	$8.95
☐ Barcelona	$7.95	☐ Paris	$8.95
☐ Belgium	$7.95	☐ Philadelphia	$8.95
☐ Boston	$8.95	☐ Rio	$8.95
☐ Cancún/Cozumel/Yucatán	$8.95	☐ Rome	$8.95
☐ Chicago	$8.95	☐ Salt Lake City	$8.95
☐ Denver/Boulder/Colorado Springs	$7.95	☐ San Diego	$8.95
☐ Dublin/Ireland	$8.95	☐ San Francisco	$8.95
☐ Hawaii	$8.95	☐ Santa Fe/Taos/Albuquerque	$8.95
☐ Hong Kong	$7.95	☐ Seattle/Portland	$7.95
☐ Las Vegas	$8.95	☐ Sydney	$8.95
☐ Lisbon/Madrid/Costa del Sol	$8.95	☐ Tampa/St. Petersburg	$8.95
☐ London	$8.95	☐ Tokyo	$7.95
☐ Los Angeles	$8.95	☐ Toronto	$8.95
☐ Mexico City/Acapulco	$8.95	☐ Vancouver/Victoria	$7.95
☐ Minneapolis/St. Paul	$8.95	☐ Washington, D.C.	$8.95

SPECIAL EDITIONS

☐ Beat the High Cost of Travel	$6.95	☐ Motorist's Phrase Book (Fr/Ger/Sp)	$4.95
☐ Bed & Breakfast—N. America	$11.95	☐ Paris Rendez-Vous	$10.95
☐ California with Kids	$14.95	☐ Swap and Go (Home Exchanging)	$10.95
☐ Caribbean Hideaways	$14.95	☐ The Candy Apple (NY with Kids)	$12.95
☐ Honeymoon Destinations (US, Mex &		☐ Travel Diary and Record Book	$5.95
Carib)	$14.95	☐ Where to Stay USA (From $3 to $30 a	
☐ Manhattan's Outdoor Sculpture	$15.95	night)	$10.95

☐ Marilyn Wood's Wonderful Weekends (CT, DE, MA, NH, NJ, NY, PA, RI, VT) $11.95

☐ The New World of Travel (Annual sourcebook by Arthur Frommer for savvy travelers) $16.95

GAULT MILLAU

(The only guides that distinguish the truly superlative from the merely overrated.)

☐ The Best of Chicago	$15.95	☐ The Best of Los Angeles	$16.95
☐ The Best of France	$16.95	☐ The Best of New England	$15.95
☐ The Best of Hong Kong	$16.95	☐ The Best of New York	$16.95
☐ The Best of Italy	$16.95	☐ The Best of Paris	$16.95
☐ The Best of London	$16.95	☐ The Best of San Francisco	$16.95

☐ The Best of Washington, D.C. $16.95

ORDER NOW!

In U.S. include $2 shipping UPS for 1st book; $1 ea. add'l book. Outside U.S. $3 and $1, respectively.

Allow four to six weeks for delivery in U.S., longer outside U.S.

Enclosed is my check or money order for $_____

NAME _____

ADDRESS _____

CITY _____ STATE _____ ZIP _____

0690